The Risks of Financial Institutions

**A National Bureau
of Economic Research
Conference Report**

The Risks of
Financial Institutions

Edited by **Mark Carey and
René M. Stulz**

The University of Chicago Press

Chicago and London

MARK CAREY is finance project manager in the Division of International Finance at the Federal Reserve Board and codirector of the National Bureau of Economic Research (NBER) Working Group on Risks of Financial Institutions. RENÉ M. STULZ is the Everett D. Reese Chair of Banking and Monetary Economics at Ohio State University, codirector of the NBER Working Group on Risks of Financial Institutions, and a research associate of the NBER.

The University of Chicago Press, Chicago 60637
The University of Chicago Press, Ltd., London
© 2006 by the National Bureau of Economic Research
All rights reserved. Published 2006
Printed in the United States of America

15 14 13 12 11 10 09 08 07 06   1 2 3 4 5
ISBN-13: 978-0-226-09285-0 (cloth)
ISBN-10: 0-226-09285-2 (cloth)

Library of Congress Cataloging-in-Publication Data

The risks of financial institutions / edited by Mark Carey and René M. Stulz.
    p.   cm. — (NBER conference report)
    Papers presented at a conference held in Woodstock, Vt., on Oct. 22–23, 2004.
    Includes bibliographical references and index.
    ISBN-13: 978-0-226-09285-0 (cloth : alk. paper)
    ISBN: 10: 0-226-09285-2 (cloth : alk. paper)
    1. Financial institutions—Congresses. 2. Risk—Congresses.
  3. Financial crises—Congresses. I. Carey, Mark S. (Mark Steven)
II. Stulz, René M. III. Series.
HG173 .R562 2006
332.1068'1—dc22

                             2006044550

Relation of the Directors to the
Work and Publications of the
National Bureau of Economic Research

1. The object of the NBER is to ascertain and present to the economics profession, and to the public more generally, important economic facts and their interpretation in a scientific manner without policy recommendations. The Board of Directors is charged with the responsibility of ensuring that the work of the NBER is carried on in strict conformity with this object.

2. The President shall establish an internal review process to ensure that book manuscripts proposed for publication DO NOT contain policy recommendations. This shall apply both to the proceedings of conferences and to manuscripts by a single author or by one or more co-authors but shall not apply to authors of comments at NBER conferences who are not NBER affiliates.

3. No book manuscript reporting research shall be published by the NBER until the President has sent to each member of the Board a notice that a manuscript is recommended for publication and that in the President's opinion it is suitable for publication in accordance with the above principles of the NBER. Such notification will include a table of contents and an abstract or summary of the manuscript's content, a list of contributors if applicable, and a response form for use by Directors who desire a copy of the manuscript for review. Each manuscript shall contain a summary drawing attention to the nature and treatment of the problem studied and the main conclusions reached.

4. No volume shall be published until forty-five days have elapsed from the above notification of intention to publish it. During this period a copy shall be sent to any Director requesting it, and if any Director objects to publication on the grounds that the manuscript contains policy recommendations, the objection will be presented to the author(s) or editor(s). In case of dispute, all members of the Board shall be notified, and the President shall appoint an ad hoc committee of the Board to decide the matter; thirty days additional shall be granted for this purpose.

5. The President shall present annually to the Board a report describing the internal manuscript review process, any objections made by Directors before publication or by anyone after publication, any disputes about such matters, and how they were handled.

6. Publications of the NBER issued for informational purposes concerning the work of the Bureau, or issued to inform the public of the activities at the Bureau, including but not limited to the NBER Digest and Reporter, shall be consistent with the object stated in paragraph 1. They shall contain a specific disclaimer noting that they have not passed through the review procedures required in this resolution. The Executive Committee of the Board is charged with the review of all such publications from time to time.

7. NBER working papers and manuscripts distributed on the Bureau's web site are not deemed to be publications for the purpose of this resolution, but they shall be consistent with the object stated in paragraph 1. Working papers shall contain a specific disclaimer noting that they have not passed through the review procedures required in this resolution. The NBER's web site shall contain a similar disclaimer. The President shall establish an internal review process to ensure that the working papers and the web site do not contain policy recommendations, and shall report annually to the Board on this process and any concerns raised in connection with it.

8. Unless otherwise determined by the Board or exempted by the terms of paragraphs 6 and 7, a copy of this resolution shall be printed in each NBER publication as described in paragraph 2 above.

Contents

Acknowledgments

This volume contains papers and comments presented at a conference held in Woodstock, Vermont, 22–23 October 2004. We thank Martin Feldstein, president of the National Bureau of Economic Research (NBER), for his advice and support over the course of this project and for his ongoing support of work on risk management and financial institutions risk. Those who have supported this NBER project over the course of many meetings are too numerous to name. We thank them all, but especially NBER research associates Charles Calomiris, Frank Diebold, Darrell Duffie, and Andrew Lo. We thank Carl Beck and Denis Healy of the NBER Conference Department for efficient support of the conference, and Robyn Scholl of Ohio State and Helena Fitz-Patrick of the NBER Publication Department for excellent assistance with the publication process.

Introduction

Mark Carey and René M. Stulz

About twenty years ago, the intellectual and practical dynamics of under-standing and managing the risks of financial system distress began to change. The consensus view, which was that runs on solvent banks were at the heart of banking panics—and that panics were the main problem—ironically began to unravel around the time Diamond and Dybvig (1983) published their theory of runs. The consensus was challenged by a series of events, including the emerging-market debt crisis of the early 1980s, the 1987 and 1989 stock market crashes, waves of failures of U.S. savings and loan associations (S&Ls) and banks in the late 1980s and early 1990s, the junk bond and U.S. municipal bond meltdowns of the early 1990s, the Long-term Capital Management (LTCM) crisis, and a new wave of emerging-market crises. Bank runs played a negligible role in most of these events. While new financial instruments (such as derivatives), new partici-pants (e.g., hedge funds), and new technologies (like electronic trading), typically have improved the informational efficiency of markets and have facilitated the matching of savings with investment opportunities, they have also changed the speed with which new information is incorporated into prices, often giving little time for institutions to adjust to new infor-mation before they see their financial soundness imperiled by new balance sheet weaknesses or by liquidity problems.

The traditional public policy prescription also became less satisfactory. The prescription was that financial system distress can be prevented or managed by a combination of banking supervision and regulation (to pre-

This introduction and book represents the authors' opinions, not necessarily those of the Board of Governors of the Federal Reserve System or the NBER. We thank an anonymous referee, Frank Diebold, Jan Krahnen, and especially Jim O'Brien for comments.

serve bank solvency and to permit central banks to identify solvent banks in a panic), lender-of-last-resort advances (to solvent banks experiencing liquidity problems during a panic), and deposit insurance. But none of the new crises fit the old mold.[1] Some of the new events featured sharp movements in asset prices and sharp contractions in market liquidity. Others featured massive credit losses due to concentrations of poorly underwritten loans or failure to appreciate credit risk concentrations. Moreover, numerous emerging-market countries experienced banking crises, but deposit insurance does not seem to have reduced the probability of banking crises and perhaps even contributed to them (see Demirgüç-Kunt and Detragiache [2001]).[2] Facing events at variance with the prevailing intellectual framework, policymakers were forced to feel their way toward crisis solutions and toward new preventive measures.

Developments in capital markets, especially the growth in derivatives markets, increased the tools available to firms to take on and manage risks.[3] These developments also made traditional accounting numbers, which regulators used to assess financial institutions and executives used to manage such institutions, much less relevant to measurement of exposures to various risks. Through the trading of derivatives, for instance, a bank can take large risks that are nearly invisible when investors look at its balance sheet. For instance, banks would traditionally take interest rate exposures by taking deposits or making loans and buying bonds. However, with derivatives, a bank can use an interest-rate swap to take the same interest rate risk as if it bought a bond, but the acquisition of the swap, in contrast to the acquisition of the bond, is not recorded on the balance sheet at inception because the value of a swap at inception is zero.[4] After inception of the swap, mark-to-market accounting requires the bank to record the market value of the swap, but that market value provides little information about the bank's interest rate exposure. Moreover, bank managers discovered that they could boost traditional accounting performance measures through trading, which requires little funding capital. A traditional measure of performance such as return on equity would improve through trading revenue or revenue from fees because such activities typically required little incremental equity.[5] However, such activities can sharply increase the risks

1. Of course, runs on solvent banks might have occurred had authorities been less vigilant or credible, and insolvency rates might have been worse without bank supervision and regulation. Our argument is that the traditional intellectual foundations do not seem to predict many of the problems that have occurred, and that some of the policies these foundations imply may no longer be appropriate.

2. Banks experiencing runs in Demirgüç-Kunt and Detragiache's (2001) sample of crises were often insolvent at the time of the runs and thus such crises, while very important, did not fit the Diamond and Dybvig paradigm of runs on solvent banks.

3. See Stulz (2004) for a review of the growth of derivatives markets.

4. A swap is an exchange of cash flows. With an interest rate swap, one party pays a fixed rate on a notional amount and receives a floating rate on the same amount.

5. See Merton and Perold (1993) for an early discussion of this issue and an analysis of the role of risk capital in financial firms.

taken by the institution, and broker-dealers and investment banks traditionally backed such activities with substantial capital. These developments forced both bank regulators and market participants to focus on approaches that would capture the risks borne by institutions in a way that accounting numbers could not.

Market participants chose to address these changes in markets, and the increased frequency and variety of financial crises that threatened their investments and earnings, by developing formalized, quantitative risk measurement and management technologies. It was becoming increasingly clear that prevailing, mostly informal, seat-of-the-pants ways of managing risk were inadequate. The goal of the new measurement technologies is to produce realistic conditional forecasts of the distribution of returns to a financial institution, especially of the tail of the distribution corresponding to adverse outcomes. Given such forecasts, the institution can make informed decisions about its portfolio and capital structure and can also design internal incentive and control systems to help ensure that decisions are implemented properly. It has become typical for up-to-date, large financial institutions to take into account the impact of each activity on their overall risk when they evaluate the profitability of activities. Typically, a firm identifies a charge for an activity proportional to some measure of the impact of that activity on the firm's risk. In principle, risks associated with financial crises can be incorporated in the modeling. Such new technologies are having a profound impact on financial institution risk and financial system risk and have already made it necessary to develop new ways of thinking about such risk and new public policy regimes. Pressure for such developments will increase in the future.

An example may help illustrate how the new techniques are being used. Suppose a bank is considering an expansion of lending to investment-grade, large corporate borrowers. Such loans pay relatively low interest rate spreads, but loss rates are very low in a typical year, so profit margins may appear positive and overall accounting profits may seem boosted by large volumes of such lending. Traditionally, senior bank managers might make a strategic decision to expand such lending, and implement the decision by rewarding loan officers based on the volume of loans made. Many new loans would be individually large.

More recently, the bank would make decisions based on how the new loans contribute to the risk of its portfolio of credits in relation to their contribution to the bank's expected profits. It would measure the risk of a portfolio of credits by estimating the distribution of the portfolio's aggregate loss, focusing in particular on the loss that might be expected to be exceeded rarely—say, once in 200 bank years (the 99.5th percentile). To produce such estimates, the bank would use a portfolio credit risk model. The reason for the focus on such loss rates is that their distribution is crucially important for maximization of franchise value, since the distribution of tail losses directly impacts a financial institution's probability of financial distress. Such tail-loss forecasts are often generically referred to as "value-at-risk" (VaR) measures. Value-at-risk measures for credit portfolios are generally referred to as credit VaRs. In our example, the new loans, particularly if they are large, may have a material impact on the firm's credit VaR. If they do, the risk of bank insolvency increases. To keep the probability of insolvency unchanged, the bank would have to allocate extra equity capital, which it would typically call risk capital, as protection. Though finance theories that assume markets to be frictionless find that there are no deadweight costs to equity finance, finance theories that take into account information asymmetries and agency problems find equity to be an expensive source of finance (see, for instance, Myers 1977, Myers and Majluf 1984). Consequently, even if mean loss rates on the new loans are low, the loans might still be unprofitable, because their spreads might be too small to cover both expected losses and the required return to the extra equity that is needed.

Portfolio models can also be useful in implementing decisions. Lending officers can be provided incentives based on the marginal profit flowing from a new loan rather than on volume. The models can be used to include in measures of marginal profit the costs of allocated risk capital as well as expected credit losses and other costs. Particularly where portfolio models include fine-grained diversification effects (where the model correlates the risks posed by individual new loans with the risks of individual loans already in the portfolio), such risk-adjusted profitability measures can (in principle) be embedded in internal control and incentive systems in such a way that the bank's target risk posture is almost automatically maintained. Such systems are especially important to the operations of very large financial institutions, where many operational decisions must be decentralized.

Although the example focuses on credit risk, the approach is used by financial institutions for other risks as well. For instance, the risks assumed by a trading desk can be evaluated by estimating the VaR of the trading desk as well as the contribution of these risks to the market risk of the financial institution or to its enterprise-wide risk.

The new risk measurement and management techniques are associated with, and in some cases are driving, a number of important changes in financial systems, including:

- A better appreciation of the types of risk to be considered and of the relationships among them.
- A better understanding of the drivers and dynamics of each type of risk and of how to model and manage risk.
- New instruments and markets that support risk transformation and risk shifting, such as securitization and derivative products.
- Changes in the industrial organization of financial systems:
  —Larger financial institutions can be more efficiently managed, adding impetus to trends toward greater concentration.

—New kinds of institutions, such as hedge funds and boutique securitization sponsors.

—A blurring of traditional classifications of types of institutions by the type of risk borne, aided by new instruments and by entry into each other's markets.

- Greater attention to legal, accounting, regulatory, and other financial infrastructure. The new techniques flourish in environments that support good data and enforceable contracts.
- Changes in the nature and incidence of risks that affect the stability and soundness of the financial system—so-called systemic risks.
- Changes in the appropriate structure of regulatory and central bank policy.

Taken together, such developments are likely to change risks of distress and crisis for individual financial institutions and for national and international financial systems.

The papers and their discussants' remarks in this volume make new contributions to the understanding, measurement, and management of financial institution risk. While some papers focus on the determinants and measurement of risks at the level of individual institutions, others focus on the determinants of systemic risk in a world where individual financial institutions measure and manage risk using approaches developed over the last twenty years. Perhaps more importantly, taken together, the papers and remarks demonstrate how interrelated the changes that are in progress are, and support the importance of continuing efforts to understand them. Another contribution, felt most forcefully by the conference participants, is the utility of bringing together academic researchers, market participants, regulators, and central bank people. All have much to contribute, and progress is particularly tangible when they are brought together.

The order in which the papers appear in the volume is somewhat arbitrary. Each paper makes contributions to an understanding of more than one of the issues in the previous list, so many different orderings can be imagined. In the remainder of this introduction, we discuss in a bit more detail each of the issues and show how the papers in this volume contribute. We hope this will help readers to better understand the overall contribution of this volume and to place these papers in a more general context. We also hope readers focusing on one or a few issues will be able to more easily find contributions of particular interest to them.

Risk Management and Firm Value Maximization

Financial institutions choose the level of risk that maximizes the objectives of those who run them, subject to constraints and penalties imposed by those who regulate them and by capital markets. If the incentives of managers are well aligned with the interests of shareholders, managers maximize shareholder wealth. Observers who emphasize the moral hazard created by deposit insurance sometimes conclude that deposit insurance leads banks to take as much risk as regulators will let them take. It is now clear that such a view is much too simple.

Many financial institutions have substantial franchise value that could be lost if they are viewed as too risky. As has been emphasized by Merton (1993) and others, risk management is uniquely important for financial institutions because, in contrast to firms in other industries, their liabilities are a source of wealth creation for their shareholders. For instance, a financial institution that writes long-dated derivatives would usually be shut out of the market if the credit rating of the vehicle it uses to write such derivatives fell below an A rating. Another example is a life insurance company writing policies on its general account. Its customers would disappear if its rating fell to a junk rating, and most likely before that (few life insurance companies have ratings below A–). Because its franchise value depends on the risk of its insolvency, a financial institution has an optimal level of risk that maximizes its value for its shareholders. Risk minimization is never optimal, because there cannot be a franchise value without taking risks, so that the firm always faces costs and benefits when its risk level increases.[6]

To maximize shareholder wealth, managers of financial institutions therefore have to be able to measure and manage the risk of their institution. In principle, they would want to take into account the whole distribution of firm value. In practice, they focus on measures of downward risk, because adverse outcomes are those that endanger franchise value. Value-at-risk is a measure of downward risk: it measures the maximum value loss at some confidence level. For instance, a firmwide daily VaR of $100 million at the 95 percent confidence level means that in five days out of a hundred, the bank expects to have a loss that exceeds $100 million. Cash flow at risk or earnings at risk are similar measures of downward risk for cash flows and earnings. For instance, cash flow at risk is the shortfall in cash flow at a given percentile of the cash flow distribution, such as the 95th percent percentile.

The level of risk that has to be measured and managed is the level of risk for the whole institution. In practice, this has proved difficult. Initially, firms focused mostly on the risk of specific activities and on specific types of risks. However, lately, firms are increasingly focusing on aggregating risks firmwide.

Once a firm has measured its level of risk, it has to decide whether it is optimal for that level to be maintained, increased, or decreased. Taking on risk enables a firm to make profits, but it also endangers franchise value. To take more risks, a firm therefore has to protect franchise value by holding

---

6. For more details on this tradeoff see Stulz (2002).

on to more capital or by hedging. Both are costly, so firms that can manage risks better are more profitable.

With this logic, risk management may lead a financial institution to hold more capital than required by its regulators because it maximizes the wealth of its shareholders by doing so. However, the ability to manage risks also enables financial institutions to take complex risks that will be hard to detect by regulators. If the downside of such risks is likely to materialize in states of the world where governments will be tempted to bail out the financial institution, such risks may be taken even where they nominally endanger franchise value. Safety nets can therefore lead to inefficient risk taking.

Understanding the Range and Types of Risks

Managing expected firmwide risk, though necessary, is hard to do in practice. Measuring risk at the firm level would be drastically simplified if risk managers could simply model firmwide cash flow or firmwide value using time-series or cross-sectional data for these variables, or cross-sectional information. There is some evidence that time-series models of the lower tail of aggregate profit-and-loss (P&L; used as a benchmark in Berkovitz and O'Brien, 2002), and measures of cash flow risk based on comparables (Stein et al. 2001) can be reasonably successful. However, such approaches are difficult to implement in a way that appropriately reflects the risks of the financial institution at the time the measure is computed. They can be misleading if risks have changed significantly in the recent past. More importantly, such measures are not useful for the purpose of actually managing a firm's risk because they cannot be used to evaluate how various actions by the firm change its risk. Nor are they useful for monitoring risk taking, because they do not reveal which risks are large and which are small.

Instead, firms have focused on measuring risk from the bottom up, starting at the level of individual positions, business units, and individual trading desks. As a result, risk measurement is organized according to a taxonomy of risk types that has become richer as risk management has matured, but that remains incomplete.

Established Risks: Market, Credit, and Operational

Before the late 1980s, only interest rate risk was modeled quantitatively at the portfolio level. The modeling was usually crude, often consisting of simple interest rate sensitivity measures such as a one-year duration gap, but it was sufficient to keep most institutions out of trouble in an environment when most assets and liabilities were straight debt. As interest rate derivatives became more important, simulation of changes in portfolio value in response to different interest rate scenarios became more widespread.

Market risk modeling grew up in response to the stock market crashes of the late 1980s, to high-profile losses suffered by institutions victimized by "rogue traders," to the expanding scope of trading and market-making activities, and to the growing importance of derivatives positions.[7] Market risks are generally defined to be risks associated with fluctuations in prices of traded financial instruments. Increasingly, interest rate risk is often thought of as just one form of market risk that has an impact on the balance sheet that goes beyond its impact on the trading book.

As banks acquired more exposures to currencies, equities, and commodities through market-making in the spot markets and through derivatives trading, focusing most of their risk measurement efforts on their exposure to interest rates was no longer appropriate. They had to find ways to measure exposure to other factors and to aggregate their market-risk exposures to different factors. To do so, following the lead of Bankers Trust and JP Morgan, firms started using portfolio risk measures for their trading books. However, the standard portfolio risk measure—volatility—was not adequate, because the distributions of returns for portfolios, including derivatives, are generally not symmetric, so that volatility might hide substantial downside risk. To assess downside risk directly, banks focused on forecasting the VaR of a portfolio. With that approach, the VaR at the 5 percent probability level is the loss that will be exceeded with probability 0.05. Because trading books can change so quickly in liquid markets, most banks measured VaR over a one-day horizon. Though in principle all trading-book positions (and perhaps some less-liquid positions) could be included in VaR measures, achieving this goal was often difficult because different traders and trading groups had different computer systems and data architectures.[8]

Today, market VaR models are ubiquitous at all kinds of financial institutions, especially those that actively trade. They are used to assess portfolio risk, allocate capital internally, and evaluate alternative investment strategies. They are also part of internal control systems designed to detect excessive risk taking by individual units or traders, and often are part of incentive systems designed to optimize the level of risk taken by individual units or traders.

Portfolio credit risk modeling was only five years or so behind market risk modeling in the timing of the explosive phase of its adoption, but it represented a much larger cultural innovation in the financial community. Quantitative analysis of investment portfolios, based on financial theories such as the capital asset pricing model, became common decades before VaR models, and thus the growth of VaR models represented an expansion

7. Although a few VaR systems were implemented in the 1980s, the main watershed events were in the 1990s, including a Group of Thirty (1993) report and JP Morgan's 1994 launch of its RiskMetrics model.

8. Harmonizing data management across operations within large financial institutions, even if limited to trading activities, often involves extremely large IT expenditures.

of the toolkit rather than a wholesale change. In contrast, even through the early 1990s, credit risk was generally managed using intuition and rough approximations. Most commercial bank managers were aware that credit risk is the big gorilla for commercial banks, completely dominating other risk types as a source of bank insolvencies. But most of their efforts were focused on traditional analysis of financial statements to support appraisals of the default risk of individual borrowers. Perhaps this was because portfolio credit risk is far more difficult to model than market risk. Much of the important variation is at relatively low business-cycle frequencies, and data are sparse and harder to obtain than in the case of market risk. Moreover, distributions of returns on credit portfolios are highly skewed.

Early adopters of portfolio credit risk modeling in the United States were motivated by their near-death experiences during the 1990–91 recession. Others began to seriously incorporate credit risk modeling into their operations at least partly in response to the Basel Committee's (1999, 2001, 2004) proposals to embed credit VaR techniques in bank capital regulations. Some firms focused on measuring losses associated with default events, thus focusing on default rates and loss-given-default (so-called default-mode modeling). Others focused on measuring changes in the mark-to-market value of credit portfolios caused by any event.[9] Both approaches remain in widespread use.

Operational risk is a relative newcomer to the taxonomy. At this point, there is not even a generally accepted definition of operational risk. Some practitioners call operational risk all the risks that are not market and credit risks. Others follow the Basel II definition of operational risk: "the risk of direct or indirect loss resulting from inadequate or failed processes, people and systems or from external events."[10] Operational risk has become an important part of financial institution risk management efforts, partly because it was highlighted by the Basel Committee (2001), because of Section 404 of Sarbanes-Oxley and related regulations about internal controls, and because of the disruptions associated with the September 11, 2001, attacks. Though some still doubt whether it is material or even can be measured, financial institutions increasingly allocate capital to operational risk. For instance, a survey by Oliver Wyman and Company of ten large international banks found that they allocate 53 percent of their economic capital to credit risk, 21 percent to market risk and asset-liability rate risks, and 26 percent to operational and other risks.[11] One contribu-

---

9. The earliest models were CreditMetrics from JP Morgan, which focused on the mark-to-market value of credits, and CreditRisk+ from CSFB, which focused only on losses associated with default. See Stulz (2002), chapter 18, for a description of these models. Basel II is a prominent example of the default-mode approach.

10. See Basel Committee (2001), page 2.

11. See Kuritzkes, Schuermann, and Weiner (2002).

tion of this volume is de Fontnouvelle, Jordan, and Rosengren's evidence that operational risk is material. In addition to methodological contributions described subsequently, their evidence implies that operational-risk VaR is on the order of market-risk VaR for typical commercial banks, consistent with the survey results just cited.

Still-Early Days: Liquidity, Strategic, and Business Risk

Taken together, do market, credit, and operational risks represent the entirety of risk in financial institutions? If operational risk is defined so that it includes everything that is not market and credit risk, the three types of risk would represent the entirety of risk in financial institutions. But as a practical matter, operational risk modeling has come to focus on a subset of event types that are susceptible to internal measurement by individual financial institutions. Regulators have also chosen a narrow definition of operational risk. The definition of operational risk in the Basel II accord excludes risks such as strategic risks, reputational risks, and liquidity risks. Though operational risk includes many facets of what people would call business risk, many definitions of operational risk do not include the business cycle and fluctuations of the fee income of banks.

If one presumes that anything can be bought and sold for a price, an implication follows that financial institutions can raise liabilities or sell assets as needed, so liquidity risk would be subsumed by market risk. Periods characterized by liquidity problems would simply be periods when prices move a lot, and a good market risk model would capture the risk of such price movements. Such a view would be correct if the only dimension of liquidity risk is changing bid-ask spreads.[12] In this case, risk management modeling of changes in bid prices for long positions and ask prices for short positions would properly take into account liquidity. However, in general, this view is flawed, because when liquidity is imperfect the price at which an asset or a liability can be quickly sold depends on the quantity sold.[13] In practice, sometimes assets cannot be sold, and liabilities cannot be raised, at any price close to fundamental value in a timely fashion. Perhaps more unnerving, worries about future liquidity can lead to crashes as investors rush for the exits.[14] Commercial and central banks have worried about liquidity risk for centuries, and have evolved various mechanisms to deal with it. Indeed, Gatev, Schuermann, and Strahan's article in this volume offers evidence that the core business lines of banks (deposits and lines of credit) act as a kind of automatic stabilizer for the whole financial system during periods of stress, with liquid deposits flowing in from some clients just at the time when other clients need to make drawdowns on their lines.

12. Bangia, Diebold, Schuermann, and Stroughair (1999) extend the traditional VaR risk measurement model for changes in bid-ask spreads.
13. See Grossman and Miller (1988).
14. Bernardo and Welch (2004) provide a model of this phenomenon.

However, at the level of individual financial institutions, to our knowledge, liquidity risks have not yet been quantitatively analyzed in the same manner as market, credit, or operational risk. Perhaps because liquidity shortages are relatively rare and often are associated with other events, data are difficult to obtain and conceptual models are lacking. Thus, progress toward VaR-like models of liquidity risk or toward a careful incorporation of liquidity risk in market risk models may be slow.[15]

Business risk and strategic risk modeling are a little bit further along. Measures that focus on cash flow at risk (CaR) or earnings at risk (EaR) capture business risk.[16] Though similar to VaR measures in that the loss rate at a percentile of a loss distribution is measured, CaR or EaR measures assume that a firm's cash flows or earnings provide the correct measure of its capacity to finance investments and repay debt, whereas VaR measures implicitly assume that all the assets and liabilities included in the measure are liquid.[17] The modeling horizon of these measures is different for business and for strategic risk. For business risk, the horizon is usually a single accounting period; for example, a quarter. But strategic decisions cannot be evaluated in the context of one accounting period. Instead, one has to look over time to see how decisions will contribute to the value of the firm and how they will affect the risk of the firm. More generally, quantification of the risk of strategic decisions forces firms to make their assumptions precise and to more directly understand the risks involved in making such decisions.

Model Risk and Systemic Risk

A final part of the risk taxonomy—model risk—is a consequence of the growth of the new risk technologies. Model risk denotes the risk institutions face because of model errors. These errors can have a wide variety of causes. For instance, a pricing model could have a coding error, could have an assumption that leads to substantial biases in some states of the world, or wrong data could have been used as input. Concerns about model risk have been raised at both individual-institution and systemic levels. In the former case, the concern is that by building models into its management and control systems a financial institution may be led by a bad model to take large risks that it would never have taken in the absence of the model. This is a legitimate concern, but the practical solutions are obvious: human review of strategies and positions, use of multiple models, and simulation of the impact of hypothetical model errors.

15. Persaud (2003) includes some attempts at analyzing liquidity risk events.
16. Unfortunately, the alphabet soup used in risk management is not standardized. As a result, at some banks CaR means "capital-at-risk," essentially VaR, and not cash-flow-at-risk. At some other banks, EaR is the abbreviation used for P&L at risk, which again is VaR, not earnings-at-risk in the sense used here.
17. See Stulz (2002), chapter 4.

Systemic model risks have recently received more attention. The most common concern is that if financial institutions adopt a common risk-modeling framework, their tendency to herd will be amplified and markets may be destabilized (see Basak and Shapiro 2001, Danielsson, Shin, and Zigrand 2002, Persaud 2000, and Scholes 2000 for this and related ideas). Existing risk management models treat the risks of positions as exogenous, and are therefore of little use to financial institutions in evaluating the risks created by model-driven behavior, either their own behavior or that of other institutions. The current volume makes contributions to this debate on both sides. Adding to the concerns in the literature are Allen and Gale's model, which might be interpreted as raising concerns about inefficient regulatory use of risk management models. The papers of Jorion and Berkowitz and O'Brien assuage such concerns. Their papers show that there is little evidence that commercial bank market VaR forecasts are highly correlated, that banks take large exposures to market risks, or that P&L exposures to risk factors are highly correlated across banks—except, perhaps, for interest rate risks. The findings are strong enough and robust enough to support rejection of hypotheses that the use of VaR measures, either internally or for regulatory purposes, will be automatically destabilizing. This is an extremely important finding because it strengthens the case for moving forward with use and improvement of risk management techniques.

Similarly, Chan, Getmansky, Haas, and Lo do not find strong evidence of commonalities in the sensitivities of hedge fund indexes to risk factors, even though risk measures like VaR are used widely among hedge funds. However, they do find evidence that bank stock returns are correlated with hedge fund returns, suggesting that further investigation into channels of contagion is needed.

Measuring Firmwide Risk

Although analyzing each type of risk in isolation allows measures to be customized to suit the properties of the risk, and thus improves their quality as stand-alone measures, at some point the different risk measures must be combined to give a view of risk for a whole financial institution—a firmwide risk measure. As noted previously, this has proved challenging. Often, financial institutions attempting to measure firmwide risk found that they had information systems that could not talk to one another, that they had little computer-readable historical data (except in their trading activities), and that they had no records at all of information important to the assessment of risks. Even partial solutions to these problems can require huge investments in information technology.

More fundamentally, however, financial institutions find it difficult to aggregate firmwide risks for three important reasons:

1. The shapes of distributions differ for different types of risk, so that the analysis of the aggregated risks is not straightforward. Whereas distributions for market risks are typically close to symmetric but with fat tails, distributions for credit risks and for operational risks are extremely skewed. With debt, the most the financial institution can receive is the promised payments—but it can lose the whole position. With operational risks, the high-frequency losses are typically small, but there is also the potential for extremely large losses, which have a low probability of occurring. Such differences in risk distribution typically make it inappropriate to use simple portfolio risk formulas to aggregate market, credit, and operational risks because means, variances, and covariances are not sufficient statistics for these risk distributions.

2. Conditional correlations of different types of risk are hard to measure with confidence. For instance, the historical record suggests that bad-tail market and credit risk outcomes are correlated—but not perfectly—and historical data do not cover enough potential states of the world. Further, correlation may not be the appropriate measure of dependence between these various types of risks because of their fat tails.[18] In particular, it is possible that tail outcomes of different types of risks are more highly correlated than other outcomes. Chan, Getmansky, Haas, and Lo in this volume discuss the phenomenon of "phase-locking," meaning states of the world where many variables become very highly correlated that otherwise tend not to be.

3. As discussed previously, risk tends to be measured over different horizons for different types of risks, but to aggregate risks at the firm level they need to be forecasted over comparable periods. For market risk, the focus is generally on days; for operational risk and credit risk, it is often on one budget year. We lack clear foundations for existing choices of horizon. They appear to be empirical compromises, driven by the nature of the positions being modeled, the needs of internal control systems, and the nature of available data. But we have little idea of how to do things differently. One approach to the problem is a framework advocated by a consulting firm, Algorithmics, named Mark-to-Future. This framework differs from traditional VaR calculations in that the simulations are computed over multiple periods and allow for actions by firms to be path dependent. However, in practice, implementation of such a framework faces a multitude of obstacles.

Firms and regulators have often approached the firmwide risk aggregation problem by using ad hoc assumptions about correlations. An example is the National Association of Insurance Commissioners' (NAIC) risk-based capital regime for insurance companies, in which risks are aggregated by a formula based on relatively simple but rather arbitrary cor-

---

18. The existence of fat tails explains the growing importance of the copula measure of dependence used in the extreme-value literature. See Rosenberg and Schuermann (2006).

relation assumptions. Another possibility is to stop short of aggregating bottom-up risk measures, turning instead to alternative measures of risk at the whole-institution level.

How to Model Risks, Including Systemic Risks

Especially if model-induced herding is less of a concern, it seems obvious that better measurement is good. Both practitioners and researchers seem to have agreed with this view over the past couple of decades. Much attention has been given to details of measurement, but much remains to be done. The papers in this volume make a number of new contributions.

Market Risk

The RiskMetrics approach proposed by JP Morgan became especially popular as JP Morgan made the methodology and the daily data freely available. This approach forecasts volatilities and correlations for a number of risk factors, assuming returns to be conditionally normal, and uses exponential weighting for the forecasts. The risks of positions are then represented in terms of exposures to the risk factors, so that the return of the portfolio becomes a weighted average of the returns of the risk factors. The volatility of a portfolio can then be computed using the formula for the variance of a portfolio. The approach is mostly focused on forecasting the risk of the portfolio over the next day, making the assumption that expected returns equal zero reasonable. Under such assumptions, the VaR at the 95 percent confidence interval is simply 1.65 times the volatility of the portfolio. Andersen, Bollerslev, Christoffersen, and Diebold in this volume discuss some of the weaknesses of this approach (and other approaches that ignore serial correlation in volatilities) and show ways to overcome them.

Early users of RiskMetrics soon began to focus more on simulations of portfolio values, because portfolio risk formulas could not handle well the risks of derivatives. Moreover, the normal distribution that was used almost exclusively in early implementations of VaR proved flawed for market risk because relevant empirical distributions have fat tails. However, parametric distributions that could be used to replace the normal distribution were generally viewed as impractical for large portfolios. The basic idea of simulation methods is to estimate portfolio value in a realistic array of circumstances, conditional on the details of portfolio positions. This led firms to either simulate risk factors using estimated distributions for each factor, an approach involving Monte Carlo simulation, or to use so-called historical simulation, wherein portfolio returns are simulated from historical realizations of risk factors.[19] Historical simulation became an espe-

19. For a detailed description of these approaches, see Jorion (2000).

cially practical way to address the problem of the inadequacies of the normal distribution.

In practical applications, the historical simulation approach is often insufficiently conditional—that is, it does not take sufficiently into account the recent past, so that sharp increases in volatility that will persist in the near future are not given sufficient weight.[20] Existing evidence on the performance of VaR models at large banks shows that they had an unusual number of days where the VaR was exceeded ("exceedances") in August and September 1998 (see Berkovitz and O'Brien 2002), demonstrating that the models fail to adequately capture the changes in the joint distribution of returns that took place during that period. Chan, Getmansky, Haas, and Lo point out that inferences about risk can be acutely sensitive to the sample period used to generate risk measures. As a result, quiet periods will lead to low VaRs. Andersen, Bollerslev, Christoffersen, and Diebold show how important it is to recognize time-varying volatility and correlation in VaR estimation. They demonstrate how this can be done using parametric generalized autoregressive conditional heteroskedasticity (GARCH) modeling, filtered historical simulation, and high-frequency data.

The model risks of risk measurement make it essential for institutions to use additional risk measures and not focus on VaR only. One contribution of Chan, Getmansky, Haas, and Lo is to provide an array of alternative risk measures in the context of their analysis of hedge fund risk.

In recent years, practitioners and regulators have put much emphasis on the use of stress tests as an alternative to VaR. Stress tests measure the impact on portfolio value of shocks to key risk factors. For example, a stress test might investigate how a bank would perform if an earlier market disruption, such as the events of August and September 1998, were repeated; any scenario, however, including one outside the boundaries of historical experience, can be used.[21] Stress test methods essentially make no use of statistical and econometric theory. They became popular because of generic concerns about model inadequacies and especially because it is difficult to model volatility and correlation behavior in times of market stress. Much has been made in the literature of correlation breakdowns in such times; the principals at LTCM are on record in stating that their correlation assumptions fell apart in August and September 1998.[22]

After describing the problems that arise in capturing time-varying volatility when there are a large number of factors, Andersen, Bollerslev, Christoffersen, and Diebold show how new techniques in multivariate time-series estimation could be usefully brought to bear to address some of the problems that pushed banks toward historical simulation and stress test-

20. Pritsker (2001) analyzes this issue in detail.
21. The Committee on the Global Financial System (2001) provides a detailed survey of stress tests across financial institutions.
22. See McKenzie (2003).

ing. They argue for an evolution of market-risk modeling of asset-return volatility and correlations away from both parametric (RiskMetrics-like) and historical-simulation methods. Instead, where feasible, they suggest the use of nonparametric volatility measurement, using high-frequency data, paired with parametric volatility models designed to support computationally efficient solutions to high-dimensional problems. Strikingly, they propose the development of risk management systems with a limited number of risk factors (less than thirty), but for which intraday data would be available and hence volatility and correlation forecasts more reliable. It remains to be seen whether such an approach could capture the risks that financial institutions now model using a much larger number of factors.

Andersen, Bollerslev, Christoffersen, and Diebold also point out the practical problems of dimensionality that arise when the number of positions is large and large numbers of factors must be used, as is common at the largest banks today. A large bank active in trading may use more than 1,000 risk factors and have more than 100,000 positions, each of which must be repriced for each draw of the underlying factors. Computational burdens of repricing are high because of nonlinear sensitivities of prices to factors. Even with RiskMetrics-style parametric modeling using a normal distribution, 1,000 factors requires modeling over 500,000 variances and covariances. Dimension reduction methods help, but they also introduce estimation errors and still require a large number of parameters to be estimated.

Credit Risk

Using a multifactor portfolio credit risk model that includes explicit dynamic modeling of macroeconomic dynamics, Pesaran, Schuermann, and Treutler offer evidence of considerably larger benefits of credit diversification than are implied by current workhorse models. The simplest portfolio credit risk model, which is widely used, has only a single systematic factor and is a model in which all borrowers have the same exposure to the factor (Gordy 2003). Commonly used model implementations, such as Credit-Metrics, are multifactor to some extent (multiple equity indexes may be included as factors and each firm may have different factor loadings), but for large portfolios an overall average equity factor often drives model results. Moreover, examination of implications of intuitively generated scenarios can be difficult. In contrast, Pesaran, Schuermann, and Treutler's setup features explicit and observable macroeconomic and industry factors and has a built-in small macroeconomic model. It can be used to study the implications of a variety of shock types. The model implies that credit VaR for a globally and industrially diversified portfolio is quite a bit smaller than credit VaR from one of the standard models for the same portfolio.

Operational Risk

As noted previously, de Fontnouvelle, Jordan, and Rosengren offer evidence that operational risk is a quantitatively important element of the risk management taxonomy. They also examine the properties of different estimators of operational VaR. They consider parametric approaches to estimating quantiles of the operational loss distribution and find that fat-tailed distribution functions perform well in some respects but not in others (thin-tailed functions perform poorly in almost every respect). In contrast, a technique from the extreme value theory (EVT) literature performs well in the most important respects.

Systemic Risk

Practitioners rarely model crisis events or systemic risk, preferring to turn to scenario analysis when they consider such events at all. In contrast, public policymakers are most concerned with such events. Hartmann, Straetmans, and de Vries offer methods and evidence that should be useful to both audiences. Using techniques from EVT, they measure bad-tail comovements of equity returns of major banks in the United States and in euro-area countries. Where the amplitude of such comovements is large but not associated with catastrophic deteriorations in bank condition, the comovements can be thought of as a form of systematic risk that is of particular interest to credit-risk modelers at bank counterparties and also to market-risk modelers with significant major bank exposures in their portfolios. Where the comovements are very large or indicative of bank distress, the authors' measures can be thought of as indicators of systemic risk. Though surely not capturing all aspects of systemic risk, any such measures remain useful to students of a subject that has proved resistant to empirical analysis.

Risk Shifting, Risk Transformation, and the Industrial Organization of Finance

It is axiomatic that diversification in portfolios is good, and thus that new opportunities to cost-effectively diversify portfolios are desirable. The creation of new instruments, and entry of formerly specialized financial institutions into each other's markets (insurance companies into syndicated loans, banks into investment banking, etc.) are to some extent a result of better measurement, which has revealed previously underappreciated opportunities for diversification. Such developments also are a result of the greater transparency and greater feasibility of new instruments that better risk measurement confers.

However, axioms that diversification and innovation are good are subject to qualification. Diversification of activities as opposed to diversification of portfolios has costs. There is now a large literature that shows that diversified firms are valued less than specialized firms. Recent evidence on diversification within the financial industry shows that it is not clear that shareholders benefit from diversification.[23] At the same time, however, the new ways of managing risk have an impact on the optimal size of institutions. First, modern risk management involves large fixed costs. For example, once a risk measurement and monitoring system is in place to measure the risk of a trading desk, the cost of the system is mostly unaffected by the scale of the positions of the desk. Second, to the extent that a cost of conglomeration is that it is harder to manage a multidivision firm than a single-division firm, the new practices in risk management make it easier to measure and manage risks in conglomerates.

Rather than taking on diversifying activities, firms can shed risks and take on risks within existing activities to increase their level of diversification within these activities. However, managing risks through risk transfer has beneficial systemic effects only to the extent that those who take on the risks are in a better position to bear them than those who shed them. It is not always clear that this is the case when risk transfer is motivated mainly by regulation. Further, the amount of risk transferred may be less than meets the eye because of implicit commitments and because of structures that lack transparency.

In this volume, Allen and Gale's paper shows that inefficient regulation can lead to risk-transfer activity that is focused on evasion of regulation, and that such activity can increase systemic risk. Gorton and Souleles offer evidence that credit card securitizations do not transfer as much risk as a literal interpretation of such structures might imply, because sponsors enter into an implicit contract to make up the losses suffered by external investors in many states of the world. Considerable tail risk is still transferred, because sponsors will default on the implicit contract when they are near insolvency themselves. However, one can imagine scenarios involving serially correlated shocks to the sponsor's solvency in which support of securitizations early in the game weakens the sponsor enough that later shocks push it into insolvency.

Franke and Krahnen offer evidence that European securitizations increase the systematic risk exposure of sponsoring banks. Sponsors retain the equity tranche, which absorbs the first losses on the securitized pool of assets. A large fraction of the default risk is retained by the sponsor. The net effect of a securitization on a sponsor's risk posture depends on the associated investment behavior. If, in a true sale, the sponsor reinvests the proceeds in risk-free assets or to pay down debt, then systematic risk will fall, because the bank has less asset risk or less leverage. If, however, the

---

23. See Laeven and Levine (2005).

sponsor reinvests the proceeds in risky loans of comparable quality, then the sponsor's systematic risks increases, because it has a similar portfolio to the one it had before plus exposure to first losses, which is a high beta asset. By examining changes in bank betas, Franke and Krahnen offer evidence that systematic risk rises. Although systematic risk is not the same as systemic risk, so it is not clear that there is a public policy concern, their finding implies that common assumptions that securitization is risk reducing for the sponsor may need to be qualified.

As noted previously, modern risk management is providing some of the impetus for changes in the industrial organization of finance. This volume's only study that touches upon consolidation is Beck, Demirgüç-Kunt, and Levine's examination of the relationship between systemic stability and concentration. We discuss their work later rather than here because it does not examine the effect of risk management on concentration. But Chan, Getmansky, Haas, and Lo's paper illuminates the increasing role of hedge funds, a type of institution that has grown dramatically in recent years. The evolution in risk measurement no doubt had a role in the growth of hedge funds. A better understanding of the implications of proprietary trading risks within diversified financial institutions probably made it less attractive for such institutions to bear some of these risks. Improvements in risk measurement also made it easier for stand-alone hedge funds to borrow, because their lenders could better monitor the risk in hedge fund positions.

Legal Regime, Regulation, Disclosure, and Systemic Stability

The changes in capital markets and the crisis events that led to the new risk management techniques, as well as the techniques themselves, both depend upon and influence the legal and regulatory environment in which they are used. They depend on the environment, because good data and enforceable contracts are essential to risk measurement and to the engineering of new financial products. They are influencing the environment by changing how regulators and central bankers think about systemic risk, and by supporting the development of more risk-sensitive regulatory regimes, such as Basel II.

Possible Unintended Effects of Regulation and Disclosure

The dramatic progress in financial engineering technology has made regulation that simplistically specifies required capital for specific positions increasingly ineffective. As discussed in the context of the Allen and Gale paper, it may well be that such regulation leads to more rather than less systemic risk. It also forces the regulators to constantly play catch-up. As a result, regulation has evolved so that capital requirements depend on measures of the overall risk taken by an institution rather than on positions taken by that institution. The obvious difficulty then becomes how risk can be measured for the purpose of setting capital requirements. Since financial institutions measure risk, it made sense for regulators to try to use their risk measures to set capital. Regulators did so first for market risk with the market risk amendment to the Basel Accord, which came into effect in 1998. Now, with Basel II, they will make some use of internal measures for credit and operational risks.

If banks can use their own risk models, there is a risk that they will manipulate them to lower their capital requirements. Similarly, if risk measures become a part of an institution's public disclosures, incentives arise to choose measures that window-dress the institution's risk posture. There is danger that the dialectic between external users and internal incentives can cause risk measures to be less effective tools for management of the institution.

For example, to prevent manipulation of measures that drive capital requirements for market risk, bank regulators have introduced many safeguards, including mandatory backtesting of the VaR model used for regulatory capital. Banks that are too optimistic in their VaR forecasts are penalized, giving banks an incentive to be pessimistic, rather than rewarding precision in VaR estimates by penalizing banks for being too pessimistic as well. Moreover, as discussed in Jorion's paper, for the measurement of market risk, regulators specify the dataset banks can use as well as how observations can be weighted. For credit risk, under Basel II, regulators will not permit banks to use their internal credit VaR models to set capital, but instead will let them use some inputs to their models as inputs to a simplified regulatory credit VaR model. In none of these cases are banks required to use the regulatory measures for internal management purposes, so perhaps undesirable side effects of regulatory use of internal measures in these cases are modest.

But supporting the general concern, Berkovitz and O'Brien (2002) show that the market risk VaR measures of very large banks in the United States seem to be systematically too conservative. While conservative risk measures might please regulators, since they mean that banks face higher capital requirements, such measures are less useful for managing institutions, since they do not provide an unbiased estimate of risk.

Use of internal measures in regulation also creates concern that the use of similar risk models to satisfy regulators as well as for the management of firms, perhaps as a means of limiting risk-management costs, will stifle innovation in risk management and make risk models less useful. For instance, some of the techniques advocated by Andersen, Bollerslev, Christoffersen, and Diebold would not meet current regulatory requirements, because they put too much weight on recent observations, even though the evidence marshaled by the authors shows that such techniques produce superior measures of risk.

Cost pressures to adopt regulatory measures for internal use could be especially material if regulators specify types of measures not used internally. Although VaR measures are useful for measuring and managing the distress probability of firms, they may not be the best measures for use in regulation. To see this, consider a firm that faces financial distress if its equity capital falls below a threshold, say $10 billion. If that firm wants its probability of financial distress to be 0.05 percent at the end of the fiscal year, then it should have equity capital above its threshold at least equal to its 0.05 percent VaR at the beginning of its fiscal year. The firm then has a probability of losing its buffer of 0.05 percent and hence a probability of financial distress of 0.05 percent. However, VaR measures are questionable as instruments to set capital requirements. After all, two banks with the same VaR could have vastly different expected losses if the VaR is exceeded. These expected losses have led to a new risk measure, the expected tail loss if VaR is exceeded, called conditional VaR, or CVaR. If two banks have a VaR of $100 million but one bank has a CVaR of $1 billion while the other has a CVaR of $1 million, these two banks would not pose equal threats to the financial system. In many ways, CVaR would be a better risk measure from the perspective of measuring potential systemic threats. However, to date regulators have stuck with measures similar to those in common use at financial institutions, perhaps because CVaR is harder to estimate than VaR, since it requires an estimate of the whole tail of the firmwide loss distribution.

Financial institutions have been prodded toward greater risk transparency by bank regulators, but nonbank institutions have also chosen to be more transparent. Risk transparency has considerable benefits, since it makes it easier for outsiders to monitor the safety of financial institutions and create incentives for those who run them to manage risk well. Unfortunately, transparency has costs also. Rather than focusing institutions on producing unbiased and precise risk measures, it may give them incentives to produce conservative but less useful risk measures. Such an attitude leads to the odd development, in the context of scientific risk measurement, of having institutions declare victory when the number of VaR breaches is too low compared to the expected number.

Stepping back to examine welfare, Pelizzon and Schaefer's paper reveals that optimal safety-and-soundness regulatory design is sensitive to the sophistication of available risk management and regulatory monitoring and intervention technologies, and to the ability of banks to quickly shift their portfolio risk posture. The relationship between the economic environment and the nature of optimal regulation is not simple. In what might be called the prerisk-management environment, say thirty or more years ago in the United States, bank risk postures were relatively transparent to regulators but also were hard to change, so that a bank in trouble could not quickly shed risk in order to increase the chance of staying solvent. Capital regulations, though crude by modern standards, were relatively hard to evade. Pelizzon and Schaefer's results imply that in the old environment, the existence of risk-based capital requirements was more important to welfare than precise calibration of the requirements, and the welfare benefit of early bank-closure rules was not obvious, so that the regulatory environment of the time was perhaps appropriate. But then the new risk measurement and management techniques changed the world drastically. In what one might call a 1990s environment, in which banks could use new instruments and risk-management technologies to easily evade archaic capital regulations, capital regulation itself arguably was welfare-reducing, but early-closure rules were importantly welfare-enhancing (and were implemented in the United States). It is difficult to know the practical implications of Pelizzon and Schaefer's results for the coming Basel II environment. Much depends on whether the new capital regulations are sufficiently responsive to risk so that they once again become difficult to evade, and also on whether banks will be able to quickly shed risk at low cost in response to an early intervention by regulators.

Systemic Stability

Beck, Demirgüç-Kunt, and Levine's paper examines the relationship between bank concentration at the national level and systemic stability, wherein instability is measured by the incidence of banking crises. They find that concentration is associated with more stability, not less, as is often claimed, but that the relationship is not a result of the competitive environment. Neither do features of the bank regulatory regime influence stability. They speculate that larger banks are more diversified and thus systems composed of large banks are more stable. We believe their results are also consistent with a view that if risk measurement and management techniques make management of very large banks more feasible, and more such banks appear, systemic stability will be enhanced. But our hypothesis cannot be tested with their data because few banks in the emerging-market nations that dominate their sample employed modern risk management techniques during the sample period.

As noted previously, other papers in this volume contribute to an understanding of the relationship between risk management, regulation, and systemic stability. Jorion offers evidence that practitioner and regulatory use of market VaR measures is not likely to be destabilizing. Berkovitz and O'Brien show that exposures to market risk are typically limited and not highly correlated across firms. Gorton and Souleles, Franke and Krahnen, and Allen and Gale offer evidence and models showing that the details of how securitizations are structured and used are important to their net effect on bank insolvency risk and systemic risk. Hartmann, Straetmans, and de Vries offer measures of the size of systematic relationships among United States and euro-area banks.

Some Speculations about Ways Forward

We believe the new risk measurement and management technology is best viewed as a kind of machinery that, overall, improves welfare by improving the efficiency of financial institutions and by reducing systemic risks in the financial sector. It should be neither feared nor deified. Like any machinery, methods and models that work poorly in the sense of being unrealistic might be harmful in that they might lead to decisions inferior to those associated with better methods and models. It is likely that much more time and experience will be needed before many kinds of crisis events can be adequately captured in risk measures, and it is even possible that risk models will, in effect, malfunction during some crises. These will be growing pains. The way forward is to diagnose weaknesses in measures, models, and management methods, fix them as necessary, and improve them when possible.

The machinery we have discussed creates risks also, however. An institution that is well equipped to measure and manage risks can increase risk, as well as decrease it, more efficiently than an institution that is not well equipped. While risk transparency would seem to make it harder for institutions to take on too much risk, risk measures can be manipulated and transparency has costs. There is always a danger that measuring risk carefully, with well-defined risk measures, just pushes risk where it is not measured. More-detailed regulations of risk measurement are unlikely to prevent these problems, as the resourcefulness of financial engineers knows few bounds. Ultimately, a financial institution's governance plays a key role in ensuring that its risk position is optimal from the perspective of its owners. As long as regulations do not make excessive risk taking optimal and as long as financial institutions are well governed, we would expect improved risk measurement and management to enhance welfare.

Better risk measurement should be a continuing part of the research agenda, as well as better understanding of how to optimize the legal environment and regulatory policies and practices. Though VaR and stress tests dominate risk management now, the motivation for the use of these tools is mostly practical. In principle, risk management should help firms take risks that make money for them and shed those that do not. It is not clear that VaR and stress tests are the best solution for profit maximization.

Though regulators and central banks have been ready to deal with the classic systemic crisis involving bank runs, they are acquiring new roles as they are called upon to ensure systemic liquidity in all kinds of crisis situations and to act as coordinating agents in the diagnosis and repair of systemic problems. Often such coordination does not involve regulation but rather a fostering of technical and institutional advances. In the past decade or so, both regulators and market participants seem to have become increasingly comfortable with such a role for the official sector, and the official sector has played a significant role in the developments we have discussed. Yet this role of the official sector does raise a troubling issue. If the official sector is an instrument of progress in risk management, why is it that private firms could not make such progress on their own? Is it because the official sector values risk management more than private firms because of externalities, so that there is an implicit subsidy from the public sector to the development of risk management? Or is it that many private firms value risk management too little because of governance failures? Or that free-rider problems interfere with the uncoordinated development of certain kinds of risk management innovations?

References

Bangia, A., F. X. Diebold, T. Schuermann, and J. Stroughair. 2001. Modeling liquidity risk, with implications for traditional market risk measurement and management. In *Risk Management: The State of the Art,* ed. S. Figlewski and R. Levich, 1–13. Amsterdam: Kluwer Academic. (Originally published in 1999 in abridged form as "Liquidity on the outside," *Risk Magazine* 12:68–73.)

Basak, S., and A. Shapiro. 2001. Value-at-risk-based risk management: Optimal policies and asset prices. *Review of Financial Studies* 14:371–405.

Basel Committee on Banking Supervision. 1999. *A new capital adequacy framework.* Basel: Bank for International Settlements.

———. 2001. *The new Basel capital accord: Second consultative paper.* Basel: Bank for International Settlements.

———. 2004. *Basel II: International convergence of capital measurement and capital standards: A revised framework.* Basel: Bank for International Settlements.

Berkowitz, J., and J. O'Brien. 2002. How accurate are value-at-risk models at commercial banks? *Journal of Finance* 57:1093–1111.

Bernardo, A., and I. Welch. 2004. Liquidity and financial market runs. *Quarterly Journal of Economics* 119:135–58.

Committee on the Global Financial System. 2001. A survey of stress tests and current practice at major financial institutions. Basel: Bank for International Settlements.

Danielsson, J., H.-S. Shin, and J.-P. Zigrand. 2002. The impact of risk regulation on price dynamics. Financial Markets Group, London School of Economics. Unpublished working paper.

Demirgüç-Kunt, A., and E. Detragiache. 2001. Does deposit insurance increase banking system stability? An empirical investigation. *Journal of Monetary Economics* 49:1373–1406.

Diamond, D. W., and P. H. Dybvig. 1983. Bank runs, deposit insurance, and liquidity. *Journal of Political Economy* 91:401–19.

Gordy, M. 2003. A risk-factor model foundation for ratings-based capital rules. *Journal of Financial Intermediation* 12:199–232.

Grossman, S. J., and M. H. Miller. 1988. Liquidity and market structure. *Journal of Finance* 43:617–33.

Group of Thirty. 1993. *Derivatives: Practices and Principles.* Washington, DC: Group of Thirty.

Jorion, P. 2000. *Value-at-risk: The new benchmark.* New York: McGraw-Hill.

Kuritzkes, A., T. Schuermann, and S. M. Weiner. 2002. Risk measurement, risk management and capital adequacy in financial conglomerates. Financial Institutions Center, Wharton School, University of Pennsylvania, Philadelphia. Working paper.

Laeven, L., and R. Levine. 2005. Is there a diversification discount in financial conglomerates. University of Minnesota, Minneapolis. Unpublished working paper.

MacKenzie, D. 2003. Long-Term Capital Management and the sociology of arbitrage. *Economy and Society* 32:349–80.

Merton, R. C. 1992. Operation and regulation in financial intermediation: A functional perspective. HBS Working Paper 93-020. Cambridge, MA: Harvard Business School.

Merton, R. C., and A. F. Perold. 1993. Theory of risk capital in financial firms. *Journal of Applied Corporate Finance* 6(3): 16–32.

Myers, S. C. 1977. Determinants of corporate borrowing. *Journal of Financial Economics* 5:147–75.

Myers, S. C., and N. S. Majluf. 1984. Corporate financing and investment decisions when firms have information that investors do not have. *Journal of Financial Economics* 13:187–221.

Persaud, A. D. 2000. Sending the herd off the cliff edge: The disturbing interaction between herding and market-sensitive risk management practices. *Journal of Risk Finance* 2:59–65.

———, ed. 2003. *Liquidity black holes.* London: Risk Books.

Pritsker, M. 2001. The hidden dangers of historical simulation. Washington, DC: Federal Reserve Board. Unpublished working paper.

Rosenberg, J., and T. Schuermann. 2006. A general approach to integrated risk management with skewed, fat-tailed risk. *Journal of Financial Economics,* forthcoming.

Scholes, M. S. 2000. Crisis and risk management. *American Economic Review* 90: 17–21.

Stein, J., S. Usher, D. LaGattuta, and J. Youngen. 2001. A comparables approach to measuring cashflow-at-risk for non-financial firms. *Journal of Applied Corporate Finance,* Winter, 100–109.

Stulz, René. 2002. *Risk management and derivatives.* Cincinnati, OH: South-Western Publishing.

———. 2004. Should we fear derivatives? *Journal of Economic Perspectives* 18: 173–92.

I

Market Risk, Risk Modeling, and Financial System Stability

1

Bank Trading Risk and Systemic Risk

Philippe Jorion

1.1 Introduction

The last decade has witnessed a revolution in financial risk management. Quantitative techniques such as option pricing, portfolio insurance, and value at risk (VaR) have become essential tools of portfolio management. The generalized use of these techniques, however, has raised concerns that they could induce similar trading patterns, or "herding," across banks using VaR systems to limit their risks. As the argument goes, some exogenous shock to volatility could push VaR above the limit, forcing banks to liquidate their positions, further depressing falling prices.

If so, the generalized use of risk management systems could cause higher volatility in times of stress, perversely making financial markets less safe than before. This could raise the prospect of systemic risk, which arises when a shock threatens to create multiple simultaneous failures in financial institutions.

Various theories have been advanced to explain herding behavior. A necessary precondition for herding is that investors within a group tend to buy (or sell) when similar participants buy (or sell). This could reflect the belief that other investors have superior information, as in informational cascade theories.[1] Alternatively, another class of contagion theories emphasizes the effect of liquidity shocks, which force some market participants to liquidate their holdings to obtain cash, perhaps due to a call for additional collateral.[2] This applies to participants with high leverage, such as bank-

1. See Bikhchandani, Hirshleifer, and Welch (1992), Banerjee (1992), or more recently Morris and Shin (1998). Bikhchandani, Hirshleifer, and Welch (1998) provide a useful survey of contagion models based on information asymmetries.
2. See Kodres and Pritsker (2002).

proprietary trading desks or hedge funds. The herding effect due to VaR is closest to this latter explanation. We can classify these herding theories into "information-based" and "constraint-based" theories.

In practice, the VaR-induced herding effect depends on commonalities in the positions in financial institutions. As Morris and Shin (1999, p. 141) have stated, "One theme which has emerged in the subsequent debate on the performance of the risk management systems has been the criticism that many financial entities entered the period of turbulence with very similar trading positions."

Thus, VaR herding requires similar positions across VaR-constrained institutions. This study tests this hypothesis by investigating the ex ante and ex post trading risk profile of U.S. commercial banks, based on quarterly banking reports over the period 1995 to 2003. These reports contain information on quarterly trading revenues broken down by risk factor category as well as the overall VaR-based market risk charge. Using segment information, broken down into fixed income, currencies, equities, and commodities categories should prove useful to detect commonalities in positions. To my knowledge, this is the first paper to do so.

Similar positions should be revealed by high correlations between banks' trading revenues as well as between banks' VaR measures. We also examine correlation patterns across risk categories to assess diversification effects. Finally, we examine the variance of aggregate trading returns from banks in the sample and break it down into different components to examine diversification effects across the industry. As a by-product of the analysis, this paper also evaluates the profitability of bank trading revenues, thus contributing to the literature on diversification in banking.[3]

This paper is structured as follows. Section 1.2 provides a review of VaR and herding theories. Section 1.3 presents the empirical analysis, and section 1.4 concludes.

1.2   VaR and Systemic Risk

In recent years, VaR has become a universally accepted benchmark for measuring market risk. The Basel Committee on Banking Supervision (BCBS), for example, provides annual descriptions of market risk disclosures by banks and securities houses. In 1993, only 5 percent of the sample reported VaR information. By 2001, this proportion had gone up to 98 percent. In addition to its role as a ubiquitous *passive* risk measure, VaR has become a tool for the *active* management of risk, including setting risk limits and capital charges. Much of this development was spurred by regulatory standards for capital requirements.

---

3. Stiroh (2004) provides a review of this literature. He shows that noninterest income has increased in importance for U.S. banks and is much more volatile than traditional interest income, based on accounting data.

1.2.1   The VaR Capital Charge

The use of internal VaR models was officially sanctioned by the BCBS, which amended the 1988 Basel Accord to include a charge for market risk (BCBS 1995, 1996). Since January 1998, banks have had a choice between using a standardized method, using predefined rules, or their own internal VaR measure as the basis for their capital charge for market risk. Because in practice the internal-model approach leads to lower capital charges than the standardized model, this has led to the generalized use of VaR methods.

To use the internal-model approach, a bank must first satisfy various qualitative requirements. The bank must demonstrate that it has a sound risk-management system, which must be integrated into management decisions. Notably, the bank has to use the regulatory VaR forecast directly for management decisions. This point is important, as it forces commercial banks to use the same parameters as dictated by the Basel rules.

When the qualitative requirements are satisfied, the market risk charge is based on the following quantitative parameters for VaR: (1) a horizon of ten trading days, or two calendar weeks, (2) a 99 percent confidence interval, and (3) an observation period based on at least a year of historical data and updated at least once a quarter.[4] In practice, banks are allowed to compute their ten-day VaR by scaling up their one-day VaR by the square root of 10.

The market risk charge (MRC) is then computed as the sum of a general market risk charge and a specific risk charge (SRC). The latter represents the risk of individual issues that is not reflected in the general market risk measure. The general market risk charge is taken as the higher of the previous day's VaR, or the average VaR over the last sixty business days, times a multiplicative factor k:

$$(1) \qquad \mathrm{MRC}_t = \mathrm{Max}\!\left(k\frac{1}{60}\sum_{t=1}^{60}\mathrm{VAR}_{t-i}, \mathrm{VAR}_{t-1}\right) + \mathrm{SRC}_t,$$

where k is to be determined by local regulators, subject to an absolute floor of three.[5] In practice, the first term in the parentheses is binding because it is multiplied by a factor of at least three. Banks are also subject to a backtest that compares the daily VaR to the subsequent profit and loss (P&L). Banks that fail the backtest can be subject to an increase in k from three to four.[6]

In this application, VaR is used to determine the minimum amount of

---

4. More precisely, the average duration of historical observations must be at least six months.

5. The specific risk charge is explained in more detail in the Basel Amendment (1996).

6. The backtesting procedure consists of matching daily VaR with the subsequent P&L. If a loss exceeds the VaR, an exception is said to have occurred. Banks can have up to four exceptions over the previous year. Beyond four exceptions, k is increased progressively, subject to the regulator's evaluation of the cause for the exception, and reaches four for ten or more exceptions.

equity capital that the bank must carry as protection against market risk. It can be viewed as a measure of economic capital to support the trading activities.

1.2.2   The VaR Vicious Circle Hypothesis

Some recent literature has emphasized the limitations of VaR. VaR is a single summary measure of downside loss. Because VaR only represents one quantile of the P&L distribution, it gives no indication about the tail loss, beyond the quantile. In theory, traders could willfully attempt to game their VaR limit by altering the distribution of P&L to satisfy a fixed VaR at the expense of a small probability of large losses.[7]

Other authors argue that widespread use of VaR could actually increase systemic risk. The novel aspect of the Basel market risk charge is that, for the first time, it creates capital requirements that are risk sensitive. The internal model approach was put into operation in January 1998. It so happened that 1998 was a tumultuous year.

The Russian default of 1998 triggered turbulences in financial markets that eventually led to the collapse of the hedge fund Long-term Capital Management (LTCM). In the search for culprits, fingers have pointed to the generalized use of risk measures such as VaR. Some observers claimed that the application of strict VaR limits led to position-cutting by traders, which put additional downward pressures on prices. These claims have been advanced by Dunbar (2000) in his book on LTCM, by Persaud (2000), and have also been echoed in the press. Likewise, Scholes (2000, p. 20) states that "banks and financial entities . . . add to the volatility in financial crises."

The argument is that some shock in volatility, say due to the Russian default, increases the VaR of outstanding positions. In 1999, *The Economist* (June 10; pp. 65–66) has argued that, as VaR goes up, a "bank is then faced with two choices: put in extra capital or reduce its positions, whatever and wherever they may be. This is what happened last autumn." As the argument goes, several banks could sell the same asset at the same time, creating higher volatility and correlations, which exacerbates the initial effect, forcing additional sales. This VaR "vicious circle" hypothesis is described in figure 1.1. The troubling conclusion is that VaR tools increase volatility and are inherently dangerous.[8]

---

7. See for instance Ju and Pearson (1999) for an analysis at the trader's level. Basak and Shapiro (2001) examine the effect of this gaming at the level of the institution on financial markets. They show that strict VaR limits could induce banks to take on more risk in bad states of the world, that is, after VaR limits have been breached, which could cause higher volatility in financial markets. On the other hand, Cuoco and Liu (2006) argue that the VaR limit should be implemented on a dynamic basis. They find that capital requirements advocated by the Basel Committee can be very effective in curbing the risk of trading portfolio and inducing truthful revelation of this risk.

8. Even so, many other reasons can also contribute to a practice of selling in a falling market. Typical examples are positive feedback technical trading rules or stop-loss rules. Margin

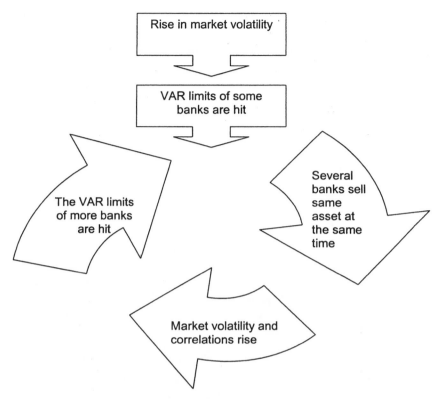

Fig. 1.1   The VaR vicious circle hypothesis
Source: Persaud (2000).

This line of argument should be a serious source of concern given the generalized trend toward risk-sensitive capital adequacy requirements. The current revisions of the Basel credit risk charges, dubbed "Basel II," also go in the direction of more sensitive risk charges. The worry is that the design of such capital-adequacy requirements might destabilize the financial system by inducing banks to tighten credit as credit risk increases— precisely at the wrong time in a recession. This prospect of procyclicality is an important issue facing bank regulation today. While it is beyond the scope of this paper to discuss procyclicality of credit risk rules, the question is whether this vicious circle argument does in fact apply to the market risk charges.

This argument requires most VaR-constrained traders to start from similar positions. Otherwise, they could simply cross their trades with little

---

calls can also lead to liquidation sales after prices have fallen. Schinasi and Smith (2000) also argue that the practice of rebalancing to fixed weights with leverage creates similar trading patterns.

effect on prices. Ultimately, positions cannot be directly compared, as these data are proprietary and jealously guarded. Instead, we can examine correlations in trading revenues.

1.2.3   Correlations in Positions and Returns

This section reviews empirical approaches to theories of herding. Realized returns reflect positions and innovations in risk factors. Consider a daily horizon indexed by t. Call $x(i, t - 1)$ the dollar position on asset i at the end of day $t - 1$. This is the number of units $n(i, t - 1)$ times the unit value $S(i, t - 1)$. The position is assumed unchanged until the next day. Define $R(i, t - 1) = [S(i, t) - S(i, t - 1)]/S(i, t - 1)$ as the rate of return on the asset, which is unitless. The dollar return on the position is then

$$x(i, t - 1)R(i, t) = n(i, t - 1)S(i, t - 1)R(i, t).$$

Contemporaneous correlations across portfolios can arise for a number of reasons. With fixed positions, correlations in dollar returns can arise because of correlations in the risk factors (R). Or, correlations could occur because positions change together (n). This could reflect herding.

It is axiomatic that every trade has a buyer and seller. Herding therefore must refer to a subset of participants; for example, financial institutions. It is often thought that institutions are more likely to herd because their information set may be more homogeneous. *Information-based* herding implies that movements in the positions depend on actions of other investors k

(2) $$\Delta n(i, t) = f[\Delta n^k(i, t) \ldots],$$

which should be reflected in positive correlations. Herding implies buying or selling an asset when others are doing the same. One class of herding models emphasizes information asymmetries as the source of herding. Investors may imitate the transactions of others whom they think have a special information advantage.

Tests of herding usually focus on portfolio positions for a subgroup of investors. Unfortunately, these tests are contaminated by other effects. Portfolio positions could change together because of common new information I:

(3a) $$\Delta n(i, t) = f[I(i, t - 1) \ldots].$$

For instance, a positive shock to interest rates may make stocks less attractive, leading to simultaneous sales by many investors. Alternatively, correlations in portfolio adjustments could be due to similar trading patterns. Technical trading rules, for instance, are defined as movements in the positions that depend on previous movements in the risk factor

(3b) $$\Delta n(i, t) = f[R(i, t - 1) \ldots].$$

As an example, momentum investors will tend to buy an asset that just went up in value. This creates positive correlations across momentum investors, which has nothing to do with herding. Alternatively, arbitrage trading can take place if the current basis, or difference between the cash and forward prices S and F, is out of line with the cash-and-carry relationship. Arbitrageurs will buy the cheap asset at the same time, creating positive correlations across their positions that have nothing to do with herding:

(3c) $$\Delta n(i, t) = f[S(i, t - 1), F(i, t - 1) \ldots].$$

Empirical tests are bedeviled by this contamination effect. Among others, Kodres and Pritsker (1996) examine the behavior of institutional investors with large positions on major U.S. futures contracts. They compute correlations between changes in daily positions within each group (broker-dealers, pension funds, commercial banks, foreign banks, and hedge funds). For a fixed contract i and two investors k and l within the same group, this is measured as

(4) $$\rho[\Delta n^k(i, t), \Delta n^l(i, t)].$$

They report that average correlations within each group are close to zero, with a range of -0.30 to $+0.34$. This provides no evidence of herding. Even with positive correlations, however, these results would have been difficult to interpret, because common movements could be due to similar trading strategies; for example, momentum strategies or stock-index arbitrage for broker-dealers, as explained previously.

Alternatively, constraint-based herding theories can be tested by examining correlations among trading returns directly (or xR). The VaR vicious circle hypothesis postulates that banks start from similar positions because they are forced to sell similar positions after the VaR limits are hit. If so, correlations among ex post trading revenues and ex ante risk measures based on VaR forecasts should be high. But first, the issue is whether large-scale VaR models successfully predict the risk of trading portfolios.

1.2.4   Empirical Evidence on VaR and Trading Revenues

Berkowitz and O'Brien (2002) provide the first empirical study of the accuracy of banks' internal VaR models. Their paper uses daily VaR and trading revenue data for six U.S. commercial banks over the period January 1998 to March 2000, or approximately 500 trading days. The data are confidential because they are provided in the course of the bank's regulatory examinations. To preserve the confidential nature of the data, the numbers are scaled, which makes it impossible to conduct cross-sectional tests.

Instead, the authors perform time-series tests of unconditional and conditional coverage. Their main conclusion is that, relative to their actual P&L, banks report VaR measures that are conservative, or too large. For four out of six banks, the average VaR is 1.6 to 3 times the actual 99th percentile of the P&L distribution. Put differently, the number of exceptions is too low. Only one bank had more than three exceptions over this period, when the expected number was five. Furthermore, most of these exceptions occurred during a short period, from August to October 1998. These results are surprising because they imply that the banks' VaR, and hence their market risk charge, is too high. Banks therefore allocate too much regulatory capital to their trading activities.

Berkowitz and O'Brien (2002) give two explanations for this observation. First, P&L include not only changes in mark-to-market positions, but also income from market-making activities, such as fees and spread, as well as net interest income. This increases the P&L, reducing the number of violations.[9] In theory, VaR should be measured against hypothetical income, taken as the change in the market value of a frozen portfolio, ignoring other effects. This is in fact the procedure in place in Germany. Jaschke, Stahl, and Stehle (2003) also compare the VaRs for thirteen German banks to the 99th percentile. They find that these VaR measures are, on average, less conservative than with U.S. data.[10]

Second, they report that some VaR models are obtained by aggregating different sectors without taking correlations into account. By neglecting diversification effects, this practice overestimates VaR. These drawbacks, however, are straightforward to correct by the internal-risk measurement system. By doing so, the banks would be releasing additional risk capital, or alternatively could be taking on more trading risk with the same amount of capital.[11] We would also expect VaR models to improve over time.

Yet another explanation is that capital requirements are currently not binding. The amount of economic capital U.S. banks currently hold is in excess of their regulatory capital. As a result, banks prefer to report high VaR numbers so as to avoid the possibility of regulatory intrusion. This is possible because the market risk capital represents a small fraction—about only two percent—of total regulatory capital.[12] Still, these practices impoverish the informational content of VaR numbers.

---

9. On the other hand, intraday trading will typically increase the portfolio risk relative to close-to-close positions because trading positions are typically cut down toward the close of the day.

10. Berkowitz and O'Brien (2002) find that 83 percent of their banks reported higher values of VaRs, which exceeded the 99th percentile by an average of 70 percent. In contrast, Jaschke, Stahl, and Stehle (2003) find that 67 percent of their banks had higher values of VaRs, which were on average actually less than the 99th percentile by 4 percent. So, VaR measures are less biased when using hypothetical P&L measures.

11. Ewerhart (2002) advances another explanation attributed to adverse selection. Assuming all banks are well capitalized, banks can be separated into prudent and less prudent ones. Because the regulator cannot differentiate among banks, more prudent ones have an incentive to report conservative capital requirements.

12. Hirtle (2003) reports a median ratio of MRC to total capital requirement of approximately 1.9 percent for large U.S. banks.

Berkowitz and O'Brien (2002) also find that a simple generalized autoregressive conditional heteroskedastic (GARCH) model appears to capture risk much better than the banks' structural models. This is not astonishing, however, because the one-year observation period requirement imposed by the Basel rules disallows fast-moving GARCH models and leads to slowly changing capital requirements.[13]

This analysis, however, is limited in time and ignores cross-sectional information. Using daily data also has drawbacks. GARCH processes decay relatively fast. Christoffersen and Diebold (2000) show that there is scant evidence of volatility predictability at horizons longer than ten days.[14] Thus, there is little point in forecasting time variation in volatility over longer horizons. In addition, daily marking-to-market introduces pricing errors for illiquid positions and positions across time zones that tend to disappear over longer horizons. Finally, daily data are provided for total trading revenues and are not disaggregated at the level of business lines.

Instead, Jorion (2002b) analyzes the informativeness of quarterly VaR numbers disclosed in financial reports. These are the only numbers available to the public. VaR measures appear to be useful forecasts of trading risks, especially in cross-sections. Time-series results for individual banks are less strong. VaR forecasts are significant only for four out of the eight banks in the sample.

Yet another approach is to focus directly on the market risk charge, as described in equation (1). Hirtle (2003) finds that market risk charges (MRCs) provide useful information about future trading risks. The MRC, however, differs from end-of-period VaR because of the averaging process, changes in the multiplier, and in the specific risk charge.

The current paper also focuses on movements in market risk charges. Commonalities in positions should be reflected in high correlations in changes in MRCs across banks. The paper will also examine correlations across trading revenues. Apparently the only other paper that deals with this issue is that by Berkowitz and O'Brien (2002), who report an average correlation of 0.17 only over the period January 1998 to March 2000. They also indicate that these correlations double over a five-day horizon. This is why it is useful to examine a quarterly horizon, a longer sample period, and different types of trading activities.

---

13. See Jorion (2002a) for a description of the movements in the market risk charge. The standard RiskMetrics model, for instance, based on exponentially weighted moving average volatility forecast, is not Basel compliant because it places too much weight on recent data.

14. This conclusion is based on daily forecasts, which tend to lose forecasting power after more than fifteen days. Andersen et al. (chapter 11, this volume), however, show that realized volatility, based on intraday data, is highly persistent up to sixty days.

1.3   Empirical Evidence

1.3.1   Data Sample

This study uses trading income and risk data reported by large U.S. bank holding companies (BHC) to the Federal Reserve. All BHCs file quarterly balance sheet and income statement reports on forms Y-9C. Trading income is reported on Schedule HI, consolidated income statement, and the MRC is reported on Schedule HC-R, regulatory capital. These are large, internationally active banks that are most likely to raise systemic risk concerns.

An advantage of this dataset is that the MRC data are measured consistently across institutions, using the same parameters, and are reported as quarter-end figures. Banks also report VaR data in their quarterly and annual reports filed with the SEC. These financial reports often have more detail by risk categories but are less consistent across banks and across time. Banks differ in their choice of confidence level and in their reporting of quarter-average or quarter-end figures. In addition, the BHC database is more comprehensive, as it covers institutions that do not file SEC reports.

The database reports quarterly MRC data starting in March 1998 and ending in September 2003.[15] In addition, we collect total assets, equity, trading assets and liabilities, derivatives notional, and total trading revenues. Trading revenues are broken down into fixed-income, currency, equity, and commodity categories. The detailed trading revenue series start in March 1995.

There is a total of forty BHCs that have nonzero entries in the MRC data field over the 1998–2003 sample period. For the correlation analysis, this study requires a continuous sample over the same period. Hence, the sample is restricted to the eleven BHCs with complete histories over the 1998–2003 period. This is the most important group, anyway. It accounts for 95 percent of the value of the aggregate market risk charge in March 1998 and 92 percent at the end of the period.

Mergers and acquisitions, however, are frequent occurrences that require special treatment. We reconstructed the time series of the merged entity by adding up the series for the separate institutions. For instance, total assets for JP Morgan Chase before September 2000 are taken as the sum of assets for the two banks before the merger. This is only an approximation,

---

15. In practice, the MRC is reported as a market risk equivalent asset figure, which is the MRC divided by 8 percent. The rationale for this is that the market risk charge is added to the credit risk charge, which is taken as 8 percent of (credit) risk-weighted assets. Thus, adding the market risk equivalent asset figure to the (credit) risk-weighted assets gives a single number, which after multiplication by 8 percent gives the total minimum capital requirement. For our purposes, the numbers we report are the reported market risk equivalent assets (item 1651) multiplied by 8 percent and translated into millions of dollars.

because it ignores transactions between the two banks. This procedure also overestimates the VaR of the merged entity, which is likely to be less than the sum of the separate VaRs, due to diversification effects.[16] This procedure is conservative, however, for the purpose of measuring the information content of VaR.

1.3.2   Summary Statistics

Table 1.1 displays the eleven BHCs with a complete time-series history over the twenty-three quarters.[17] Over this five-year period, nearly all banks have increased in size. Total assets have grown by 34 percent, equity by 56 percent, and derivatives notional amounts by 118 percent. The major exception is Deutsche Bankers Trust (DBT), whose operations were wound down after its acquisition by Deutsche Bank.

Table 1.2 displays trading position data for the bank sample. It shows the size of trading assets, trading liabilities, and of the MRC. Comparing the two tables, we see that trading assets account for approximately 14 percent of total assets as of 2002. Three banks, JP Morgan Chase, Bank of America, and DBT, have large trading operations in terms of relative size of trading assets. Overall, trading liabilities amount to approximately half of trading assets. These numbers, however, like derivatives notional amounts, are not very informative, because they fail to capture the risk and correlations of positions, which is better measured by the MRC.

1.3.3   The Market Risk Charge

We now turn to the description of the market risk charge. This amounted to $6.7 billion in total for these eleven banks as of 2002. In relation to total assets or equity, however, this is a small number. The MRC averages about 1.4 percent of total trading assets, or 2.4 percent of total book equity. This masks differences across banks, however. As of December 2002 JP Morgan Chase and Bank of America had the biggest trading operations, with an MRC/equity ratio of 6.3 percent and 4.6 percent, respectively. At the other extreme, Keycorp's MRC is only 0.2 percent of equity.

The aggregate MRC hardly changed over this five-year period, increasing from $6.5 to only $6.7 billion. This number, however, is mainly driven by large banks, and is partly offset by a large drop in the MRC for DBT. Figure 1.2 displays the MRC for all eleven banks. Apart from DBT, MRCs steadily increase over time. Some banks with low initial MRC, such as Mellon Bank, State Street, and Wells Fargo, do increase their market risk substantially in relative terms. To abstract from size, we compound the average

16. Strictly speaking, the VaR of a portfolio can only be less than the sum of the individual VaRs for elliptical distributions. Artzner et al. (2001) show pathological cases where this so-called coherence property is not satisfied.

17. This sample includes all eight banks analyzed by Jorion (2002b), of which two disappeared due to mergers (JP Morgan and NationsBank).

Table 1.1   Summary information for bank holding companies (BHCs; in millions of dollars)

Bank holding company	Total assets		Equity		Derivatives notional		Mergers
	March 1998	Dec. 2002	March 1998	Dec. 2002	March 1998	Dec. 2002	
Deutsche Bank Trust	157,537	58,083	5,812	4,545	2,005,662	48,276	
Bank of NY	59,611	77,564	4,812	6,684	242,253	413,133	
J P Morgan Chase	637,254	758,800	33,638	42,306	13,980,827	28,201,736	Chase & JPM to Sept. 2000
Citicorp	330,414	727,337	21,471	73,540	2,768,682	8,043,202	
Keycorp	73,269	84,710	5,338	6,835	31,159	64,368	
Bank One	231,666	277,383	18,472	22,440	1,116,818	1,049,397	Banc One & First Chi. to Sept. 1998
Mellon Financial	47,543	36,306	4,086	3,395	52,399	81,566	
Wachovia	237,090	341,839	17,586	32,078	127,431	1,794,589	Wachovia & First Union to June 2001
Bank of America	579,939	660,458	45,104	50,319	3,505,507	12,100,962	Bank Am. & NationsBank to June 1998
State Street	39,010	85,794	2,077	4,788	111,079	232,264	
Wells Fargo	190,913	349,259	19,909	30,358	3,406	198,837	Wells Fargo & Norwest to Sept. 1998
Total	2,584,247	3,457,533	178,303	277,288	23,945,223	52,228,331	
Growth in total (%)		34		56		118	

Notes: Sample of 11 BHCs with continuous market risk data from March 1998 to September 2003. Data for merged banks are obtained by adding up data for separate entities.

Table 1.2   **Trading positions for bank holding companies (in millions of dollars)**

Bank holding company	Trading assets		Trading liabilities		Market risk charge		Ratios, Dec. 2002 (%)			
	March 1998	Dec. 2002	March 1998	Dec. 2002	March 1998	Dec. 2002	TrA/A	TrL/TrA	MRC/TrA	MRC/Eq
Deutsche Bank Trust	60,363	10,529	29,118	2,876	1,419	66	18.1	27.3	0.6	1.4
Bank of NY	2,225	7,309	1,591	2,800	78	43	9.4	38.3	0.6	0.6
J P Morgan Chase	194,570	248,301	120,063	133,091	1,903	2,663	32.7	53.6	1.1	6.3
Citicorp	39,740	49,042	31,291	26,371	456	505	6.7	53.8	1.0	0.7
Keycorp	640	2,561	705	2,088	11	15	3.0	81.5	0.6	0.2
Bank One	9,321	11,000	6,442	4,921	222	140	4.0	44.7	1.3	0.6
Mellon Financial	650	1,911	524	1,240	25	60	5.3	64.9	3.1	1.8
Wachovia	7,879	33,155	6,597	22,903	362	505	9.7	69.1	1.5	1.6
Bank of America	54,425	95,829	31,004	48,459	1,905	2,313	14.5	50.6	2.4	4.6
State Street	1,118	3,435	1,078	2,373	11	27	4.0	69.1	0.8	0.6
Wells Fargo	2,223	10,167	124	4,774	69	374	2.9	47.0	3.7	1.2
Total	373,153	473,240	228,538	251,897	6,461	6,710	13.7	53.2	1.4	2.4
Average of ratios (%)							10.0	54.5	1.5	1.8

Notes: The table reports trading assets (TrA), trading liabilities (TrL), and the market risk charge (MRC) at two points in time. The MRC is obtained by multiplying the reported market risk equivalent assets by 8 percent. The ratios are for trading assets over total assets (A), trading liabilities over trading assets, MRC to TrA, and MRC over equity (Eq). For the ratios, "Total" refers to the ratio of the dollar sum of trading assets over the sum of assets, for example. "Average" refers to the arithmetic average of entries (ratios) for all 11 banks.

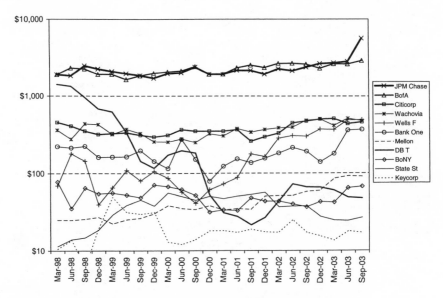

Fig. 1.2   Market risk charge (millions of dollars)

of the quarterly rate of growth for various series across banks. Figure 1.3 compares the growth of the MRC, trading assets, bank equity, and bank assets. For the average bank, trading has become more important over the last five years.[18]

We now examine the time-series behavior of the MRC, an ex ante measure of risk. Table 1.3 displays the quarterly *relative* change in the MRC, along with the value-weighted and equally weighted averages across banks. The bottom of the first panel displays the mean and standard deviation of each time series. Note that the mean is systematically smaller than the standard deviation. For JP Morgan Chase, for instance, the mean is 7.0 percent, and the standard deviation 23.9 percent. As a result, tests have little statistical power. The *t*-statistics do not allow us to reject the hypothesis of zero mean change in the MRC.[19]

Since some observers have blamed VaR for the volatility experienced in the third quarter of 1998, we would expect to see a sharp increase in the aggregate VaR from June to September 1998. Instead, the relative change in total VaR is only 4.5 percent, which is within the range of typical fluctuations in VaR. There is no evidence that the market risk charge went up

18. This could be explained by an increase in general market risk, as measured by VaR, or in specific risk. Casual observation from annual reports, however, indicates that these banks have increased their VaR over this period. See the *Financial Times* (March 25, 2004), "The balancing act that is Value at Risk."

19. The only exception is Mellon Bank, for which the *t*-statistic is 2.1.

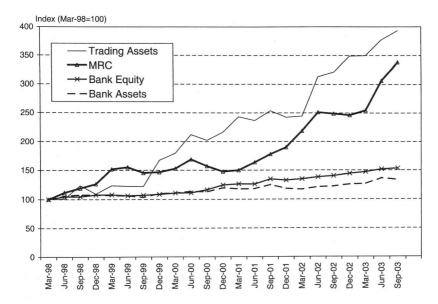

Fig. 1.3   Relative growth in trading (equally weighted)

sharply during this period. Perhaps market volatility went up and positions were cut, however.

Finally, the bottom of table 1.3 displays the correlation matrix between changes in VaR. The average correlation is –0.033, which is close to zero.[20] Only one correlation among the fifty-five entries is significantly different from zero. This highest correlation is 0.625, between Citicorp and DBT. The correlation between the two biggest trading operations, JP Morgan (JPM) Chase and Bank of America (BofA), is 0.302, which is still small. Thus, a single high correlation is not evidence of general VaR-induced herding.

To assess the economic implication of diversification effects, we can compare volatility measures under different assumptions. Define x_i as the variable of interest, say the relative change in the MRC. The volatility of the average (equally weighted) is derived from:

$$(5) \qquad \sigma^2\left[(1/N)\sum x_i\right] = (1/N)^2\left[\sum_i \sigma_i^2 + 2\sum_i\sum_{i\neq j}\sigma_i\sigma_j\rho_{ij}\right]$$

The volatility of the average, which is shown in the last column, is only 7.8 percent.

We can then compare this volatility with what we would obtain under

20. The pairwise correlation coefficients are not independent because the correlation matrix must obey positive-definiteness conditions. We also report the average of positive entries and the average of negative entries. These must obviously be greater than the grand average, and reflect the average correlation between banks that have positive or negative correlations.

Table 1.3 Properties of relative changes in market risk charges (%)

						Bank							
	DBT	BoNY	JPM Chase	Citicorp	Keycorp	Bank One	Mellon	Wachovia	BofA	State St	Wells F	VW total	EW average
June 1998	-5.5	-54.7	-3.5	-10.5	-30.1	-4.2	-0.6	-23.6	21.9	22.1	157.1	3.1	11.7
Sept. 1998	-28.3	89.9	35.0	-13.7	-55.4	4.9	3.4	58.1	-2.9	5.8	-19.4	4.5	6.5
Dec. 1998	-29.1	-15.5	-9.0	-9.1	217.4	-27.7	5.8	-2.2	-14.9	25.9	-72.4	-14.9	6.3
March 1999	-8.4	2.2	-7.2	2.5	152.3	0.9	-17.8	-25.1	-0.1	56.3	65.1	-4.3	20.1
June 1999	-45.8	-6.0	-6.5	2.4	-35.9	0.8	12.7	16.0	-14.6	34.1	67.3	-10.7	2.2
Sept. 1999	-57.6	-7.3	-5.9	-7.1	-5.6	19.6	5.0	-11.5	11.8	17.1	-26.6	-3.5	-6.2
Dec. 1999	-18.2	45.8	-7.5	-5.1	5.6	-27.0	14.1	-21.7	7.7	-16.6	32.1	-2.4	0.8
March 2000	46.6	-4.8	14.8	5.4	-58.7	-19.1	28.2	-1.2	4.3	47.5	-18.4	7.6	4.0
June 2000	14.2	-8.4	2.4	17.9	-7.1	137.1	-8.6	9.8	3.2	-10.1	-33.8	6.5	10.6
Sept. 2000	-7.2	-16.5	18.9	-4.3	15.8	-44.9	-3.3	-10.2	13.9	-10.8	-28.4	8.4	-7.0
Dec. 2000	-71.3	-39.4	-19.2	0.0	29.4	-47.8	-12.0	30.3	-20.8	12.0	49.1	-18.1	-6.0
March 2001	-41.4	7.4	-0.4	0.0	0.6	56.1	-12.4	-6.1	0.6	-6.7	18.7	0.3	1.5
June 2001	-10.4	-2.2	12.7	4.5	-5.2	24.4	4.2	23.8	20.9	7.7	20.9	16.1	9.2
Sept. 2001	-22.1	45.4	-0.3	-29.1	10.0	-10.7	-2.2	-9.7	8.7	4.9	101.6	2.4	8.8
Dec. 2001	24.3	-9.4	-10.5	14.4	-7.9	14.3	47.9	8.0	-7.0	6.6	-7.2	-5.4	6.7
March 2002	63.4	-0.3	17.5	11.3	-1.2	16.6	1.4	5.1	13.2	-35.2	79.9	15.5	15.1
June 2002	66.2	-8.1	-5.4	35.5	45.1	17.6	0.2	2.2	0.8	1.9	7.7	1.8	14.9
Sept. 2002	-8.5	-8.3	11.5	5.5	-31.4	-10.6	13.1	22.3	-2.6	0.7	-1.6	4.0	-0.9
Dec. 2002	-0.8	16.8	11.4	6.3	-10.3	-26.9	3.2	4.1	-11.6	-27.1	23.4	0.5	-1.1
March 2003	-8.4	-1.8	1.9	1.7	-11.7	28.1	42.9	-17.5	14.2	-10.4	-0.9	5.2	3.5
June 2003	-19.0	54.3	4.6	-14.0	31.7	102.4	8.0	23.6	-0.6	-1.2	33.0	6.6	20.3
Sept. 2003	-2.6	4.2	98.7	5.1	-4.6	2.1	-1.6	-6.8	10.9	9.8	0.4	41.0	10.5
Mean	-7.7	3.5	7.0	0.9	13.8	9.4	7.1	3.1	2.6	6.1	20.1	2.9	6.0
SD	34.8	30.6	23.9	13.1	62.0	43.8	15.8	20.2	11.6	22.1	51.2	12.0	7.8
Average of SD													29.9

Correlation matrix

	DBT	BoNY	JPM Chase	Citicorp	Keycorp	Bank One	Mellon	Wachovia	BofA	State St	Wells F
DBT	1.000										
BoNY	-0.073	1.000									
JPM Chase	0.182	0.238	1.000								
Citicorp	0.625**	-0.386	0.013	1.000							
Keycorp	-0.104	-0.225	-0.296	-0.093	1.000						
Bank One	0.141	0.188	-0.008	0.203	-0.130	1.000					
Mellon	0.128	-0.066	-0.162	0.115	-0.321	-0.145	1.000				
Wachovia	-0.134	0.334	0.119	0.034	-0.343	0.145	0.094	1.000			
BofA	0.293	-0.038	0.302	-0.103	-0.222	0.169	-0.122	-0.432	1.000		
State St	-0.197	-0.238	-0.123	-0.135	0.318	-0.193	-0.012	-0.107	-0.178	1.000	
Wells F	-0.026	-0.105	-0.175	-0.252	-0.057	-0.107	-0.209	-0.228	0.227	0.057	1.000

Average	-0.033
Average, 20 positive values	0.196
Average, 35 negative values	-0.170

Notes: The top part of the table reports the quarterly rate of change in the banks' market risk charge (MRC), as well as that of the total for the 11 banks. "VW total" refers to the sum of the dollar MRCs. "EW average" refers to the arithmetic average of entries for all 11 banks. The table also reports the mean value, the standard deviation (SD), and the correlation matrix for these entries. Asymptotic standard error of correlation is 0.229.

**Significant at the 5 percent level

different correlation scenarios. With perfect correlations, equation (5) simplifies to a volatility measured as $(1/N)[\Sigma_i \sigma_i]$, which is the average of volatilities across banks. This is 29.9 percent in our sample, which is much greater than what we observe. On the other hand, with zero correlations, the volatility of the average should be $(1/N)[\Sigma_i \sigma_i^2]^{1/2}$, which is 10.2 percent in our sample. The fact that the actual volatility of 7.8 percent is even lower than this last number reflects the many negative correlations across series. In other words, there seems to be substantial idiosyncratic movement in the market risk charge. Thus, there is no support for the hypothesis that VaR measures move strongly together.

1.3.4   Trading Revenues

Next, table 1.4 reports measures of trading revenues. The first column reports the average annual trading revenue in dollars. This is annualized by multiplying the quarterly average by four. The numbers are all positive but are hard to compare to each other because the scale of the operations are so different. Instead, the second column reports the average of the quarterly trading revenue deflated by beginning-of-quarter trading assets, which is similar to a return-on-assets measure (rather, revenue-on-assets, since expenses are not taken into account). The range of values is striking. Many banks return less than 5 percent. Two banks, however, return more than 10 percent. These banks, Mellon Financial and State Street, have relatively small values for trading assets.

The next column deflates trading revenues by book equity instead, giving a metric similar to return-on-equity. This is also an incomplete measure, because equity supports not only market risk but also other risks. Here also, there is a wide dispersion in ratios. The ordering of banks is generally similar to that in the previous column, except for JP Morgan Chase, which now ranks with the highest ratio, because the bank has a large trading operation relative to its other activities.

We verify whether these results still hold when using the market risk charge as the denominator instead of trading assets. The next column reports the average of trading revenue deflated by the beginning-of-quarter MRC, which can be interpreted as the economic risk capital required to support the trading activity. The ratios are all very high, reaching 1,069 percent per annum for State Street. The ratio for the total is 184 percent. Even after deduction of expenses, these ratios seem high.

Assume for instance that costs account for 80 percent of revenues, which is a high but conservative number.[21] This gives a net return before taxes to the MRC of 184 percent $\times$ (1 – 80 percent) = 37 percent, which is still very

---

21. Goldman Sachs, for example, reports segment information for proprietary trading. Over the last three years, operating expenses for this segment ranged from 66 percent to 76 percent of net revenues.

Table 1.4   Annual trading revenues for bank holding companies (June 1998 to September 2003)

Bank holding company	Average total trading revenue				Trading revenue by category ($)			
	TrR ($)	TrR/TrA (%)	TrR/Eq (%)	TrR/MRC (%)	Fixed income	Currency	Equity	Commodity
Deutsche Bank Trust	2	0.4	0.4	149.9	−43	70	−36	11
Bank of NY	253	5.4	4.3	552.1	77	175	2	
J P Morgan Chase	4,590	2.3	12.0	219.0	2,154	1,081	1,041	315
Citicorp	3,058	7.8	8.0	851.5	786	1,965	285	22
Keycorp	133	9.5	2.1	820.5	91	33		9
Bank One	183	1.9	0.9	110.1	60	98	4	20
Mellon Financial	178	19.4	4.7	503.5	11	157	10	0
Wachovia	274	1.7	1.2	83.4	172	86	16	0
Bank of America	1,116	1.8	2.4	54.1	191	490	380	56
State Street	321	15.3	10.5	1068.7	−16	337		
Wells Fargo	287	8.2	1.1	267.0	168	119		−1
Total	10,396	2.78	4.73	183.77	3,651	4,612	1,701	432
Average entry	945	6.69	4.31	425.43	332	419	213	48

Notes: The table reports trading revenue (TrR) data averaged over the June 1998 to September 2003 period and expressed in annual terms. Trading revenue data are measured in millions of dollars and as a fraction of beginning-of-quarter trading assets (TrA), book equity (Eq), and the market risk charge (MRC). "Total" refers to the aggregated series, which is the ratio of the sum of trading revenues over the sum of trading assets, equity, or MRC. "Average entry" refers to the arithmetic average of entries for all 11 banks.

high. For Citicorp, for instance, the table implies a net return on MRC of 852 percent × (1 – 80 percent) = 170 percent. This is much higher than its total return to equity of about 30 percent over recent years. For this sample, seven out of eleven banks show a ratio of trading revenue to MRC above 184 percent. Either proprietary trading has been very profitable over these years, or the MRC is too low as a measure of economic capital.

The right side of table 1.4 decomposes trading revenues into its four categories. Based on total dollar revenues, fixed-income trading accounts for 35 percent of the total; currency trading accounts for 45 percent, equity trading for 16 percent, and commodity trading for 4 percent. Smaller banks tend to specialize in currency and fixed-income trading and are thus less diversified.

Next we turn to a correlation analysis of trading revenues. To increase the sample size, the analysis starts in March 1995, for a total of thirty-five quarters instead of twenty-three as in the previous sample. Trading revenues are deflated by trading assets at the beginning of each quarter to produce a rate of return. Table 1.5 presents the volatility of scaled trading revenues and their correlations. The next-to-last column is the total aggregate number. This is a value-weighted aggregate obtained by scaling the total dollar trading revenues by total dollar trading assets. The last column represents the arithmetic, or equally-weighted average for the eleven banks.

The table shows that correlations are generally low. The average correlation is only 0.163, which does not support a generalized theory of herding. Note that there is substantial imprecision in these numbers. Under the null of zero correlation, for example, the standard error is 0.177. Thus, there is no evidence that trading activities for these banks are highly correlated, on average. Even the average of positive values is still relatively low, at 0.275; the average of negative entries is –0.167, which is also low. The main exception is for the two largest trading operations, JPM Chase and BofA, which have a high correlation coefficient of 0.709. These banks account for 52 percent and 17 percent, respectively, of total trading assets for this sample. So the two largest banks in the sample have commonalities in trading revenues. This might be a source of concern but still does not create systemic risk, as market risk represents only a small fraction of the risks incurred by U.S. commercial banks.

Figure 1.4 plots the quarterly scaled trading revenue for the industry as a whole. The top line represents the equal-weighted average, the bottom line the value-weighted average. The equal-weighted average is higher, reflecting the higher profitability of smaller banks when scaling by trading assets. The value-weighted index drops to a slightly negative value only once, during the third quarter of 1998. This reflects the losses suffered by the larger banks during the LTCM crisis. The equal-weighted index, however, only registers a small drop during this quarter.

As before, we can measure the diversification effect by comparing the

Table 1.5 Volatility and correlation of trading revenues (scaled by trading assets; March 1995 to September 2003)

	DBT	BoNY	JPM Chase	Citicorp	Keycorp	Bank One	Mellon	Wachovia	BofA	State St	Wells F	VW total	EW total
							Bank						
Volatility	0.0041	0.0078	0.0026	0.0062	0.0233	0.0036	0.0176	0.0046	0.0038	0.0162	0.0350	0.0026	0.0064
Average													0.0113
						Correlation matrix							
DBT	1.000												
BoNY	0.064	1.000											
JPM Chase	0.421**	0.198	1.000										
Citicorp	0.233	−0.364**	0.245	1.000									
Keycorp	0.442**	0.308	0.456**	−0.127	1.000								
Bank One	−0.098	−0.297	−0.019	0.464**	−0.245	1.000							
Mellon	0.109	0.217	0.143	0.102	0.335	−0.109	1.000						
Wachovia	0.249	0.387**	0.422**	−0.183	0.432**	−0.163	0.124	1.000					
BofA	0.442**	−0.028	0.709**	0.343	0.330	0.187	0.244	0.435**	1.000				
State St	0.197	0.344	0.051	−0.228	0.375**	−0.214	0.714**	0.261	0.083	1.000			
Wells F	0.204	0.174	0.041	−0.180	0.225	−0.081	0.031	0.102	0.156	0.282	1.000		
Average												0.163	
Average, 41 positive values												0.275	
Average, 14 negative values												−0.167	
						Memo: Trading assets (millions of $)							
Mean ($)	32,438	4,925	184,231	38,739	1,203	11,181	898	16,527	60,259	1,878	3,313	355,591	
Fraction (%)	9.1	1.4	51.8	10.9	0.3	3.1	0.3	4.6	16.9	0.5	0.9	100.0	

Notes: The table describes the quarterly trading revenue scaled by beginning-of-quarter trading assets over the period March 1995 to September 2003. The table reports the quarterly volatility and the correlation matrix. "VW total" refers to the value-weighted series, obtained as the ratio of the sum of trading revenues over the sum of trading assets. "EW total" refers to the equal-weighted series, obtained as the average of ratios of trading revenues over trading assets. "Average" refers to the cross-sectional average of entries for all 11 banks; for the correlation matrix, this is the average of nondiagonal entries. Mean of trading assets gives the time-series average for each bank and its fraction of the total. Asymptotic standard error of correlation is 0.177.

**Significant at the 5 percent level.

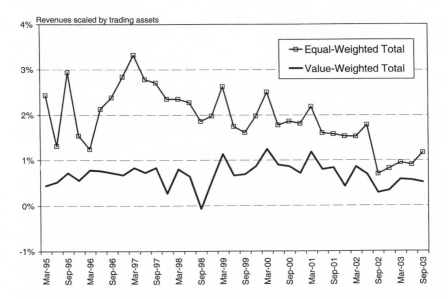

Fig. 1.4   Aggregate trading revenues

average volatility and the volatility of the equally-weighted average. The average volatility, which assumes no diversification effects, is 1.13 percent. If the series were totally uncorrelated, the volatility of an equally-weighted portfolio should be 0.46 percent. Instead, the volatility of the average, which is shown in the last column, is only 0.64 percent. This number is slightly higher than the uncorrelated volatility but still much lower than the undiversified volatility of 1.13 percent, confirming that the trading risk of the commercial banking system is rather well diversified, on average.

Perhaps these results mask high correlations for some categories of trading. To check this, table 1.6 provides a more detailed analysis by trading category. The bottom of the table describes the distribution of correlation coefficients for fixed-income, currency, equity, and commodity trading.[22] The averages are all low, ranging from –0.039 to 0.149, indicating little commonality in trading positions within each category. Even the fixed-income positions, often thought to be similar to those assumed by LTCM, have low correlations.[23] Equity trading portfolios have the highest correlation, which averages 0.149, still a low number.

Table 1.6 also shows diversification effects across categories for each

22. Not all banks engage in trading activities across all categories. All banks were active in fixed-income and currencies, but only eight banks report equity trading, and nine banks report commodity trading.

23. Notably, JPM Chase and BofA have a correlation of 0.512, 0.157, 0.680, and 0.322, for fixed-income, currency, equity, and commodity risk, respectively. So, the high correlation of 0.709 for their total trading is not driven by fixed-income positions alone. Note that because correlations are not linear operators the correlation for the sum may be greater than the correlations for the four business lines.

Table 1.6   Risk analysis and correlation of trading revenues by category (March 1995 to September 2003)

	Bank												
	DBT	BoNY	JPM Chase	Citicorp	Keycorp	Bank One	Mellon	Wachovia	BofA	State St	Wells F	VW total	Average
Volatility	0.0041	0.0078	0.0026	0.0062	0.0233	0.0036	0.0176	0.0046	0.0038	0.0162	0.0350	0.0026	0.0113
					Risk decomposition (percent of total volatility)								
Fixed income	72.8	52.0	62.6	65.0	81.0	68.3	13.0	92.3	96.6	115.5	94.9	61.9	74.0
Currency	33.3	91.7	29.6	58.0	35.8	31.0	97.1	21.2	35.0	159.6	26.7	25.8	56.3
Equity	50.2	5.9	34.5	29.9		15.1	13.0	41.2	33.6			33.0	27.9
Commodity	8.6		30.0	30.2	91.0	82.0	1.9	2.1	9.8		5.0	17.2	28.9
Sum	164.9	149.6	156.7	183.1	207.8	196.3	125.0	156.7	175.1	275.1	126.6	137.9	174.3
Diversification	−64.9	−49.6	−56.7	−83.1	−107.8	−96.3	−25.0	−56.7	−75.1	−175.1	−26.6	−37.9	−74.3
Total	100.0	100.0	100.0	100.0	100.0	100.0	100.0	100.0	100.0	100.0	100.0	100.0	100.0

Correlation statistics

	Average	Median	SD	Max.	Min.
All	0.163	0.197	0.245	0.714	−0.364
Fixed income	0.069	0.049	0.180	0.512	−0.513
Currency	0.073	0.133	0.317	0.649	−0.672
Equity	0.149	0.131	0.321	0.680	−0.597
Commodity	−0.039	0.019	0.306	0.560	−0.735

Notes: The table describes the quarterly trading revenue scaled by beginning-of-quarter trading assets over the period March 1995 to September 2003 for each of the subcategories, fixed-income instruments, currencies, equities, and commodities. "VW total" refers to the series constructed as the ratio of the sum of trading revenues over the sum of trading assets, using dollar amounts. "Average" refers to the arithmetic average of entries for all 11 banks. The top line reports the volatility over the sample period. The middle panel provides a risk decomposition of volatility by category, as a percentage of total revenues. The bottom panel describes the distribution of correlation coefficients within each trading category and the total.

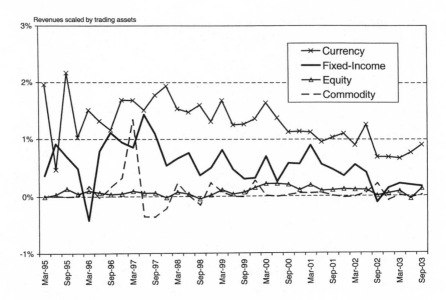

Fig. 1.5   Components of average trading revenues

bank. The risk decomposition panel lists volatilities scaled as a percentage of each bank's total trading risk. The first four categories correspond to the individual risk of each trading line. For JPM Chase, for instance, the trading risk is 62.6 percent of the total for fixed-income, 29.6 percent for currencies, 34.5 percent for equities, and 30.0 percent for commodities. These numbers are representative of the industry as a whole, with more trading risk coming from fixed-income products. These numbers sum to an undiversified risk of 156.7 percent of the actual risk. The difference, or 56.7 percent, is a diversification effect. The table shows substantial diversification effects across trading categories. The average diversification effect across banks is 74 percent. This effect is visually confirmed by figure 1.5, which shows that the four components of the equally-weighted bank index behave relatively independently of each other. Thus, these banks are fairly diversified across risk categories.

Next, we provide a direct test of the hypothesis that the risk of trading portfolio has increased since the internal models approach, based on VaR, was put in place in 1998. Table 1.7 compares the volatility of scaled trading revenues before and after 1998. The evidence is inconclusive. Six banks had increased risk, five had lower risk, a few significantly so in either direction. Based on the value-weighted data, trading risk seems to have increased. Based on an equal-weighted portfolio, however, volatility went down post-1998. Similarly, the average of individual volatilities dropped from 0.0128 to 0.0084 in the post-1998 period. This does not suggest the average volatility of trading bank portfolios has increased over time.

Table 1.7 Tests of stability in volatility of trading revenues

						Bank							
Volatility	DBT	BoNY	JPM Chase	Citicorp	Keycorp	Bank One	Mellon	Wachovia	BofA	State St	Wells F	VW total	EW total
1995–97	0.0029	0.0061	0.0022	0.0033	0.0259	0.0018	0.0194	0.0048	0.0017	0.0197	0.0534	0.0017	0.0067
1998–2003	0.0044	0.0082	0.0028	0.0059	0.0149	0.0041	0.0171	0.0042	0.0045	0.0132	0.0133	0.0030	0.0053
F-test	0.428	0.557	0.589	0.327	3.017*-	0.191	1.284	1.302	0.140*+	2.211*-	16.234*-	0.337	1.602
p-value	(0.936)	(0.853)	(0.829)	(0.976)	(0.011)	(0.998)	(0.292)	(0.282)	(0.999)	(0.049)	(0.000)	(0.973)	(0.160)

Notes: The table describes tests of equality of variance across two subperiods for the quarterly trading revenue scaled by beginning-of-quarter trading assets. The significance level for the F-test is in parentheses. "VW total" refers to the series constructed as the ratio of the sum of trading revenues over the sum of trading assets, using dollar amounts. "EW total" refers to the series constructed from the arithmetic average of scaled trading revenues for all 11 banks. One-tailed significance at the 5 percent level indicated by *- for decreases and *+ for increases.

Finally, table 1.8 revisits the trading performance of this bank sample, now adjusting for risk. The cross-sectional average of mean scaled trading revenues was 7.68 percent and the average volatility was 2.27 percent. The last columns show that these correspond to very high Sharpe ratios. The average Sharpe ratio based on dollars trading revenues is 3.54 for this sample (from the cross-sectional average of the average trading revenue divided by its volatility). Using trading revenues scaled by trading assets gives a similar ratio of 3.42. These numbers are much higher than the Sharpe ratio of 1.30 for an aggregate hedge fund index reported by Asness, Krail, and Liew (2001), although they do not take costs into account.[24]

Perhaps these results are due to the shape of distribution of trading revenues. Table 1.8 also reports skewness and excess kurtosis. The average skewness is close to zero; none is significant. Excess kurtosis is generally positive, with four significant entries. These numbers are similar to those for hedge funds. Even so, risk adjustments based on volatility alone should be viewed with caution, as they ignore tail risks.

These results are in line with those of Kwan (1997). He finds that trading is more profitable, but riskier, than banking activities.[25] Interestingly, he also reports that trading by primary dealer subsidiaries, which overlap with the large banks in our sample, has a negative correlation with banking activities, providing diversification benefits to bank holding companies. No doubt this explains the increased focus on proprietary trading.

1.4   Conclusions

VaR systems and the discipline of risk-sensitive capital charges have focused the attention of financial institutions on improving risk management practices. No doubt this helps explain the resilience of the banking system in the face of the recent recession and ever-bigger corporate and sovereign defaults. A nagging concern, however, is whether the generalized use of these techniques could increase volatility in financial markets.

This study provides a first attempt at addressing this issue. In the absence of position data, it relies on the time-series behavior of market risk charges and trading revenues broken down by line of activity. This analysis must be qualified, however, by the use of quarterly returns that could mask the risk of proprietary trading portfolios, which follow dynamic trading strategies with even higher turnover than hedge funds. In addition, the relatively short sample periods do not allow investigating correlations in the tails, which may be different from the average correlations used here.

---

24. The data are over a similar period, January 1994 to September 2000. The Sharpe ratio for the S&P index is 1.39, also expressed in raw rather than excess returns.

25. Over the period 1990.II to 1997.II. Kwan (1997) reports average trading revenues over trading assets for primary dealers of 6.0 percent, with a volatility of 2.3 percent, using annual data.

Table 1.8   Risk-adjusted performance of trading activities (March 1995 to September 2003; annualized)

Bank holding company	Average trading revenue		Volatility		Skewness	Excess kurtosis	Sharpe ratio	
	TrR ($)	TrR/TrA (%)	TrR ($)	TrR/TrA (%)	TrR/TrA	TrR/TrA	TrR	TrR/TrA
Deutsche Bank Trust	281	0.8	355	0.8	-1.17	1.92	0.79	0.98
Bank of NY	193	6.0	51	1.6	0.53	-0.93	3.81	3.88
J P Morgan Chase	4,149	2.4	960	0.5	-0.46	0.06	4.32	4.60
Citicorp	2,542	6.7	508	1.2	0.45	-0.61	5.00	5.40
Keycorp	98	13.5	40	4.7	1.25	4.42**	2.48	2.90
Bank One	170	1.6	65	0.7	1.61	4.34**	2.62	2.26
Mellon Financial	149	19.8	23	3.5	-0.04	-0.70	6.56	5.61
Wachovia	226	2.2	109	0.9	0.27	0.23	2.08	2.37
Bank of America	1,057	2.0	403	0.8	-1.39	5.85**	2.62	2.62
State Street	270	17.2	46	3.2	0.79	0.21	5.90	5.28
Wells Fargo	218	12.3	79	7.0	1.13	5.61**	2.75	1.76
Total	9,355	2.74	1,846	0.52	-0.40	1.44	5.07	5.29
Average entry	850	7.68	240	2.27	0.27	1.85	3.54	3.42

Notes: The table reports trading revenue (TrR) data averaged over the March 1995 to September 2003 period and expressed in annual terms. Trading revenue data are measured in millions of dollars and as a fraction of beginning-of-quarter trading assets (TrA). The total reports the annualized average, volatility, and Sharpe ratio, or ratio of average to volatility. "Total" refers to the series constructed as the ratio of the sum of trading revenues over the sum of trading assets, using dollar amounts. "Average entry" refers to the arithmetic average of entries for all 11 banks. Asymptotic standard error of skewness and excess kurtosis is 2.42 and 1.21, respectively.

**Significant at the 5 percent level.

Nevertheless, the overall picture from these preliminary results is that there is a fair amount of diversification across banks, and within banks across business lines. There is also no evidence that the post-1998 period has witnessed an increase in volatility. Thus, arguments that bank trading and VaR systems contribute to volatility due to similar positions has no empirical support. As Fed Vice-Chairman Roger Ferguson (2002) said in a recent speech, these concerns seem "overestimated."

References

Artzner, Philippe, Freddy Delbaen, Jean-Marc Eber, and David Heath. 1999. Coherent measures of risk. *Mathematical Finance* 9 (July): 203–28.

Asness, Clifford, Robert Krail, and John Liew. 2001. Do hedge funds hedge? *Journal of Portfolio Management* 28 (Fall): 6–19.

Banerjee, A. V. 1992. A simple model of herd behavior. *Quarterly Journal of Economics* 93 (3): 797–817.

Basak, Suleyman, and Alex Shapiro. 2001. Value-at-Risk based risk management: Optimal policies and asset prices. *Review of Financial Studies* 14 (Summer): 371–405.

Basel Committee on Banking Supervision. 1995. *An internal model-based approach to market risk capital requirements.* Basel, Switzerland: Bank for International Settlements.

———. 1996. *Amendment to the Basel Capital Accord to Incorporate Market Risk.* Basel, Switzerland: Bank for International Settlements.

Berkowitz, Jeremy, and James O'Brien. 2002. How accurate are Value-at-Risk models at commercial banks? *Journal of Finance* 57 (June): 1093–1111.

Bikhchandani, Sushil, David Hirshleifer, and Ivo Welch. 1992. A theory of fads, fashion, custom, and cultural change in informational cascades. *Journal of Political Economy* 100 (October): 992–1026.

———. 1998. Learning from the behavior of others: Conformity, fads, and informational cascades. *Journal of Economic Perspectives* 12 (Summer): 151–70.

Christoffersen, Peter, and Francis Diebold. 2000. How relevant is volatility forecasting for financial risk management? *Review of Economics and Statistics* 82 (February): 12–22.

Cuoco, Domenico, and Hong Liu. 2006. Forthcoming. An analysis of VaR-based capital requirements. *Journal of Financial Intermediation.*

Dunbar, Nicholas. 2000. *Inventing money.* New York: Wiley.

Ewerhart, Christian. 2002. Banks, internal models, and the problem of adverse selection. Mimeograph, University of Bonn, Germany.

Ferguson, Roger. 2002. Financial engineering and financial stability. Speech presented at the Annual Conference on the Securities Industry. Washington, DC: Board of Governors of the Federal Reserve System, November.

Hirtle, Beverly J. 2003. What market risk capital reporting tells us about bank risk. *Federal Reserve Bank of New York Economic Policy Review* 9 (September): 37–54.

Jaschke, Stefan, Gerhard Stahl, and Richard Stehle. 2003. Evaluating VaR forecasts under stress. The German experience. Working paper. Center for Financial Studies, Frankfurt, Germany.

Jorion, Philippe. 2002a. Fallacies about the effects of market risk management systems. *Journal of Risk* 5 (Fall): 75–96.

―――. 2002b. How informative are Value-at-Risk disclosures? *Accounting Review* 77 (October): 911–31.

Ju, Xiongwi, and Neil Pearson. 1999. Using value at risk to control risk taking: How wrong can you be? *Journal of Risk* 1 (Winter): 5–36.

Kodres, Laura, and Matthew Pritsker. 1996. Directionally similar position taking and herding by large futures market participants. In *Risk measurement and systemic risk: Proceedings of a joint central bank research conference,* pp. 271–72. Washington, DC: Board of Governors of the Federal Reserve Systems.

―――. 2002. A rational expectations model of financial contagion. *Journal of Finance* 57 (April): 769–99.

Kwan, Simon. 1997. Securities activities by commercial banking firms' Section 20 subsidiaries: Risk, return, and diversification benefits. Federal Reserve Bank of San Francisco Working Paper.

Morris, Stephen, and Hyun Song Shin. 1999. Risk management with interdependent choice. *Financial Stability Review* 7 (November): 141–50.

―――. 1998. Unique equilibrium in a model of self-fulfilling currency attacks. *American Economic Review* 88 (June): 587–97.

Persaud, Avinash. 2000. Sending the herd off the cliff edge: The disturbing interaction between herding and market-sensitive risk management practices. *Journal of Risk Finance* 2:59–65.

Schinasi, Garry, and R. Todd Smith. 2000. Portfolio diversification, leverage, and financial contagion. *International Monetary Fund Staff Papers* 47 (December): 159–76.

Scholes, Myron. 2000. Crisis and risk management. *American Economic Review* 90 (May): 17–21.

Stiroh, Kevin. 2004. Diversification in banking: Is noninterest income the answer? *Journal of Money, Credit, and Banking* 36 (October): 853–82.

Estimating Bank Trading Risk
A Factor Model Approach

James O'Brien and Jeremy Berkowitz

2.1 Introduction

Bank dealers play a central role in securities and derivatives markets and are active traders in their own right. Their trading risks and risk management are important to the banks' soundness and the functioning of securities and derivatives markets. In this paper, we use proprietary daily trading revenues of six large bank dealers to study their market risks using a market factor model approach. We estimate the bank dealers' exposures to exchange rate, interest rate, equity, and credit market factors.

Traditionally, the safety and soundness of the banking system has been the principal focus of interest in bank dealer risk. Important for this purpose is the level of market risk taken by bank dealers and the level of commonality in their risk exposures. In recent literature, the focus has been extended to the effects of bank dealers' and other trading institutions' risk-management policies on market stability. In using risk measures based on market volatility, and in particular value at risk (VaR), it has been argued that institutions' demands for risky assets will move simultaneously, which will lead to exaggerated price movements and market instability. When market volatility is low, institutions will increase demands to hold risky assets, putting upward pressure on prices and, when market volatility becomes high, institutions will attempt to reduce their positions in risky assets, putting downward pressure on prices. This behavior is said to have

We are grateful for the substantial help of Mathew Chesnes in developing programs and compiling databases and to Anthony Cho for valuable research assistance. For helpful suggestions, we would like to thank Andy Lo, Sean Campbell, Paul Kupiec (our discussant), Ken Abbott (our discussant), Peter Christoffersen, Mark Flannery, Bill English, Egon Zakrajsek, Alexandre Baptista, Andrew Karolyi, and the editors, Mark Carey and René Stulz. The views expressed are solely those of the authors.

exaggerated market instability in the late summer and fall of 1998, following the Russian ruble devaluation and debt moratorium and the near failure of Long-term Capital Management (LTCM).[1]

Despite the strong interest, there has been little study of bank dealer risks and risk management, and there appears to be little formal evidence on the size, variation, or commonality in dealer risks. In significant measure, this owes to limited public information on dealer positions and income, which limits the study of dealer risks and risk management. Individual banks report on trading positions and revenues only quarterly, and reporting is limited to securities and derivatives in broad market categories. While there is weekly reporting, it includes security positions and transactions—but only limited information on derivatives, and data is reported only for aggregated primary (bank and nonbank) dealers.[2]

Bank VaRs, which forecast the maximum loss on the trading portfolio with a given confidence, provide a direct measure of market risk. However, VaRs do not reveal the dealers' underlying market exposures or their size. Berkowitz and O'Brien (2002) also found the risk forecast performance of the daily VaRs for the banks examined in this study to be weak. Further, there was no common pattern in the correlation of VaRs across banks.

Here we apply a factor model to the daily trading revenues of six large bank dealers to estimate their market risk exposures. Factor models have long been used to study portfolio and firm market risks (e.g., Chen, Roll, and Ross 1986, Flannery and James 1984). Closer to our objectives is their application to mutual fund and hedge fund returns to characterize the market risks in the funds' portfolios (e.g., Sharpe 1992, Fung and Hsieh 1997).

With daily trading revenues, we can study the effects of daily market price moves on the banks' trading portfolios. Also, the sample sizes are large, about 1,200 daily observations per bank. However, the trading revenue data is subject to significant limitations as well. Risk exposures can be inferred only through effects on trading revenues. Trading revenues include fee and spread income and net interest income, as well as market gains and losses on positions. Further, while used by the banks internally and required for VaR model testing, the daily trading revenues lack the accounting scrutiny accorded to quarterly reports.

---

1. For dynamic analyses of market effects of a VaR constraint, see Basak and Shapiro (2001), Danielsson, Shin, and Zigrand (2002), Persaud (2000), and Morris and Shin (1999). For different analyses of the risk-taking incentives and portfolio choice effects of a VaR constraint, see Basak and Shapiro (2001), Cuoco and Liu (2003), and Alexander and Baptista (2004).

2. Jorion (2005) analyzes bank dealer trading risks and VaRs and implications for systemic market risk using quarterly reported trading revenues and VaR-based market risk capital requirements. Adrian and Fleming (2005) provide a description of data collected and reported for primary securities dealers and present some evidence on dealer risk taking based on dealer financing data.

In the standard factor model, factor coefficients represent estimates of fixed portfolio exposures. For bank dealers, exposures are variable, as dealers actively trade their positions and are not buy-and-hold investors. Thus, the standard factor model approach may not apply here. This leads us to first consider a factor model framework and estimation issues when positions are variable. The framework is used in implementing two empirical modeling approaches where trading positions are variable.

One approach is a random coefficient model, where the factor coefficients represent randomly varying market factor exposures. Using the random coefficient framework of Hildreth and Houck (1968), the dealers' mean exposures to different market factors and the variances of exposures are estimated. Estimates of average daily market risk exposures are small relative to average trading revenues and cannot account for much of the trading revenue variation. The signs of the exposures also differ across the banks, indicating heterogeneity in average exposures. A notable exception is the interest rate factor, where all banks but one exhibit small net long exposures to interest rate risk.

Even with small average exposures risk taking could still be large, since dealers could vary positions between large long exposures and large short exposures. Our estimates indicate significant variation in market exposures that include both long and short positions. Nonetheless, the ranges of potential variation in trading revenues due to variation in market exposures do not appear large relative to the total variation in trading revenues.

The random coefficient model is based on highly simplifying assumptions about the variability in exposures. Especially important is the assumption that exposures are independent of the market factors, which conflicts with portfolio strategies that are related to market prices. This issue has also been important in hedge fund studies, some of whom have tailored the functional form of the factor model to certain types of portfolio strategies. It is subsequently argued that specifying an appropriate functional form requires a good deal of specificity on the portfolio strategy. However, our information on bank dealer strategies is too sparse to formulate a specific portfolio strategy or unambiguously interpret results from alternative functional forms that might be used.

A more limited approach to considering market price-dependent trading strategies is taken here. For each bank, a linear factor model with a 150-day rolling sample is estimated. Using historical plots, the six banks' rolling regression factor coefficients are compared to the respective factors' contemporaneous 150-day rolling means. The latter will reflect periods of rising and declining market prices. Of interest is whether the rolling coefficients move systematically with the factors. This would indicate that the dealers' market exposures vary with the market factors and, hence, a possible price-dependent trading strategy.

For all factors but interest rates, the six banks' rolling factor coefficients show no common movement with the factors' rolling means. For the interest rate factor, the banks' rolling factor coefficients tend to vary inversely with the level of the interest rate. This would be consistent with the interest rate durations for their trading portfolios becoming larger (smaller) when rates are declining (rising).

The samples for the factor regressions include many days when factor changes are small. However, the conclusions are basically the same if we restrict the analysis to days of large price movements. The banks' trading revenues do not show a common systematic relation with large price changes for the noninterest rate factors, but trading revenues tend to be abnormally low on days of relatively large interest rate increases.

In sum, our principal findings are: significant heterogeneity across dealers in their market exposures, relatively small exposures on average, and a limited range of long or short exposures. Commonality in dealer exposures is limited to interest rate risk, with exposure levels inversely related to the level of rates. The implications of these results for aggregate bank dealer risk and market stability are discussed in the concluding section of the paper.

The remaining sections are as follows. In the next section, the bank data and the distribution of trading revenues are described. The factor model framework and empirical model specifications are developed in section 2.3. The estimation and results for the random coefficient model are presented in section 2.4, the rolling regressions in section 2.5, and the relation between trading revenues and large market price changes in section 2.6.

2.2   Bank Trading Revenues

The Basel Market Risk Amendment (MRA) sets capital requirements for the market risk of bank holding companies with large trading operations. The capital requirements are based on the banks' internal 99th percentile VaR forecasts with a one-day horizon. Banks are required to maintain records of daily trading revenue for testing their VaR models. The daily trading revenue for six large trading banks is used in this study.[3]

All of the banks in the study meet the Basel MRA "large trader" criterion and are subject to market risk capital requirements. Four of the six banks are among the largest derivatives dealers worldwide, and the other two are among the largest in the United States. The six trading banks and the sample periods for each bank were selected so as to exclude banks or periods for which there was a major merger, which could substantially change the size and mix of trading. So as not to reveal dollar magnitudes, trading revenues are divided by the sample standard deviations of the respective banks' trading revenues.

---

3. The six banks were studied in Berkowitz and O'Brien (2002), using a shorter sample period.

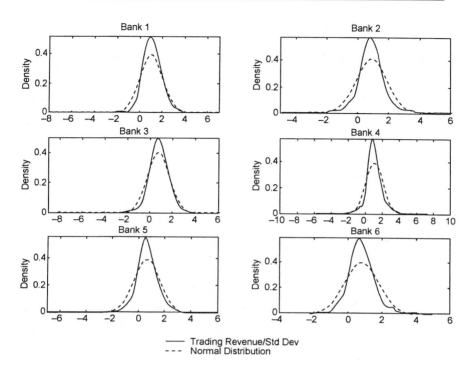

Trading Revenue/Std Dev
--- Normal Distribution

Fig. 2.1   Densities for bank trading revenues

Trading revenues are for the consolidated bank holding company and include gains and losses on trading positions, fee and spread income from customer transactions, and net interest income. Trading positions are required to be marked-to-market daily. Some smoothing of daily valuations is possible, although this would conflict with mark-to-market accounting rules. In this study, pricing inaccuracies are necessarily treated as a residual item. An attempt is made to represent the effects of fee and spread income and net interest income on trading revenues using proxy variables.

In figure 2.1, kernel densities for the banks' trading revenues (divided by trading revenue standard deviations) are presented. A normal distribution having the same means and standard deviations as the banks' distributions is provided for reference. Descriptive statistics are presented in table 2.1. As figure 2.1 and table 2.1 show, trading revenues are typically positive. For the median bank, mean daily trading revenues equal .78 trading revenue standard deviations. As shown in the bottom of table 2.1, losses occurred on less than 20 percent of trading days for any bank. The typically positive trading revenues likely reflect the importance of fee and spread income and net interest income.

The trading revenue distributions also have high peaks and heavy tails, as revealed in figure 2.1 and by the excess kurtosis statistics in table 2.1. The

Table 2.1   **Daily trading revenue descriptive statistics**

Bank	Dates	No. of obs.	Mean	Excess kurtosis	Skewness
1	Jan. 1998–Dec. 2000	762	1.05	10.75	–0.60
2	Jan. 1998–Sept. 2000	711	0.79	4.82	0.16
3	Jan. 1998–Sept. 2001	1524	0.77	13.13	1.49
4	Jan. 1998–Dec. 2003	1544	0.90	4.17	0.46
5	Jan. 1998–Dec. 2003	1551	0.62	6.46	–0.62
6	Jan. 1998–June 2002	1166	0.72	79.64	–3.98

				Quantiles		
	Loss rate	0.005	0.01	0.05	0.95	0.99	0.995
1	0.074	–2.29	–1.83	–0.22	2.72	3.77	4.15
2	0.132	–3.05	–1.98	–0.63	2.39	3.93	5.15
3	0.146	–2.99	–2.18	–0.60	2.24	3.11	3.89
4	0.111	–1.83	–1.63	–0.54	2.71	4.08	4.57
5	0.188	–3.41	–2.45	–0.84	2.15	3.40	4.15
6	0.147	–1.87	–1.40	–0.55	2.16	3.49	3.90

Notes: Trading revenues in both panels are divided by bank's sample standard deviations. Loss rate is the fraction of days when reported trading revenues were negative.

5 percent and 95 percent quantiles for the banks' trading revenues in the bottom panel of table 2.1 lie inside 5 percent and 95 percent quantiles, which would be consistent with a normal distribution. The 1 percent and 99 percent and the 0.05 percent and 99.5 percent quantiles lie outside quantiles consistent with a normal distribution. There also is no indication of any common skewness in the banks' trading revenue distributions.

To provide more information on the heavy tails, the lowest and highest 10 percent returns for each bank are plotted by historical dates in figure 2.2. The plotted values are expressed as deviations from trading revenue means and are divided by sample standard deviations. With some exceptions for bank 1, the lowest 10 percent returns are all losses. Several features of figure 2.2 are notable.

One is that, while there is temporal clustering in both high and low returns, the clustering tends to be greater for low returns. This asymmetry in temporal clustering may be due to periodic large fees earned by dealers from customer transactions that are more evenly dispersed through time. In contrast, low returns are likely to reflect mostly portfolio losses from adverse market moves and persistency in market volatility (operational costs are not included in trading revenues).

A second and related feature of figure 2.2 is that all of the banks encountered loss clustering, with some also experiencing positive spikes, during the market turmoil in the late summer and fall of 1998. The market in-

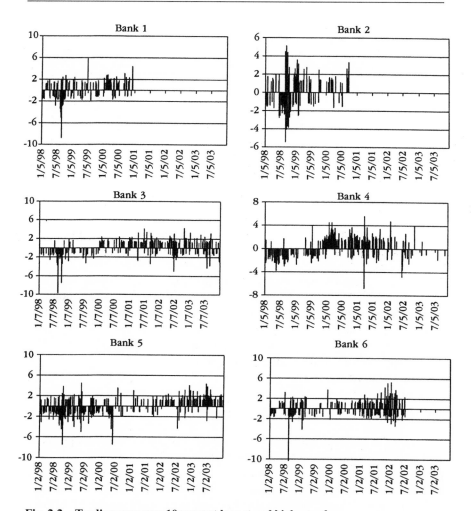

Fig. 2.2   Trading revenues: 10 percent lowest and highest values

Notes: Values are expressed as deviations from the banks' sample means and in terms of the sample standard deviations. The large negative spike for bank 6 exceeds 10 standard deviations.

stability during this period had important common effects on the banks' trading revenues. For all six banks, daily averages of trading revenues for the second half of 1998 were low and this period had a large effect on the full sample trading revenue kurtosis for banks 1, 2, 3, and especially 6.[4]

It should be noted that variation in dealer positions is also a potentially

4. For the second half of 1998, daily averages of trading revenues for banks 1 to 6 were respectively 0.55, 0.39, 0.22, 0.15, 0.15, and 0.39. If the second half of 1998 is excluded from the sample, the excess kurtosis for banks 1 through 6 are respectively 4.30, 2.63, 2.84, 4.42, 6.07, and 4.64. See table 2.1 for comparable statistics for the full-period samples.

Table 2.2   **Cross-bank trading revenue correlations and VAR (trading revenue above the diagonal and VAR below the diagonal)**

	Bank					
Bank	1	2	3	4	5	6
1		0.415	0.210	0.182	0.028	0.145
2	−0.027		0.112	0.070	0.158	0.147
3	0.99	−0.151		0.243	0.169	0.145
4	0.060	−0.812	0.130		0.048	0.146
5	−0.119	0.684	0.097	−0.503		0.094
6	−0.314	−0.300	−0.271	0.627	−0.330	

important determinant of the trading return distribution. The dependency of the trading return distribution on the dynamic management of positions under a VaR constraint is a major feature in Basak and Shapiro (2001).

Table 2.2 presents cross-bank correlations for daily trading revenues above the diagonal and, for comparison, cross-bank daily VaR correlations below the diagonal. The trading revenue correlations are all positive and significant using a standard t-test. The potential contribution of exposures to market factors on the trading revenue correlations is considered in the following. In contrast, the bank VaR correlations show no common pattern, as correlations are both positive and negative and vary widely.

2.3   Factor Model with Varying Positions

A factor model framework when positions are variable is developed here and is used to guide the empirical specifications. Consider a portfolio with positions in K risky securities and a risk-free asset. Positions in securities and the risk-free asset may be long or short and include those held indirectly through derivatives. For measuring the portfolio's sensitivity to market factors, bid-ask spreads are abstracted from and the values of short or long positions are measured at a single price, for example, the midmarket price. The portfolio can be adjusted continuously, but returns are observed only for discrete time units.

Let t denote time measured in discrete units. At the start of t, the bank holds an amount x_{kt}^0 in risky security categories $k = 1, \{\ldots\}, K$ and x_{0t}^0 in the risk-free asset, which are referred to as the bank's positions. Positions may be carried over from $t - 1$ or new positions may be set at the start of t prior to any price changes since $t - 1$. Positions and prices measured at the end of period t are denoted by $x_k(t)$, $x_0(t)$, and $p_k(t)$. The price of the risk-free asset is fixed at 1. Using this notation, the values of the portfolio at the start of t and at the end of t are respectively

(1a)
$$W_t^0 \equiv \sum_{k=1}^{K} x_{kt}^0 p_k(t-1) + x_{0t}^0$$

(1b)
$$W(t) \equiv \sum_{k=1}^{K} x_k(t) p_k(t-1) \left(\frac{p_k(t)}{p_k(t-1)} \right) + x_0(t).$$

For the factor model, we want to express the 1-period change in the portfolio value as a function of 1-period changes in market prices $r_k(t) \equiv [p_k(t) - p_k(t-1)]/p_k(t-1)$. If positions are fixed, the change in the portfolio value will be determined by the 1-period market price changes. However, if positions are variable, the change in the portfolio value can be affected by intraperiod price movements not revealed in the 1-period price changes. Thus, the suitability of a factor model when portfolio values are observed only discretely requires restrictions on intraperiod position and/or possibly price changes. A highly simplifying assumption made here is that intraperiod changes in security positions and prices are uniform over the period. This assumption becomes accurate for very short periods and it may be a reasonable approximation for one-day returns. It implies that the intraperiod position and price changes can be measured from the full period changes.

A second assumption is made to avoid complications from outside cash infusions or withdrawals: there are no exogenous intraperiod capital flows to the portfolio, and intraperiod cash payments and accrued interest on positions are accumulated in a separate account. Under this assumption, changes in positions at any time τ within period t, $dx_{kt}(\tau)$, made at prices $p_{kt}(\tau)$, will satisfy a self-financing constraint: $\Sigma_{k=1}^{K} dx_{kt}(\tau)p_{kt}(\tau) + dx_{0t}(\tau) = 0$.

Using the self-financing constraint and (1), the change in the portfolio value over the period, $w(t) \equiv W(t) - W^0(t)$, is

(2)
$$w(t) = \sum_{k=1}^{K} \left[x_{kt}^0 p_k(t-1) + \frac{1}{2} \Delta x_k(t) p_k(t-1) \right] r_k(t),$$

where $\Delta x_k(t)$ is the change in the position over period t (see appendix). Note that $x_{kt}^0 p_k(t-1) + [1/2\Delta x_k(t)p_k(t-1)]$ is the average position in the period valued at the price of k at the end of $t-1$.

The change in the portfolio value can be expressed using a factor model form:

(3)
$$w(t) = \sum_{k=1}^{K} V_k(t) r_k(t)$$

where $V_k(t) \equiv [x_k^0(t) + 1/2\Delta x_k(t)]p_k(t-1)$. $V_k(t)$ is the value of the portfolio position in factor k and measures the portfolio's exposure to factor shock $r_k(t)$. Unlike the standard factor model assumption, the factor exposures are not constant. With daily data, they would reflect time-varying daily average positions. Two specifications of equation (3) will be considered.

For the first specification, $V_k(t)$ is assumed to be a random draw from a stationary process with mean $\overline{V}_k$. Further, the positions' values, $V_k(t)$, are assumed to be independent of market factor changes and mutually independent. Under these conditions, the portfolio return in equation (3) satisfies the random coefficient models developed in Hildreth and Houck (1968).

With $\overline{V}_k$ as the mean position value in factor k and $v_k(t) \equiv V_k(t) - \overline{V}_k$ as the random change in the position value, the details of the factor model can be expressed by

(4a)
$$w(t) = \sum_{k=1}^{K} r_k(t)\overline{V}_k + u(t)$$

(4b)
$$u(t) \equiv \sum_{k=1}^{K} r_k(t)v_k(t)$$

(4c)
$$E[w(t)] = \sum_{k=1}^{K} \mu_k(t)\overline{V}_k$$

(4d)
$$\sigma_{ww} = \sum_{k=1}^{K}\sum_{l=1}^{K} \overline{V}_k\overline{V}_l\omega_{kl} + \sum_{k=1}^{K} \sigma_{v_kv_k}\omega_{kk},$$

where $\mu_k \equiv E[r_k(t)]$ is the expected change in the market price represented by factor k, $\sigma_{v_kv_k}$ is the variance for factor position k; σ_{ww} is the unconditional variance of changes in the value of the portfolio, and ω_{kl} is the covariance (variance) for individual factors $r_k(t)$ and $r_l(t)$. For the following analysis, it is assumed that $\mu_k = 0$.

Equation (4a) expresses the change in the value of the portfolio as the sum of change in value conditioned on average positions and the change in value conditioned on the positions' realized random components, the latter being defined in equation (4b). Equations (4c) and (4d) are the portfolio's unconditional mean change and variance. The unconditional variance is the sum of the variances for $\sum_{k=1}^{K} r_k(t)\overline{V}_k$ and $u(t)$. The variance is the sum of the factor variances and covariances weighted by the mean positions plus the sum of the products of the factor variances and position variances. Thus, with variable positions, the volatility of positions interacts with the volatility of the factors in determining the dispersion of portfolio returns.

The factor model in equations (4a)–(4d) also provides for the correlation between the changes in banks' i and j portfolio values that come from market factor shocks. This correlation represents a measure of cross-bank commonality in market risks. Using subscripts for banks i and j, we have (see appendix)

(5)
$$\rho_{w_iw_j} = \rho_{\hat{w}_i\hat{w}_j} \sqrt{RS_i} \sqrt{RS_j} + \rho_{u_iu_j} \sqrt{1 - RS_i} \sqrt{1 - RS_j},$$

where $w_i(t) = \hat{w}_i(t) + u_i(t)$, $\hat{w}_i(t) \equiv r(t)\overline{V}_i$ and $u_i(t)$ is the residual for bank i in equation (4b).

Equation (5) describes two sources of commonality in banks' market risks. $\rho_{\hat{w}_i\hat{w}_j}$ is the correlation between changes in i and j's portfolio values when factor exposures are conditioned on the mean positions. One source of commonality is similar mean positions, which would make $\rho_{\hat{w}_i\hat{w}_j}$ positive. $\rho_{u_iu_j}$ is the correlation associated with the variation in positions, as reflected in $u_i(t)$ and $u_j(t)$. A second source is common variation in positions. RS_i and RS_j determine the relative importance of these two sources of correlated returns. RS_i is the (population) R-square from a regression of i's portfolio value changes on market factors with factor coefficients set at their means $(RS_i \equiv \sigma_{\hat{w}_i\hat{w}_j}/\sigma_{w_iw_j})$.

Using the random coefficient model and with observations on trading portfolio value changes and market factors, it is possible to estimate the bank dealers' average factor positions and their variances and some components of the cross-bank correlations.

The assumptions, of course, are restrictive and limit the generality of results. The assumption that position changes are mutually independent is one of notational convenience but potentially important for empirical tractability if there are many factors. Dropping this assumption would require recognizing all the covariances between position changes in equation (4d).

Assuming that market exposures are independent of factor changes is particularly limiting because portfolio management may be related to market price movements. As discussed earlier, such policies have been said to adversely affect market stability. Dropping the assumption of independence has important effects on the factor model formulation and, specifically, can make portfolio returns nonlinear in the factor changes, $r_k(t)$.

An illustration of this is when the portfolio is managed such that returns resemble a call or put option on, say, security k. The optionlike portfolio implies a position in the security and a cash position. Changes in the security price have both first-order and higher-order effects on the portfolio return. The higher-order effects imply changes in the security and cash positions that are related to the factor price change. For security k, $\Delta x_k(t)$ in equation (2) is positive and depends on the price change, $r_k(t)$. A second-degree polynomial provides a second-order approximation to the effect of the market factor on the portfolio value.

$$(6) \qquad\qquad w(t) = a_k^0(t)r_k(t) + b_k^0(t)[r_k(t)]^2$$

The coefficient for the linear component in equation (6) is analogous to the option's delta and that for the quadratic component to the option's gamma.

Nonlinear portfolio return equations such as (6) and returns expressed as functions of traded option values have been used in hedge fund studies to capture positions that vary with market returns.[5] However, a particular

5. Chan et al. (2005) use higher-order polynomials in market factors to capture nonlinearity in hedge fund returns. Agarwal and Naik (2004) use returns to call and put options as the

portfolio strategy, including the strategy horizon, is needed to specify or interpret a particular functional form. For example, the strategy specified in the preceding illustration implies that the squared market factor in equation (6) reflects the nonlinear sensitivity of the portfolio to the market factor, that is, the option's "gamma." Without this specification, the interpretation of the squared factor would be ambiguous (e.g., it might represent the sensitivity of the portfolio value to market volatility). Further, the coefficients $a_k^0(t)$ and $b_k^0(t)$ expressed in equation (6) are for period t. They depend on the security value at the start of the period and also the portfolio management horizon (option's time to expiration). Treating the two coefficients as constants implies that the portfolio is being rebalanced to a constant composition and horizon at the start of each sample observation, for example, each month if observations are monthly.

We have little specific information on bank dealers' portfolio strategies and we are not testing a specific strategy. This lack of specificity includes the time dimension of the dealer's strategy as it relates to our daily observation period.

A less formal approach to price-dependent strategies is taken here. For each bank, we estimate a linear regression of trading revenues on market factor changes (and nonmarket factor variables) with 150-day daily rolling samples. For the six banks, the estimated rolling coefficients are plotted along with coincidental 150-day rolling means for the respective factors (factor price levels, not changes). The 150-day rolling means will reflect periods of rising or declining market prices. Of interest is whether the rolling factor coefficients move systematically with the factors. This would indicate dealers' market exposures vary with the market factors and, hence, a possible price-dependent strategy. The significance of any comovement will be judged according to whether it is common among the six banks.

While observed comovement between the factor coefficients and the factors would indicate that the dealers' market exposures are related to the market factors, this may still not uniquely identify the price-dependent portfolio strategy. We consider this issue in evaluating the rolling regression results.

Before presenting the empirical factor models, the treatment of other components of trading revenues needs to be mentioned. (1) Portfolio revenues include accrued and explicit interest payments and payments for risk-bearing. (2) Trading revenues also includes fee and spread income from market-making. We do not have direct measures of these additional components. Proxy variables are used to capture the effects of trading volume and net interest income on dealer trading revenues. (3) Portfolio revenues also are affected by (interperiod) changes in the portfolio's capital.

---

factors in hedge fund factor regressions to capture the nonlinearity between the hedge fund's returns and the underlying market factors that arise from option-type trading strategies. Mitchel and Pulvino (2001) apply a piecewise linear factor model in returns to risk arbitrage strategies.

Changes in the capital of the portfolio are not explicitly accounted for other than what can be represented by a trend variable.

2.4 Random Coefficient Model

We first describe the explanatory variables used in the empirical analysis.

2.4.1 Explanatory Variables

In selecting market factors, four broad market categories are represented: exchange rates, interest rates, equity, and credit spreads. For exchange rates, equities, and credit spreads multiple factors are used for each category. A ten-year U.S. Treasury rate is used to capture interest rate risk in the trading portfolio. In an earlier version, a ten-year rate and a three-month rate were used, with qualitatively similar coefficients estimated for both factors. There are a total of eleven market factors, which are identified in panel A of table 2.3 with descriptive statistics.

For exchange rate factors, regional exchange rate indices were constructed. They are weighted averages of log changes in individual country exchange rates. The exception is Russia, the only Eastern Europe country for which we had historical data. The weights are shown in panel B of table 2.3. They were constructed from worldwide dealer foreign exchange (FX) spot and derivatives turnover reported in Bank of International Settlements (BIS) Central Bank Surveys in 1998 and 2001.

Exchange rate and equity factors are measured as log differences; interest rate and credit spread factors are first differences. For the exchange rate and equity market factors, positive differences indicate increases in asset values and, for the interest rate and credit spreads, positive differences indicate decreases in asset values.

In addition to the market factors, a proxy variable is used to represent trading volume that generates fee and spread income. We do not have direct information on dealers' daily transactions and use detrended daily volume on the New York Stock Exchange (NYSE) plus NASDAQ to represent a market volume influence on trading revenue. Also, we do not have data on net interest income from trading positions. To proxy for net interest income, we use a monthly lagged moving average of the ten-year U.S. Treasury rate. This is intended to represent the gradual realization in the portfolio of upward and downward movements in interest rate levels.

A trend variable is used to capture any trend in the level of the bank's activity. Lagged trading revenue is also included. If dealers smooth position revaluations, this could produce serially correlated returns.

2.4.2 Market Risk Estimates

We use the generalized least squares (GLS) random coefficient estimators developed by Hildreth and Houck (1968) to estimate the banks' mean exposures to the market factors, $\overline{V}_k$, shown in equation (4a), and the exposure

Table 2.3   **Market factors**

A. Market factors: Daily changes, 1998–2003[a]

Exchange rates	Mean	Equity	Mean	Interest rates	Mean	Credit spreads[b]	Mean
Western Europe	0.00009 (0.00558)	NYSE	0.00012 (0.01156)	10-yr U.S. Treasury rate	−0.00084 (0.06302)	10-yr Baa	0.00050 (0.03497)
Russia	−0.00107 (0.02274)	NASDAQ	0.00015 (0.02222)			5-yr high yield	0.00049 (0.09338)
Asian Pacific	0.00012 (0.00603)					10-yr swap	−0.00007 (0.03185)
South America	−0.00037 (0.00611)					EMBI+	−0.00060 (0.24070)

B. Exchange rates with U.S. dollar: Construction of regional indices[c]

Western Europe (1998)		Western Europe (1999–2002)		Asian Pacific		South America	
Country	Weight	Country	Weight	Country	Weight	Country	Weight
Germany	0.54	Europe	0.633	Japan	0.727	Mexico	0.658
United Kingdom	0.198	United Kingdom	0.222	Australia	0.136	Brazil	0.342
France	0.092	Switzerland	0.102	Hong Kong	0.075		
Switzerland	0.127	Sweden	0.043	Singapore	0.035		
Sweden	0.043			Korea	0.027		

[a]Standard deviations are in parentheses. Units for factor means and standard deviations: Exchange rates and equity means are daily log differences of levels; interest rates and credit spreads are daily first differences of levels expressed as percentage points.

[b]Credit spreads are spreads from treasury rates with the same maturity. EMBI+ is JP Morgan's Emerging Markets Bond Spread Index Plus.

[c]Regional exchange rates are weighted log differences. Weights are based on worldwide dealer FX spot and derivatives turnover volume reported for different currencies. Turnover volume is taken mostly from the 2002 BIS Central Bank Survey. The survey date is June April 2001. June 1998 turnover volume from the 1999 Central bank Survey is used to determine weights for Western Europe currencies for pre-Euro 1998 (country coverage in the 1998 survey is limited).

Table 2.4   **Summary statistics for factor model and coefficient variances regressions**

	Bank					
	1	2	3	4	5	6
Factor model regressions[a]						
Regression R^2	0.18	0.15	0.22	0.32	0.15	0.07
Regression F-values	10.09	7.64	27.44	45.36	17.93	5.33
Market factor F-values	1.84	1.05	2.36	7.93	0.97	1.88
Sample size (n)	728	681	1,484	1,485	1,483	1,109
Coefficient variance regressions[b]						
Regression R^2	0.06	0.18	0.08	0.03	0.04	0.02
Regression F-values	3.82	13.73	11.07	4.16	5.59	1.98
Sample size (n)	728	681	1,484	1,485	1,483	1,109

[a] .05 critical F-values: for regression $F(16,n-16) = 1.65$; for market factors $F(11,n-16) = 1.80$.
[b] .05 critical F-values: $F(12,n-12) = 1.76$.

variances, $\sigma_{v_k v_k}$, shown in equations (4d) and (4e).[6] For the estimation we are assuming that $v_k(t)$ is i.i.d. independent of the market factors, and that $v_k(t)$ and $v_l(t)$ are independent for $k \neq l$. The residual in the trading revenue equation will include the residual that arises from random position changes, that is, $u(t)$ in equation (4b), as well as any independent sources of trading revenue not accounted for in the model. Under these assumptions, Hildreth and Houck provide unbiased and consistent estimators of the mean coefficients and coefficient variances. Here, we allow only the eleven market factors to have variable coefficients.

Appendix tables 2A.1 and 2A.2 contain the detailed regression results. Reported coefficients are estimated using trading revenues divided by sample standard deviations and thus measure trading revenue effects in terms of trading revenue standard deviations. The estimates are discussed here using several summary tables. In the top part of table 2.4, summary statistics for the regressions estimating mean exposures to the market factors and including other regressors are presented. As shown, the full set of regressors has significant explanatory power based on F-values and regression R-squares. However, the F-values measuring the joint explanatory power for the eleven market factors are not very high and do not exceed the 0.05 critical value for two banks. Thus the market factors do not have a lot of explanatory power (excluding these factors from the regressions, causes the R-squares to drop by about four basis points). Since the factor coefficients reflect the estimated mean factor exposures, this implies

6. Specifically, we use (14), p. 587, to estimate the coefficient variances and $\tilde{\beta}$ estimator in (25), p. 589, to estimate the mean market factor positions.

that average market exposures cannot account for much of the variability of trading revenues.

In contrast, equity volume, used as a proxy for market transactions volume, is positive for all banks and highly significant for all but one bank (appendix table 2A.1). Trading revenues also have a significant positive trend. The estimated coefficients for the moving-average interest rate (to proxy interest income) and lagged trading revenue have mixed signs and significance across the banks.

The bottom part of table 2.4 presents summary statistics for the regressions estimating the variances of the market factor coefficients. While R-squares are low, the F-values are highly significant, implying significant variability in the market factor coefficients. The estimator used for the variances of the market factor coefficients is unbiased under the model assumptions. While Hildreth and Houck suggest constraining the coefficient estimates to nonnegative values (pp. 587–89), this constraint was not imposed here. A little more than a third of the estimated coefficients are negative, although only two are significant at a 0.05 level and one at a 0.01 level (appendix table 2A.2). We regard the negative coefficients as reflecting sampling error and exclude them in evaluating the variability of the dealers' market exposures. We have no reason to believe that this biases our interpretation of the results.

In table 2.5, two measures of the dealers' potential exposures to large market factor shocks are constructed using appendix tables 2A.1 and 2A.2. The top number in each cell is equal to the respective factor's coefficient from table 2A.1—the estimate of the bank's mean exposure to the factor—multiplied by a 2 standard deviation shock to the factor. Recall that the coefficient estimates measure trading revenue effects in terms of trading revenue standard deviations. Hence, the top number in the cell measures trading revenue effects in terms of trading revenue standard deviations from a 2 standard deviation factor shock.

The two numbers underneath are the 2.5 percent and 97.5 percent estimated quantiles for factor exposures, that is, 95 percent intervals. The quantile estimates use the estimated mean coefficients (table 2A.1) and coefficient variances (table 2A.2), and assume the coefficients are normally distributed. The quantile estimates also are multiplied by 2 standard deviation factor shocks. The italic numbers indicate where coefficient variance estimates are negative (a zero interval is reported but is not used in the following analysis).

Consider first the estimated mean factor exposures (the top number in each cell). The estimates are small compared to the mean trading revenues shown in table 2.1. For all factors, a 2 standard deviation market factor shock produces less than a 0.3 standard deviation change in a bank's trading revenue and less than a 0.1 standard deviation change in trading revenue for two-thirds of the factors. For the median bank, mean trading revenues

Table 2.5   Scaled factor coefficients with 2.5 percent and 97.5 percent quantiles[a] (estimated coefficient quantiles)

Factors[b]	Bank					
	1	2	3	4	5	6
fx w eur	0.062 (0.062, 0.062)	0.063 (0.063, 0.192)	0.051 (−0.732, 0.833)	*0.076 (0.076, 0.076)*	−0.082 (−0.813, 0.648)	*0.062 (0.062, 0.062)*
fx russia	0.041 (−0.087, 0.169)	0.082 (−0.066, 0.575)	0.228 (−0.586, 1.042)	*−0.004 (−0.004, −0.004)*	0.028 (−0.461, 0.516)	*−0.047 (−0.047, −0.047)*
fx asia pac	−0.216 (−1.413, 0.982)	−0.103 (−0.410, 1.215)	−0.024 (−0.909, 0.861)	*0.046 (0.046, 0.046)*	0.034 (−1.261, 1.329)	*0.007 (0.007, 0.007)*
fx so amer	−0.049 (−0.049, −0.049)	−0.071 (−1.422, −0.071)	−0.006 (−0.688, 0.676)	*0.057 (−0.932, 1.046)*	−0.080 (−0.080, −0.080)	*0.164 (0.164, 0.164)*
nyse	−0.126 (−1.295, 1.043)	−0.118 (−1.087, 0.850)	0.052 (0.052, 0.052)	*0.237 (−0.414, 0.887)*	−0.149 (−0.149, −0.149)	*−0.045 (−1.334, 1.243)*
nasdaq	0.082 (−0.650, 0.815)	0.108 (0.108, 0.108)	0.007 (−0.081, 0.094)	*−0.072 (−1.083, 0.939)*	0.044 (0.044, 0.044)	*−0.063 (−0.063, −0.063)*
10-yr treas	−0.276 (−1.356, 0.803)	0.101 (0.101, 0.101)	−0.190 (−1.970, 1.590)	*−0.204 (−0.204, −0.204)*	−0.071 (−1.979, 1.836)	*−0.088 (−1.063, 0.888)*
Baa sprd	−0.041 (−0.041, −0.041)	0.165 (−0.938, 1.268)	−0.083 (−0.083, −0.083)	*0.022 (0.022, 0.022)*	−0.021 (−0.021, −0.021)	*0.162 (0.162, 0.162)*
hi yld sprd	−0.081 (−0.081, −0.081)	0.011 (−1.406, 1.428)	−0.168 (−1.219, 0.883)	*−0.189 (−1.085, 0.708)*	−0.037 (−0.037, −0.037)	*−0.227 (−0.910, 0.455)*
10-yr swap sprd	−0.017 (−1.193, 1.159)	−0.015 (−0.266, 0.236)	0.075 (−0.554, 0.705)	*0.012 (0.012, 0.012)*	0.025 (0.025, 0.025)	*−0.037 (−0.037, −0.037)*
embi+ sprd	0.006 (−1.954, 1.966)	0.081 (−1.879, 2.041)	−0.134 (−2.094, 1.826)	*−0.347 (−2.307, 1.613)*	−0.032 (−1.992, 1.928)	*0.047 (−1.913, 2.007)*

[a]Scaled coefficients equal the change in trading revenue measured in terms of trading revenue standard deviations due to 2 standard deviation factor shocks. Italic numbers indicate the estimated variance was negative.

[b]Factors expressed as log changes for exchange rates and equity and first differences for interest rate and credit spreads.

equal 0.78 standard deviations. Thus, 2 standard deviation shocks to individual factors and even to multiple factors would still leave a positive expected trading revenue.

Among individual market categories, the estimated mean exposures for the interest rate factor are negative for five of six banks. The negative exposures would imply bank dealers have (small) net long exposures to interest rate changes on average; that is, the portfolio duration is positive. For the three other broad market categories, however, there does not appear to be a clear pattern of directional mean exposures to these market categories, although coefficients are mostly positive for the Western Europe exchange index. Generally, the coefficients vary in sign across broad market categories for a given bank and for the most part across banks for a given factor.

Now consider the estimated 95-percentile intervals for the market factor exposures reported under the mean exposure estimates in table 2.5. The interval estimates cover both positive and negative values, indicating that factor exposures can vary between long and short positions. Also, for the factor variances with nonnegative estimates, the 95 percent coefficient bounds are large relative to the estimated mean coefficients. However, the bounds do not appear to be particularly large when measured against the trading revenue quantiles shown in the bottom panel of table 2.1.

Specifically, the 95 percent bounds in table 2.5 measure potential trading revenue variation from 2 standard deviation market factor shocks. Conditioned on a 2 standard deviation factor shock, they represent 95 percent bounds on portfolio gains and losses. The trading revenue quantiles in table 2.1 measure trading revenue variation due to market factor shocks *and* variation from other influences, such as market-making revenues. The bounds in table 2.5 tend to be within the 1 percent and 99 percent quantiles for trading revenues shown in table 2.1. Also, the bounds in table 2.5 are for 2 standard deviation market factor shocks. Thus, trading revenues conditioned on estimates of relatively large factor exposures and factor shocks do not produce extreme outliers relative to the unconditional variability of the trading revenues.

Overall, the results from the random coefficient model do not indicate that bank dealers take large market risks relative to the size of average trading revenues and trading revenue volatility, and there is significant cross-dealer heterogeneity in exposures. However, at times dealers may still have large exposures to particular factors, creating the potential for significant losses on days of extreme market conditions.

2.4.3 Cross-Bank Trading Revenue Correlations

As described earlier in section 2.2, cross-bank trading revenues show small but consistently positive correlations (table 2.2). As shown in equation (5), cross-bank trading return correlation due to market risk exposures can come from dealers either having common average exposures to market factors or common variation in exposures. Based on the random coefficient regression results, average factor exposures seem unlikely to be an important source of cross-bank trading revenue correlation. This can be determined by applying the mean and variance estimates of the random coefficients for the market factors to estimate $\rho_{\hat{w}_i\hat{w}_j}\sqrt{RS_i}\sqrt{RS_j}$ in equation (5) for banks' i and j.[7] The cross-bank correlation component reflecting positions at their mean values was calculated for each pair of banks. For all but one bank this component is less than 0.02 (for banks 2 and 4, it is –0.04).

If market exposures account for most of the observed trading revenue correlations, it must be mainly due to common changes in banks' exposures; that is, the component $\rho_{u_iu_j}\sqrt{1 - RS_i}\sqrt{1 - RS_j}$ in equation (5). To determine this component requires estimates of the variable exposure component $u_i(t)$ in each bank's residual revenue (equation [4b]). The best that can be done is to use the factor model regression residuals for $u_i(t)$ to calculate $\rho_{u_iu_j}\sqrt{1 - RS_i}\sqrt{1 - RS_j}$ for each combination of banks. Unfortunately, the regression residuals will include both $u_i(t)$ and other unspecified components of trading revenues.

Nonetheless, correlations reported in the bottom panel of table 2.6 were obtained by calculating $\rho_{u_iu_j}\sqrt{1 - RS_i}\sqrt{1 - RS_j}$ using the regression equation residuals (correlations above the diagonal are the trading revenue correlations displayed in table 2.2). The correlations below the diagonal typically are slightly more than half the trading revenue correlations above the diagonal. Whether the former represent a small commonality in trading revenue due to common market exposures or due to other common influences on trading revenues not controlled for in the regressions is difficult to say. Employing different approaches, further consideration is given to dealer commonality in market exposures in the next two sections.

2.5   Rolling Regressions

In this section, we present estimates of market factor coefficients for daily rolling regressions. Using ordinary least squares (OLS), each bank's trading revenue is regressed on the market factors and other explanatory variables, including our proxy variables for trading volume and net interest payment effects on trading revenues. The rolling window is 150 days. The first 150-day regression ends on August 11, 1998 (August 14, 1998, for bank 1). The regression equations are reestimated daily, dropping the last day and adding a new day using each bank's available sample period.

In figures 2.3–2.6, plots of rolling coefficients that are representative of

---

7. $\rho_{\hat{w}_i\hat{w}_j}$ is generated by historically simulating $\hat{w}_i$ for each bank, using the estimated factor coefficients and historical factor data. For $RS_i = \sigma_{\hat{w}_i\hat{w}_i}/\sigma_{w_iw_i}$, $\sigma_{\hat{w}_i\hat{w}_j}$ is similarly obtained. $\sigma_{w_iw_i}$ can be generated from equation (4.e) in the text, using the estimated factor coefficients for V_k, the sample factor variances for ω_{kk}, and the estimated factor coefficient variances used for $\sigma_{v_kv_k}$.

Table 2.6   Cross-bank trading revenue correlation due to market factors (unconditional trading revenue correlations above diagonal; correlations due to market factors below diagonal)

	Bank					
Bank	1	2	3	4	5	6
1		0.415	0.21	0.182	0.028	0.145
2	0.301		0.112	0.070	0.158	0.147
3	0.139	0.064		0.243	0.169	0.145
4	−0.011	−0.028	0.138		0.048	0.146
5	0.029	0.121	0.042	0.017		0.094
6	0.123	0.107	0.056	0.063	0.045	

Notes: The cross-bank correlations due to market factors were calculated using equation (5). For details of the calculations, see the explanation in text.

the results for the different broad market categories are presented along with 150-day coincidental moving averages of the respective factors. The coefficients for each factor are in the same units as the random coefficient model estimates in appendix table 2A.1 (average values of the rolling coefficients are of the same order of magnitude as those in the random coefficient model in table 2A.1). The rolling means of factors are expressed as factor levels (not differences). They show large ranges of variation over the sample period, which includes a business cycle peak in March 2000 and a trough in November 2001. The interest rate, equity, and credit spread factors (Baa and high yield) show evidence of business cycle influences.

Our interest is in whether the rolling coefficients vary systematically with the factors, which would indicate that the dealers' market exposures are related to market prices.

Consider first the coefficients for the interest rate factor plotted in figure 2.3. The coefficients for all but bank 4 show a rising and declining pattern that roughly tracks the rising and declining interest rate pattern. The pattern implies a tendency for the portfolio's interest rate exposure to move inversely with interest rates to the point where exposures may go from long to short or short to long.

This pattern would be consistent with dealers' reducing net long positions in longer-term securities when interest rates are rising, even to the point of taking short positions. When interest rates decline, dealers increase their net long positions so that, in low interest rate environments, they tend to have relatively large interest rate exposures.

A more passive strategy also might be consistent with the results in figure 2.3. As shown in equation (3), the factor coefficients measure factor exposures in terms of position values. Rather than actively alter positions, dealers might have simply held their same positions and allowed position values to deteriorate, even becoming negative, as rates increased (prices de-

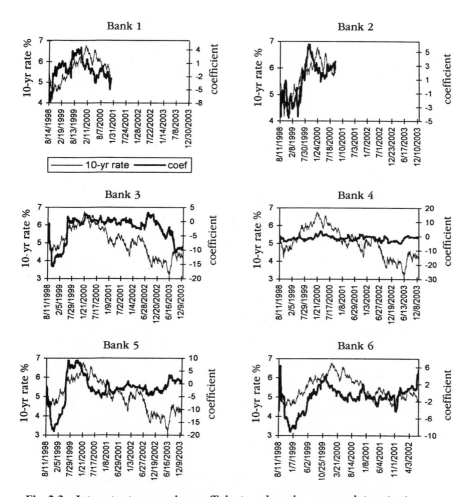

Fig. 2.3   Interest rate regression coefficients and moving-average interest rate

clined) and then increase as rates subsequently declined. Against this explanation, however, market analysts suggested that dealers were increasing their long-term positions as interest rates declined to low levels in the early 2000s.[8]

Aside from the explanation for the rolling interest rate coefficients, it is shown in table 2.7 that cross-bank correlations for the coefficients are all positive. This reinforces the impression from figure 2.3 of common variation in the dealers' interest rate exposures.

For the most part, the rolling coefficients for the other factors do not

8. See *Financial Times* article by Jenny Wiggins, March 11, 2004. Also see Adrian and Fleming (2005), p. 4.

Table 2.7   **Cross-bank correlations for rolling regression coefficients**

	xwe	xru	xap	xsa	nyse	nasdaq	r10yr	Baa	hy yld	swap	embi
Median correlation	0.09	0.03	0.18	0.28	0.18	0.20	0.74	0.16	0.59	0.25	0.13
Percent positive correlation	53	53	53	67	73	60	100	60	80	67	67

Note: There are 15 cross-bank correlations for each market factor.

show any clear patterns of comovement with their respective factors that are common to all or most banks. In figures 2.4 and 2.5, plots are presented for the rolling coefficients and factors for the NYSE and high yield spreads. These results are representative of results for the other factors as well, excluding the Russian ruble (see the following). For some individual banks, comovement is observed between the coefficients and factors—for example, the NYSE rolling coefficients and NYSE factor for bank 2. Whether this represents an underlying relationship for a particular bank or just a chance realization of the data can't be determined. Nonetheless, for the non-interest rate factors, the results do not indicate any covariation between the factor exposures and the factors that is common among the dealers.

Something of an exception to these results is the behavior of the Russian ruble coefficients shown in figure 2.6. For all six banks, the coefficients move toward zero in late August and early September 1998 as the ruble declined precipitously. The estimated coefficients remain close to zero until mid-1999 (several months after the August–October 1998 period passed out of the rolling samples). This behavior would be consistent for the banks becoming insulated against the ruble.[9]

2.6   Dealer Trading Revenues on Days of Large Market Moves

The results from the two-factor model approaches suggest that, in the aggregate, bank dealers are not consistently on one side of the market, except possibly for (default-free) interest rate exposures. However, as described in section 2.2, all six banks had abnormally low, though still mostly positive, trading revenues in the latter part of 1998. This was a period that included both high market volatility and sharp declines in credit and other risky asset prices and increases in U.S. Treasury security prices. In a final exercise, we look to see whether dealer trading revenues might be commonly related to price movements on days of large price changes. This may

9. While difficult to see in the figure, prior to convergence to zero, the rolling coefficients across the six banks were quite different and included both positive and negative coefficient values, implying long and short exposures in the ruble. Note also that the volatility of the ruble (measured as absolute daily log changes) remained above pre-August 1998 levels over the rest of the year and into the first half of 1999.

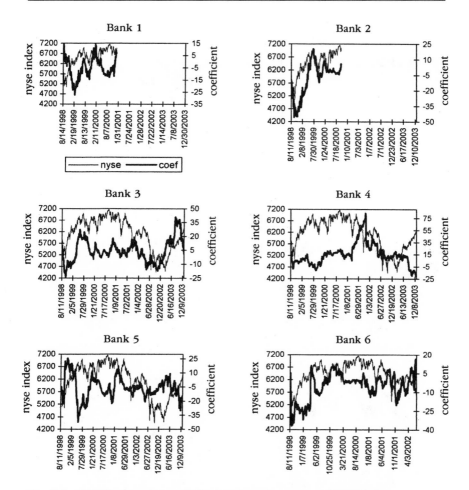

Fig. 2.4   NYSE regression coefficients and moving-average NYSE index

not be evident in the factor model regressions based on the full samples where, on many days, price changes are small.

For simplicity, days of relatively large price increases and, separately, price declines are identified only for the broad market categories—exchange rate, equity, interest rate, and credit. For each market factor, days where factor shocks fall into the first quintile and the fifth quintile are separately sorted. For a market category, a large market decline day (or a large market increase day) is defined as a day when at least one factor in the category is in the first (the fifth) quintile and none is in the fifth (the first) quintile. For example, a day when the change in the NYSE index is in the first quintile and the NASDAQ index is not in the fifth quintile is a large equity market decline day. Typically, when one factor in a market category expe-

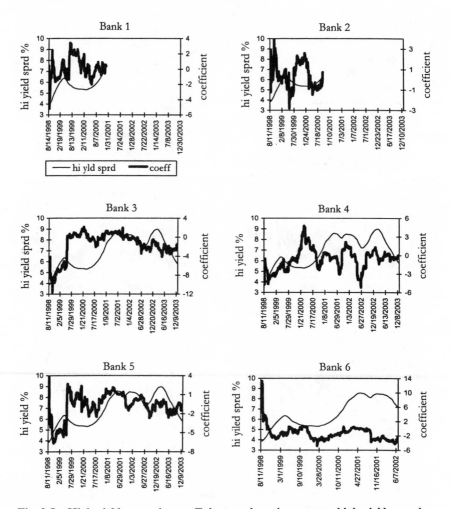

Fig. 2.5   High-yield regression coefficients and moving-average high-yield spread

riences a large change, other factor(s) in that category change in the same direction, although this is less true for exchange rates (further description of the large factor changes is provided in table 2.8). Large market move days span the entire six-year sample period, but with a higher frequency in the second half of 1998.

Mean and median bank trading revenues for low and high market return days for each of the four market categories are reported in table 2.8. Except for the interest rate category, mean and median trading revenues for the six banks on low return days in each of the other market categories are not uniformly lower, or higher, than on high return days. For these market categories, this comparison does not indicate that dealers' market exposures bear a common systematic relation to market prices. For the interest rate

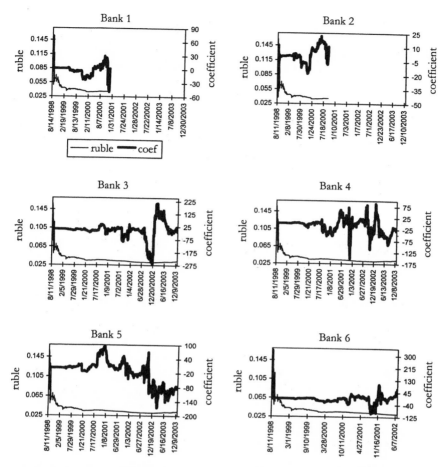

Fig. 2.6   Russian ruble regression coefficients and moving-average exchange rate

category, on days of large rate increases, trading revenues are uniformly lower across the six banks than on days of large rate declines, suggesting long (positive duration) interest rate exposures are typical. These results are consistent with the results from the factor models.

While heterogeneity in exposures will reduce the likelihood of large aggregate dealer losses, the chance realization of losses (or abnormally high returns) for a group of dealers is still more likely during a period when volatility is high across markets. The summer and autumn of 1998 was such a period, and the higher volatility in the banks' trading revenues is apparent from figure 2.2.[10] Nonetheless, with cross-bank heterogeneity in expo-

10. We also looked at absolute trading revenues on days of high and low absolute changes in market factors, where absolute values are used to measure the size of daily fluctuations or volatility. Days of high and low volatility were defined at the market category level using an analogous procedure to that followed in determining days of large market declines and large

Table 2.8   **Bank trading revenues conditioned on large one-day market moves**

	Exchange rate change				Interest rate change			
	Trading revenue: Mean		Trading revenue: Median		Trading revenue: Mean		Trading revenue: Median	
Bank	Decline	Increase	Decline	Increase	Decline	Increase	Decline	Increase
1	1.14	1.04	1.07	0.97	1.29**	1.00	1.22**	0.90
2	0.87	0.85	0.82	0.78	0.93	0.85	0.82	0.80
3	0.70	0.81	0.70	0.75	0.86**	0.71	0.90*	0.72
4	0.85	0.98**	0.81	0.81	0.95	0.93	0.87	0.78
5	0.60	0.61	0.55	0.59	0.69**	0.57	0.70**	0.55
6	0.63	0.69	0.63	0.68	0.87**	0.63	0.81**	0.64

	Equity price change				Credit spread changes			
	Trading revenue: Mean		Trading revenue: Median		Trading revenue: Mean		Trading revenue: Median	
	Decline	Increase	Decline	Increase	Decline	Increase	Decline	Increase
1	1.17	1.06	1.06	0.89	1.00	1.13	0.93	1.13
2	0.93	0.77	0.86	0.78	0.72**	0.92	0.64**	0.84
3	0.74	0.86	0.78	0.85	0.84	0.73	0.76	0.78
4	0.83	1.20**	0.80	0.93**	1.01	0.91	0.85	0.83
5	0.60	0.51	0.59	0.45	0.68	0.63	0.64	0.61
6	0.82	0.72	0.75	0.75	0.73	0.73	0.66	0.77

Notes: Bank trading revenue is normalized by full sample bank trading revenue standard deviations. Sample sizes for each of the "Decline" and "Increase" categories range from 167 to 606, with a median of 323. For individual factors (e.g., NYSE for equity category), their mean values for the "Decline" quintile is 1 to 2 standard deviations below the mean values for the "Increase" quintile. Means test is a standard difference of two means. Medians test uses the Mann-Whitney-Wilcoxon rank sum test for large samples.

**Significant at .05 for the difference between "Decline" and "Increase" day trading revenue mean (median) values.

sures, losses are likely to come from positions in different markets. For the 1998 third and fourth quarters, major U.S. bank dealers reported quarterly losses or low revenues in different market categories—interest rate (including credit), equity, and commodities.[11] For the six banks studied here, it was also the case that different banks reported quarterly losses or low returns in different markets.

increases (table 2.8), except in terms of the size of absolute factor changes. For each of the six banks, mean and median absolute one-day trading revenues are consistently higher on high market volatility days than on low market volatility days for all four market categories, with significance at the 0.05 level for almost 75 percent of the mean and median calculations.

11. For large bank dealers, see "Bank Derivatives Report, Fourth Quarter 2001," Office of the Comptroller of the Currency, p. 13. Note that the quarterly revenue reports include fee and spread income as well as changes in position market values.

2.7   Conclusions

To recap the main results, bank dealers do not consistently maintain exposures on one side of the market, with the exception of small average long exposures to interest rate risk. They vary their exposures in size and direction but, except for interest rate exposures, the variation is heterogeneous across the dealers. Interest rate exposures tend to vary inversely with the level of interest rates. Variation in trading revenues from market exposures also does not seem large relative to the variation in total trading revenues, which also include fee, spread, and net interest income.

These results are subject to important limitations imposed by limitations of the trading revenue data that were used, inherent factor model limitations, and to a small sample of bank dealers. Also, the two-factor modeling approaches employ different underlying assumptions whose consequences have not been examined. If these limitations are put aside, a number of points can be made about the relation between dealer market risks, VaR, and market prices based on the results.

Heterogeneity in dealers' market exposures reduces the likelihood that dealers as a group will incur large losses in periods of market stress or that their aggregate risk-taking behavior contributes significantly to a herding phenomenon. The heterogeneity in exposures also applies to arguments that dealers' common use of VaR for risk management leads to herding behavior. Shifts in market volatility could produce common changes in dealers' VaRs and desired risk exposures but without leading to common directional shifts in risky asset demands because dealers have both short and long positions. A potential exception is commonality in adjustments to interest rate risk exposures.

While heterogeneity in dealers' market exposures reduces the likelihood of large aggregate dealer losses, the chance occurrence of common losses (or abnormally high returns) among banks is still more likely in a period of generally high market volatility. The summer and autumn of 1998 was such a period, when volatility was high across markets and dealers' losses or low returns occurred in different markets.

Especially during periods of extreme market conditions, there are areas of dealer activity other than securities trading that may be more important to financial market stability and bank risk. This would include dealers' market-making role under extreme market conditions. For example, see Routledge and Zinn (2004), with some empirical evidence on the summer and autumn of 1998 in Furfine and Remolona (2002). Also potentially important is dealer (including parent bank), credit exposures to hedge funds, and other important market players. The issue of bank credit exposures to hedge funds and large market players is taken up in Kho, Lee, and Stulz (2000), Furfine and Remolona (2002), and Chan, Getmansky, Hass, and Lo (2005).

Appendix

Factor Model Derivations

Factor Model Portfolio Value (equation [2])

Here the 1-period change in the value of the portfolio shown in equation (2) is derived. Two assumptions are used. One is a self-financing constraint within the period, $\Sigma_{k=1}^{K} dx_{kt}(\tau)p_{kt}(\tau) + dx_{0t}(\tau) = 0$. The second is that price and position changes within the period are uniform: $dp_{kt}(\tau) = \Delta p_k(t)d\tau$ and $dx_{kt}(\tau) = \Delta x_k(t)d\tau$ for $t-1 < \tau < t$. The starting position for security k is x_{kt}^0. The derivation uses continuous price and position changes within the period. The change in the value of the portfolio is $w(t) \equiv W(t) - W_t^0$.

Using the above assumptions and notation:

$$(A.1) \quad w(t) = \int_{t-1}^{t} \left[\sum_{k=1}^{K} x_k(\tau)dp_k(\tau) + p_k(\tau)dx_k(\tau) + dx_0(\tau) \right] d\tau$$

$$= \sum_{k=1}^{K} \int_{t-1}^{t} x_k(\tau)dp_k(\tau) \qquad \text{(using the self-financing constraint)}$$

$$= \sum_{k=1}^{K} \int_{t-1}^{t} \left[x_{kt}^0 + \int_{t-1}^{\tau} dx_k(\varsigma)d\varsigma \right] dp_k(\tau)d\tau$$

$$= \sum_{k=1}^{K} \left[x_{kt}^0 + \frac{1}{2}\Delta x(t) \right] \Delta p(t) \qquad \text{(using uniform price and position changes)}$$

$$= \sum_{k=1}^{K} \left[x_{kt}^0 p_k(t-1) + \frac{1}{2}\Delta x(t)p_k(t-1) \right] r_k(t)$$

where $r_k(t) \equiv \Delta p_k(t)/p_k(t-1)$.

Cross-Bank Portfolio Value Correlation Due to Market Factors (equation [5])

The correlation in portfolio value changes between bank i and j due to market factor shocks is derived under the assumptions used for the random coefficient model presented in equations (4a)–(4d). The following vector notation is used here: $r(t)$, $V_i(t)$, $\bar{V}_i$ and $v_i(t)$ are $K \times 1$ vectors of the market factors, factor coefficients, mean coefficients and random coefficient components, respectively. The factor shocks $r(t)$ are assumed to have a zero expected value.

Using equation (4a) in the text, $w(t) = \sum_{k=1}^{K} r_k(t)\overline{V}_k + u(t)$ and equation (4b), $u(t) \equiv \sum_{k=1}^{K} r_k(t)v_k(t)$, the expected cross-product of returns for banks i and j, conditioned on $r(t)$, is:

(A.2) $\quad E(w_i(t)w_j(t)\,|\,r(t)) = E_{v_i, v_j}\{[\overline{V}_i'r(t) + v_i'(t)r(t)][\overline{V}_j'r(t) + v_j'(t)r(t)]\,|\,r(t)\},$

where $E_{v_i, v_j}[g(v_i, v_j)\,|\,r(t)] \equiv \int_{v_{i1}} \ldots \int_{v_{jK}} g[v_{i1} \ldots, v_{jK}, r(t)] f[v_{i1} \ldots, v_{jK}\,|\,r(t)]dv_{i1} \ldots, dv_{jK}$. Using $E[v_i(t)] = 0$ and independence between $v_i(t)$ and $r(t)$, $E_{v_i}[\overline{V}_i'r(t)r'(t)v_j(t)\,|\,r(t)] = E_{v_i}[v_j'(t)r(t)r'(t)\overline{V}_j\,|\,r(t)] = 0$. Using this orthogonality, (A.2) becomes

(A.3) $\quad E(w_i(t)w_j(t)\,|\,r(t)) = \overline{V}_i'r(t)r'(t)\overline{V}_j + E_{v_i, v_j}[v_i'(t)r(t)r'(t)v_j(t)\,|\,r(t)]$

$$= \overline{V}_i'r(t)r'(t)\overline{V}_j + \sum_{k=1}^{K}\sum_{l=1}^{K}\sigma_{v_{ik}v_{jl}}r_k(t)r_i(t).$$

Since the factor shocks are zero mean, the (unconditional) covariance between portfolio returns to i and j is $\sigma_{w_i w_j} \equiv E[w_i w_j] = E_r\{E[w_i(t)w_j(t)\,|\,r(t)]\}$. Applying $E_r\{E[w_i(t)w_j(t)\,|\,r(t)]\}$ to (A.3) yields

(A.4) $\qquad \sigma_{w_i w_j} = E_r[\overline{V}_i'r(t)r'(t)\overline{V}_j] + E_r\left[\sum_{k=1}^{K}\sum_{l=1}^{K}\sigma_{v_{ik}v_{jl}}r_k(t)r_i(t)\right]$

$$= \overline{V}_i'\Omega\overline{V}_j + \sum_{k=1}^{K}\sum_{l=1}^{K}\sigma_{v_{ik}v_{jl}}\omega_{kl},$$

where $\Omega \equiv E[r(t)r'(t)]$ is the covariance matrix for $r(t)$ and $\omega_{kl} \equiv E[r_k(t)r_i(t)]$ the covariance for $r_k(t)$ and $r_l(t)$. $\overline{V}_i'\Omega\overline{V}_j$ is the covariance between changes in bank i and bank j's portfolio values conditioned on market exposures set at their mean values. $\sum_{k=1}^{K}\sum_{l=1}^{K}\sigma_{v_{ik}v_{jl}}\omega_{kl}$ is the covariance between changes in i and j's portfolio values due to the interaction between the random shifts in the coefficients and the market factors. Note the sign for $\sigma_{v_{ik}v_{jk}}\omega_{kk}$ is the same as that for $\sigma_{v_{ik}v_{jk}}$.

To obtain the correlation coefficient for $w_i(t)$ and $w_j(t)$, define $\sigma_{\hat{w}_i\hat{w}_j} \equiv \overline{V}_i'\Omega\overline{V}_j$ and $\sigma_{u_iu_j} \equiv \sum_{k=1}^{K}\sum_{l=1}^{K}\sigma_{v_{ik}v_{jl}}\omega_{kl}$. Define $\rho_{w_i w_j}$ as the correlation between $w_i(t)$ and $w_j(t)$. Using this notation, we can express the various correlations and covariances between changes in i and j's portfolio values as follows:

(A.5a) $\qquad\qquad \rho_{w_i w_j} \equiv \sigma_{w_i w_j}/\sqrt{\sigma_{w_i w_i}}\sqrt{\sigma_{w_j w_j}}$

(A.5b) $\qquad\qquad \sigma_{\hat{w}_i\hat{w}_j} \equiv \rho_{\hat{w}_i\hat{w}_j}\sqrt{\sigma_{\hat{w}_i\hat{w}_i}}\sqrt{\sigma_{\hat{w}_j\hat{w}_j}}$

(A.5c) $\qquad\qquad \sigma_{u_iu_j} \equiv \rho_{u_iu_j}\sqrt{\sigma_{\hat{w}_i\hat{w}_i}}\sqrt{\sigma_{\hat{w}_j\hat{w}_j}}$

Also, from equation (A.4), we have $\sigma_{w_i w_j} = \sigma_{\hat{w}_i\hat{w}_i} + \sigma_{u_iu_i}$. Using this result with the definitions in equations (A.5a)–(A.5c) gives the unconditional correlation between changes in i and j's portfolio values, shown in equation (5) in the text:

$$(A.6) \quad \rho_{w_i w_j} = \rho_{\hat{w}_i \hat{w}_j} \sqrt{\frac{\sigma_{\hat{w}_i \hat{w}_i}}{\sigma_{w_i w_i}}} \sqrt{\frac{\sigma_{\hat{w}_j \hat{w}_j}}{\sigma_{w_j w_j}}} + \rho_{u_i u_j} \sqrt{\frac{1 - \sigma_{\hat{w}_i \hat{w}_i}}{\sigma_{w_i w_i}}} \sqrt{\frac{1 - \sigma_{\hat{w}_j \hat{w}_j}}{\sigma_{w_j w_j}}}$$

$$= \rho_{\hat{w}_i \hat{w}_i} \sqrt{RS_i} \sqrt{RS_j} + \rho_{u_i u_j} \sqrt{1 - RS_i} \sqrt{1 - RS_j}.$$

Table 2A.1   **Market factor model for bank trading revenue**

	Bank					
Variable	1	2	3	4	5	6
constant						
β_0	−0.105	1.152	−0.575	−2.632	1.397	0.422
t-value	−0.26	2.81	−2.54	−11.24	5.51	1.44
fx we						
β_1	5.568	5.652	4.528	6.771	−7.380	5.575
t-value	0.92	0.94	1.02	1.64	−1.52	1.13
fx russia						
β_2	0.901	1.814	5.011	−0.088	0.605	−1.038
t-value	0.56	0.97	2.57	−0.08	0.35	−0.72
fx asia pac						
β_3	−17.873	−8.553	−2.006	3.794	2.843	0.550
t-value	−3.02	−1.45	−0.47	1.01	0.58	0.13
fx s amer						
β_4	−3.993	−5.830	−0.506	4.637	−6.527	13.453
t-value	−0.60	−0.91	−0.12	1.03	−1.43	2.43
nyse						
β_5	−5.437	−5.112	2.241	10.230	−6.432	−1.959
t-value	−1.19	−1.14	0.79	3.50	−2.06	−0.53
nasdaq						
β_6	1.855	2.440	0.148	−1.621	0.985	−1.410
t-value	0.92	1.19	0.10	−1.07	0.62	−0.89
10-yr treas						
β_7	−2.192	0.804	−1.507	−1.618	−0.566	−0.696
t-value	−2.23	0.78	−2.38	−2.89	−0.85	−0.99
Baa sprd						
β_8	−0.593	2.355	−1.184	0.314	−0.305	2.312
t-value	−0.41	1.58	−1.30	0.36	−0.31	2.12
hi yld sprd						
β_9	−0.434	0.059	−0.901	−1.011	−0.200	−1.218
t-value	−0.62	0.07	−2.06	−2.46	−0.48	−2.48
swap sprd						
β_{10}	−0.268	−0.234	1.181	0.191	0.397	−0.582
t-value	−0.21	−0.21	1.53	0.28	0.51	−0.64
embi+ sprd						
β_{11}	0.013	0.168	−0.279	−0.722	−0.066	0.097
t-value	0.07	0.86	−2.12	−5.55	−0.44	0.52
equity vol						
β_{12}	0.353	0.418	0.223	0.363	0.083	0.236
t-value	3.78	4.21	4.97	8.07	1.71	4.00

Table 2A.1   (continued)

	Bank					
Variable	1	2	3	4	5	6
10-yr treas move ave						
β_{13}	0.143	−0.124	0.150	0.529	−0.206	0.024
t-value	1.91	−1.60	4.07	13.42	−5.03	0.47
PL_{t-1}						
β_{14}	0.142	0.181	0.203	0.227	−0.081	−0.028
t-value	4.03	5.09	8.30	9.65	−3.17	−1.07
trend						
β_{15}	0.001	0.001	0.001	0.001	0.001	0.000
t-value	3.59	3.45	9.05	12.08	6.71	4.37
F-Stat2	9.236	6.081	22.368	44.293	14.593	4.576
R^2	0.172	0.128	0.196	0.325	0.137	0.063
N	728	681	1,484	1,485	1,483	1,109

Notes: Trading revenues are divided by the banks' sample standard deviations. Equity volume has been scaled by 1 million. Coefficients are estimated for equation (4.a) in the text with additional explanatory variables described in the text. A GLS estimator is used, which is described in Hildreth and Houck (1968). See their description for β, second equation in (25), p. 589.

Table 2A.2   **Estimates of coefficient variances for market factors**

	Bank					
Variable	1	2	3	4	5	6
constant						
α_0	0.48	0.40	0.44	0.57	0.56	0.90
t-value	3.25	3.89	5.86	8.21	5.76	2.41
fx w eur						
α_1	−528.20	34.75	1281.02	−87.84	1114.55	−2052.03
t-value	−0.26	0.02	1.19	−0.09	0.80	−0.39
fx russia						
α_2	2.05	30.54	83.44	−19.82	30.01	−108.13
t-value	0.10	2.18	5.85	−1.51	1.62	−1.75
fx asia pac						
α_3	2567.56	3111.68	1401.34	−240.30	3002.21	−449.13
t-value	3.00	5.26	2.43	−0.45	4.00	−0.18
fx s amer						
α_4	−1526.15	−333.83	810.87	1705.42	−862.05	−2801.47
t-value	−1.71	−0.54	1.57	3.58	−1.28	−1.13
nyse						
α_5	665.46	456.79	−301.12	206.31	−35.02	808.70
t-value	1.28	1.19	−1.22	0.90	−0.11	0.56

continued

Table 2A.2   (continued)

Variable	Bank					
	1	2	3	4	5	6
nasdaq						
α_6	70.81	−80.79	1.01	134.72	−38.89	−154.61
t-value	0.56	−0.70	0.02	2.23	−0.46	−0.51
10-yr treas						
α_7	19.11	−4.55	51.94	−8.02	59.64	15.60
t-value	0.74	−0.25	5.87	−0.98	5.10	0.31
Baa sprd						
α_8	−58.85	64.78	−78.46	−29.95	−16.59	−69.86
t-value	−0.86	1.44	−3.07	−1.27	−0.50	−0.55
hi yld sprd						
α_9	−0.15	15.00	8.25	6.00	−0.55	3.48
t-value	−0.02	1.52	3.24	2.56	−0.17	0.28
swap sprd						
α_{10}	88.76	4.04	25.43	−15.60	−15.92	−24.42
t-value	2.49	0.16	1.42	−0.95	−0.68	−0.25
embi+ sprd						
α_{11}	1.39	1.68	0.19	0.37	0.56	4.73
t-value	3.11	5.73	0.78	1.68	1.79	4.44
F-Stat	3.82	13.73	11.07	4.16	5.59	1.98
R^2	0.06	0.18	0.08	0.03	0.04	0.02
N	728	681	1,484	1,485	1,483	1,109

Note: The coefficients (variances) and their standard errors use an unbiased least-squares estimator developed in Hildreth and Houck (1968), equation (14), p. 587.

References

Adrian, T., and M. Fleming. 2005. What financing data reveal about dealer leverage. *Federal Reserve Bank of New York Current Issues in Economics and Finance* 11(3): 1–7.

Agarwal, V., and N. Naik. 2004. Risks and portfolio decisions involving hedge funds. *The Review of Financial Studies* 17(1): 63–98.

Alexander, G., and A. Baptista. 2004. A comparison of VaR and CVaR constraints on portfolio selection with the mean-variance model. *Management Science* 50 (9): 1261–73.

Basak, S., and A. Shapiro. 2001. Value-at-Risk based risk management: Optimal policies and asset prices. *Review of Financial Studies* 14:371–405.

Berkowitz, J., and J. O'Brien. 2002. How accurate are Value-at-Risk models at commercial banks? *Journal of Finance* 57:1093–1112.

Chan, N., M. Getmansky, S. Hass, and A. Lo. 2005. Systematic risk and hedge funds. Paper presented at NBER Conference on the Risks of Financial Institutions. 22–23 October, Woodstock, VT.

Chen, N., R. Roll, and S. Ross. 1986. Economic forces and the stock market: Testing the APT and alternate asset pricing theories. *Journal of Business* 53:383–404.

Cuoco, D., and H. Liu. 2003. An analysis of VaR-based capital requirements. Forthcoming. *Journal of Financial Intermediation.*

Danielsson, J., H. S. Shin, and J.-P. Zigrand. 2002. The impact of risk regulation on price dynamics. Available at http://www.riskresearch.org.

Flannery, M., and C. James. 1984. The effect of interest rate changes on the common stock returns of financial institutions. *The Journal of Finance* 39:1141–53.

Fung, W., and D. A. Hsieh. 1997. Empirical characteristics of dynamic trading strategies: The case of hedge funds. *Review of Financial Studies* 10:275–302.

Furfine, C., and E. Remolona. 2002. Price discovery in a market under stress: The U.S. Treasury market in fall 1998. Paper presented at Bocconi Centennial Conference. June, Milan, Italy.

Hildreth, C., and J. Houck. 1968. Some estimators for a linear model with random coefficients. *Journal of the American Statistical Association* 63:584–95.

Jorion, P. 2004. Bank trading risk and systematic risk. Paper presented at NBER Conference on the Risks of Financial Institutions. 22–23 October, Woodstock, VT.

Koh, B., D. Lee, and R. M. Stulz. 2000. U.S. banks, crises, and bailouts: From Mexico to LTCM. *American Economic Review* (May): 28–31.

Mitchel, M., and T. Pulvino. 2001. Characteristics of risk and return in risk arbitrage. *The Journal of Finance* 56 (6): 2135–75.

Morris, S., and H. S. Shin. 1999. Risk management with independent choice. *Oxford Economic Policy* 15:52–62.

Persaud, A. 2000. Sending the herd off the cliff. Available at http://www.erisk.com/ResourceCenter/ERM/persaud.pdf.

Routledge, B., and S. Zin. 2001. Model uncertainty and liquidity. NBER Working Paper no. 8683. Cambridge, MA: National Bureau of Economic Research.

Sharpe, W. 1992. Asset allocation: Management style and performance measurement. *Journal of Portfolio Management* (Winter): 7–19.

Comment on Chapters 1 and 2   Kenneth C. Abbott

First of all, I want to thank the NBER for inviting me to this conference. Among the attendees are professors from my student days, academics whose works I've admired for years, and regulators whose role I have come to respect more and more. I also thank the authors of the two papers for their work in this important field.

For years, value-at-risk (VaR) has had both its supporters and its detractors in the academic and regulatory communities. The detractors have been quick to point out that VaR fails to capture extreme market movements and does not react quickly enough to changes in market conditions. Supporters, on the other hand, simply look to its simplicity of purpose (to gain some crude measure of likely trading loss) and, more importantly, to the degree of uniformity it has imposed on the risk measurement processes used at banks and brokerages. I agree that it's far from perfect, but it does serve a very useful purpose.

As a practitioner, my concern has always been (and continues to be) that those studying the numbers emanating from banks' risk processes view

These comments reflect the opinion of the author alone and do not represent the views of Morgan Stanley.

those numbers as being similar to the random variables coming from some natural, or at least stationary, statistical process. While it is certainly not my intention to throw mud at the risk processes that financial institutions have spent so much time, effort, and money to put in place, I feel the need to make clear to everyone some of the problems inherent in those processes.

First, there is a considerable lack of consistency in the measurement of VaR across financial institutions. The Market Risk Amendment of 1996 standardized some aspects of VaR calculation, including the confidence level, the time frame of the loss estimate, the minimum amount of historical data required, and the minimum number of yield curve points necessary, to name but a few. It did not, however, say which methodology should be used (variance/covariance, Monte Carlo simulation, or Historical Simulation), nor did it specify exactly how much data should be used in the process.

I recently conducted an informal poll of fifteen major financial institutions and found that Historical Simulation is used by about 80 percent of them. One institution still used variance/covariance, while the rest did Monte Carlo simulations. What surprised me, however, was that the amount of data used ranged from one year to five years, with the mode of the distribution being two years. What this suggests is that banks' risk measurements will show varying degrees of sensitivity to short-term (and possibly short-lived) changes in market volatility. Most institutions update their datasets quarterly. The addition of one quarter to a rolling four-quarter dataset will be significantly greater than that to a twenty-quarter dataset.

Equally important, the Market Risk Amendment did not clearly define the standards for profit and loss (P&L) calculation for use in VaR backtests. While the recently released Consultative Paper makes some reference to the standardization of P&L, it has remained unclear. Regulators have been known to differ on the definition of the "clean" P&L required for backtests.

A major issue I see with studying VaR in conjunction with trading P&L in a time series framework (e.g., autoregressive integrated moving average [ARIMA], generalized autoregressive conditional heteroskedastic [GARCH], etc.) regards the stationarity of the measures themselves. VaR is clearly a function of the underlying trading position in a given trading book. Some books are very stable or change slowly over time. Certain proprietary books, for example, will hold on to sets of positions for extended periods of time. Other books, however, will show very high degrees of turnover. I have seen certain trading books used for intraday positioning that have shown no end-of-day positions. As a result, they would have no VaR attributed to them. (As a practical matter, for days when the book was flat, I assigned a certain *de minimus* VaR to them based on the average level of risk taking over a period of time.)

This is especially important in the context of very liquid derivatives markets. These portfolios are often very large and frequently represent the plurality of the risk taking going on within a financial institution. These positions can go from hugely long to hugely short in the course of minutes. As a result, these desks are often the risk "steering wheels" for banks' trading portfolios.

Another area where the changing composition of trading books is important to note involves books used to contain large syndication or block trading positions. Here, the book might go from levels of risk near zero to ones of tens of millions of dollars of VaR in an afternoon. Their risk might be reduced quickly, or it might be worked off gradually over time. Either way, the risk of these types of books is anything but stationary.

A third area of concern involves changing risk appetites within firms. Certain trading books may be cut back, often drastically, by senior management. This may take place during market crises, or it may reflect management's lack of confidence in a strategy or a trader. It would be difficult to account or correct for this in any time series analysis of VaR.

A fourth consideration involves the tendency of banks to err on the side of conservatism in their VaR measures. Given a choice between a highly accurate measure that might occasionally understate the VaR and a more conservative metric, all banks are likely to choose the conservative measure. This is because there is a severe penalty for an excess number of outliers (i.e., more than 1 percent at the 99 percent confidence level) in the regulatory capital calculation. In fact, it is not uncommon for books to show no outliers over extended periods of time. This is pointed out in earlier work (2002) by Berkowitz and O'Brien.

A final consideration regarding methodology involves changes in the methodology itself. Firms are constantly upgrading the techniques used to estimate their risk. Notably, these are not uniformly to reduce VaR. In fact, a casual examination of changes in bank's methodologies are likely to reveal as many VaR-increasing changes as decreasing ones. Usually, one does not go back to restate earlier trading days' VaR to reflect the new methodology unless the change took place near the beginning of a quarter. These changes are likely to manifest themselves as jumps in the VaR that have nothing to do with true trading risk.

The measurement of P&L presents still more issues relevant in this context. Some recent work has suggested that time series analysis of actual trading P&L be used as a measure of VaR. While this would certainly reflect market volatility better, it presents a number of difficulties.

First, one has to define trading P&L. While Financial Accounting Standard 133 has helped to define what should be marked-to-market, the actual definition of marked-to-market varies from book to book. In most cases it is fairly easy. Cash equity books have prices that are posted daily. These prices are used (among other things) to set margin levels, so they can probably be counted on to be reasonable.

Second, other trading books have less transparent pricing. Consider the U.S. corporate bond market, for example. Pricing is available every day for most bonds, but much of that is matrix pricing and does not necessarily represent where a bond would trade in the market. Even if the price were "real" it might be a bid for an odd lot and not for size.

Third, firms are likely to use trader marks for positions, checking them periodically with outside sources for veracity. Many of these books have positions within them that have poor price discovery. Many high-yield bonds, for example, are only repriced weekly. Other trading books have positions which are clearly "trading" positions, inasmuch as they are there to capture short-term gains, but for which there is no pricing available at all. It is not uncommon for banks to have distressed debt positions for which one will observe no price changes for weeks or even months at a time. As a result, all measures of P&L on these portfolios must be viewed as approximations of changes in value.

Fourth, the timing of certain P&L events may be subjective. For example, one may observe that a bond spread has widened 10 basis points between day 1 and day 10. Is it safe to assume that the widening took place gradually, suggesting that the loss be recognized on a straight-line basis? Or is it more appropriate to take the loss all at once, perhaps when there was another trade on the market to justify the new price?

The subjectivity of P&L events is exaggerated in the mark-to-model framework, which may affect many derivative transactions. Model changes for derivative books may result in P&L events in dealer portfolios. While some of these events may be covered by reserves set aside for such purposes, other losses may not. This may be due to models behind large positions that are based primarily upon variables that cannot be observed directly.

I think that one possible way of addressing all of these issues is to make bank regulators much more aware of all of the issues involved in the calculation of P&L and the estimation of VaR. I think it would be enormously instructive for bank examiners to study P&L time series to come to an understanding of which pieces of it are purely objective (i.e., based upon prices and/or model input parameters clearly observed in the market) and which pieces less so.

On the VaR side, regulators need to remember that VaR is simply an order statistic—a (sometimes) crude heuristic used to estimate the shape of a loss distribution.

While I'm sure that many firms would be hesitant to release detailed P&L and risk data freely into the academic community, there are probably ways to normalize the data and obfuscate the exact source (i.e., which desk produced the results) that would pass banks' data security rules. This might help all involved gain more insight into how it can be used more effectively.

Comment on Chapters 1 and 2   Paul Kupiec

Let me begin by thanking the NBER for the opportunity to participate in the Woodstock financial regulatory conference. I would also like to thank the authors, Philippe Jorion, James O'Brien, and Jeremy Berkowitz for the opportunity to discuss their papers.

Both of the papers I have been asked to discuss are motivated by the conjecture that the widespread adoption of value-at-risk (VaR) measurement and risk management techniques leads to increased market volatility. The mechanism causing excess volatility is herding behavior among market participants who identically measure and manage risk. Groupthink in risk measurement and management practices, it is alleged, leads investors to construct similar exposures and display a uniform reaction to unanticipated market developments. Presumably this leads to overreactions in market clearing prices, as liquidity providers are ill-prepared to absorb the sales demand of the stampeding VaR-driven investors. The corollary to this conjecture is that unless there is diversity among investor risk measurement and management practices, the buy side of the capital markets are in danger of evaporating when unanticipated market events create sell signals for VaR-focused investors.

In considering the merits of this conjecture, it is unclear to me what special role VaR has to do with creating herdlike behavior. Value at risk is not a trading strategy—it is a specific way of measuring risk. VaR has no direct link with expected return and so it cannot play a defining role in the construction of profitable trading strategies. There is no theoretical or empirical literature of which I am aware that suggests that there is a market price for bearing VaR exposure.[1] VaR limits can be used to control trading losses, but the use of VaR limits does not create positive feedback trading demands that are, for example, required by portfolio insurance dynamic hedges.

VaR is a useful way of measuring and monitoring the exposure of agents that trade risk on behalf of a financial institution. It may, moreover, also be convenient for an institution to use VaR to set limits on these agents' capacity to assume risk. But VaR is not unique in this regard. Risk measures and limits based on durations, convexity, and fixed shocks to the yield curve have long been used to monitor and place limits on the interest rate risks taken by fixed-income traders. Similarly, before the popularization of VaR, options traders' positions were monitored and limited according to rules that used the aggregate delta and vega values of their portfolios. What

These comments reflect the opinion of the author alone and do not represent the views of the FDIC.
1. Yet many investors have used VaR measures in the denominator of pseudo-Sharpe measures of ex post trading performance.

is unclear to me is why the use of VaR should be unique in its power to cause herding and excess volatility. If risk management encourages herding, then any measure of risk that facilitates monitoring and control of trading activity could give rise to the excess volatility concerns that have been voiced regarding the use of VaR.

It is possible that VaR could be a stronger stimulant for herding behavior than would be the case for other risk and control measures. Unlike duration-based or other methods for limiting risk, VaR estimates are a direct determinant of a bank's minimum regulatory capital requirement. The Basel Market Risk Amendment sets a bank's capital requirement for market risks using the bank's VaR estimates in a formula for minimum regulatory capital (MRC; this formula is well described in Jorion's paper). It is possible that unanticipated changes in asset prices, correlations, or volatilities could result in pressure on regulatory capital capacities in a manner that encourages banks to initiate portfolio adjustments. No other widely used risk monitoring measure has a direct link to minimum regulatory capital needs. The problem with this line of reasoning is that, to date, no U.S. bank has been at risk of becoming less than adequately capitalized due to an unanticipated increase in MRC for market risk.

Quantitative requirements surrounding the construction of banks' MRCs ensure that a bank's daily VaR estimate reacts sluggishly to increases in market volatility.[2] As a consequence, it is highly improbable that unanticipated increases in market factor volatilities can increase daily VaR to a point that it dominates the sixty-day moving average component of the MRC formula, given the attached multiplier of three.[3] Thus, spikes in market volatilities alone are unlikely to cause large daily trading rebalancing demands. For daily VaR to dominate in the MRC calculation, a bank must increase its exposures to market factors by a substantial amount. Absent large changes in bank positions, MRC requirements move only sluggishly from day to day. Moreover, even when banks change positions substantially, the sixty trading-day moving average component of the MRC formula ensures that minimum regulatory capital can only decline gradually. This feature limits the effectiveness of stop-loss trading and wholesale position liquidations as a capital minimization feature.

Even if banks exhibit herdlike reactions to changes in market conditions,

---

2. The Basel Committee on Banking Supervision (1996a, p. 46) specifies quantitative standards for the implicit calculation of market factor volatilities and correlations in regulatory VaR calculations: "The choice of *historical observation period* (sample period) for calculating value-at-risk will be constrained to a minimum length of one year. For banks that use a weighting scheme or other methods for the historical observation period, the "effective" observation period must be at least one year (that is, the weighted average time lag of the individual observations cannot be less than 6 months)."

3. A 3 multiplier on the sixty-day moving average VaR component applies to a bank with satisfactory backtest results. The multiplier can be increased should a bank's VaR perform poorly in backtests (see the Basel Committee on Banking Supervision 1996a).

bank MRC requirements provide only a weak signal of banks' position adjustments. The signal will be further diminished if banks reallocate the proceeds of their liquidated positions to other positions in the trading book. Bank trading desks may, moreover, also rebalance away from troubled markets but attempt to maintain internal VaR utilization targets.[4] All of these issues make MRC a less-than-ideal medium for studying bank herding behavior. It is perhaps not surprising that Jorion finds very little evidence of a strong positive correlation in bank's market risk minimum capital requirements. While the evidence that Jorion presents is consistent with diversity among bank trading positions and strategies, given MRC construction, the lack of strong positive correlation among bank MRCs is not strong evidence against the possibility of herding behavior in at least some trading markets.

Since unanticipated increases in market volatility are unlikely to increase a bank's market risk capital requirement in a manner that would cause significant shedding of risky positions, the regulatory risk to a bank would seem to be driven by the bank's performance on VaR backtests. For backtesting, daily VaR estimates must be compared against daily trading book profits and losses (Basel Committee on Banking Supervision 1996b). If losses exceed a bank's daily VaR estimate, an exception is recorded. An excessive number of exceptions within a 250-day window is cause for an increase in the bank's regulatory multiplier.

In their 2002 paper, Berkowitz and O'Brien document that daily VaR exceptions are rare events. In a sample that includes six large U.S. banks over the period January 1998 through March 2000, only sixteen exceptions were recorded. Of these, fourteen occurred during the period August 1989–October 1998. Only one bank in their sample experienced enough exceptions during this interval to qualify it for an elevated regulatory capital multiplier.[5] To date, it appears that banks have experienced few, if any, situations where an unanticipated movement in markets has caused losses that put banks at risk of insufficient or higher regulatory capital requirements for market risk. Still, if VaR-based capital regulations are a cause of herding, one would expect capital regulations to have caused risk control sales during the August 1998–October 1998 period. In an earlier draft of their paper, Berkowitz and O'Brien focused on bank daily trade revenue data from this period. While they found some commonalities among bank trading revenues during this episode, they did not find strong evidence of trading behavior consistent with VaR-driven herding behavior.

Market risk capital regulations alone seem unlikely to make VaR a spe-

---

4. In my experience, many banks set VaR limits for trading activities and monitor desks according to their utilization of a given VaR limit.

5. Some individual bank exceptions documented in the Berkowitz and O'Brien study appear to be large enough so that the bank's daily loss exceeded the bank's MRC, but these losses were still small relative to the bank's overall capital position.

cial attractor that encourages herding among institutional investors. Institutional investors may, however, still exhibit herding tendencies, yet these tendencies may not be very apparent when examining banks' quarterly MRCs and trading revenues (as in Jorion), or even when examining bank daily trading revenues (as in Berkowitz and O'Brien).

If investors follow similar trading strategies and have stop-loss control measures in place, unanticipated market movements could periodically trigger sympathetic rebalancing behavior that is unrelated to regulatory capital constraints. Again, this has nothing to do with VaR, even though VaR measures may be used by banks to measure and monitor risk exposure. If institutions exhibit such behavior, positive fee and interest income components recorded in trading operations revenues and the revenue diversification benefits gained from multiple trading activities (equity, FX, fixed income, etc.) may make it difficult to detect, in quarterly data, the commonality of trading patterns generated by herding. If herding is a feature of these markets, one might anticipate finding stronger evidence of its existence in the daily profit and loss (P&L) trading account data analyzed by Berkowitz and O'Brien. In the remainder of this discussion, we consider issues associated with the analysis of daily trading revenues.

Berkowitz and O'Brien (2005) analyze the daily trading P&Ls for a sample of six large U.S. banks from January 1998 to March 2003. They analyze these data by interpreting the estimates from both a random coefficient linear-factor model and a 150-day rolling window linear-factor model that generates time-varying factor loadings. The authors discuss a number of limiting issues associated with the interpretation of the random coefficient factor-model estimates, and, for me at least, the exercise only confirms that bank positions (factor loadings) vary daily, and sometimes by substantial magnitudes. The random coefficients approach turns out to be less than ideal for drawing inferences about bank herding behavior, and Berkowitz and O'Brien focus on estimates from a rolling factor model regression approach. They argue that time series comovements between factor loading estimates and the level of the risk factors is evidence that banks rebalance as factors move. After analyzing the relationship between rolling regression-factor loading estimates and the level of market risk factors, Berkowitz and O'Brien find only fragmentary evidence of commonalities in banks' factor-loading movements. They conclude that there is no strong evidence that supports the VaR-herding hypothesis in their sample data. Even here, however, the interpretation of the rolling-regression model estimates presented by Berkowitz and O'Brien is difficult, and it is unclear what their results imply regarding the herding hypothesis.

Berkowitz and O'Brien estimate a model where trading revenue is a linear function of percentage changes in some market risk factors (exchange rate and equity market factors) and changes in the levels of other market factors (the ten-year Treasury rate, and four credit spread measures). In a typical linear factor model for equity positions, asset returns are modeled as linear functions of the returns on common market factors. Ignoring dividend income, a linear factor model with a single factor, $\tilde{F}_t$, for equity returns is typically written

(1)
$$\frac{\Delta P_t}{P_{t-1}} = \alpha_0 + \beta \frac{\Delta F_t}{F_{t-1}} + \tilde{e}_t.$$

If expression (1) holds, trading revenue in a mark-to-market book that is not rebalanced is given by

(2)
$$\Delta \tilde{P}_t = \alpha_0 + (\beta P_{t-1})\frac{\Delta F_t}{F_{t-1}} + \tilde{e}_t P_{t-1}.$$

If the return-factor model beta coefficient is positive, we would expect the estimated factor loadings in the 150-day rolling Berkowitz and O'Brien trading revenue model to be positively related to the level of the factor. When the market risk factor increases over time, the estimated rolling regression coefficient should also increase if the linear-factor *return* model correctly describes asset price dynamics.

In the fixed income setting, relationships between daily trading revenues and interest rate changes are harder to predict, even if bank fixed-income positions are not rebalanced. If a bank's positions are not rebalanced and are exclusively floating rate (for simplicity, assume rates are continuously reset), accrued interest will decline in proportion with rates, and the mark-to-market change in the floating rate position's value will be zero. A bank with such exposures should exhibit a constant negative coefficient in a linear regression of fixed-income trading revenue on the change in the level of interest rates. Alternatively, at the other end of the spectrum, should a bank's fixed income instruments be exclusively long-term discount instruments, the Berkowitz and O'Brien factor model specification should produce factor loading estimates that are larger (in absolute value) the lower are ten-year Treasury rates, owing to the convexity of long-dated discount instruments.

These issues complicate the interpretation of the time-series relationship between the market risk factors (measured in levels) and the factor loading estimates from the 150-day rolling regressions in the Berkowitz and O'Brien paper. A strong correlation between movements in the rolling-window trading revenue-factor model loading estimates and the level of market risk factors does not necessarily imply that a bank has altered its trading book positions in response to a change in the market factor. Information on changes in daily trading revenues and market risk factors by themselves may not be sufficient to identify bank rebalancing activities.

To summarize my discussion let me reiterate that I do not stay up nights worrying about whether the widespread adoption of VaR techniques has increased the potential for herding behavior. Based on my professional experience—which is clearly limited, but includes studying, working in, and examining financial institutions—I think that capital market participants may at times demonstrate what appears to be fadlike behavior in their investment strategies. In my view, apparent commonalities in bank trading activities have nothing to do with the institutions' use of VaR measurement. Value at risk is just one of many risk management and control tools available, and its widespread adoption will not increase the tendency for risk-takers to herd. I think it is fair to say that the authors of both papers share my views regarding the use of VaR. While both authors claim to find little systematic evidence in their respective datasets that links the use of VaR to herdlike behavior among dealer banks, it is also clear that the available data may not be adequate to produce powerful tests of the herding hypothesis.

References

Basel Committee on Banking Supervision. 1996a. Amendment to the Capital Accord to Incorporate Market Risks. Basel: Bank for International Settlements.
———. 1996b. Supervisory Framework for the Use of "Backtesting" in Conjunction with the Internal Models Approach to Market Risk Capital Requirements. Basel: Bank for International Settlements.
Berkowitz, J., and J. O'Brien. 2002. How accurate are Value-at-Risk models at commercial banks? *Journal of Finance* 57 (3): 1093–1112.
———. 2005. "Estimating bank trading risk: A factor model approach." Memo.
Jorion, P. 2004. "Bank Trading Risk and Systemic Risk." Memo.

Discussion Summary

A single general discussion of these two related papers was conducted. Part of the discussion centered on whether herding by banks, especially in crisis situations, is a material concern, and on how the authors might better present evidence about it. In their responses, both *Jorion* and *O'Brien* agreed that the extent of herding is an interesting and important question but noted that it is largely beyond the scope of their papers, which are focused on whether the use of VaR measures is likely to cause herding. They interpreted the remarks as being consistent with their own conclusions—that it does not. They agreed that their data and methods are not ideal for addressing the broader questions.

Andrew Lo suggested some additional measures would be informative. Noting that outliers matter more to systemic risk than average correlations, he suggested looking at averages of absolute value of correlations. He also suggested a greater focus on the experience of individual banks, since a systemic event need involve a failure of only one or two major banks.

Richard Evans suggested that the VaR data used by all of the authors, while different in the details of sources and construction, may suffer from a lack of comparability across institutions. The assets that are included in the portfolios for which VaR measures are disclosed differ cross-sectionally and over time at a given financial institution. Profit-and-loss results are badly distorted, especially at a daily frequency, for a number of reasons, such as the impact of accounting reserves. Some institutions that appear in the samples are relatively small; the behavior of their VaR measures may be different and of less interest than at the major dealer banks. Overall, although he believes that better data would reveal higher correlations of VaR and returns than the authors find, use of VaR measures does not itself cause herding by the dealer banks.

II

Systemic Risk

How Do Banks Manage Liquidity Risk?
Evidence from the Equity and Deposit Markets in the Fall of 1998

Evan Gatev, Til Schuermann, and Philip E. Strahan

3.1 Introduction

The rise of the commercial paper market and the subsequent growth of the junk bond market in the 1980s and 1990s have seemingly reduced the role of banks in the financing of large businesses (Mishkin and Strahan 1998). This much-remarked-upon evolution away from banks and toward the securities markets has not rendered banks irrelevant (Boyd and Gertler 1994). While they do provide less funding than before, banks remain important to large firms as providers of liquidity support to the commercial paper market. Banks act as the "liquidity provider of last resort" by promising to offer cash on demand through commercial paper backup lines of credit.[1] This liquidity insurance role became especially notable in the fall of 1998, when many firms turned to their banks to provide liquidity normally supplied by the commercial paper market. During this episode, banks faced a *systematic* increase in the demand for liquidity. This paper studies how banks were able to manage this systematic liquidity risk and thus weather the 1998 crisis successfully.

Banks have traditionally provided liquidity, not only to borrowers with open lines of credit and loan commitments (we use these terms interchangeably), but also to depositors in the form of checking and other transactions accounts. Both contracts allow customers to receive liquidity (cash) on short

We would like to thank participants at the NBER Conference on Risk at Financial Institutions, our discussant Randy Kroszner, and Brian Madigan for comments. We also thank Gretchen Weinbach for help with the data and Kristin Wilson for her excellent research assistance. Any views expressed represent those of the authors only, and not necessarily those of the Federal Reserve Bank of New York or the Federal Reserve System.

1. Banks also continue to bear significant credit risk through off–balance sheet guarantees such as standby letters of credit.

notice. In fact, a financial intermediary combining these two products offers a reasonable definition of what most scholars and regulators mean by "bank." This liquidity insurance role exposes banks to the risk that they will have insufficient cash to meet random demands from their depositors and borrowers.[2]

To the extent that liquidity demands are *idiosyncratic* and therefore independent across customers, a bank can use scale to mitigate its need to hold cash to meet unexpected liquidity shocks.[3] In fact, Kashyap, Rajan, and Stein (2002) present a model in which a risk-management motive explains the combination of transactions deposits and loan commitments: as long as the demand for liquidity from depositors through the checking account is not highly correlated with liquidity demands from borrowers, an intermediary will be able to reduce its need to hold cash by serving both customers. Thus, their model yields a diversification synergy between demand deposits (or transactions deposits more generally) and loan commitments. As evidence, they show that banks offering more transaction deposits (as a percentage of total deposits) tend also to make more loan commitments (also scaled appropriately). The correlation is robust across all sizes of banks.

A bank offering liquidity insurance may face a problem if, rather than facing *idiosyncratic* demands for cash, it sometimes faces *systematic* increases in liquidity demand. For example, during the first week of October 1998, following the coordinated restructuring of the hedge fund Long-term Capital Management (LTCM), spreads between safe Treasury securities and risky commercial paper rose dramatically. Many large firms were unable to roll over their commercial paper as it came due, leading to a sharp reduction in the amount of commercial paper outstanding and a corresponding increase in takedowns on preexisting lines of credit (Saidenberg and Strahan 1999).[4] As a result of this liquidity shock, banks faced a systematic spike in demand for cash because many of their largest customers wanted funds all at once. Because funding flowed into the banking system, however, this systematic increase in demand was easily met. Gatev and Strahan (2003) show that funding supply to banks moves inversely with market liquidity—that is, when commercial paper spreads widen, banks face a greater *supply* of funds (especially transactions deposits). Thus, when

2. Liquidity risk has been used to justify government deposit insurance (e.g., Diamond and Dybvig, 1983).

3. In a Modigliani-Miller world, holding cash is not costly. However, in a world with taxes, financial distress, or agency costs, holding cash or other liquid assets is costly for banks and other firms (e.g., Myers and Rajan, 1998). Garber and Weisbrod (1990) argue that banks also have an advantage due to their ability to move liquid assets between banks efficiently, thereby lowering the amount of cash that any individual bank needs to hold.

4. Commercial paper often has maturity as short as one week. Firms, however, routinely roll over their paper as it matures.

liquidity demands are at their highest, so is funding supply. Gatev and Strahan argued that banks can weather a liquidity storm due to their perceived status as a safe haven for funds.

In this paper, we study the 1998 crisis to investigate differences *across* banks in their ability to manage systematic liquidity risk. We show that during the 1998 crisis, loan commitments exposed banks to liquidity risk, whereas transactions deposits insulated them from this risk. First, we report evidence from the equity market that transactions deposits reduce bank risk exposure, whereas unused loan commitments increase their exposure. We measure risk using stock return volatility observed during the three-month period beginning in the middle of August, when the crisis began with the announcement of the Russian default. During this period, bank stock prices were buffeted by news of the Russian crisis, followed by the demise of the hedge fund LTCM in late September, and finally by the drying up of the commercial paper market in the first week of October. Banks with more unused loan commitments had higher risk, whereas those with more transactions deposits had lower risk. We compare this pattern with the three months prior to the Russian default, and show a much smaller correlation between risk and loan commitments or risk and transactions deposits.

Second, we extend the Kashyap, Rajan, and Stein (2002) and Gatev and Strahan (2003) results by exploring in greater detail how bank deposit growth responded to the 1998 liquidity crisis. We argue that the synergy between deposits and loan commitments emphasized by Kashyap, Rajan, and Stein—that banks can reduce risk through diversification by holding demand deposits and loan commitments—becomes especially powerful during crises, because investors tend to move funds from the capital markets into their bank during these times. The conditional correlation between liquidity demanded from depositors and liquidity demanded by borrowers becomes *negative* during crises, thereby dramatically increasing the diversification benefit of combining these two products. This negative correlation shows up as an increase in funds flowing into bank transaction deposit accounts at the same time that funds are flowing out of the bank as borrowers take down funds from preexisting lines of credit.

As evidence, we test how funding behaved during the first weeks of October 1998, when banks faced a dramatic increase in demand for funds from firms unable to roll over their commercial paper. This increase in liquidity demand obligated banks to supply funds because firms had established their commercial paper backup lines prior to the onset of the crisis. We find that banks with more transactions deposits as a share of total deposits (based on data just *before* the onset of the crisis) had much greater inflows of deposits, and that all of those inflows were concentrated among transactions deposits rather than other deposits. Banks with more unused loan commitments before the onset of the crisis also experienced increased growth of deposits, which reflected their greater demand for funds (resulting from takedown demand by their borrowers). We find that these relationships reversed sign at the end of October, as the commercial paper spreads fell and the market began to function as it normally does—that is, as the crisis subsided funds flowed out of bank transactions deposit accounts and, presumably, back into the capital markets.

Our results show that transactions deposits play a critically important role in allowing banks to manage their liquidity risk. The findings strengthen the Kashyap, Rajan, and Stein theoretical argument, and they can help explain the robust positive correlation across banks between transaction deposits and loan commitments.

The remainder of the paper proceeds as follows. Section 3.2 following, provides some background by describing banks' liquidity insurance role in the commercial paper market, and describes the chronology of the 1998 crisis. The key issue for our test is finding the right week(s) when banks faced a systematic increase in liquidity demand. Section 3.3 then describes our data, empirical methods, and results. Section 3.4 concludes the paper.

3.2   The 1998 Liquidity Crisis

The focus of this paper is how the banking system in the United States survived the dramatic decline in risky asset prices during the fall of 1998. The episode has been called a liquidity crisis mainly because the widespread decline in asset prices did not seem to be fully explainable based on cash-flow fundamentals. But for our purposes, these events did lead to a well-defined liquidity crisis in the commercial paper market, because a large number of borrowers were unable to refinance their paper as it matured. In response, many of these issuers turned to their bank for funds.

In our first set of results, we focus on bank stock return volatility during the whole three-month period, beginning when Russia defaulted (August 17) and ending after spreads in the commercial paper market returned to normal levels (November 17). As shown in Kho, Lee, and Stulz (2000), bank stock prices were hit throughout this period by news about conditions in credit markets around the world. We do not model changes in the level of stock prices, which would require us to pinpoint exactly which events were viewed as harmful (e.g., Russia's default and subsequent deviation) or helpful (e.g., announcements that the International Monetary Fund [IMF] would intervene in Brazil). Instead, we focus on explaining how the cross-section of stock return volatility, measured throughout the whole three-month period, reflects exposure to liquidity risk as well as a bank's ability to manage that risk.

We then analyze the cross-section of deposit changes, focusing specifically on the one-week period ending on October 5. While the whole three-month period following the Russian default did raise uncertainty for banks and bank stock prices (fig. 3.1), it was *only* during October that banks in fact faced a sharp increase in liquidity demands. Thus, while forward-looking stock prices (and hence volatility) over the whole period reflected the effects of the liquidity crisis, bank balance sheets only reacted during the weeks when liquidity demand spiked.

Bad news began on August 17, 1998, when the Russian government announced its intention to default on its sovereign debt, floated the exchange rate, and devalued the ruble (Chiodo and Owyang 2002). The announcement was followed by a steep drop in U.S. equity prices during the last two weeks of August, and a sustained period of high volatility in asset markets around the world (fig. 3.1).

Outside of the U.S. equity market, the prices of risky debt securities across the whole credit spectrum and across markets began to fall sharply after Russia's announcement. As an example, the spread between speculative grade and investment grade debt in the U.S. bond market rose from about 1.8 percentage points in mid-August to 2.5 percentage points by October. Spreads of risky bonds outside the United States, as well as swap spreads, also widened dramatically (Saidenberg and Strahan, 1999).

Partly as a result of the simultaneous collapse in the prices of risky assets across many markets, the hedge fund LTCM announced to its shareholders on September 2 that the fund had sustained large losses. These losses mounted as credit spreads continued to widen, moving well beyond levels that had been observed during the 1990s. LTCM was unable to secure additional investment from its owners or liquidity support from its creditors (Lowenstein, 2000). As a result, the hedge fund faced the possibility of an uncoordinated unwinding of its large positions in the bond and swaps markets. The Federal Reserve Bank of New York, fearing the potential systemic consequences of a rapid liquidation of LTCM's large positions in the face of already falling asset prices, brokered a private-sector restructuring of the fund. The news of the restructuring became public on Wednesday, September 23.[5]

The effects of these events can be seen clearly in tracking bank stock prices over this period. Panel A of figure 3.1 reports the change in an equally weighted index of bank stock prices and the Standard and Poor's (S&P) 500 from the middle of May 1998 through the middle of November. Panel B reports the conditional volatility over the same period for this bank-stock index.[6] Bank stock prices began to fall in the summer and then

---

5. See Edwards (1999) for an evaluation of the policy implications of the Fed's actions.

6. The conditional volatility (standard deviation) is estimated from an exponential generalized autoregressive EGARCH (1,1) model with a first-order auto-regressive process for the mean (Nelson, 1991).

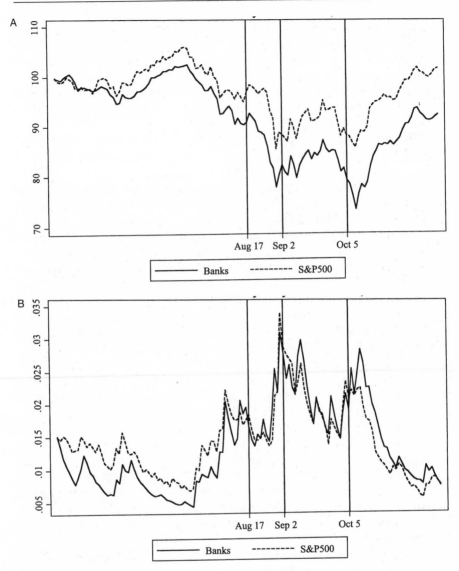

Fig. 3.1   Bank performance from May 14 to November 17, 1988: *A*, Stock-price index; *B*, Conditional stock-return volatility

dropped sharply after the Russian default on August 17. Prices stabilized in September until the announcement of the restructuring of LTCM and the pull-back in the commercial paper market, then fell sharply again. The conditional volatility of bank stocks also spiked just after the Russian default, stabilized in September, and spiked again in the beginning of October. Both the level and volatility of bank stock prices quickly recovered in

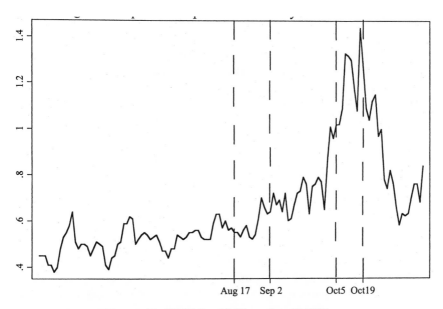

Fig. 3.2   Paper-bill spread in BPS May 14–November 17 1998

the second half of October. While these patterns are also evident for the S&P 500, the effects of the 1998 crisis appear larger for banks' stocks, both in terms of price levels and return volatility.[7]

The U.S. commercial paper (CP) market also began to feel the effects of investors' pulling back from risky assets during the week following LTCM's collapse. Spreads on short-term, high-grade CP over Treasury securities of comparable maturity had risen gradually throughout the end of August and through September, from about 55 basis points to about 70 basis points just prior to LTCM's demise. Spreads then jumped sharply, rising to more than 100 basis points and remaining at that level for the first three weeks of October (fig. 3.2). Spreads on low-grade commercial paper increased even more than spreads on high-grade paper. The jump in these spreads reflected rationing in the commercial paper market, as the stock of outstanding commercial paper declined by more than 2 percent during the month of October.[8] Credit rationing places issuers in the position of facing a liquidity crisis as their paper comes due.[9] Chava and Purnanadam

7. Note that bank stock volatility was lower than the S&P 500 before the crisis, but equal to or larger during the crisis.

8. Stiglitz and Weiss (1981) show that equilibrium credit rationing is possible when borrowers are better informed than lenders.

9. Such crises had happened before 1998. Banks' role in offering liquidity insurance originated early in the development of the commercial paper market when the Penn Central Transportation Company defaulted on more than $80 million in commercial paper outstanding. As a result of this default, investors lost confidence in *other* large commercial paper issuers, mak-

(2005) provide evidence that the CP market ceased to function at the beginning of October, by comparing abnormal returns for firms with and without access to this market. They show first that stock prices of CP issuers fell much less than other firms in response to the decline in bank financial condition during September of 1998 (while markets continued to function). During the first two weeks of October, however, the stock prices of *all* firms, regardless of their ability to access the CP market, fell equally. Thus, *all* firms became bank dependent—even CP issuers—during these weeks (because markets ceased to function).

At the same time that the CP market was drying up, growth in bank lending accelerated dramatically, because the commercial paper issuers began to draw funds from their backup lines of credit. This growth in lending was concentrated at banks with high levels of undrawn loan commitments prior to the onset of the crisis. For example, among the top fifty banks, those with above-average levels of undrawn loan commitments (scaled by total loans plus commitments) saw lending rise three times as fast as banks with below-average undrawn loan commitments (Saidenberg and Strahan 1999). Moreover, press reports suggest that most of the bank loan growth during the beginning of October occurred because of strong takedown demand by commercial paper issuers drawing funds from preexisting credit lines rather than because of new loan originations. The *New York Times* reported, for example, that "rather than signaling a flow of new loans, much of the lending appears to be borrowers' drawing on existing lines of credit" (Uchitelle 1998). Thus, the liquidity crisis moved seamlessly from CP issuers to their banks. As we show next, banks with larger transaction deposits were better positioned to face this crisis: they experienced less volatility in their stock prices and, when the liquidity demands hit hardest, they experienced the greatest inflows of funds.

Expressing concern that "growing caution by lenders and unsettled conditions in financial markets more generally [were] likely to be restraining aggregate demand in the future," the Federal Reserve decreased the target Fed Funds rate by 25 basis points on September 29 and again on October 15, 1998.[10] The rate was dropped another 25 basis points on November 17. It did not stay low for long, however, going back up to 5 percent in two steps by November 1999.

---

ing it difficult for some of these firms to refinance their paper as it matured. The Federal Reserve responded to the Penn Central crisis by lending aggressively to banks through the discount window and encouraging them, in turn, to provide liquidity to their large borrowers (Kane, 1974). In response to this difficulty, commercial paper issuers thereafter began purchasing backup lines of credit from banks to insure against future funding disruptions.

10. The announcement can be found at http://www.federalreserve.gov/boarddocs/press/monetary/1998.

3.3   Empirical Methods, Data, and Results

In this section, we report our results linking stock return volatility and changes in bank deposits to bank characteristics during the 1998 crisis. We first describe our empirical methods, then our data, and last we report the results.

3.3.1   Empirical Methods

We test how preexisting open lines of credit and preexisting levels of transactions deposits affect both risk (stock returns) and deposit flows. Unused loan commitments expose banks to liquidity risk. Thus, we expect banks with more open credit lines to face greater liquidity risk (higher stock return volatility) and to face a greater demand for loans when the commercial paper market dried up in the beginning of October 1998 (faster deposit growth). Kashyap, Rajan, and Stein argue that *combining* loan commitments with transactions deposits lowers risk due to diversification (because demands are less-than-perfectly correlated). This force is especially powerful during liquidity crises like the autumn of 1998, because uninformed investors put funds into banks as a safe haven for their wealth. Thus, banks with more transactions deposits ought to have had lower risk than other banks. And when the CP market dried up, such banks ought to have experienced faster growth of deposits, as funds flowed into their transactions accounts from investors that would normally buy commercial paper.

To be more precise, we estimate two sets of cross-sectional regressions with the following structure:

(1) $\text{Stock Return Volatility}_i = \alpha_1 + \gamma_1 \text{Loan Commitment Ratio}_i$
$$+ \gamma_2 \text{Transaction Deposit Ratio}_i$$
$$+ \text{Control Variables}_i + \varepsilon_{1,i}$$

(2) $\text{Deposit Change}_i = \alpha_2 + \beta_1 \text{Loan Commitment Ratio}_i$
$$+ \beta_2 \text{Transaction Deposit Ratio}_i$$
$$+ \text{Control Variables}_i + \varepsilon_{2,i},$$

where i refers to the bank. We estimate each of these regressions during the crisis period and during a noncrisis period. For the crisis period, we expect the following: $\gamma_1 > 0$ and $\gamma_2 < 0$; $\beta_1 > 0$ and $\beta_2 > 0$. For equation (1), we estimate a noncrisis period that ends in the middle of August; we expect similar qualitative results but much smaller magnitudes. For equation (2), we estimate the relationships during the weeks when the CP market dried up (crisis weeks), and again during the weeks when this market recovered.

In this case, we would expect opposite relationships during the noncrisis period. Funds should flow into banks as the CP market dries up, and back out as it rebounds.

3.3.2   Data

Explanatory Variables

To construct measures of liquidity risk exposure and transactions deposits we follow the procedures outlined by Kashyap, Rajan, and Stein (2002). We use the level of unused loan commitments as of June 1998 (that is, before the onset of the crisis), scaled by the sum of unused loan commitments plus total on–balance sheet loans.[11] This variable is our measure of a bank's potential exposure to a liquidity shock.[12] In our deposit flow regressions, the unused commitments ratio can be thought of as a proxy for the high level of demand for funds that a bank may need to meet from CP issuers unable to roll over their paper.

To measure the size of a bank's transactions deposit base, we use total transactions deposits divided by total deposits. We take this variable from the Federal Reserve's FR2900 (Report of Transaction Accounts, Other Deposits, and Vault Cash) as of August 10, 1998, the last date prior to the onset of the crisis. The FR2900 provides confidential and detailed weekly data on bank deposits used to measure levels and changes in the money supply.[13] Some of the deposit components are also used to calculate reserve requirements. Using a separate data source, Kashyap, Rajan, and Stein show that transaction deposits are highly correlated with the loan commitment variable across banks, regardless of bank size. (Note that we also find a very strong positive correlation between transactions deposits and loan commitments in our data.) They do not, however, test whether transactions deposits in fact help banks hedge against the risks of a liquidity shock. That is, they do not measure the correlation of liquidity demands across these two classes of customers. This is where our approach extends and sharpens their empirical findings.

Our sample includes all domestic banking organizations with assets over $1 billion (as of the June 1998 Call Report). We exclude the smaller banks because most of the commercial paper backup lines of credit are issued by large banks, and, as we have said, the liquidity shock was driven by the absence of liquidity in the commercial paper market. Again following

11. We alter this definition slightly relative to what Kashyap, Rajan, and Stein use by taking out unused loan commitments to retail customers (i.e., credit card lines). These retail exposures did not create liquidity problems for banks in the fall of 1998.

12. Unfortunately, we know of no data that would allow us to observe the amount of funds actually taken down off of preexisting lines of credit, which would be the best ex post measure of the shock to loan demand.

13. The confidential data were processed solely within the Federal Reserve for the analysis presented in this paper.

Kashyap, Rajan, and Stein, we aggregate the bank-level data from the June 1998 Call Report up to the level of the highest holding corporation. This aggregation takes account of the possibility that affiliated banks can pool their resources to hedge against unexpected liquidity shocks.

Beyond the two variables of interest, we also control for a series of additional bank characteristics, including the log of total assets, the capital-asset ratio, an indicator equal to 1 for banks with a credit rating, the ratio of liquid assets (cash plus securities) to total assets, the ratio of Fed Funds purchased to total assets, and an indicator equal to 1 if the bank's stock is publicly traded. We include bank size and capital to test whether risk or deposit inflows are affected by insolvency risk—larger and better-capitalized banks are less likely to fail, all else being equal. Larger banks may also have been viewed as safer than smaller ones if the implicit government safety net is more readily available to them. We control for asset liquidity for the obvious reason that banks with more liquid balance sheets will be better able to meet the demands of borrowers taking down funds from preexisting loan commitments. Similarly, banks with greater access to the Fed Funds market may be better able to weather a liquidity shock. The publicly traded and rated indicators are included to test whether less opaque banks fared better during the crisis. Last, we include indicator variables equal to 1 for banks exposed to Russia and to LTCM (see Kho, Lee, and Stulz, 2000).

Dependent Variables

To measure bank risk, we use three months of daily stock return data from the Center for Research in Security Prices (CRSP) to construct the standard deviation of each bank's stock return from the onset of the crisis on August 17, 1998. We construct the same volatility measure during the three-month period *ending* on August 14 to obtain a benchmark set of results to make sure that the relationships we observe during the fall really have something to do with the liquidity crisis, rather than some time-invariant characteristics of banks.

For deposit flows, we construct the change in total deposits during the week ending on October 5, 1998. This first week of October follows the restructuring of LTCM at the end of September, and was the critical week in which CP spreads first spiked (fig. 3.2). Spreads remained high for an additional two weeks, so we also report as a robustness test the change in deposits during the three-week period ending on October 19.

For each of our deposit change results, we also report a parallel set of regressions for the week ending on October 26 (the week the spreads began to subside), and the three-week period ending on November 6, 1998. These weeks represent a resumption of normal conditions in the commercial paper market. Spreads began to fall after October 16, from a high of 150 basis points to below 100 basis points by October 26, and then fell below 60 basis points by November 4. We also split the change in total deposits into the change in transactions deposits and the change in all other deposits to test whether these two kinds of products responded differently when liquidity demanded by the commercial paper issuers peaked.[14] Each of these changes is normalized by the bank's total assets as of June 1998.[15] As with the level of preexisting transactions deposits, the data for deposit changes come from the Federal Reserve's FR2900 data.

3.3.3   Results

Summary Statistics

Table 3.1 reports summary statistics for our dependent variables (panel A) and for our explanatory variables (panel B). Bank stocks clearly became significantly more volatile during the fall of 1998, rising from a daily standard deviation of 2.0 percent for the average bank before the crisis to 3.4 percent during the crisis.[16] Moreover, the bank deposit change variable was much higher during the crisis weeks at the beginning of October than during the weeks at the end of the month. For example, the change in deposits relative to assets averaged 1.4 percent during the first week of October (crisis period), whereas deposits actually shrank by 0.4 percent of assets during the week ending on October 26 (noncrisis period). Deposit change during that first week of October annualizes to a change of about *70 percent* of assets.

As noted, we take most of our explanatory variables from the June 1998 Call Report, to be sure that they are predetermined with respect to the onset of crisis, with one exception: the transactions deposit ratio is taken from the August 10, 1998, FR2900 data, both to ensure comparability with the deposit changes, and because we wanted to measure a bank's transaction deposit franchise as close to the onset of the crisis as possible.

As reported in table 3.1, a typical bank held unused loan commitments equal to about 19 percent of its total credit exposure (on–balance sheet loans plus unused commitments). The transactions deposit variable averaged 0.189, and exhibited a wide range (from zero to 0.49). These are the two explanatory variables of greatest interest, because they allow us to test

14. Transaction accounts is the sum of demand deposits, Automatic Transfer Service (ATS) accounts, NOW accounts/share drafts and telephone pre-authorized transfers.

15. We considered looking at deposit growth, but this variable displays some large outliers, especially when we disaggregate the deposits (e.g., transaction versus nontransaction deposits, and demand versus other transaction deposits). Normalizing the change in deposits by total assets reduces the outlier problems, but we also trim the deposit changes at the 1st and 99th percentiles in the regressions reported in this paper. The results do not change materially for the crisis weeks if we do not trim, but the coefficient on deposit changes during the noncrisis period becomes much larger (as does its standard error) due to the influence of one observation.

16. These volatility figures are higher than the conditional volatilities plotted in figure 3.1 because they include bank-specific idiosyncratic risk. The data in figure 3.1 are based on an equally weighted index of bank stocks.

Table 3.1   **Summary statistics**

	Crisis period		Noncrisis period	
	Mean (1)	Standard deviation (2)	Mean (3)	Standard deviation (4)
A. Dependent variables				
Stock return volatility	0.034	0.011	0.020	0.006
Change in total deposits/assets$_{6/98}$	0.014	0.011	−0.004	0.013
Change in transactions deposits/assets$_{6/98}$	0.004	0.009	−0.002	0.008
Change in nontransaction deposits/assets$_{6/98}$	0.011	0.015	−0.003	0.012
B. Explanatory variables				
Transactions deposits/total deposits	0.189	0.100		
Unused commitments/(Commitments + Loans)	0.187	0.127		
Log of assets	15.23	1.38		
Russia exposure indicator	0.022			
LTCM exposure indicator	0.013			
Capital/Assets	0.092	0.039		
Fed funds purchased/assets	0.068	0.066		
(Cash + Securities)/assets	0.324	0.141		
Has a credit rating indicator	0.349			
Is publicly traded indicator	0.838			

Notes: Dependent variables: Stock return volatility equals the standard deviation of daily stock returns. The change in deposits is taken from the Federal Reserve's FR2900 data.

Explanatory variables: With the exception of the transactions deposit ratio, explanatory variables are taken from the June 1998 Call Report. The transactions deposit/total deposits ratio is taken from the August 10, 1998, FR2900 data, as are the deposit change rates (the dependent variables).

Crisis/Noncrisis periods: For stock return volatility, the crisis period begins on August 17, 1998, (when Russia defaulted) and ends three months later. The noncrisis period is the three-month period ending on August 14, 1998. For deposit change, the crisis week is the week ending on October 5, 1998 (the week that commercial paper spreads began to subside).

the Kashyap, Rajan, and Stein model, which implies that exposure to take-down risk on loan commitments can be partly hedged with transactions deposits. Means for the other controls variables are also reported in table 3.1. Average bank size in the sample was $16.5 billion (log of assets averaged 15.23). Two percent of the banks in the sample had exposure to Russia, and a little more than 1 percent (four banks) of the banks had exposure to LTCM. Most of the banks are publicly traded (84 percent), but fewer than half have a credit rating (35 percent).

Bank Stock Return Volatility

Table 3.2 reports the regression estimates for equation (1), where bank stock return volatility is the dependent variable. During the crisis period, there is a positive association between the unused loan commitments and volatility (although not statistically significant at conventional levels), and a significant negative association between the size of a bank's transactions deposit ratio and volatility. That is, loan commitments seem to have *ex-*

Table 3.2   **Bank liquidity risk declines with size of bank's transactions deposit franchise**

	Dependent variables	
Explanatory variables	Crisis period stock return volatility: 8/17/98–11/17/98 (1)	Noncrisis stock return volatility: 5/14/98–8/14/98 (2)
Transactions deposits/Total deposits	−0.037**	−0.008*
	(0.011)	(0.004)
Unused commitments/(Commitments + Loans)	0.010	0.001
	(0.011)	(0.004)
Log of assets	0.001	−0.001
	(0.001)	(0.001)
Russia exposure indicator	0.003	0.001
	(0.004)	(0.001)
LTCM exposure indicator	0.017**	0.011
	(0.006)	(0.006)
Capital/Assets	0.039**	0.003
	(0.014)	(0.007)
Fed funds purchased/Assets	−0.001	0.010
	(0.010)	(0.006)
(Cash + Securities)/Assets	0.002	−0.004
	(0.007)	(0.004)
Has a credit rating indicator	−0.001	−0.002
	(0.002)	(0.001)
N	175	178
R^2	0.18	0.12

Notes: All regressions include an intercept, which is not reported. Coefficients reported with robust standard errors in parentheses. With the exception of the deposit ratio, explanatory variables are from the June 1998 Call Report. The transactions deposit/total deposits ratio is taken from the August 10, 1998, FR2900 data.

**Indicates statistical significance at the 5 percent level.

*Indicates statistical significance at the 10 percent level.

posed banks to risk (weakly), while transactions deposits helped them *hedge* that risk. The coefficient on the transaction deposits variable is especially striking. For example, a 1 standard deviation increase in this variable came with a decrease in stock return volatility of 0.004, which is about 40 percent of the cross-sectional standard deviation in stock return volatility. During the 1998 crisis a bank with a large transaction deposit base experienced much lower stock return volatility because, as we will show, it received a large inflow of new deposits. This result highlights how banking has changed in recent years. Before the introduction of government safety nets, transactions deposits could sometimes expose a bank to liquidity risk when consumers simultaneously removed deposits to increase consumption. This bank-run problem has traditionally been viewed as the primary source of bank liquidity risk and lies behind bank reserve requirements for demand deposits. Rather than open banks to liquidity risk, however, deposits now seem to insulate them from that risk.

Table 3.2 also shows that the relationships observed during the 1998 crisis *do not* reflect the normal links from liquidity exposure to risk. The coefficients on both loan commitments and transactions deposits in the volatility regressions are much smaller during the noncrisis period, and this difference is statistically significant at the 5 percent level.[17] The effect of transactions deposits falls by a factor of about five, and the effect of loan commitments falls by a factor of ten. Thus, the extent to which combining loan commitments with transactions deposits helps banks hedge risk was *dramatically larger during the 1998 liquidity crisis than during normal times.* This is consistent with our argument that the conditional correlation between liquidity demands of depositors and borrowers goes negative during liquidity crises—depositors put their money in banks just as borrowers draw money out. In other words, the diversification synergy of combining loan commitments and transactions deposits is especially powerful during crises.

Banks with LTCM exposure also had much higher stock return volatility than other banks during the crisis months. Sensibly, LTCM investments increased bank equity risk, both before and after the Russian default was announced. This result is consistent with Kho, Lee, and Stulz (2000), who show that LTCM-exposed banks experienced a relatively large decline in stock prices compared to other banks when the hedge fund's problems first became public, and again when the coordinated restructuring occurred.[18] Our results suggest that the market was aware of potential LTCM risk even before the news of the fund's difficulties became widely recognized (i.e., the coefficient is positive even during our precrisis period). This coefficient, of course, could be capturing more than just LTCM risk, to the extent that these banks were engaged in other risk-enhancing activities, such as proprietary trading.

Somewhat to our surprise we find no effect on volatility of bank size or the other measures of liquidity risk (the fed funds purchased-to-assets or liquid assets-to-total-assets ratios). We find that banks with more capital had higher, rather than lower, stock-return volatility. The small coefficient on bank size indicates that large banks were not viewed as relatively safer during the crisis, as might be expected if government safety nets become relatively more valuable for large banks at these times. These results are

---

17. In addition, we have estimated the volatility model for the crisis period, with the noncrisis volatility (i.e., the lagged dependent variable) included as a right-hand side variable. In these models, the fit (R^2) increases, but the magnitude and statistical significance of the other regressors remain similar to those reported in column 1 of table 3.2.

18. The LTCM-exposed banks became equity holders in LTCM after the restructuring. Note that despite the higher equity risk for these banks, they were probably not close to insolvency. Furfine (2002) shows that LTCM-exposed banks continued to have access to borrowing in the unsecured Fed Funds market during this period.

consistent with our subsequent deposit-flow evidence and with the findings of Gatev and Strahan (2003), who show that funds flowed into banks across the board rather than to large (or well-capitalized) banks.[19]

Bank Deposit Inflows

In tables 3.3–3.6, we report estimates of the links from banks' transactions deposits base and their total unused loan commitments to deposit inflows during the crisis and recovery weeks of the commercial paper market. Table 3.3 focuses first on total deposit flows. During the first week of October, banks with more transactions deposits (as of the beginning of the crisis) experienced *larger inflows of funds* than other banks (column [1]).[20] Moreover, these funds seemed to have flowed *out* of banks as the CP market recovered during the week ending October 26 (column [2]). Similarly, we find that banks with higher levels of preexisting unused or open loan commitments had greater inflows during the crisis week, and greater levels of outflows during the recovery week. Banks with high levels of open credit lines thus seem to have experienced the greatest takedown demand, as CP issuers turned to their banks for liquidity. This liquidity shock is reflected by deposits that were pulled into the bank by high loan demand. Banks with higher levels of transactions deposits, however, also experienced greater inflows. We interpret this latter inflow as a deposit-supply response to the crisis: when investors lost their nerve, two things happened. First, the CP market dried up. Second, funds normally invested in commercial paper flowed temporarily into bank accounts. Thus, banks with high levels of both open commitments and transactions accounts experienced *offsetting flows of funds.*[21]

Table 3.4 sharpens this result by looking at the flows into bank transaction deposit accounts and into nontransaction deposit accounts separately. During the crisis week, the positive correlation between preexisting transaction deposits and deposits flow shows up *only* in the transactions deposits accounts (panel A). That is, banks with a large base of transactions deposit accounts experienced flows of funds into those accounts. In contrast, there is a *negative* correlation between the size of a bank's trans-

---

19. Gatev and Strahan (2003) use call report data to analyze the effects of CP spreads and loan commitments on balance sheet changes at quarterly frequency. Hence, they are not able to focus specifically on how deposit growth behaved during the critical weeks in October when takedown demand by commercial paper issuers spiked.

20. We have also included an indicator variable for four large banks involved in wholesale payments processing to our model (Bank of New York, State Street Bank, Northern Trust, and Mellon Bank). These banks did not experience greater inflows than other banks.

21. We have also estimated our model for subsamples of above- and below-median size banks. In both samples, we find that deposit flows were greater for banks with more transactions deposits (significant for large banks) and more unused loan commitments (significant for smaller banks). The transactions deposit coefficient was slightly larger for the above-median banks, whereas the coefficient on preexisting unused loan commitments was slightly larger for the below-median banks.

Table 3.3   **Deposits flow more into banks with larger transactions deposit franchise**

Explanatory variables	Dependent variables	
	Crisis period change in deposits/Assets$_{6/98}$: 9/28/98–10/05/98 (1)	Noncrisis change in deposits/Assets$_{6/98}$: 10/19/98–10/26-98 (2)
Transactions deposits/Total deposits	0.020*	−0.024*
	(0.011)	(0.010)
Unused commitments/(Commitments + Loans)	0.022**	−0.016**
	(0.010)	(0.007)
Log of assets	−0.001	−0.002
	(0.001)	(0.001)
Russia exposure indicator	−0.010**	0.003
	(0.004)	(0.004)
LTCM exposure indicator	−0.005	0.009*
	(0.005)	(0.005)
Capital/Assets	−0.026	−0.006
	(0.016)	(0.014)
Fed funds purchased/Assets	−0.002	−0.007
	(0.011)	(0.010)
(Cash + Securities)/Assets	0.001	0.001
	(0.006)	(0.006)
Has a credit rating indicator	0.004	0.006
	(0.003)	(0.004)
Is publicly traded indicator	−0.002	0.001
	(0.002)	(0.002)
N	223	222
R^2	0.12	0.14

Notes: All regressions include an intercept, which is not reported. Coefficients reported with robust standard errors in parentheses. With the exception of the deposit ratio, explanatory variables are from the June 1998 Call Report. The transactions deposit/total deposits ratio is taken from the August 10, 1998, FR2900 data, as are the deposit change rates (the dependent variables). The change in deposits is trimmed at the 1st and 99th percentiles.

**Indicates statistical significance at the 5 percent level.
*Indicates statistical significance at the 10 percent level.

actions deposit base and flows into nontransaction deposits. Also, there is no correlation between unused loan commitments and flows into transactions deposits.

The results in table 3.4 validate our interpretation of unused loan commitments as controlling for shocks to loan *demand* (and hence bank demand for funds), whereas the size of the transactions deposit base controls for shocks to deposit *supply*. The deposit-supply response to shocks at high frequency affects the transactions accounts, but demand shocks do not (hence the lack of correlation between unused lines and flows into transactions accounts). Banks are not likely to be able to fund high-frequency

Table 3.4   **Deposits flow more into bank transactions-deposit accounts**

	Dependent variables	
Explanatory variables	Change in transactions deposits/Assets$_{6/98}$: 9/28/98–10/05/98 (1)	Change in nontransactions deposits/Assets$_{6/98}$: 9/28/98–10.05/98 (2)
A. Transactions versus Nontransactions deposit		
Transactions deposits/Total deposits	0.044**	−0.035**
	(0.009)	(0.016)
Unused commitments/(Commitments + Loans)	−0.009	0.038**
	(0.006)	(0.015)
Log of assets	0.001	−0.001
	(0.001)	(0.001)
Russia exposure indicator	−0.004	−0.007
	(0.003)	(0.004)
LTCM exposure indicator	0.001	−0.006
	(0.003)	(0.006)
Capital/Assets	0.009	−0.046*
	(0.016)	(0.027)
Fed funds purchased/Assets	0.009	−0.010
	(0.012)	(0.016)
(Cash + Securities)/Assets	−0.008	0.002
	(0.005)	(0.008)
Has a credit rating indicator	0.002	0.001
	(0.002)	(0.004)
Is publicly traded indicator	−0.003	0.002
	(0.001)	(0.002)
N	222	223
R^2	0.22	0.09

	Dependent variables	
	Change in demand deposits/Assets$_{6/98}$: 9/28/98–10/05/98 (3)	Change in other transactions deposits/Assets$_{6/98}$: 9/28/98–10/05/98 (4)
B. Demand deposits versus all other transactions deposit		
Transactions deposits/Total deposits	0.039**	0.004
	(0.007)	(0.004)
Unused commitments/(Commitments + Loans)	−0.005	−0.004
	(0.006)	(0.003)
Log of assets	0.001	0.001
	(0.001)	(0.001)
Russia exposure indicator	−0.004	−0.001
	(0.003)	(0.001)
LTCM exposure indicator	−0.001	0.001*
	(0.003)	(0.001)
Capital/Assets	0.003	0.006
	(0.012)	(0.007)

Table 3.4   (continued)

	Dependent variables	
	Change in demand deposits/Assets$_{6/98}$: 9/28/98–10/05/98 (3)	Change in other transactions deposits/Assets$_{6/98}$: 9/28/98–10/05/98 (4)
Fed funds purchased/Assets	0.005	0.005
	(0.010)	(0.005)
(Cash + Securities)/Assets	–0.004	–0.003
	(0.004)	(0.003)
Has a credit rating indicator	0.002	0.001
	(0.001)	(0.001)
Is publicly traded indicator	–0.002*	–0.001
	(0.001)	(0.001)
N	222	222
R^2	0.24	0.03

Notes: See table 3.3.

**Indicates statistical significance at the 5 percent level.

*Indicates statistical significance at the 10 percent level.

demand shocks with transaction deposits unless they experience inflows into preexisting accounts. Banks without such supplies of funds need to resort to other sources when takedowns increase unexpectedly. Hence, in column (2) of table 3.4 we estimate a positive and significant effect of unused loan commitments and change in nontransactions deposits. Moreover, the negative coefficient on the transaction deposits/total deposits variable also makes sense, because banks with more transactions account ex ante experienced large increases in funding supply into these accounts (column [1]); hence, their demand to raise nontransactions deposits was lower (column [2]).

Next, we test whether banks are paying higher interest rates for the funds that flow into their transactions accounts. In table 3.4, panel B, we disaggregate the transactions deposit change into the change-in-demand deposits versus the change in all other transaction accounts. These other accounts include such interest-bearing accounts as negotiable order of withdrawal (NOW) accounts. Because banks pay no interest on demand deposit accounts, we can be sure that the flows into these accounts do *not* reflect an increase in a bank's willingness to pay for funds. That is, any change in these accounts (especially at high frequency, such as one week) must reflect shifts in *deposit supply* rather than shifts in the bank's demand for funds. In fact, we find that all of the increased funding flows are concentrated in demand deposit accounts rather than other kinds of transactions deposit accounts.

Table 3.5   **Deposits flow more into banks with larger transactions deposit franchise (three week changes)**

	Dependent variables	
Explanatory variables	Crisis period change in deposits/Assets$_{6/98}$: 9/28/98–10/19/98 (1)	Noncrisis change in deposits/Assets$_{6/98}$: 10/19/98–11/09/98 (2)
Transactions deposits/Total deposits	0.036**	0.058
	(0.015)	(0.052)
Unused commitments/(Commitments + Loans)	0.006	−0.012
	(0.010)	(0.016)
Log of assets	−0.001	−0.005*
	(0.001)	(0.003)
Russia exposure indicator	0.063	−0.010
	(0.048)	(0.017)
LTCM exposure indicator	−0.067	0.019
	(0.048)	(0.017)
Capital/Assets	0.014	−0.025
	(0.041)	(0.097)
Fed funds purchased/Assets	0.029	−0.040
	(0.019)	(0.030)
(Cash + Securities)/Assets	−0.016*	−0.009
	(0.010)	(0.017)
Has a credit rating indicator	0.002	0.011
	(0.004)	(0.008)
Is publicly traded indicator	−0.001	−0.006
	(0.003)	(0.005)
N	223	222
R^2	0.17	0.07

Notes: See table 3.3.
**Indicates statistical significance at the 5 percent level.
*Indicates statistical significance at the 10 percent level.

Tables 3.5 and 3.6 report the same tests as tables 3.3 and 3.4, but now we expand the length of the crisis and noncrisis periods from one week to three weeks. We consider this test less powerful because the most dramatic changes in the CP market occurred rapidly. Nevertheless, we again find a positive correlation between banks' transaction deposit base and subsequent flows of deposit funds during the crisis weeks. As the crisis subsided at the end of October, the regression coefficient remained positive but lost statistical significance. That is, there is no statistically significant relationship between deposit flows and a bank's transaction deposit base as the commercial paper market recovered. (This result contrasts with the sign reversals observed at one-week frequency in table 3.4.) Table 3.6 again shows that the funding inflows related to a banks preexisting level of transactions deposits occurred into transactions accounts rather than non-

Table 3.6   **Deposits flow more into banks with larger transactions deposit franchise (three-week changes; transactions versus nontransactions deposits)**

	Dependent variables	
	Change in transactions deposits/Assets$_{6/98}$: 9/28/98–10/19/98	Change in nontransactions deposits/Assets$_{6/98}$: 9/28/98–10/19/98
Explanatory variables	(1)	(2)
Transactions deposits/Total deposits	0.055**	−0.012
	(0.016)	(0.027)
Unused commitments/(Commitments + Loans)	−0.020	0.033
	(0.010)	(0.022)
Log of assets	0.001	−0.001
	(0.001)	(0.001)
Russia exposure indicator	0.013	0.049
	(0.008)	(0.041)
LTCM exposure indicator	−0.012	−0.057
	(0.009)	(0.041)
Capital/Assets	0.019	−0.033
	(0.020)	(0.052)
Fed funds purchased/Assets	0.010	−0.003
	(0.014)	(0.029)
(Cash + Securities)/Assets	−0.015**	0.013
	(0.007)	(0.016)
Has a credit rating indicator	−0.001	−0.002
	(0.001)	(0.005)
Is publicly traded indicator	−0.003	0.004
	(0.002)	(0.003)
N	222	223
R^2	0.18	0.08

Notes: See table 3.3.

**Indicates statistical significance at the 5 percent level.

transactions accounts.[22] Overall, the results based on the three-week changes point in the same direction as the one-week changes, but the differences between the crisis and noncrisis periods are somewhat muted.

3.4 Conclusions

This paper tests how bank equity risk and the supply of deposit funds reacted to the liquidity crisis of 1998. During this period, bank stock price

22. We also find some evidence of a negative correlation between balance-sheet liquidity and flows into bank transactions accounts during the three-week crisis window. It is hard to explain why bank liquidity would be negatively related to the supply of funds, and since this result is not robust to our choice of the crisis period, we are hesitant to draw strong conclusions from it.

volatility increased sharply in response to global shocks to credit markets. These shocks, which began when Russia defaulted, led to declining asset prices and widening spreads on risky debt across many markets in response to an investor "flight to quality." Spreads on safe securities, such as U.S. government securities, therefore fell sharply, while the supply of funds to banks increased. We show that this increase in funding supply was greatest at banks with large preexisting transactions deposit accounts. This seems sensible to the extent that investors expected the market uncertainty to be relatively short in duration. We also show that banks with greater transactions deposit accounts had much lower stock return volatility than other banks.

Our results extend and deepen our understanding of the deposit-lending synergy suggested by Kashyap, Rajan, and Stein (2002). According to their model, banks will combine liquidity provision to both depositors (through transactions deposits) and borrowers (through unused loan commitments) to reduce risk as long as liquidity demands from these two classes of customers are not highly correlated. The motivation for this combination is to diversify away some liquidity risk and thus reduce the need to hold cash. Our results suggest that this diversification effect becomes especially powerful during periods of crisis, when the correlation in demand for liquidity by depositors and by borrowers becomes *negative*. Depositors become net suppliers of liquidity during crises because they view banks as a safe haven, just as borrower demands for liquidity are at their highest. We find little relation between observable measures of bank safety, such as size, rating, or deposit flows. Thus, investors seem to view *all* banks as equally safe during liquidity crises (or at least during the 1998 crisis), presumably because of the presence of government safety nets and backup liquidity from the central bank.

References

Boyd, John, and Mark Gertler. 1994. Are banks dead? Or, are the reports greatly exaggerated? Federal Reserve Bank of Minneapolis, *Quarterly Review* (Summer): 1–19.

Chava, Sudheer, and Amiyatosh Purnanandam. 2006. The effect of banking crisis on bank-dependent borrowers. Social Science Research Network. Available at http://ssrn.com/abstract-821804.

Chiodo, Abbigail, and Michael T. Owyang. 2002. A case study of a currency crisis: The Russian default of 1998. *St. Louis Federal Reserve Review* (November): 7–17.

Diamond, Douglas, and Philip Dybvig. 1983. Bank runs, deposit insurance, and liquidity. *Journal of Political Economy* 91 (3): 401–19.

Edwards, Franklin. 1999. Hedge funds and the collapse of Long-Term Capital Management. *Journal of Economic Perspectives* 13 (2): 189–209.

Furfine, Craig. 2002. The costs and benefits of moral suasion: Evidence from the rescue of Long-Term Capital Management. Federal Reserve Bank of Chicago Working Paper no. 2002-11.

Garber, Peter, and David Weisbrod. 1990. Banks in the market for liquidity. NBER Working Paper no. 3381. Cambridge, MA: National Bureau of Economic Research, June.

Gatev, Evan, and Philip E. Strahan. 2006. Banks' advantage in hedging liquidity risk: Theory and evidence from the commercial paper market. *Journal of Finance* 61 (2): 867–92.

Kane, Edward. 1974. All for the best: The Federal Reserve Board's 60th Annual Report. *American Economic Review* (December): 835–50.

Kashyap, Anil K., Raghuram G. Rajan, and Jeremy C. Stein. 2002. Banks as liquidity providers: An explanation for the co-existence of lending and deposit-taking. *Journal of Finance* 57 (1): 33–74.

Kho, Bong-Chan, Dong Lee, and René M. Stulz. 2000. US banks, crises and bailouts: From Mexico to LTCM. *American Economic Review* 90 (2): 28–31.

Lowenstein, Roger. 2000. *When genius failed: The rise and fall of Long-Term Capital Management.* New York: Random House.

Mishkin, Frederic, and Philip E. Strahan. What will technology do to financial structure? 1998. In *The effect of technology on the financial sector,* ed. Robert Litan and Anthony Santomero, 249–87. Washington, DC: Brookings-Wharton Papers on Financial Services.

Myers, Stewart C., and Raghuram G. Rajan. 1998. The paradox of liquidity. *Quarterly Journal of Economics* 113:733–71.

Nelson, Daniel. 1991. Conditional heteroskedasticity in asset returns: A new approach. *Econometrica* 59:247–70.

Saidenberg, Marc R., and Philip E. Strahan. 1999. Are banks still important for financing large businesses? 1999. Federal Reserve Bank of New York's *Current Issues in Economics and Finance* 5 (12): 1–6.

Stiglitz, Joseph, and Andrew Weiss. 1981. Credit rationing in markets with imperfect information. *American Economic Review* 71 (3): 393–410.

Uchitelle, Louis. 1998. "Sure banks are lending, but will they keep it up?" *New York Times,* November 1, 1998.

Comment   Mark Carey

Gatev, Schuermann, and Strahan's paper is first-class research that persuasively argues that large commercial banks are uniquely positioned to act as a stabilizing force during systemic liquidity crises. They present compelling evidence that a large volume of funds flowed into demand deposit accounts at U.S. banks at the same time that corporations were drawing large amounts on their lines of credit, and that the volatility of bank stock prices was smaller for banks with a larger share of transaction deposits among their liabilities. The evidence is from the period around what is arguably the largest pure liquidity crisis of recent years, the Russian default

This discussion represents my own opinions, which are not necessarily those of the Board of Governors, other members of its staff, or the Federal Reserve System.

and subsequent collapse of Long-term Capital Management (LCTM) during 1998. The authors interpret their results as further evidence of a special role for banks that only recently has begun to receive more attention in papers such as Gatev and Strahan (2003) and Kashyap, Rajan, and Stein (2002). In this view, banks are special because they buffer idiosyncratic and systematic liquidity shocks, both for individual borrowers and depositors and for the financial system as a whole. Banks are able to do so because both demand for and supply of liquid funds shift in tandem such that individual banks are able to manage the net liquidity risk at relatively low cost.

I have no suggestions for improvements to this excellent paper. Instead, in the remainder of this discussion, I offer observations that amount to suggestions for future research.

One surprise in the empirical results is that very large banks were not more likely than medium-size banks to experience large flows during the crisis period. It is my impression that "money center" banks disproportionately serve financial market participants who might have been among those engaged in a flight to quality, and that they also meet the borrowing needs of the large corporations that were unable to roll over commercial paper (or were unwilling to do so, given that commercial paper [CP] market spreads were higher than the spreads specified in their backup lines of credit). Even though they are not among the largest banks, some "processing" banks, like State Street or Bank of New York, might experience large deposit inflows from entities for which they process financial transactions and might balance the liquidity risk by participating in the syndicates that typically provide large backup lines of credit. Such banks might introduce enough noise into the relationship between size and flows to make it undetectable in a regression context. It is more difficult to believe that purely regional banks that serve mainly small and middle-market business customers and that rarely participate in syndicated loans would experience the same impact of a LTCM-style liquidity crisis on loan and deposit flows. One way to shed light on this issue would be to simply publish a table that ranks banks by the proportional size of the flows they experience, but I suspect that Gatev, Schuermann, and Strahan could not do this because of the confidential data they use. Another possibility would be to use loan syndication data to identify the exposure of each bank to drawdowns on commercial paper backup lines, using this information in specifications similar to Gatev, Schuermann, and Strahan's.

Regardless of the empirical method, a more detailed understanding of which economic agents are responsible for systemic *and* systematic deposit and loan flows is a key area for future research. We need to know more about which kinds of events will feature offsetting deposit and loan flows and which will be more one-sided. For example, what if the events of a crisis lowered rates and spreads on all short-term instruments, including commercial paper, while still causing a flight-to-quality on the part of investors in other financial assets, like bonds or equities? Flows of bank liabilities and assets might not be offsetting in such a case. Similarly, loss of confidence in one or more major banks almost surely would lead to withdrawals of deposits, but might not lead to paydowns of existing loan balances. Case studies of different kinds of events and panel-data studies are likely to be helpful, and I hope that these and other authors will produce such studies in the future.

Similarly, systematic relationships between deposit and loan flows might differ across nations and institutional structures. The U.S. institutional structure might be particularly supportive of the behavior revealed in Gatev, Schuermann, and Strahan's paper because commercial paper plays an important role and because, at least at the time, the details of CP backup lines of credit locked banks into lending at what turned out to be below-market spreads. In an environment where banks have more discretion about making advances and about the rates charged, it is possible that corporations facing rationing in one capital market might find it more difficult or costly to replace the lost funds. And in an environment where firms depend on banks for almost all debt finance, rapid flows of deposits into banks might not be offset by additional lending. This might happen, for example, if individuals in a nation of bank-dependent firms were placing significant amounts of savings in foreign vehicles, such as foreign bonds or mutual funds, and then the individuals lost confidence in the foreign vehicles.

I was also surprised at the authors' finding that bank equity volatility was negatively related to the share of total deposits in transaction deposits, but was not significantly positively related to the share of unused loan commitments in total loans and commitments. I can easily imagine a positive relationship between unused commitments and volatility: during the crisis, equity investors might reasonably fear that events would lead to a recession and that unused commitments might turn into loans to firms that eventually default, reducing bank earnings down the road.

It is harder to imagine why the relationship between volatility and transaction deposits is so economically large. Even without the deposit inflows, banks in the authors' sample would surely have been able to fund loan commitment drawdowns in interbank markets or through discount window advances at the Federal Reserve (in a period when the Federal Reserve was targeting the federal funds rate, excess demand in the interbank market would simply have led to monetary policy operations that would have the effect of satisfying the demand). Thus, it is difficult to believe that large ex ante transaction balances implied smaller "liquidity risk," because there was essentially no liquidity risk anyway.

It is possible that volatility in transaction deposit volume translates into volatility in bank profits and, as noted, the evidence is persuasive that larger ex ante transaction balances were associated with more volatile balances during the crisis. By construction, transaction deposits in the authors' data pay no interest, so an increase in such balances must reduce a bank's average cost of funds. Even if the bank is forced to place incremental balances in the interbank market, which is a relatively low-margin investment, every extra dollar of transaction deposits should add to the bank's bottom line. Thus, more volatile transaction deposit balances translate into more volatile profits and more volatile equity prices. But in this story, the volatility is all on the upside. And it is hard to believe the effect is nearly as large as the authors find, because had the inflows into banks been more long-lived, depositors surely would have shifted into interest-bearing accounts. Overall, the authors' findings represent a significant puzzle of interpretation. I hope future research will replicate the result for other episodes and be able to shed light on the details of the relationship between bank equity volatility and transaction deposit volumes.

References

Gatev, Evan, and Philip E. Strahan. 2003. Banks' advantage in hedging liquidity risk: Theory and evidence from the commercial paper market. *Journal of Finance* 61 (2): 867–92.
Kashyap, Anil K., Raghuram G. Rajan, and Jeremy C. Stein. 2002. Banks as liquidity providers: An explanation for the co-existence of lending and deposit taking. *Journal of Finance* 57 (1): 33–74.

Discussion Summary

The general discussion opened with a number of questions of clarification. Discussion then turned to intuition about exactly how liquidity flows are embodied during a crisis and whether bank transaction deposits capture them. *Martin Feldstein* asked whether the price of liquidity changes; that is, whether flows represent a shift in supply or demand. *Richard Evans* gave examples of his experience during the LTCM crisis and around September 11, 2001. In both cases, institutions he worked for and other major dealer banks were flooded with liquid liabilities, and the systemic problem for commercial and central banks was to rapidly recycle such liquidity to where it was needed. *Ken Abbott* observed that the recent appearance of contingent put options and market-disruption put options may compel dealer banks that write such options to make substantial payouts during crisis periods, and thus inflows of liquidity would be helpful. *Peter Garber* observed that many wholesale depositors likely would turn to repos as a safe-haven asset during crises rather than deposits, if only because of the ease with which repos can be arranged. *Til Schuermann* noted that large

CD volumes increased sharply at the time of the LTCM crisis, but only at the shortest maturities.

The remainder of the discussion included a number of suggestions for the authors, flowing from skepticism that refinancing of commercial paper is the whole story, as well as technical concerns. *Casper de Vries* suggested excluding the banks that had financed LTCM in order to limit concerns about simultaneity bias. *Eric Rosengren* suggested close attention to the experience of banks that specialize in transaction processing, noting that many banks in the authors' sample are small and are unlikely to serve commercial paper issuers. *Hashem Pesaran* suggested including trailing volatility in regressions, and *David Modest* suggested using measures of excess volatility; that is, individual equity volatility net of the change in market-wide volatility.

Banking System Stability
A Cross-Atlantic Perspective

Philipp Hartmann, Stefan Straetmans, and
Casper G. de Vries

4.1 Introduction

A particularly important sector for the stability of financial systems is
the banking sector. Banks play a central role in the money creation process
and in the payment system. Moreover, bank credit is an important factor
in the financing of investment and growth. Faltering banking systems have
been associated with hyperinflations and depressions in economic history.
Hence, to preserve monetary and financial stability central banks and supervisory authorities have a special interest in assessing banking system
stability.

This is a particularly complex task in very large economies with highly
developed financial systems, such as the United States and the euro area.
Moreover, structural changes in the financial systems of both these economies make it particularly important to track risks over time. In Europe,

We benefited from suggestions and criticism by many participants in the NBER conference
on "Risks of Financial Institutions," in particular by the organizers Mark Carey and René
Stulz (also involving Dean Amel and Allen Berger), by our discussant Tony Saunders, and by
Patrick de Fontnouvelle, Gary Gorton, Andy Lo, Jim O'Brien, and Eric Rosengren. Further-
more, we are grateful for comments we received at the 2004 European Finance Association
Meetings in Maastricht, in particular by our discussant Marco da Rin and by Christian
Upper, at the 2004 Ottobeuren seminar in economics, notably the thoughts of our discussant
Ernst Baltensberger, of Friedrich Heinemann and of Gerhard Illing, as well as at seminars
of the Max Planck Institute for Research on Collective Goods, the Federal Reserve Bank of
St. Louis, the European Central Bank (ECB) and the University of Frankfurt. Gabe de Bondt
and David Marques Ibanez supported us enormously in finding yield spread data, and Lieven
Baele and Richard Stehle kindly made us aware of pitfalls in Datastream equity data. Very
helpful research assistance by Sandrine Corvoisier, Peter Galos and Marco Lo Duca as well
as editorial support by Sabine Wiedemann are gratefully acknowledged. Any views expressed
reflect only those of the authors and should not be interpreted as the ones of the ECB or the
Eurosystem.

gradually integrating financial systems under a common currency increase the relationships between banks across borders. This development raises the question of how banking systems should be monitored in a context where banking supervision—in contrast to monetary policy—remains a national responsibility. In the United States, tremendous consolidation as well as the removal of regulatory barriers to universal and cross-state banking has led to the emergence of large and complex banking organizations (LCBOs), whose activities and interconnections are particularly difficult to follow. For all these reasons we present a new approach in this paper of how to assess banking system risk, and apply it to the euro area and the United States.

A complication in assessing banking system stability is that, in contrast to other elements of the financial system, such as securities values, interbank relationships that can be at the origin of bank contagion phenomena or the values of and correlations between loan portfolios are particularly hard to measure and monitor.[1] Hence, a large part of the published banking stability literature has resorted to more indirect market indicators. In particular, spillovers in bank equity prices have been used for this purpose. Pioneered by Aharony and Swary (1983), a series of papers has examined the effects of specific bank failures or bad news for certain banks on other banks' stock prices (see also Wall and Petersen 1990, or Docking, Hirschey, and Jones 1997).[2] In another series of papers various regression approaches are used in order to link abnormal bank stock returns to asset-side risks (e.g., Smirlock and Kaufold 1987, Musumeci and Sinkey 1990). In fact, some authors point out that most banking crises have been related to macro-economic fluctuations rather than to prevalent contagion (e.g., Gorton 1988, Demirgüç-Kunt and Detragiache 1998).[3]

An issue in the previously noted literature is that any form of stock market reaction is considered. The extreme-value approach for assessing banking system risk advocated in this paper also employs equity prices, but focuses only on crisis propagations, that is, relationships between extremely large negative returns. We want to make three main contributions compared to the previous literature. First, we use the novel multivariate extreme value techniques applied by Hartmann, Straetmans, and de Vries (2003a, 2003b, and 2004) and Poon, Rockinger, and Tawn (2004) to esti-

1. Even central banks and supervisory authorities usually do not have continuous information about interbank exposures. For the Swedish example of a central bank monitoring interbank exposures at a quarterly frequency, see Blavarg and Nimander (2002).
2. Chen (1999), Allen and Gale (2000), and Freixas, Parigi, and Rochet (2002) develop the theoretical foundations of bank contagion.
3. Hellwig (1994) argues that the observed vulnerability of banks to macroeconomic shocks may be explained by the fact that deposit contracts are not conditional on aggregate risk.

For a comprehensive survey of the theoretical and empirical contagion and systemic risk literature, see De Bandt and Hartmann (2000). We list the most recent contributions in the accompanying working paper (Hartmann, Straetmans, and de Vries 2005).

mate the strength of banking system risks. In particular, we distinguish conditional co-crash probabilities between banks from crash probabilities conditional on aggregate shocks. While extreme value theory (EVT)—both univariate and multivariate—has been applied to general stock indices before, it has not yet been used to assess the extreme dependence between bank stock returns with the aim to measure banking system risk. Second, we cover both euro area countries and the United States to compare banking system stability internationally. We are not aware of any other study that tries to compare systemic risk in these major economies. Third, we apply the test of structural stability for tail indexes by Quintos, Fan, and Phillips (2001) to the multivariate case of extreme linkages and assess changes in banking system stability over time with it. Again, whereas a few earlier papers addressed the changing correlations between bank stock returns (e.g., de Nicoló and Kwast 2002), none focused on the extreme interdependence we are interested in in the present paper.

The idea behind our approach is as follows. We assume that bank stocks are efficiently priced, in that they reflect all publicly available information about (1) individual banks' asset and liability side risks and (2) relationships between different banks' risks (be it through correlations of their loan portfolios, interbank lending, or other channels). We identify the risk of a problem in one or several banks spilling over to other banks (contagion risk) with extreme negative comovements between individual bank stocks (similar to the conditional co-crash probability in our earlier stock, bond, and currency papers). In addition, we identify the risk of banking system destabilization through aggregate shocks with the help of the "tail-β" proposed by Straetmans, Verschoor, and Wolf (2003). The tail-β is measured by conditioning our co-crash probability on a general stock index (or another measure of systematic risk) rather than on individual banks' stock prices. Therefore, in some respects it reflects the tail equivalent to standard asset pricing models. In this paper we further extend the analysis of tail-β by also using high-yield bond spreads as measures of aggregate risk. Based on the estimated individual co-crash probabilities and tail-βs, we can then test for the equality of banking system risk between the United States and the euro area and for changes in systemic risk over time.

Our work is also related to the broader literature examining which phenomena constitute financial contagion and how they can be empirically identified. In our reading, the main criteria proposed so far to identify contagion are that (1) a problem at a financial institution adversely affects other financial institutions or that a decline in an asset price leads to declines in other asset prices (e.g., Bae, Karolyi, and Stulz 2003); (2) the relationships between failures or asset price declines must be different from those observed in normal times (regular interdependence; see Forbes and Rigobon 2002); (3) the relationships are in excess of what can be explained by economic fundamentals (Pindyck and Rotemberg 1993, and Bekaert,

Harvey, and Ng, forthcoming); (4) the events constituting contagion are negative extremes, such as full-blown institution failures or market crashes, so that they correspond to crisis situations (Longin and Solnik 2001, and Hartmann et al. 2004); (5) the relationships are the result of propagations over time rather than being caused by the simultaneous effects of common shocks. Most empirical approaches proposed in the recent literature on how to measure contagion capture the first criterion (1), but this is where the agreement usually ends. Authors differ in their views of which of the other criteria (2) through (5) are essential for contagion. The reason why we particularly focus on criterion (4) is that it allows us to concentrate on events that are severe enough to always be of a concern for policy. Other criteria are also interesting and have their own justifications, but more regular propagations or changes in them are not necessarily a concern for policies that aim at the stability of financial systems.

The data we use in this work are daily bank stock excess returns in euro-area countries and the United States between April 1992 and February 2004. For each area or country we chose twenty-five banks based on the criteria of balance-sheet size and involvement in interbank lending. So, our sample represents the most systemically relevant financial institutions, but neglects a large number of smaller banks. During our sample period several of the banks selected faced failure-like situations; also, global markets passed through several episodes of stress. All in all, we have about 3,100 observations per bank.

Our results suggest that the risk of multivariate extreme spillovers between U.S. banks is higher than between European banks. Hence, despite the fact that available balance-sheet data show higher interbank exposures in the euro area, the U.S. banking system seems to be more prone to contagion risk. The lower spillover risk among European banks is mainly related to relatively weak cross-border linkages among a certain number of countries. Domestic linkages in France, Germany, and Italy, for example, are of the same order as domestic U.S. linkages. One interpretation of this result is that further banking integration in Europe could lead to higher cross-border contagion risk in the future, with the more integrated U.S. banking system providing a benchmark. Second, cross-border spillover probabilities tend to be smaller than domestic spillover probabilities, but only for a few countries is this difference statistically significant. For example, among the banks from a number of larger countries—such as France, Germany, the Netherlands, and Spain—extreme cross-border linkages are statistically indistinguishable from domestic linkages. In contrast, the effects of banks from these larger countries on the main banks from some smaller countries—including Finland and Greece in particular, and sometimes Ireland or Portugal—tend to be significantly weaker than the effects on their domestic banks. Hence, those smaller countries located further away from the center of Europe seem to be more insulated from European cross-border contagion.

Third, the effects of macro shocks emphasized by the estimated tail-βs are similar for the euro area and the United States, and they illustrate the relevance of aggregate risks for banking system stability. While stock market indices perform well as indicators of aggregate risk, we find that high-yield bond spreads capture extreme systematic risk for banks relatively poorly, both in Europe and the United States. Fourth, structural stability tests for our indicators suggest that systemic risk, both in the form of interbank spillovers and in the form of aggregate risk, has increased in Europe and in the United States. Our tests detect the break points during the second half of the 1990s, but graphic illustrations of our extreme dependence measures show that this was the result of developments spread out over time. In particular in Europe the process was very gradual, in line with what one would expect during a slowly advancing financial integration process. Interestingly, the introduction of the euro in January 1999 seems to have had a reductionary or no effect on banking system risk in the euro area. This may be explained by the possibility that stronger cross-border crisis transmission channels through a common money market could be offset by better risk sharing and the better ability of a deeper market to absorb shocks.

The paper is structured as follows. The next section describes our two theoretical indicators of banking system stability. Section 4.3 briefly outlines the estimation procedures for both measures; section 4.4 sketches the tests for their stability over time and across countries and continents. Section 4.5 describes the data we employ. Section 4.6 then presents the empirical results on extreme bank spillover risks; section 4.7 turns to the empirical results for aggregate banking system risk (tail-βs). Section 4.8 asks the question whether systemic risk has changed over time. The final section concludes. We have five appendices. Appendix A describes in greater depth our estimation procedures and appendix B the structural stability test. Appendix C discusses small sample properties of estimators and tests. Appendix D lists the banks in our sample and the abbreviations used for them in the paper. Finally, appendix E discusses the relevance of volatility modeling for financial stability policy-oriented research and examines the importance of volatility clustering for extreme dependence in bank stock returns.

4.2   Indicators of Banking System Stability

Our indicators of banking system stability are based on extreme stock price movements. They are constructed as conditional probabilities, conditioning single or multiple bank stock price crashes on other banks' stock price crashes or on crashes of the market portfolio. Extreme comovements, as measured by multivariate conditional probabilities between individual banks' stock returns, are meant to capture the risk of contagion from one bank to another. Extreme comovements between individual banks' stock returns and the returns of a general stock market index or another measure of nondiversifiable risk (the so-called "tail-β") are used to assess the risk of banking system instability through aggregate shocks. The two forms of banking system instability are theoretically distinct, but in practice they may sometimes interact. Both have been extensively referred to in the theoretical and empirical banking literature.

4.2.1   Multivariate Extreme Spillovers: A Measure of Bank Contagion Risk

Let us start by describing the measure of multivariate extreme bank spillovers. The measure can be expressed in terms of marginal (univariate) and joint (multivariate) exceedance probabilities. Consider an N-dimensional banking system, that is, a set of N banks from, for example, the same country or continent. Denote the log first differences of the price changes in bank stocks minus the risk-free interest rate by the random variables $X_i (i = 1, \ldots, N)$. Thus, X_i describes a bank i's excess return. We adopt the convention to take the negative of stock returns, so that we can define all used formulae in terms of upper tail returns. The crisis levels or extreme quantiles $Q_i (i = 1, \ldots, N)$ are chosen such that the tail probabilities are equalized across banks; that is,

$$P(X_1 > Q_1) = \ldots = P(X_i > Q_i) = \ldots = P(X_N > Q_N) = p.$$

With the probability level in common, crisis levels Q_i will generally not be equal across banks, because the marginal distribution functions $P(X_i > Q_i) = 1 - F_i(Q_i)$ are bank specific. The crisis levels can be interpreted as "barriers" that will on average only be broken once in $1/p$ time periods, that is, p^{-1} days if the data frequency is daily. Suppose now that we want to measure the propagation of severe problems throughout the European and U.S. banking sectors by calculating the probability of joint collapse in an arbitrarily large set of N bank stocks, conditional on the collapse of a subset $L < N$ banks:

$$(1) \qquad P_{N|L} = P\left[\bigcap_{i=1}^{N} X_i > Q_i(p) \,\middle|\, \bigcap_{j=1}^{L} X_j > Q_j(p)\right]$$

$$= \frac{P[\bigcap_{i=1}^{N} X_i > Q_i(p)]}{P[\bigcap_{j=1}^{L} X_j > Q_j(p)]}.$$

Clearly, the right-hand side immediately follows from the definition of conditional probability. With independence the measure reduces to p^{N-L}. This provides a benchmark against which the dependent cases are to be judged.

Equation (1) is very flexible in terms of the conditioning set on the right-hand side. For example, the conditioning banks do not necessarily have to be a subset of the bank set on the left-hand side. Moreover, the conditioning random variables could also be other than just bank stock prices.[4]

4.2.2   Tail-βs: A Measure of Aggregate Banking System Risk

Our second measure of banking system risk is from a methodological point of view a bivariate variant of equation (1), in which $N = 1$ and the conditioning set is limited to extreme downturns of the market portfolio or another indicator of aggregate risk ($L = 1$).[5] This tail-β measure is inspired by portfolio theory and has been used before by Straetmans, Verschoor, and Wolff (2003) to examine the intraday effects of the September 11 catastrophe on U.S. stocks. Let X_M be the excess return on the market portfolio (e.g., using a stock market index) and let p be the common tail probability; then this measure can be written as:

$$(2) \quad P[X_k > Q_k(p) \mid X_M > Q_M(p)] = \frac{P[X_k > Q_k(p), X_M > Q_M(p)]}{P[X_M > Q_M(p)]}$$

$$= \frac{P[X_k > Q_k(p), X_M > Q_M(p)]}{p}.$$

The measure captures how likely it is that an individual bank's (k) value declines dramatically if there is an extreme negative systematic shock. Analogous to the multivariate spillover probability (1), the tail-β (2) reduces to $p^2/p = p$ under the benchmark of independence. We extend the analysis of extreme aggregate risk in this paper by also experimenting with high-yield bond spreads as a measure X_M of systematic shocks.[6]

4.3   Estimation of the Indicators

The joint probabilities in (1) and (2) have to be estimated. Within the framework of a parametric probability law, the calculation of the proposed multivariate probability measures is straightforward, because one can estimate the distributional parameters by (for example) maximum likelihood techniques. However, if one makes the wrong distributional assumptions, the linkage estimates may be severely biased due to misspecification. As there is no clear evidence that all stock returns follow the same distribution—even less so for the crisis situations we are interested in here—we

4. In Hartmann, Straetmans, and de Vries (2003a), we applied an analogous measure to assess the systemic breadth of currency crises.
5. Technically, it is also possible to derive and estimate this measure for $N > 1$, but we do not do this in the present paper.
6. In the present paper we limit ourselves to the measures (1) and (2) of banking system risk. In future research, the approach could be extended by also including further economic variables in the conditioning set, such as interest rates or exchange rates.

want to avoid very specific assumptions for bank stock returns. Therefore, we implement the semiparametric EVT approach proposed by Ledford and Tawn (1996; see also Draisma et al. 2001, and Poon, Rockinger, and Tawn 2004, for recent applications). Loosely speaking, their approach consists of generalizing some "best practice" in univariate extreme value analysis.

After a transformation of the return data to unit Pareto marginals, which removes any influence of the marginal distributions on the probabilities of interest, we can rewrite the joint tail probability that occurs in equations (1) and (2):

$$P\left[\bigcap_{i=1}^{N} X_i > Q_i(p)\right] = P\left[\bigcap_{i=1}^{N} \tilde{X}_i > q\right].$$

$\tilde{X}_i$ is the excess return of X_i after the transformation, and $q = 1/p$. We describe the details of this step in appendix A. The consequence is that differences in joint tail probabilities across different banking systems (e.g., United States versus Europe) can now be attributed solely to differences in the tail-dependence structure of the extremes.

The multivariate estimation problem is thus reduced to estimating a univariate exceedance probability for the cross-sectional minimum of the N bank excess return series; that is, it is always true that

(3) $$P\left[\bigcap_{i=1}^{N} \tilde{X}_i > q\right] = P[\min_{i=1}^{N} (\tilde{X}_i) > q] = P[\tilde{X}_{min} > q].$$

The estimation exploits the fact that under fairly general conditions the auxiliary variable $\tilde{X}_{min}$ has a regularly varying tail (Ledford and Tawn 1996).[7] Assuming that the tail index of $\tilde{X}_{min}$ is $\alpha = 1/\eta$, the univariate probability in equation (3) exhibits a tail descent of the Pareto type:

(4) $$P(\tilde{X}_{min} > q) \approx q^{-1/\eta}, \eta \leq 1,$$

with q large (p small). The higher η the more dependent are the components $(\tilde{X}_1, \ldots, \tilde{X}_i, \ldots, \tilde{X}_N)$ from (3) far out in their joint tail. As we argue in appendix A, if the return series $\tilde{X}_i$ are asymptotically dependent then $\eta = 1$, and if they are asymptotically independent then $\eta < 1$.

We estimate equation (4) with the semiparametric probability estimator from de Haan et al. (1994):

(5) $$\hat{P}(\tilde{X}_{min} > q) = \frac{m}{n}\left(\frac{C_{n-m,n}}{q}\right)^{1/\eta},$$

---

7. A function $F(x)$ is said to have a regularly varying left tail if

$$\lim_{u \to \infty} F(-ux)/F(-u) = x^{-\alpha}$$

for any $x > 0$ and tail index $\alpha > 0$.

where n is the sample size and the "tail cut-off point" $C_{n-m,n}$ is basically the $(n - m)$-th largest return from the cross-sectional minimum series $\tilde{X}_{min}$. Equation (5) extends the empirical distribution function of $\tilde{X}_{min}$ for more extreme returns q than the ones observed in the sample. It is conditional upon the tail dependence parameter η and a choice of the threshold parameter m.

To estimate η we use the popular Hill (1975) estimator for the index of regular variation:

$$(6) \qquad \hat{\eta} = \frac{1}{m} \sum_{j=0}^{m-1} \ln\left(\frac{C_{n-j,n}}{C_{n-m,n}}\right) = \frac{1}{\hat{\alpha}}.$$

m is the number of most extreme returns that enter the estimation. Appendix A contains a discussion on how it is chosen optimally. Draisma et al. (2001) derive asymptotic normality of $\sqrt{m}(\hat{\eta}/\eta - 1)$ under fairly general conditions. The asymptotic normality will prove convenient for the tests implemented later on. We discuss small-sample properties of our tail-dependence estimator $\hat{\eta}$ in the first section of appendix C.

4.4   Hypothesis Testing

In this section we introduce some tests that can be used to assess various hypotheses regarding the evolution and structure of systemic risk in the banking system. The first one allows to test for the structural stability of the amount of risk found with our two indicators. In the first subsection we present the rationale for using this test and the intuition of how it works. Appendix B contains a more detailed technical exposition. The second test in subsection 4.4.2 allows us to compare systemic risk across countries and continents.

4.4.1   Time Variation

The multivariate linkage estimator (1) and its bivariate counterpart in (2) were presented so far as assuming stationarity of tail behavior over time. From a policy perspective, however, it is important to know whether systemic risk in the banking system—either in terms of contagion risk (1) or in terms of extreme systematic risk (2)—has changed over time. As the discussion of the Ledford and Tawn approach toward estimating (1) or (2) has shown, the structural (in)stability of systemic risk will critically depend on whether the tail dependence parameter η is constant or not. We study the occurrence of upward and downward swings in η with a recently developed structural stability test for the Hill statistic (6).

Quintos, Fan, and Phillips (2001) present a number of tests for identifying single unknown breaks in the estimated tail index $\hat{\alpha}$. As our estimation approach allows us to map the multivariate dependence problem into a univariate estimation problem, we can choose from them the best test procedures for our tail dependence parameter η. Balancing the prevention of type I and type II errors, we opt for their recursive test.

This test takes a window of the data at the start of the sample and estimates the respective $\hat{\eta}$. It then reestimates the tail dependence parameter, successively increasing the data window until the end of the sample is reached. One calculates the (appropriately scaled) ratios of the subsample ηs and the full sample equivalent and chooses the date with the maximum ratio as a candidate break point. The null hypothesis of the test is that there is no change in η over time. The alternative hypothesis is that asymptotic dependence has either increased or decreased at some point in time.

Asymptotic critical values of the suprema of the ratio series have been derived by Quintos, Fan, and Phillips (2001). They are 1.46, 1.78, and 2.54 for the 10 percent, 5 percent, and 1 percent significance levels, respectively. If the data exhibit nonlinear intertemporal dependencies, such as the well-known autoregressive conditional heteroskedasticity (ARCH) effects (volatility clustering) in financial returns, then some additional scaling of the test statistic is needed to avoid erroneous inference. In contrast to Quintos, Fan, and Phillips, we estimate the asymptotic variance of the dependence parameter that is used for the scaling with a block bootstrap, which accounts for more general dependencies than ARCH. If the supremum of the scaled ratio exceeds the critical values, the test rejects the null hypothesis of constant extreme dependence.

Quintos, Fan, and Phillips report a Monte Carlo study that indicates good small sample power, size, and bias properties of the recursive break test. Only in the case of a decrease of extreme tail dependence under the alternative hypothesis ($\eta_1 > \eta_2$) do they detect less-acceptable power properties. We solve this problem by executing the recursive test both in a "forward" version and a "backward" version. The forward version calculates the subsample ηs in calendar time, and the backward version in reverse calendar time. If a downward break in η occurs and the forward test does not pick it up, then the backward test corrects for this. The second section of appendix C provides a further Monte Carlo study of the small-sample properties of the recursive structural break test.

4.4.2 Cross-sectional Variation

We would also like to know whether cross-sectional differences between various groups of banks or different banking systems, say between the United States and Europe or between different European countries, are statistically and economically significant. The asymptotic normality of $\hat{\eta}$ referred to earlier enables some straightforward hypothesis testing. A test for the equality of tail-dependence parameters (null hypothesis) is based on the following T-statistic:

(7)
$$T = \frac{\hat{\eta}_1 - \hat{\eta}_2}{\text{s.e.}(\hat{\eta}_1 - \hat{\eta}_2)},$$

which converges to a standard normal distribution in large samples.[8] Accordingly, the asymptotic critical values are 1.65, 1.96, and 2.58 for the 10 percent, 5 percent, and 1 percent significance levels, respectively. In the following empirical applications, the asymptotic standard error in the test's denominator (7) is estimated using a block bootstrap.[9] Similar to the previous structural stability test, we opt for bootstrapping in blocks because of the nonlinear dependencies that might be present in the return data.

4.5 Data and Descriptive Statistics

We collected daily stock price data (total return indexes including dividends) for twenty-five euro area banks and twenty-five U.S. banks. Excess returns are constructed by taking log first differences and deducting three-month London Interbank Offered Rate (LIBOR) rates (adjusted linearly to derive daily from annual rates). They are expressed in local currency so that they do not vary directly with exchange rates. The market risk factor or aggregate shocks to the euro area and U.S. banking systems are proxied by several measures, with an eye toward some sensitivity analysis. First, we employ a general stock index and the banking sector subindex for the euro area and the United States, respectively. Second, we use the spread between below-investment-grade and treasury bond yields for each of these economies. Finally, we use a global stock index and the global banking sector subindex.

All series, except one, start on 2 April, 1992, and end on 27 February, 2004, rendering 3,106 return observations per bank. The euro area high-yield bond spread is only available from 1 January, 1998, onward, yielding 1,497 observations. All series are downloaded from Datastream, whose source for high-yield bond spreads is Merrill Lynch.[10] The stock indices are the total return indexes calculated by the data provider.

The following subsection provides information about how the fifty banks were chosen, based on balance sheet items for European and U.S. banks. The subsequent section discusses the return data, in particular their negative extremes.

---

8. One can safely assume that T comes sufficiently close to normality for empirical sample sizes as the one used in this paper (see, e.g., Hall 1982, or Embrechts, Klüppelberg, and Mikosch 1997).

9. As for the test of time variation (see appendix B), we follow Hall, Horowitz, and Jing (1995) and set the optimal block length equal to $n^{1/3}$.

10. See de Bondt and Marques (2004) for an in-depth discussion of high-yield bond spreads.

4.5.1   Bank Selection and Balance Sheet Information

The time dimension of this dataset was very much constrained by the unavailability of longer stock price series for European banks. Before the 1990s fewer large European banks were privately quoted on stock exchanges; also, many banks disappeared as a consequence of mergers.[11] Roughly in proportion to the sizes of their economies in terms of gross domestic product (GDP) and the sizes of their banking systems in terms of assets, we have six banks from Germany, four banks from France, four banks from Italy, three banks from Spain, two banks each from the Netherlands and from Belgium, and one bank from Finland, Greece, Ireland, and Portugal, respectively. Appendix D contains the full list of banks, the abbreviations used in the tables, and their country of origin.

Apart from those constraints, banks were chosen on the basis of two main criteria: first, their size (as measured mainly by assets and deposits) and, second, their involvement in interbank lending (as measured by interbank loans, amounts due to and due from other banks, and total money market funding). The necessary balance-sheet information was taken from Bureau van Dijk's Bankscope database (considering end-of-year values between 1992 and 2003). For the United States, the choice of banks was double-checked on the basis of the Federal Reserve Bank of Chicago commercial bank and bank holding company databases.

We used this balance-sheet information to identify the "systemically most important" banks across all the twelve years. By using several criteria, some choices naturally had to be made. We showed the data and discussed the choices in detail in the accompanying working paper (see subsection 4.5.1 and appendix C in Hartmann, Straetmans, and C. de Vries 2005). Here we just list two interesting observations from this: (1) while in Europe bank size and interbank lending activity are quite aligned, in the United States a number of smaller banks (such as State Street, Northern Trust, Bank of New York, or Mellon) have very large interbank exposures. We are careful to have these clearing banks in our sample of twenty-five U.S. banks, as the failure of one or several of them may constitute a particularly severe source of contagion risk,[12] and (2) the sizes of euro area and U.S. banks chosen are similar, but the data also show much larger interbank exposures among European than among U.S. banks. To our knowledge, this difference has not been noted in the literature on banking system

---

11. Ten out of twelve euro area countries have banks in our sample. There is no Austrian bank, as we could not construct a long enough stock price series for any of the two largest banks from this country. We deliberately excluded banks from Luxembourg, as they are considerably smaller than the larger banks from all other euro area countries.

12. For example, the failure of Continental Illinois in 1983–84 and the computer problem of Bank of New York in 1985 raised major concerns and were accompanied by public action in order to prevent those incidents from spreading through the banking system.

risk before. It will be interesting to subsequently verify whether it translates into larger systemic risk in the European banking system.

4.5.2   Stock Returns and Yield Spreads

The accompanying working paper presents an extensive discussion of the typical host of descriptive statistics for our fifty bank stock return series and the factors capturing aggregate risk (see subsection 4.5.2 and appendix D in Hartmann, Straetmans, and C. de Vries 2005). As the results are pretty standard, we list here only two observations: (1) while individual bank stock returns are highly correlated with stock indices, the same does not apply to high-yield bond spreads. This provides first evidence that yield spreads might not be a good predictor of aggregate banking system risk, and (2) correlations between individual bank stock returns are generally positive and of similar order of magnitude in the euro area and in the United States. For the United States, however, correlation coefficients appear to be much more uniform across bank pairs.

For the purpose of the present paper, we are particularly interested in extreme negative returns. The left-hand sides of tables 4.1 and 4.2 report the three largest negative excess returns (in absolute value) for all the banks in the sample and for the two banking sector stock indices. Starting with Europe, the largest stock price decline in the sample (a massive daily collapse of 85 percent) happens for Banco Espanol de Credito (Banesto) in February 1994. Around that time, this Spanish bank faced major difficulties and was rescued by an initial public intervention in December 1993. Another bank in major difficulties during our sample period is Berliner Bankgesellschaft from Germany. This is reflected in two consecutive stock price crashes of 38 percent and 27 percent during the summer of 2001. Ultimately this bank was also saved by the federal state of Berlin. As regards the United States, the largest daily stock price slump happens to Unionbancal Corporation. The market value of this troubled California bank declined in June 2000 by as much as 36 percent, as a consequence of credit quality problems. The next most significant corrections of just above 20 percent occur for Comerica Inc. and AmSouth Bancorporation. These examples illustrate that we have a number of individual bank crises in the sample.

In contrast to the stock returns, the high-yield bond spreads reported at the bottom of tables 4.1 and 4.2 are maxima, as extreme positive values indicate a situation of high risk. One can see that in times of stress, noninvestment grade corporate debt can trade at yields of more than 10 percent above government debt.

There is also some first evidence of clustering in extreme bank stock declines, as many of them happen around a number of well-known crisis episodes. For example, a significant number of European and U.S.-based banks faced record downward corrections around the end of the summer

Table 4.1   Historical minima, tail indexes and quantile estimates for excess stock returns of euro area banks (%)

| Bank | | Extreme negative returns | | | $\|\hat{Q}(p)\|$ | |
	$X_{1,n}$ (date)	$X_{2,n}$ (date)	$X_{3,n}$ (date)	$\hat{\alpha}$	$p = 0.05$	$p = 0.02$
DEUTSCHE	12.4 (09/11/01)	12.0 (03/09/00)	10.1 (09/19/01)	3.3	13.8	18.2
HYPO	17.3 (10/23/02)	14.3 (09/30/02)	11.5 (09/11/01)	3.1	17.9	24.0
DRESDNER	11.1 (10/28/97)	9.9 (07/22/02)	9.7 (03/09/00)	3.2	16.1	21.5
COMMERZ	13.3 (09/11/01)	13.1 (09/20/01)	13.1 (10/23/02)	2.9	15.9	21.9
BGBERLIN	37.9 (08/30/01)	27.0 (09/10/01)	17.1 (01/17/94)	2.	23.4	34.2
DEPFA	16.5 (11/29/00)	10.4 (10/08/98)	10.3 (07/23/02)	3.2	13.4	17.6
BNPPAR	12.5 (09/30/98)	11.2 (09/30/02)	11.0 (10/04/02)	3.0	15.4	20.8
CA	19.6 (11/19/01)	12.4 (07/12/01)	10.5 (09/12/02)	2.4	13.3	19.4
SGENERAL	12.5 (09/10/98)	11.6 (09/30/02)	10.4 (07/19/02)	2.7	17.1	23.6
NATEXIS	13.6 (10/08/97)	10.8 (09/25/96)	10.6 (03/25/94)	3.6	9.6	12.3
INTESA	12.7 (11/07/94)	12.2 (09/20/01)	11.6 (10/28/97)	3.9	13.7	17.4
UNICREDIT	10.9 (07/20/92)	10.3 (09/10/98)	9.9 (10/21/92)	3.6	12.9	16.7
PAOLO	9.9 (12/04/00)	9.7 (09/10/98)	9.5 (09/20/01)	3.5	13.3	17.3
CAPITA	18.2 (03/07/00)	12.0 (10/01/98)	11.5 (06/20/94)	3.3	16.7	24.6
SANTANDER	15.9 (10/01/98)	12.8 (01/13/99)	11.4 (07/30/02)	3.0	15.8	21.4
BILBAO	14.5 (01/13/99)	11.8 (09/10/98)	10.7 (09/24/92)	2.6	17.4	24.8
BANESP	84.8 (02/02/94)	18.9 (11/27/02)	15.5 (08/28/98)	2.2	20.1	30.6
ING	16.1 (10/15/01)	14.0 (10/02/98)	13.9 (09/11/01)	2.4	23.4	34.4
ABNAMRO	12.6 (09/14/01)	11.9 (09/11/01)	11.3 (09/30/02)	2.5	19.6	28.3
FORTIS	11.0 (08/01/02)	10.6 (09/30/02)	10.6 (09/11/01)	3.1	14.6	19.7
ALMANIJ	8.7 (11/26/99)	8.0 (04/30/92)	6.2 (08/01/02)	3.8	0.7	12.4
ALPHA	9.4 (04/27/98)	9.4 (09/09/93)	9.1 (01/13/99)	3.1	14.4	19.3
BCP	17.1 (10/23/02)	9.9 (02/25/03)	9.1 (04/16/99)	2.5	13.8	19.8
SAMPO	20.7 (08/17/92)	18.3 (12/21/92)	15.6 (08/26/92)	2.6	23.8	33.7
IRBAN	18.2 (02/06/02)	10.3 (10/08/98)	10.1 (10/28/97)	2.9	12.7	17.4
Bank index	6.9 (09/11/01)	6.7 (10/01/98)	6.3 (09/10/98)	2.5	11.2	16.1
Stock index	6.3 (09/11/01)	5.3 (10/28/97)	5.0 (09/14/01)	3.2	7.7	10.2
Yield spread	16.6 (10/02/01)	16.5 (10/03/01)	16.3 (10/01/01)	9.1	22.3	24.7

Source: The source of raw data is Datastream.

Notes: Returns and quantiles are reported in absolute values and therefore positive. $X_{1,n}$, $X_{2,n}$, and $X_{3,n}$ are the three smallest daily excess returns in the sample for each bank or each index. The last line describes the largest values (maxima) for high-yield bond spreads. Dates in parentheses are denoted XX/YY/ZZ, where XX = month, YY = day, and ZZ = year. $\hat{\alpha}$ is the tail index, estimated with the method by Hill (1975). $\hat{Q}(p)$ is the estimated quantile (crisis level) for each bank, as implied by the estimated tail index and the assumed percentile (crisis probability). The quantiles are calculated for two percentiles p that correspond to an in-sample quantile ($p = 0.05$) and an out-of-sample quantile ($p = 0.02$). Data are from 2 April, 1992, to 27 February, 2004. See table 4D.1 for list of abbreviations.

of 1998. This is the infamous episode related to the Long-term Capital Management (LTCM) collapse (and perhaps also to the Russian default). Another similar episode, very much limited to U.S. banks, happened in spring and summer 2000, potentially related to the burst of the technology bubble. Interestingly, record bank stock crashes around 11 September, 2001—the time of the New York terrorist attack—are registered for a num-

Table 4.2   Historical minima, tail indexes, and quantile estimates for excess stock returns of U.S. banks (%)

Bank	Extreme negative returns				$\|\hat{Q}(p)\|$	
	$X_{1,n}$ (date)	$X_{2,n}$ (date)	$X_{3,n}$ (date)	$\hat{\alpha}$	$p = 0.05$	$p = 0.02$
CITIG	17.1 (07/23/02)	11.7 (07/22/02)	11.5 (10/27/97)	3.3	13.7	18.0
JP MORGAN	20.0 (07/23/02)	10.8 (09/03/98)	10.1 (09/13/00)	3.7	12.9	16.6
BAMERICA	11.6 (10/14/98)	10.7 (10/27/03)	9.1 (06/16/00)	3.6	12.0	15.5
WACHOVIA	9.2 (11/14/00)	9.1 (05/25/99)	9.0 (01/27/99)	3.5	10.9	14.1
FARGO	9.2 (06/16/00)	7.5 (06/08/98)	7.3 (04/14/00)	3.7	9.6	12.3
BONE	25.8 (08/25/99)	11.4 (11/10/99)	9.5 (10/27/97)	3.0	13.5	18.4
WASHING	11.7 (10/17/01)	10.3 (09/04/98)	9.3 (12/09/03)	3.5	12.7	16.5
FLEET	11.2 (07/16/02)	10.2 (02/21/95)	8.0 (07/23/02)	3.7	11.7	15.0
BNYORK	16.9 (12/18/02)	13.9 (07/16/01)	11.1 (10/03/02)	3.4	12.6	16.5
SSTREET	19.7 (04/14/93)	12.1 (03/21/03)	11.9 (10/12/00)	3.0	14.8	20.0
NTRUST	10.6 (10/03/02)	9.1 (04/14/00)	8.5 (05/25/00)	3.5	11.8	15.4
MELLON	13.0 (10/27/97)	10.6 (01/22/03)	9.8 (03/08/96)	3.3	12.7	16.7
BCORP	17.4 (10/05/01)	15.9 (06/30/92)	10.7 (10/04/00)	2.9	14.4	19.8
CITYCO	9.5 (04/14/00)	8.2 (10/27/97)	7.7 (02/04/00)	3.1	11.3	15.2
PNC	16.1 (07/18/02)	10.3 (10/17/02)	9.8 (01/29/02)	3.4	10.9	14.3
KEYCO	8.9 (08/31/98)	8.3 (03/07/00)	8.2 (06/30/00)	3.4	11.4	14.9
SOTRUST	10.6 (04/26/93)	10.3 (01/03/00)	9.7 (03/17/00)	3.1	12.0	16.2
COMERICA	22.7 (10/02/02)	9.1 (04/17/01)	9.1 (04/14/00)	3.4	10.7	14.0
UNIONBANK	36.4 (06/16/00)	15.5 (03/17/00)	10.9 (12/15/00)	3.0	15.1	20.6
AMSOUTH	20.9 (09/22/00)	15.0 (06/01/99)	6.9 (01/10/00)	3.5	9.4	12.2
HUNTING	18.3 (09/29/00)	10.4 (01/18/01)	10.0 (08/31/98)	3.1	13.2	17.8
BBT	8.2 (01/21/03)	7.2 (06/15/00)	7.0 (04/14/00)	3.4	10.1	13.2
53BANCO	8.5 (11/15/02)	7.3 (01/14/99)	7.0 (04/14/00)	3.8	9.6	12.3
SUTRUST	10.2 (0720/98)	9.5 (04/14/00)	8.9 (06/16/00)	3.2	10.6	14.2
REGIONS	11.2 (12/15/03)	9.1 (08/31/98)	8.5 (06/15/00)	3.5	10.2	13.2
Bank index	7.0 (04/14/00)	6.8 (07/23/02)	6.7 (10/27/97)	3.4	9.1	12.0
Stock index	7.0 (08/31/98)	6.8 (04/14/00)	6.8 (10/27/97)	3.7	6.3	8.0
Yield Spread	10.8 (10/10/02)	10.7 (10/09/02)	10.7 (10/11/02)	15.8	12.1	12.9

Source: The source of raw data is Datastream.
Notes: See table 4.1.

ber of European banks, but not for U.S. banks.[13] Finally, some American and European banks were hit significantly by the onset of the Asian crisis in fall 1997. These examples illustrate, first, that our sample covers a number of stress situations in global and national markets,[14] and second, that they also indicate the relevance of systematic shocks for banking stability, which motivates our tail-β indicator.

13. The less extreme reactions of U.S. bank stocks may, however, also have to do with a four-day suspension of trading at the New York Stock Exchange.
14. The presence of single and aggregate crisis situations in our sample is reassuring, as the focus of our paper is financial stability. At the same time, however, we would like to note that extreme-value methods do not require the presence of individual or aggregate failures in the

We also report in tables 4.1 and 4.2 the estimated tail indexes $\hat{\alpha}$ for individual banks and for the stock indices. It turns out that they vary around 3, which is in line with the evidence presented in Jansen and de Vries (1991), illustrating the well known nonnormality of stock returns and the nonexistence of higher-order moments. If anything, the tails of a number of European banks seem to be slightly fatter (smaller α) than the ones of U.S. banks. In addition to the larger interbank lending in Europe referred to earlier, this observation raises again the issue of whether systemic risk on the European side of the Atlantic is more pronounced than on the other. Another observation is that the yield spreads have much thinner tails than stock index returns.

The right-hand sides of tables 4.1 and 4.2 show the estimated quantiles for all the banks when assuming a common percentile (or crash probability). In this paper, we experiment with percentiles p between 0.02 percent and 0.05 percent (explicitly reporting results for the latter), as for these values the implied crisis levels tend to be close to or slightly beyond the historical extremes (see left-hand side). In other words, there cannot be any doubt about the fact that the phenomena considered constitute critical situations for banks. In terms of sensitivity analysis, all our qualitative results reported subsequently are robust to varying the crash probability p, at least within this range.

4.6   Bank Contagion Risk

In this section we report the results from our multivariate bank spillover measure. We are trying to answer two main sets of questions: (1) how large is bank contagion risk in euro area countries, and, in particular, what do our stock market indicators suggest about the relative importance of the risk of domestic spillovers between banks as compared to the risk of cross-border spillovers? Answers to the latter question are particularly important for macroprudential surveillance and for the ongoing debate about supervisory cooperation and the structure of supervisory authorities in Europe. (2) What do our indicators say about the relative size of bank contagion risk when comparing the euro area with the United States? Is one banking system more at risk than the other? The former set of questions is addressed in subsection 4.6.1 and the latter in subsection 4.6.2. In the present section we still abstract from extreme systematic risk for the euro area and U.S. banking system, as this is addressed in the following section (section 4.7). For expositional reasons, we also abstract here from changes of spillover risk over time, which are addressed in section 4.8.

---

sample. In contrast to fully nonparametric and parametric approaches, our semiparametric approach allows us to estimate reliably extremal behavior even beyond the sample boundaries.

4.6.1 Euro Area

In order to assess the exposure of euro area banks to each other, as derived from their extreme stock price comovements, we report in table 4.3 the estimation results for our measure (1). To keep the amount of information manageable, we do not show the extreme dependence parameters η that enter in the estimation of (1), and we only display the spillovers to the largest banks of the countries listed on the left-hand side. We calculate the co-crash probabilities conditional on the second (column $\hat{P}_1$), second and third (column $\hat{P}_2$), second, third, and fourth (column $\hat{P}_3$), and so on largest banks from Germany (upper panel), from Spain (upper middle panel), from Italy (lower middle panel) and from France (lower panel). All probabilities refer to the crisis levels (extreme quantiles) reported in table 4.1 for $p = 0.05$ percent.

For example, the value 22.4 percent in the row "Germany" and the column "$\hat{P}_1$" in the upper panel refers to the probability that Deutsche Bank (the largest German bank) faces an extreme spillover from HypoVereinsbank (the second largest German bank). Going a few cells down, the value 11.2 percent describes the probability that Banco Santander Central Hispano (the largest Spanish bank) faces an extreme spillover from HypoVereinsbank. The difference between these two values would suggest that the likelihood of cross-border contagion could only be half of the likelihood of domestic contagion. When going through the table more systematically (in particular through the columns for more than one conditioning bank crash), it turns out that cross-border contagion risk is indeed generally estimated to be smaller than domestic contagion risk in the euro area banking system. To pick just another example, the probability that the largest French bank (BNP Paribas) faces an extreme stock price slump given that the second (Crédit Agricole) and third largest French bank (Société Générale) have experienced one is a nonnegligible 35.9 percent (see column $\hat{P}_2$, upper middle panel, row "France"). The same probability for the largest Italian bank (Banca Intesa) is 7.5 percent (see column $\hat{P}_2$, upper middle panel, row "Italy"). The probabilities in the first row of each panel are very often higher than the probabilities in the rows underneath.

There are also some exceptions, in particular among the bivariate probabilities reflecting linkages between two large banks (column $\hat{P}_1$). This is not too surprising, as the largest players will have more extensive international operations, implying more scope for cross-border contagion. In particular, Algemene Bank Nederland-Amsterdam Roterdam (ABN AMRO)—the largest Dutch bank—is more affected by problems of HypoVereinsbank than Deutsche Bank (26.5 percent > 22.4 percent). Actually, the linkages between Dutch and German banks tend to be among the largest cross-border linkages in our sample. Other important cross-border linkages exist between the top banks of France, Germany, the Netherlands,

Table 4.3 **Domestic versus cross-border extreme spillover risk among euro area banks: Estimations**

Largest bank	$\hat{P}_1$	$\hat{P}_2$	$\hat{P}_3$	$\hat{P}_4$	$\hat{P}_5$
Conditioning banks: German					
Germany	22.4	65.1	74.3	72.7	55.4
The Netherlands	26.5	54.1	70.1	43.0	34.2
France	8.2	25.2	35.8	31.0	16.2
Spain	11.2	17.4	24.2	44.1	40.3
Italy	7.5	13.6	12.9	7.5	10.8
Belgium	16.1	44.2	42.6	28.5	9.2
Ireland	4.0	5.5	5.4	24.7	16.5
Portugal	7.7	13.6	21.7	25.1	18.0
Finland	0.9	1.7	2.3	4.0	4.5
Greece	0.9	1.4	1.3	1.3	2.1
Conditioning banks: French					
France	2.9	35.9	76.6		
Germany	3.1	23.9	69.5		
The Netherlands	8.2	48.7	71.8		
Italy	1.5	7.5	13.1		
Spain	3.3	27.4	70.1		
Belgium	6.7	38.0	56.3		
Ireland	1.0	1.8	6.9		
Portugal	2.5	6.5	26.5		
Finland	0.0	0.2	0.7		
Greece	0.2	0.3	0.6		
Conditioning banks: Italian					
Italy	9.6	16.4	16.6		
Germany	5.1	12.4	18.8		
The Netherlands	7.2	16.1	18.0		
Spain	4.6	11.7	14.6		
France	5.2	7.3	8.6		
Belgium	4.7	12.0	11.4		
Ireland	1.6	2.6	5.1		
Portugal	1.8	2.5	3.3		
Finland	1.9	3.2	2.5		
Greece	0.8	0.8	0.7		
Conditioning banks: Spanish					
Spain	45.4	31.6			
Germany	22.4	13.9			
The Netherlands	26.5	15.6			
France	25.8	21.6			
Italy	8.3	9.0			
Belgium	13.7	5.6			
Ireland	4.1	3.3			
Portugal	6.2	6.5			
Finland	1.1	1.4			
Greece	1.7	1.1			

Notes: The table reports estimated extreme spillover probabilities between banks, as defined in (1). Each column $\hat{P}_j$ shows the spillover probabilities for the largest bank of the country mentioned on the left-hand side conditional on a set of banks j from either the same country

Table 4.3   (continued)

or other countries. The number of conditioning banks varies from one to five for Germany (top panel), one to three for France (upper middle panel), one to three for Italy (lower middle panel), and one to two for Spain (bottom panel). For example, the $\hat{P}_2$ column contains probabilities for a stock market crash of the largest bank in each country, conditional on crashes of the second and third largest bank in Germany, France, Italy, or Spain. All probabilities are estimated with the extension of the approach by Ledford and Tawn (1996) described in section 4.3 and reported in percentages. Univariate crash probabilities (crisis levels) are set to $p = 0.05$ percent.

and the top Spanish bank. Moreover, as in the case of BNP Paribas, Crédit Agricole, and Société Générale, the largest institutions of a country must not always be very strongly interlinked in the home market. As a consequence, the French panel shows that ABN AMRO and Fortis—the largest Belgian bank—are more exposed to the second and third largest French bank than is BNP Paribas. The fact that Belgian and Dutch banks are associated with the largest cross-border spillover risks is also intuitive, since the banking sectors of these countries are dominated by a small number of very large international financial conglomerates. Also, the results of Degryse and Nguyen (2004) and van Lelyveld and Liedorp (2004) suggest their special exposure to cross-border risk.

Another observation from table 4.3 is that the main Finnish and Greek banks, located in two countries next to the outside border of the euro area, tend to be least affected by problems of large banks from other euro area countries. Something similar, but to a lesser extent, can be observed for Ireland and, with exceptions, for Portugal. Apparently, smaller banking systems located more in the periphery of the euro area are more insulated from foreign spillovers than larger systems in the center. Overall, the level of spillover risk seems to be economically relevant, both domestically and across borders, in particular when more than one large bank faces a stock price crash. Contagion risk for single crashes tends, however, to be markedly lower.

An interesting exception is Italy. While being a larger core country in the euro area, it is much less affected by problems in French, German, or Spanish banks than other core countries. This is also consistent with the findings of Mistrulli (2005). In addition, spillovers from the largest Italian banks to other main banking systems in Europe seem also quite limited. One explanation for this phenomenon could be the low penetration of the Italian banking system from abroad and the limited number of acquisitions by Italian banks in other European countries.[15]

The test results in table 4.4 show whether the differences between domestic and cross-country contagion risk are statistically significant or not.

---

15. This must, however, not remain like this, as the recent acquisition of HypoVereinsbank by UniCredito suggests.

Table 4.4 **Domestic versus cross-border extreme spillover risk among euro area banks: Tests**

Largest bank	T_1	T_2	T_3	T_4	T_5
Conditioning banks: German					
The Netherlands	−1.01	0.00	−0.50	0.66	0.59
France	1.61	1.58	1.20	0.83	1.52
Spain	0.98	2.51**	2.19**	0.50	0.21
Italy	1.56	2.58***	3.10***	2.59***	1.91*
Belgium	0.12	0.26	0.83	0.98	1.86*
Ireland	2.08**	−2.15**	3.78***	1.36	1.51
Portugal	1.28	2.9**	1.90*	0.91	1.17
Finland	3.93***	4.82***	4.32***	3.09***	2.62***
Greece	3.61***	4.47***	4.44***	3.28***	2.66***
Conditioning banks: French					
Germany	−0.31	0.86	−0.39		
The Netherlands	−2.50**	−1.11	−0.75		
Spain	−0.24	0.48	0.08		
Italy	1.03	2.75***	1.92*		
Belgium	−1.85*	−0.51	0.37		
Ireland	1.32	3.20***	2.58***		
Portugal	0.11	2.36**	1.04		
Finland	3.56***	3.96***	3.93***		
Greece	2.56**	3.73***	3.65***		
Conditioning banks: Italian					
Germany	1.11	0.42	−0.09		
The Netherlands	0.41	−0.17	−0.56		
Spain	1.33	0.45	−0.01		
France	0.96	1.27	−0.09		
Belgium	1.01	0.31	−0.36		
Ireland	2.50**	2.52**	1.46		
Portugal	2.70***	2.57**	2.07**		
Finland	2.33**	2.10**	2.16**		
Greece	3.90***	3.59***	3.34***		
Conditioning banks: Spanish					
Germany	1.41	1.04			
The Netherlands	0.89	1.00			
France	0.68	0.31			
Italy	2.83***	1.51			
Belgium	1.83*	1.91*			
Ireland	4.21***	3.00***			
Portugal	3.47***	2.05**			
Finland	5.40***	3.92***			
Greece	4.58***	3.39***			

Notes: The table reports the statistics for the cross sectional test (4.4.1). Within each panel the degree of extreme domestic spillover risk is compared with the degree of extreme cross-border spillover risk for a given fixed number of conditioning banks. So, each T-statistic describes whether the differences between domestic and cross-border values of η that entered the estimations in table 4.3 are statistically significant. For example, in the top panel the test statistic in the row "The Netherlands" and the column T_1 indicates whether the difference between the η for the spillover probability between ABN AMRO and HypoVereinsbank and the η be-

Table 4.4   (continued)

tween Deutsche Bank and HypoVereinsbank is statistically significant. The null hypothesis is that the respective two ηs are equal. Insignificant T-statistics imply that the domestic and cross-border spillover risks are indistinguishable. A significant rejection with positive sign implies that cross-border spillover risk is statistically smaller than its domestic counterpart; a rejection with negative sign implies that cross-border risk is larger than domestic risk. The critical values of the test are 1.65, 1.96, and 2.58 for the 10 percent, 5 percent, and 1 percent levels, respectively.
***Indicates rejection of the null hypothesis at 1 percent significance.
**Indicates rejection of the null hypothesis at 5 percent significance.
*Indicates rejection of the null hypothesis at 10 percent significance.

Rows and columns refer to the same banks as in table 4.3, but the cells now show T-statistics of the cross-sectional test described in subsection 4.4.2. The null hypothesis is that domestic spillovers equal cross-border spillovers.[16] The test statistics partly qualify the interpretation of some of the contagion probabilities in table 4.3. Extreme cross-border linkages between Belgian, Dutch, French, German, and Spanish banks are not (statistically) significantly different from domestic linkages within the major countries. In contrast, for Finland and Greece the null hypothesis is rejected in all cases. Moreover, the same happens in many cases for Ireland and Portugal. So, severe problems of larger French, German, Italian, and Spanish banks may create similar problems for other large banks at home or in other central euro area countries, but often would do much less so for the largest banks of those smaller countries close to the outside border of the euro area. Hence, for the latter countries the tests of table 4.4 confirm the impression from the estimations in table 4.3.

The T-tests also confirm the special situation of Italy among the larger euro area countries. In many cases the exposure of Italian banks to foreign problems is significantly lower than domestic exposures in the other main countries. In addition, the greater exposure of ABN AMRO to Crédit Agricole (cross-border) than BNP Paribas to Crédit Agricole (domestic) is statistically significant at the 1 percent level. And, similarly, the greater exposure of Fortis to Crédit Agricole (cross-border) than BNP Paribas to Crédit Agricole (domestic) is significant at the 10 percent level.

The probabilities in table 4.3 allow one to derive a relationship between

16. The T-statistics result from comparing cross-border η-values with domestic η-values (ceteris paribus the number of conditioning banks), as used for the spillover probabilities of table 4.3. The estimation of tail dependence parameters η have been described in equation (7). For example, the T-statistic in row Netherlands and column T_1 in table 4.4 results from testing whether the η-value for the largest Dutch bank (ABN AMRO) with respect to the second largest German bank (HypoVereinsbank) significantly differs from the domestic η-value of the largest German bank (Deutsche Bank) with respect to the second largest German bank (HypoVereinsbank).

the likelihood of a bank crash as a function of the number of other banks crashing. In our previous paper on currencies, we have denoted this relationship between the probability of crises and the number of conditioning events as "contamination function" (see Hartmann, Maddaloni, and Manganelli 2003, figs. 1 to 7). Bae, Karolyi, and Stulz (2003) speak in their international equity market contagion paper of "co-exceedance response curves." Gropp and Vesala (2004) apply the latter concept to European banks. While the results in table 4.3 suggest that most contamination functions in European banking are monotonously increasing (as for currencies), at least over certain ranges of conditioning events, there are also some exceptions. Witness, for example, the exposure of Banco Commercial Portugues (the largest Portuguese bank) to problems of German banks. Going from $\hat{P}_4$ to $\hat{P}_5$ implies a reduction in the crash probability of BCP.

Potential explanations for this phenomenon are "flight to quality," "flight to safety," or "competitive effects." Some banks may benefit from the troubles at other banks, as, for example, depositors withdraw their funds from the bad banks to put them in good banks. Such behavior has been referred to by Kaufman (1988) in relation to U.S. banking history, and Saunders and Wilson (1996) provide some evidence for it during two years of the Great Depression. For a more recent time period, Slovin, Sushka, and Polonchek (1999) find regional "competitive effects" in response to dividend reduction and regulatory action announcements. Nonmonotonicity of contamination functions might also occur for the curse of dimensionality, as very few observations may enter the joint failure area for more than two banks.

The finding of statistically similar spillover risk between major euro area banks within and between some large countries could be important for surveillance of the banking system and supervisory policies. One explanation for it may be the strong involvement of those banks in the unsecured euro interbank market. As these large players interact directly with each other, and in large amounts, one channel of contagion risk could be the exposures resulting from such trading. For example, Gropp and Vesala (2004) find interbank exposures at the country level to be a variable explaining part of spillovers in default risk between European banks. One implication of the similarity of domestic and cross-border spillover risks for some countries is that macroprudential surveillance and banking supervision need to have a cross-border dimension in the euro area. This is currently happening through the Eurosystem monitoring of banking developments, through the application of the home-country principle (the home supervisor considers domestic and foreign operations of a bank), through the existence of various bilateral memoranda of understanding between supervisory authorities, through multilateral "colleges" of supervisors for specific groups, and now also through the newly established "Lamfalussy Committees" in banking. The results could provide some arguments in favor of an increasing European-wide component in macroprudential surveillance and supervisory structures over time.

It is also interesting to see that in some smaller and less-central countries in the area cross-border risk is more contained. This could suggest that even the larger players from those countries are still less interlinked with the larger players from the bigger countries. The existence of significant differences in the degree of cross-border risks between different groups of European countries could make the development of homogenous supervisory structures more complicated.

Overall, one could perhaps conclude that the results so far suggest that the still relatively limited cross-border integration of banking in the euro area does not seem to eliminate any contagion risk among the larger players from some key countries to levels that are so low that they can be simply ignored. This conclusion is also consistent with Degryse and Nguyen (2004) and Lelyveld and Liedorp (2004), whose analyses of interbank exposures suggest that risks from abroad may be larger than domestic risks in the Belgian and Dutch banking systems. One explanation for the relevance of cross-border bank risks could be that while bank mergers have been mainly national and traditional loan and deposit business of banks are only to a very limited extent expanding across national borders (see, e.g., the recent evidence provided in Hartmann, Maddaloni, and Manganelli 2003, figs. 10 and 11), much of the wholesale business of these large players happens in international markets that are highly interlinked.

4.6.2 Cross-Atlantic Comparison

The next step in examining interbank spillovers consists of comparing them between the euro area and U.S. banking systems. To do so, we calculate for each system the tail dependence parameter η that governs the estimate of the multivariate contagion risk measure (1). Notice that for each continent η_{US} and η_{EA} are derived from all the extreme stock return linkages (bilateral and multilateral) between the respective $N = $ twenty-five banks, following the estimation procedure described in section 4.3.

As indicated in table 4.5, we obtain $\hat{\eta}_{US} = 0.39$ and $\hat{\eta}_{EA} = 0.17$. The evidence thus suggests that overall contagion risk in the U.S. banking system is higher than contagion risk among euro area banks (about two times).[17] Moreover, knowing that for the case of independence $\eta = 1/N = 0.04$, the amount of multivariate linkage is of economically relevant magnitude. The $\hat{P}$ values in the table describe the probability that all twenty-five banks in the euro area or the United States crash, given that any of them crashes. These probabilities illustrate that overall systemic risk related to the crash

17. Strictly speaking, this and subsequent related statements in the main text make the plausible assumption that the dependence structure is sufficiently similar on both sides of the Atlantic for the slowly varying function $\ell(q)$ described in appendix A not to have a large impact on relative probabilities.

Table 4.5   **Multivariate extreme spillover risk among euro area and U.S. banks**

Country/Area	Estimations		Cross-sectional test T
	$\hat{\eta}$	$\hat{P}$	
United States ($N = 25$)	0.39	2.8E-4	$H_0 : \eta_{U.S.} = \eta_{EA}$
Euro area ($N = 25$)	0.17	6.7E-15	$T = 7.25$
Germany ($N = 6$)	0.42	1.5E-3	
France ($N = 4$)	0.48	1.4E-2	
Italy ($N = 4$)	0.62	0.6	

Notes: The table reports in the column $\hat{\eta}$ the coefficient that governs the multivariate extreme tail dependence for all the banks of the countries/areas detailed on the left-hand side. In the column $\hat{P}$ it shows the probability that all banks of a specific country/area crash given that one of them crashes. Both statistics are estimates of systemwide extreme spillover risks. Univariate crash probabilities (crisis levels) are set to $p = 0.05$ percent. The right-hand column describes the cross-sectional test (4.4.1) for the whole United States and euro area banking system. A positive (negative) test statistic indicates that the United States (euro area) η is larger than the euro area (United States) η. The critical values of the test are 1.65, 1.96, and 2.58 for the 10 percent, 5 percent, and 1 percent levels, respectively. Note that η values for countries/areas with different numbers of banks may not be comparable.

of a single bank is extremely low. Of course, multivariate contagion risk increases for multiple bank crashes.

Is this difference between the United States and the euro area statistically significant? We apply the cross-sectional stability test (7) described in subsection 4.4.2, with the following null hypothesis:

$$H_0 : \eta_{US} = \eta_{EA}$$

It turns out that the T-statistic reaches $T = 7.25$. In other words, our indicators and tests suggest that the difference in systemic spillover risk between the United States and the euro area is statistically significant, way beyond the 1 percent confidence level.

One explanation could be that in a much more integrated banking system, such as that of the United States, areawide systemic risk is higher, as banking business is much more interconnected. We examine this hypothesis by also estimating the multivariate contagion risk for individual European countries. If the previous explanation was true, then overall systemic spillover risk should not be lower within France, Germany, or Italy than it is in the United States.[18] The bottom part of table 4.5 shows that this is actually the case. Overall, domestic spillover risk in France and Germany is about the same as in the United States; in Italy it is even larger than in the United States (see also fig. 4.1 in subsection 4.8.1). Our cross-sectional test cannot reject parameter equality between France and the United States or between Germany and the United States, but it rejects it between Italy

18. We thank Christian Upper for suggesting this exercise to us.

and the United States (as Italy is even more risky). In other words, the lower overall spillover risk in Europe is explained by the quite weak extreme cross-border linkages.

Having said this, we note that there is some structural instability in the extreme dependence of bank stock returns on both sides of the Atlantic. As we will discuss in depth in section 4.8 following, the risk of spillovers has quite generally increased in the course of our sample period. We will, however, also show that all our conclusions here are robust for taking structural instability into account. The only caveat we have to keep in mind is that the probabilities in table 4.3 represent averages across the whole sample period, so that they tend to overestimate the risk of spillovers at the start of the sample and underestimate it towards the end of the sample.

Looking ahead, the analysis in the present section suggests that—as the European banking system integrates further over time—it could become more similar to the U.S. system in terms of contagion risk. In other words, the ongoing and gradual integration process should be accompanied by appropriate changes in macroprudential surveillance and supervisory structures.

4.7   Aggregate Banking System Risk

Next we turn to the analysis based on our measure of extreme systematic risk. We are interested in assessing the extent to which individual banks and banking systems are vulnerable to an aggregate shock, as captured by an extreme downturn of the market risk factor or an extreme upturn of high-yield bond spreads. Across this section we assume stability of estimated tail-βs over time. The same caveat applies as in the previous section, as structural breaks of extreme systematic banking system risk are only considered in section 4.8.

The results are summarized in tables 4.6 and 4.7 for the euro area and the United States, respectively, and for all measures of aggregate risk listed in subsection 4.5.2. The different stock indexes capture market risk, as in traditional asset pricing theory. The high-yield bond spread is also tested as a measure of aggregate risk. For example, Gertler and Lown (1999) have shown that it can be a good predictor of the business cycle, at least in the United States, and fluctuations in economic activity are the most important determinant of banks' asset quality. Some might also regard high-yield spreads as a particularly suitable indicator for crisis situations.

The upper part of the tables report tail-βs for individual banks. To take an example, the value 12.1 in the row "IRBAN" and column "stock index" of table 4.6 means that a very large downturn in the general euro area stock index is usually associated with a 12 percent probability that Allied Irish Banks, a top Irish bank, faces an extreme stock price decline. The value 30.2 in row "BNPPAR" and column "stock index" suggests that the same

Table 4.6   Extreme systematic risk (tail-βs) of euro area banks

Bank	Aggregate risk factor				
	Bank index	Stock index	Global bank	Global stock	Yield spread
DEUTSCHE	51.1	35.0	25.6	13.0	3.8E-5
HYPO	22.3	20.8	9.3	5.5	0.1
DRESDNER	37.9	27.7	19.1	11.6	0.3
COMMERZ	39.5	30.8	15.2	13.9	0.2
BGBERLIN	2.8	1.6	0.8	0.7	0.8
DEPFA	6.2	7.3	3.0	2.9	3.4E-2
BNPPAR	42.1	30.2	23.2	13.2	2.7E-2
CA	9.2	6.7	1.6	2.0	0.4
SGENERAL	45.8	30.0	22.7	16.0	6.9E-2
NATEXIS	1.8	1.9	2.2	1.7	9.1E-3
INTESA	19.1	11.2	7.2	5.9	0.4
UNICREDIT	14.5	9.5	10.5	5.0	0.3
PAOLO	36.7	28.5	15.2	10.2	0.3
CAPITA	16.5	9.3	9.4	6.4	0.3
SANTANDER	36.4	33.4	17.4	14.5	0.6
BILBAO	41.6	31.1	20.4	13.4	0.6
BANESP	2.6	1.2	1.4	0.6	2.7E-3
ING	61.7	46.0	23.1	14.1	0.5
ABNAMRO	50.3	46.3	23.7	13.9	0.2
FORTIS	48.5	36.3	11.8	10.9	0.1
ALMANIJ	11.9	11.1	7.4	4.5	0.2
ALPHA	3.7	4.1	1.5	1.2	8.0E-3
BCP	17.0	11.9	9.3	7.5	0.3
SAMPO	2.7	2.2	3.4	1.4	2.1E-2
IRBAN	13.9	12.1	6.9	4.6	0.1
Average	25.4	19.4	11.6	7.8	0.2
Standard deviation	18.8	14.5	8.3	5.3	0.2

Note: The table exhibits the estimates of extreme systematic risk (2; tail-βs) for individual euro area banks and for the euro area banking system as a whole. The entries show the probability that a given bank crashes given that a market indicator of aggregate risk crashes (or in the case of the yield spread, booms). Results are reported for five different aggregate risk factors: the euro area banking sector subindex, the euro area stock index, the world banking sector subindex, the world stock index, and the euro area high-yield bond spread. Data for the euro area yield spread are only available from 1998 to 2004. All probabilities are estimated with the extension of the approach by Ledford and Tawn (1996) described in section 4.3 and reported in percentages. Univariate crash probabilities (crisis levels) are set to $p = 0.05$ percent. The average and the standard deviation at the bottom of the table are calculated over the twenty-five individual tail-βs in the upper rows, respectively. See table 4D.1 for list of abbreviations.

probability for the largest French bank is substantially higher. Going more systematically up and down the columns as well as moving to the right and left in the rows, one can see (1) that tail-βs can be quite different across banks, both in Europe and in the United States, and (2) that the relative sizes of tail-β seem to be quite similar for different measures of aggregate risk. For example, a number of banks from some more peripheral and

Table 4.7   **Extreme systematic risk (tail-βs) of U.S. banks**

Bank	Aggregate risk factor				
	Bank index	Stock index	Global bank	Global stock	Yield spread
CITIG	41.1	26.5	16.5	17.4	0.3
JPMORGAN	39.4	18.0	15.2	16.4	1.3
BOA	37.7	12.4	6.4	7.1	0.2
WACHO	27.2	9.6	8.6	9.3	0.5
FARGO	17.1	7.1	4.5	3.8	2.4E-2
BONEC	31.0	14.0	9.7	10.0	0.4
WASHMU	9.5	2.8	4.7	1.8	0.1
FLEET	38.8	13.1	10.6	10.1	0.6
BNYORK	25.2	12.9	10.9	11.3	1.0
STATEST	26.8	19.0	10.9	18.3	1.0
NOTRUST	26.7	17.4	12.0	10.0	0.9
MELLON	29.4	16.4	10.6	10.4	0.8
USBANC	19.6	6.6	7.8	4.8	0.3
CITYCO	32.3	8.9	7.4	6.7	0.2
PNC	25.8	12.7	10.2	8.9	0.3
KEYCO	24.9	8.4	6.1	6.1	0.2
SUNTRUST	32.0	11.7	8.9	7.8	0.3
COMERICA	24.0	13.5	7.1	7.1	0.5
UNIONBAN	11.2	3.9	5.9	3.8	0.1
AMSOUTH	15.1	7.5	8.7	6.4	0.3
HUNTING	17.5	7.0	8.3	6.0	0.1
BBT	19.9	6.6	5.3	5.4	0.2
53BANCO	21.7	8.6	4.9	3.6	0.2
SOTRUST	33.3	7.3	6.8	4.4	0.3
RFCORP	26.5	11.6	8.4	7.8	0.2
Average	26.2	11.3	8.6	8.2	0.4
Standard deviation	8.5	4.4	3.0	4.2	0.3

Notes: The table exhibits the estimates of extreme systematic risk (2; tail-βs) for individual U.S. banks and for the U.S. banking system as a whole. The entries show the probability that a given bank crashes given that a market indicator of aggregate risk crashes (or in the case of the yield spread, booms). Results are reported for five different aggregate risk factors: the U.S. banking sector subindex, the U.S. stock index, the world banking sector subindex, the world stock index, and the U.S. high-yield bond spread. All probabilities are estimated with the extension of the approach by Ledford and Tawn (1996) described in section 4.3 and reported in percentages. Univariate crash probabilities (crisis levels) are set to $p = 0.05$ percent. The average and the standard deviation at the bottom of the table are calculated over the twenty-five individual tail-βs in the upper rows, respectively. See table 4D.1 for list of abbreviations.

smaller euro area countries or smaller banks from large euro area countries can have quite low tail-βs. One interpretation of this result is that the more local business of the latter banks exposes them less to aggregate euro area risk. Similar cases can be found for the United States in table 4.7. For example, some players focusing on regional or local retail business, such as a savings and loans association like Washington Mutual, have relatively low tail-βs (in this specific case, 3 percent for the U.S. stock index as aggregate risk factor). In contrast, large and geographically broad banks—such as Deutsche Bank, BNP Paribas, Citigroup, or JP Morgan Chase—exhibit larger tail-βs, as they are much more diversified.

The bottoms of tables 4.6 and 4.7 report the means and standard deviations of tail-βs across the twenty-five banks for each continent. Overall, tail-βs in Europe and in the United States are of similar order of magnitude, although the U.S. tail-βs tend to be slightly less variable (except for yield spreads). We can use a cross-sectional T-test to compare aggregate banking risk across the Atlantic. Table 4.8 shows the average extreme dependence parameters $\bar{\eta}$ derived from the individual η parameters governing the tail-βs of the twenty-five banks on each continent. It also shows the T-values for a test with the following null hypothesis:

$$H_0 : \bar{\eta}_{US} = \bar{\eta}_{EA}$$

The equality of extreme dependence between stock returns and the market risk factor in Europe and the United States cannot be rejected.

When turning to extreme systematic risk associated with high-yield

Table 4.8   Comparisons of extreme systematic risk across different banking systems

Banking system	Aggregate risk factor				
	Bank index	Stock index	Global bank	Global stock	Yield spread
$\bar{\eta}_{US}$	0.87	0.79	0.78	0.77	0.55
$\bar{\eta}_{EA}$	0.86	0.83	0.80	0.76	0.53
$\bar{\eta}_{FR}$	0.85	0.82	0.79	0.76	0.50
$\bar{\eta}_{GE}$	0.86	0.84	0.80	0.76	0.53
$\bar{\eta}_{IT}$	0.88	0.83	0.82	0.78	0.57
Null hypothesis					
$\bar{\eta}_{US} = \bar{\eta}_{EA}$	0.19	−0.94	−0.44	0.21	0.30
$\bar{\eta}_{US} = \bar{\eta}_{FR}$	0.34	−0.59	−0.32	0.14	1.18
$\bar{\eta}_{US} = \bar{\eta}_{GE}$	0.20	−1.05	−0.47	0.30	0.48
$\bar{\eta}_{US} = \bar{\eta}_{IT}$	−0.08	−0.63	−0.81	−0.16	−0.48

Notes: The table exhibits the average tail dependence parameters η that govern the tail-β estimates reported in tables 4.6 and 4.7 for the United States, euro area, French, German, and Italian banking system (upper panel) and the statistics of tests examining differences in extreme systematic risk between the United States and euro area banking systems (lower panel). Each $\bar{\eta}$ is calculated as the mean of tail-β dependence parameters across all the banks in our sample for the respective country/area. The tests are applications of the cross-sectional test (7). The null hypothesis is that extreme systematic risk in the U.S. banking system is the same as in the other banking systems. A positive (negative) test statistic indicates that extreme systematic risk in the U.S. banking system (in the respective euro area banking system) is larger than in the respective euro area (United States) banking system. The critical values of the test are 1.65, 1.96, and 2.58 for the 10 percent, 5 percent, and 1 percent levels, respectively. All results are reported for the five different aggregate risk factors: the euro area/United States banking sector subindex, the euro area/United States stock index, the world banking sector subindex, the world stock index, and the euro area/United States high-yield bond spread. Univariate crash probabilities (crisis levels) are set to $p = 0.05$ percent.

bond spreads (see the right-hand side of tables 4.6 and 4.7), the results are different. Tail-βs for spreads are extremely small. Extreme positive levels of spreads on average do not seem to be associated with a high likelihood of banking problems. Quite the contrary—the probabilities are almost zero. This also confirms the simple correlation analysis referred to in subsection 4.5.2.

Accordingly, the tail dependence parameters $\bar{\eta}$ for spreads in table 4.8 are much smaller than the ones for stock indexes. Note that the mean dependence parameters for yield spreads are all estimated to be quite close to the level associated with asymptotic independence for this two-dimensional measure, $\eta_{indep} = 1/N = 0.5$. Thus, it is no surprise that the T-tests show that—as for the market risk factor—the level of extreme aggregate risk in the United States and in the euro area is statistically indistinguishable.

We conclude from this that high-yield bond spreads are not very informative about extreme aggregate banking system risk on both sides of the Atlantic. This finding could mean, for example, that credit spreads are a less-good predictor of business cycle fluctuations—in particular of severe ones—than previously thought. It could also mean that the banks in our sample hold only a very limited amount of loans from borrowers that are rated below investment grade. Still, future research could address whether they have at least some incremental explanatory value for banking problems when other variables are controlled for as well.

4.8   Has Systemic Risk Increased?

A crucial issue for macroprudential surveillance and supervisory policies is whether banking system risks change over time. In particular, it would be important to know whether they may have increased lately. Therefore, we apply in the present section our multivariate application of the structural stability test by Quintos, Fan, and Phillips (2001; see subsection 4.4.2) to the estimators of multivariate spillovers and systematic risk (see subsections 4.8.1 and 4.8.2, respectively).

4.8.1   Time Variation of Bank Contagion Risk

We apply the recursive structural stability test described in subsection 4.4.1 and equations (B.1) through (B.4) of appendix B to the extreme tail dependence parameters η that govern the spillover probabilities reported in table 4.3. The null hypothesis of constancy of η for the cases in the table is given by equation (B.3). The test results are reported in table 4.9, with the different cases structured in the same way as in tables 4.3 and 4.4.

Each entry first shows the endogenously estimated break point, if any, and then the value of the test statistic in parentheses. It turns out that the forward version of the recursive test discovers a significant upward break

Table 4.9 **Domestic and cross-border extreme spillover risk among euro area banks: Time variation**

Largest bank	$\hat{\eta}_1$	$\hat{\eta}_2$	$\hat{\eta}_3$	$\hat{\eta}_4$	$\hat{\eta}_5$
	Conditioning banks: German				
Germany	3/31/97 (43.5)	8/1/97 (62.0)	4/2/97 (38.4)	8/15/97 (7.2)	7/23/97 (17.3)
The Netherlands	3/31/97 (81.1)	4/2/97 (77.9)	4/2/97 (66.2)	8/21/97 (16.9)	4/2/97 (7.3)
France	7/23/97 (25.6)	8/1/97 (37.5)	9/9/97 (41.2)	7/23/97 (19.3)	8/15/97 (8.4)
Spain	7/21/97 (68.8)	5/27/97 (39.7)	5/29/97 (55.9)	7/23/97 (18.9)	8/14/97 (5.5)
Italy	7/21/97 (49.2)	9/9/97 (46.2)	9/9/97 (41.4)	8/21/97 (20.2)	8/21/97 (9.3)
Belgium	8/21/97 (62.2)	4/2/97 (50.1)	3/27/97 (56.7)	7/23/97 (25.9)	6/12/98 (6.9)
Ireland	8/20/97 (43.0)	10/16/97 (24.3)	8/15/97 (21.9)	8/14/97 (11.3)	8/15/97 (4.7)
Portugal	9/9/97 (27.5)	1/14/94 (37.1)	1/25/94 (50.1)	7/23/97 (23.2)	7/23/97 (7.5)
Finland	10/16/97 (30.5)	10/16/97 (26/3)	5/23/94 (37.2)	8/22/97 (23.6)	7/23/97 (9.6)
Greece	3/27/97 (64.0)	3/27/97 (58.8)	4/2/97 (47.8)	3/27/97 (18.8)	8/15/97 (7.4)
	Conditioning banks: French				
France	2/15/02 (25.3)	9/19/00 (32.8)	6/17/94 (22.5)		
Germany	10/9/00 (52.6)	11/21/00 (36.3)	5/21/96 (4.4)		
The Netherlands	10/10/00 (54.4)	9/20/00 (44.9)	10/22/97 (39.0)		
Italy	1/11/02 (20.1)	1/31/01 (37.8)	10/22/97 (32.5)		
Spain	10/10/00 (34.3)	9/19/00 (40.6)	10/13/97 (32.1)		
Belgium	9/1/00 (47.7)	11/27/01 (52.4)	6/9/98 (40.8)		
Ireland	9/20/00 (13.8)	11/21/00 (19.4)	12/7/01 (12.2)		
Portugal	1/25/02 (24.8)	1/29/02 (30.4)	10/22/97 (20.4)		
Finland	4/14/00 (6.1)	5/31/94 (26.0)	11/4/96 (27.5)		
Greece	6/11/98 (15.5)	2/28/97 (32.5)	2/28/97 (19.2)		
	Conditioning banks: Italian				
Italy	9/30/97 (5.4)	9/25/97 (9.0)	9/30/97 (3.6)		
Germany	7/25/97 (23.9)	7/25/97 (31.7)	10/8/97 (18.8)		
The Netherlands	10/7/97 (16.6)	8/1/97 (27.7)	8/7/97 (18.7)		
Spain	6/27/97 (7.6)	7/14/97 (19.9)	9/9/97 (12.1)		
France	10/8/97 (9.9)	10/22/97 (8.3)	9/9/97 (7.9)		
Belgium	7/31/97 (25.8)	8/1/97 (44.8)	10/8/97 (30.2)		
Ireland	8/22/97 (4.9)	10/8/97 (7.0)	8/7/97 (6.7)		
Portugal	8/1/97 (9.1)	8/1/97 (18.2)	8/7/97 (13.6)		
Finland	—	7/25/97 (8.5)	10/24/97 (5.9)		
Greece	9/9/97 (15.3)	10/17/97 (19.2)	8/15/97 (13.4)		
	Conditioning banks: Spanish				
Spain	7/16/97 (33.1)	7/16/97 (4.0)			
Germany	3/17/97 (88.0)	5/21/97 (9.0)			
The Netherlands	7/21/97 (39.0)	7/3/97 (7.3)			
France	10/22/97 (34.6)	5/27/97 (5.4)			
Italy	7/28/97 (33.2)	6/18/97 (3.8)			
Belgium	7/17/97 (47.7)	2/25/97 (12.4)			
Ireland	7/16/97 (22.7)	—			
Portugal	6/16/97 (42.7)	3/31/97 (12.8)			
Finland	10/24/97 (21.3)	7/23/97 (3.9)			
Greece	6/2/97 (37.9)	3/27/97 (12.4)			

Notes: The table reports the results of tests examining the structural stability of the extreme spillover risks documented in table 4.3. This is done by testing for the constancy of the η tail-dependence param-

Table 4.9   (continued)

eters (null hypothesis) that govern the spillover probabilities in table 4.3. Applying the recursive test (B1) through (B4) by Quintos, Fan, and Phillips (2001) described in appendix B and subsection 4.4.1, each cell shows the endogenously found break date and the test value in parentheses. Dates are denoted XX/YY/ZZ, where XX = month, YY = day, and ZZ = year. The critical values of the test are 1.46, 1.78, and 2.54 for the 10 percent, 5 percent, and 1 percent levels, respectively. A test value exceeding these numbers implies an increase in extreme dependence over time. The absence of a break over the sample period is marked with a dash.

in spillover risk in almost every case, be it a domestic linkage or a cross-border linkage. For spillovers conditioned on German, Italian, and Spanish banks, almost all increases in risk occur sometime during the year 1997. If crashes of French banks are the conditioning events, breaks tend to occur somewhat later, most often around the year 2000. While there have been economic events in the vicinity of the break point times found by the test that could have contributed to increases in spillover risks (e.g., the Asian financial crisis, the end of the technology boom), we would not pay too much attention to the exact dates. The reason is that further evidence, presented subsequently, suggests that changes in risk exhibit fairly gradual patterns, so that just singling out the most important break point could be misleading.

These results suggest that there was also an increase in systemwide spillover risks. We examine this question in table 4.10. We first calculate the 25-dimensional ($N = 25$) tail-dependence parameter values that span the whole U.S. block $\hat{\eta}_{US}$ and the whole euro area block $\hat{\eta}_{EA}$ (as in subsection 4.6.2, table 4.5) and test for structural change. We do the same for Germany ($N = 6$), France ($N = 4$), and Italy ($N = 4$), separately. The null is again as in equation (B3). Table 4.10 shows on the left-hand side break points and test statistics for the full sample; in the middle of table 4.10 estimated subsample values for the different ηs are reported. Finally, the right-hand side of the table also displays the results of two further structural stability tests, limited to the second half of the sample after the first endogenous break. The first test is another Quintos, Fan, and Phillips endogenous stability test, and the second an exogenous stability test (T_{EMU}), in which the break point is chosen to be 1 January, 1999, the start of economic and monetary union in Europe.

The tests indicate a significant upward break in euro area systemic risk around mid-1996 (test value 4.9) and in U.S. systemic risk at the end of 1995 (test value 18.5). These breaks are both slightly earlier than the lower-dimensional ones in table 4.9.[19] The extreme dependence parameter $\hat{\eta}_{US}$ increases from 0.20 to 0.41, and parameter $\hat{\eta}_{EA}$ from 0.13 to 0.20. Gropp and

---

19. One explanation for the earlier increase in fully systemic risk could be that the (many) cases not covered in table 4.9 have earlier breaks than the ones shown.

Table 4.10   **Multivariate extreme spillover risk among euro area and U.S. banks: Time variation**

Country/Area	Full sample break test	Subsample estimates		Second subsample break tests	
		$\hat{\eta}_1$	$\hat{\eta}_2$	Endogenous	Exogenous
United States ($N = 25$)	11/22/95 (18.5)	0.20	0.41	3/11/97 (2.2)	n.a.
Euro area ($N = 25$)	12/5/96 (4.9)	0.13	0.20	(B) 1/18/99 (3.2)	(1.4)
Germany ($N = 6$)	7/23/97 (17.6)	0.24	0.52	—	(1.9)
	(B) 4/2/97 (2.1)			(B) 1/22/99 (3.9)	
France ($N = 4$)	6/17/94 (21.9)	0.19	0.52	12/7/01 (12.8)	(−3.0)
	(B) 5/21/96 (4.3)			(B) 2/24/97 (3.0)	
Italy ($N = 4$)	09/30/97 (3.4)	0.45	0.72	(B) 4/11/03 (2/2)	(2.1)

Notes: The table reports tests and estimations assessing time variation in the multivariate spillover probabilities of table 4.5. The column on the left displays estimated break dates and values from the recursive Quintos, Fan, and Phillips (2001) test (B.1) through (B.4) described in appendix B and subsection 4.4.1 applied to the η parameter governing the extreme tail dependence of the banks located in the countries/areas displayed on the extreme left. Dates are denoted XX/YY/ZZ, where XX = month, YY = day, and ZZ = year. The forward recursive version of the test is used, unless marked otherwise. (B) marks the backward recursive version of the test. The critical values of the test are 1.46, 1.78, and 2.54 for the 10 percent, 5 percent, and 1 percent levels, respectively. The middle columns show pre- and postbreak estimates for η. The columns on the right display two tests that assess the occurrence of further breaks in the second half of the sample. The first one is the same as the one on the left-hand side. The second one is a simple differences-in-means test based on (7). The exogenous break point is chosen to be 1/1/99, the time of the introduction of the euro. Critical values for this test are 1.65, 1.96, and 2.58 for the 10 percent, 5 percent, and 1 percent significance levels. Note that η values for countries/areas with different numbers of banks may not be comparable.

Vesala (2004) also find an increase in bank spillover risk in Europe, using a different methodology, but they impose the break point at the time of the introduction of the euro. For France, Germany, and Italy, our test also indicates strong domestic upward breaks, but in addition France and Germany experience a (weaker) downward break (as indicated by the backward version of the test). In sum, we detect a significant increase of multivariate spillover risk both in the euro area and in the U.S. banking system. Both systems seem to be more vulnerable to contagion risk today than they have been in the early 1990s, the United States even more so than the euro area.

The increase of spillover risk found for the United States is consistent with the findings of de Nicoló and Kwast (2002), who detect an upward trend of regular correlations between U.S. LCBOs during the period 1988 to 1999 and interpret it as a sign of increasing systemic risk.[20] The authors estimate that part of the increase is likely to be related to consolidation among LCBOs. The timing of structural change in de Nicoló and Kwast's

---

20. Within the group of about twenty-two LCBOs, however, most of the increase in correlations is concentrated among the less-complex banks.

paper is not exactly the same as in ours but quite similar, as they find most correlation changes during 1996 and perhaps 1997. Mistrulli (2005) argues that some increase in domestic contagion risk in the Italian banking sector has been caused by new interbank lending structures that emerged from consolidation. And the risk seems to pick up around 1997, similar to our break points. Hence, banking consolidation may be one important explanation for a higher contagion risk *within* the countries discussed. It is, however, a less likely explanation for the increase in η for the euro area banking system as a whole. The reason is that cross-border bank mergers are still relatively rare in Europe (see, e.g., Hartmann, Maddaloni, and Manganelli 2003, figure 10).

In order to get a better view of the evolution of multivariate contagion risk over time, we plot in figure 4.1 the recursive estimates of η for the euro area, the United States, France, Germany, and Italy. In addition to unfiltered results (solid lines), we also display results for GARCH-filtered return data (dotted lines). For the reasons given in the first subsection of appendix E, however, one should focus on the unfiltered results. Comparing the two upper panels of the figure, we can see the smaller and gradual character of the increase in spillover risk in the euro area. Notice the consistency of this evolution with a slowly advancing integration process. Multivariate risk in the United States starts at a higher level and begins to rise later, but at a much faster pace. The lower panels of the figure confirm the results discussed in subsection 4.6.2, insofar as general spillover risk within France, Germany, and Italy is higher than in the euro area as a whole and, on average, of a similar order of magnitude as within the United States. (The results are qualitatively the same for filtered data, although the strength of changes is sometimes muted.[21]) All these findings are consistent with the hypothesis advanced in section 4.6—that banks are more exposed to each other within a country than across borders. So far, this remains true even in the euro area, which shares a common currency and a common interbank market.

Figure 4.2 shows the recursive statistics of the cross-sectional tests comparing U.S. multivariate spillover risk with euro area, French, German, and Italian spillover risk. We would like to learn from this whether the similarities and differences in multivariate risk across those banking systems established in section 4.6 generally hold across our sample period. Each panel exhibits the difference in η between the first country (always the United States) and the second area or country. The straight dashed lines describe two standard deviation confidence intervals. So, when a solid curve moves out of a confidence interval, then the test rejects the equality

---

21. A similar phenomenon for general stock market data has already been observed by Poon, Rockinger, and Tawn (2004). In the working paper version of the present paper we display a larger number of the results for filtered data (Hartmann, Straetmans, and C. de Vries 2005, appendix E). The second section of appendix E briefly summarizes them.

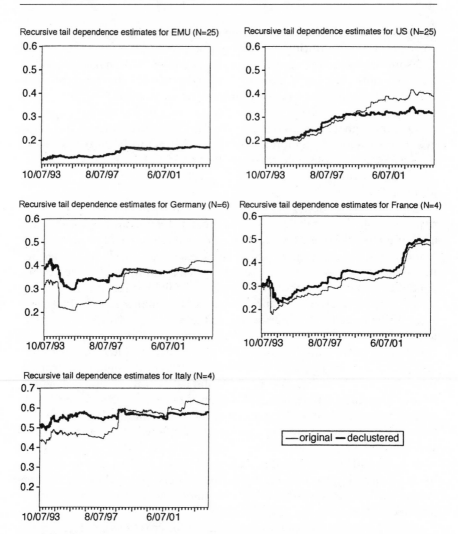

Fig. 4.1   Evolution of multivariate extreme spillover risk among euro area and U.S. banks

of multivariate tail-dependence parameters between the two countries. If a curve is above the confidence interval, then the first country is more susceptible to contagion. In the opposite case, the second country is the more risky one. We can immediately confirm from the upper left-hand chart in figure 4.2 that the United States is more risky than the euro area, except for the very start of the sample. The lower right-hand chart illustrates that Italy is more risky than the United States.

Finally, we turn to the results of the two structural stability tests for the second half of the sample on the right of table 4.10. Interestingly enough, the endogenous test (backward version) finds a second break point for the

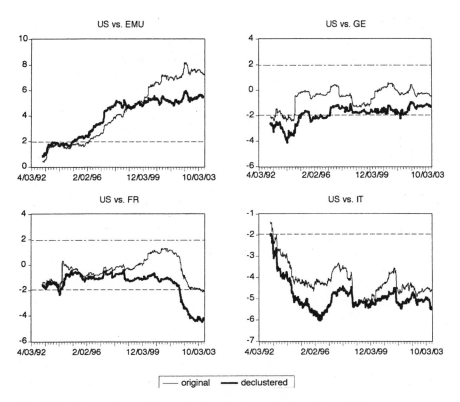

Fig. 4.2   Comparisons of the evolution of extreme bank spillover risk across countries

euro area in January 1999 reducing η (test value 3.2 compared to a critical value of 2.6 for a significant change at the 1 percent level). In other words, it indicates that multivariate contagion risk decreased in parallel with the introduction of the euro. As we are concerned about the validity of the asymptotic properties of the Quintos, Fan, and Phillips test when it is applied in a sequential way, we also conduct an exogenous stability test for which we impose 1 January, 1999, as the break point. This test exploits the asymptotic normality of the tail dependence parameter, as in the case of cross-sectional differences discussed earlier. It confirms that there is some decline in η_{EA} at the time of the euro changeover, but this decline is not statistically significant (test value 1.4 compared to a critical value of 1.9 for a significant change at the 5 percent level).

While it is often assumed that the introduction of the euro with a common money market should have led to an increase in contagion risk in the euro area, our results do not provide any evidence of that actually happening. On the contrary, if anything there was a slight decrease of multivariate extreme dependence between all euro area banks. One explanation for such a development would be as follows. Whereas the introduction of a single currency with a common (and fully integrated) money market could increase the interbank linkages between banks across borders, and thereby the risk of contagion, on the other hand the much larger and more liquid money market as well as the wider access to different contingent claims under a single currency could also increase the money market's resilience against shocks and improve risk sharing. If the latter effects dominate the former, then the banking system could well become less prone to extreme spillovers.

As for the three larger euro area countries, Germany experiences a similar reduction in risk as the area as a whole. But in this case the reduction is also statistically significant for the exogenous break test, at least at the 10 percent level. France and Italy also have some further breaks. While statistically significant, they do not happen in the vicinity of the euro changeover. The United States banking system faces a further increase in multivariate spillover risk at the end of 1997.

We close this subsection with a word of caution. While the evidence supporting increases in multivariate extreme dependencies among banks in both the euro area and the United States seems statistically relatively strong, we should not forget that our sample period extends only over twelve years. This means, first, that we cover only a small number of economic cycles.[22] Since there was a relatively long upturn during the 1990s, there may be a risk that this had an impact on extreme bank stock return dependence. More generally, similar to correlation, extreme dependence can oscillate over time. Obviously, we cannot know whether there was already a period of higher extreme linkages between banks before our sample starts or whether the high linkages observed toward the end of our sample will come down again in the future.

4.8.2   Time Variation of Aggregate Banking System Risk

Lastly, we apply the structural stability test to extreme systematic risk in banking systems. More precisely, we study whether the bivariate extreme dependence parameters η that enter our estimates of tail-βs have changed between 1992 and 2004. Table 4.11 reports the results for each euro area bank in our sample and table 4.12 for each U.S. bank. Each table shows for the respective banks the estimated break points, if any, with test values in parentheses. Tests are performed for all aggregate risk measures on which we condition the tail-βs.

The general result is that extreme systematic risk has increased over time. In other words, both the euro area and the U.S. banking system seem to be more exposed to aggregate shocks today than they were in the early 1990s. We further illustrate this at the systemwide level in figure 4.3, which gives us a better insight into the time evolution of extreme systematic risk.

22. Following the NBER and CEPR business cycle dating programs, we cover at most two full cycles; see http://www.nber.org/cycles.html and http://www.cepr.org/data/Dating/.

Table 4.11   **Extreme systematic risk (tail-βs) of euro area banks: Time variation**

	Aggregate risk factor				
Bank	Bank index	Stock index	Global bank	Global stock	Yield spread
DEUTSCHE	3/12/97 (45.3)	3/12/97 (57.7)	8/15/97 (53.3)	12/5/96 (86.1)	9/14/00 (153.4)
HYPO	7/21/97 (40.1)	10/22/97 (60.0)	9/9/97 (62.8)	10/22/97 (60.5)	10/4/00 (124.1)
DRESDNER	8/1/97 (69.1)	12/5/96 (53.1)	12/5/96 (48.5)	12/5/96 (59.5)	8/22/00 (44.1)
COMMERZ	7/21/97 (22.8)	3/19/97 (34.8)	8/1/97 (30.4)	8/21/97 (70.4)	10/3/00 (142.7)
BGBERLIN	12/3/96 (7.9)	12/3/96 (10.9)	12/5/96 (11.8)	7/3/97 (19.2)	1/4/01 (496.6)
DEPFA	7/5/96 (33.7)	7/15/96 (37.6)	8/21/97 (19.4)	8/12/97 (33.6)	9/13/00 (97.5)
BNPPAR	8/15/97 (34.7)	7/17/97 (41.1)	10/22/97 (27.5)	8/27/97 (34.0)	9/15/00 (77.3)
CA	10/5/00 (50.4)	9/19/00 (52.7)	10/9/00 (26.6)	9/19/00 (31.7)	7/21/00 (127.3)
SGENER	10/22/97 (40.9)	10/22/97 (35.4)	10/22/97 (37.4)	10/22/97 (42.6)	9/21/00 (114.5)
NATEXIS	12/5/96 (6.0)	12/3/96 (8.5)	8/28/97 (11.0)	8/28/97 (21.1)	9/15/00 (155.1)
INTESA	7/31/97 (25.6)	7/28/97 (39.7)	9/9/97 (14.5)	7/31/97 (24.4)	7/24/00 (183.9)
UNICRED	10/8/97 (23.8)	9/25/97 (14.2)	10/8/97 (18.7)	9/9/97 (18.0)	9/11/00 (123.4)
PAOLO	7/28/97 (52.6)	9/25/97 (51.4)	10/24/97 (43.8)	10/8/97 (58.7)	8/17/00 (218.4)
CAPITA	8/12/97 (17.0)	9/10/97 (15.7)	9/9/97 (13.1)	9/9/97 (16.0)	9/15/00 (170.6)
SANTANDER	7/23/97 (60.3)	5/27/97 (64.0)	8/21/97 (28.3)	10/8/97 (51.5)	9/15/00 (207.3)
BILBAO	10/8/97 (54.0)	10/16/97 (58.7)	10/7/97 (36.2)	10/22/97 (68.7)	9/11/00 (209.3)
BANESP	5/16/97 (6.3)	10/16/97 (5.3)	10/22/97 (2.5)	10/22/97 (2.3)	7/21/00 (29.3)
ING	11/26/96 (43.7)	10/22/96 (36.4)	8/21/97 (57.2)	7/5/96 (51.7)	9/20/00 (186.5)
ABNAMRO	11/26/96 (48.1)	12/5/96 (56.3)	7/4/96 (73.9)	7/4/96 (61.6)	9/15/00 (132.5)
FORTIS	3/17/97 (65.4)	12/10/96 (41.1)	12/10/96 (33.0)	7/17/97 (36.7)	9/15/00 (161.2)
ALMANIJ	3/14/97 (59.4)	1/23/97 (56.7)	1/23/97 (54.5)	8/7/97 (77.1)	9/14/00 (238.2)
ALPHA	2/24/97 (52.7)	2/27/97 (64.5)	1/8/97 (36.6)	2/6/97 (66.1)	9/29/00 (80.7)
BCP	6/16/97 (37.8)	7/3/97 (42.2)	8/26/97 (28.7)	7/17/97 (57.6)	9/15/00 (129.0)
SAMPO	10/16/97 (15.2)	10/24/97 (15.6)	10/24/97 (6.0)	10/16/97 (11.5)	8/16/00 (151.6)
IRBAN	8/12/97 (22.4)	3/12/97 (25.2)	8/21/97 (16.5)	8/20/97 (25.3)	9/29/00 (164.7)

Notes: The table reports the results of tests examining the structural stability of the extreme systematic risks of euro area banks documented in table 4.6. This is done by testing the constancy of the η tail-dependence parameters (null hypothesis) that govern the tail-βs in table 4.6. Applying the recursive test (B1) through (B4) by Quintos, Fan, and Phillips (2001) described in appendix B and subsection 4.4.1, each cell shows the endogenously found break date and the test value in parentheses. Dates are denoted XX/YY/ZZ, where XX = month, YY = day, and ZZ = year. The critical values of the test are 1.46, 1.78, and 2.54 for the 10 percent, 5 percent, and 1 percent levels, respectively. A test value exceeding these numbers implies an increase in extreme dependence over time. See table 4D.1 for list of abbreviations.

The lines in the two panels refer to averages of ηs across the twenty-five euro area and twenty-five United States banks, respectively. We choose the general local stock indexes as aggregate risk factors, but the picture is unchanged for other stock indexes. Similar to figure 4.1 for interbank spillover risk, the η-values entering the figure are calculated recursively. One can see that the increase in aggregate banking system risk is also economically significant, both in the euro area and in the United States.[23] While results corrected for time-varying volatility (GARCH-filtered returns) are

---

23. Notice that these results are different from the ones by de Nicoló and Kwast (2002) using standard market model βs among U.S. LCBOs. They do not identify any increase of the

Table 4.12   Extreme systematic risk (tail-βs) of U.S. banks: Time variation

	Aggregate risk factor				
Bank	Bank index	Stock index	Global bank	Global stock	Yield spread
CITIG	12/20/96 (28.0)	12/15/95 (17.8)	10/22/97 (34.0)	10/23/97 (30.8)	10/20/00 (93.5)
JPMORGAN	2/25/97 (34.1)	3/11/97 (28.3)	10/13/97 (33.1)	10/16/97 (40.0)	10/17/00 (87.4)
BOA	12/2/96 (27.4)	12/10/96 (27.9)	11/29/96 (33.1)	12/2/96 (38.6)	9/15/00 (64.7)
WACHO	3/10/97 (14.9)	12/10/96 (22.0)	2/26/97 (66.4)	2/26/97 (41.3)	10/10/00 (64.5)
FARGO	1/3/96 (14.4)	12/15/95 (14.7)	2/27/97 (23.4)	2/26/97 (15.6)	10/5/00 (35.4)
BONEC	12/6/95 (23.7)	12/13/95 (32.3)	11/29/96 (47.6)	2/19/96 (40.3)	10/5/00 (98.8)
WASHMU	2/27/97 (8.1)	2/23/96 (10.6)	10/16/97 (20.2)	2/24/97 (9.9)	11/21/00 (33.6)
FLEET	4/22/98 (33.8)	12/10/96 (25.5)	4/17/98 (39.2)	12/10/96 (36.2)	11/30/00 (52.6)
BNYORK	2/19/96 (20.2)	1/8/96 (17.7)	12/11/96 (41.3)	2/6/97 (47.0)	9/19/00 (77.8)
STATEST	3/11/97 (35.8)	12/2/96 (49.4)	12/2/96 (41.7)	10/16/97 (58.2)	10/5/00 (158.3)
NOTRUST	11/29/96 (33.8)	12/2/96 (51.7)	10/22/97 (35.3)	12/5/96 (52.8)	9/29/00 (107.8)
MELLON	12/4/95 (13.4)	12/13/95 (25.4)	10/24/97 (38.3)	10/24/97 (26.0)	10/11/00 (108.6)
USBANC	2/25/97 (40.1)	1/23/97 (48.3)	9/25/97 (57.9)	9/25/97 (39.5)	11/10/00 (37.0)
CITYCO	11/29/96 (26.7)	12/2/96 (28.8)	11/29/96 (45.9)	12/2/96 (44.7)	10/10/00 (38.9)
PNC	12/10/96 (24.3)	12/13/95 (26.3)	12/10/96 (34.6)	3/7/96 (34.5)	11/30/00 (51.6)
KEYCO	12/2/96 (12.1)	12/6/95 (18.1)	12/5/96 (19.5)	12/2/96 (27.3)	9/28/00 (56.7)
SUNTRUST	12/2/96 (29.0)	12/13/95 (38.7)	12/5/96 (31.8)	12/5/96 (31.6)	10/20/00 (40.8)
COMERICA	1/3/96 (11.3)	12/13/95 (17.9)	2/25/97 (27.8)	1/8/96 (23.4)	10/11/00 (64.2)
UNIONBAN	7/21/97 (29.6)	10/24/97 (44.6)	6/26/97 (6.4)	10/23/97 (17.2)	9/26/00 (19.6)
AMSOUTH	12/19/95 (18.4)	1/8/96 (24.9)	12/10/96 (23.8)	1/1/97 (17.5)	9/19/00 (45.4)
HUNTING	2/6/97 (34.2)	1/22/97 (67.3)	10/13/97 (29.9)	10/16/97 (40.9)	10/5/00 (30.3)
BBT	3/28/97 (22.3)	3/28/97 (24.7)	10/22/97 (16.7)	10/29/97 (19.4)	9/19/00 (24.6)
53BANCO	12/2/96 (31.6)	12/2/96 (26.2)	12/5/96 (59.2)	4/9/97 (34.3)	10/16/00 (42.0)
SOTRUST	2/26/97 (47.4)	2/24/97 (36.6)	10/13/97 (35.6)	10/8/97 (44.2)	12/1/00 (41.5)
RFCORP	3/7/96 (36.4)	2/23/96 (40.7)	12/10/96 (23.3)	12/10/96 (33.9)	10/10/00 (24.0)

Notes: The table reports the results of tests examining the structural stability of the extreme systematic risks of U.S. banks documented in table 4.7. This is done by testing for the constancy of the η tail-dependence parameters (null hypothesis) that govern the tail-βs in table 4.7. Applying the recursive test (B1) through (B4) by Quintos, Fan, and Phillips (2001) described in appendix B and subsection 4.4.1, each cell shows the endogenously found break date and the test value in parentheses. Dates are denoted XX/YY/ZZ, where XX = month, YY = day, ZZ = year. The critical values of the test are 1.46, 1.78, 2.54 for the 10 percent, 5 percent, and 1 percent levels, respectively. A test value exceeding these numbers implies an increase in extreme dependence over time. See table 4D.1 for list of abbreviations.

somewhat more muted, qualitatively they are unchanged (see also the second subsection of appendix E). Moreover, the similarity of extreme aggregate banking system risk in the euro area and the United States established in section 4.7 seems to be valid for the entire sample period.

Table 4.11 locates the timing of most European break points for the stock indexes around 1997 and for some cases in 1996. In the United States

---

impact of the general market index on LCBO stock returns between 1992 and 1999. They only observe an increase of the impact of a special sectoral LCBO index in late 1992/early 1993, conditional on the general market index.

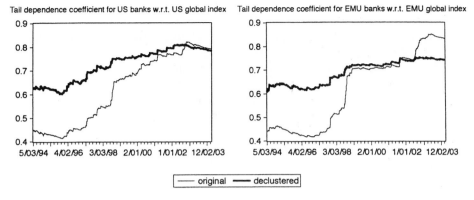

Tail dependence coefficient for US banks w.r.t. US global index   Tail dependence coefficient for EMU banks w.r.t. EMU global index

— original — declustered

Fig. 4.3   Evolution of extreme systematic risk in the euro area and the U.S. banking systems

they happen somewhat earlier, with many breaks in 1996 (table 4.12). For Europe the timing is roughly in line with, but not identical to, interbank spillover risks (see the previous subsection). For the United States the tail-β breaks happen somewhat later than the contagion breaks. Similar to the spillover risks discussed earlier, the time evolution visible in figure 4.3, however, suggests that not too much importance should be given to the exact break dates.

We just mention that economically relevant tail-β changes occur for some of the most important players, such as the largest U.S. banks (Citigroup and JP Morgan Chase). The βs of important clearing banks, such as Bank of New York, State Street, or Northern Trust, changed as well, sometimes by even more than the former. The main U.S. clearers also have some of the statistically most significant breaks (table 4.12). Similarly significant changes can also be observed for the euro area.

Both in Europe and in the United States there are also breaks in tail-βs for yield spreads. They happen, however, with surprising regularity in 2000, the time of the burst of the technology bubble. In any case, given the very low extreme systematic risk associated with yield spreads, not too much importance should be given to this result. Finally, the same words of caution about business cycles and time-varying comovements should be kept in mind as for the previous subsection.

4.9   Conclusions

In this paper we made a new attempt to assess banking system risk by applying recent multivariate extreme-value estimators and tests to excess returns of the major banks in the euro area and the United States. We distinguish two types of measures, one capturing extreme spillovers among banks (contagion risk) and another capturing the exposure of banks to extreme systematic shocks (which we denote as tail-β). We compare the importance of those forms of systemic risk across countries and over time.

Our results suggest that bank spillover risk in the euro area is significantly lower than in the United States. As domestic linkages in the euro area are comparable to extreme linkages among U.S. banks, this finding appears to be related to weak cross-border linkages in Europe. For example, the largest banks of some smaller countries at the periphery of the area seem to be more protected from cross-border contagion risk than some of the major European banks originating from some central European countries. Extreme systematic risk for banks seems to be roughly comparable across the Atlantic. In contrast to stock indexes, high-yield bond spreads in general do not seem to be very informative about aggregate banking risks. Structural stability tests for both our banking system risk indicators suggest a general increase in systemic risk taking place over the second half of the 1990s, both in Europe and the United States. We do not find, however, that the introduction of the euro had any adverse effect on cross-border banking risks, quite the contrary. Overall, the increase of risk in the euro area as a whole seems to have happened extremely gradually, as one would expect from the slow integration of traditional banking business. For the United States it may be noteworthy that some of the strongest increases in extreme systematic risk seem to be concentrated among the largest players and the main clearing banks.

Our results provide some interesting perspectives on the ongoing debate on financial stability policies in Europe. For example, the benchmark of the United States seems to indicate that cross-border risks may further increase in the future, as banking business becomes better integrated. At the same time, it should be recognized that the direction of this process is not unique to Europe. And in addition, our twelve-year sample period includes one long economic cycle that may have overemphasized commonality in banking risks. Keeping these caveats in mind, the results in this paper underline the importance of macroprudential surveillance that takes a cross-border perspective, in particular in Europe. They also encourage further thinking about the best institutional structures for supervision in a European banking system that slowly overcomes the barriers imposed by national and economic borders. While important steps have already been taken in this regard, if one thinks for example of the newly established Lamfalussy Committees in banking, it is nevertheless important to prepare for a future that may be different from the status quo.

Appendix A

Estimation of the Indicators of Banking System Stability: Details

In this appendix we discuss a number of more technical issues describing the estimators for (1) and (2) that had to be left out in section 4.3.

The first issue concerns the variable transformation from X_i to $\tilde{X}_i$. It is important to stress that the dependence between two random variables and the shape of the marginal distributions are unrelated concepts. To extract the dependence, given by the copula function, it is convenient to transform the data and remove any possible influences of marginal aspects on the joint tail probabilities. One can transform the different original excess returns to ones with a common marginal distribution (see, e.g., Ledford and Tawn, 1996; Draisma et al., 2001). After such a transformation, differences in joint tail probabilities across banking systems (e.g., Europe versus the United States) can be solely attributed to differences in the tail-dependence structure of the extremes. This is different, for example, from correlation-based measures that are still influenced by the differences in marginal distribution shapes.

In this spirit we transform the bank stock excess returns $(X_1, \ldots, X_i, \ldots, X_N)$ to unit Pareto marginals:

$$\tilde{X}_i = \frac{1}{1 - F_i(X_i)}, i = 1, \ldots, N,$$

with $F_i(\cdot)$ representing the marginal cumulative distribution function (cdf) for X_i. However, since the marginal cdfs are unknown, we have to replace them with their empirical counterparts. For each X_i this leads (with a small modification to prevent division by 0) to:

(A.1) $$\tilde{X}_i = \frac{n + 1}{n + 1 - R_{X_i}}, i = 1, \ldots, N,$$

where $R_{X_i} = \text{rank}(X_{il}, l = 1, \ldots, n)$. Using this variable transform, we can rewrite the joint tail probability that occurs in (1) and (2):

$$P\left[\bigcap_{i=1}^{N} X_i > Q_i(p)\right] = P\left(\bigcap_{i=1}^{N} \tilde{X}_i > q\right),$$

where $q = 1/p$.[24]

In this way the multivariate estimation problem can be reduced to estimating a univariate exceedance probability for the cross-sectional minimum of the N bank excess return series:

---

24. The multivariate probability stays invariant under the variable transformation $(X_1, \ldots, X_i, \ldots, X_N) \rightarrow (\tilde{X}_1, \ldots, \tilde{X}_i, \ldots, \tilde{X}_N)$, because the determinant of the Jacobian matrix can be shown to be equal to 1.

(A.2) $$P\left(\bigcap_{i=1}^{N} \tilde{X}_i > q\right) = P[\min_{i=1}^{N} (\tilde{X}_i > q] = P(\tilde{X}_{min} > q).$$

The marginal tail probability at the right-hand side can be calculated, provided the following additional assumption on the univariate tail behavior of $\tilde{X}_{min}$ is made. Ledford and Tawn (1996) argue that the bivariate dependence structure is a regular varying function under fairly general conditions. Peng (1999) and Draisma et al. (2001) give sufficient conditions and further motivation. Therefore, we assume that the auxiliary variable $\tilde{X}_{min}$ has a regularly varying tail. Notice, however, that in contrast to Ledford and Tawn (1996) we often consider more than two dimensions.[25]

Another issue is the approximate nature of equation (4), as described in section 4.3. Assuming that $\tilde{X}_{min}$ exhibits heavy tails with tail index $\alpha = 1/\eta$, then the regular variation assumption for the auxiliary variables implies that the univariate probability in equations (3) or (A.2) exhibits a tail descent of the Pareto type:

(A.3) $$P(\tilde{X}_{min} > q) \approx \ell(q)q^{-1/\eta}, \eta \leq 1,$$

with q large (p small) and where $\ell(q)$ is a slowly varying function (i.e., $\lim_{q\to\infty} \ell[xq]/\ell[q] = 1$ for all fixed $x > 0$). As $\ell(q)$ is unlikely to have significant effects on our results, we neglected it in the main body of the paper.

From equations (4) and (A.3) one sees that a higher η implies, ceteris paribus (given the slowly varying function $\ell[q]$), a higher degree of dependence among the components $(\tilde{X}_1, \ldots, \tilde{X}_i, \ldots, \tilde{X}_N)$ from equations (4) or (A.2) far out in their joint tail. We can distinguish the two extreme cases in which the $\tilde{X}_i$, are *asymptotically dependent* and asymptotically independent. In the former case $\eta = 1$ and

$$\lim_{q\to\infty} \frac{P(\tilde{X}_{min} > q)}{P(\tilde{X}_{max} > q)} = 0.$$

with $P(\tilde{X}_{max} > q) = P(\max_{i=1}^{N}[\tilde{X}_i] > q]$. Examples of asymptotically dependent random variables include the multivariate Student-T distribution, for example. For *asymptotic independence* of the random variables $\eta < 1$, we have that

---

25. Equations (3) and (A.2) require a common quantile q. This can, however, be easily generalized to the case where q differs across the marginals. Assume that we allow both the quantiles of the original distribution function Q_1 and Q_2 and the corresponding marginal probabilities p_1 and p_2 to be different from each other. For the bivariate case this would imply, for example, that

$$P[X_1 > Q_1(p_1), X_2 > Q_2(p_2)] = P(\tilde{X}_1 > q_1, \tilde{X}_2 > q_2),$$

with $q_i = 1/p_i (i = 1, 2)$. By multiplying $\tilde{X}_2$ with q_1/q_2 the above joint probability again reduces to a probability with a common quantile q_1 and we are back to the framework described previously, where the loading variable $\tilde{X}_{min}$ can be calculated.

(A.4)
$$\lim_{q \to \infty} \frac{P(\tilde{X}_{min} > q)}{P(\tilde{X}_{max} > q)} > 0.$$

An example of this case is the bivariate standard normal distribution with correlation coefficient ρ. For this distribution $\eta = (1 + \rho)/2$ and the limit (A.4) applies. When the normal random variables are independent ($\rho = 0$), one immediately obtains that $\eta = 1/2$. In general, whenever the $\tilde{X}_i$ are fully independent in the N-dimensional space, $\eta = 1/N$ and $P(\tilde{X}_{min} > q) = p^N$. But the reverse is not true; that is, there are joint N-dimensional distributions with nonzero pairwise correlation that nevertheless have $\eta = 1/N$. The Morgenstern distribution constitutes an example of this tail behavior. (A bivariate version is employed in a Monte Carlo exercise in appendix C.1.)

The estimation of equation (4) with the de Haan et al. estimator (5) and the Hill estimator (6) has already been sketched in the main text. One may still want to remark that, technically, the "tail cut-off point" $C_{n-m,n}$ in equation (5) is the $(n - m)$-th ascending order statistic from the cross-sectional minimum series $\tilde{X}_{min}$. Similarly, m is the number of higher-order extremes that enter the estimation of (6). The estimator (5) basically extends the empirical distribution function of $\tilde{X}_{min}$ outside the domain of the sample by means of its asymptotic Pareto tail from equation (4). An intuitive derivation of the estimator is provided in Danielsson and de Vries (1997). For discussions of alternative estimators and proper convergence behavior, see for example Draisma et al. (2001), Peng (1999), and Beirlandt and Vandewalle (2002). Further details on the Hill estimator can be found in Jansen and de Vries (1991), for example, and in the monograph by Embrechts, Klüppelberg, and Mikosch (1997).

The optimal choice of the threshold parameter m is a point of concern in the extreme value theory literature. Goldie and Smith (1987) suggest to select the nuisance parameter m so as to minimize the asymptotic mean-squared error. A widely used heuristic procedure plots the tail estimator as a function of m and selects m in a region where $\hat{\eta}$ from equation (6) is stable. Double bootstrap techniques based upon this idea have been developed recently (see, e.g., Danielsson et al., 2001), but these are only advisable for sample sizes that are larger than the ones we have available for this paper. For simplicity, and in accordance with the minimization criterion of Goldie and Smith (1987), we select $m = \kappa n^\gamma$ with $\gamma = 2/3$, sample size n, where κ is derived from the widely used Hill plot method.[26]

---

26. Minimizing the asymptotic mean-squared error for the Hill estimator by balancing bias and variance renders this nonlinear selection rule. For convenience, we impose the parameter restriction $\gamma = 2/3$. While simplifying, it can be shown to hold for a wide variety of distribution functions. Moreover, establishing stable and accurate estimates of γ is notoriously difficult (see, e.g., Gomes, de Hann, and Peng 2002, for a recent example). κ is calibrated by means of the heuristic Hill plot method. Once a value of m^* is selected in a horizontal range of $\hat{\eta} = \hat{\eta}(m)$, the scale factor immediately follows from $\kappa = m^*/n^{2/3}$.

Appendix B

Test for Time Variation in the Indicators of Banking System Stability: Details

In this appendix we discuss a number of more technical issues that had to be left out from the description of the Quintos, Fan, and Phillips recursive structural break test presented in subsection 4.4.1.

Let t denote the endpoint of a subsample of size $w_t < n$. The recursive estimator for the tail-dependence parameter η is calculated from equation (6) for subsamples $[1; t] \subset [1; n]$:

$$(\text{B.1}) \qquad \hat{\eta}_t = \frac{1}{m_t} \sum_{j=0}^{m_t-1} \ln\left(\frac{X_{t-j,t}}{X_{t-m_t,t}}\right),$$

with $mt = \kappa t^{2/3}$.[27]

The value of the recursive test statistic equals the supremum of the following time series:

$$(\text{B.2}) \qquad Y_n^2(t) = \left(\frac{tm_t}{n}\right)\left(\frac{\hat{\eta}_n}{\hat{\eta}_t} - 1\right)^2.$$

Expression (B.2) compares the recursive value of the estimated tail parameter (6) or (B.1) to its full sample counterpart $\hat{\eta}_n$. The null hypothesis of interest is that the tail-dependence parameter does not exhibit any temporal changes. More specifically, let η_t be the dependence in the left tail of X. The null hypothesis of constancy then takes the form

$$(\text{B.3}) \qquad H_0 : \eta_{(nr)} = \eta, \quad \forall r \in R_\varepsilon = (\varepsilon; 1 - \varepsilon) \subset (0; 1),$$

with $[nr]$ representing the integer value of nr. Without prior knowledge about the direction of a break, one is interested in testing the null against the two-sided alternative hypothesis $H_A : \eta_{(nr)} \neq \eta$. For practical reasons this test is calculated over compact subsets of $(0; 1)$; that is, t equals the integer part of nr for $r \in R_\varepsilon = (\varepsilon; 1 - \varepsilon)$ and for small $\varepsilon > 0$. Sets like R_ε are often used in the construction of parameter constancy tests (see, e.g., Andrews 1993).[28] In line with Quandt's (1960) pioneering work on endogenous breakpoint determination in linear time series models, the candidate break date r can be selected as the maximum value of the test statistic (B.2)

---

27. See the end of appendix A for a discussion of how to choose m.

28. The restricted choice of r implies that $\varepsilon n \leq t \leq (1 - \varepsilon)n$. When the lower bound would be violated the recursive estimates might become too unstable and inefficient because of too-small subsample sizes. On the other hand, the test will never find a break for t equal or very close to n, because the test value (B.2) is close to zero in that latter case. Thus, for computational efficiency one might stop calculating the tests beyond the upper bound of $(1 - \varepsilon)n < n$. We search for breaks in the $[0.15n; 0.85n]$ subset of the total sample, as Andrews (1993) does.

because at this point in time the constancy hypothesis is most likely to be violated.

Asymptotic critical values can be derived for the sup-value of equation (B.2), but if the data are temporally dependent the test sequence Y_n^2 needs to be scaled in order to guarantee convergence to the same limiting distribution function as in the case of absence of temporal dependence. It is well known that financial returns exhibit nonlinear dependencies like, for example, ARCH effects (volatility clustering). It is likely that the loading variable $\tilde{X}_{min}$, previously defined as the cross-sectional minimum of the bank stock returns (transformed using their proper empirical distribution function), partly inherits these nonlinearities. The nonlinear dependence implies that the asymptotic variance of the Hill estimator $1/\hat{\eta}$ is s^2/η^2, with s some scaling factor. If the scaling factor differs from 1 (presence of temporal dependence), the asymptotic critical values of the test statistic will depend on the scaling. Quintos, Fan, and Phillips suggest to premultiply the test statistic with the inverse of the scaling factor in order to let it converge to the same critical values as in the i.i.d. case. However, their scaling estimator is based upon the ARCH assumption for univariate time series. As we do not want to make very specific assumptions on the precise structure of the nonlinear dependence in the marginals, we apply a block bootstrap to the asymptotic variance of the Hill statistic $1/\hat{\eta}$ and thus the scaling factor s.[29] Following Hall, Horowitz, and Jing (1995), the optimal block length is set equal to $n^{1/3}$. One now selects r for the recursive test such that $Y_n^2(t)$—appropriately scaled—is maximal:

$$(B.4) \qquad\qquad \Omega_{r \in R_\tau} = \sup \hat{s}^{-1} Y_n^2(t),$$

with $\hat{s}$ the estimate of the scaling factor. The null of parameter constancy is rejected if this sup-value exceeds the asymptotic critical values.

Appendix C

Small Sample Properties of Estimators and Tests

Small Sample Properties of the Bivariate Estimator

In this section we investigate the small sample properties of our estimators. We limit our attention to the bivariate version, which could either be a spillover probability between two banks or a tail-β, and the respective de-

---

29. The scale is estimated by $s = \hat{\eta} m \hat{\sigma}^2 (1/\hat{\eta})$ with $\hat{\sigma}^2$ the block bootstrapped variance of the Hill statistic.

pendence parameter. Without loss of generality, we will always refer to tail-β in the following discussion. Three different data-generating processes are investigated: the bivariate Pareto distribution (C.1), the bivariate Morgenstern distribution (1956) with Pareto marginals (C.2), and the bivariate standard normal distribution (C.3). The first two distributions both have Pareto marginals, but only the first distribution exhibits asymptotic dependence (in which case $\eta = 1$). The bivariate normal is also asymptotically independent (as long as $|\rho| \neq 1$). The normal distribution has a dependence parameter η that varies with the correlation coefficient, and we investigate different configurations. The precise specifications of the distributions are as follows:

Bivariate Pareto

(C.1) $F(x, y) = 1 - x^{-\alpha} - y^{-\alpha} + (x + y - 1)^{-\alpha},$

$\rho = 1/\alpha$ for $\alpha > 2,$

$\eta = 1.$

Bivariate Morgenstern Distribution with Pareto Marginals

(C.2) $F(x, y) = (1 - x^{-\alpha})(1 - y^{-\alpha})(1 + \delta x^{-\alpha} y^{-\alpha}), \quad -1 \leq \delta \leq 1,$

$\rho = \delta\alpha(\alpha - 2)(2\alpha - 1)^{-2}$ for $\alpha > 2,$

$\eta = 1/2.$

Bivariate Normal with Correlation Coefficient ρ and Dependence Parameter

(C.3) $\eta = \dfrac{1 + \rho}{2}$

The three specific distributions have the advantage that they allow us to calculate the true value of η and the tail-β (τ_β). Thus, the estimation bias and asymptotic mean-squared error can be calculated explicitly. The true "benchmark" values of the tail-βs are:

$\tau_\beta = (2 - p^{1/\alpha})^{-\alpha}$ (bivariate Pareto),

$\tau_\beta = (1 + \delta)p - 2\delta p^2 + \delta p^3$ (bivariate Morgenstern),

$\tau_\beta = \dfrac{\Phi(-x, -x, \rho)}{p},$ (bivariate standard normal),

where $p = P(X > x)$. In the following tables we evaluate the tail-βs and dependence parameters at $p = 0.05$ percent, which is one of the marginal significance levels we also use in the empirical applications. Two different sample sizes are considered: a truly small sample of 500 observations and a larger sample of 3,106, corresponding to the actual sample size in the empirical application to bank stocks.

The following three tables report true values of τ_β as well as estimates of the average, bias, and standard deviation of η and τ_β for 5,000 Monte Carlo replications. Notice that biases are reported in absolute and not in percentage terms. Back-of-the-envelope calculations of the relative (percentage) biases may nevertheless be handy for the sake of comparing the bias across different parametrizations, but were omitted because of space considerations.[30] Averages, biases, and standard deviations are multiplied by 100 for the sake of convenience. The estimates are conditioned on cutoff points m^* that minimize the Asymptotic Mean Squared error (AMSE). The AMSE is calculated for 5,000 Monte Carlo replications.[31]

We start with an evaluation for the Morgenstern distribution with Pareto marginals (see table 4C.1).

Analytic tail-β values are small, which makes this model the least realistic as a benchmark for comparison with the tail-βs we found in practice. We let both the tail index α and the parameter δ vary. The table shows that the Morgenstern bias in η and τ_β does depend on δ but not on α. This is not surprising, given that α does not enter the analytic expression of the Morgenstern tail-β; that is the tail-β is independent from marginal properties in this case.[32] Biases are small for small δ but become substantial in both absolute and relative terms when δ is large. Also, the estimation accuracy—as reflected by the standard errors s.e.—is found to be higher for small values of δ.

Next, we turn to the results for the Pareto distribution. The results are in table 4C.2. In contrast to table 4C.1, there now appears a considerable downward bias in absolute terms for both η and τ_β. However, the relative (percentage) biases can be shown to be smaller than in the Morgenstern case. Recall that the true value of η is equal to the boundary value of 1 in this case, so that in any empirical exercise one expects at least some downward bias. Moreover, (absolute and relative) biases and standard errors decrease with a decrease in correlation (an increase in α).

Last, we consider the small-sample performance for the bivariate nor-

---

30. Relative or percentage measures of the bias can be calculated as $100 \times (E[\hat{\eta}] - \eta/\eta)$ and $100 \times (E[\hat{\tau}_\beta] - \tau_\beta)/\tau_\beta$ for the tail dependence parameter and the tail-β, respectively.

31. If two (unit Pareto) random variables are independent, we previously noted that $P(X > q, Y > q) = p^2$ with $p = P(X > q) = P(Y > q)$. This exact Pareto tail allows the use of all extreme observations in estimation because of the unbiasedness of the Hill statistic under the Pareto law, that is, $m^* = n - 1$.

32. It can be easily shown that the analytic expressions for Morgenstern bias and asymptotic mean squared error (AMSE) do not depend on the marginal distributional properties like scale and tail indices.

Table 4C.1   Small sample behavior of tail betas for bivariate Morgenstern distribution

		$\hat{\eta}$			$\hat{\tau}_\beta (\times 100)$			
$(\alpha; \delta)$	m^*	Average	Bias	Standard error	Average	Bias	Standard error	$\tau_\beta (\times 100)$
				A. n = 500				
(2; 0.0)	499	0.499	−0.001	0.013	0.052	0.002	0.021	0.050
(3; 0.0)	499	0.499	−0.001	0.013	0.052	0.002	0.021	0.050
(4; 0.0)	499	0.499	−0.001	0.013	0.052	0.002	0.021	0.050
(2; 0.5)	150	0.546	0.046	0.034	0.231	0.156	0.190	0.075
(3; 0.5)	150	0.545	0.045	0.034	0.226	0.151	0.189	0.075
(4; 0.5)	150	0.546	0.046	0.034	0.232	0.157	0.198	0.075
(2; 0.9)	134	0.570	0.070	0.036	0.424	0.329	0.338	0.095
(3; 0.9)	134	0.570	0.070	0.037	0.427	0.332	0.349	0.095
(4; 0.9)	134	0.570	0.070	0.037	0.419	0.324	0.327	0.095
				B. n = 3,106				
(2; 0.0)	3,105	0.500	0.000	0.005	0.050	0.000	0.008	0.050
(3; 0.0)	3,105	0.500	0.000	0.005	0.050	0.000	0.008	0.050
(4; 0.0)	3,105	0.500	0.000	0.005	0.050	0.000	0.008	0.050
(2; 0.5)	376	0.532	0.032	0.023	0.152	0.077	0.083	0.075
(3; 0.5)	376	0.532	0.032	0.023	0.151	0.076	0.083	0.075
(4; 0.5)	376	0.532	0.032	0.023	0.148	0.073	0.080	0.075
(2; 0.9)	335	0.543	0.043	0.025	0.225	0.130	0.121	0.095
(3; 0.9)	335	0.543	0.043	0.025	0.224	0.129	0.120	0.095
(4; 0.9)	335	0.543	0.043	0.025	0.225	0.130	0.120	0.095

Notes: The table reports estimated values and true (analytic) values of the tail dependence parameter η and the tail-β (τ_β) for different sample sizes and different parameter configurations (α, δ). Tail-βs and corresponding biases and accuracy are expressed in percentage terms (%). Moreover, the linkage estimates are conditioned on the cutoff point m^* that minimizes the asymptotic mean squared error of $\hat{\eta}$. The conditioning quantiles for the tail-β are chosen such that the corresponding marginal excess probabilities are equal to 0.05 percent.

mal distribution (see table 4C.3). For the normal distribution the estimators appear to behave quite reasonably. Absolute and relative biases are found to be smaller than in the Pareto case. Moreover, it may be difficult to distinguish the normal distribution from the Pareto distribution just on the basis of, say, the dependence parameter estimate. To this end it would be helpful to investigate the tail properties of the marginals as well.

Small-Sample Properties of the Endogenous Break Test

In this part of the appendix we investigate the small-sample properties of the recursive test for a single endogenous break in η. This is done through a simulation study in which we use the bivariate normal as the data-generating process (see table 4C.4).

Table 4C.2 **Small sample behavior of tail betas for bivariate Pareto distribution**

α	m^*	$\hat{\eta}$ Average	Bias	Standard error	$\tau_\beta\ (\times 100)$ Average	Bias	Standard error	$\tau_\beta\ (\times 100)$	η
					A. n = 500				
2	31	0.831	−0.169	0.113	15.44	−10.12	13.15	25.56	1
3	26	0.763	−0.237	0.126	8.32	−5.79	9.49	14.11	1
4	22	0.719	−0.281	0.134	5.49	−3.04	7.40	8.53	1
Indep.	499	0.498	−0.002	0.013	0.05	0.00	0.02	0.05	1/2
					B. n = 3,106				
2	89	0.889	−0.111	0.073	19.19	−6.38	8.73	25.57	1
3	45	0.832	−0.168	0.106	10.61	−3.50	7.51	14.11	1
4	42	0.777	−0.223	0.110	6.28	−2.25	5.37	8.53	1
Indep.	3,105	0.500	0.000	0.005	0.05	0.00	0.00	0.05	1/2

Notes: The table reports estimated values and true (analytic) values of the tail-dependence parameter η and the tail-β (τ_β) for different sample sizes and different values of α. Tail-βs and corresponding biases and accuracy are expressed in percentage terms (%). Moreover, the linkage estimates are conditioned on the cutoff point m^* that minimizes the Asymptotic Mean Squared Error of $\hat{\eta}$. The conditioning quantiles for the tail-β are chosen such that the corresponding marginal excess probabilities are equal to 0.05 percent.

Table 4C.3 **Small sample behavior of tail betas for bivariate normal distribution**

ρ	m^*	$\hat{\eta}$ Average	Bias	Standard error	$\hat{\tau}_\beta\ (\times 100)$ Average	Bias	Standard error	$\tau_\beta\ (\times 100)$	$\eta = \dfrac{1+\rho}{2}$
					A. n = 500				
3/4	138	0.795	−0.080	0.038	13.55	−4.59	5.11	18.14	0.875
1/2	154	0.684	−0.066	0.038	3.09	−1.12	1.69	4.21	0.75
1/4	233	0.583	−0.042	0.026	0.47	−0.20	0.27	0.67	0.625
0	499	0.499	−0.001	0.013	0.05	0.00	0.02	0.05	0.05
					B. n = 3,106				
3/4	299	0.815	−0.060	0.031	15.74	−2.40	4.10	18.14	0.875
1/2	403	0.699	−0.051	0.027	3.47	−0.74	1.20	4.21	0.75
1/4	574	0.594	−0.031	0.020	0.54	−0.12	0.20	0.66	0.625
0	3,105	0.500	0.000	0.005	0.05	0.00	0.00	0.05	0.5

Notes: The table reports estimated values and true (analytic) values of the tail-dependence parameter η and the tail-β (τ_β) for different sample sizes and different correlations ρ. Tail-βs and corresponding biases and accuracy are expressed in percentage terms (%). Moreover, the linkage estimates are conditioned on the cutoff point m^* that minimizes the Asymptotic Mean Squared Error of $\hat{\eta}$. The conditioning quantiles for the tail-β are chosen such that the corresponding marginal excess probabilities are equal to 0.05 percent.

Table 4C.4   **Simulated breakpoints**

$(\eta_1; \eta_2)$	Estimated breakpoints (standard error)		
	$r = 1/3$	$r = 1/2$	$r = 2/3$
(0.5; 0.7)	0.364	0.514	0.617
	(0.190)	(0.166)	(0.117)
(0.5; 0.9)	0.264	0.485	0.636
	(0.095)	(0.078)	(0.092)
(0.7; 0.9)	0.394	0.508	0.587
	(0.209)	(0.172)	(0.194)

Notes: Estimated breakpoints are reported for the tail dependence parameter of the bivariate normal df. The break estimates are reported for varying locations of the true breakpoints ($r = 1/3, 1/3, 2/3$). The number of Monte Carlo replications is set to 1,000. The accompanying sampling errors are reported between brackets. Q-tests are calculated starting with a minimum sample size of 500. For sake of convenience, we set the number of upper-order extremes used in estimating the tail index equal to $2_{n2/3}$.

Recall that in this case $\eta = (1 + \rho)/2$. By changing the correlation coefficient, we can easily change the dependence parameter η.

The breaks are engineered at five different points in the sample (see r-columns in the table). Three different combinations of pre- and postbreak ηs are considered (see rows of the table). The sample size is 3,000. Table 4C.4 shows that the test has more difficulty in accurately locating the break if it is close to the start or the end of the sample. The reason is that in these cases one has fewer observations available for one of the two subsamples. When the change in the dependence parameter is small, then the standard errors tend to be more sizable. For example, the standard errors in the first and third scenario are about twice as large as in the second scenario. In sum, the cases in which we have to be more cautious in interpreting the test results are when the changes in η are small and when they occur close to the boundaries of the sample.

Appendix D

Table 4D.1   **List of banks in the sample**

Euro area		United States	
Bank name	Abbreviation	Bank name	Abbreviation
Germany		Citigroup	CITIG
Deutsche Bank	DEUTSCHE	JP Morgan Chase	JP MORGAN
Bayerische Hypo- und Vereinsbank	HYPO	Bank of America BOA	BAMERICA
Dresdner Bank	DRESDNER	Wachovia Corporation	WACHOVIA
Commerzbank	COMMERZ	Wells Fargo and Company	FARGO
Bankgesellschaft Berlin	BGBERLIN	Bank One Corporation	BONE
DePfa Group	DEPFA	Washington Mutual, Inc.	WASHING
		Fleet Boston Financial Corporation	FLEET
France		Bank of New York	BNYORK
BNP Paribas	BNPPAR	State Street	SSTREET
Crédit Agricole	CA	Northern Trust	NTRUST
Societe Generale	SGENER	Mellon	MELLON
Natexis Banques Populaires	NATEXIS	US Bancorp	BCORP
		National City Corporation	CITYCO
Italy		PNC Financial Services Group	PNC
Banca Intesa	INTESA	Keycorp	KEYCO
UniCredito Italiano	UNICREDIT	Sun Trust	SUTRUST
Sanpaolo IMI	PAOLO	Comerica Incorporated	COMERICA
Capitalia	CAPITA	Unionbancal Corporation	UNIONBANK
		AmSouth Bancorp	AMSOUTH
Spain		Huntington Bancshares, Inc.	HUNTING
Banco Santander Central Hispano	SANTANDER	BBT Corporation	BBT
Banco Bilbao Vizcaya Argentaria	BILBAO	Fifth Third Bancorp	53BANCO
Banco Espagnol de Credito	BANESP	Southtrust	SOTRUST
		Regions Financial Corporation	REGIONS
The Netherlands			
ABN AMRO	ABNAMRO		
ING Bank	ING		
Belgium			
Fortis	FORTIS		
Almanij	ALMAIJ		
Finland			
Sampo Leonia	SAMPO		
Greece			
Alpha Bank	ALPHA		
Ireland			
Allied Irish Banks	IRBAN		
Portugal			
Banco Commercial Portugues	BCP		

Appendix E

Volatility Modeling and the Analysis of Banking System Stability

A widely recognized feature of financial market returns is volatility clustering (see, e.g., Bollerslev, Chou, and Kroner, 1992). So a question that comes to mind is to which extent the extreme dependence between bank stock returns and its changes we discover in this paper is associated with persistence and changes in volatility. Before providing some answers to this question, we need to establish first the relationship between the manner in which volatility of bank stock returns is modeled and the objectives of our paper. So, in the first section of this appendix we discuss whether financial stability policy oriented research should focus on conditional volatility modeling or not. In the second section we summarize some results for our indicators of banking system stability when the return data are cleaned for GARCH effects.

How Useful Is Conditional Volatility Modeling for Financial Stability Policy?

The main objective of our work is to measure systemic risk in banking on the basis of market data. The amount of systemic risk in banking is instrumental for the assessment of financial stability and for the design of policies to preserve the stability of financial systems, such as banking regulation and crisis management. The indicators of banking system stability we are using are designed to satisfy the demand by policymakers, who need to have a view about the likelihood of crises and who need to devise the best financial regulations to preserve financial stability.

To assess system stability, banking supervisors need to know the likelihood that one or several banks break down given that other banks break down, or how likely it is that one or several banks break down given that there is an adverse macroeconomic shock. They are not interested in two-sided volatility of bank stock returns per se or in its persistence. In addition, banking regulations are determined in advance for longer periods of time. They cannot be changed within a few days. So, they need to be based on long-term structural risk assessments, not on the likelihood of volatility tomorrow given today's volatility. This is why, for the questions we are interested in, straight returns are preferable to volatility of returns and unconditional modeling is preferable to conditional models. In contrast, conditional models will be preferable for short-term volatility forecasting, as today's volatility is informative for tomorrow's volatility. This type of analysis may be more important for short-term pricing of financial instruments.

Summary of Results for GARCH-Filtered Data

Although the indicators (1) and (2) are the right ones for answering the questions of interest in this paper, we may learn from unclustered return data more about the statistical components of spillover and extreme systematic risk in banking. For example, Poon, Rockinger, and Tawn (2004) argue that conditional heteroskedasticity is an important source of extreme dependence in stock markets in general, but not the only one. Thus, in this section we ask to which extent the extreme dependence of bank stock returns uncovered in the main body of the paper results from univariate volatility clustering or multivariate dependence in volatilities. We do this by filtering our bank excess returns with standard GARCH(1,1) processes and by recalculating the results for our estimators of banking system risk and related tests.

Appendix E.1 in the accompanying working paper (Hartmann, Straetmans, and C. de Vries 2005) reports the results for multivariate spillover probabilities (equation [1]) using the unclustered return data. Tables E.1 through E.5 there reproduce tables 4.3, 4.4, 4.5, 4.9, and 4.10 in the main text here for GARCH-filtered returns. While extreme dependence generally tends to decrease, the qualitative results are quite similar to the ones for plain bank returns. Only very few of the spillover risk changes in Europe (table 4.9) seem to be entirely related to volatility clustering. But clustering plays more of a role in the differences between domestic and cross-border spillovers (table 4.4). Multivariate spillover risk in the United States and Europe, as well as its changes over time, seem little related to volatility clustering (tables 4.5 and 4.10). This is also confirmed by the dotted lines in figures 4.1 and 4.2, which describe the same statistics as the solid lines for GARCH-filtered returns.

Appendix E.2 in the working paper does the same for tail-βs (equation [2]). Tables E.6 through E.10 there reproduce tables 4.6, 4.7, 4.8, 4.11, and 4.12 in the main text here for unclustered returns. As for the previously noted spillover risk, dependencies generally decrease, but none of the qualitative results is fundamentally changed. Again this is also confirmed by the dotted lines in figure 4.3, which illustrate the more muted changes in GARCH-filtered tail-βs and the same direction of their movements.

Overall, we can conclude that in line with the results of Poon, Rockinger, and Tawn (2004) for stock markets in general, part of the extreme dependencies in bank stock returns we find in this paper are related to time-varying volatility and volatility clustering. From the exercises summarized in this appendix we can not ascertain whether this phenomenon is related to the marginal distributions or to multivariate dependence of volatilities. Nevertheless, the primary results that supervisors should pay attention to in order to assess general banking system stability and decide upon regulatory policies are the unadjusted spillover and systematic risk probabilities.

References

Aharony, J., and I. Swary. 1983. Contagion effects of bank failures: Evidence from capital markets. *Journal of Business* 56 (3): 305–17.

Allen, F., and D. Gale. 2000. Financial contagion. *Journal of Political Economy* 108 (1): 1–33.

Andrews, D. 1993. Tests for parameter stability and structural change with unknown change point. *Econometrica* 59:817–58.

Bae, K., A. Karolyi, and R. Stulz. 2003. A new approach to measuring financial contagion. *Review of Financial Studies* 16 (3): 717–63.

Beirlant, J., and B. Vandewalle. 2002. Some comments on the estimation of a dependence index in bivariate extreme values statistics. *Statistics and Probability Letters* 60:265–78.

Bekaert, G., C. Harvey, and A. Ng. 2005. Market integration and contagion. *Journal of Business* 78 (1): 39–70.

Blavarg, M., and P. Nimander. 2002. Interbank exposures and systemic risk. In *Risk Measurement and Systemic Risk,* 287–305. Proceedings of the Third Joint Central Bank Research Conference. Basel: Bank for International Settlements.

Bollerslev, T., R. T. Chou, and K. F. Kroner. 1992. ARCH modeling in finance: A selective review of the theory and empirical evidence. Journal of Econometrics 52:5–59.

Chen, Y. 1999. Banking panics: The role of the first-come, first-served rule and information externalities. *Journal of Political Economy* 107 (5): 946–68.

Danielsson, J., and C. de Vries. 1997. Tail index and quantile estimation with very high frequency data. *Journal of Empirical Finance* 4:241–57.

Danielsson, J., L. de Haan, L. Peng, and C. de Vries. 2001. Using a bootstrap method to choose the sample fraction in tail index estimation. *Journal of Multivariate Analysis* 76:226–48.

De Bandt, O., and P. Hartmann. 2000. Systemic risk: A survey. European Central Bank Working Paper no. 35, November.

de Bondt, G., and D. Marques. 2004. The high-yield segment of the corporate bond market: A diffusion modelling approach for the United States, the United Kingdom and the euro area. European Central Bank Working Paper no. 313, February.

Degryse, H., and G. Nguyen. 2004. Interbank exposures: An empirical examination of systemic risk in the Belgian banking system. Paper presented at the Symposium of the ECB-CFS research network on Capital Markets and Financial Integration in Europe. 10–11 May, European Central Bank, Frankfurt am Main.

Demirgüç-Kunt, A., and E. Detragiache. 1998. The determinants of banking crises in developing and developed countries. *International Monetary Fund Staff Papers* 45:81–109.

De Nicoló, G., and M. Kwast. 2002. Systemic risk and financial consolidation: Are they related? *Journal of Banking and Finance* 26:861–80.

Docking, D., M. Hirschey, and E. Jones. 1997. Information and contagion effects of bank loan-loss reserve announcements. *Journal of Financial Economics* 43 (2): 219–40.

Draisma, G., H. Drees, A. Ferreira, and L. de Haan. 2001. Tail dependence in independence. EURANDOM report 2001-014.

Embrechts, P., C. Klüppelberg, and T. Mikosch. 1997. *Modelling extremal events.* Berlin: Springer.

Forbes, K., and R. Rigobon. 2002. No contagion, only interdependence: Measuring stock market comovements. *Journal of Finance* 57:2223–62.

Freixas, X., B. Parigi, and J.-C. Rochet. 2002. Systemic risk, interbank relations and liquidity provision by the central bank. *Journal of Money, Credit, and Banking* 32 (3/2): 611–40.

Gertler, M., and C. Lown. 1999. The information in the high-yield bond spread for the business cycle: Evidence and some implications. *Oxford Review of Economic Policy* 15 (3): 132–50.

Goldie, C., and R. Smith. 1987. Slow variation with remainder: Theory and applications. *Quarterly Journal of Mathematics* 38:45–71.

Gomes, I., L. de Haan, and L. Peng. 2002. Semi-parametric estimation of the second order parameter in statistics of extremes. *Extremes* 5 (4): 387–414.

Gorton, G. 1988. Banking panics and business cycles. *Oxford Economic Papers* 40:751–81.

Gropp, R., and J. Vesala. 2004. Bank contagion in Europe. Paper presented at the Symposium of the ECB-CFS research network on Capital Markets and Financial Integration in Europe. 10–11 May, European Central Bank, Frankfurt am Main.

Haan, L. de, D. W. Jansen, K. Koedijk, and C. G. de Vries. 1994. Safety first portfolio selection, extreme value theory and long run asset risks. In *Extreme Value Theory and Applications,* ed. J. Galambos, J. Lehner, and E. Simiu, 471–87. Dordrecht: Kluwer Academic Publishers.

Hall, P. 1982. On some simple estimates of an exponent of regular variation. *Journal of the Royal Statistical Society, B* 44 (1): 37–42.

Hall, P., J. Horowitz, and B. Jing. 1995. On blocking rules for the bootstrap with dependent data. *Biometrika* 82 (3): 561–74.

Hartmann, P., A. Maddaloni, and S. Manganelli. 2003. The euro area financial system: Structure, integration and policy initiatives. *Oxford Review of Economic Policy* 19 (1): 180–213.

Hartmann, P., S. Straetsmans, and C. de Vries. 2003a. The breadth of currency crises. Paper presented at the Center for Financial Studies/Wharton School conference on Liquidity Concepts and Financial Instabilities, Eltville, Germany, June.

———. 2003b. A global perspective on extreme currency linkages. In *Asset Price Bubbles: The Implications for Monetary, Regulatory and International Policies,* ed. W. Hunter, G. Kaufman and M. Pomerleano, 361–82. Cambridge: MIT Press.

———. 2004. Asset market linkages in crisis periods. *Review of Economics and Statistics* 86 (1): 313–26.

———. 2005. Banking system stability: A cross-Atlantic perspective. NBER Working Paper no. 11698, Cambridge, MA: National Bureau of Economic Research, September.

Hellwig, M. 1994. Liquidity provision, banking, and the allocation of interest rate risk. *European Economic Review* 38 (7): 1363–89.

Hill, B. 1975. A simple general approach to inference about the tail of a distribution. *The Annals of Statistics* 3 (5): 1163–73.

Jansen, D., and C. de Vries. 1991. On the frequency of large stock returns: Putting booms and busts into perspective. *Review of Economics and Statistics* 73:19–24.

Kaufman, G. 1988. Bank runs: Causes, benefits and costs. *Cato Journal* 7 (3): 559–87.

Ledford, A., and J. Tawn. 1996. Statistics for near independence in multivariate extreme values. *Biometrika* 83 (1): 169–87.

Lelyveld, I., and F. Liedorp. 2004. Interbank contagion in the Dutch banking sector. De Nederlandsche Bank Working Paper no. 005, July.

Longin, F., and B. Solnik. 2001. Extreme correlation of international equity markets. *Journal of Finance* 56:649–76.

Mistrulli, P. 2005. Interbank lending patterns and financial contagion. Banca d'Italia, May. Mimeograph.

Morgenstern, D. 1956. Einfache Beispiele zweidimensionaler Verteilungen. *Mitteilungsblatt fur Mathematische Statistik* 8:234–35.

Musumeci, J., and J. Sinkey. 1990. The international debt crisis, investor contagion, and bank security returns in 1987: The Brazilian experience. *Journal of Money, Credit, and Banking* 22 (2): 210–33.

Peng, L. 1999. Estimation of the coefficient of tail dependence in bivariate extremes. *Statistics and Probability Letters* 43:399–409.

Pindyck, R., and J. Rotemberg. 1993. The comovements of stock prices. *Quarterly Journal of Economics* 108:1073–1104.

Poon, S.-H., M. Rockinger, and J. Tawn. 2004. Extreme value dependence in financial markets: Diagnostics, models, and financial implications. *Review of Financial Studies* 17 (2): 581–610.

Quandt, R. 1960. Test of the hypothesis that a linear regression system obeys two separate regimes. *Journal of the American Statistical Association* 55:324–30.

Quintos, C., Z. Fan, and P. Phillips. 2001. Structural change tests in tail behaviour and the Asian crisis. *Review of Economic Studies* 68:633–63.

Saunders, A. 1986. An examination of the contagion effect in the international loan market. *Studies in Banking and Finance* 3:219–47.

Saunders, A., and B. Wilson. 1996. Contagious bank runs: Evidence from the 1929–33 period. *Journal of Financial Intermediation* 5 (4): 409–23.

Slovin, M., M. Sushka, and J. Polonchek. 1999. An analysis of contagion and competitive effects at commercial banks. *Journal of Financial Economics* 54:197–225.

Smirlock, M., and H. Kaufold. 1987. Bank foreign lending, mandatory disclosure rules, and the reaction of bank stock prices to the Mexican debt crisis. *Journal of Business* 60 (3): 347–64.

Straetmans, S., W. Verschoor, and C. Wolff. 2003. Extreme US stock market fluctuations in the wake of 9/11. Paper presented at the 2004 American Finance Association Meetings, San Diego, 3–5 January.

Wall, L., and D. Peterson. 1990. The effect of Continental Illinois' failure on the financial performance of other banks. *Journal of Monetary Economics* 26:77–99.

Comment   Anthony Saunders

Introduction

The topic of banking contagion and crash risk has spawned a voluminous literature, exceeding more than 100 papers. Yet despite apparent extreme events, such as September 11th, 2001, the banking systems of Europe and the United States seem robust, and have survived such events in a remarkably intact way. One possible explanation is that central bankers have been highly skilled in using policy instruments—such as the discount window during the September 11th event—to deter contagious runs and crashes. Nevertheless, the possibility remains that there will be an event that overwhelms even the most sophisticated and adaptable policymakers. Thus, the question of what is the probability of a crash occurring in the current United States and euro area banking contexts is of some importance.

This essentially is the focus of this excellent and comprehensive paper by Hartmann, Straetmans, and de Vries.

The Authors' Approach

To date, a large number of approaches have been employed to examine bank contagion risk. These include: (1) event study analysis on stock returns, (2) correlation analysis, (3) fund withdrawal behavior, and (4) logit/ probit analysis. This literature is amply reviewed in an earlier paper by De-Bant and Hartmann and I will not go over the strengths and weaknesses of these approaches again here. What has been missing is a detailed examination of the tails of bank failure probability distributions. Put simply, what is the probability that an extreme event (e.g., far worse than September 11th) will have such a strong systematic impact that we will get the long-feared crash of Western banking systems?

The authors' novel approach is to use extreme value theory (EVT)—long used in life insurance to assess extreme claims risk—to examine the probability of extreme banking events, such as a systemic collapse. To paraphrase the authors, they apply EVT to examine dependencies in the extreme tail of bank equity return distributions within countries and between countries with emphasis on the United States and Europe. This extreme risk is measured in two ways: (1) between bank stock returns and (2) between a bank's stock return and bank indexes, so as to examine the home country's systematic exposure to shocks (so-called tail-β [beta] risk). Since the focus is on large bank contagion, the banks analyzed are twenty-five United States and twenty-five European banks, chosen based on two criteria: (1) size and (2) interbank lending market presence. The basic premise—although not one tested directly in the paper—is that a primary route of contagion among banks is through the interbank market in purchased funds. Thus, the branch structures and deposit-raising powers of different banks are not explicitly explored in the paper. For example, a bank with the same interbank borrowing exposure as another bank, but with a more extensive branch network (and thus core deposit base) would likely be less susceptible to interbank market propagation of shocks. Of course, one could think of many more sample conditioning variables (see later), but to my mind the authors' focus on size and interbank lending seems a reasonable first approximation.

The Authors' Major Findings

The paper has a large number of empirical results and findings. I will leave technical issues such as their choice of tail indicator measure and estimation approaches to others to evaluate, but the choice of an appropriate estimator is not without controversy, especially in regards to parametric versus nonparametric methods of estimation (the authors apply a semiparametric method of estimation). Contingent on their choice of estimator, the authors most important findings are that the risk of a bank contagion spillover in the euro area is lower than in the United States. In addition, they find that banks in smaller countries on the periphery of the euro area, such as Finland and Greece, have lower cross-country contagion risk than those in larger, "central" euro area countries (possibly due to weaker cross-country linkages in small countries). Finally, they find that a structural increase in bank contagion risk has taken place in both the U.S. and European banking markets.

Remaining Issues

No paper can address all the issues relating to large bank contagion, although this paper comes very close to doing this. What remains to be done?

EVT and Capital Requirements

The focus of the paper is on the correlation between banks' extreme (negative) tail risks and the probability of joint crashes. The reader—or at least one interested in bank regulation—thinks about the adequacy of bank capital requirements such as those under Basel I and Basel II. There is little or no discussion of the probability of current or proposed bank capital requirements withstanding the size of the EVT-based co-crash probabilities found in the paper. For example, perhaps there is a structural increase in contagion risk—but what is the probability of joint failure under a Basel I 8 percent rule? Importantly, it should be noted that the issue of the optimum size of a systematic component to bank capital relative to the size of the bank-specific (unsystematic) component remains a relatively underresearched area. Since there seems to be a clear potential linkage between co-crash banks' EVT-measured risk and the optimal size of bank systematic risk capital, this issue could have been explored by the authors.

Interbank Loans

I'm still not convinced that interbank lending exposure as measured in the Hartman, Straetmans, and de Vries paper is really the best way (along with size) to select the samples of euro area and U.S. banks. For example, I still have a hard time convincing myself that State Street Bank or Northern Trust belong in the same contagion risk league as Citicorp. Their inclusion appears to be, in part, dependent on their prominent clearing and settlement activities. However, much of this activity is in securities markets and not the fed funds market or on the clearing house interbank payments system (CHIPS), which are most relevant for interbank lending in the United States. This suggests that additional sample conditioning variables may be worth exploring, such as branch networks, or the scope of geographic diversification of funds, both of which would provide some form of risk mitigation in the presence of a run in the interbank market.

Mergers and Acquisitions

While the authors take note of the growth in merger and acquisition (M&A) activity in enhancing interbank correlations, my feeling is that its current and future importance is somewhat underplayed in the paper. For example, the high rate of bank M&As in the United States following the passage of the Riegle-Neal Interstate Banking Act in 1994 may well explain a significant component of the higher relative contagion risk in the United States versus the euro area in the later 1990s. This is especially so in view of the relatively slow cross-border bank M&A in the euro area to date (notwithstanding the Single Capital Market legislation). In addition, the existence of M&A activity raises some important implications in terms of sample selection bias, including (1) the use of bank asset size and (2) survivorship bias over a twelve-year sample period. My feeling is that these issues are not sufficiently confronted in the paper.

Other Conditioning Variables

The authors focus on conditioning systematic risk on either general bank indexes or high-yield spreads. Thus, unsystematic bank risk is the residual excess return after such conditioning. This unsystematic risk will include all other risk effects after controlling for market indexes or yield spreads. As is well known, one- or two-factor models potentially leave a lot of systematic risk unexplained. Indeed, when I think of extreme events, my natural inclination is to think of disasters or catastrophes (including reputational), which are often put under the general rubric of "operational" risk. Indeed, one interesting EVT question is that after controlling for all reasonable systematic risk factors—including market and macro-factors— what are the co-crash probabilities across banks' operational or "extreme event" risks? While the authors have not extended their research in this direction, there is one recent working paper by Allen and Bali of Baruch College, CUNY that explores this issue by analyzing correlations across residual stock returns after controlling for a large array of market and macro-factors. In sum, one is not quite sure what remaining tail risks the Hartmann, Straetmans, and de Vries paper explores.

Good News Contagion

The focus of this paper, as in much of the bank contagion literature, is on contagion due to bad news or negative events. This is, of course, natural, given the "specialness" of banks and the downside macro-risk and externalities from systemic failure. Nevertheless, there is often good news, such as an individual bank announcing record earnings that may well (also) favorably impact other banks' stock return distributions. For example, is bank-specific good news sufficiently contagious across banks that it enhances the safety and soundness of the banking system overall? For example, in good-news periods banks may exploit the higher stock returns associated with such news by issuing more equity to bolster capital reserves against bad times. To my knowledge upside contagion or extreme positive event risk is a relatively unexplored area.

Conclusion

This is an excellent paper. The authors should be commended for proposing and employing a novel way of thinking about event and co-crash risk across banks. As noted earlier, the results of the paper have important implications for policymakers, encompassing M&A, cross-border policy, capital requirements, and safety net design in general. I'm sure that there will be many future papers extending the Hartmann, Straetmans, and de Vries EVT methodology, including ones analyzing developing banking systems such as those in Asia, Africa, and elsewhere.

Discussion Summary

René Stulz opened the general discussion by asking whether what the authors measure as contagion simply reflects an increase in volatility of a factor that affects the equity returns of all banks. *Philipp Hartmann* noted that results of some preliminary robustness checks employing GARCH models imply that this is not the whole story, but even if it is, the vulnerability of the banking system to extreme shocks is of interest. This issue is now discussed in detail in the revised version of the paper. *Jan Krahnen* asked about the experience of healthy versus unhealthy banks, and Hartmann replied that extreme moves appear to be larger for the latter.

Eric Rosengren suggested segmenting the sample by market-makers versus other banks, rather than using geography, as the relative vulnerability of the major dealer banks is of considerable interest. *Hashem Pesaran* suggested systematic pairwise comparison of banks in the sample, to see if most of the average results are coming from a few banks. *Philipp Hartmann* noted that a pairwise approach would not capture higher-order dependencies, which are captured by the authors' method.

In response to a query about practitioner use of extreme value theory, *Ken Abbott* noted that although the methods used by risk managers generally have to be understandable by nonspecialists, and EVT does not yet meet that standard, he intends to train his staff to understand EVT.

Bank Concentration and Fragility
Impact and Mechanics

Thorsten Beck, Asli Demirgüç-Kunt, and Ross Levine

5.1   Purposes and Motivation

Public policy debates and theoretical disputes motivate this paper's examination of the relationship between bank concentration and banking system fragility and the mechanisms underlying this relationship. The rapid consolidation of banks around the world is intensifying concerns among policymakers about bank concentration, as reflected in major reports by the Bank for International Settlements (2001), International Monetary Fund (2001), and the Group of Ten (2001). These reports note that concentration may reduce competition in and access to financial services, increase the market power and political influence of financial conglomerates, and destabilize financial systems as banks become too big to discipline and use their influence to shape banking regulations and policies. These reports also provide countervailing arguments. Consolidation may improve banking system efficiency and enhance stability as the best banks succeed, diversify, and boost franchise value. Further, some may question whether bank concentration is a reliable indicator of competition in the banking industry.

Theoretical disputes parallel these public policy deliberations. Some models yield a "concentration-stability" prediction that banking system concentration reduces fragility (Allen and Gale 2000, 2003). In terms of

We received very helpful comments from John Boyd, Maria Carkovic, George Clarke, Gianni DeNicolo, Peter Garber, and seminar participants at the University of Minnesota, the World Bank, and the NBER Conference on the Risks of Financial Institutions. This paper's findings, interpretations, and conclusions are entirely those of the authors and do not necessarily represent the views of the World Bank, its executive directors, or the countries they represent.

mechanisms, concentration may signal less competition and hence greater market power and profits. Higher profits provide a buffer against adverse shocks and increase the franchise value of the bank, which reduces incentives for bankers to take excessive risk.[1] Also, some hold that it is substantially easier for supervisors to monitor a few banks in a concentrated banking system than it is to monitor lots of banks in a diffuse banking system, so that in equilibrium, concentrated banking systems will suffer fewer banking crises. Some proponents of the "concentration-stability" view note that if (1) concentrated banking systems have larger banks and (2) larger banks hold more diversified portfolios than smaller banks, then concentrated banking systems will tend to be more stable.[2]

In contrast, some models produce a "concentration-fragility" prediction, where concentration increases fragility. Boyd and De Nicoló (2005) stress that banks in less competitive environments charge higher interest rates to firms, which induces firms to assume greater risk. Their model predicts that if concentration is positively associated with banks having market power, then concentration will increase both the expected rate of return on bank assets and the standard deviation of those returns. Also, proponents of the concentration-fragility view disagree with the proposition that a few large banks are easier to monitor than many small banks. If size is positively correlated with complexity, then large banks may be more difficult to monitor than small banks, not less. Finally, some researchers argue that larger banks are protected by implicit "too-big-to-fail" policies that small banks do not enjoy. This protection intensifies risk-taking incentives beyond any diversification advantages enjoyed by large banks (Boyd and Runkle 1993; Mishkin 1999; O'Hara and Shaw 1990).[3] From this perspec-

---

1. See Boot and Greenbaum (1993), Besanko and Thakor (1993), Hellman, Murdoch, and Stiglitz (2000), and Matutes and Vives (2000). Also, Smith (1984) shows that less competition in banking leads to more stability if information about the probability distribution of depositors' liquidity needs is private and lower competition allows banking relationships to endure for longer periods. Matutes and Vives (1996), however, argue that concentration is not a consistent signal of competition, so that bank illiquidity can arise in any market structure.

2. Each of these conditions is debatable. Models by Diamond (1984), Ramakrishnan and Thakor (1984), Boyd and Prescott (1986), Williamson (1986), Allen (1990), and others predict economies of scale in intermediation. As discussed by Calomiris (2000) and Calomiris and Mason (2000), research finds an inverse relationship between bank size and bank failure in the United States. However, Chong (1991) and Hughes and Mester (1998) indicate that bank consolidation tends to increase the risk of bank portfolios. Moreover, Boyd and Runkle (1993) examine 122 U.S. bank holding companies and find an inverse relationship between size and the volatility of assets returns, but not evidence that large banks fail less frequently than small banks. In contrast, De Nicoló (2000) finds a positive relationship between bank size and the probability that the bank will fail in the United States, Japan, and several European countries. We control for bank size in our regressions, but the focus of our research is on the relationship between the concentration and fragility of national banking systems.

3. A large literature indicates that implicit or explicit deposit insurance creates incentives for banks to increase risk (e.g., Merton 1977, Sharpe 1978, Flannery 1989, Kane 1989, and Chan, Greenbaum, and Thakor 1992). If this insurance were the same for banks of all sizes, these models would predict no relationship between bank size and bank fragility. Since regu-

tive, concentrated banking systems with a few large banks will tend to be more fragile than diffuse banking system with many small banks.

Given these conflicting theoretical predictions and policy disputes, there are surprisingly few cross-country examinations of banking system concentration and fragility.[4] Although there is a growing cross-country empirical literature that uses time series data to examine the determinants of banking crises, this research does not examine concentration (Demirgüç-Kunt and Detragiache 1998, 1999, henceforth DD; Gonzalez-Hermosillo, Pazarbasioglu, and Billings 1997; Kaminsky and Reinhart 1999). Although Barth, Caprio, and Levine (2004) examine the relationship between bank regulations and crises, they do not examine bank concentration, and they use pure cross-country comparisons rather than panel analyses. De Nicoló et al. (2003) find a positive relationship between banking system concentration and the fragility of the largest five banks in a country. They do not, however, examine systemic crises.

This paper (1) assesses the relationship between bank concentration and the probability that a country will suffer a systemic crisis and (2) provides evidence on whether particular hypothesized mechanisms linking concentration and fragility—competition, diversification, and the ease of monitoring—account for the identified relationship between concentration and stability. We focus on these three mechanisms because of their prominence in policy and academic discussions.

To investigate systemic crises, we use annual data on sixty-nine countries over the period 1980–1997. While no single, unambiguous definition of a systemic crisis exists, we use the DD (2002) classification and confirm the results with other definitions. DD (2002) consider a country to be in a systemic crisis if (1) authorities use emergency measures, such as bank holidays, deposit freezes, blanket guarantees, and so forth to assist the banking industry, (2) countries undertake large-scale nationalizations of banks, (3) nonperforming loans top 10 percent of total banking assets, or (4) the fiscal costs of rescue operations exceed two percent of Gross Domestic Product (GDP). Using logit regressions, we analyze the association between banking system concentration and the probability that a country experi-

---

lators may fear potential macroeconomic consequences of large bank failures, many countries have implicit "too-large-to-fail" policies that protect large banks more than small banks. Thus, the largest banks frequently receive a greater net insurance subsidy from the government. This subsidy may in turn increase the risk-taking incentives of the larger banks more than smaller banks. For an analysis of the corporate governance of banks, see Macey and O'Hara (2003). Note, however, that even in the absence of deposit insurance, banks are prone to excessive risk taking due to limited liability for their equity holders and to their high leverage (Stiglitz 1972).

4. For the United States, Keeley (1990) provides evidence that increased competition following the relaxation of state branching restrictions in the 1980s increased the risk of large banks. However, Jayaratne and Strahan (1998) find that deregulation in the 1980s lowered loan losses, and Dick (2006) finds higher loan loss provisions following deregulation in the 1990s.

ences a systemic crisis. In the analyses we condition on many country characteristics, including bank supervisory and regulatory practices, institutional development, and macroeconomic controls, such as the level of economic development, economic growth, inflation, interest rates, terms of trade changes, and credit growth.

The results are inconsistent with the concentration-fragility view. We do not find a positive relationship between banking system concentration and the likelihood that the country suffers a systemic crisis. Using different conditioning information sets, different sample periods, different definitions of crises, and different measures of concentration, we never find a significant, positive link between concentration and crises. Thus, our analyses lend no support to the view that concentration increases the fragility of banks.

Rather, the findings are broadly consistent with the concentration-stability view. Concentration enters the crises regressions negatively and significantly across a wide array of specifications. Thus, although we will emphasize numerous qualifications, the data consistently indicate a positive relationship between national bank concentration and banking system stability.

Furthermore, we provide exploratory evidence on the potential mechanisms—competition, diversification, and ease of monitoring—underlying the positive relationship between concentration and stability. First, to assess whether concentration proxies for competition, we include bank regulatory indicators and measures of national institutional development. More specifically, we control for national policies toward bank entry, bank activities, and bank ownership, as well as several indicators of national institutions that affect competition. If (1) these variables measure the competitive environment in banking and (2) concentration proxies for competition, then including these variables should eliminate the significance of concentration in the fragility regressions. Moreover, these assessments provide independently valuable information on the linkages between banking system fragility and bank regulations. Second, to assess whether concentration proxies for diversification or ease of monitoring, we include numerous indicators that attempt to proxy for these mechanisms. For diversification, we control for (a) the size of the economy, which may correlate positively with the ability of banks to diversify domestically, (b) restrictions on making loans abroad, which may correlate negatively with the ability of banks to diversify internationally, and (c) mean bank size, which some argue is positively correlated with diversification. For ease of monitoring, we control for (a) the number of banks, (b) regulatory restrictions on banks' ability to engage in nonlending services, since the complexity of banks may hinder monitoring, (c) mean bank size, since larger banks may be more complex than smaller banks, (d) capital regulatory requirements, deposit insurance, and other prudential regulations, and (e) the average cash flow rights of the controlling owner, if any, of the largest, listed banks in the country, which may reflect the incentives of the largest owner to govern the bank effectively. Again, if including these variables eliminates the relationship between concentration and fragility, then this provides circumstantial evidence that concentration acts as a proxy for diversification or the cost of monitoring banks.

In terms of regulatory policies and institutional development, we find that (1) fewer regulatory restrictions on banks—lower barriers to bank entry, fewer restrictions on bank activities, and fewer impediments to bank operations in general—reduce banking system fragility, and (2) countries with national institutions that foster competition have lower banking system fragility. Thus, policies and institutions that facilitate competition in banking are associated with less—not *more*—banking system fragility. Furthermore, capital requirements, reserve requirements, and prudential regulations do not affect the results on concentration and, interestingly, do not reduce the likelihood of suffering a systemic crisis. Regarding specific mechanisms associated with the concentration-stability view, the findings that (1) banking system concentration is associated with *lower* fragility and (2) policies that foster competition are associated with *lower* fragility suggest that concentration is proxying for something else besides a lack of competition.

In terms of diversification, we find some support for the view that one of the mechanisms underlying the negative relationship between concentration and banking system fragility is that concentrated banking systems tend to have larger, better-diversified banks. While recognizing that the measures of diversification are both indirect and potentially imprecise, we find that controlling for proxies of diversification substantially reduces the ties between concentration and crises. More specifically, we find that (1) controlling for the size of the domestic economy eliminates the connection between concentration and systemic crises, (2) controlling for the mean size of banks weakens the link between concentration and crises, and (3) controlling for mean bank size and restrictions on foreign loans eliminates the negative relationship between banking system concentration and the probability of suffering a systemic crisis. The results are consistent with arguments that countries with, on average, larger banks tend to have a lower likelihood of suffering a systemic crisis and inconsistent with the view that large banks distort public policies in a manner that increases banking system fragility.

In contrast, we find no support for any of the views suggesting that concentration is a proxy for the degree of difficulty in monitoring banks. When controlling for the number of banks, or regulatory restrictions on banks, or capital requirements, or prudential regulations, or the cash flow rights of the bank's controlling owner (if any), this does not change the finding of a negative relationship between concentration and crises. In sum, we did not find much support that a distinguishing characteristic of concentrated banking systems is that they are easier to monitor than more diffuse systems.

The analyses in this paper are subject to considerable qualifications and interpretational limitations.

First, as our own results emphasize, concentration is not necessarily a reliable indicator of competition (Tirole 1988; Sutton 1991, 1998). Mergers and acquisitions that increase concentration could reflect competition, not the absence of competition. A country with a few banks in a contestable market may be more competitive than a country with lots of banks in segmented monopolies. This does not invalidate this paper's usefulness. Around the world, policymakers, in forming bank regulations, and courts, in assessing antitrust challenges to bank consolidation, use banking system concentration as a signal. Toward this end, our work suggests that (1) banking system concentration is not associated with greater bank instability; rather, it is associated with less fragility and (2) policies and regulations that ease competition lower banking system fragility.

Second, although we use different measures of banking system crises, any examination of systemic crises is constrained by the difficulty in defining and dating a "systemic" crisis. Thus, we interpret these results cautiously and trust that this information is one useful input into assessing the linkages between the market structure of the banking industry, bank regulations, and banking system fragility. Future research that examines the interactions between concentration, bank regulations, and bank fragility at the microeconomic level will provide a very valuable addition to the crises analyses that we provide.

Third, the absence of time series data on bank regulations lowers confidence in the finding that regulatory impediments to bank competition increase fragility. The regulatory indicators are measured toward the end of the sample period, so that these indicators are sometimes measured *after* the crisis. This data limitation is difficult to correct because it is only very recently that detailed data have been collected on bank regulations around the world (Barth, Caprio, and Levine 2001a, 2001b, 2004, 2006). More importantly for the purposes of this paper, this timing issue does not affect the core finding supporting the concentration-stability view, as these results hold when including or excluding the regulatory indicators. Furthermore, sensitivity checks suggest that regulatory impediments to competition did not grow after systemic crises, so that reverse causality does not seem to drive the results.

Finally, our exploratory evidence that (1) supports the view that concentrated banking systems tend to have larger, better-diversified banks and (2) contradicts the view that concentrated banking systems with a few large banks are easier to monitor is just that, exploratory. The measures that we use are highly imperfect measures of diversification and the ease of monitoring. Nevertheless, when including imperfect indicators of diversification, this reduces the significance of concentration in the fragility regressions, suggesting that concentration may proxy for banking systems with larger, better-diversified banks. Given the natural skepticism about our proxies, however, considerably more evidence is required before one can draw confident conclusions about the mechanisms underlying the negative relationship between concentration and fragility.

The remainder of the paper is organized as follows. Section 5.2 analyzes the relationship between banking system concentration and systemic crises. Section 5.3 provides additional information on the mechanisms explaining the positive relationship between concentration and banking system stability. Section 5.4 briefly lists conclusions.

5.2   Does Bank Concentration Enhance the Risk of Systemic Failure?

In this section, we examine the impact of national bank concentration on the likelihood of a country suffering a systemic banking crisis. Using data on sixty-nine countries over the period 1980–1997, we assess the connection between banking system concentration and the incidence of systemic banking failures.[5] To assess the robustness of our analyses, we (1) use a range of different measures of bank concentration and crises, (2) control for an array of country characteristics, (3) use different estimation procedures and samples of countries, and (4) allow for potential nonlinearities in the relationship between concentration and crises. After describing data and methodology in the first two subsections, we present the regression results.

5.2.1   Data

Data: Crises and Concentration

Following Lindgren, Garcia, and Saal (1996), Caprio and Klingebiel (1999), and Demirgüç-Kunt and Detragiache (2002), we identify and date episodes of banking sector distress by using information on individual bank failures and reports by national supervisory agencies. Then, these episodes of distress are classified as systemic if (1) emergency measures were taken to assist the banking system (such as bank holidays, deposit freezes, blanket guarantees to depositors or other bank creditors), or (2) large-scale nationalizations took place, or (3) nonperforming assets reached at least 10 percent of total assets at the peak of the crisis, or (4) the cost of the rescue operations was at least 2 percent of GDP. In sum, our sample of sixty-nine countries contains forty-seven crisis episodes. Table 5.1 lists this information.

Crisis is a dummy variable that equals 1 if the country is going through

---

5. Demirgüç-Kunt, Laeven, and Levine (2004) investigate the impact of bank concentration on bank net interest margins, but they do not examine bank fragility.

Table 5.1   **Bank concentration and competition and banking crises**

Country	GDP per capita	Crisis period	Concentration
Australia	17,913		0.65
Austria	25,785		0.75
Bahrain	9,398		0.93
Belgium	24,442		0.64
Benin	362	(1988–1990)	1.00
Botswana	2,781		0.94
Burundi	186		1.00
Cameroon	790	(1987–1993, 1995–1998)	0.95
Canada	18,252		0.58
Chile	3,048	(1981–1987)	0.49
Colombia	1,802	(1982–1985)	0.49
Congo	940		1.00
Côte d'Ivoire	843	(1988–1991)	0.96
Cyprus	9,267		0.88
Denmark	31,049		0.78
Dominican Republic	1,426		0.65
Ecuador	1,516	(1995–1997)	0.40
Egypt	905		0.67
El Salvador	1,450	(1989)	0.84
Finland	23,204	(1991–1994)	0.85
France	24,227		0.44
Germany	27,883		0.48
Ghana	356	(1982–1989)	0.89
Greece	10,202		0.79
Guatemala	1,415		0.37
Guyana	653	(1993–1995)	1.00
Honduras	694		0.44
India	313	(1991–1997)	0.47
Indonesia	761	(1992–1997)	0.44
Ireland	13,419		0.74
Israel	13,355	(1983–1984)	0.84
Italy	17,041	(1990–1995)	0.35
Jamaica	1,539	(1996–1997)	0.82
Japan	35,608	(1992–1997)	0.24
Jordan	1,646	(1989–1990)	0.92
Kenya	336	(1993)	0.74
Korea	6,857	(1997)	0.31
Lesotho	356		1.00
Malaysia	3,197	(1985–1988, 1997)	0.54
Mali	260	(1987–1989)	0.91
Mauritius	2,724		0.94
Mexico	3,240	(1982, 1994–1997)	0.63
Nepal	179	(1988–1997)	0.90
The Netherlands	22,976		0.76
New Zealand	15,539		0.77
Nigeria	251	(1991–1995)	0.83
Norway	28,843	(1987–1993)	0.85
Panama	2,824	(1988–1989)	0.42
Papua New Guinea	1,024	(1989–1997)	0.87

Table 5.1   (continued)

Country	GDP per capita	Crisis period	Concentration
Peru	2,458	(1983–1990)	0.69
Philippines	1,070	(1981–1987)	0.49
Portugal	8,904	(1986–1989)	0.46
Senegal	562	(1988–1991)	0.94
Sierra Leone	260	(1990–1997)	1.00
Singapore	20,079		0.71
South Africa	3,680	(1985)	0.77
Sri Lanka	588	(1989–1993)	0.86
Swaziland	1,254	(1995)	0.95
Sweden	24,845	(1990–1993)	0.89
Switzerland	42,658		0.77
Thailand	1,886	(1983–1987, 1997)	0.54
Togo	366		1.00
Tunisia	1,831		0.63
Turkey	2,451	(1982, 1991, 1994)	0.45
United Kingdom	16,883		0.57
United States	24,459	(1980–1992)	0.19
Uruguay	5,037	(1981–1985)	0.87
Venezuela	3,558	(1993–1997)	0.52
Zambia	464		0.84

Source: See table 5A.1 for sources.

Notes: GDP per capita is in constant dollars, averaged over the entire sample period, 1980–1997. Crisis period denotes the years in which each country experienced a systemic banking crisis and the duration of said crisis. Concentration is a measure of concentration in the banking industry, calculated as the fraction of assets held by the three largest banks in each country, averaged over 1988–1997.

a systemic crisis, and 0 if it is not. We experiment with different ways of dating and defining crises.[6] First, since crises run for multiple years and since crises may influence concentration and other explanatory variables, implying reverse causality, most of the regressions reported in the tables exclude observations classified as crises after the initial year of the crisis. That is, we only include the initial year of a multiyear crisis. We do include the years after a multiyear crisis is over, which are noncrisis observations.[7] If the country suffers a second crisis, this is included as well. Second, we also conducted the analyses when including crisis observations following the initial year of a multiyear banking crisis. The results are robust to including these years and classifying them as either crisis observations or noncrisis observations. Thus, the results are not sensitive to the classification of

6. Clearly, there may be disagreements about the dating of major crises. For example, the database we are using classifies the United States as having a crisis from 1980–1992, and many may dispute this dating. Nevertheless, we use different dating conventions and we use different subsamples to reduce fears that dating problems drive the results.

7. The results also hold when dropping all postcrisis years for each country experiencing a crisis.

the crisis years following the initial year of multiyear crisis. Again, once each crisis is over, we include the noncrisis years that follow a multiyear crisis in all of the specifications. Third, this paper's findings are robust to changing the definition of a crisis to also include borderline crises as defined by Caprio and Klingebiel (1999). Specifically, borderline cases do not meet the definition of a systemic crisis described previously and instead include cases where a large bank fails. We do not believe it is appropriate to include borderline cases because we are assessing the impact of banking system concentration on systemic banking crises, not the failure of a large bank. In sum, while recognizing that there is no single, unanimous definition of a systemic banking crisis, the primary goal of this section is to provide a cross-country, time series assessment of the relationship between national bank concentration and crises. The identified relationship is robust to using these different definitions of a systemic crisis.

Concentration equals the share of total banking system assets held by the three largest banks. The data are from the Bankscope database. Since the sample of banks covered in Bankscope increased over the sample period, changes in the concentration measure could reflect changes in coverage. To reduce biases stemming from the coverage problem, we average the concentration measure over the period 1988–1997. As reported in tables 5.1 and 5.2, most countries have concentrated banking systems with a sample mean of 72 percent. Still, there is wide cross-country variation in the sample, with concentration levels ranging from less than 20 percent for the United States to 100 percent for many African countries. Simple correlations show a significant negative relationship between the crisis dummy and bank concentration.

In robustness tests, we consider a number of different concentration measures. This paper's results hold when using (1) annual concentration values, (2) concentration from Bankscope measured at the beginning of the sample period (1988), and (3) a measure of concentration based on the Barth, Caprio, and Levine (2004) survey of bank supervisory agencies regarding deposits in banks.[8] Moreover, by confirming our results using the initial level of concentration at the start of the sample period, we reduce reverse causality concerns. Unfortunately, using initial values cuts the number of observations in half. Thus, we focus on the data averaged over the entire period.

Data: Core Control Variables

To investigate the relationship between systemic banking crises and banking system concentration, we condition on an assortment of macro-

---

8. This alternative measure of concentration is from the Barth, Caprio, and Levine (2004) survey database, which defines bank concentration as the share of deposits of the largest five banks. The correlation between the concentration measures calculated from Bankscope data and from Barth, Caprio, and Levine is 52 percent, and is significant at the 1 percent level.

economic and regulatory factors that may also influence banking system fragility.

We start with the explanatory variables from DD's (2002) examination of the determinants of banking system crises. DD (2002) include four contemporary explanatory variables to control for macroeconomic factors that may affect the quality of bank assets and bank profitability: (1) national economic growth (*real GDP growth*), (2) changes in the external terms of trade (*terms of trade change*), (3) the rate of inflation (*inflation*), and (4) the short-term real interest rate (*real interest rate*). DD (2002) include two variables to control for international forces influencing bank vulnerability: (1) the rate of exchange rate depreciation (*depreciation*) and (2) the ratio of M2 to foreign exchange reserves (*M2/reserves*). Since rapid credit growth may signal an asset price bubble, DD (2002) include lagged credit growth (*credit growth$_{t-2}$*). To condition on the overall level of economic development, DD (2002) also include the level of real per capita GDP (*GDP per capita*). In robustness tests, we also include DD's (2002) measure of deposit insurance generosity (*moral hazard*). To build an aggregate index of moral hazard, DD (2002) estimate the first principal component of various deposit insurance design features. Specifically, they use coinsurance, coverage of foreign currency and interbank deposits, type of funding, source of funding, management, membership, and the level of explicit coverage to create this aggregate index, which increases with the generosity of the deposit insurance regime. The index varies over time, since different countries adopted deposit insurance or revised its design features at different points in time.

Simple correlations in table 5.2 suggest that banking crises are more likely in countries with less concentrated banking systems, higher levels of inflation and exchange rate depreciation, and less likely in growing countries with higher GDP per capita and higher real interest rates. Crises are more likely in countries with more generous deposit insurance.

Data: Bank Regulation and Supervision Control Variables

We augment the benchmark specification from DD (2002) by including measures of bank regulation and supervision from Barth, Caprio, and Levine (2001a, 2001b, 2004). These data on bank supervision and regulation around the world were collected through surveys of government officials from over 100 countries in 1999. This is a problem, because the crises regressions are run over the period 1980–1997. Thus, the regulatory indicators are measured *after* the dependent variable. Besides the fact that no other dataset has the level of cross-country detail on bank regulations, we offer three additional defenses for using these data in the crisis regressions (despite the timing problem). First, Barth, Caprio, and Levine (2001b) show that the regulatory restrictions on bank activities did not change much following systemic crises. Moreover, in the few cases when they did change,

Table 5.2   Summary statistics and correlations

A. Summary statistics

	Mean	Median	Standard deviation	Maximum	Minimum	Observations
Banking crisis	0.04	0.00	0.20	1.00	0.00	1,230
Real GDP growth	3.41	3.45	4.25	23.60	−17.15	1,216
Terms of trade change	0.15	0.01	10.30	63.24	−51.45	1,191
Real interest rate	1.58	2.68	19.34	151.21	−283.00	1,160
Inflation	14.07	7.75	23.42	350.56	−29.17	1,220
M2/reserves	19.87	6.56	68.86	1,289.31	0.19	1,222
Depreciation	0.10	0.04	0.22	2.62	−0.35	1,238
Credit growth$_{t-2}$	6.01	5.09	15.84	115.42	−54.62	1,203
Real GDP per capita	7,813.94	2,302.37	10,299.92	45,950.46	134.54	1,222
Moral hazard	−1.09	−2.49	2.24	3.98	−2.49	1,238
Concentration	0.72	0.77	0.21	1.00	0.19	1,106
Banking freedom	3.36	3.00	0.88	5.00	1.00	1,184

B. Correlations: Banking crisis, concentration, macro indicators, and institutions

	Banking crisis	Real GDP growth	Terms of trade change	Real interest rate	Inflation	M2/reserves	Depreciation	Credit growth$_{t-2}$	Real GDP per capita	Moral hazard	Concentration
Real GDP growth	0.158***	1.000									
Terms of trade change	−0.032	0.029	1.000								
Real interest rate	0.079***	0.093***	−0.053*	1.000							

Inflation	0.103***	−0.117***	0.043	−0.980***	1.000							
M2/reserves	0.094***	−0.117***	0.015	0.011	−0.017	1.000						
Depreciation	0.171***	−0.194***	0.002	−0.561***	0.642***	−0.035	1.000					
Credit growth$_{t-2}$	−0.023	0.040	0.008	0.004	−0.015	−0.097***	−0.103***	1.000				
Real GDP per capita	0.090***	−0.084***	0.015	0.029	−0.051*	−0.053*	−0.226***	−0.014	1.000			
Moral hazard	0.078***	−0.004	0.030	0.028	−0.037	−0.058**	−0.096***	−0.015	0.459***	1.000		
Concentration	−0.062**	−0.061**	−0.004	0.004	−0.002	0.093***	0.040	−0.054*	0.263***	−0.399***	1.000	
Banking freedom	0.183***	0.019	−0.012	0.018	−0.022	0.098***	0.070**	−0.020	0.456***	−0.142***	0.257***	1.000

Source: See table 5A.1 for sources.

Notes: Summary statistics are presented in Panel A and correlations in Panel B. Banking crisis is a crisis dummy, which takes on the value of 1 if there is a systemic crisis and the value of zero otherwise. Growth is the rate of growth of real GDP. Real interest rate is the nominal interest rate minus the contemporaneous rate of inflation. Inflation is the rate of change of the GDP deflator. M2/reserves is the ratio of M2 to international reserves. Credit growth is the real growth of domestic credit, lagged two periods. Depreciation is the rate of change of the exchange rate. Moral hazard is an aggregate index of moral hazard associated with varying deposit insurance schemes. Concentration is a measure of concentration in the banking industry, calculated as the fraction of assets held by the three largest banks in each country, averaged over the sample period. Banking freedom is an indicator of the relative openness of the banking system.

***Indicates significance at the 1 percent level.

**Indicates significance at the 5 percent level.

*Indicates significance at the 10 percent level.

there was a change toward fewer regulatory restrictions. Thus, the timing of the Barth, Caprio, and Levine (2001b) data actually biases the results against finding a positive relationship between regulatory restrictions on bank activities and the likelihood of suffering a systemic crisis. Second, Carkovic and Levine (2002) show that the bank regulations that compose the Barth, Caprio, and Levine (2001b) survey have remained virtually unchanged in Chile during the decade of the 1990s. Third, Barth, Caprio, and Levine's (2006) follow-up survey indicates that there have been remarkably few substantive changes in bank regulatory regimes since the initial survey in 1999, which advertises the stability of bank supervisory and regulatory policies. Nevertheless, timing issues are an important constraint on our ability to draw confident conclusions on the market power, diversification, and easier monitoring explanations of why concentration is associated with more stable banking systems.

We include bank regulation indicators to accomplish three objectives. First, controlling for differences in national policies provides a simple robustness test of the relationship between concentration and crises. Second, controlling for regulations provides additional information on the concentration-fragility relationship. If concentration is proxying for regulations that impede competition, then controlling for the regulatory environment will drive out the significance of concentration in the crisis regression. Finally, examining the relationship between bank regulations and banking system stability is independently valuable, since countries may implement regulations to promote banking system stability. The timing problem primarily, though not necessarily exclusively, affects this last motivation for including the regulatory controls: the fact that regulations are measured after crises reduces the confidence we have in the results on regulations.

Fraction of entry denied equals the number of entry applications denied as a fraction of the number of applications received from domestic and foreign entities, which is a measure of entry restrictions in banking and thus the contestability of the market. If entry restrictions only increase bank profits, this would be associated with a lower rate of fragility. If, however, entry restrictions induce inefficiencies in the banking market, then they could lead to greater fragility.

Activity restrictions is an index of regulatory restrictions on bank activities. This includes information on regulations regarding bank activities in the securities, insurance, real estate markets, and banks owning nonfinancial firms. For each of these four categories of bank activities each country is given a score of 1 through 4, depending on the degree to which regulations restrict bank activity in each area: (1) unrestricted, (2) permitted, (3) restricted, or (4) prohibited. The aggregate indicator has therefore a range from 4 to 16, with higher numbers indicating more restrictions on bank activities. If these activity restrictions keep banks from entering risky lines of business, then Activity Restrictions will tend to reduce the probability of crises. If, however, regulatory restrictions on bank activities prevent firms from diversifying risks, then higher values of Activity Restrictions will tend to increase the probability of suffering a systemic crisis.

Required reserves equals the ratio of bank deposits that regulators require banks to hold as reserves. Banking systems with higher ratios of required reserves may be more stable, since they would have a greater buffer to absorb liquidity shocks. However, greater required reserves are also a tax on the banking system, which may lower profits and raise fragility.

Capital regulatory index is a summary measure of each country's capital stringency requirements, taken from Barth, Caprio, and Levine (2004). To the extent that book capital is an accurate measure of bank solvency we expect better-capitalized banks to be less fragile. Also, capital regulations are a focus of Basel agreements to reduce systemic risk. Thus, including an index of national capital regulations will provide information on whether cross-country differences in one of the three pillars of the Basel II Accord on prudential bank supervision and regulation actually explain differences in banking system fragility. Problematically, however, Barth, Caprio, and Levine (2006) stress that Basel's success and the lack of historical data on capital regulations makes it difficult to assess the impact of capital regulations. Specifically, because Basel has successfully harmonized capital regulations over the past decade, there may be insufficient cross-country variation in the Capital Regulatory Index to explain systemic crises.

Official supervisory power is an index of the power of the commercial bank supervisory agency to monitor and discipline banks (Barth, Caprio, and Levine 2004). It includes information on the legal power of the supervisory authority to (1) meet with, demand information from, and impose penalties on auditors, (2) force a bank to change its internal organizational structure, managers, directors, and so on, (3) oblige the bank to provision against potential bad loans, suspend dividends, bonuses, management fees, and to supersede the rights of shareholders, and (4) intervene a bank and/or declare a bank insolvent. The appendix provides a more detailed definition of Official Supervisory Power. An emphasis of the Basel II accord on prudential supervision and regulation is to strengthen official monitoring of banks. We use this indicator of the power of the supervisory authority to assess the robustness of the results on concentration and to examine the relationship between Official Supervisory Power and the probability that a country suffers a systemic crisis.

Data: Bank Ownership Control Variables

Next, we also control for ownership.

State ownership equals the percentage of banking system assets controlled by banks that are 50 percent or more government owned, which is taken from the Barth, Caprio, and Levine (2001a, 2001b) database.[9] If government-owned banks enjoy greater government support than private banks, then banking systems with a larger share of public banks may experience fewer banks runs and fewer (overt) banking crises. However, inefficiencies in public banks may also make them more fragile, as argued by Caprio and Martinez-Peria (2000). While providing evidence on the relationship between ownership and crises, we use State Ownership as a control variable to test the robustness of the results between concentration and crises. There is not a significant correlation between State Ownership and crises.

Foreign ownership equals the percentage of the banking system's assets in banks that are 50 percent or more foreign owned, which is also taken from the Barth, Caprio, and Levine (2001a, 2001b) database. Foreign banks may bring better banking practices that improve the operation and safety of the banking system (Claessens, Demirgüç-Kunt, and Huizinga 2001). On the other hand, greater openness to foreign banks could intensify competition, reduce profits, and hurt stability. Thus, it is an empirical question as to whether, on net, foreign bank ownership stabilizes or destabilizes a banking system. Again, our goal is to assess the robustness of the relationship between concentration and crises, not to fully explore the impact of foreign banks on the operation of a domestic financial system. The simple correlation between Foreign Ownership and crises is insignificant.

Data: Openness, Competition, Institutional Control Variables

Finally, we include additional control variables for the general openness, competitiveness, and institutional development of the banking sector in particular and the economy more generally. There is overlap between some of these general indexes and the individual regulatory and ownership variables defined earlier. Also, there is overlap between these general indicators. Thus, we note these overlaps in defining the variables and do not include them simultaneously in the regressions that follow.

Banking freedom is an indicator of the relative openness of the banking system. We obtain these data from the Heritage Foundation and use an average over the period 1995–1997. It is a composite index of the barriers foreign banks and financial services firms face in conducting banking operations, how difficult it is to open domestic banks and other financial services firms, how heavily regulated the financial system is, the presence of state-owned banks, whether the government influences allocation of credit, and

---

9. As a robustness check, we employ a different measure of state ownership than La Porta, Lopez-de-Silanes, and Shleifer (2002), which equals the percentage of government ownership (voting rights) of the assets of the ten largest banks in each country where ownership of each bank is weighted by the assets of that bank. Thus, the La Porta, Lopez-de-Silanes, and Shleifer (2002) measure does not define bank ownership in terms of voting rights greater than 50 percent. We get the same results with both measures.

whether banks are restricted from providing insurance and securities market services to clients. Higher values indicate fewer restrictions on banking freedoms. This aggregate Banking Freedom indicator also uses information from the regulatory restrictions, entry restrictions, and ownership indicators discussed previously. We include this for two reasons. First, debate exists on the impact of official restrictions on bank operations. On the one hand, fewer official impediments to bank operations and entry could stimulate efficiency and diversification, which promotes stability. On the other hand, greater banking freedom could induce destabilizing competition. We provide information on this debate. Second, official impediments to banking freedom could influence both concentration and fragility. Since our goal is to assess the independent link between concentration and crises, we test the robustness of the findings to controlling for banking freedom.

Economic freedom is an indicator of how a country's policies rank in terms of providing economic freedoms. It is a composite of ten indicators ranking policies in the areas of trade, government finances, government interventions, monetary policy, capital flows and foreign investment, banking and finance, wages and prices, property rights, regulation, and black market activity. We obtain these data from the Heritage Foundation and use an average over the period 1995–1997. Higher scores indicate policies more conducive to competition and economic freedom. Also, Banking Freedom is a subcomponent of Economic Freedom, which includes information on economic freedom beyond the banking industry. To the extent that freedoms allow banks to improve efficiency and to engage in different activities and diversify their risks, we expect an increased level of freedoms to reduce fragility. However, it is also true that greater freedoms allow banks to undertake greater risks, particularly if the underlying institutional environment and existing regulations and supervision distort risk-taking incentives. Thus, overall greater freedom may also lead to greater bank fragility. Thus, we (1) examine the relationship between economic freedom and crises and (2) assess the strength of the relationship between concentration and crises conditional on overall economic freedom.

KKZ composite is an index of the overall level of institutional development constructed by Kaufman, Kraay, and Zoido-Lobaton (1999). The underlying indicators are voice and accountability, government effectiveness, political stability, regulatory quality, rule of law, and control of corruption. This index is available for 1998. We expect better institutions to lead to reduced bank fragility, controlling for all other factors. Simple correlations indicate that the crisis dummy is negatively and significantly correlated with the two freedom indicators and the institutions variable. Countries with better institutions also tend to have more competitive banking systems with fewer regulatory restrictions. Thus, it is independently valuable to examine the relationship between institutional development and banking system stability. At the same time, we use *KKZ* Composite to gauge the strength of the independent relationship between concentration and crises.

5.2.2 Methodology

Methodologically, to estimate the crisis model we follow Cole and Gunther (1995), Gonzalez-Hermosillo, Pazarbasioglu, and Billings (1997), Demirgüç-Kunt (1989), and DD (1998, 2002) and use a logit probability model with standard errors that are robust to heteroskedasticity. Specifically, we estimate the probability that a systemic crisis will occur at a particular time in a particular country, assuming that this probability is a function of explanatory variables $(X[i, t])$. Let $P(i, t)$ denote a dummy variable that takes the value of 1 when a banking crisis occurs in country i and time t and a value of zero otherwise. β is a vector of n unknown coefficients and $F(\beta' X[i, t])$ is the cumulative probability distribution function evaluated at $\beta' X(i, t)$. Then, the log-likelihood function of the model is

$$\text{Ln } L = \sum_{t=1...T} \sum_{i=1...n} (P(i, t)\ln\{F[\beta'X(i, t)]\} + (1 - P[i, t])\ln\{1 - F[\beta'X(i, t)]\}.$$

We also conducted robustness tests using alternative estimation procedures. First, this core specification allows for heteroskedasticity but assumes that the errors are independent. We confirm the results, however, when allowing for clustering of the errors within countries, which requires that the error terms are independent across countries but not within countries. Second, the results hold when estimating a logit model with random country effects.

5.2.3 Results

The paper finds that crises are less likely in more concentrated banking systems using different measures of concentration and conditioning on different country characteristics. As shown in table 5.3, concentration always enters with a negative and significant coefficient. Regression 1 presents our baseline specification, where we exclude observations classified as crises after the first year of a multiyear banking crisis. Regressions 2 and 3 include crisis observations after the initial crisis year. In column 2, crisis observations following the initial year of a multiyear crisis are classified as crises.[10] In column 3, crisis observations after the initial year of a multiyear crisis are classified as noncrisis observations.[11] In all three regressions, concentration enters negatively and significantly.

The negative relationship between concentration and crises is robust to

10. This explains the entry of 202 crises in column 2 of table 5.3. When we include all of the years of each multiyear banking crisis, this adds an additional 155 crisis observations to the number reported in regressions 1 and 3.

11. In all three specifications, we include observations after the crisis is over. Thus, we include the switch from crisis to the noncrisis state.

Table 5.3 **Banking crisis and concentration**

	Specification					
	(1)	(2)	(3)	(4)	(5)	(6)
Real GDP growth	−0.163***	−0.088***	−0.136***	−0.306***	−0.164***	−0.164***
	(0.035)	(0.020)	(0.030)	(0.074)	(0.035)	(0.033)
Terms of trade change	−0.013	−0.008	−0.011	−0.034	−0.015	−0.012
	(0.012)	(0.007)	(0.012)	(0.024)	(0.013)	(0.012)
Real interest rate	0.010***	0.006**	0.002	0.009	0.010***	0.010***
	(0.004)	(0.003)	(0.004)	(0.009)	(0.004)	(0.004)
Inflation	0.009	0.006**	−0.002	−0.016	0.009	0.008
	(0.009)	(0.003)	(0.005)	(0.024)	(0.008)	(0.009)
M2/reserves	0.002*	0.002**	0.001	0.001	0.002*	0.002
	(0.001)	(0.001)	(0.001)	(0.002)	(0.001)	(0.001)
Depreciation	0.453	0.624	0.706	1.802	0.777	0.491
	(1.142)	(0.425)	(0.991)	(2.696)	(1.133)	(1.151)
Credit growth$_{t-2}$	0.014*	−0.001	0.012	0.028***	0.015*	0.014
	(0.009)	(0.005)	(0.009)	(0.012)	(0.009)	(0.009)
Real GDP per capita	−0.004*	−0.000***	−0.000*	−0.006*		−0.002
	(0.002)	(0.000)	(0.000)	(0.004)		(0.002)
Concentration	−1.946***	−1.479***	−1.696**	−3.744***	−1.607**	−1.845***
	(0.797)	(0.415)	(0.747)	(1.430)	(0.805)	(0.797)
G10 countries						1.011
						(2.332)
G10 countries × concentration						−3.287
						(5.091)
No. of crises	47	202	47	20	47	47
No. of observations	989	1,144	1,144	410	989	989
Percent crises correct	68	57	64	70	68	70
Percent correct	73	66	67	76	72	72
Model χ²	47.83***	75***		37.37***	40.34***	38.19***	46.38***

Sources: See table 5A.1 for sources.

Notes: The logit probability model estimated is Banking Crisis$_{[Country=j, \, Time=t]}$ = α + β₁ Real GDP growth$_{j,t}$ + β₂ Terms of trade change$_{j,t}$ + β₃ Real interest rate$_{j,t}$ + β₄ Inflation$_{j,t}$ + β₅ M2/reserves$_{j,t}$ + β₆ Depreciation$_{j,t}$ + β₇ Credit growth$_{j,t-2}$ + β₈ Real GDP per capita$_{j,t}$ + β₉ Average concentration$_{j,t}$ + β₁₀ G10 countries$_{j,t}$ + ε$_{j,t}$. The dependent variable is a crisis dummy that takes on the value of one if there is a systemic crisis and the value of zero otherwise. Growth is the rate of growth of real GDP. Real interest rate is the nominal interest rate minus the contemporaneous rate of inflation. Inflation is the rate of change of the GDP deflator. M2/reserves is the ratio of M2 to international reserves. Credit growth is the real growth of domestic credit, lagged two periods. Depreciation is the rate of change of the exchange rate. G10 country is a dummy variable that takes the value 1 for G10 countries and zero otherwise. Concentration is a measure of concentration in the banking industry, calculated as the fraction of assets held by the three largest banks in each country, averaged over the sample period. Banking freedom measures the relative openness of the banking and financial system. The sample period is 1980–1997. Specification (1) excludes all crisis observations after the initial year of crisis. Specification (2) includes the crisis periods (after the initial crisis year) as crisis observations. Specification (3) includes the crisis periods (after the initial crisis year) as non-crisis observations. In specification (4) Average Concentration is replaced by the Initial Concentration, and is restricted to the actual starting date and years following that date. Specification (5) omits real GDP per capita. Specification (6) includes G10 country dummy and its interaction with concentration. White's heteroskedasticity consistent standard errors are given in parentheses. See table 5A.1 for detailed variable definitions.

***Indicates significance at the 1 percent level.

**Indicates significance at the 5 percent level.

*Indicates significance at the 10 percent level.

alternative specifications and to controlling for reverse causality. If systemic crises reduce concentration, then it would be inappropriate to interpret our early results as implying that concentration reduces banking system fragility. Thus, in regression 4, we use the value of banking system concentration measured at the beginning of the sample period instead of concentration averaged over the period. Even when using initial concentration, however, we continue to find a negative relationship between concentration and crises. Regression 5 shows that the results do not depend on including or excluding real GDP per capita. Regression 6 assesses whether the results change if the country is a Group of Ten (G10) country. We see that country membership in the G10 does not alter the results on concentration. Further, the insignificant interaction between concentration and membership in G10 indicates that the relationship between concentration and systemic banking fragility does not vary between the G10 countries and the remainder of the sample.

Among the control variables in table 5.3, annual real GDP growth enters negatively and significantly throughout. This suggests that macroeconomic success reduces the likelihood of suffering a crisis. Or, to phrase this differently, recessions increase banking system fragility. The estimates also indicate that real interest rate enters positively, which confirms earlier research (DD 1999).

Furthermore, the economic impact of banking system concentration on the likelihood of a country suffering a systemic crisis is large. We evaluate the marginal impact of concentration on the probability of crisis at the mean values for all variables using regression 1 from table 5.3. The estimates indicate that a 1 standard deviation increase in concentration leads to a decrease in crisis probability of 1 percent. Since crisis probabilities at any point in time are quite low, with a mean value of 4 percent, this is a substantial reduction. We have recalculated the economic impact of a marginal increase in bank concentration when using a sample that includes the year after the initial year of the crisis. Using this larger sample, we find an even larger economic impact of concentration on crises than in the core regression presented in table 5.3.

This paper's findings hold when allowing for a potential nonlinear relationship between concentration and crises. First, we added a simple quadratic term and found no evidence of a nonlinear relationship. Next, we estimated piecewise regressions, where concentration was broken into (a) quintiles and then (b) deciles. The results indicate that the stabilizing effect of concentration becomes significant after the first quintile (second decile), where the quintile and decile analyses identify consistent cutoffs. The data indicate that there is a statistically significant, negative relationship between concentration and banking system fragility for levels of concentration above 35 percent, and the marginal impact of a change in concentration does not vary significantly beyond this 35 percent cutoff. This cutoff is low, considering that the sample mean value of national banking system concentration is 72 percent. There is never a positive relationship between concentration and fragility. Third, we examine whether concentration has different effects in different institutional settings by interacting concentration and our measures of institutional development (Economic Freedom and KKZ composite). Again, this did not change the result of a negative relationship between bank concentration and the probability of suffering a systemic crisis.

The negative relationship between crises and concentration also holds when using different samples of countries. Specifically, we excluded all countries with populations less than 1 million, less than 10 million, and less than 20 million, respectively. The coefficient on concentration remains negative and significant across these three different samples of countries. Next, we excluded all sub-Saharan African countries, since they tend to have very high bank concentration ratios, and we eliminated the G10 countries because their high level of institutional development may not be captured appropriately with the control variables. Again, these two different samples yield the same results. Finally, we excluded a few country-year data points where the data seem to be mismeasured, because the values are extraordinarily different from the country's average value over the sample.[12] The results do not change.

In sum, these results are consistent with the concentration-stability theory's argument that banking systems characterized by a few large banks are more stable than less concentrated banking markets. There is certainly no evidence that banking system concentration increases banking sector fragility. Furthermore, the inverse relationship between banking system concentration and the likelihood of suffering a systemic crisis holds when allowing for possible nonlinear links between concentration and fragility and when using different samples of countries. Next, we assess the robustness of these results to conditioning on additional country-specific traits.

5.2.4 Additional Sensitivity Tests and Discussion

Additional Country Level Controls

In table 5.4, we confirm the findings on the relationship between banking sector concentration and systemic crises when controlling for (1) moral hazard associated with deposit insurance, (2) different bank regulations, (3) the ownership of banks, and (4) general indicators of banking freedom, economic freedom, and institutional development. The results hold when controlling for moral hazard, fraction of entry applications denied, activity

---

12. Specifically, we eliminate Côte d'Ivoire (1993) because their M2/reserves values are very different for that year. Similarly, in these outlier tests, we exclude Peru (1991) because its inflation and real interest rate values are so different from other years.

Table 5.4   Banking crisis, regulation, and concentration

	(1)	(2)	(3)	(4)	(5)	(6)	(7)	(8)	(9)	(10)	(11)
Concentration	-1.467**	-2.556*	-2.285***	-2.472***	-2.847***	-2.533**	-2.796***	-2.524***	-1.953***	-1.930***	-1.881***
	(0.565)	(1.552)	(0.939)	(1.060)	(1.142)	(1.096)	(1.091)	(1.083)	(0.806)	(0.809)	(0.769)
Moral hazard	0.037										
	(0.075)										
Fraction of entry denied		1.885***									
		(0.737)									
Activity restrictions			0.166**								
			(0.072)								
Official Supervisory Power				-0.021							
				(0.166)							
Required reserves					0.016						
					(0.016)						
Capital regulatory index						-0.079					
						(0.129)					
State ownership							0.015*				
							(0.008)				
Foreign ownership								-0.005			
								(0.008)			
Banking freedom									-0.506***		
									(0.165)		
Economic freedom										-0.513***	
										(0.225)	
KKZ_composite											-0.439**
											(0.201)

No. of crises	47	21	34	34	27	33	32	31	47	47	47
No. of observations	989	583	767	767	572	755	686	609	955	955	989
Percent crises correct	66	62	68	62	63	61	66	68	68	66	68
Percent correct	71	81	79	78	77	79	74	73	70	70	72
Model ^{2}	37.93***	29.34***	38.21***	38***	30.46***	37.62***	30.97***	34.15***	52.41***	47.58***	49.59***

Source: See table 5A.1 for sources.

Notes: The logit probability model estimated is Banking Crisis$_{[Country=j, Time=t]} = \alpha + \beta_1$ Real GDP growth$_{j,t} + \beta_2$ Terms of trade change$_{j,t} + \beta_3$ Real interest rate$_{j,t} + \beta_4$ Inflation$_{j,t} + \beta_5$ M2/reserves$_{j,t} + \beta_6$ Depreciation$_{j,t} + \beta_7$ Credit growth$_{j,t-2} + \beta_8$ Concentration$_{j,t} + \beta_9$ Regulatory measure$_{j,t} + \varepsilon_{j,t}$. The dependent variable is a crisis dummy that takes on the value of one if there is a systemic and the value of zero otherwise. Growth is the growth rate of real GDP. Real interest rate is the nominal interest rate minus the inflation rate. Inflation is the rate of change of the GDP deflator. M2/reserves is the ratio of M2 to international reserves. Credit growth is the real growth of domestic credit, lagged two periods. Depreciation is the rate of change of the exchange rate. Concentration equals the fraction of assets held by the three largest banks in each country, averaged over the sample period. Moral Hazard is an aggregate index of moral hazard associated with variations in deposit insurance design features. Fraction of entry denied measures the number of entry applications denied as a fraction of the total received. Activity restrictions captures bank's ability to engage in business of securities underwriting, insurance underwriting and selling, and in real estate investment, management, and development. Official Supervisory Power is an index of the power of supervisory agency to enforce prudential regulations on banks. Required reserves is the percentage of deposits regulators require banks to hold as reserves. Capital regulatory index is a summary measure of capital stringency. State ownership is the percentage of banking system's assets in banks that are 50 percent or more government owned. Foreign ownership is the percentage of banking system's assets in banks that are 50 percent or more foreign owned. Banking freedom is an indicator of relative openness of banking and financial system, while economic freedom is a composite of ten institutional factors determining economic freedom. KKZ composite is an aggregate measure of six governance indicators. White's heteroskedasticity consistent standard errors are given in parentheses. The sample period is 1980–1997. See table 5A.1 for detailed variable definitions

***Indicates significance at the 1 percent level.

**Indicates significance at the 5 percent level.

*Indicates significance at the 10 percent level.

restrictions, official supervisory power, required reserves, and the capital regulatory index (regressions 1–6). The significance level on concentration falls to a 10 percent level when including fraction of entry applications denied, but data limitations on fraction of entry applications denied cuts the sample from 989 to 583 observations. Furthermore, concentration remains negatively associated with crises at the 1 percent significance level when controlling for state or foreign ownership of banks (regressions 7 and 8). In terms of broad measures such as banking freedom or general indicators of economic freedom and institutional development (KKZ composite), concentration continues to enter the crisis regressions negatively and significantly at the 1 percent level (regression 9–11). The regressions in table 5.4 do not include GDP per capita because (1) the regulatory/institutional variables are highly correlated with the level of development and (2) GDP per capita is often used to proxy for institutional development. However, including GDP per capita in table 5.4 does not change the conclusions on concentration.

Beyond concentration, the table 5.4 results indicate that tighter entry restrictions and more severe regulatory restrictions on bank activities boost bank fragility. These are consistent with the results obtained by Barth, Caprio, and Levine (2004), who examine the impact of entry restrictions and regulatory restrictions on bank activities on crises in a purely cross-country investigation that does not control for bank concentration. A higher fraction of entry applications denied—a proxy for tighter entry regulations—leads to higher levels of fragility in the banking system. This is consistent with the argument that restricted entry reduces the efficiency of the banking system, also making it more vulnerable to external shocks. Similarly, we find that restrictions on bank activities increase crisis probabilities. This result indicates that overall these restrictions prevent banks from diversifying outside their traditional business, reducing their ability to reduce the riskiness of their portfolios.

Overall, the results do not provide support for Basel II's emphasis on capital regulations and more stringent regulations. We do not find that stricter capital regulations or greater official supervisory power lowers the probability that a country will suffer a systemic crisis. While it is natural and appropriate to question these results because of the timing issues emphasized earlier, we are unaware of cross-country research that finds that banking system stability is enhanced by countries adopting official supervisory and regulatory regimes that impose stricter capital regulations or more stringent prudential regulations. Indeed, a growing body of evidence suggests that strengthening official supervisory power can actually increase corruption in lending and reduce banking system efficiency (Barth, Caprio, and Levine 2006; Beck, Demirgüç-Kunt, and Levine 2006; Demirgüç-Kunt, Laeven, and Levine 2004). Finally, confirming earlier research, we also see that state ownership is associated with greater fragility, albeit significant only at 10 percent (Caprio and Martinez-Peria 2000).

Furthermore, the results in table 5.4 suggest that openness, competition, and institutional development foster greater banking system stability. Countries with greater freedoms in banking (banking freedom) and generally more competitive economic systems (economic freedom) are less likely to experience banking crises (regressions 9 and 10). This finding suggests that concentration is not simply proxying for the degree of competition in the banking industry. Better institutional environment is also associated with a lower probability of systemic crisis (regression 11). The evidence is consistent with theories that emphasize the stabilizing effects of openness and competition, but inconsistent with the many models that stress the destabilizing effects from competition.[13]

Costs of Banking Crises

We also assessed whether countries with concentrated banking systems have bigger, more costly banking crises. If (1) concentrated banking systems are more likely to have too-big-to-fail policies and (2) too-big-to-fail policies induce greater risk-taking and (3) too-big-too fail policies can operate for only some fixed period of time, then this suggests that crises will be larger, though less frequent, in concentrated banking systems. If this were the case, then our findings that concentration is associated with a lower probability of suffering a systemic crisis may provide a misleading impression of the concentration-stability relationship.

Thus, in table 5.5, we examine the relationship between banking system concentration and the costs of banking crises. To include countries that suffered no crises in the sample, we use a Tobit model, where zero implies that the country did not experience a banking crisis. We use three different measures of banking crisis costs.

As shown in table 5.5, we find no evidence for the contention that more concentrated banking systems have more costly crises. Concentration does not enter significantly at the 5 percent level in any of the regressions. It enters with a negative coefficient across the different cost measures. Given the lack of a robust relationship, however, we do not draw the conclusion that concentration reduces both the likelihood and the size of crises.

5.3   Why Is Concentration Stabilizing?
Additional Evidence from Crisis Data

Although the finding of a negative relationship between banking system concentration and the likelihood of suffering a systemic crisis is consistent

---

13. Boyd and De Nicoló (2005) stress that competition exerts a stabilizing impact on banks because more competitive banks charge lower interest rates to firms and these lower rates reduce the likelihood of default. This prediction is consistent with our results. However, Boyd and De Nicoló (2005) use bank concentration as an indicator of bank competition. Thus, they stress that concentration will exert a destabilizing impact on banks, which is inconsistent with our results.

Table 5.5   Banking crisis and concentration: Cost of crises

	Specification		
	(1)	(2)	(3)
Real GDP growth	3.821***	3.614***	1.553**
	(0.811)	(0.857)	(0.814)
Terms of trade change	−0.929*	−0.832	0.047
	(0.489)	(0.593)	(0.444)
Real interest rate	0.235	0.591**	−0.139
	(0.191)	(0.291)	(0.257)
Inflation	1.050***	1.198***	0.316
	(0.196)	(0.272)	(0.225)
M2/reserves	0.144***	0.080**	0.126***
	(0.029)	(0.036)	(0.029)
Depreciation	−57.818***	−141.172***	−26.592
	(16.742)	(32.809)	(21.046)
Credit growth$_{t-2}$	0.217	0.185	0.087
	(0.141)	(0.155)	(0.178)
Real GDP per capita	0.000**	0.000	−0.000
	(0.000)	(0.000)	(0.000)
Moral hazard index	0.408	0.764	1.343*
	(0.887)	(0.912)	(0.820)
Concentration	−8.261	−15.006*	−2.269
	(7.499)	(9.207)	(9.355)
No. of observations	47	49	69

Notes: The Tobit model estimated takes the form: Cost of crisis$_{[Country=j]}$ = α + β_1 Real GDP growth$_j$ + β_2 Terms of trade change$_j$ + β_3 Real interest rate$_j$ + β_4 Inflation$_j$ + β_5M2/reserves$_j$ + β_6Depreciation$_j$ + β_7 Credit growth$_j$ + β_8 Moral hazard index$_j$ + β_9 Concentration$_j$ + ε_j. The dependent variables capture the fiscal cost of crisis. In specification (1) we focus on one variation of the Klingebiel-Honohan fiscal cost measure, while in specifications (2) focus is on the second variation of the Klingebiel-Honohan fiscal cost measure. Specification (3) examines the Boyd and Smith measure of cost of crisis. Growth is the rate of growth of real GDP. Real interest rate is the nominal interest rate minus the contemporaneous rate of inflation. Inflation is the rate of change of the GDP deflator. M2/reserves is the ratio of M2 to international reserves. Depreciation is the rate of change of the exchange rate. Credit growth is the real growth of domestic credit, lagged two periods. Moral hazard is an aggregate index of moral hazard associated with varying deposit insurance schemes. Concentration is a measure of concentration in the banking industry, calculated as the fraction of assets held by the three largest banks in each country, averaged over the sample period. White's heteroskedasticity-consistent standard errors are given in parentheses. Detailed variable definitions and sources are given in the data appendix.

***Indicates significance at the 1 percent level.

**Indicates significance at the 5 percent level.

*Indicates significance at the 10 percent level.

with the concentration-stability view (tables 5.3 and 5.4), the results do not distinguish among possible explanations of this finding. Why is concentration stabilizing? This section explores the validity of different explanations for why bank concentration lowers banking system fragility.

5.3.1   Is It Market Power and Bank Profits?

One possible argument is that the level of bank concentration proxies for the degree of competition in the banking industry. According to this market power view, powerful banks (either directly or through policymakers) restrict competition, which boosts bank profits, lowers incentives for risk taking, and thus reduces systemic risk. Thus, the finding of a negative relationship between banking system concentration and systemic crises is consistent with the view that banking sector concentration increases banking system stability by reducing the openness and competitiveness of the banking industry.

In contrast to this market power explanation of how concentration promotes banking system stability, however, note that concentration remains negatively associated with crises even when controlling for regulatory restrictions on bank activities and measures of the openness and competitiveness of the banking industry and the economy more generally. Thus, to the extent that these variables adequately control for competition, the findings suggest that something else besides market power is driving the negative relationship between bank concentration and bank fragility.

The findings on bank regulations, banking freedom, economic freedom, and institutional development also run counter to the view that competition intensifies fragility. Restrictions on competition and openness—such as regulatory impediments to the entry of new banks, or regulatory barriers to banks engaging in nonlending services, or general indicators of the openness of the banking industry or the overall economy—do not reduce the probability of suffering a systemic banking crisis (table 5.4). Thus, the findings that (1) concentration lowers banking system fragility and (2) low competition raises banking system fragility imply that concentration is not proxying for the degree of competition in the banking industry.

However, the measures of bank regulation, bank freedom, economic freedom, and institutional development may not sufficiently control for competition in banking. Thus, given the difficulty in adequately controlling for the competitive environment using regulatory indicators, some may view the table 5.4 results as too weak to discard the market power explanation of why concentration is stabilizing.

5.3.2   Is It Diversification?

Next, consider the argument that banks in more concentrated banking systems are more diversified than banking systems composed of many small banks. If this argument is correct and if we include good measures of bank diversification in the systemic crises regressions, then this should drive out the significance of bank concentration.

To proxy for the diversification channel, we use three measures. First, we use *mean bank size,* which equals total bank assets divided by the number of banks.[14] The presumption is that larger banks tend to be more diversified. While clearly problematic, bank-level data on each bank's asset holdings are impossible to obtain. So, we use mean bank size in trying to assess why concentration is associated with lower levels of banking system fragility. If mean bank size does not drive out the significance of concentration, this weakens the argument that concentrated banking systems have larger, better-diversified banks than less concentrated banking systems with smaller banks. However, since bank size does not directly measure diversification, finding that mean bank size drives out concentration provides only suggestive support for the diversification argument.

Second, we include an indicator of regulatory restrictions on banks' ability to diversify risk abroad. Specifically, *no foreign loans* equals 1 if banks are prohibited from making foreign loans, and 0 otherwise. In many countries, it may be impossible for banks to sufficiently diversify their asset holding domestically. Thus, restrictions on investing abroad may doom domestic banks to holding excessively risky assets. Indeed, countries with both small banks and regulatory restrictions on those banks' lending abroad may have especially unstable banks. Again, if we control for these measures of diversification and they drive out the significance of concentration in the systemic crisis regressions, then this provides smoking gun evidence that concentration is associated with banking system stability because concentration is associated with more diversified banks.

A third potential indicator of bank diversification is the size of the economy. The presumption, albeit questionable, is that larger economies are more diversified and therefore offer banks easier means to hold diversified loan portfolios. Thus, we include the level of GDP in attempting to dissect the negative relationship between concentration and crises.[15]

The results in table 5.6 provide suggestive support for the view that concentrated banking systems are composed of bigger, more diversified banks that are hence less prone to systemic failure. As the results in table 5.6 show, the significance of the concentration coefficient drops to 10 percent when we control for bank size and completely disappears when we control for the size of the economy (regressions 1 and 2). These findings are consistent with the view that part of the reason that concentration enhances stability is that concentrated systems are composed of bigger, better-diversified banks. Regression 3 indicates that including no foreign loans does not al-

---

14. Using the mean bank size of the largest three banks does not change our results.
15. Replacing GDP by M2 to control for the size of the financial system does not change our results.

Table 5.6   **Banking crisis and concentration: Diversification versus ease of supervision**

	(1)	(2)	(3)	(4)	(5)	(6)	(7)
Concentration	−1.511*	−1.379	−2.381**	−1.653	−2.234*	−2.111**	−3.576**
	(0.854)	(0.860)	(1.095)	(1.119)	(1.162)	(1.061)	(1.651)
Mean bank size	0.004			0.007			
	(0.005)			(0.005)			
No foreign loans			0.153	−0.350			
			(0.635)	(0.617)			
No foreign loans × bank size				0.184***			
				(0.068)			
GDP ($)		0.0003					
		(0.0002)					
No. of banks					0.008	0.003	
					(0.014)	(0.013)	
Activity Restrictions						0.141	
						(0.103)	
Cashflow							0.030**
							(0.014)
No. of crises	47	47	34	34	34	34	29
No. of observations	988	989	767	767	767	767	527
Percent of crises correct	68	72	65	62	62	68	72
Percent correct	73	73	79	79	79	79	78
Model χ^2	48.36***	48.79***	49.43***	43.90***	43.90***	43.43***	48.31***

Source: See table 5A.1 for sources.

Notes: The logit probability model estimated is Banking Crisis$_{[Country=j, Time=t]}$ = α + β_1 Real GDP growth$_{j,t}$ + β_2 Terms of trade change$_{j,t}$ + β_3 Real interest rate$_{j,t}$ + β_4 Inflation$_{j,t}$ + β_5M2/reserves$_{j,t}$ + β_6Depreciation$_{j,t}$ + β_7 Credit growth$_{j,t-2}$ + β_8 Real GDP per capita$_{j,t}$ + β_9 Moral hazard index$_{j,t}$ + β_{10} Concentration$_{j,t}$ + β_{11} Mean Bank Size$_{j,t}$ + β_{12} No foreign loans$_{j,t}$ + β_{13} GDP$_{j,t}$ + β_{14} No. of Banks$_{j,t}$ + β_{15} Activity Restrictions$_{j,t}$ + β_{16} Cashflow rights$_{j,t}$ + $\varepsilon_{j,t}$. The dependent variable is a crisis dummy that takes on the value of one if there is a systemic crisis and the value of zero otherwise. Growth is the rate of growth of real GDP. Real interest rate is the nominal interest rate minus the contemporaneous rate of inflation. Inflation is the rate of change of the GDP deflator. M2/reserves is the ratio of M2 to international reserves. Credit growth is the real growth of domestic credit, lagged two periods. Depreciation is the rate of change of the exchange rate. Moral hazard is an aggregate index of moral hazard associated with varying deposit insurance schemes. Concentration is a measure of concentration in the banking industry, calculated as the fraction of assets held by the three largest banks in each country, averaged over the sample period. The sample period is 1980–1997. Mean bank size is given by average bank asset size (in billions of U.S. dollars). No foreign loans takes the value one if banks are prohibited from investing abroad and 0 otherwise. GDP is real GDP in billions of US$. Number of banks is given in hundreds and activity restrictions captures bank's ability to engage in business of securities underwriting, insurance underwriting and selling, and in real estate investment, management, and development. Both are from Barth, Caprio, and Levine (2001a, 2001b) database. Cashflow is the fraction of a bank's total cash-flow rights held by each bank's main owner, averaged across each country's banks (Caprio, Laeven, and Levine 2003). White's heteroskedasticity consistent standard errors are given in parentheses. See table 5A.1 for detailed variable definitions.

***Indicates significance at the 1 percent level.
**Indicates significance at the 5 percent level.
*Indicates significance at the 10 percent level.

ter the findings on banking system concentration. In regression 4, the concentration effect becomes completely insignificant when including the (1) mean bank size, (2) no foreign loans, and (3) the interaction term between bank size and no foreign loans. The result in column 4 indicates that countries with larger banks become significantly more prone to systemic crises if they prohibit their banks from investing abroad. This finding on the interaction between bank size and regulatory restrictions on foreign loans runs counter to our prediction that restrictions on foreign lending would be particularly destabilizing for small (presumably less diversified) banks. Nevertheless, while these measures of diversification are highly imperfect, including these proxies for diversification drives out the significance of banking system concentration and suggests that the diversification explanation has some merit.

5.3.3   Is It Easier Monitoring?

A third argument for why concentration is stabilizing is that (1) concentrated banking systems tend to have a few large banks and (2) a few large banks are easier to monitor than many small ones. As earlier, if this easier monitoring argument is correct and if we include good measures of monitoring in the crisis regressions, then this should drive out the significance of bank concentration. Of course, there are countervailing views. Large banks may be substantially more complex than small banks. So, supervision may be more difficult with a few complex banks than with a higher number of simple banks.[16]

We use three measures to attempt to capture empirically the ease of monitoring banks. First, we use the *number of banks,* which equals the number of banks in the economy. The easier monitoring argument relies on the presumption that concentrated banking systems have a few large banks, and this is crucial in explaining better monitoring and greater banking system stability. Second, *activity restrictions* equals regulatory restrictions on the ability of banks to engage in securities market, insurance, and real estate activities as well as restrictions on banks owning nonfinancial firms. The presumption is that greater regulatory restrictions will make it easier to monitor banks. So, to the extent that regulatory restrictions are correlated with bank concentration, this would help account for the negative relationship between concentration and systemic crises. Third, *cashflow* is the fraction of a bank's total cash-flow rights held by each bank's main owner, averaged across each country's banks. As suggested by La Porta et al. (1999) and La Porta, Lopez-de-Silanes, and Shleifer (2002), countries where laws and regulations are ineffective at protecting the rights of small shareholders will tend to have corporations that do not rely on small shareholders to exert corporate control, and instead have concentrated cash-flow rights to induce the main owner to exert sound corporate governance. In terms of banks, Caprio, Laeven, and Levine (2003) show

---

16. As pointed out to us by Mark Carey and René Stulz, there is another dimension to this monitoring argument. If monitoring skills are scarce and there are economies of scope in monitoring, then concentrated banking systems may facilitate monitoring. However, the scarcity of monitoring skills, and hence the benefits of concentration, may be different across countries.

that a bank's major owner tends to have higher cash-flow rights in countries where the institutions underlying monitoring of banks are weak, such as weak shareholder protection laws or ineffective bank supervision and regulation. These weak institutions discourage diffuse ownership and produce concentrated ownership of banks. Thus, we use each country's average cash-flow rights across banks as an additional proxy of each country's monitoring regime. If including cash-flow rights eliminates the significance of concentration, concerns would naturally arise about the endogeneity of cash-flow rights. But if including cash-flow rights does not alter the results on concentration, then this simply represents an additional, if flawed, robustness check.

The results presented in table 5.6 do not provide support for the easier monitoring view of why concentration reduces the likelihood of suffering a systemic crisis. Including the number of banks reduces the significance of concentration to 10 percent, but the significance level is restored once we also control for activity restrictions. Including cash-flows does not alter the findings on concentration either. Number of banks and activity restrictions do not enter the crises regressions significantly. Cash-flow enters positively, which is consistent with the view that in countries with weak legal and corporate governance institutions and ineffective bank supervision and regulation the ownership structure adjusts such that cash-flow becomes concentrated in order to boost monitoring incentives. However, the resultant outcome is still associated with a higher likelihood of suffering a crisis. For the purposes of this paper, the point is that including proxies for the monitoring regime does not alter the results on concentration significantly. This suggests, to the extent that these are reasonable proxies, that concentration is not a simple proxy for easier monitoring.

5.4 Conclusions

To summarize, using a cross-country, time series panel of data on systemic banking crises, we find that greater bank concentration is associated with a lower likelihood of suffering a crisis. We never find that concentration increases fragility. While subject to the qualifications stressed in the introduction and throughout the paper, the negative relationship between concentration and crises is robust to including various control variables, including indicators of the macroeconomic environment, the international environment, the domestic banking environment, bank supervisory and regulatory policies, and indexes of overall economic freedom and institutional development. Furthermore, reverse causality does not seem to be driving the concentration-stability findings. Thus, the data on systemic crises are more consistent with the concentration-stability view than with the concentration-fragility view.

In searching for the mechanisms underlying the concentration-stability result, we find no support for the view that banking system concentration is a proxy for a less competitive banking environment. We draw this conclusion for two reasons. First, when we include regulatory and institutional measures of the degree of competition in banking and the overall economy, we find that crises are less—not more—likely in competitive regulatory and institutional environments. Second, even when we control for these regulatory and institutional measures of the degree of competition, we continue to find that concentration is negatively associated with systemic crises. To the extent that we have good measures of the competitive environment, these findings suggest that banking system concentration is a proxy for something else besides banking industry competition.

Furthermore, we find suggestive support that concentrated banking systems have more diversified banks, but not evidence that concentrated banking systems with a few large banks are easier to monitor and hence more stable than less concentrated banking systems. On ease of monitoring, none of our measures of the ease of monitoring enters significantly, and including them in the analyses did not alter the coefficient on bank concentration. On diversification, the data indicate that part of the reason concentrated banking systems lower the probability of suffering a systemic crisis is that concentrated banking systems tend to have larger, better-diversified banks with a correspondingly lower probability of failure. We draw this tentative conclusion because the concentration-crisis link weakens appreciably when we include proxies for diversification. We emphasize, however, that these proxies are aggregate indicators and do not directly measure individual bank asset diversification, and hence we view these results as suggestive and hope that they stimulate cross-country, bank-level research into this important policy issue.

Appendix

Table 5A.1

Variable	Definition	Source
Banking crisis	Dummy takes on value of 1 during episodes identified as a systematic banking crises	Demirgüç-Kunt and Detragiache (2001)
Real GDP growth	Rate of growth of real GDP	WDI (World Bank)
Terms of trade change	Change in the terms of trade	WDI (World Bank)
Real interest rate	Nominal interest rate minus the contemporaneous rate of inflation	IFS (IMF)
Inflation	Rate of change of GDP deflator	IFS (IMF)
M2/reserves	Ratio of M2 to international reserves	IFS (IMF)
Depreciation	Rate of depreciation	IFS (IMF)
Credit growth	Rate of growth of real domestic credit to the private sector	IFS line 32d divided by GDP deflator
GDP/CAP	Real GDP per capita	WDI (World Bank)
GDP	Real GDP in billions of U.S. dollars	WDI (World Bank)
Moral hazard index	Principal component indicator measuring the generosity of deposit insurance, based on coinsurance, coverage of foreign currency and interbank deposits, type and source of funding, management, membership, and level of explicit coverage	DD (2002)
Concentration	Degree of concentration in the banking industry, calculated as the fraction of assets held by the three largest banks. Averaged over the 1988–1997 period.	Beck, Demirgüç-Kunt, and Levine (2000)—Financial Structures Database
Initial Concentration	Initial degree of concentration in the banking industry	BankScope database
Mean Bank Size	Total banking assets divided by number of banks	BankScope database

continued

Table 5A.1   (continued)

Variable	Definition	Source
No Foreign Loans	Survey question 7.2 asks if banks are prohibited from making loans abroad (yes = 1, no = 0)	Barth, Caprio, and Levine (2001a, 2001b)—Survey of Bank Regulation and Supervision
No. of Banks	Number of banks (in hundreds)	Barth, Caprio, and Levine (2001a, 2001b)—Survey of Bank Regulation and Supervision
Banking Freedom	Indicator of relative openness of banking and financial system: specifically, whether the foreign banks and financial services firms are able to operate freely, how difficult it is to open domestic banks and other financial services firms, how heavily regulated the financial system is, the presence of state-owned banks, whether the government influences allocation of credit, and whether banks are free to provide customers with insurance and invest in securities (and vice versa). The index ranges in value from 1 (very low—banks are primitive) to 5 (very high—few restrictions). Averaged over 1995–1997 period.	Index of Economic Freedom (Heritage Foundation)
Fraction of entry denied	Number of entry applications denied as a fraction of the number of applications received from domestic and foreign entities	Barth, Caprio, and Levine (2001a, 2001b)—Survey of Bank Regulation and Supervision
Activity restrictions	Indicator of bank's ability to engage in business of securities underwriting, insurance underwriting and selling, and in real estate investment, management, and development	Barth, Caprio, and Levine (2001a, 2001b)—Survey of Bank Regulation and Supervision
Required reserves	Ratio of reserves required to be held by banks	Barth, Caprio, and Levine (2001a, 2001b)—Survey of Bank Regulation and Supervision
Capital regulatory index	Summary measure of capital stringency: sum of overall and initial capital stringency. Higher values indicate greater stringency	Barth, Caprio, and Levine (2001a, 2001b)—Survey of Bank Regulation and Supervision
Official Supervisory Power	Principal component indicator of fourteen dummy variables: 1. Does the supervisory agency have the right to meet with external auditors to discuss their report without the approval of the bank? 2. Are auditors required by	Barth, Caprio, and Levine (2001a, 2001b)—Survey of Bank Regulation and Supervision

law to communicate directly to the supervisory agency any presumed involvement of bank directors or senior managers in elicit activities, fraud, or insider abuse? 3. Can supervisors take legal action against external auditors for negligence? 4. Can the supervisory authority force a bank to change its internal organizational structure? 5. Are off–balance sheet items disclosed to supervisors? 6. Can the supervisory agency order the bank's directors or management to constitute provisions to cover actual or potential losses? 7. Can the supervisory agency suspend the directors' decision to distribute: (a) dividends? (b) bonuses? (c) management fees? 8. Can the supervisory agency legally declare—such that this declaration supersedes the rights of bank shareholders—that a bank is insolvent? 9. Does the banking law give authority to the supervisory agency to intervene; that is, suspend some or all ownership rights—in a problem bank? 10. Regarding bank restructuring and reorganization, can the supervisory agency or any other government agency do the following: (a) supersede shareholder rights? (b) remove and replace management? (c) remove and replace directors?

State ownership	Percentage of banking system's assets in banks that are 50% or more government owned	Barth, Caprio, and Levine (2001a, 2001b)—Survey of Bank Regulation and Supervision
Foreign ownership	Percentage of banking system's assets in banks that are 50% or more foreign owned	Barth, Caprio, and Levine (2001a, 2001b)—Survey of Bank Regulation and Supervision
Economic freedom	Composite of ten institutional factors determining economic freedom: trade policy, fiscal burden of government, government intervention in the economy, monetary policy, capital flows and foreign investment, banking and finance, wages and prices, property rights, regulation, and black market activity. Individual factors are weighted equally to determine overall score of economic freedom. A high score signifies an institutional or consistent set of policies that are most conducive to economic freedom, while a score close to 1 signifies a set of policies that are least conducive. Averaged over 1995–1997 period.	Index of Economic Freedom (Heritage Foundation)

continued

Table 5A.1   (continued)

Variable	Definition	Source
KKZ composite	Composite of six governance indicators (1998 data): voice and accountability, political stability, government effectiveness, regulatory quality, rule of law, and corruption. Individual factors are weighted equally to determine overall score of economic freedom. Higher values correspond to better governance outcomes.	Kaufman and Kray (1999)
G10 countries	Dummy accounting for G10 country	
Concentration	Degree of concentration in the banking industry, calculated as the fraction of assets held by the three largest banks. Averaged over the 1994–2001 period.	Bankscope database
Banking Freedom	Indicator of relative openness of banking and financial system: specifically, whether the foreign banks and financial services firms are able to operate freely, how difficult it is to open domestic banks and other financial services firms, how heavily regulated the financial system is, the presence of state-owned banks, whether the government influences allocation of credit, and whether banks are free to provide customers with insurance and invest in securities (and vice versa). The index ranges in value from 1 (very low—banks are primitive) to 5 (very high—few restrictions). Averaged over 1994–2001 period.	Index of Economic Freedom (Heritage Foundation), 2003
Cashflow	Fraction of a bank's total cash-flow rights held by each bank's main owner, averaged across each country's banks	Caprio, Laeven, and Levine (2004)

Source: Kaufman, Kraay, and Zoido-Lobaton (1999).

References

Allen, Franklin. 1990. The market for information and the origin of financial intermediation. *Journal of Financial Intermediation* 1:3–30.

Allen, Franklin, and Douglas Gale. 2000. *Comparing financial systems.* Cambridge, MA, and London: MIT Press.

———. 2003. Competition and financial stability. *Journal of Money, Credit, and Banking* 36 (3 pt. 2): 433–80.

Bank for International Settlement. 2001. The banking industry in the emerging market economies: Competition, consolidation, and systemic stability. BIS Paper no. 4. Basel, Switzerland: Bank for International Settlement.

Barth, James R., Gerard Caprio, Jr., and Ross Levine. 2001a. Banking systems around the globe: Do regulation and ownership affect performance and stability? In *Financial supervision and regulation: What works and what doesn't,* ed. F. Mishkin, 31–88. Chicago: University of Chicago Press.

———. 2001b. The regulation and supervision of banks around the world: A new database. In *Brooking-Wharton Papers on Financial Services,* ed. R. E. Litan and R. Herring, 183–250. Washington, DC: Brookings Institution.

———. 2004. Bank supervision and regulation: What works best? *Journal of Financial Intermediation* 13:205–48.

———. 2006. *Rethinking bank supervision and regulation: Until angels govern.* Cambridge: Cambridge University Press.

Beck, Thorsten, Asli Demirgüç-Kunt, and Ross Levine. 2006. Forthcoming. Bank supervision and corruption in lending. *Journal of Monetary Economics.*

Besanko, D., and Anjan V. Thakor. 1993. Relationship banking, deposit insurance and bank portfolio. In *Capital markets and financial intermediation,* ed. C. Mayer and X. Vives, 292–318. Cambridge: Cambridge University Press.

Boot, A. W., and S. Greenbaum. 1993. Bank regulation, reputation, and rents: Theory and policy implications. In *Capital markets and financial intermediation,* ed. C. Mayer and X. Vives, 262–85. Cambridge: Cambridge University Press.

Boyd, John H., and Gianni De Nicoló. 2005. The theory of bank risk-taking and competition revisited. *Journal of Finance* 60 (3): 1329–43.

Boyd, John H., and Edward C. Prescott. 1986. Financial intermediary-coalitions. *Journal of Economic Theory* 38:211–32.

Boyd, John H., and David E. Runkle. 1993. Size and performance of banking firms: Testing the predictions of theory. *Journal of Monetary Economics* 31:47–67.

Calomiris, Charles W. 2000. *U.S. bank deregulation in historical perspective.* Cambridge: Cambridge University Press.

Calomiris, Charles W., and Joseph R. Mason. 2000. Causes of bank distress during the Great Depression. NBER Working Paper no. 7919. Cambridge, MA: National Bureau of Economic Research.

Caprio, Gerard, Jr., and Daniela Klingebiel. 1999. Episodes of systematic and borderline financial distress. Unpublished manuscript. The World Bank.

Caprio, Gerard, Jr., Luc Laeven, and Ross Levine. 2003. Governance and bank valuation. Working Paper no. 10158. Cambridge, MA: National Bureau of Economic Research.

Caprio, Gerard, Jr., and Maria Soledad Martinez-Peria. 2000. Avoiding disaster: Policies to reduce the risk of banking crises. ECES discussion paper. Cairo: Egyptian Center for Economic Studies.

Carkovic, Maria, and Ross Levine. 2002. Finance and growth: New evidence and policy analyses for Chile. In *Economic growth: Sources, trends, and cycles,* ed. N. Loayza and R. Soto, 343–76. Santiago: Central Bank of Chile.

Chan, Yuk-Shee, Stuart Greenbaum, and Anjan Thakor. 1992. Is fairly priced deposit insurance possible? *Journal of Finance* 47:227–45.

Chong, Beng Soon. 1991. Effects of interstate banking on commercial banks' risk and profitability. *Review of Economics and Statistics* 73:78–84.

Claessens, Stijn, Asli Demirgüç-Kunt, and Harry Huizinga. 2001. How does foreign entry affect domestic banking markets? *Journal of Banking and Finance* 25 (5): 891–911.

Cole, R. A., and Gunther, J. W. 1995. Separating the likelihood and timing of bank failure. *Journal of Banking and Finance* 19 (6): 1073–89.

Demirgüç-Kunt, Asli. 1989. Deposit-institution failures: A review of empirical literature. *Federal Reserve Bank of Cleveland Economic Review* 25 (4): 2–18.

Demirgüç-Kunt, Asli, and Enrica Detragiache. 1998. The determinants of banking crises in developing and developed countries. *International Monetary Fund Staff Papers* 45 (1): 81–109.

———. 1999. Financial liberalization and financial fragility. In *Proceedings of the 1998 World Bank Conference on Development Economics,* ed. B. Pleskovic and J. E. Stiglitz, 303–31. Washington, DC: The World Bank.

———. 2002. Does deposit insurance increase banking system stability? An empirical investigation. *Journal of Monetary Economics* 49 (7): 1373–1406.

Demirgüç-Kunt, Asli, Luc Laeven, and Ross Levine. 2004. Regulations, market structure, institutions, and the cost of financial intermediation. *Journal of Money, Credit and Banking* 36:593–622.

De Nicoló, Gianni. 2000. Size, charter value and risk in banking: An international perspective. International Finance Discussion Paper no. 689. Washington, DC: Board of Governors of the Federal Reserve System.

De Nicoló, Gianni, Philip Batholomew, Zaman Jahanara, and Mary Zephirin. 2003. Bank consolidation, conglomeration and internationalization: Trends and implications for financial risk. IMF Working Paper no. 03/158. Washington, DC: International Monetary Fund.

Diamond, Douglas W. 1984. Financial intermediation and delegated monitoring. *Review of Economic Studies* 51:393–414.

Dick, Astrid. 2006. Nationwide branching and its impact on market structure, quality and bank performance. *Journal of Business* 79 (2): 567–92.

Flannery, Mark J. 1989. Capital regulation and insurance banks' choice of individual loan default risks. *Journal of Monetary Economics* 24:235–58.

Gonzalez-Hermosillo, Brenda, Ceyla Pazarbasioglu, and Robert Billings. 1997. Banking system fragility: Likelihood versus timing of failure: An application to the Mexican financial crisis. *IMF Staff Papers* (September): 295–314.

Group of Ten. 2001. Report on Consolidation in the Financial Sector. Basel, Switzerland: Bank for International Settlements.

Hellman, Thomas, Kevin Murdock, and Joseph E. Stiglitz. 2000. Liberalization, moral hazard in banking and prudential regulation: Are capital controls enough? *American Economic Review* 90 (1): 147–65.

Hughes, Joseph P., and Loretta Mester. 1998. Bank capitalization and cost: Evidence of scale economies in risk management and signaling. *Review of Economics and Statistics* 80:314–25.

International Monetary Fund. 2001. *Financial sector consolidation in emerging markets, chapter 5.* International Capital Market Report. Washington, DC: International Monetary Fund.

Jayaratne, Jith, and Philip Strahan. 1998. Entry restrictions, industry evolution, and dynamic efficiency: Evidence from commercial banking. *Journal of Law and Economics* 41:249–75.

Kaminsky, Graciela, and Carmen Reinhart. 1999. The twin crises: The causes of banking and balance of payments problems. *American Economic Review* 89:473–500.

Kane, Edward J. 1989. *The S&L insurance mess: How did it happen?* Washington, DC: Urban Institute Press.

Kaufman, Daniel, Aart Kraay, and P. Zoido-Lobaton. 1999. Governance matters. World Bank Policy Research Department Working Paper no. 2196. Washington, DC: The World Bank.

Keeley, Michael C. 1990. Deposit insurance, risk and market power in banking. *American Economic Review* 80:1183–1200.

La Porta, Rafael, Florencia Lopez-de-Silanes, Andrei Shleifer, and Robert W. Vishny. 1999. The quality of government. *Journal of Law, Economics, and Organization* 15:222–79.

La Porta, Rafael, Florencio Lopez-de-Silanes, and Andrei Shleifer. 2002. Government ownership of banks. *Journal of Finance* 57 (1): 265–301.

Lindgren, Carl-Johan, Gillian Garcia, and Matthew I. Saal. 1996. *Bank soundness and macroeconomic policy.* Washington, DC: International Monetary Fund.

Macey, J. R., and M. O'Hara. 2003. The corporate governance of banks. *Federal Reserve Bank of New York Economic Policy Review* 9:91–107.

Matutes, Carmen, and Xavier Vives. 1996. Competition for deposits, fragility and insurance. *Journal of Financial Intermediation* 5:184–216.

———. 2000. Imperfect competition, risk taking and regulation in banking. *European Economic Review* 44:184–216.

Merton, Robert C. 1977. An analytic derivation of the cost of deposit insurance and loan guarantees: An application of modern option pricing theory. *Journal of Banking and Finance* 1:3–11.

Mishkin, Frederic S. 1999. Financial consolidation: Dangers and opportunities. *Journal of Banking and Finance* 23:675–91.

O'Hara, Maureen, and W. Shaw. 1990. Deposit insurance and wealth effects: The value of being 'too big to fail'. *Journal of Finance* 45:1587–1600.

Ramakrishnan, Ram, and Anjan V. Thakor. 1984. Information reliability and a theory of financial intermediation. *Review of Economic Studies* 51:415–32.

Sharpe, William F. 1978. Bank capital adequacy, deposit insurance and security values. *Journal of Financial and Quantitative Analysis* 13:701–18.

Smith, B. D. 1984. Private information, deposit interest rates, and the 'stability' of the banking system. *Journal of Monetary Economics* 14:293–317.

Stiglitz, Joseph E. 1972. Some aspects of the pure theory of corporate finance: Bankruptcies and takeovers. *Bell Journal of Economics* 3:458–82.

Sutton, John. 1991. *Sunk costs and market structure.* Cambridge, MA: MIT Press.

———. 1998. *Technology and market structure.* Cambridge, MA: MIT Press.

Tirole, Jean. 1988. *The theory of industrial organization.* Cambridge, MA: MIT Press.

Williamson, Stephen D. 1986. Costly monitoring, financial intermediation, and equilibrium credit rationing. *Journal of Monetary Economics* 18:159–79.

Comment   René M. Stulz

Kwast and De Nicolo (2001) and Hartmann, Straetmans, and de Vries (chapter 4, this volume) find that interdependencies among large banks increased in the 1990s for, respectively, the United States, and the United

Kingdom and the eurozone. A plausible explanation for these findings is that bank consolidation led to an increase in systemic risk. While some observers are concerned that increases in bank concentration have led to increases in systemic risk, this belief is not universally shared. For instance, the recent Counterparty Risk Management Policy Group report concludes that systemic risk has decreased in the banking system in recent years.

The paper by Beck, Demirgüç-Kunt, and Levine makes an important contribution to this debate. They look across countries to find whether there is a relation between bank concentration and the extent to which a country spends its time in banking crises. They find that bank concentrations is associated with fewer crises across the globe. As is typical of the papers by these authors, it is hard to think of a robustness check that they have not already attempted. Consequently, it would be a waste of my time to try to argue that maybe after all there is a positive relation between banking concentration and banking crises. After reading the paper, one has to conclude that, across the world, countries with higher bank concentration have not been more likely to experience banking crises.

The strength of the paper is that it allows us to dismiss the simple argument that concentration creates systemic risk. In my discussion, I focus on three issues that the paper raises. First, it seems that welfare is lower in the high banking concentration countries, so that the frequency of banking crises may not be a good indicator of welfare. Second, it is hard to evaluate the extent to which the paper can be used to argue that concentration in the United States does not create systemic risk. Third, while it is clear that concentration does not increase the risk of crises, one has to be cautious about concluding that it decreases them.

The sample includes sixty-nine countries. A large number of countries in the sample are small and financially underdeveloped. The authors measure concentration by the fraction of assets held by the three largest banks in the country. In the sample, there is a strong negative correlation between real GDP per capita and banking concentration. The highest value of the concentration index is 1. The sample has seven countries with a concentration index of 1. They are all African countries. From 1980 through 1997, these countries spend a total of eleven years in the banking crisis state. In contrast, the United States has a concentration index of 0.19 and spends twelve years in the banking crisis state. The authors show that there results hold without the African countries and without the United States. However, the comparison points to important issues when one attempts to evaluate the results of the paper. First, though banking concentration is not associated with banking crises, it seems associated with financial underdevelopment. Perhaps most of these countries would happily trade their banking system for the U.S. banking system if the cost were to have a savings and loans crisis. Second, not all crises are alike. The U.S. savings and loans crisis was assuredly expensive. However, did it really endanger the U.S. banking system? Probably not.

There are not many banks in the world that come close to being similar to the largest U.S. banks. These banks have activities throughout the world. Their activities are quite diversified. They have extremely sophisticated risk measurement and management organizations. Increasing concentration in the United States might just bring assets under the control of the most efficient banks. However, at the same time, one has to wonder about whether such incredibly complex organizations are not more fragile than simpler and more straightforward organizations. The Challenger shuttle was brought down by an O-ring. Do we really have a good sense of what the O-rings of a major bank are? The sample the authors consider does not really help in answering that question. This it not a criticism of the paper. It is just that this type of study is well suited at answering the question of whether concentration leads to greater systemic risk for the median country in the sample but not for countries where banks are fundamentally different from typical banks in the sample.

Most banks do not use derivatives. However, in the United States, most of the notional amount of derivatives contracts held by banks is held by a handful of banks. Specifically, at the end of the third quarter of 2005, the notional amount of derivatives held by banks was $96.2 trillion, but 95 percent of that amount was held by five U.S. banks.[1] JP Morgan Chase alone accounts for close to half the notional amount of derivatives held by U.S. banks. There are good reasons why this concentration of derivatives holdings could substantially worsen the impact of losses at major banks. Suppose that JP Morgan Chase suffers a one-year-in-fifty loss on its loan portfolio. Would the problems posed by that loss be smaller or greater if it held one fourth of its derivatives? There are reasons why the problems would be smaller with a smaller portfolio of derivatives. One would expect the bank's dealings with its counterparties in the derivatives market to become substantially more complicated after such a large loss. Contracts wherein JP Morgan has to put up additional collateral would impose demands on the bank's liquidity. More importantly, its ability to trade derivatives would be impaired, which would adversely affect its ability to hedge and to generate income. All of these developments would substantially worsen the impact of the loss on its loss portfolio. Obviously, a crisis at JP Morgan Chase that prevents it from functioning normally as a bank would have far-reaching implications compared to the S&L crisis. However, whether banking concentration makes such a crisis more likely and whether it worsens its impact cannot be learned from international comparisons—very few other countries have the equivalent of JP Morgan Chase.

The authors attempt to understand why it is that concentration reduces the risk of crises. I have two reservations with that exercise. First, while it is clear that concentration does not worsen the risk of crises, it is less clear that it reduces it. The authors use a dataset of yearly observations. The ob-

1. See Comptroller of the Currency (OCC), Bank derivatives report, third quarter of 2005.

vious difficulty with such a sample is that concentration is highly autocorrelated. It seems likely that this autocorrelation leads to an overstatement of the significance of the coefficient on concentration in the logistic regressions that predict whether a country is in the crisis state or not. Second, the authors consider the impact on the coefficient on concentration of adding explanatory variables to the logistic regression. They find that concentration ceases to be significant when they add a variable corresponding to the mean bank size of a country times an interactive variable that takes value 1 if the banks in the country cannot make foreign loans. In other words, crises are more likely in countries where the banking system seems closed and where banks are large. While the authors would like to interpret this result as explaining the role of concentration, I am not convinced with that view. All they seem to show is that they added an omitted variable in the regression.

Reference

De Nicolo, Gianno, and Myron L. Kwast. 2002. System risk and financial consolidation: Are they related? *Journal of Banking and Finance* 26:861–80.

Discussion Summary

Much of the general discussion was focused on alternative stories. *Philipp Hartmann* suggested an alternative to a market-power story: Concentration increases the chance that a material portion of a nation's banking sector will be treated as too-big-to-fail, and given the definition of the crisis measure, this will reduce the measured likelihood of a crisis. *Jan Krahnen* wondered whether measured concentration may be a proxy for country size and about other measurement error, noting that the German banking system is functionally highly concentrated even though it would not be measured as such by the authors. *Patricia Jackson* observed that United Kingdom experience has taught that, at the individual bank level, concentration in the sense of a bank being locked into a single funding source, into lending to a single industry, or into operating in a small geographic area is a major factor in bank failure, but the paper does not include these types of concentration.

Hashim Pesaran and *Darrell Duffie* expressed concern about the use of a logit model in a setting where dynamic relationships within the sample may be material. Duffie suggested use of a Cox proportional hazard model for the probability of moving into a crisis as a way of dealing with such concerns. He also suggested examining the probability of moving out of a crisis.

Systemic Risk and Hedge Funds

Nicholas Chan, Mila Getmansky, Shane M. Haas, and
Andrew W. Lo

6.1 Introduction

The term *systemic risk* is commonly used to describe the possibility of
a series of correlated defaults among financial institutions—typically
banks—that occurs over a short period of time, often caused by a single
major event. A classic example is a banking panic, in which large groups of
depositors decide to withdraw their funds simultaneously, creating a run
on bank assets that can ultimately lead to multiple bank failures. Banking
panics were not uncommon in the United States during the nineteenth and
early twentieth centuries, culminating in the 1930–1933 period, with an
average of 2,000 bank failures per year during these years, according to
Mishkin (1997), and which prompted the Glass-Steagall Act of 1933 and
the establishment of the Federal Deposit Insurance Corporation (FDIC)
in 1934.

Although today banking panics are virtually nonexistent, thanks to the

The views and opinions expressed in this article are those of the authors only, and do not
necessarily represent the views and opinions of AlphaSimplex Group, MIT, the University of
Massachusetts, or any of their affiliates and employees. The authors make no representations
or warranty, either expressed or implied, as to the accuracy or completeness of the information contained in this article, nor are they recommending that this article serve as the basis for
any investment decision—this article is for information purposes only. Research support
from AlphaSimplex Group and the MIT Laboratory for Financial Engineering is gratefully
acknowledged. We thank Mark Carey, David Modest, René Stulz and participants of the
NBER Conference on The Risks of Financial Institutions for helpful comments and discussion. Parts of this paper include ideas and exposition from several previously published papers and books of some of the authors. Where appropriate, we have modified the passages to
suit the current context and composition without detailed citations and quotation marks so
as preserve continuity. Readers interested in the original sources of those passages should
consult Getmansky (2004), Getmansky, Lo, and Makarov (2004), Getmansky, Lo, and Mei
(2004), and Lo (2001, 2002).

FDIC and related central banking policies, systemic risk exposures have taken shape in other forms. In particular, the proliferation of hedge funds in recent years has indelibly altered the risk/reward landscape of financial investments. Unregulated and opaque investment partnerships that engage in a variety of active investment strategies,[1] hedge funds have generally yielded double-digit returns historically, but not without commensurate risks, and such risks are currently not widely appreciated or well understood. In particular, we argue that the risk/reward profile for most hedge funds differ in important ways from more traditional investments, and such differences may have potentially significant implications for systemic risk. This was underscored by the aftermath of the default of Russian government debt in August 1998, when Long-term Capital Management (LTCM) and many other fixed-income hedge funds suffered catastrophic losses over the course of a few weeks, creating significant stress on the global financial system and several major financial institutions—that is, creating systemic risk.

In this paper, we consider the impact of hedge funds on systemic risk by examining the unique risk-and-return profiles of hedge funds—at both the individual fund and the aggregate industry level—and proposing some new risk measures for hedge fund investments. Two major themes have emerged from August 1998: the importance of liquidity and leverage, and the capriciousness of correlations between instruments and portfolios that were thought to be uncorrelated. The precise mechanism by which these two sets of issues posed systemic risks in 1998 is now well understood. Because many hedge funds rely on leverage, their positions are often considerably larger than the amount of collateral posted to support those positions. Leverage has the effect of a magnifying glass, expanding small profit opportunities into larger ones, but also expanding small losses into larger losses. And when adverse changes in market prices reduces the market value of collateral, credit is withdrawn quickly; the subsequent forced liquidation of large positions over short periods of time can lead to widespread financial panic, as in the aftermath of the default of Russian government debt in August 1998. The more illiquid the portfolio, the larger the price impact of a forced liquidation, which erodes the fund's risk capital that much more quickly. If many funds face the same "death spiral" at a given point in time—that is, if they become more highly correlated during times of distress, and if those funds are obligors of a small number of major financial institutions—then a market event like August 1998 can cascade quickly into a global financial crisis. This is systemic risk.

---

1. Although hedge funds have avoided regulatory oversight in the past by catering only to "qualified" investors (investors that meet a certain minimum threshold in terms of net worth and investment experience) and refraining from advertising to the general public, a recent ruling by the U.S. Securities and Exchange Commission (Rule 203[b][3]-2) require most hedge funds to register as investment advisers under the Investment Advisers Act of 1940 by February 1, 2006.

Therefore, the two main themes of this study are illiquidity exposure and time-varying hedge fund correlations, both of which are intimately related to the dynamic nature of hedge fund investment strategies and their risk exposures. In particular, one of the justifications for the unusually rich fees that hedge funds charge is the fact that highly skilled hedge fund managers are engaged in active portfolio management. It is common wisdom that the most talented managers are drawn first to the hedge fund industry because the absence of regulatory constraints enables them to make the most of their investment acumen. With the freedom to trade as much or as little as they like on any given day, to go long or short on any number of securities and with varying degrees of leverage, and to change investment strategies at a moment's notice, hedge fund managers enjoy enormous flexibility and discretion in pursuing investment returns. But dynamic investment strategies imply dynamic risk exposures, and while modern financial economics has much to say about the risk of *static* investments—the market beta is a sufficient statistic in this case—there is currently no single summary measure of the risks of a *dynamic* investment strategy.[2]

To illustrate the challenges and opportunities in modeling the risk exposures of hedge funds, we provide two concrete examples in this section. In section 6.1.1, we present a hypothetical hedge fund strategy that yields remarkable returns with seemingly little risk, yet a closer examination will reveal quite a different story. And in section 6.1.2, we show that standard correlation coefficients may not be able to capture certain risk exposures that are particularly relevant for hedge fund investments.

These examples provide an introduction to the analysis in sections 6.3–6.7, and serve as motivation for developing new quantitative methods for capturing the impact of hedge funds on systemic risk. In section 6.3, we summarize the empirical properties of aggregate and individual hedge fund data used in this study, the Credit Suisse First Boston (CSFB)/Tremont hedge-fund indexes and the Tremont TASS individual hedge fund database. In section 6.4, we turn to the issue of liquidity—one of the central aspects of systemic risk—and present several measures for gauging illiquidity exposure in hedge funds and other asset classes, which we apply to individual and index data. Since systemic risk is directly related to hedge fund failures, in section 6.5 we investigate attrition rates of hedge funds in the TASS database and present a logit analysis that yields estimates of a fund's probability of liquidation as a function of various fund characteristics, such as return history, assets under management, and recent fund flows. In section 6.6, we present three other approaches to measuring systemic risk in the hedge fund industry: risk models for hedge fund indexes, regression models relating the banking sector to hedge funds, and regime-

2. Accordingly, hedge fund track records are often summarized with multiple statistics; for example, mean, standard deviation, Sharpe ratio, market beta, Sortino ratio, maximum drawdown, worst month.

switching models for hedge fund indexes. These three approaches yield distinct insights regarding the risks posed by the hedge fund industry, and we conclude in section 6.7 by discussing the current industry outlook implied by the analytics and empirical results of this study. Our tentative inferences suggest that the hedge fund industry may be heading into a challenging period of lower expected returns, and that systemic risk has been increasing steadily over the recent past.

Our preliminary findings must be qualified by the acknowledgment that all of our measures of systemic risk are *indirect,* and therefore open to debate and interpretation. The main reason for this less-than-satisfying state of affairs is the fact that hedge funds are currently not required to disclose any information about their risks and returns to the public, so empirical studies of the hedge fund industry are based only on very limited hedge fund data, provided voluntarily to TASS, and which may or may not be representative of the industry as a whole. Even after February 1, 2006, when, according to the U.S. Securities and Exchange Commission's Rule 203(b)(3)-2, all hedge funds must become Registered Investment Advisers, the regular filings of hedge funds will not include critical information such as a fund's degree of leverage, the liquidity of a fund's portfolio, the identities of the fund's major creditors and obligors, and the specific terms under which the fund's investors have committed their capital. Without this kind of information for the majority of funds in the industry, it is virtually impossible to construct direct measures of systemic risk, even by regulatory authorities like the SEC. However, as the hedge fund industry grows, the number and severity of hedge fund failures will undoubtedly increase as well, eventually moving the industry toward greater transparency.

6.1.1   Tail Risk

Consider the eight-year track record of a hypothetical hedge fund, Capital Decimation Partners, LP, first described by Lo (2001) and summarized in table 6.1. This track record was obtained by applying a specific investment strategy, to be revealed subsequently, to actual market prices from January 1992 to December 1999. Before discussing the particular strategy that generated these results, let us consider its overall performance: an average monthly return of 3.7 percent versus 1.4 percent for the Standard and Poor's (S&P) 500 during the same period, a total return of 2,721.3 percent over the eight-year period versus 367.1 percent for the S&P 500, a Sharpe ratio of 1.94 versus 0.98 for the S&P 500, and only six negative monthly returns out of ninety-six versus thirty-six out of ninety-six for the S&P 500. In fact, the monthly performance history, given in Lo (2001, table 4), shows that, as with many other hedge funds, the worst months for this fund were August and September of 1998. Yet October and November 1998 were the fund's two best months, and for 1998 as a whole the fund was up 87.3 percent versus 24.5 percent for the S&P 500! By all accounts, this is an enor-

Table 6.1   **Capital Decimation Partners, L.P.: Performance summary, January 1992 to December 1999**

Statistic	S&P 500	CDP
Monthly mean (%)	1.4	3.7
Monthly standard deviation (%)	3.6	5.8
Minimum month (%)	−8.9	−18.3
Maximum month (%)	14.0	27.0
Annual Sharpe ratio	0.98	1.94
No. of negative months	36/96	6/96
Correlation with S&P 500 (%)	100.0	59.9
Total return (%)	367.1	2,721.3

Note: Summary of simulated performance of a particular dynamic trading strategy using monthly historical market prices from January 1992 to December 1999.

mously successful hedge fund with a track record that would be the envy of most managers. What is its secret?

The investment strategy summarized in table 6.1 consists of shorting out-of-the-money S&P 500 (SPX) put options on each monthly expiration date for maturities less than or equal to three months, with strikes approximately 7 percent out of the money. The number of contracts sold each month is determined by the combination of: (1) Chicago Board Options Exchange (CBOE) margin requirements,[3] (2) an assumption that we are required to post 66 percent of the margin as collateral,[4] and (3) $10 million of initial risk capital. For concreteness, table 6.2 reports the positions and profit/loss statement for this strategy for 1992. See Lo (2001) for further details of this strategy.

The track record in table 6.1 seems much less impressive in light of the simple strategy on which it is based, and few investors would pay hedge fund-type fees for such a fund. However, given the secrecy surrounding most hedge fund strategies, and the broad discretion that managers are given by the typical hedge fund offering memorandum, it is difficult for investors to detect this type of behavior without resorting to more sophisticated risk analytics that can capture *dynamic* risk exposures.

Some might argue that this example illustrates the need for position transparency—after all, it would be apparent from the positions in table 6.2 that the manager of Capital Decimation Partners is providing little or no value added. However, there are many ways of implementing this

3. The margin required per contract is assumed to be:

$$100 \times [15\% \times (\text{current level of the SPX}) - (\text{put premium}) - (\text{amount out of the money})]$$

where the amount out of the money is equal to the current level of the SPX minus the strike price of the put.

4. This figure varies from broker to broker, and is meant to be a rather conservative estimate that might apply to a $10 million startup hedge fund with no prior track record.

Table 6.2   Capital Decimation Partners, L.P. positions and profit/loss for 1992

	S&P 500		No. of puts	Strike	Price	Expiration	Margin required ($)	Profits ($)	Initial capital + cumulative profits ($)	Capital available for investments ($)	Return (%)
12/20/91	387.04	new	2,300	360	4.625	March 1992	6,069,930		10,000,000	6,024,096	
1/17/92	418.86	mark to market	2,300	360	1.125	March 1992	654,120	805,000	10,805,000	6,509,036	8.1
	418.86	new	1,950	390	3.250	March 1992	5,990,205				
						Total margin:	6,644,325				
2/21/92	411.46	mark to market	2,300	360	0.250	March 1992	2,302,070	690,000			
	411.46	mark to market	1,950	390	1.625	March 1992	7,533,630	316,875	11,811,875	7,115,587	9.3
	411.46	liquidate	1,950	390	1.625	March 1992	0	0	11,811,875	7,115,587	
	411.46	new	1,246	390	1.625	March 1992	4,813,796				
						Total margin:	7,115,866				
3/20/92	411.30	expired	2,300	360	0.000	March 1992	0	373,750			
	411.30	expired	1,246	390	0.000	March 1992	0	202,475			
	411.30	new	2,650	380	2.000	May 1992	7,524,675		12,388,100	7,462,711	4.9
						Total margin:	7,524,675				
4/19/92	416.05	mark to market	2,650	380	0.500	May 1992	6,852,238	397,500			
	416.05	new	340	385	2.438	June 1992	983,280		12,785,600	7,702,169	3.2
						Total margin:	7,835,518				
5/15/92	410.09	expired	2,650	380	0.000	May 1992	0	132,500			
	410.09	mark to market	340	385	1.500	June 1992	1,187,399	31,875			
	410.09	new	2,200	380	1.250	July 1992	6,638,170		12,949,975	7,801,190	1.3
						Total margin:	7,825,569				

6/19/92	403.67	expired	340	385	0.000	June 1992	0	51,000			
	403.67	mark to market	2,200	380	1.125	July 1992	7,866,210	27,500	13,028,475	7,848,479	0.6
						Total margin:	7,866,210				
7/17/92	415.62	expired	2,200	380	0.000	July 1992	0	247,500			
	415.62	new	2,700	385	1.8125	September 1992	8,075,835		13,275,975	7,997,575	1.9
						Total margin:	8,075,835				
8/21/92	414.85	mark to market	2,700	385	1	September 1992	8,471,925	219,375	13,495,350	8,129,729	1.7
						Total margin:	8,471,925				
9/18/92	422.92	expired	2,700	385	0	September 1992	0				
	422.92	new	2,370	400	5.375	December 1992	8,328,891	270,000	13,765,350	8,292,380	2.0
						Total margin:	8,328,891				
10/16/92	411.73	mark to market	2,370	400	7	December 1992	10,197,992	(385,125)			
	411.73	liquidate	2,370	400	7	December 1992	0	0	13,380,225	8,060,377	-2.8
	411.73	new	1,873	400	7	December 1992	8,059,425				
						Total margin:	8,059,425				
11/20/92	426.65	mark to market	1,873	400	0.9375	December 1992	6,819,593	1,135,506	14,515,731	8,744,416	8.5
	426.65	new	529	400	0.9375	December 1992	1,926,089				
						Total margin:	8,745,682				
12/18/92	441.20	expired	1,873	400	0	December 1992	0	175,594	14,691,325	8,850,196	1.2
1992 total return											46.9

Note: Simulated positions and profit/loss statement for 1992 for a trading strategy that consists of shorting out-of-the-money put options on the S&P 500 once a month.

strategy that are not nearly so transparent, even when positions are fully disclosed. For example, Lo (2001) provides a more subtle example—Capital Decimation Partners II—in which short positions in put options are synthetically replicated using a standard "delta-hedging" strategy involving the underlying stock and varying amounts of leverage. Casual inspection of the monthly positions of such a strategy seem to suggest a contrarian trading strategy: when the price declines, the position in the underlying stock is increased, and when the price advances, the position is reduced. However, the net effect is to create the same kind of option-like payoff as Capital Decimation Partners, but for many securities, not just for the S&P 500.[5] Now imagine an investor presented with monthly position reports like table 6.2, but on a portfolio of 200 securities, as well as a corresponding track record that is likely to be even more impressive than that of Capital Decimation Partners, LP. Without additional analysis that explicitly accounts for the dynamic aspects of this trading strategy, it is difficult for an investor to fully appreciate the risks inherent in such a fund.

In particular, static methods such as traditional mean-variance analysis and the Capital Asset Pricing Model cannot capture the risks of dynamic trading strategies like Capital Decimation Partners (note the impressive Sharpe ratio in table 6.1). In the case of the strategy of shorting out-of-the-money put options on the S&P 500, returns are positive most of the time and losses are infrequent, but when they occur, they are extreme. This is a very specific type of risk signature that is not well summarized by static measures such as standard deviation. In fact, the estimated standard deviations of such strategies tend to be rather low, hence a naive application of mean-variance analysis such as risk-budgeting—an increasingly popular method used by institutions to make allocations based on risk units—can lead to unusually large allocations to funds like Capital Decimation Partners. The fact that total position transparency does not imply risk transparency is further cause for concern.

This is not to say that the risks of shorting out-of-the-money puts are inappropriate for all investors—indeed, the thriving catastrophe reinsurance industry makes a market in precisely this type of risk, often called "tail risk." However, such insurers do so with full knowledge of the loss profile and probabilities for each type of catastrophe, and they set their capital reserves and risk budgets accordingly. The same should hold true for institutional investors of hedge funds, but the standard tools and lexicon of the industry currently provide only an incomplete characterization of such risks. The need for a new set of dynamic risk analytics specifically targeted for hedge fund investments is clear.

---

5. A portfolio of options is worth more than an option on the portfolio, hence shorting puts on the individual stocks that constitute the SPX will yield substantially higher premiums than shorting puts on the index.

6.1.2 Phase-Locking Risk

One of the most compelling reasons for investing in hedge funds is the fact that their returns seem relatively uncorrelated with market indexes such as the S&P 500, and modern portfolio theory has convinced even the most hardened skeptic of the benefits of diversification (see, for example, the correlations between hedge fund indexes and the S&P 500 in table 6.4). However, the diversification argument for hedge funds must be tempered by the lessons of the summer of 1998, when the default in Russian government debt triggered a global flight to quality that changed many of these correlations overnight from 0 to 1. In the physical and natural sciences, such phenomena are examples of "phase-locking" behavior, situations in which otherwise uncorrelated actions suddenly become synchronized.[6] The fact that market conditions can create phase-locking behavior is certainly not new—market crashes have been with us since the beginning of organized financial markets—but prior to 1998, few hedge fund investors and managers incorporated this possibility into their investment processes in any systematic fashion.

From a financial-engineering perspective, the most reliable way to capture phase-locking effects is to estimate a risk model for returns in which such events are explicitly allowed. For example, suppose returns are generated by the following two-factor model:

$$(1) \qquad R_{it} = \alpha_i + \beta_i \Lambda_t + I_t Z_t + \varepsilon_{it},$$

and assume that Λ_t, I_t, Z_t, and ε_{it} are mutually independently and identically distributed (i.i.d.) with the following moments:

$$(2) \qquad E(\Lambda_t) = \mu_\lambda, \operatorname{Var}(\Lambda_t) = \sigma_\lambda^2$$

$$E(Z_t) = 0, \operatorname{Var}(Z_t) = \sigma_z^2$$

$$E(\varepsilon_{it}) = 0, \operatorname{Var}(\varepsilon_{it}) = \sigma_{\varepsilon_i}^2,$$

and let the phase-locking event indicator I_t be defined by:

$$(3) \qquad I_t = \begin{cases} 1 \text{ with probability } p \\ 0 \text{ with probability } 1 - p \end{cases}$$

According to equation (1), expected returns are the sum of three components: the fund's alpha, α_i, a "market" component, Λ_t, to which each fund has its own individual sensitivity, β_i, and a phase-locking component that is identical across all funds at all times, taking only one of two possible

---

6. One of the most striking examples of phase-locking behavior is the automatic synchronization of the flickering of Southeast Asian fireflies. See Strogatz (1994) for a description of this remarkable phenomenon as well as an excellent review of phase-locking behavior in biological systems.

values, either 0 (with probability p) or Z_t (with probability $1 - p$). If we assume that p is small, say 0.001, then most of the time the expected returns of fund i are determined by $\alpha_i + \beta_i \Lambda_t$, but every once in a while an additional term Z_t appears. If the volatility σ_z of Z_t is much larger than the volatilities of the market factor, Λ_t, and the idiosyncratic risk, ε_{it}, then the common factor Z_t will dominate the expected returns of all stocks when $I_t = 1$; that is, phase-locking behavior.

More formally, consider the *conditional* correlation coefficient of two funds i and j, defined as the ratio of the conditional covariance divided by the square root of the product of the conditional variances, conditioned on $I_t = 0$:

$$(4) \qquad \mathrm{Corr}(R_{it}, R_{jt} \,|\, I_t = 0) = \frac{\beta_i \beta_j \sigma_\lambda^2}{\sqrt{\beta_i^2 \sigma_\lambda^2 + \sigma_{\varepsilon_i}^2}\,\sqrt{\beta_j^2 \sigma_\lambda^2 + \sigma_{\varepsilon_j}^2}}$$

$$(5) \qquad \approx 0 \quad \text{for } \beta_i \approx \beta_j \approx 0,$$

where we have assumed that $\beta_i \approx \beta_j \approx 0$ to capture the market-neutral characteristic that many hedge-fund investors desire. Now consider the conditional correlation, conditioned on $I_t = 1$:

$$(6a) \quad \mathrm{Corr}(R_{it}, R_{jt} \,|\, I_t = 1) = \frac{\beta_i \beta_j \sigma_\lambda^2 + \sigma_z^2}{\sqrt{\beta_i^2 \sigma_\lambda^2 + \sigma_z^2 + \sigma_{\varepsilon_i}^2}\,\sqrt{\beta_j^2 \sigma_\lambda^2 + \sigma_z^2 + \sigma_{\varepsilon_j}^2}}$$

$$(6b) \qquad \approx \frac{1}{\sqrt{1 + \sigma_{\varepsilon_i}^2/\sigma_z^2}\,\sqrt{1 + \sigma_{\varepsilon_j}^2/\sigma_z^2}} \quad \text{for } \beta_i \approx \beta_j \approx 0.$$

If σ_z^2 is large relative to σ_{ε_i} and $\sigma_{\varepsilon_j}^2$, that is, if the variability of the catastrophe component dominates the variability of the residuals of both funds—a plausible condition that follows from the very definition of a catastrophe—then equation (6) will be approximately equal to 1! When phase-locking occurs, the correlation between two funds i and j—close to 0 during normal times—can become arbitrarily close to 1.

An insidious feature of equation (1) is the fact that it implies a very small value for the *unconditional* correlation, which is the quantity most readily estimated and most commonly used in risk reports, value-at-risk (VaR) calculations, and portfolio decisions. To see why, recall that the unconditional correlation coefficient is simply the unconditional covariance divided by the product of the square roots of the unconditional variances:

$$(7a) \qquad \mathrm{Corr}(R_{it}, R_{jt}) \equiv \frac{\mathrm{Cov}(R_{it}, R_{jt})}{\sqrt{\mathrm{Var}(R_{it})\mathrm{Var}(R_{jt})}}$$

$$(7b) \qquad \mathrm{Cov}(R_{it}, R_{jt}) = \beta_i \beta_j \sigma_\lambda^2 + \mathrm{Var}(I_t Z_t) = \beta_i \beta_j \sigma_\lambda^2 + p\sigma_z^2$$

$$(7c) \qquad \mathrm{Var}(R_{it}) = \beta_i^2 \sigma_\lambda^2 + \mathrm{Var}(I_t Z_t) + \sigma_{\varepsilon_i}^2 = \beta_i^2 \sigma_\lambda^2 + p\sigma_z^2 + \sigma_{\varepsilon_i}^2.$$

Combining these expressions yields the unconditional correlation coefficient under equation (1).

$$(8a) \qquad \text{Corr}(R_{it}, R_{jt}) = \frac{\beta_i \beta_j \sigma_\lambda^2 + p\sigma_z^2}{\sqrt{\beta_i^2 \sigma_\lambda^2 + p\sigma_z^2 + \sigma_{\varepsilon_i}^2} \sqrt{\beta_j^2 \sigma_\lambda^2 + p\sigma_z^2 + \sigma_{\varepsilon_j}^2}}$$

$$(8b) \qquad\qquad \approx \frac{p}{\sqrt{p + \sigma_{\varepsilon_i}^2/\sigma_z^2} \sqrt{p + \sigma_{\varepsilon_j}^2/\sigma_z^2}} \quad \text{for } \beta_i \approx \beta_j \approx 0$$

If we let $p = 0.001$ and assume that the variability of the phase-locking component is 10 times the variability of the residuals ε_i and ε_j, this implies an unconditional correlation of:

$$\text{Corr}(R_{it}, R_{jt}) \approx \frac{p}{\sqrt{p + 0.1}\sqrt{p + 0.1}} = 0.001/.101 = 0.0099$$

or less than 1 percent. As the variance σ_z^2 of the phase-locking component increases, the unconditional correlation (8) also increases, so that eventually the existence of Z_t will have an impact. However, to achieve an unconditional correlation coefficient of, say, 10 percent, σ_z^2 would have to be about 100 times larger than σ_ε^2. Without the benefit of an explicit risk model such as eqution (1), it is virtually impossible to detect the existence of a phase-locking component from standard correlation coefficients.

These considerations suggest the need for a more sophisticated analysis of hedge fund returns, one that accounts for asymmetries in factor exposures, phase-locking behavior, jump risk, nonstationarities, and other nonlinearities that are endemic to high-performance active investment strategies. In particular, nonlinear risk models must be developed for the various types of securities that hedge funds trade; for example, equities, fixed-income instruments, foreign exchange, commodities, and derivatives, and for each type of security, the risk model should include the following general groups of factors:

- Price factors
- Sectors
- Investment style
- Volatilities
- Credit
- Liquidity
- Macroeconomic factors
- Sentiment
- Nonlinear interactions

The last category involves dependencies between the previous groups of factors, some of which are nonlinear in nature. For example, credit factors may become more highly correlated with market factors during economic downturns and virtually uncorrelated at other times. Often difficult to detect empirically, these types of dependencies are more readily captured through economic intuition and practical experience, and should not be overlooked when constructing a risk model.

Finally, although common factors listed previously may serve as a useful starting point for developing a quantitative model of hedge fund risk exposures, it should be emphasized that a certain degree of customization will be required. To see why, consider the following list of key considerations in the management of a typical long/short equity hedge fund:

- Investment style (value, growth, and so on)
- Fundamental analysis (earnings, analyst forecasts, accounting data)
- Factor exposures (S&P 500, industries, sectors, characteristics)
- Portfolio optimization (mean-variance analysis, market neutrality)
- Stock loan considerations (hard-to-borrow securities, short "squeezes")
- Execution costs (price impact, commissions, borrowing rate, short rebate)
- Benchmarks and tracking error (T-bill rate versus S&P 500)

and compare them with a similar list for a typical fixed-income hedge fund:

- Yield-curve models (equilibrium versus arbitrage models)
- Prepayment models (for mortgage-backed securities)
- Optionality (call, convertible, and put features)
- Credit risk (defaults, rating changes, and so on)
- Inflationary pressures, central bank activity
- Other macroeconomic factors and events

The degree of overlap is astonishingly small, which suggests that the relevant risk exposures of the two types of funds are likely to be different as well. For example, changes in accounting standards are likely to have a significant impact on long/short equity funds because of their reliance on fundamental analysis, but will have little effect on a mortgage-backed securities fund. Similarly, changes in the yield curve may have major implications for fixed-income hedge funds but are less likely to affect a long/short equity fund. While such differences are also present among traditional institutional asset managers, they do not have nearly the latitude that hedge fund managers do in their investment activities—hence the differences are not as consequential for traditional managers. Therefore, the number of unique hedge fund risk models may have to match the number of hedge fund styles that exist in practice.

The point of the two examples in sections 6.1.1 and 6.1.2 is that hedge fund risks are not adequately captured by traditional measures such as market beta, standard deviation, correlation, and VaR. The two most significant risks facing hedge funds—illiquidity exposure and phase-locking behavior—are also the most relevant for systemic risk; hence we turn to these issues after reviewing the literature in section 6.2.

6.2   Literature Review

The explosive growth in the hedge fund sector over the past several years has generated a rich literature both in academia and among practitioners, including a number of books, newsletters, and trade magazines, several hundred published articles, and an entire journal dedicated solely to this industry (the *Journal of Alternative Investments*). However, none of this literature has considered the impact of hedge funds on systemic risk.[7] Nevertheless, thanks to the availability of hedge fund returns data from sources such as AltVest, Center for International Securities and Derivatives Markets (CISDM), HedgeFund.net, Hedge Fund Research (HFR), and TASS, a number of empirical studies have highlighted the unique risk/reward profiles of hedge fund investments. For example, Ackermann, McEnally, and Ravenscraft (1999), Fung and Hsieh (1999, 2000, 2001), Liang (1999, 2000, 2001), Agarwal and Naik (2000b, 2000c), Edwards and Caglayan (2001), Kao (2002), and Amin and Kat (2003a) provide comprehensive empirical studies of historical hedge fund performance using various hedge fund databases. Brown, Goetzmann, and Park (2000, 2001a, 2001b), Fung and Hsieh (1997a, 1997b), Brown, Goetzmann, and Ibbotson (1999), Agarwal and Naik (2000a, 2000d), Brown and Goetzmann (2003), and Lochoff (2002) present more detailed performance attribution and "style" analysis for hedge funds.

Several recent empirical studies have challenged the uncorrelatedness of hedge fund returns with market indexes, arguing that the standard methods of assessing their risks and rewards may be misleading. For example, Asness, Krail, and Liew (2001) show that in several cases where hedge funds purport to be market neutral—that is, funds with relatively small market betas—including both contemporaneous and lagged market returns as regressors and summing the coefficients yields significantly higher market exposure. Moreover, in deriving statistical estimators for Sharpe ratios of a sample of mutual and hedge funds, Lo (2002) proposes a better method for computing annual Sharpe ratios, based on monthly means and standard deviations, yielding point estimates that differ from the naive Sharpe ratio estimator by as much as 70 percent in his empirical application. Getmansky, Lo, and Makarov (2004) focus directly on the unusual degree of serial correlation in hedge fund returns, and argue that illiquidity exposure and smoothed returns are the most common sources of such

---

7. For example, a literature search among all abstracts in the EconLit database—a comprehensive electronic collection of the economics literature that includes over 750 journals—in which the two phrases "hedge fund" and "systemic risk" are specified yields no records.

serial correlation. They also propose methods for estimating the degree of return-smoothing and adjusting performance statistics like the Sharpe ratio to account for serial correlation.

The persistence of hedge fund performance over various time intervals has also been studied by several authors. Such persistence may be indirectly linked to serial correlation; for example, persistence in performance usually implies positively autocorrelated returns. Agarwal and Naik (2000c) examine the persistence of hedge fund performance over quarterly, half-yearly, and yearly intervals by examining the series of wins and losses for two, three, and more consecutive time periods. Using net-of-fee returns, they find that persistence is highest at the quarterly horizon and decreases when moving to the yearly horizon. The authors also find that performance persistence, whenever present, is unrelated to the type of hedge fund strategy. Brown, Goetzmann, Ibbotson, and Ross (1992), Ackermann, McEnally, and Ravenscraft (1999), and Baquero, Horst, and Verbeek (2004) show that survivorship bias—the fact that most hedge fund databases do not contain funds that were unsuccessful and which went out of business—can affect the first and second moments and cross-moments of returns, and generate spurious persistence in performance when there is dispersion of risk among the population of managers. However, using annual returns of both defunct and currently operating offshore hedge funds between 1989 and 1995, Brown, Goetzmann, and Ibbotson (1999) find virtually no evidence of performance persistence in raw returns or risk-adjusted returns, even after breaking funds down according to their returns-based style classifications.

Fund flows in the hedge fund industry have been considered by Agarwal, Daniel, and Naik (2004) and Getmansky (2004), with the expected conclusion that funds with higher returns tend to receive higher net inflows and funds with poor performance suffer withdrawals and, eventually, liquidation—much like the case with mutual funds and private equity.[8] Agarwal, Daniel, and Naik (2004), Goetzmann, Ingersoll, and Ross (2003), and Getmansky (2004) all find decreasing returns to scale among their samples of hedge funds, implying that an optimal amount of assets under management exists for each fund and mirroring similar findings for the mutual fund industry by Pérold and Salomon (1991) and the private equity industry by Kaplan and Schoar (2004). Hedge fund survival rates have been studied by Brown, Goetzmann, and Ibbotson (1999), Fung and Hsieh (2000), Liang (2000, 2001), Bares, Gibson, and Gyger (2003), Brown, Goetzmann, and Park (2001a), Gregoriou (2002), and Amin and Kat (2003b). Baquero, Horst, and Verbeek (2004) estimate liquidation probabilities of hedge funds and find that they are greatly dependent on past performance.

---

8. See, for example, Ippolito (1992), Chevalier and Ellison (1997), Goetzmann and Peles (1997), Gruber (1996), Sirri and Tufano (1998), Zheng (1999), and Berk and Green (2004) for studies of mutual fund flows, and Kaplan and Schoar (2004) for private-equity fund flows.

The survival rates of hedge funds have been estimated by Brown, Goetzmann, and Ibbotson (1999), Fung and Hsieh (2000), Liang (2000, 2001), Brown, Goetzmann, and Park (2001a,b), Gregoriou (2002), Amin and Kat (2003b), Bares, Gibson, and Gyger (2003), and Getmansky, Lo, and Mei (2004). Brown, Goetzmann, and Park (2001a) show that the probability of liquidation increases with increasing risk, and that funds with negative returns for two consecutive years have a higher risk of shutting down. Liang (2000) finds that the annual hedge fund attrition rate is 8.3 percent for the 1994–1998 sample period using TASS data, and Baquero, Horst, and Verbeek (2004) find a slightly higher rate of 8.6 percent for the 1994–2000 sample period. Baquero, Horst, and Verbeek (2004) also find that surviving funds outperform nonsurviving funds by approximately 2.1 percent per year, which is similar to the findings of Fung and Hsieh (2000, 2002b) and Liang (2000), and that investment style, size, and past performance are significant factors in explaining survival rates. Many of these patterns are also documented by Liang (2000), Boyson (2002), and Getmansky, Lo, and Mei (2004). In particular, Getmansky, Lo, and Mei (2004) find that attrition rates in the TASS database from 1994 to 2004 differ significantly across investment styles, from a low of 5.2 percent per year on average for convertible arbitrage funds to a high of 14.4 percent per year on average for managed futures funds. They also relate a number of factors to these attrition rates, including past performance, volatility, and investment style, and document differences in illiquidity risk between active and liquidated funds. In analyzing the life cycle of hedge funds, Getmansky (2004) finds that the liquidation probabilities of individual hedge funds depend on fund-specific characteristics such as past returns, asset flows, age, and assets under management, as well as category-specific variables such as competition and favorable positioning within the industry.

Brown, Goetzmann, and Park (2001a) find that the half-life of the TASS hedge funds is exactly thirty months, while Brooks and Kat (2002) estimate that approximately 30 percent of new hedge funds do not make it past thirty-six months due to poor performance; in Amin and Kat's (2003c) study, 40 percent of their hedge funds do not make it to the fifth year. Howell (2001) observed that the probability of hedge funds failing in their first year was 7.4 percent, only to increase to 20.3 percent in their second year. Poorly performing younger funds drop out of databases at a faster rate than older funds (see Getmansky 2004, and Jen, Heasman, and Boyatt 2001), presumably because younger funds are more likely to take additional risks to obtain good performance which they can use to attract new investors, whereas older funds that have survived already have track records with which to attract and retain capital.

A number of case studies of hedge fund liquidations have been published recently, no doubt spurred by the most well-known liquidation in the hedge fund industry to date: Long Term Capital Management (LTCM). The literature on LTCM is vast, spanning a number of books, journal articles, and news stories; a representative sample includes Greenspan (1998), McDonough (1998), Pérold (1999), the President's Working Group on Financial Markets (1999), and MacKenzie (2003). Ineichen (2001) has compiled a list of selected hedge funds and analyzed the reasons for their liquidations. Kramer (2001) focuses on fraud, providing detailed accounts of six of history's most egregious cases. Although it is virtually impossible to obtain hard data on the frequency of fraud among liquidated hedge funds,[9] in a study of over 100 liquidated hedge funds during the past two decades, Feffer and Kundro (2003) conclude that "half of all failures could be attributed to operational risk alone," of which fraud is one example. In fact, they observe that "The most common operational issues related to hedge fund losses have been misrepresentation of fund investments, misappropriation of investor funds, unauthorized trading, and inadequate resources" (p. 5). The last of these issues is, of course, not related to fraud, but Feffer and Kundro (fig. 2) report that only 6 percent of their sample involved inadequate resources, whereas 41 percent involved misrepresentation of investments, 30 percent involved misappropriation of funds, and 14 percent involved unauthorized trading. These results suggest that operational issues are indeed an important factor in hedge fund liquidations, and deserve considerable attention by investors and managers alike.

Collectively, these studies show that the dynamics of hedge funds are quite different than those of more traditional investments, and the potential impact on systemic risk is apparent.

6.3   The Data

It is clear from section 6.1 that hedge funds exhibit unique and dynamic characteristics that bear further study. Fortunately, the returns of many individual hedge funds are now available through a number of commercial databases such as AltVest, CISDM, HedgeFund.net, HFR, and TASS. For the empirical analysis in this paper, we use two main sources: (1) a set of aggregate hedge fund index returns from CSFB/Tremont, and (2) the TASS database of hedge funds, which consists of monthly returns and accompanying information for 4,781 individual hedge funds (as of August 2004) from February 1977 to August 2004.[10]

The CSFB/Tremont indexes are asset-weighted indexes of funds with a minimum of $10 million of assets under management (AUM), a minimum one-year track record, and current audited financial statements. An aggre-

---

9. The lack of transparency and the unregulated status of most hedge funds are significant barriers to any systematic data collection effort; hence it is difficult to draw inferences about industry norms.

10. For further information about these data see http://www.hedgeindex.com (CSFB/Tremont indexes) and http://www.tassresearch.com (TASS). We also use data from Altvest, the University of Chicago's Center for Research in Security Prices, and Yahoo!Finance.

gate index is computed from this universe, and ten subindexes based on investment style are also computed using a similar method. Indexes are computed and rebalanced on a monthly frequency and the universe of funds is redefined on a quarterly basis.

The TASS database consists of monthly returns, assets under management, and other fund-specific information for 4,781 individual funds from February 1977 to August 2004. The database is divided into two parts: "Live" and "Graveyard" funds. Hedge funds that are in the Live database are considered to be active as of August 31, 2004.[11] As of August 2004, the combined database of both live and dead hedge funds contained 4,781 funds with at least one monthly return observation. Out of these 4,781 funds, 2,920 funds are in the Live database and 1,861 in the Graveyard database. The earliest data available for a fund in either database is February 1977. TASS started tracking dead funds in 1994; hence it is only since 1994 that TASS transferred funds from the Live database to the Graveyard database. Funds that were dropped from the Live database prior to 1994 are not included in the Graveyard database, which may yield a certain degree of survivorship bias.[12]

The majority of 4,781 funds reported returns net of management and incentive fees on a monthly basis,[13] and we eliminated fifty funds that reported only gross returns, leaving 4,731 funds in the "Combined" database (2,893 in the Live and 1,838 in the Graveyard database). We also eliminated funds that reported returns on a quarterly—not monthly—basis, leaving 4,705 funds in the Combined database (2,884 in the Live and 1,821 in the Graveyard database). Finally, we dropped funds that did not report assets

11. Once a hedge fund decides not to report its performance, is liquidated, is closed to new investment, restructured, or merged with other hedge funds, the fund is transferred into the Graveyard database. A hedge fund can only be listed in the Graveyard database after being listed in the Live database. Because the TASS database fully represents returns and asset information for live and dead funds, the effects of survivorship bias are minimized. However, the database is subject to *backfill bias*—when a fund decides to be included in the database, TASS adds the fund to the Live database and includes all available prior performance of the fund. Hedge funds do not need to meet any specific requirements to be included in the TASS database. Due to reporting delays and time lags in contacting hedge funds, some Graveyard funds can be incorrectly listed in the Live database for a period of time. However, TASS has adopted a policy of transferring funds from the Live to the Graveyard database if they do not report over an eight- to ten-month period.

12. For studies attempting to quantify the degree and impact of survivorship bias, see Baquero, Horst, and Verbeek (2004), Brown, Goetzmann, Ibbotson, and Ross (1992), Brown, Goetzmann, and Ibbotson (1999), Brown, Goetzmann, and Park (1997), Carpenter and Lynch (1999), Fung and Hsieh (1997b, 2000), Horst, Nijman, and Verbeek (2001), Hendricks, Patel, and Zeckhauser (1997), and Schneeweis and Spurgin (1996).

13. TASS defines returns as the change in net asset value during the month (assuming the reinvestment of any distributions on the reinvestment date used by the fund) divided by the net asset value at the beginning of the month, net of management fees, incentive fees, and other fund expenses. Therefore, these reported returns should approximate the returns realized by investors. TASS also converts all foreign-currency denominated returns to U.S.-dollar returns using the appropriate exchange rates.

Table 6.3   **Number of funds in the TASS hedge fund Live, Graveyard, and Combined databases, from February 1977 to August 2004**

		Number of TASS funds in:		
Category	Definition	Live	Graveyard	Combined
1	Convertible arbitrage	127	49	176
2	Dedicated short bias	14	15	29
3	Emerging markets	130	133	263
4	Equity-market neutral	173	87	260
5	Event driven	250	134	384
6	Fixed-income arbitrage	104	71	175
7	Global macro	118	114	232
8	Long/short equity	883	532	1,415
9	Managed futures	195	316	511
10	Multistrategy	98	41	139
11	Fund of funds	679	273	952
Total		2,771	1,765	4,536

under management, or reported only partial assets under management, leaving a final sample of 4,536 hedge funds in the Combined database, which consists of 2,771 funds in the Live database and 1,765 funds in the Graveyard database. For the empirical analysis in section 6.4, we impose an additional filter in which we require funds to have at least five years of nonmissing returns, leaving 1,226 funds in the Live database and 611 in the Graveyard database, for a combined total of 1,837 funds. This obviously creates additional survivorship bias in the remaining sample of funds, but since the main objective is to estimate measures of illiquidity exposure and not to make inferences about overall performance, this filter may not be as problematic.[14]

TASS also classifies funds into one of eleven different investment styles, listed in table 6.3 and described in the appendix, of which ten correspond exactly to the CSFB/Tremont subindex definitions.[15] Table 6.3 also reports the number of funds in each category for the Live, Graveyard, and Combined databases; it is apparent from these figures that the representation of investment styles is not evenly distributed, but is concentrated among four categories: Long/Short Equity (1,415), Fund of Funds (952), Managed Futures (511), and Event Driven (384). Together, these four categories account for 71.9 percent of the funds in the Combined database. Figure 6.1 shows that the relative proportions of the Live and Graveyard databases are roughly comparable, with the exception of two categories: Funds of

14. See the references in footnote 12.
15. This is no coincidence—TASS is owned by Tremont Capital Management, which created the CSFB/Tremont indexes in partnership with Credit Suisse First Boston.

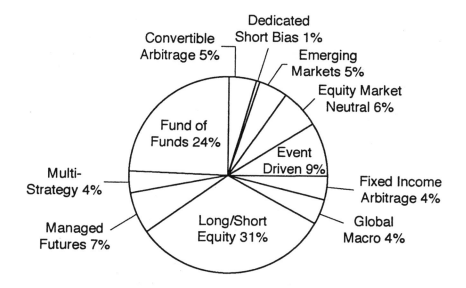

Live Funds

Graveyard Funds

Fig. 6.1 Breakdown of TASS Live and Graveyard funds by category

Funds (24 percent in the Live and 15 percent in the Graveyard database), and Managed Futures (7 percent in the Live and 18 percent in the Graveyard database). This reflects the current trend in the industry toward funds of funds, and the somewhat slower growth of managed futures funds.

6.3.1   CSFB/Tremont Indexes

Table 6.4 reports summary statistics for the monthly returns of the CSFB/Tremont indexes from January 1994 to August 2004. Also included for purposes of comparison are summary statistics for a number of aggregate measures of market conditions, which we will use later as risk factors for constructing explicit risk models for hedge fund returns in section 6.6; their definitions are given in table 6.23.

Table 6.4 shows that there is considerable heterogeneity in the historical risk and return characteristics of the various categories of hedge fund investment styles. For example, the annualized mean return ranges from –0.69 percent for Dedicated Shortsellers to 13.85 percent for Global Macro, and the annualized volatility ranges from 3.05 percent for Equity Market Neutral to 17.28 percent for Emerging Markets. The correlations of the hedge fund indexes with the S&P 500 are generally low, with the largest correlation at 57.2 percent for Long/Short Equity, and the lowest correlation at –75.6 percent for Dedicated Shortsellers—as investors have discovered, hedge funds offer greater diversification benefits than many traditional asset classes. However, these correlations can vary over time. For example, consider a rolling sixty-month correlation between the CSFB/Tremont Multi-Strategy Index and the S&P 500 from January 1999 to December 2003, plotted in figure 6.2. At the start of the sample in January 1999, the correlation is –13.4 percent, then drops to –21.7 percent a year later, and increases to 31.0 percent by December 2003 as the outliers surrounding August 1998 drop out of the sixty-month rolling window.

Although changes in rolling correlation estimates are also partly attributable to estimation errors,[16] in this case an additional explanation for the positive trend in correlation is the enormous inflow of capital into multistrategy funds and fund-of-funds over the past five years. As assets under management increase, it becomes progressively more difficult for fund managers to implement strategies that are truly uncorrelated with broadbased market indexes like the S&P 500. Moreover, figure 6.2 shows that the correlation between the Multi-Strategy Index return and the lagged S&P 500 return has also increased in the past year, indicating an increase in the illiquidity exposure of this investment style (see Getmansky, Lo, and Makarov 2004, and section 6.4). This is also consistent with large inflows of capital into the hedge fund sector.

---

16. Under the null hypothesis of no correlation, the approximate standard error of the correlation coefficient is $1/\sqrt{60} = 13$ percent.

Table 6.4 Summary statistics for monthly CSFB/Tremont hedge fund index returns and various hedge fund risk factors from January 1994 to August 2004 (except for Fund of Funds, which begins in April 1994, and S&P 500, which ends in December 2003)

Variable	Sample size	Annual mean	Annual standard deviation	Correlation with S&P 500	Minimum	Median	Maximum	Skewness	Kurtosis	ρ_1	ρ_2	ρ_3	p-value of LB-Q
CSFB/Tremont indexes													
Hedge funds	128	10.51	8.25	45.9	−7.55	0.78	8.53	0.12	1.95	12.0	4.0	−0.5	54.8
Convertible arbitrage	128	9.55	4.72	11.0	−4.68	1.09	3.57	−1.47	3.78	55.8	41.1	14.4	0.0
Dedicated shortseller	128	−0.69	17.71	−75.6	−8.69	−0.39	22.71	0.90	2.16	9.2	−3.6	0.9	73.1
Emerging markets	128	8.25	17.28	47.2	−23.03	1.17	16.42	−0.58	4.01	30.5	1.6	−1.4	0.7
Equity-market neutral	128	10.01	3.05	39.6	−1.15	0.81	3.26	0.25	0.23	29.8	20.2	9.3	0.0
Event driven	128	10.86	5.87	54.3	−11.77	1.01	3.68	−3.49	23.95	35.0	15.3	4.0	0.0
Distressed	128	12.73	6.79	53.5	−12.45	1.18	4.10	−2.79	17.02	29.3	13.4	2.0	0.3
Event-driven multistrategy	128	9.87	6.19	46.6	−11.52	0.90	4.66	−2.70	17.63	35.3	16.7	7.8	0.0
Risk arbitrage	128	7.78	4.39	44.7	−6.15	0.62	3.81	−1.27	6.14	27.3	−1.9	−9.7	1.2
Fixed income arbitrage	128	6.69	3.86	−1.3	−6.96	0.77	2.02	−3.27	17.05	39.2	8.2	2.0	0.0
Global macro	128	13.85	11.75	20.9	−11.55	1.19	10.60	0.00	2.26	5.5	4.0	8.8	65.0
Long/short equity	128	11.51	10.72	57.2	−11.43	0.78	13.01	0.26	3.61	16.9	6.0	−4.6	21.3
Managed futures	128	6.48	12.21	−22.6	−9.35	0.18	9.95	0.07	0.49	5.8	−9.6	−0.7	64.5
Multistrategy	125	9.10	4.43	5.6	−4.76	0.83	3.61	−1.30	3.59	−0.9	7.6	18.0	17.2
S&P 500	120	11.90	15.84	100.0	−14.46	1.47	9.78	−0.61	0.30	−1.0	−2.2	7.3	86.4
Banks	128	21.19	13.03	55.8	−18.62	1.96	11.39	−1.16	5.91	26.8	6.5	5.4	1.6
LIBOR	128	−0.14	0.78	3.5	−0.94	−0.01	0.63	−0.61	4.11	50.3	32.9	27.3	0.0
USD	128	−0.52	7.51	7.3	−5.35	−0.11	5.58	0.00	0.08	7.2	−3.2	6.4	71.5
Oil	128	15.17	31.69	−1.6	−22.19	1.38	36.59	0.25	1.17	−8.1	−13.6	16.6	7.3
Gold	128	1.21	12.51	−7.2	−9.31	−0.17	16.85	0.98	3.07	−13.7	−17.4	8.0	6.2
Lehman bond	128	6.64	4.11	0.8	−2.71	0.50	3.50	−0.04	0.05	24.6	−6.3	5.2	3.2
Large minus small cap	128	−1.97	13.77	7.6	−20.82	0.02	12.82	−0.82	5.51	−13.5	4.7	6.1	36.6
Value minus growth	128	0.86	18.62	−48.9	−22.78	0.40	15.85	−0.44	3.01	8.6	10.2	0.4	50.3
Credit spread (not annual)	128	4.35	1.36	−30.6	2.68	3.98	8.23	0.82	−0.30	94.1	87.9	83.2	0.0
Term spread (not annual)	128	1.65	1.16	−11.6	−0.07	1.20	3.85	0.42	−1.25	97.2	94.0	91.3	0.0
VIX (not annual)	128	0.03	3.98	−67.3	−12.90	0.03	19.48	0.72	4.81	−8.2	−17.5	−13.9	5.8

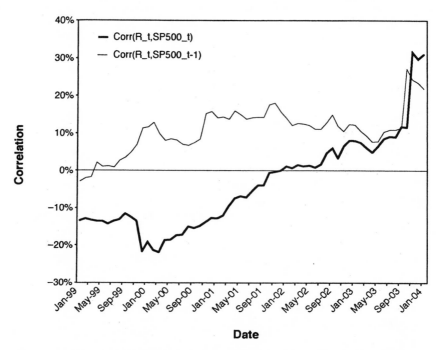

Date

Fig. 6.2   Sixty-month rolling correlations between CSFB/Tremont Multi-Strategy Index returns and the contemporaneous and lagged return of the S&P 500, from January 1999 to December 2003

Notes: Under the null hypothesis of no correlation, the approximate standard error of the correlation coefficient is $1/\sqrt{60} = 13$ percent, hence the differences between the beginning-of-sample and end-of-sample correlations are statistically significant at the 1 percent level.

Despite their heterogeneity, several indexes do share a common characteristic: negative skewness. Convertible Arbitrage, Emerging Markets, Event Driven, Distressed, Event-Driven Multi-Strategy, Risk Arbitrage, Fixed-Income Arbitrage, and Fund of Funds all have skewness coefficients less than zero, in some cases substantially so. This property is an indication of tail risk exposure, as in the case of Capital Decimation Partners (see section 6.1.1), and is consistent with the nature of the investment strategies employed by funds in those categories. For example, Fixed-Income Arbitrage strategies are known to generate fairly consistent profits, with occasional losses that may be extreme; hence a skewness coefficient of –3.27 is not surprising. A more direct measure of tail risk or "fat tails" is kurtosis—the normal distribution has a kurtosis of 3.00, so values greater than this represent fatter tails than normal. Not surprisingly, the two categories with the most negative skewness—Event Driven (–3.49) and Fixed-Income Arbitrage (–3.27)—also have the largest kurtosis, 23.95 and 17.05, respectively.

Several indexes also exhibit a high degree of positive serial correlation, as measured by the first three autocorrelation coefficients ρ_1, ρ_2, and ρ_3, as well as the p-value of the Ljung-Box Q-statistic, which measures the degree of statistical significance of the first three autocorrelations.[17] In comparison to the S&P 500, which has a first-order autocorrelation coefficient of -1.0 percent, the autocorrelations of the hedge fund indexes are very high, with values of 55.8 percent for Convertible Arbitrage, 39.2 percent for Fixed-Income Arbitrage, and 35.0 percent for Event Driven, all of which are significant at the 1 percent level, according to the corresponding p-values. Serial correlation can be a symptom of illiquidity risk exposure, which is particularly relevant for systemic risk, and we shall focus on this issue in more detail in section 6.4.

The correlations between the hedge fund indexes are given in table 6.5, and the entries also display a great deal of heterogeneity, ranging from -71.9 percent (between Long/Short Equity and Dedicated Shortsellers) and 93.6 percent (between Event Driven and Distressed). However, these correlations can vary through time, as table 6.6 illustrates, both because of estimation error and through the dynamic nature of many hedge fund investment strategies and the changes in fund flows among them. Over the sample period from January 1994 to December 2003, the correlation between the Convertible Arbitrage and Emerging Market indexes is 31.8 percent, but during the first half of the sample this correlation is 48.2 percent, and during the second half it is -5.8 percent. A graph of the sixty-month rolling correlation between these two indexes from January 1999 to December 2003 provides a clue as to the source of this nonstationarity: figure 6.3 shows a sharp drop in the correlation during the month of September 2003. This is the first month for which the August 1998 data point—the start of the LTCM event—is not included in the sixty-month rolling window. Table 6.7 shows that in August 1998 the returns for the Convertible Arbitrage and Emerging Market Indexes were -4.64 percent and -23.03, respectively. In fact, ten out of the thirteen style-category indexes yielded negative returns in August 1998, many of which were extreme outliers relative to the entire sample period; hence rolling windows containing this month can yield dramatically different correlations than those without it.

---

17. Ljung and Box (1978) propose the following statistic to measure the overall significance of the first k autocorrelation coefficients:

$$Q = T(T + 2) \sum_{j=1}^{k} \hat{\rho}_j^2 / (T - j)$$

which is asymptotically χ_k^2 under the null hypothesis of no autocorrelation. By forming the sum of squared autocorrelations, the statistic Q reflects the absolute magnitudes of the $\hat{\rho}_j$s irrespective of their signs; hence funds with large positive or negative autocorrelation coefficients will exhibit large Q-statistics. See Kendall, Stuart, and Ord (1983, chapter 50.13) for further details.

Table 6.5   Correlation matrix for CSFB/Tremont hedge fund index returns, in percent, based on monthly data from January 1994 to August 2004

Correlation matrix	Hedge funds	Convertible arbitrage	Dedicated shortseller	Emerging markets	Equity-market neutral	Event driven	Distressed	Event-driven multi-strategy	Risk arbitrage	Fixed income arbitrage	Global macro	Long/ Short equity	Managed futures	Multi-strategy
Hedge funds	100.0													
Convertible arbitrage	39.1	100.0												
Dedicated shortseller	−46.7	−22.3	100.0											
Emerging markets	65.7	32.0	−56.8	100.0										
Equity-market neutral	32.0	30.0	−34.6	24.8	100.0									
Event driven	66.1	59.0	−62.9	66.5	39.3	100.0								
Distressed	56.5	50.7	−62.3	57.7	35.7	93.6	100.0							
Event-driven multistrategy	69.0	60.1	−54.0	67.1	37.3	93.0	74.9	100.0						
Risk arbitrage	39.6	41.8	−50.6	44.1	32.1	69.7	58.0	66.6	100.0					
Fixed income arbitrage	40.7	53.0	−4.6	27.1	5.7	37.3	28.3	43.3	13.2	100.0				
Global macro	85.4	27.5	−11.0	41.5	18.6	36.9	29.5	42.7	12.9	41.5	100.0			
Long/short equity	77.6	25.0	−71.9	58.9	34.2	65.2	57.0	63.9	51.7	17.0	40.6	100.0		
Managed futures	12.4	−18.1	21.1	−10.9	15.3	−21.2	−14.6	−24.4	−21.1	−6.7	26.8	−3.6	100.0	
Multistrategy	16.0	35.0	−5.8	−3.2	20.6	15.9	10.9	19.7	5.9	27.3	11.3	14.5	−2.4	100.0

Table 6.6

Correlation matrices for five CSFB/Tremont hedge fund index returns, in percent, based on monthly data from January 1994 to December 2003

	Dedicated short	Emerging markets	Equity-market neutral	Event driven	Distressed
January 1994 to December 2003					
Convertible arbitrage	−23.0	31.8	31.2	58.7	50.8
Dedicated short		−57.1	−35.3	−63.4	−63.2
Emerging markets			22.0	67.8	59.2
Equity-market neutral				37.9	34.9
Event-driven					93.8
January 1994 to December 1998					
Convertible arbitrage	−25.2	48.2	32.1	68.4	61.6
Dedicated short		−52.6	−43.5	−66.2	−69.1
Emerging markets			22.1	70.8	65.4
Equity-market neutral				43.4	44.9
Event-driven					94.9
January 1999 to December 2003					
Convertible arbitrage	−19.7	−5.8	32.3	41.8	33.5
Dedicated short		−67.3	−22.9	−63.0	−56.8
Emerging markets			22.1	60.6	45.2
Equity-market neutral				20.8	6.4
Event-driven					91.4

Source: AlphaSimplex Group.

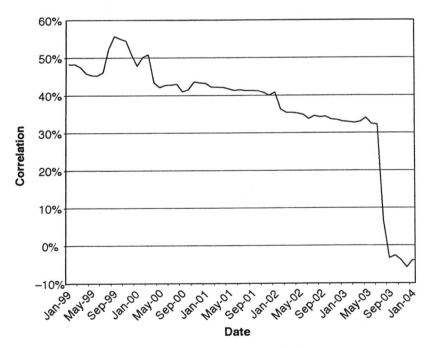

Fig. 6.3 **Sixty-month rolling correlations between CSFB/Tremont Convertible Arbitrage and Emerging Market Index returns, from January 1999 to December 2003**

Note: The sharp decline in September 2003 is due to the fact that this is the first month in which the August 1998 observation is dropped from the sixty-month rolling window.

Table 6.7   **CSFB/Tremont hedge fund index and market-index returns from August to October 2003**

Index	August 1998	September 1998	October 1998
Aggregate index	−7.55	−2.31	−4.57
Convertible arbitrage	−4.64	−3.23	−4.68
Dedicated short	22.71	−4.98	−8.69
Emerging markets	−23.03	−7.40	1.68
Equity-market neutral	−0.85	0.95	2.48
Event-driven	−11.77	−2.96	0.66
Distressed	−12.45	−1.43	0.89
Event driven multistrategy	−11.52	−4.74	0.26
Risk arbitrage	−6.15	−0.65	2.41
Fixed income arbitrage	−1.46	−3.74	−6.96
Global macro	−4.84	−5.12	−11.55
Long/short equity	−11.43	3.47	1.74
Managed futures	9.95	6.87	1.21
Multistrategy	1.15	0.57	−4.76
Ibbotson S&P 500	−14.46	6.41	8.13
Ibbotson Small Cap	−20.10	3.69	3.56
Ibbotson LT Corporate Bonds	0.89	4.13	−1.90
Ibbotson LT Government Bonds	4.65	3.95	−2.18

Source: AlphaSimplex Group.

Note: Monthly returns of CSFB/Tremont hedge-fund indexes and Ibbotson stock and bond indexes during August, September, and October 1998, in percent.

6.3.2 TASS Data

To develop a sense of the dynamics of the TASS database, in table 6.8 we report annual frequency counts of the funds added to and exiting from the TASS database each year. Not surprisingly, the number of hedge funds in both the Live and Graveyard databases grows over time. Table 6.8 shows that despite the start date of February 1977, the database is relatively sparsely populated until the 1990s, with the largest increase in new funds in 2001 and the largest number of funds exiting the database in the most recent year, 2003. TASS began tracking fund exits starting only in 1994, and for the unfiltered sample of all funds, the average attrition rate from 1994–1999 is 7.51 percent, which is very similar to the 8.54 percent attrition rate obtained by Liang (2001) for the same period. See section 6.5 for a more detailed analysis of hedge fund liquidations.

Table 6.9 contains basic summary statistics for the funds in the TASS Live, Graveyard, and Combined databases. Not surprisingly, there is a great deal of variation in mean returns and volatilities both across and within categories and databases. For example, the 127 Convertible Arbitrage funds in the Live database have an average mean return of 9.92 percent and an average standard deviation of 5.51 percent, but in the Graveyard database,

Table 6.8　　Annual frequency counts of entries into and exits out of the TASS hedge fund database from February 1977 to August 2004

Number of funds added to the TASS database each year

Year	All funds	Convertible arbitrage	Dedicated short	Emerging markets	Equity-market neutral	Event driven	Fixed income arbitrage	Global macro	Long/Short equity	Managed futures	Multi-strategy	Fund of funds
1977	3	0	0	0	0	2	0	0	0	1	0	0
1978	2	0	0	0	0	0	0	0	0	1	0	1
1979	2	0	0	0	0	0	0	0	0	1	0	0
1980	3	0	0	0	0	0	0	1	0	3	0	0
1981	3	0	0	0	0	0	0	0	1	1	0	1
1982	4	0	0	0	0	0	1	0	1	1	0	1
1983	9	0	0	0	0	1	0	1	3	3	0	1
1984	15	0	1	0	0	1	1	0	6	2	0	5
1985	9	0	0	0	0	1	0	1	0	1	0	5
1986	22	0	0	0	0	2	1	2	5	8	0	4
1987	28	0	0	0	0	2	0	2	10	7	1	6
1988	33	4	2	0	0	6	0	1	2	9	1	8
1989	43	1	0	3	3	7	1	2	7	10	0	9
1990	102	4	3	5	1	11	0	7	24	18	2	27
1991	89	2	2	5	1	11	1	11	17	20	1	18
1992	155	8	0	10	4	9	7	10	37	31	2	37
1993	247	7	3	21	3	18	10	12	55	64	10	44
1994	251	13	1	25	7	16	16	11	52	52	5	53
1995	299	12	0	34	10	27	12	19	74	41	7	63
1996	332	14	3	25	10	29	16	16	116	42	14	47
1997	356	10	3	40	14	31	15	19	118	37	13	56
1998	346	14	1	22	29	28	16	20	117	25	8	66

continued

Table 6.8 (continued)

Year	All funds	Convertible arbitrage	Dedicated short	Emerging markets	Equity-market neutral	Event driven	Fixed income arbitrage	Global macro	Long/Short equity	Managed futures	Multi-strategy	Fund of funds
1999	403	10	4	26	36	29	13	12	159	35	10	69
2000	391	17	2	20	17	38	9	18	186	13	10	61
2001	460	25	1	5	49	34	20	15	156	18	16	121
2002	432	22	1	4	41	40	23	26	137	22	14	102
2003	325	11	1	12	23	21	12	15	83	23	14	110
2004	1	0	0	0	0	0	0	0	0	0	0	1
Number of funds exiting the TASS database each year												
1994	25	0	0	0	1	0	3	3	2	9	4	3
1995	62	0	1	1	0	1	2	5	7	30	2	13
1996	129	7	1	4	0	3	4	17	23	51	1	18
1997	106	3	1	8	0	3	5	7	17	37	3	22
1998	171	5	0	26	4	3	14	9	35	37	6	32
1999	190	3	1	18	15	20	8	16	45	41	2	21
2000	243	3	6	27	13	15	11	33	60	35	3	42
2001	263	5	1	28	9	22	7	9	112	19	1	45
2002	255	6	1	11	16	32	5	9	112	32	5	26
2003	297	10	1	14	32	24	9	9	112	23	18	45
2004	88	10	2	1	5	15	4	1	27	5	0	18

Note: Prior to January 1994, exits were not tracked.

Table 6.9   Means and standard deviations of basic summary statistics for hedge funds in the TASS Hedge Fund Live, Graveyard, and Combined databases from February 1977 to August 2004

Category	Sample size	Annualized mean (%)		Annualized SD (%)		ρ_1 (%)		Annualized Sharpe ratio		Annualized adjusted Sharpe ratio		Ljung-Box p-value (%)	
		Mean	SD	Mean	SD	Mean	SD	Mean	SD	Mean	SD	Mean	SD
				Live funds									
Convertible arbitrage	127	9.92	5.89	5.51	4.15	33.6	19.2	2.57	4.20	1.95	2.86	19.5	27.1
Dedicated shortseller	14	0.33	11.11	25.10	10.92	3.5	10.9	−0.11	0.70	0.12	0.46	48.0	25.7
Emerging markets	130	17.74	13.77	21.69	14.42	18.8	13.8	1.36	2.01	1.22	1.40	35.5	31.5
Equity-market neutral	173	6.60	5.89	7.25	5.05	4.4	22.7	1.20	1.18	1.30	1.28	41.6	32.6
Event driven	250	12.52	8.99	8.00	7.15	19.4	20.9	1.98	1.47	1.68	1.47	31.3	34.1
Fixed income arbitrage	104	9.30	5.61	6.27	5.10	16.4	23.6	3.61	11.71	3.12	7.27	36.6	35.2
Global macro	118	10.51	11.55	13.57	10.41	1.3	17.1	0.86	0.68	0.99	0.79	46.8	30.6
Long/short equity	883	13.05	10.56	14.98	9.30	11.3	17.9	1.03	1.01	1.01	0.95	38.1	31.8
Managed futures	195	8.59	18.55	19.14	12.52	3.4	13.9	0.48	1.10	0.73	0.63	52.3	30.8
Multistrategy	98	12.65	17.93	9.31	10.94	18.5	21.3	1.91	2.34	1.46	2.06	31.1	31.7
Fund of funds	679	6.89	5.45	6.14	4.87	22.9	18.5	1.53	1.33	1.48	1.16	33.7	31.6
				Graveyard funds									
Convertible arbitrage	49	10.02	6.61	8.14	6.08	25.5	19.3	1.89	1.43	1.58	1.46	27.9	34.2
Dedicated shortseller	15	1.77	9.41	27.54	18.79	8.1	13.2	0.20	0.44	0.25	0.48	55.4	25.2
Emerging markets	133	2.74	27.74	27.18	18.96	14.3	17.9	0.37	0.91	0.47	1.11	48.5	34.6
Equity-market neutral	87	7.61	26.37	12.35	13.68	6.4	20.4	0.52	1.23	0.60	1.85	46.6	31.5
Event driven	134	9.07	15.04	12.35	12.10	16.6	21.1	1.22	1.38	1.13	1.43	39.3	34.2
Fixed income arbitrage	71	5.51	12.93	10.78	9.97	15.9	22.0	1.10	1.77	1.03	1.99	46.0	35.7
Global macro	114	3.74	28.83	21.02	18.94	3.2	21.5	0.33	1.05	0.37	0.90	46.2	31.0

continued

Table 6.9   (continued)

Category	Sample size	Annualized mean (%)		Annualized SD (%)		ρ_1 (%)		Annualized Sharpe ratio		Annualized adjusted Sharpe ratio		Ljung-Box p-value (%)	
		Mean	SD	Mean	SD	Mean	SD	Mean	SD	Mean	SD	Mean	SD
Long/short equity	532	9.69	22.75	23.08	16.82	6.4	19.8	0.48	1.06	0.48	1.17	47.8	31.3
Managed futures	316	4.78	23.17	20.88	19.35	−2.9	18.7	0.26	0.77	0.37	0.97	48.4	30.9
Multistrategy	41	5.32	23.46	17.55	20.90	6.1	17.4	1.10	1.55	1.58	2.06	49.4	32.2
Fund of funds	273	4.53	10.07	13.56	10.56	11.3	21.2	0.62	1.26	0.57	1.11	40.9	31.9
				Combined funds									
Convertible arbitrage	176	9.94	6.08	6.24	4.89	31.4	19.5	2.38	3.66	1.85	2.55	21.8	29.3
Dedicated shortseller	29	1.08	10.11	26.36	15.28	5.9	12.2	0.05	0.59	0.19	0.46	52.0	25.2
Emerging markets	263	10.16	23.18	24.48	17.07	16.5	16.2	0.86	1.63	0.84	1.31	42.2	33.7
Equity-market neutral	260	6.94	15.94	8.96	9.21	5.1	21.9	0.97	1.24	1.06	1.53	43.3	32.3
Event driven	384	11.31	11.57	9.52	9.40	18.4	21.0	1.71	1.48	1.49	1.48	34.1	34.3
Fixed income arbitrage	175	7.76	9.45	8.10	7.76	16.2	22.9	2.59	9.16	2.29	5.86	40.4	35.6
Global macro	232	7.18	22.04	17.21	15.61	2.3	19.3	0.60	0.92	0.70	0.90	46.5	30.8
Long/short equity	1415	11.79	16.33	18.02	13.25	9.5	18.8	0.82	1.06	0.81	1.07	41.7	31.9
Managed futures	511	6.23	21.59	20.22	17.07	−0.6	17.4	0.34	0.91	0.50	0.88	49.8	30.9
Multistrategy	139	10.49	19.92	11.74	15.00	14.7	20.9	1.67	2.16	1.49	2.05	36.7	32.9
Fund of funds	952	6.22	7.17	8.26	7.75	19.6	20.0	1.27	1.37	1.21	1.22	35.8	31.8

Note: The columns "*p*-value (*Q*)" contain means and standard deviations of *p*-values for the Ljung-Box *Q*-statistic for each fund, using the first eleven autocorrelations of returns. SD = standard deviation.

the forty-nine Convertible Arbitrage funds have an average mean return of 10.02 percent and a much higher average standard deviation of 8.14 percent. Not surprisingly, average volatilities in the Graveyard database are uniformly higher than those in the Live database because the higher-volatility funds are more likely to be eliminated.[18]

Average serial correlations also vary considerably across categories in the Combined database, but six categories stand out: Convertible Arbitrage (31.4 percent), Fund of Funds (19.6 percent), Event Driven (18.4 percent), Emerging Markets (16.5 percent), Fixed-Income Arbitrage (16.2 percent), and Multi-Strategy (14.7 percent). Given the descriptions of these categories provided by TASS (see the appendix) and common wisdom about the nature of the strategies involved—these categories include some of the most illiquid securities traded—serial correlation seems to be a reasonable proxy for illiquidity and smoothed returns (see Lo, 2001; Getmansky, Lo, and Makarov, 2004; and section 6.4). Alternatively, equities and futures are among the most liquid securities in which hedge funds invest, and not surprising, the average first-order serial correlations for Equity Market Neutral, Long/Short Equity, and Managed Futures are 5.1 percent, 9.5 percent, and –0.6 percent, respectively. Dedicated Shortseller funds also have a low average first-order autocorrelation, 5.9 percent, which is consistent with the high degree of liquidity that often characterize shortsellers (by definition, the ability to short a security implies a certain degree of liquidity).

These summary statistics suggest that illiquidity and smoothed returns may be important attributes for hedge fund returns, which can be captured to some degree by serial correlation and the time series model of smoothing in section 6.4.

Finally, table 6.10 reports the year-end assets under management for funds in each of the eleven TASS categories for the Combined database from 1977 to 2003; the relative proportions are plotted in figure 6.4. Table 6.10 shows that the total assets in the TASS combined database is approximately $391 billion, which is a significant percentage—though not nearly exhaustive—of the estimated $1 trillion in the hedge fund industry today.[19] The two dominant categories in the most recent year are Long/Short Equity ($101.5 billion) and Fund of Funds ($76.8 billion), but figure 6.4 shows that the relative proportions can change significantly over time (see Getmansky 2004 for a more detailed analysis of fund flows in the hedge fund industry).

---

18. This effect works at both ends of the return distribution—funds that are wildly successful are also more likely to leave the database, since they have less of a need to advertise their performance. That the Graveyard database also contains successful funds is supported by the fact that in some categories, the average mean return in the Graveyard database is the same as or higher than in the Live database—for example, convertible arbitrage, equity market neutral, and dedicated shortseller.

19. Of course, part of the $391 billion is Graveyard funds, hence the proportion of current hedge fund assets represented by the TASS database is less.

Table 6.10 Assets under management at year end in millions of U.S. dollars for funds in each of the eleven categories in the TASS combined hedge fund database from 1977 to 2003

Year	Convertible arbitrage	Dedicated shortseller	Emerging markets	Equity-market neutral	Event driven	Fixed income arbitrage	Global macro	Long/Short equity	Managed futures	Multi-strategy	Fund of funds	Total
1977					16.2			42.9	5.4			64.4
1978					22.1			53.2	18.0		32.2	125.5
1979					34.5		0.0	77.6	44.3		46.9	203.4
1980					52.7		0.1	110.6	55.1		76.9	295.4
1981					55.5		0.2	125.6	62.4		80.0	323.7
1982	3.5				76.9	13.5	0.3	174.3	72.2		172.0	512.8
1983	4.1				114.9	20.4	5.8	249.7	68.9		233.0	696.9
1984	3.7				168.7	23.0	6.2	345.0	68.8		245.6	860.9
1985	4.4	44.2			274.0	18.0	4.8	510.8	114.7		386.3	1,357.3
1986	5.2	63.4			387.5	64.9	132.6	737.3	180.7		641.9	2,213.4
1987	5.7	72.6			452.0	96.7	248.5	925.2	484.7	1,830.0	898.2	5,013.6
1988	27.5	108.5	17.9		1,012.1	95.1	265.2	1,324.8	775.4	1,821.6	1,318.7	6,766.9
1989	82.4	133.8	169.3	134.6	1,216.5	152.0	501.6	2,025.5	770.5	2,131.2	1,825.5	9,143.0
1990	188.2	260.4	330.3	156.5	1,383.4	289.0	1,964.9	2,609.8	1,006.6	2,597.8	2,426.2	13,213.2
1991	286.9	221.7	696.4	191.0	2,114.7	605.6	4,096.2	3,952.2	1,183.3	3,175.6	3,480.4	20,004.0
1992	1,450.7	237.0	1,235.4	316.2	2,755.3	928.2	7,197.0	5,925.5	1,466.8	3,778.0	4,941.8	30,231.9
1993	2,334.9	260.2	3,509.6	532.1	4,392.4	1,801.7	14,275.5	11,160.6	2,323.2	5,276.0	10,224.3	56,090.6
1994	2,182.4	388.2	5,739.4	577.2	5,527.6	2,237.5	11,822.6	12,809.7	2,965.4	4,349.9	10,420.2	59,020.2
1995	2,711.1	342.8	5,868.8	888.3	7,025.5	3,279.6	12,835.3	17,257.1	2,768.8	6,404.2	11,816.1	71,197.5
1996	3,913.3	397.4	8,439.8	2,168.7	9,493.3	5,428.4	16,543.2	23,165.7	2,941.0	7,170.1	14,894.0	94,554.9
1997	6,488.7	581.5	12,780.2	3,747.4	14,508.8	9,290.5	25,917.6	31,807.0	3,665.0	10,272.4	21,056.9	140,116.1
1998	7,802.7	868.2	5,743.9	6,212.5	17,875.4	8,195.3	23,960.9	36,432.9	4,778.5	9,761.3	22,778.5	144,410.3
1999	9,228.6	1,061.2	7,991.5	9,165.5	20,722.1	8,052.1	15,928.3	62,817.2	4,949.3	11,520.2	26,373.3	177,809.3
2000	13,365.2	1,312.7	6,178.7	13,507.5	26,569.6	8,245.0	4,654.9	78,059.0	4,734.8	10,745.2	31,378.5	198,751.0
2001	19,982.4	802.8	6,940.1	18,377.9	34,511.9	11,716.3	5,744.1	88,109.3	7,286.4	13,684.2	40,848.5	248,003.9
2002	23,649.4	812.8	8,664.8	20,008.2	36,299.0	17,256.8	8,512.8	84,813.5	10,825.4	16,812.1	51,062.7	278,717.4
2003	34,195.7	503.8	16,874.0	23,408.4	50,631.1	24,350.1	21,002.2	101,461.0	19,449.1	22,602.6	76,792.4	391,270.5

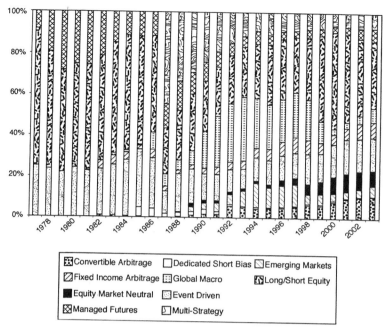

Fig. 6.4   Relative proportions of assets under management at year-end in the eleven categories of the TASS Hedge Fund Combined database, from 1977 to 2003

6.4   Measuring Illiquidity Risk

The examples of section 6.1 highlight the fact that hedge funds exhibit a heterogeneous array of risk exposures, but a common theme surrounding systemic risk factors is credit and liquidity. Although they are separate sources of risk exposures for hedge funds and their investors—one type of risk can exist without the other—nevertheless, liquidity and credit have been inextricably intertwined in the minds of most investors because of the problems encountered by Long Term Capital Management and many other fixed-income relative-value hedge funds in August and September of 1998. Because many hedge funds rely on leverage, the size of the positions are often considerably larger than the amount of collateral posted to support those positions. Leverage has the effect of a magnifying glass, expanding small profit opportunities into larger ones, but also expanding small losses into larger losses. When adverse changes in market prices reduce the market value of collateral, credit is withdrawn quickly, and the subsequent forced liquidation of large positions over short periods of time can lead to widespread financial panic, as in the aftermath of the default of Russian government debt in August 1998.[20] Along with the many benefits

20. Note that in the case of Capital Decimation Partners in section 6.1.1, the fund's consecutive returns of –18.3 percent and –16.2 percent in August and September 1998 would have

of a truly global financial system is the cost that a financial crisis in one country can have dramatic repercussions in several others—that is, contagion.

The basic mechanisms driving liquidity and credit are familiar to most hedge fund managers and investors, and there has been much progress in the recent literature in modeling both credit and illiquidity risk.[21] However, the complex network of creditor/obligor relationships, revolving credit agreements, and other financial interconnections is largely unmapped. Perhaps some of the newly developed techniques in the mathematical theory of networks will allow us to construct systemic measures for liquidity and credit exposures and the robustness of the global financial system to idiosyncratic shocks. The "small-world" networks considered by Watts and Strogatz (1998) and Watts (1999) seem to be particularly promising starting points.

6.4.1   Serial Correlation and Illiquidity

A more immediate method for gauging the illiquidity risk exposure of a given hedge fund is to examine the autocorrelation coefficients ρ_k of the fund's monthly returns, where $\rho_k \equiv \mathrm{Cov}(R_t, R_{t-k})/\mathrm{Var}(R_t)$ is the k-th order autocorrelation of (R_t),[22] which measures the degree of correlation between month t's return and month $t - k$'s return. To see why autocorrelations may be useful indicators of liquidity exposure, recall that one of the earliest financial asset pricing models is the martingale model, in which asset returns are serially uncorrelated ($\rho_k = 0$ for all $k \neq 0$). Indeed, the title of Samuelson's (1965) seminal paper—"Proof that Properly Anticipated Prices Fluctuate Randomly"—provides a succinct summary for the motivation of the martingale property: in an informationally efficient market, price changes must be unforecastable if they are properly anticipated—that is, if they fully incorporate the expectations and information of all market participants.

This extreme version of market efficiency is now recognized as an idealization that is unlikely to hold in practice.[23] In particular, market frictions such as transactions costs, borrowing constraints, costs of gathering and processing information, and institutional restrictions on shortsales and

---

made it virtually impossible for the fund to continue without a massive injection of capital. In all likelihood, it would have closed down along with many other hedge funds during those fateful months, never to realize the extraordinary returns that it would have earned had it been able to withstand the losses in August and September (see Lo 2001, table 6.4).

21. See, for example, Bookstaber (1999, 2000) and Kao (1999), and their citations.

22. The k-th order autocorrelation of a time series (R_t) is defined as the correlation coefficient between R_t and R_{t-k}, which is simply the covariance between R_t and R_{t-k} divided by the square root of the product of the variances of R_t and R_{t-k}. But since the variances of R_t and R_{t-k} are the same under the assumption of stationarity, the denominator of the autocorrelation is simply the variance of R_t.

23. See, for example, Farmer and Lo (1999) and Lo (2004).

other trading practices do exist, and they all contribute to the possibility of serial correlation in asset returns, which cannot easily be arbitraged away precisely because of the presence of these frictions. From this perspective, the degree of serial correlation in an asset's returns can be viewed as a proxy for the magnitude of the frictions, and illiquidity is one of most common forms of such frictions. For example, it is well known that the historical returns of residential real estate investments are considerably more highly autocorrelated than, say, the returns of the S&P 500 indexes during the same sample period. Similarly, the returns of S&P 500 futures contracts exhibit less serial correlation than those of the index itself. In both examples, the more liquid instrument exhibits less serial correlation than the less liquid, and the economic rationale is a modified version of Samuelson's (1965) argument—predictability in asset returns will be exploited and eliminated only to the extent allowed by market frictions. Despite the fact that the returns to residential real estate are highly predictable, it is impossible to take full advantage of such predictability because of the high transactions costs associated with real estate transactions, the inability to shortsell properties, and other frictions.[24]

A closely related phenomenon that buttresses this interpretation of serial correlation in hedge-fund returns is the "nonsynchronous trading" effect, in which the autocorrelation is induced in a security's returns because those returns are computed with closing prices that are not necessarily established at the same time each day (see, for example, Campbell, Lo, and MacKinlay 1997, chapter 3). But in contrast to the studies by Lo and MacKinlay (1988, 1990b) and Kadlec and Patterson (1999), in which they conclude that it is difficult to generate serial correlations in weekly U.S. equity portfolio returns much greater than 10 percent to 15 percent through nonsynchronous trading effects alone, Getmansky, Lo, and Makarov (2004) argue that in the context of hedge funds, significantly higher levels of serial correlation can be explained by the combination of illiquidity and performance smoothing (see the following), of which nonsynchronous trading is a special case. To see why, note that the empirical analysis in the nonsynchronous-trading literature is devoted exclusively to exchange-traded equity returns, not hedge fund returns, hence the corresponding conclusions may not be relevant in this context. For example, Lo and MacKinlay (1990b) argue that securities would have to go without trading for several days on average to induce serial correlations of 30 percent, and they dismiss such nontrading intervals as unrealistic for most exchange-traded U.S. equity issues. However, such nontrading intervals are considerably more realistic for the types of securities held by many hedge funds;

---

24. These frictions have led to the creation of real estate investment trusts (REITs), and the returns to these securities—which are considerably more liquid than the underlying assets on which they are based—exhibit much less serial correlation.

for example, emerging-market debt, real estate, restricted securities, control positions in publicly traded companies, asset-backed securities, and other exotic over-the-counter (OTC) derivatives. Therefore, nonsynchronous trading of this magnitude is likely to be an explanation for the serial correlation observed in hedge fund returns.

But even when prices are synchronously measured—as they are for many funds that mark their portfolios to market at the end of the month to strike a net asset value at which investors can buy into or cash out of the fund— there are several other channels by which illiquidity exposure can induce serial correlation in the reported returns of hedge funds. Apart from the nonsynchronous-trading effect, naive methods for determining the fair market value or "marks" for illiquid securities can yield serially correlated returns. For example, one approach to valuing illiquid securities is to extrapolate linearly from the most recent transaction price (which, in the case of emerging-market debt, might be several months ago), which yields a price path that is a straight line, or at best a series of straight lines. Returns computed from such marks will be smoother, exhibiting lower volatility and higher serial correlation than true economic returns; that is, returns computed from mark-to-market prices where the market is sufficiently active to allow all available information to be impounded in the price of the security. Of course, for securities that are more easily traded and with deeper markets, mark-to-market prices are more readily available, extrapolated marks are not necessary, and serial correlation is therefore less of an issue. But for securities that are thinly traded, or not traded at all for extended periods of time, marking them to market is often an expensive and time-consuming procedure that cannot easily be frequently performed.[25] Therefore, serial correlation may serve as a proxy for a fund's liquidity exposure.

Even if a hedge fund manager does not make use of any form of linear extrapolation to mark the securities in his portfolio, he may still be subject to smoothed returns if he obtains marks from broker-dealers that engage in such extrapolation. For example, consider the case of a conscientious hedge fund manager attempting to obtain the most accurate mark for his or her portfolio at month end by getting bid/offer quotes from three independent broker-dealers for every security in his portfolio, and then marking each security at the average of the three quote midpoints. By averaging the quote midpoints, the manager is inadvertently downward-biasing price volatility, and if any of the broker-dealers employ linear extrapolation in formulating their quotes (and many do, through sheer necessity because they have little else to go on for the most illiquid securities), or if they fail to update their quotes because of light volume, serial correlation will also be induced in reported returns.

Finally, a more prosaic channel by which serial correlation may arise in

25. Liang (2003) presents a sobering analysis of the accuracy of hedge fund returns that underscores the challenges of marking a portfolio to market.

the reported returns of hedge funds is through "performance smoothing," the unsavory practice of reporting only part of the gains in months when a fund has positive returns so as to partially offset potential future losses and thereby reduce volatility and improve risk-adjusted performance measures such as the Sharpe ratio. For funds containing liquid securities that can be easily marked to market, performance smoothing is more difficult and, as a result, less of a concern. Indeed, it is only for portfolios of illiquid securities that managers and brokers have any discretion in marking their positions. Such practices are generally prohibited by various securities laws and accounting principles, and great care must be exercised in interpreting smoothed returns as deliberate attempts to manipulate performance statistics. After all, as discussed previously, there are many other sources of serial correlation in the presence of illiquidity, none of which is motivated by deceit. Nevertheless, managers do have certain degrees of freedom in valuing illiquid securities—for example, discretionary accruals for unregistered private placements and venture capital investments—and Chandar and Bricker (2002) conclude that managers of certain closed-end mutual funds do use accounting discretion to manage fund returns around a passive benchmark. Therefore, the possibility of deliberate performance smoothing in the less regulated hedge fund industry must be kept in mind in interpreting any empirical analysis of serial correlation in hedge fund returns.

Getmansky, Lo, and Makarov (2004) address these issues in more detail by first examining other explanations of serial correlation in hedge fund returns that are unrelated to illiquidity and smoothing—in particular, time-varying expected returns, time-varying leverage, and incentive fees with high-water marks—and show that none of them can account for the magnitudes of serial correlation in hedge fund returns. They propose a specific econometric model of smoothed returns that is consistent with both illiquidity exposure and performance smoothing, and they estimate it using the historical returns of individual funds in the TASS hedge fund database. They find that funds with the most significant amount of smoothing tend to be the more illiquid—for example, emerging market debt, fixed income arbitrage, and so forth, and after correcting for the effects of smoothed returns, some of the most successful types of funds tend to have considerably less attractive performance characteristics.

However, for the purpose of developing a more highly aggregated measure to address systemic risk exposure, a simpler approach is to use serial correlation coefficients and the Ljung-Box Q-statistic (see footnote 17). To illustrate this approach, we estimate these quantities using monthly historical total returns of the ten largest (as of February 11, 2001) mutual funds, from various start dates through June 2000, and twelve hedge funds from various inception dates to December 2000. Monthly total returns for the mutual funds were obtained from the University of Chicago's Center for Research in Securities Prices. The twelve hedge funds were selected from the Altvest database to yield a diverse range of annual Sharpe ratios (from

1 to 5) computed in the standard way ($\sqrt{12}\widehat{SR}$, where $\widehat{SR}$ is the Sharpe ratio estimator applied to monthly returns), with the additional requirement that the funds have a minimum five-year history of returns.[26] The names of the hedge funds have been omitted to maintain their privacy, and we will refer to them only by their stated investment styles; for example, Relative Value Fund, Risk Arbitrage Fund.

Table 6.11 reports the means, standard deviations, $\hat{\rho}_1$ to $\hat{\rho}_6$, and the p-values of the Q-statistic using the first six autocorrelations for the sample of mutual and hedge funds. The first subpanel shows that the ten mutual funds have very little serial correlation in returns, with first-order autocorrelations ranging from –3.99 percent to 12.37 percent, and with p-values of the corresponding Q-statistics ranging from 10.95 percent to 80.96 percent, implying that none of the Q-statistics is significant at the 5 percent level. The lack of serial correlation in these ten mutual fund returns is not surprising. Because of their sheer size, these funds consist primarily of highly liquid securities and, as a result, their managers have very little discretion in marking such portfolios. Moreover, many of the SEC regulations that govern the mutual-fund industry—for example, detailed prospectuses, daily net asset value calculations, and quarterly filings—were enacted specifically to guard against arbitrary marks, price manipulation, and other unsavory investment practices.

The results for the twelve hedge funds are considerably different. In sharp contrast to the mutual fund sample, the hedge fund sample displays substantial serial correlation, with first-order autocorrelation coefficients that range from –20.17 percent to 49.01 percent, with eight out of twelve funds that have Q-statistics with p-values less than 5 percent, and ten out of twelve funds with p-values less than 10 percent. The only two funds with p-values that are not significant at the 5 percent or 10 percent levels are the Risk Arbitrage A and Risk Arbitrage B funds, which have p-values of 74.10 percent and 93.42 percent, respectively. This is consistent with the notion of serial correlation as a proxy for illiquidity risk because among the various types of funds in this sample, risk arbitrage is likely to be the most liquid, since, by definition, such funds invest in securities that are exchange-traded and where trading volume is typically heavier than usual because of the impending merger events on which risk arbitrage is based.

To develop further intuition for serial correlation in hedge fund returns, we reproduce a small portion of the analysis in Getmansky, Lo, and Makarov (2004), in which they report the serial correlation coefficients of the returns of the Ibbotson stock and bond indexes, the Merrill Lynch Convertible Securities Index,[27] the CSFB/Tremont hedge-fund indexes, and

---

26. See http://www.investorforce.com for further information about the Altvest database.

27. This is described by Merrill Lynch as a "market value-weighted index that tracks the daily price only, income and total return performance of corporate convertible securities, including U.S. domestic bonds, Eurobonds, preferred stocks and Liquid Yield Option Notes."

Table 6.11 Autocorrelations of mutual fund and hedge fund returns: Monthly data, various sample periods

Fund	Start date	T	$\hat{\mu}$ (%)	$\hat{\sigma}$ (%)	$\hat{\rho}_1$ (%)	$\hat{\rho}_2$ (%)	$\hat{\rho}_3$ (%)	$\hat{\rho}_4$ (%)	$\hat{\rho}_5$ (%)	$\hat{\rho}_6$ (%)	p-value of Q_6 (percent)
Mutual funds											
Vanguard 500 Index	76.10	286	1.30	4.27	−3.99	−6.60	−4.94	−6.38	10.14	−3.63	31.85
Fidelity Magellan	67.01	402	1.73	6.23	12.37	−2.31	−0.35	0.65	7.13	3.14	17.81
Investment Company of America	63.01	450	1.17	4.01	1.84	−3.23	−4.48	−1.61	6.25	−5.60	55.88
Janus	70.03	364	1.52	4.75	10.49	−0.04	−3.74	−8.16	2.12	−0.60	30.32
Fidelity Contrafund	67.05	397	1.29	4.97	7.37	−2.46	−6.81	−3.88	2.73	−4.47	42.32
Washington Mutual Investors	63.01	450	1.13	4.09	−0.10	−7.22	−2.64	0.65	11.55	−2.61	16.73
Janus Worldwide	92.01	102	1.81	4.36	11.37	3.43	−3.82	−15.42	−21.36	−10.33	10.95
Fidelity Growth and Income	86.01	174	1.54	4.13	5.09	−1.60	−8.20	−15.58	2.10	−7.29	30.91
American Century Ultra	81.12	223	1.72	7.11	2.32	3.35	1.36	−3.65	−7.92	−5.98	80.96
Growth Fund of America	64.07	431	1.18	5.35	8.52	−2.65	−4.11	−3.17	3.43	0.34	52.45
Hedge funds											
Convertible/Option Arbitrage	92.05	104	1.63	0.97	42.59	28.97	21.35	2.91	−5.89	−9.72	0.00
Relative Value	92.12	97	0.66	0.21	25.90	19.23	−2.13	−16.39	−6.24	1.36	3.32
Mortgage-Backed Securities	93.01	96	1.33	0.79	42.04	22.11	16.73	22.58	6.58	−1.96	0.00
High Yield Debt	94.06	79	1.30	0.87	33.73	21.84	13.13	−0.84	13.84	4.00	1.11
Risk Arbitrage A	93.07	90	1.06	0.69	−4.85	−10.80	6.92	−8.52	9.92	3.06	74.10
Long/Short Equities	89.07	138	1.18	0.83	−20.17	24.62	8.74	11.23	13.53	16.94	0.05
Multistrategy A	95.01	72	1.08	0.75	48.88	23.38	3.35	0.79	−2.31	−12.82	0.06
Risk Arbitrage B	94.11	74	0.90	0.77	−4.87	2.45	−8.29	−5.70	0.60	9.81	93.42
Convertible Arbitrage A	92.09	100	1.38	1.60	33.75	30.76	7.88	−9.40	3.64	−4.36	0.06
Convertible Arbitrage B	94.07	78	0.78	0.62	32.36	9.73	−4.46	6.50	−6.33	−10.55	8.56
Multistrategy B	89.06	139	1.34	1.63	49.01	24.60	10.60	8.85	7.81	7.45	0.00
Fund of Funds	94.10	75	1.68	2.29	29.67	21.15	0.89	−0.90	−12.38	3.01	6.75

Source: AlphaSimplex Group.

Notes: Means, standard deviations, and autocorrelation coefficients for monthly total returns of mutual funds and hedge funds from various start dates through June 2000 for the mutual fund sample and various start dates through December 2000 for the hedge fund sample. "$\hat{\rho}_k$" denotes the k-th auto-correlation coefficient, and "p-value of Q_6" denotes the significance level of the Ljung-Box (1978) Q-statistic $T(T+2)\sum_{k=1}^{6} \hat{\rho}_k^2/(T-k)$, which is asymptotically χ_6^2 under the null hypothesis of no serial correlation.

two mutual funds: the highly liquid Vanguard 500 Index Fund and the considerably less liquid American Express Extra Income Fund.[28] Table 6.12 contains the autocorrelations as well as market betas (where the market return is taken to be the S&P 500 total return) and contemporaneous and lagged market betas.[29]

Consistent with our interpretation of serial correlation as an indicator of illiquidity, the returns of the most liquid portfolios in table 6.12—the Ibbotson Large Company Index, the Vanguard 500 Index Fund (which is virtually identical to the Ibbotson Large Company Index, except for sample period and tracking error), and the Ibbotson Long-Term Government Bond Index—have small autocorrelation coefficients: 9.8 percent for the Ibbotson Large Company Index, –2.3 percent for the Vanguard 500 Index Fund, and 6.7 percent for the Ibbotson Long-Term Government Bond Index. The lagged market betas of these indexes are also statistically indistinguishable from 0. However, first-order autocorrelations of the less liquid portfolios are: 15.6 percent for the Ibbotson Small Company Index, 15.6 percent for the Ibbotson Long-Term Corporate Bond Index, 6.4 percent for the Merrill Lynch Convertible Securities Index, and 35.4 percent for the American Express Extra Income Fund, which, with the exception of the Merrill Lynch Convertible Securities Index, are considerably higher than those of the more liquid portfolios.[30] Also, the lagged market betas are statistically significant at the 5 percent level for the Ibbotson Small Company Index (a t-statistic for $\hat{\beta}_1$: 5.41), the Ibbotson Long-Term Government

28. As of January 31, 2003, the net assets of the Vanguard 500 Index Fund (ticker symbol: VFINX) and the AXP Extra Income Fund (ticker symbol: INEAX) are given by http://finance.yahoo.com/ as $59.7 billion and $1.5 billion, respectively, and the descriptions of the two funds are as follows:

> The Vanguard 500 Index Fund seeks investment results that correspond with the price and yield performance of the S&P 500 Index. The fund employs a passive management strategy designed to track the performance of the S&P 500 Index, which is dominated by the stocks of large U.S. companies. It attempts to replicate the target index by investing all or substantially all of its assets in the stocks that make up the index.
>
> AXP Extra Income Fund seeks high current income; capital appreciation is secondary. The fund ordinarily invests in long-term high-yielding, lower-rated corporate bonds. These bonds may be issued by U.S. and foreign companies and governments. The fund may invest in other instruments such as: money market securities, convertible securities, preferred stocks, derivatives (such as futures, options and forward contracts), and common stocks.

29. Market betas were obtained by regressing returns on a constant and the total return of the S&P 500, and contemporaneous and lagged market betas were obtained by regressing returns on a constant, the contemporaneous total return of the S&P 500, and the first two lags. Asness, Krail, and Liew (2001) observe that many hedge funds that claim to be market neutral are, in fact, not neutral with respect to a lagged market factor, and Getmansky, Lo, and Makarov (2004) show that this is consistent with illiquidity exposure and performance smoothing.

30. However, note that the second-order autocorrelation of the Merrill Lynch Convertible Securities Index is 12.0 percent, which is second only to the AXP Extra Income Fund in absolute magnitude, two orders of magnitude larger than the second-order autocorrelation of the Ibbotson bond indexes, and one order of magnitude larger than the Ibbotson stock indexes.

Table 6.12   Autocorrelations and market betas for various indexes and mutual funds

Series	Period	T	Mean (%)	SD (%)	$\hat{\rho}_1$ (%)	$\hat{\rho}_2$ (%)	$\hat{\rho}_3$ (%)	Market model $\hat{\beta}$	SE($\hat{\beta}$)	R^2 (%)	Contemporaneous and lagged market model $\hat{\beta}_0$	SE($\hat{\beta}_0$)	$\hat{\beta}_1$	SE($\hat{\beta}_1$)	$\hat{\beta}_2$	SE($\hat{\beta}_2$)	R^2 (%)
Ibbotson Small Company	192601–200112	912	1.35	8.63	15.6	1.7	-10.6	1.27	0.03	66.9	1.25	0.03	0.16	0.03	0.03	0.03	68.0
Ibbotson Long-Term Government Bonds	192601–200112	912	0.46	2.22	6.7	0.3	-8.3	0.07	0.01	2.8	0.07	0.01	-0.03	0.01	-0.02	0.01	3.6
Ibbotson Long-Term Corporate Bonds	192601–200112	912	0.49	1.96	15.6	0.3	-6.0	0.08	0.01	5.2	0.08	0.01	-0.01	0.01	-0.01	0.01	5.3
Ibbotson Large Company	192601–200112	912	1.03	5.57	9.8	-3.2	-10.7	1.00	0.00	100.0	1.00	0.00	0.00	0.00	0.00	0.00	100.0
Merrill Lynch Convertibles Index	199401–200210	168	0.99	3.43	6.4	12.0	5.1	0.59	0.05	48.6	0.60	0.05	0.15	0.05	0.07	0.04	52.2
AXP Extra Income Fund (INEAX)	198401–200112	216	0.67	2.04	35.4	13.1	2.5	0.21	0.03	20.7	0.21	0.03	0.12	0.03	0.04	0.03	28.7
Vanguard 500 Index Trust (VFINX)	197609–200112	304	1.16	4.36	-2.3	-6.8	-3.2	1.00	0.00	100.0	1.00	0.00	0.00	0.00	0.00	0.00	100.0
CSFB/Tremont Indexes																	
Aggregate hedge fund index	199401–200210	106	0.87	2.58	11.2	4.1	-0.4	0.31	0.05	24.9	0.32	0.05	0.06	0.05	0.16	0.05	32.1
Convertible arbitrage	199401–200210	106	0.81	1.40	56.6	42.6	15.6	0.03	0.03	1.1	0.04	0.03	0.09	0.03	0.06	0.03	12.0
Dedicated short bias	199401–200210	106	0.22	5.29	7.8	-6.3	-5.0	-0.94	0.08	58.6	-0.93	0.08	-0.06	0.08	0.08	0.08	59.3
Emerging markets	199401–200210	106	0.54	5.38	29.4	1.2	-2.1	0.62	0.11	24.0	0.63	0.11	0.19	0.11	0.03	0.12	26.2
Equity-market neutral	199401–200210	106	0.89	0.92	29.4	18.1	8.4	0.10	0.02	21.1	0.10	0.02	0.02	0.02	0.00	0.02	22.1
Event driven	199401–200210	106	0.83	1.81	34.8	14.7	3.8	0.23	0.04	30.2	0.23	0.03	0.11	0.03	0.04	0.03	38.2
Fixed income arbitrage	199401–200210	106	0.55	1.18	39.6	10.8	5.4	0.02	0.03	0.7	0.03	0.03	0.05	0.03	0.09	0.03	12.9
Global macro	199401–200210	106	1.17	3.69	5.6	4.6	8.3	0.24	0.09	7.5	0.26	0.09	-0.01	0.09	0.23	0.09	14.1
Long/Short	199401–200210	106	0.98	3.34	15.9	5.9	-4.6	0.48	0.06	36.7	0.49	0.06	0.06	0.06	0.15	0.06	40.7
Managed futures	199401–200210	106	0.55	3.44	3.2	-6.3	0.7	-0.12	0.06	2.5	-0.13	0.08	-0.17	0.08	0.02	0.08	7.8

Notes: Autocorrelations and contemporaneous and lagged market betas for the returns of various indexes and two mutual funds, the Vanguard 500 Index Trust (which tracks the S&P 500 index), and the AXP Extra Income Fund (which focuses on high current income and invests in long-term, high-yielding, lower-rated corporate bonds). Total returns of the S&P 500 index are used for both market models. SD = standard deviation; SE = standard error.

Bond Index (t-statistic for $\hat{\beta}_1$: –2.30), the Merrill Lynch Convertible Securities Index (t-statistic for $\hat{\beta}_1$: 3.33), and the American Express (AXP) Extra Income Fund (t-statistic for $\hat{\beta}_1$: 4.64).

The results for the CSFB Hedge Fund Indexes in the second panel of table 6.12 are also consistent with the empirical results in table 6.11—indexes corresponding to hedge fund strategies involving less liquid securities tend to have higher autocorrelations. For example, the first-order autocorrelations of the Convertible Arbitrage, Emerging Markets, and Fixed-Income Arbitrage Indexes are 56.6 percent, 29.4 percent, and 39.6 percent, respectively. In contrast, the first-order autocorrelations of the more liquid hedge fund strategies such as Dedicated Short Bias and Managed Futures are 7.8 percent and 3.2 percent, respectively.

While these findings are generally consistent with the results for individual hedge funds in Getmansky, Lo, and Makarov (2004), it should be noted that the process of aggregation can change the statistical behavior of any time series. For example, Granger (1980, 1988) observes that the aggregation of a large number of stationary autoregressive processes can yield a time series that exhibits long-term memory, characterized by serial correlation coefficients that decay very slowly (hyperbolically, as opposed to geometrically as in the case of a stationary autoregressive moving average [ARMA] process). Therefore, while it is true that the aggregation of a collection of illiquid funds will generally yield an index with smoothed returns,[31] the reverse need not be true—smoothed index returns need not imply that all of the funds comprising the index are illiquid. The latter inference can only be made with the benefit of additional information—essentially identification restrictions—about the statistical relations among the funds in the index; that is, covariances and possibly other higher-order comoments, or the existence of common factors driving fund returns.

It is interesting to note that the first lagged market beta, $\hat{\beta}_1$, for the CSFB/Tremont indexes is statistically significant at the 5 percent level in only three cases (Convertible Arbitrage, Event Driven, and Managed Futures), but the second lagged beta, $\hat{\beta}_2$, is significant in five cases (the overall index, Convertible Arbitrage, Fixed Income Arbitrage, Global Macro, and Long/Short). Obviously, the S&P 500 index is likely to be inappropriate for certain styles—for example, Emerging Markets—and these somewhat inconsistent results suggest that using a lagged market-beta adjustment may not completely account for the impact of illiquidity and smoothed returns.

Overall, the patterns in table 6.12 confirm our interpretation of serial correlation as proxies for illiquidity, and suggest that there may be broader

---

31. It is, of course, possible that the smoothing coefficients of some funds may exactly offset those of other funds so as to reduce the degree of smoothing in an aggregate index. However, such a possibility is extremely remote and pathological if each of the component funds exhibits a high degree of smoothing.

applications of this model of smoothed returns to other investment strategies and asset classes.

Of course, there are several other aspects of liquidity that are not captured by serial correlation, and certain types of trading strategies can generate serial correlation even though they invest in highly liquid instruments. In particular, conditioning variables such as investment style, the types of securities traded, and other aspects of the market environment should be taken into account, perhaps through the kind of risk models proposed in section 6.6. However, for the purpose of developing a measure of systemic risk in the hedge fund industry, autocorrelation coefficients and Q-statistics provide a great deal of insight and information in a convenient manner.

6.4.2   An Aggregate Measure of Illiquidity

Having established the relevance of serial correlation as a proxy for illiquidity, we now turn to the measurement of illiquidity in the context of systemic risk. To that end, let $\rho_{1t,i}$ denote the first-order autocorrelation coefficient in month t for fund i using a rolling window of past returns. Then an aggregate measure of illiquidity ρ_t^* in the hedge fund sector may be obtained by a cross-sectional weighted average of these rolling autocorrelations, where the weights ω_{it} are simply the proportion of assets under management for fund i:

$$(9) \qquad \qquad \rho_t^* \equiv \sum_{i=1}^{N_t} \omega_{it} \rho_{1t,i}$$

$$(10) \qquad \qquad \omega_{it} \equiv \frac{\mathrm{AUM}_{it}}{\sum_{j=1}^{N_t} \mathrm{AUM}_{jt}},$$

where N_t is the number of funds in the sample in month t, and AUM_{jt} is the assets under management for fund j in month t.

Figure 6.5 plots these weighted correlations from January 1980 to August 2004, using all funds in the TASS Combined database with at least thirty-six consecutive trailing months of nonmissing returns, along with the number of funds each month (at the bottom, measured by the right vertical axis), and the median correlation in the cross-section (in gray).[32] The median correlation is quite different from the asset-weighted correlation in the earlier part of the sample, but as the number of funds increases over time, the behavior of the median becomes closer to that of ρ_t^*.

Figure 6.5 also shows considerable swings in ρ_t^* over time, with dynamics that seem to be related to liquidity events. In particular, consider the fol-

---

32. The number of funds in the early years is relatively low, reaching a level of fifty or more only in late 1988; therefore the weighted correlations before then may be somewhat less informative.

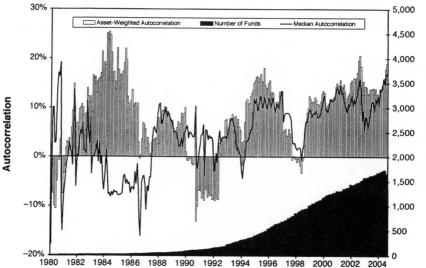

Fig. 6.5   Monthly cross-sectional median and weighted-mean first-order autocorrelation coefficients of individual hedge funds in the TASS Combined hedge-fund database with at least thirty-six consecutive trailing months of returns, from January 1980 to August 2004

lowing events: between November 1980 and July 1982, the S&P 500 dropped 23.8 percent; in October 1987 the S&P 500 fell by 21.8 percent; in 1990, the Japanese "bubble economy" burst; in August 1990, the Persian Gulf War began with Iraq's invasion of Kuwait, ending in January 1991 with Kuwait's liberation by coalition forces; in February 1994, the U.S. Federal Reserve started a tightening cycle that caught many hedge funds by surprise, causing significant dislocation in bond markets worldwide; the end of 1994 witnessed the start of the "Tequila Crisis" in Mexico; in August 1998 Russia defaulted on its government debt; and between August 2000 and September 2002 the S&P 500 fell by 46.3 percent. In each of these cases, the weighted autocorrelation rose in the aftermath, and in most cases abruptly. Of course, the fact that we are using a thirty-six-month rolling window suggests that as outliers drop out of the window, correlations can shift dramatically. However, as a coarse measure of liquidity in the hedge fund sector, the weighted autocorrelation seems to be intuitively appealing and informative.

6.5   Hedge Fund Liquidations

Since the collapse of LTCM in 1998, it has become clear that hedge fund liquidations can be a significant source of systemic risk. In this section, we consider several measures of liquidation probabilities for hedge funds in the TASS database, including a review of hedge fund attrition rates documented in Getmansky, Lo, and Mei (2004) and a logit analysis of hedge fund liquidations in the TASS Graveyard database. By analyzing the factors driving hedge fund liquidations, we may develop a broader understanding of the likely triggers of systemic risk in this sector.

Because of the voluntary nature of inclusion in the TASS database, Graveyard funds do not consist solely of liquidations. TASS gives one of seven distinct reasons for each fund that is assigned to the Graveyard, ranging from "Liquidated" (status code 1) to "Unknown" (status code 9). It may seem reasonable to confine our attention to those Graveyard funds categorized as Liquidated or perhaps to drop those funds that are closed to new investment (status code 4) from our sample. However, because our purpose is to develop a broader perspective on the dynamics of the hedge fund industry, we argue that using the entire Graveyard database may be more informative. For example, by eliminating Graveyard funds that are closed to new investors, we create a downward bias in the performance statistics of the remaining funds. Because we do not have detailed information about each of these funds, we cannot easily determine how any particular selection criterion will affect the statistical properties of the remainder. Therefore, we choose to include the entire set of Graveyard funds in our analysis, but caution readers to keep in mind the composition of this sample when interpreting our empirical results.

For concreteness, table 6.13 reports frequency counts for Graveyard funds in each status code and style category, as well as assets under management at the time of transfer to the Graveyard.[33] These counts show that 1,571 of the 1,765 Graveyard funds, or 89 percent, fall into the first three categories, categories that can plausibly be considered liquidations, and within each of these three categories, the relative frequencies across style categories are roughly comparable, with Long/Short Equity being the most numerous and Dedicated Shortseller being the least numerous. Of the remaining 194 funds with status codes 4–9, only status code 4—funds that are closed to new investors—is distinctly different in character from the other status codes. There are only seven funds in this category, and these funds are all likely to be success stories, providing some counterbalance to the many liquidations in the Graveyard sample. Of course, this is not to say that seven out of 1,765 is a reasonable estimate of the success rate in the hedge fund industry, because we have not included any of the Live funds in this calculation. Nevertheless, these seven funds in the Graveyard sample do underscore the fact that hedge fund data are subject to a variety of biases that do not always point in the same direction, and we prefer to leave

---

33. Of the 1,765 funds in the Graveyard database, four funds did not have status codes assigned, hence we coded them as 9's ("Unknown"). They are 3882 (Fund of Funds), 34053 (Managed Futures), 34054 (Managed Futures), 34904 (Long/Short Equity).

Table 6.13   Frequency counts and assets under management (in millions of dollars) of funds in the TASS Graveyard database by Category and Graveyard status code

Code	All funds	Convertible arbitrage	Dedicated short	Emerging markets	Equity-market neutral	Event driven	Fixed income arbitrage	Global macro	Long/Short equity	Managed futures	Multi-strategy	Fund of funds
					Frequency count							
1	913	19	7	78	65	50	29	53	257	190	30	135
2	511	21	4	34	12	56	26	29	187	43	7	92
3	147	4	1	7	8	17	3	17	54	18	1	17
4	7	0	0	0	0	1	2	0	3	0	0	1
5	56	2	1	5	0	6	3	6	16	9	1	7
7	2	0	0	0	0	1	0	0	1	0	0	0
9	129	3	2	9	2	3	8	9	14	56	2	21
Total	1,765	49	15	133	87	134	71	114	532	316	41	273
					Assets under management							
1	18,754	1,168	62	1,677	1,656	2,047	1,712	2,615	4,468	975	641	1,732
2	36,366	6,420	300	848	992	7,132	2,245	678	10,164	537	882	6,167
3	4,127	45	34	729	133	1,398	50	115	931	269	2	423
4	487	0	0	0	0	100	31	0	250	0	0	106
5	3,135	12	31	143	0	222	419	1,775	473	33	3	24
7	8	0	0	0	0	6	0	0	2	0	0	0
9	3,052	42	18	222	9	159	152	32	193	1,671	18	538
Total	65,931	7,686	445	3,620	2,789	11,063	4,610	5,215	16,482	3,484	1,546	8,991

Note: Graveyard status code: 1 = fund liquidated; 2 = fund no longer reporting to TASS; 3 = TASS has been unable to contact the manager for updated information; 4 = fund closed to new investment; 5 = fund has merged into another entity; 7 = fund dormant; 9 = unknown assets under management are at the time of transfer into the graveyard database.

them in so as to reflect these biases as they occur naturally rather than to create new biases of our own. For the remainder of this article, we shall refer to all funds in the TASS Graveyard database as "liquidations" for expositional simplicity.

Figure 6.6 provides a visual comparison of average means, standard deviations, Sharpe ratios, and first-order autocorrelation coefficients ρ_1 in the Live and Graveyard databases (table 6.9 contains basic summary statistics for the funds in the TASS Live, Graveyard, and Combined databases). Not surprisingly, there is a great deal of variation in mean returns and volatilities, both across and within categories and databases. For example, the 127 Convertible Arbitrage funds in the Live database have an average mean return of 9.92 percent and an average standard deviation of 5.51 percent, but in the Graveyard database, the forty-nine Convertible Arbitrage funds have an average mean return of 10.02 percent and a much higher average standard deviation of 8.14 percent. As expected, average volatilities in the Graveyard database are uniformly higher than those in the Live database because the higher-volatility funds are more likely to be eliminated. This effect operates at both ends of the return distribution—funds that are wildly successful are also more likely to leave the database, since they have less motivation to advertise their performance. That the Graveyard database also contains successful funds is supported by the fact that in some categories, the average mean return in the Graveyard database is the same as or higher than in the Live database—for example, Convertible Arbitrage, Equity Market Neutral, and Dedicated Shortseller.

Figure 6.7 displays the histogram of year-to-date returns at the time of liquidation. The fact that the distribution is skewed to the left is consistent with the conventional wisdom that performance is a major factor in determining the fate of a hedge fund. However, note that there is nontrivial weight in the right half of the distribution, suggesting that recent performance is not the only relevant factor.

Finally, figure 6.8 provides a summary of two key characteristics of the Graveyard funds: the age distribution of funds at the time of liquidation, and the distribution of their assets under management. The median age of Graveyard funds is forty-five months, hence half of all liquidated funds never reached their fourth anniversary. The mode of the distribution is 36 months. The median assets under management for funds in the Graveyard database is $6.3 million, not an uncommon size for the typical startup hedge fund.

In section 6.5.1, we document the attrition rates of funds in the TASS database, both in the aggregate and for each style category. These attrition rates provide crude baseline measures of the likelihood of liquidation for a given fund. To develop a more precise measure that allows for cross-sectional variability in the likelihood of liquidation—as a function of fund characteristics such as assets under management and recent performance—we estimate a logit model for hedge fund liquidations in section 6.5.2.

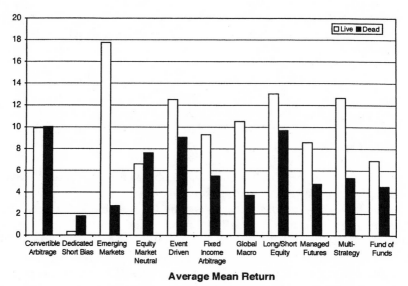

Average Mean Return

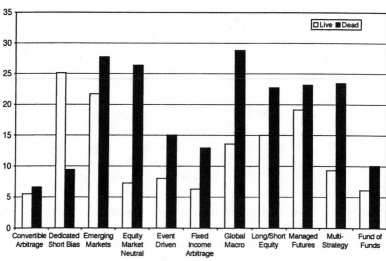

Average Standard Deviation

Fig. 6.6   Comparison of average means, standard deviations, Sharpe ratios, and first-order autocorrelation coefficients for categories of funds in the TASS Live and Graveyard databases from January 1994 to August 2004

6.5.1   Attrition Rates

To develop a sense of the dynamics of the TASS database and the birth and death rates of hedge funds over the past decade,[34] in table 6.14 we re-

34. Recall that TASS launched their Graveyard database in 1994, hence this is the beginning of our sample for table 6.14.

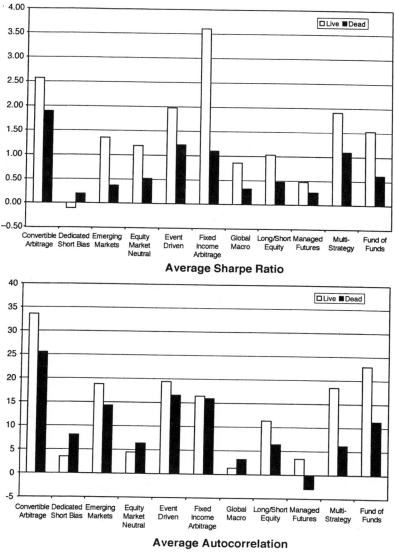

Fig. 6.6   (cont.)

port annual frequency counts of the funds in the database at the start of each year, funds entering the Live database during the year, funds exiting during the year and moving to the Graveyard database, and funds entering and exiting within the year. The panel labelled "All Funds" contains frequency counts for all funds, and the remaining eleven panels contain the same statistics for each category. Also included in table 6.14 are attrition rates, defined as the ratio of funds exiting in a given year to the number of

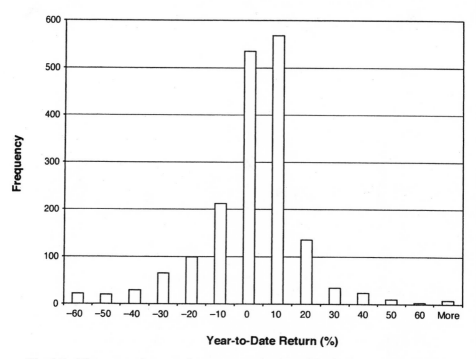

Fig. 6.7   Histogram of year-to-date return at the time of liquidation of hedge funds in the TASS Graveyard database, January 1994 to August 2004

existing funds at the start of the year, and the performance of the category as measured by the annual compound return of the CSFB/Tremont Index for that category.

For the unfiltered sample of all funds in the TASS database, and over the sample period from 1994 to 2003, the average attrition rate is 8.8 percent.[35] This is similar to the 8.5 percent attrition rate obtained by Liang (2001) for the 1994-to-1999 sample period. The aggregate attrition rate rises in 1998, partly due to LTCM's demise and the dislocation caused by its aftermath. The attrition rate increases to a peak of 11.4 percent in 2001, mostly due to

35. We do not include 2004 in this average because TASS typically waits eight to ten months before moving a nonreporting fund from the Live to the Graveyard database. Therefore, the attrition rate is severely downward biased for 2004, since the year is not yet complete, and many nonreporting funds in the Live database have not yet been classified as Graveyard funds (we use the TASS database from February 1997 to August 2004). Also, note that there is only 1 new fund in 2004—this figure is grossly downward biased as well. Hedge funds often go through an "incubation period" where managers trade with limited resources to develop a track record. If successful, the manager will provide the return stream to a database vendor like TASS, and the vendor usually enters the entire track record into the database, providing the fund with an "instant history." According to Fung and Hsieh (2000), the average incubation period—from a fund's inception to its entry into the TASS database—is one year.

Fig. 6.8 Histograms of age distribution and assets under management at the time of liquidation for funds in the TASS Graveyard database, January 1994 to August 2004

Table 6.14   Attrition rates for all hedge funds in the TASS hedge fund database, and within each style category, from January 1994 to August 2004

All funds

Year	Existing funds	New entries	New exits	Intra-year entry and exit funds	Total funds	Attrition rate (%)	Index return (%)
1994	769	251	23	2	997	3.0	−4.4
1995	997	299	61	1	1,235	6.1	21.7
1996	1,235	332	120	9	1,447	9.7	22.2
1997	1,447	356	100	6	1,703	6.9	25.9
1998	1,703	346	162	9	1,887	9.5	−0.4
1999	1,887	403	183	7	2,107	9.7	23.4
2000	2,107	391	234	9	2,264	11.1	4.8
2001	2,264	460	257	6	2,467	11.4	4.4
2002	2,467	432	246	9	2,653	10.0	3.0
2003	2,653	325	285	12	2,693	10.7	15.5
2004	2,693	1	87	1	2,607	3.2	2.7

Convertible arbitrage

Year	Existing funds	New entries	New exits	Intra-year entry and exit funds	Total funds	Attrition rate (%)	Index return (%)
1994	26	13	0	0	39	0.0	−8.1
1995	39	12	0	0	51	0.0	16.6
1996	51	14	7	0	58	13.7	17.9
1997	58	10	3	0	65	5.2	14.5
1998	65	14	5	0	74	7.7	−4.4
1999	74	10	3	0	81	4.1	16.0
2000	81	17	3	0	95	3.7	25.6
2001	95	25	5	0	115	5.3	14.6
2002	115	22	6	0	131	5.2	4.0
2003	131	11	10	0	132	7.6	12.9
2004	132	0	10	0	122	7.6	0.6

Equity-markets neutral

Year	Existing funds	New entries	New exits	Intra-year entry and exit funds	Total funds	Attrition rate (%)	Index return (%)
1994	12	7	1	0	18	8.3	−2.0
1995	18	10	0	0	28	0.0	11.0
1996	28	10	0	0	38	0.0	16.6
1997	38	14	0	0	52	0.0	14.8
1998	52	29	2	2	79	3.8	13.3
1999	79	36	14	1	101	17.7	15.3
2000	101	17	13	0	105	12.9	15.0
2001	105	49	9	0	145	8.6	9.3
2002	145	41	14	2	172	9.7	7.4
2003	172	23	32	0	163	18.6	7.1
2004	163	0	5	0	158	3.1	4.7

Event driven

Year	Existing funds	New entries	New exits	Intra-year entry and exit funds	Total funds	Attrition rate (%)	Index return (%)
1994	71	16	0	0	87	0.0	−8.1
1995	87	27	1	0	113	1.1	18.4
1996	113	29	3	0	139	2.7	23.0
1997	139	31	3	0	167	2.2	20.0
1998	167	28	2	1	193	1.2	−4.9
1999	193	29	19	1	203	9.8	22.3
2000	203	38	15	0	226	7.4	7.2
2001	226	34	19	3	241	8.4	11.5
2002	241	40	30	2	251	12.4	0.2
2003	251	21	23	1	249	9.2	20.0
2004	249	0	15	0	234	6.0	5.7

Long/Short equity

Year	Existing funds	New entries	New exits	Intra-year entry and exit funds	Total funds	Attrition rate (%)	Index return (%)
1994	168	52	2	2	218	1.2	−8.1
1995	218	74	7	0	285	3.2	23.0
1996	285	116	21	2	380	7.4	17.1
1997	380	118	15	2	483	3.9	21.5
1998	483	117	33	2	567	6.8	17.2
1999	567	159	42	3	684	7.4	47.2
2000	684	186	55	5	815	8.0	2.1
2001	815	156	109	3	862	13.4	−3.7
2002	862	137	107	5	892	12.4	−1.6
2003	892	83	110	2	865	12.3	17.3
2004	865	0	27	0	838	3.1	1.5

Managed futures

Year	Existing funds	New entries	New exits	Intra-year entry and exit funds	Total funds	Attrition rate (%)	Index return (%)
1994	181	52	8	1	225	4.4	11.9
1995	225	41	30	0	236	13.3	−7.1
1996	236	42	49	2	229	20.8	12.0
1997	229	37	36	1	230	15.7	3.1
1998	230	25	37	0	218	16.1	20.7
1999	218	35	40	1	213	18.3	−4.7
2000	213	13	35	0	191	16.4	4.3
2001	191	18	19	0	190	9.9	1.9
2002	190	22	32	0	180	16.8	18.3
2003	180	23	21	2	182	11.7	14.2
2004	182	0	5	0	177	2.7	−7.0

Dedicated shortseller

Year	No. of funds (start)	New	Dissolved	No. of funds (end)	Attrition (%)	Return (%)
1994	11	1	0	12	0.0	14.9
1995	12	0	1	11	8.3	−7.4
1996	11	3	1	13	9.1	−5.5
1997	13	3	1	15	7.7	0.4
1998	15	1	0	16	0.0	−6.0
1999	16	4	1	19	6.3	−14.2
2000	19	2	1	20	5.3	15.8
2001	20	1	6	15	30.0	−3.6
2002	15	1	1	15	6.7	18.2
2003	15	1	1	15	6.7	−32.6
2004	15	0	2	13	13.3	9.1

Emerging markets

Year	No. of funds (start)	New	Dissolved	No. of funds (end)	Attrition (%)	Return (%)
1994	44	25	0	69	0.0	12.5
1995	69	34	1	102	1.4	−16.9
1996	102	25	4	123	3.9	34.5
1997	123	40	8	155	6.5	26.6
1998	155	22	25	152	16.1	−37.7
1999	152	26	18	160	11.8	44.8
2000	160	20	25	155	15.6	−5.5
2001	155	5	28	132	18.1	5.8
2002	132	4	11	125	8.3	7.4
2003	125	12	13	124	10.4	28.7
2004	124	0	1	123	0.8	3.1

Fixed income arbitrage

Year	No. of funds (start)	New	Dissolved	No. of funds (end)	Attrition (%)	Return (%)
1994	22	16	3	35	13.6	0.3
1995	35	12	2	45	5.7	12.5
1996	45	16	4	57	8.9	15.9
1997	57	15	4	68	7.0	9.4
1998	68	16	14	70	20.6	−8.2
1999	70	13	8	75	11.4	12.1
2000	75	9	11	73	14.7	6.3
2001	73	20	7	86	9.6	8.0
2002	86	23	5	104	5.8	5.7
2003	104	12	9	107	8.7	8.0
2004	107	0	4	103	3.7	4.7

Global macro

Year	No. of funds (start)	New	Dissolved	No. of funds (end)	Attrition (%)	Return (%)
1994	50	11	3	58	6.0	−5.7
1995	58	19	5	72	8.6	30.7
1996	72	16	13	75	18.1	25.6
1997	75	19	6	88	8.0	37.1
1998	88	20	7	101	8.0	−3.6
1999	101	12	15	98	14.9	5.8
2000	98	18	33	83	33.7	11.7
2001	83	15	9	89	10.8	18.4
2002	89	26	9	106	10.1	14.7
2003	106	15	8	113	7.5	18.0
2004	113	0	1	112	0.9	4.4

Multistrategy

Year	No. of funds (start)	New	Dissolved	No. of funds (end)	Attrition (%)	Return (%)
1994	17	5	3	19	17.6	
1995	19	7	2	24	10.5	11.9
1996	24	14	1	37	4.2	14.0
1997	37	13	3	47	8.1	18.3
1998	47	8	5	50	10.6	7.7
1999	50	10	2	58	4.0	9.4
2000	58	10	2	66	3.4	11.2
2001	66	16	1	81	1.5	5.5
2002	81	14	5	90	6.2	6.3
2003	90	14	14	90	15.6	15.0
2004	90	0	0	90	0.0	2.8

Fund of funds

Year	No. of funds (start)	New	Dissolved	No. of funds (end)	Attrition (%)
1994	167	53	3	217	1.8
1995	217	63	12	268	5.5
1996	268	47	17	298	6.3
1997	298	56	21	333	7.0
1998	333	66	32	367	9.6
1999	367	69	21	415	5.7
2000	415	61	41	435	9.9
2001	435	121	45	511	10.3
2002	511	102	26	587	5.1
2003	587	110	44	653	7.5
2004	653	1	17	637	2.6

Note: Index returns are annual compound returns of the CSFB/Tremont hedge fund indexes. Attrition rates for 2004 are severely downward-biased because TASS typically waits 8 to 10 months before moving a nonreporting fund from the Live to the Graveyard database; therefore, as of August 2004, many nonreporting funds in the Live database have not yet been moved to the Graveyard.

the Long/Short Equity category—presumably the result of the bursting of the technology bubble.

Although 8.8 percent is the average attrition rate for the entire TASS database, there is considerable variation in average attrition rates across categories. Averaging the annual attrition rates from 1994–2003 within each category yields the following:

Convertible Arbitrage:	5.2%	Global Macro:	12.6%
Dedicated Shortseller:	8.0%	Long/Short Equity:	7.6%
Emerging Markets:	9.2%	Managed Futures:	14.4%
Equity Market Neutral:	8.0%	Multi-Strategy:	8.2%
Event Driven:	5.4%	Fund of Funds:	6.9%
Fixed Income Arbitrage:	10.6%		

These averages illustrate the different risks involved in each of the eleven investment styles. At 5.2 percent, Convertible Arbitrage enjoys the lowest average attrition rate, which is not surprising since this category has the second-lowest average return volatility of 5.89 percent (see table 6.9). The highest average attrition rate is 14.4 percent for Managed Futures, which is also consistent with the 18.55 percent average volatility of this category, the highest among all eleven categories.

Within each category, the year-to-year attrition rates exhibit different patterns, partly attributable to the relative performance of the categories. For example, Emerging Markets experienced a 16.1 percent attrition rate in 1998, no doubt because of the turmoil in emerging markets in 1997 and 1998, which is reflected in the –37.7 percent return in the CSFB/Tremont Emerging Markets Index for 1998. The opposite pattern is also present— during periods of unusually good performance, attrition rates decline, as in the case of Long/Short Equity from 1995 to 2000, when attrition rates were 3.2 percent, 7.4 percent, 3.9 percent, 6.8 percent, 7.4 percent, and 8.0 percent, respectively. Of course, in the three years following the bursting of the technology bubble—2001 to 2003—the attrition rates for Long/Short Equity shot up to 13.4 percent, 12.4 percent, and 12.3 percent, respectively. These patterns are consistent with the basic economic of the hedge fund industry: good performance begets more assets under management, greater business leverage, and staying power; poor performance leads to the Graveyard.

To develop a better sense of the relative magnitudes of attrition across categories, table 6.15 and figure 6.9 (panel A) provide a decomposition by category, where the attrition rates in each category are renormalized so that when they are summed across categories in a given year, the result equals the aggregate attrition rate for that year. From these renormalized figures, it is apparent that there is an increase in the proportion of the total attrition rate due to Long/Short Equity funds beginning in 2001. In fact, table 6.15 shows that of the total attrition rates of 11.4 percent, 10.0 per-

Table 6.15　Decomposition of attribution rates by category for all hedge funds in the TASS hedge fund database from January 1994 to August 2004, and corresponding CSFB/Tremont hedge fund index returns and assets under management

Year	All funds	Convertible arbitrage	Dedicated short	Emerging markets	Equity-market neutral	Event driven	Fixed income arbitrage	Global macro	Long/Short equity	Managed futures	Multi-strategy	Fund of funds
				Total attrition rates and components by category (In percent)								
1994	3.0	0.0	0.0	0.0	0.1	0.0	0.4	0.4	0.3	1.0	0.4	0.4
1995	6.1	0.0	0.1	0.1	0.0	0.1	0.2	0.5	0.7	3.0	0.2	1.2
1996	9.7	0.6	0.1	0.3	0.0	0.2	0.3	1.1	1.7	4.0	0.1	1.4
1997	6.9	0.2	0.1	0.6	0.0	0.2	0.3	0.4	1.0	2.5	0.2	1.5
1998	9.5	0.3	0.0	1.5	0.1	0.1	0.8	0.4	1.9	2.2	0.3	1.9
1999	9.7	0.2	0.1	1.0	0.7	1.0	0.4	0.8	2.2	2.1	0.1	1.1
2000	11.1	0.1	0.0	1.2	0.6	0.7	0.5	1.6	2.6	1.7	0.1	1.9
2001	11.4	0.2	0.3	1.2	0.4	0.8	0.3	0.4	4.8	0.8	0.0	2.0
2002	10.0	0.2	0.0	0.4	0.6	1.2	0.2	0.4	4.3	1.3	0.2	1.1
2003	10.7	0.4	0.0	0.5	1.2	0.9	0.3	0.3	4.1	0.8	0.5	1.7
2004	3.2	0.4	0.1	0.0	0.2	0.6	0.1	0.0	1.0	0.2	0.0	0.6
Mean	8.8	0.2	0.1	0.7	0.4	0.5	0.4	0.6	2.4	1.9	0.2	1.4
Standard deviation	2.7	0.2	0.1	0.5	0.4	0.4	0.2	0.4	1.6	1.0	0.2	0.5
				Annual returns of CSFB/Tremont hedge fund indexes by category (In percent)								
1994	-4.4	-8.1	14.9	12.5	-2.0	0.7	0.3	-5.7	-8.1	11.9		
1995	21.7	16.6	-7.4	-16.9	11.0	18.4	12.5	30.7	23.0	-7.1	11.9	
1996	22.2	17.9	-5.5	34.5	16.6	23.0	15.9	25.6	17.1	12.0	14.0	
1997	25.9	14.5	0.4	26.6	14.8	20.0	9.4	37.1	21.5	3.1	18.3	
1998	-0.4	-4.4	-6.0	-37.7	13.3	-4.9	-8.2	-3.6	17.2	20.7	7.7	
1999	23.4	16.0	-14.2	44.8	15.3	22.3	12.1	5.8	47.2	-4.7	9.4	
2000	4.8	25.6	15.8	-5.5	15.0	7.2	6.3	11.7	2.1	4.3	11.2	
2001	4.4	14.6	-3.6	5.8	9.3	11.5	8.0	18.4	-3.7	1.9	5.5	

continued

Table 6.15   (continued)

Year	All funds	Convertible arbitrage	Dedicated short	Emerging markets	Equity-market neutral	Event driven	Fixed income arbitrage	Global macro	Long/Short equity	Managed futures	Multi-strategy	Fund of funds
2002	3.0	4.0	18.2	7.4	7.4	0.2	5.7	14.7	-1.6	18.3	6.3	
2003	15.5	12.9	-32.6	28.7	7.1	20.0	8.0	18.0	17.3	14.2	15.0	
2004	2.7	0.6	9.1	3.1	4.7	5.7	4.7	4.4	1.5	-7.0	2.8	
Mean	11.6	11.0	-2.0	10.0	10.8	11.8	7.0	15.3	13.2	7.5	11.0	
Standard deviations	11.3	10.5	15.5	25.2	5.6	10.4	6.8	13.9	16.5	9.4	4.3	
	Total assets under management (In $MM) and percent breakdown by category (In percent)											
1994	57,684	3.8	0.7	9.3	1.0	9.5	3.9	20.5	20.7	5.1	7.5	18.0
1995	69,477	3.9	0.5	8.1	1.3	10.0	4.7	18.5	22.9	4.0	9.2	17.0
1996	92,513	4.2	0.4	8.7	2.3	10.1	5.9	17.9	23.4	3.2	7.8	16.1
1997	137,814	4.7	0.4	8.9	2.7	10.4	6.7	18.8	21.9	2.7	7.5	15.3
1998	142,669	5.5	0.6	4.0	4.4	12.5	5.7	16.8	24.4	3.3	6.8	16.0
1999	175,223	5.3	0.6	4.6	5.2	11.7	4.6	9.1	34.5	2.8	6.6	15.1
2000	197,120	5.4	0.5	2.5	5.5	10.6	3.3	1.9	31.1	1.9	4.4	12.7
2001	246,695	8.1	0.3	2.8	7.4	13.9	4.7	2.3	35.3	3.0	5.5	16.6
2002	277,695	8.5	0.3	3.1	7.2	13.0	6.2	3.1	30.2	3.9	6.1	18.4
2003	389,965	8.8	0.1	4.3	6.0	13.0	6.2	5.4	25.7	5.0	5.8	19.7
2004	403,974	8.8	0.2	4.2	5.9	13.5	7.1	6.6	26.3	5.3	6.8	15.3
Mean	178,685	5.8	0.5	5.6	4.3	11.5	5.2	11.4	27.0	3.5	6.7	16.5
Standard deviation	103,484	1.9	0.2	2.8	2.4	1.5	1.1	7.8	5.3	1.0	1.4	2.0

Note: Attrition rates for 2004 are severely downward biased, because TASS typically waits eight to ten months before moving a nonreporting fund from the Live to the Graveyard database; therefore, as of August 2004, many nonreporting funds in the Live database have not yet been moved to the Graveyard. Consequently, the reported means and standard deviations in all three panels are computed over the 1994–2003 period.

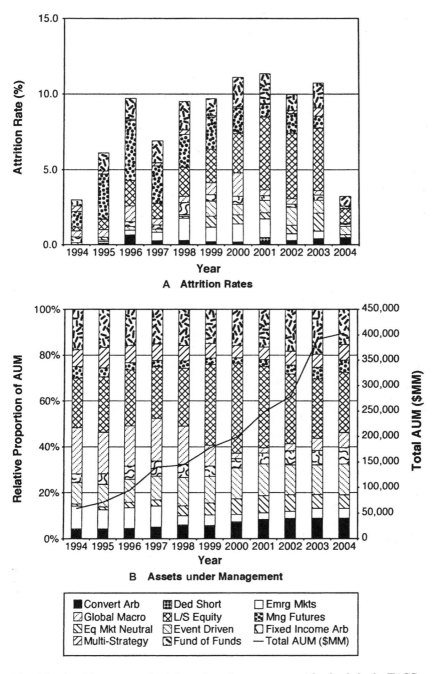

Fig. 6.9   Attrition rates and total assets under management for funds in the TASS Live and Graveyard database from January 1994 to August 2004.

Note: The data for 2004 is incomplete, and attrition rates for this year are severely downward biased because of an eight- to ten-month lag in transferring nonreporting funds from the Live to the Graveyard database.

cent, and 10.7 percent in years 2001–2003, the Long/Short Equity category was responsible for 4.8, 4.3, and 4.1 percentage points of those totals, respectively. Despite the fact that the average attrition rate for the Long/Short Equity category is only 7.6 percent from 1994 to 2003, the funds in this category are more numerous; hence they contribute more to the aggregate attrition rate. Figure 9 (panel B) provides a measure of the impact of these attrition rates on the industry by plotting the total assets under management of funds in the TASS database along with the relative proportions in each category. Long/Short Equity funds are indeed a significant fraction of the industry, hence the increase in their attrition rates in recent years may be cause for some concern.

6.5.2   Logit Analysis of Liquidations

To estimate the influence of various hedge-fund characteristics on the likelihood of liquidation, in this section we report the results of a logit analysis of liquidations in the TASS database. Logit can be viewed as a generalization of the linear regression model to situations where the dependent variable takes on only a finite number of discrete values (see, for example, Maddala 1983 for details).

To estimate the logit model of liquidation, we use the same sample of TASS Live and Graveyard funds as in section 6.5.1: 4,536 funds from February 1977 to August 2004, of which 1,765 are in the Graveyard database and 2,771 are in the Live database. As discussed in sections 6.3.2 and 6.5.1, the Graveyard database was initiated only in January 1994, hence this will be the start date of our sample for purposes of estimating the logit model of liquidation. For tractability, we focus on annual observations only, so the dependent variable Z_{it} indicates whether fund i is live or liquidated in year t.[36] See table 6.8 for a frequency count of the funds entering and exiting the TASS database in each year. Over the sample period from January 1994 to August 2004, we have 23,925 distinct observations for Z_{it}, and after filtering out funds that do not have at least two years of history, we are left with 12,895 observations.

Associated with each Z_{it} is a set of explanatory variables listed in table 6.16. The motivation for AGE, ASSETS, and RETURN are well-known—older funds, funds with greater assets, and funds with better recent performance are all less likely to be liquidated, hence we would expect negative coefficients for these explanatory variables (recall that a larger conditional

---

36. Note that a fund cannot die more than once, hence liquidation occurs exactly once for each fund i in the Graveyard database. In particular, the time series observations of funds in the Graveyard database will always be $(0,0, \ldots, 0,1)$. This suggests that a more appropriate statistical technique for modeling hedge fund liquidations is survival analysis, which we plan to pursue in a future study. However, for purposes of summarizing the impact of certain explanatory variables on the probability of hedge fund liquidations, logit analysis is a reasonable choice.

Table 6.16   Definition of explanatory variables in logit analysis of hedge fund liquidations in the TASS database from January 1994 to August 2004

Variable	Definition
AGE	The current age of the fund (in months).
ASSETS	The natural logarithm of current total assets under management.
ASSETS_{-1}	The natural logarithm of total assets under management as of December 31 of the previous year.
RETURN	Current year-to-date total return.
RETURN_{-1}	Total return last year.
RETURN_{-2}	Total return two years ago.
FLOW	Fund's current year-to-date total dollar inflow divided by previous year's assets under management, where dollar inflow in month τ is defined as $\text{FLOW}_{\tau} \equiv \text{AUM}_{\tau} - \text{AUM}_{\tau-1}(1 + R_{\tau})$ and AUM_{τ} is the total assets under management at the beginning of month τ, R_{τ} is the fund's net return for month τ, and year-to-date total dollar inflow is simply the cumulative sum of monthly inflows since January of the current year.
FLOW_{-1}	Previous year's total dollar inflow divided by assets under management the year before.
FLOW_{-2}	Total dollar inflow two years ago divided by assets under management the year before.

mean for Z^* implies a higher probability that $Z_{it} = 1$ or liquidation). The FLOW variable is motivated by the well-known "return-chasing" phenomenon, in which investors flock to funds that have had good recent performance, and leave funds that have underperformed (see, for example, Chevalier and Ellison 1997; Sirri and Tufano 1998; and Agarwal, Daniel, and Naik 2004).

Table 6.17 contains summary statistics for these explanatory variables as well as for the dependent variable Z_{it}. Note that the sample mean of Z_{it} is 0.09, which may be viewed as an unconditional estimate of the probability of liquidation, and is consistent with the attrition rate of 8.8 percent reported in section 6.5.1.[37] The objective of performing a logit analysis of Z_{it} is, of course, to estimate the *conditional* probability of liquidation, conditional on the explanatory variables in table 6.16.

The correlation matrix for Z_{it} and the explanatory variables are given in table 6.18. As expected, Z_{it} is negatively correlated with age, assets under management, cumulative return, and fund flows, with correlations ranging from –26.2 percent for AGE to –5.8 percent for RETURN_{-2}. Table 6.18 also shows that the assets under management variable is highly persistent, with a correlation of 94.3 percent between its contemporaneous and lagged values. To avoid multicollinearity problems, we include only the lagged

37. A slight discrepancy should be expected, since the selection criterion for the sample of funds in this section is not identical to that of section 6.5.1 (e.g., funds in the logit sample must have nonmissing observations for the explanatory variables in table 6.16).

Table 6.17 Summary statistics for dependent and explanatory variables of a logit analysis of hedge fund liquidations in the TASS database from 1994 to 2004

Variable	Mean	SD	Skewness	Kurtosis	Min.	10%	25%	50%	75%	90%	Max.
Z	0.09	0.28	2.88	6.32	0.00	0.00	0.00	0.00	0.00	0.00	1.00
AGE	108.20	48.94	1.02	1.50	27	52	72	101	135	175	331
ASSETS	17.25	1.88	−0.33	0.32	7.67	14.82	16.06	17.34	18.53	19.58	23.01
ASSETS$_{-1}$	17.20	1.79	−0.29	0.29	8.11	14.87	16.07	17.28	18.42	19.42	23.01
RETURN	0.09	0.24	2.81	30.81	−0.96	−0.12	−0.01	0.06	0.16	0.31	4.55
RETURN$_{-1}$	0.12	0.26	2.83	28.24	−1.00	−0.11	0.01	0.10	0.20	0.37	4.55
RETURN$_{-2}$	0.13	0.32	22.37	1,340.37	−0.95	−0.10	0.01	0.10	0.22	0.38	20.85
FLOW	0.84	66.32	112.48	12,724.87	−1.98	−0.39	−0.16	0.00	0.21	0.71	7,505.99
FLOW$_{-1}$	1.07	67.34	108.00	11,978.17	−3.15	−0.38	−0.15	0.00	0.30	1.01	7,505.99
FLOW$_{-2}$	0.85	15.82	74.41	5,857.91	−3.15	−0.33	−0.11	0.02	0.46	1.55	1,323.53

Notes: The dependent variable Z takes on the value 1 in the year a hedge fund is liquidated, and is 0 in all prior years. The units of measurement for the explanatory variables are: months for AGE, the natural logarithm of millions of dollars for ASSETS, and raw ratios (not percentages) for RETURN and FLOW.

Table 6.18   Correlation matrix of dependent and explanatory variables of a logit analysis of hedge fund liquidations in the TASS database from 1994 to 2004

Variable	Z	AGE	ASSETS	ASSETS$_{-1}$	RETURN	RETURN$_{-1}$	RETURN$_{-2}$	FLOW	FLOW$_{-1}$	FLOW$_{-2}$
Z	100.0	-26.2	-21.4	-17.3	-20.4	-14.6	-5.8	-13.0	-11.6	-6.8
AGE	-26.2	100.0	13.8	13.2	15.9	8.5	5.5	-3.8	-9.7	-21.4
ASSETS	-21.4	13.8	100.0	94.3	15.0	17.8	15.2	27.6	28.9	22.1
ASSETS$_{-1}$	-17.3	13.2	94.3	100.0	1.4	11.1	14.0	2.6	23.8	22.1
RETURN	-20.4	15.9	15.0	1.4	100.0	4.2	8.9	16.3	-0.7	1.0
RETURN$_{-1}$	-14.6	8.5	17.8	11.1	4.2	100.0	3.3	29.2	16.6	-2.9
RETURN$_{-2}$	-5.8	5.5	15.2	14.0	8.9	3.3	100.0	7.4	29.1	17.0
FLOW	-13.0	-3.8	27.6	2.6	16.3	29.2	7.4	100.0	28.7	9.0
FLOW$_{-1}$	-11.6	-9.7	28.9	23.8	-0.7	16.6	29.1	28.7	100.0	28.6
FLOW$_{-2}$	-6.8	-21.4	22.1	22.1	1.0	-2.9	17.0	9.0	28.6	100.0

Note: The dependent variable Z takes on the value 1 in the year a hedge fund is liquidated, and is 0 in all prior years.

variable ASSETS$_{-1}$ in our logit analysis, yielding the following final specification, which we call Model 1:

$$(11) \quad Z_{it} = G(\beta_0 + \beta_1 AGE_{it} + \beta_2 ASSETS_{it-1} + \beta_3 RETURN_{it}$$
$$+ \beta_4 RETURN_{it-1} + \beta_5 RETURN_{it-2} + \beta_6 FLOW_{it}$$
$$+ \beta_7 FLOW_{it-1} + \beta_8 FLOW_{it-2} + \varepsilon_{it}).$$

Table 6.19 contains maximum-likelihood estimates of equation (11) in the first three columns, with statistically significant parameters in bold. Note that most of the parameter estimates are highly significant. This is due to the unusually large sample size, which typically yields statistically significant estimates because of the small standard errors implied by large samples (recall that the standard errors of consistent and asymptotically normal estimators converge to 0 at a rate of $1/\sqrt{n}$ where n is the sample size). This suggests that we may wish to impose a higher threshold of statistical significance in this case, so as to provide a better balance between Type I and Type II errors.[38]

The negative signs of all the coefficients other than the constant term confirm our intuition that age, assets under management, cumulative return, and fund flows all have a negative impact on the probability of liquidation. The fact that RETURN$_{-2}$ is not statistically significant suggests that the most recent returns have the highest degree of relevance for hedge fund liquidations, a possible indication of the short-term, performance-driven nature of the hedge fund industry. The R^2 of this regression is 29.3 percent, which implies a reasonable level of explanatory power for this simple specification.[39]

To address fixed effects associated with the calendar year and hedge fund style category, in Model 2 we include indicator variables for ten out of eleven calendar years, and ten out of eleven hedge fund categories, yielding the following specification:

$$(12) \quad Z_{it} = G\left[\beta_0 + \sum_{k=1}^{10} \zeta_k I(YEAR_{k,i,t}) + \sum_{k=1}^{10} \xi_k I(CAT_{k,i,t}) + \beta_1 AGE_{it} \right.$$
$$+ \beta_2 ASSETS_{it-1} + \beta_3 RETURN_{it} + \beta_4 RETURN_{it-1}$$
$$+ \beta_5 RETURN_{it-2} + \beta_6 FLOW_{it} + \beta_7 FLOW_{it-1}$$
$$\left. + \beta_8 FLOW_{it-2} + \varepsilon_{it} \right]$$

38. See Leamer (1978) for further discussion of this phenomenon, known as "Lindley's Paradox."

39. This R^2 is the adjusted generalized coefficient of determination proposed by Nagelkerke (1991), which renormalizes the Cox and Snell's (1989) R^2 measure by its maximum (which is less than unity) so that it spans the entire unit interval. See Nagelkerke (1991) for further discussion.

Table 6.19   Maximum likelihood estimates of a logit model for hedge fund liquidations using annual observations of liquidation status from the TASS database from January 1994 to August 2004

Variable	Model 1 β	Model 1 SE(β)	Model 1 p-value (%)	Model 2 β	Model 2 SE(β)	Model 2 p-value (%)	Model 3 β	Model 3 SE(β)	Model 3 p-value (%)	Model 4 β	Model 4 SE(β)	Model 4 p-value (%)	Model 5 β	Model 5 SE(β)	Model 5 p-value (%)
Sample size	12,895			12,895			12,895			12,846			12,310		
R^2 (%)	29.3			34.2			34.2			34.5			35.4		
Constant	4.73	0.34	<.01	2.31	0.41	<.01	-5.62	0.18	<.01	-5.67	0.18	<.01	-7.04	0.26	<.01
AGE	-0.03	0.00	<.01	-0.03	0.00	<.01	-1.62	0.07	<.01	-1.66	0.07	<.01	-2.08	0.10	<.01
ASSETS$_{-1}$	-0.26	0.02	<.01	-0.19	0.02	<.01	-0.34	0.04	<.01	-0.36	0.04	<.01	-0.38	0.06	<.01
RETURN	-2.81	0.19	<.01	-2.86	0.20	<.01	-0.67	0.05	<.01	-0.67	0.05	<.01	-0.61	0.06	<.01
RETURN$_{-1}$	-1.39	0.16	<.01	-1.40	0.17	<.01	-0.36	0.04	<.01	-0.36	0.04	<.01	-0.44	0.06	<.01
RETURN$_{-2}$	-0.04	0.09	67.5	-0.38	0.14	0.7	-0.12	0.04	0.7	-0.12	0.05	1.1	-0.17	0.07	1.3
FLOW	-0.63	0.08	<.01	-0.49	0.07	<.01	-32.72	4.91	<.01	-33.27	5.04	<.01	-32.93	6.74	<.01
FLOW$_{-1}$	-0.13	0.04	0.0	-0.11	0.03	0.1	-7.53	2.33	0.1	-7.60	2.37	0.1	-19.26	4.71	<.01
FLOW$_{-2}$	-0.09	0.02	<.01	-0.11	0.02	<.01	-1.74	0.36	<.01	-1.64	0.36	<.01	-1.83	0.51	0.0
I(1994)				0.79	0.38	3.9	0.79	0.38	3.9	0.82	0.39	3.4	1.01	0.54	5.9
I(1995)				1.24	0.27	<.01	1.24	0.27	<.01	1.18	0.28	<.01	1.37	0.37	0.0
I(1996)				1.83	0.20	<.01	1.83	0.20	<.01	1.83	0.21	<.01	1.92	0.28	<.01
I(1997)				1.53	0.21	<.01	1.53	0.21	<.01	1.52	0.21	<.01	2.03	0.27	<.01
I(1998)				1.81	0.18	<.01	1.81	0.18	<.01	1.80	0.19	<.01	2.29	0.24	<.01
I(1999)				2.10	0.18	<.01	2.10	0.18	<.01	2.05	0.18	<.01	2.25	0.24	<.01
I(2000)				2.25	0.17	<.01	2.25	0.17	<.01	2.19	0.17	<.01	2.08	0.24	<.01
I(2001)				1.97	0.17	<.01	1.97	0.17	<.01	1.96	0.17	<.01	1.80	0.25	<.01
I(2002)				1.46	0.16	<.01	1.46	0.16	<.01	1.41	0.16	<.01	1.50	0.22	<.01
I(2003)				1.55	0.16	<.01	1.55	0.16	<.01	1.53	0.16	<.01	1.71	0.22	<.01
I(ConvertArb)				0.44	0.20	2.9	0.44	0.20	2.9	0.43	0.20	3.4	0.16	0.34	62.5
I(DedShort)				0.05	0.37	88.9	0.05	0.37	88.9	-0.03	0.39	94.3	0.20	0.49	68.0
I(EmrgMkt)				0.25	0.15	10.2	0.25	0.15	10.2	0.24	0.15	11.7	0.54	0.20	0.7
I(EqMktNeut)				0.12	0.20	54.7	0.12	0.20	54.7	0.15	0.20	46.7	0.53	0.25	3.4
I(EventDr)				0.33	0.15	3.0	0.33	0.15	3.0	0.31	0.15	4.7	-0.01	0.24	97.4
I(FixedInc)				0.50	0.19	1.1	0.50	0.19	1.1	0.45	0.20	2.3	0.33	0.30	26.8
I(GlobMac)				0.32	0.18	7.4	0.32	0.18	7.4	0.24	0.18	20.2	0.33	0.25	17.9
I(LongShortEq)				0.18	0.11	10.2	0.18	0.11	10.2	0.15	0.11	16.6	0.14	0.15	36.4
I(MgFut)				0.49	0.12	<.01	0.49	0.12	<.01	0.49	0.13	0.0	0.71	0.16	<.01
I(Multistrat)				0.17	0.25	49.4	0.17	0.25	49.4	0.18	0.25	48.5	0.85	0.29	0.3

Note: The dependent variable Z takes on the value 1 in the year a hedge fund is liquidated, and is zero in all prior years.

where

(13a) $I(\mathrm{YEAR}_{k,i,t}) \equiv \begin{cases} 1 \text{ if } t = k \\ 0 \text{ otherwise} \end{cases}$

(13b) $I(\mathrm{CAT}_{k,i,t}) \equiv \begin{cases} 1 \text{ if fund } i \text{ is in Category } k \\ 0 \text{ otherwise} \end{cases}$

The columns labelled "Model 2" in table 6.19 contain the maximum-likelihood estimates of equation (12) for the same sample of funds as Model 1. The coefficients for AGE, ASSETS, and RETURN exhibit the same qualitative properties as in Model 1, but the fixed-effect variables do provide some additional explanatory power, yielding an R^2 of 34.2 percent. In particular, the coefficients for the 1999 and 2000 indicator variables are higher than those of the other year indicators, a manifestation of the impact of August 1998 and the collapse of LTCM and other fixed-income, relative-value hedge funds. The impact of the LTCM collapse can also be seen from the coefficients of the category indicators—at 0.50, Fixed-Income Relative Value has the largest estimate among all ten categories. Managed Futures has a comparable coefficient of 0.49, which is consistent with the higher volatility of such funds and the fact that this category exhibits the highest attrition rate, 14.4 percent, during the 1994–2003 sample period (see section 6.5.1). However, the fact that Convertible Arbitrage and Event-Driven categories are the next largest, with coefficients of 0.44 and 0.33, respectively, is somewhat surprising given their unusually low attrition rates of 5.2 percent and 5.4 percent, respectively, reported in section 6.5.1. This suggests that the conditional probabilities produced by a logit analysis—which control for assets under management, fund flows, and performance—yields information not readily available from the unconditional frequency counts of simple attrition statistics. The remaining category indicators are statistically insignificant at the 5 percent level.

To facilitate comparisons across explanatory variables, we standardize each of the nonindicator explanatory variables by subtracting its mean and dividing by its standard deviation and then reestimating the parameters of equation (12) via maximum likelihood. This procedure yields estimates that are renormalized to standard deviation units of each explanatory variable, and are contained in the columns labelled "Model 3" of table 6.19. The renormalized estimates show that fund flows are an order of magnitude more important in determining the probability of liquidation than assets under management, returns, or age, with normalized coefficients of –32.72 and –7.53 for FLOW and FLOW_{-1}, respectively.

Finally, we reestimate the logit model (12) for two subsets of funds using standardized explanatory variables. In Model 4, we omit Graveyard funds that have either merged with other funds or are closed to new investments (status codes 4 and 5), yielding a subsample of 12,846 observations. In Model 5, we omit all Graveyard funds except those that have liquidated (status code 1), yielding a subsample of 12,310 observations. The last two sets of columns in table 6.19 show that the qualitative features of most of the estimates are unchanged, with the funds in Model 5 exhibiting somewhat higher sensitivity to the lagged FLOW variable. However, the category fixed-effects in Model 5 does differ in some ways from those of Models 2–4, with significant coefficients for Emerging Markets, Equity Market Neutral, and Multi-Strategy, as well as for Managed Futures. This suggests that there are significant differences between the full Graveyard sample and the subsample of funds with status code 1, and bears further study.

Because of the inherent nonlinearity of the logit model, the coefficients of the explanatory variables cannot be as easily interpreted as in the linear regression model. One way to remedy this situation is to compute the estimated probability of liquidation implied by the parameter estimates $\hat{\boldsymbol{\beta}}$ and specific values for the explanatory variables, which is readily accomplished by observing that:

$$(14a) \qquad p_{it} \equiv \text{Prob}(Z_{it} = 1) = \text{Prob}(Z_{it}^* > 0)$$

$$(14b) \qquad = \text{Prob}(\mathbf{X}_{it}'\boldsymbol{\beta} + \varepsilon_{it} > 0 = \frac{\exp(\mathbf{X}_{it}'\boldsymbol{\beta})}{1 + \exp(\mathbf{X}_{it}'\boldsymbol{\beta})}$$

$$(14c) \qquad \hat{p}_{it} = \frac{\exp(\mathbf{X}_{it}'\hat{\boldsymbol{\beta}})}{1 + \exp(\mathbf{X}_{it}'\hat{\boldsymbol{\beta}})}.$$

Table 6.20 reports year-by-year summary statistics for the estimated liquidation probabilities ($\hat{p}_{it}$) of each fund in our sample, where each $\hat{p}_{it}$ is computed using values of the explanatory variables in year t. The left panel of table 6.20 contains summary statistics for estimated liquidation probabilities from Model 1, and the right panel contains corresponding figures from Model 5. We have also stratified the estimated liquidation probabilities by their liquidation status—Live funds in the top panel, Graveyard funds in the middle panel, and the Combined sample of funds in the bottom panel.[40]

For both Models 1 and 5, the mean and median liquidation probabilities are higher for Graveyard funds than for Live funds, a reassuring sign that the explanatory variables are indeed providing explanatory power for the liquidation process. For Model 1, the Combined sample shows an increase in the mean and median liquidation probabilities in 1998 as expected, and another increase in 2001, presumably due to the bursting of the technology

---

40. Note that the usage of "Graveyard funds" in this context is somewhat different, involving a time dimension as well as liquidation status. For example, in this context the set of Graveyard funds in 1999 refers to only those funds that liquidated in 1999, and does not include liquidations before or after 1999.

Table 6.20 Year-by-year summary statistics for the probabilities of liquidation implied by the parameter estimates of two specifications of a logit model for hedge fund liquidations using annual observations of the liquidation status of individual hedge funds in the TASS database from January 1994 to August 2004

Model 1

Statistic	1994	1995	1996	1997	1998	1999	2000	2001	2002	2003	2004
Live funds											
Mean	4.19	5.47	5.84	5.04	6.32	5.17	5.59	6.84	8.92	7.11	11.04
SD	7.49	9.33	11.15	9.74	9.66	8.61	8.15	9.23	10.15	8.00	10.91
Min.	0.01	0.01	0.00	0.00	0.00	0.00	0.00	0.00	0.00	0.00	0.00
10%	0.13	0.19	0.19	0.18	0.31	0.20	0.35	0.44	0.68	0.41	0.89
25%	0.43	0.51	0.52	0.56	0.99	0.79	1.10	1.39	2.05	1.45	2.66
50%	1.16	1.46	1.52	1.59	2.71	2.18	2.80	3.69	5.62	4.49	7.55
75%	4.21	6.03	5.11	4.83	7.20	5.55	6.54	8.39	12.01	10.22	16.31
90%	12.13	16.17	16.85	13.27	16.76	12.80	13.78	16.23	21.61	17.26	26.33
Max.	52.49	58.30	72.97	90.06	77.63	87.06	75.83	92.36	79.02	92.44	79.96
Count	357	483	629	773	924	1,083	1,207	1,317	1,480	1,595	1,898
Graveyard funds											
Mean	36.59	32.85	31.89	39.75	30.64	27.68	22.78	28.17	25.22	21.55	17.01
SD	24.46	22.77	18.86	22.70	21.67	19.24	17.67	20.03	18.22	15.91	14.30
Min.	4.91	2.50	1.05	0.25	0.00	0.53	0.22	0.98	0.13	0.02	0.25
10%	6.08	8.39	10.63	9.29	6.86	4.98	2.41	5.94	5.50	2.64	2.26
25%	22.06	16.28	17.47	21.81	12.13	12.84	9.14	12.07	10.58	8.32	6.43
50%	32.82	28.53	27.44	39.78	25.20	24.03	19.81	23.28	21.50	19.18	13.35
75%	48.40	49.79	43.36	56.94	46.21	39.62	34.92	41.01	37.98	32.28	25.26
90%	71.63	58.62	60.08	71.13	61.74	50.75	45.84	58.90	48.81	45.42	34.67
Max.	77.37	97.42	79.51	88.70	85.41	84.87	87.89	78.68	94.65	72.29	67.10
Count	10	27	73	62	104	129	176	175	167	158	68
Combined funds											
Mean	5.07	6.92	8.55	7.61	8.78	7.56	7.77	9.35	10.57	8.42	11.24
SD	9.86	12.10	14.53	14.44	13.59	12.39	11.41	13.01	12.26	9.90	11.10
Min.	0.01	0.01	0.00	0.00	0.00	0.00	0.00	0.00	0.00	0.00	0.00
10%	0.14	0.20	0.22	0.20	0.38	0.22	0.39	0.53	0.77	0.43	0.93
25%	0.45	0.55	0.62	0.62	1.10	0.91	1.20	1.62	2.28	1.60	2.72
50%	1.23	1.72	1.84	1.88	3.34	2.63	3.35	4.49	6.31	4.97	7.69
75%	4.89	7.67	8.96	6.25	9.81	7.92	9.03	11.28	13.94	11.74	16.46
90%	14.96	20.53	27.36	22.94	25.11	21.39	20.97	24.21	25.98	21.48	26.97
Max.	77.37	97.42	79.51	90.06	85.41	87.06	87.89	92.36	94.65	92.44	79.96
Count	367	510	702	835	1,028	1,212	1,383	1,492	1,647	1,753	1,966

Model 5

Statistic	1994	1995	1996	1997	1998	1999	2000	2001	2002	2003	2004
Live funds											
Mean	1.06	2.22	4.30	3.43	4.70	4.05	3.80	3.40	4.07	4.45	1.76
SD	3.28	6.01	10.97	8.70	9.51	8.87	7.72	6.76	6.58	6.33	2.70
Min.	0.00	0.00	0.00	0.00	0.00	0.00	0.00	0.00	0.00	0.00	0.00
10%	0.00	0.01	0.02	0.02	0.06	0.04	0.07	0.07	0.09	0.07	0.03
25%	0.02	0.04	0.09	0.10	0.27	0.23	0.33	0.33	0.44	0.43	0.15
50%	0.07	0.16	0.36	0.45	1.03	0.96	1.18	1.26	1.74	2.04	0.72
75%	0.52	1.25	2.61	2.26	4.03	3.22	3.49	3.63	4.75	6.01	2.31
90%	2.61	5.85	11.24	9.12	14.21	10.09	9.88	8.10	10.52	12.03	4.71
Max.	35.62	42.56	76.54	86.91	77.72	80.45	75.95	91.82	73.06	81.10	29.28
Count	357	483	629	773	924	1,083	1,207	1,317	1,480	1,595	1,898
Graveyard funds											
Mean	24.23	23.50	34.07	42.30	36.17	31.46	32.55	22.82	20.68	20.18	4.60
SD	24.12	20.12	25.19	26.95	25.12	21.96	22.47	19.84	18.94	16.27	6.20
Min.	1.00	4.92	1.88	1.49	0.00	0.11	0.02	0.51	0.03	0.03	0.04
10%	5.31	5.53	5.25	8.61	4.49	2.12	3.95	2.00	2.61	3.02	0.13
25%	11.79	7.99	11.28	21.29	15.56	12.66	15.91	6.43	5.29	6.42	0.97
50%	18.02	17.66	33.94	37.54	28.92	30.16	27.57	19.11	14.32	14.03	3.16
75%	26.24	32.58	54.36	64.53	60.14	46.31	48.38	33.10	33.19	30.61	5.51
90%	48.95	51.10	68.87	80.97	69.54	64.68	61.91	55.75	46.84	43.06	10.17
Max.	64.10	69.64	82.29	93.17	87.67	89.00	90.90	76.34	90.02	67.86	33.31
Count	5	14	41	46	68	64	68	58	76	89	35
Combined funds											
Mean	1.38	2.82	6.12	5.62	6.85	5.58	5.33	4.22	4.88	5.29	1.81
SD	4.94	7.62	14.21	13.84	13.79	11.85	11.17	8.68	8.44	8.01	2.82
Min.	0.00	0.00	0.00	0.00	0.00	0.00	0.00	0.00	0.00	0.00	0.00
10%	0.00	0.01	0.02	0.03	0.06	0.05	0.07	0.07	0.09	0.08	0.03
25%	0.02	0.04	0.10	0.11	0.30	0.24	0.35	0.35	0.48	0.49	0.15
50%	0.08	0.19	0.43	0.54	1.24	1.06	1.32	1.42	1.93	2.28	0.73
75%	0.56	1.38	3.58	3.02	5.57	4.27	4.40	4.15	5.36	6.63	2.36
90%	3.06	7.02	19.05	16.84	22.27	17.07	15.37	9.65	12.50	13.79	4.85
Max.	64.10	69.64	82.29	93.17	87.67	89.00	90.90	91.82	90.02	81.10	33.31
Count	362	497	670	819	992	1,147	1,275	1,375	1,556	1,684	1,933

bubble in U.S. equity markets. Most troubling from the perspective of systemic risk, however, is the fact that the mean and median liquidation probabilities for 2004 (which only includes data up to August) are 11.24 percent and 7.69 percent, respectively, the highest levels in our entire sample. This may be a symptom of the enormous growth that the hedge fund industry has enjoyed in recent years, which increases both the number of funds entering and exiting the industry, but may also indicate more challenging market conditions for hedge funds in the coming months. Note that the mean and median liquidation probabilities for Model 5 do not show the same increase in 2004—this is another manifestation of the time lag with which the Graveyard database is updated (recall that Model 5 includes only those funds with status code 1, but a large number of funds that eventually receive this classification have not yet reached their eight- to ten-month limit by August 2004). Therefore, Model 1's estimated liquidation probabilities are likely to be more accurate for the current year.[41]

The logit estimates and implied probabilities suggest that a number of factors influence the likelihood of a hedge fund's liquidation, including past performance, assets under management, fund flows, and age. Given these factors, our estimates imply that the average liquidation probability for funds in 2004 is over 11 percent, which is higher than the historical unconditional attrition rate of 8.8 percent. To the extent that a series of correlated liquidations stresses the capital reserves of financial counterparties, this is yet another indirect measure of an increase in systemic risk from the hedge fund industry.

6.6   Other Hedge Fund Measures of Systemic Risk

In addition to measures of liquidity exposure, there are several other hedge fund related metrics for gauging the degree of systemic risk exposure in the economy. In this section, we propose three alternatives: (1) risk models for hedge funds; (2) regressions of banking sector indexes on hedge fund and other risk factors; and (3) a regime-switching model for hedge fund indexes. We describe these alternatives in more detail in sections 6.6.1–6.6.3.

6.6.1   Risk Models for Hedge Funds

As the examples in section 6.1 illustrate, hedge fund returns may exhibit a number of nonlinearities that are not captured by linear methods such as correlation coefficients and linear factor models. An example of a simple nonlinearity is an asymmetric sensitivity to the S&P 500; that is, different beta coefficients for down-markets versus up-markets. Specifically, consider the following regression:

---

41. The TASS reporting delay affects Model 1 as well, suggesting that its estimated liquidation probabilities for 2004 are biased downward as well.

(15) $$R_{it} = \alpha_i + \beta_i^+ \Lambda_t^+ + \beta_i^- \Lambda_t^- + \varepsilon_{it},$$

where

(16) $$\Lambda_t^+ = \begin{cases} \Lambda_t & \text{if } \Lambda_t > 0 \\ 0 & \text{otherwise,} \end{cases} \qquad \Lambda_t^- = \begin{cases} \Lambda_t & \text{if } \Lambda_t \leq 0 \\ 0 & \text{otherwise,} \end{cases}$$

and Λ_t is the return on the S&P 500 index. Since $\Lambda_t = \Lambda_t^+ + \Lambda_t^-$, the standard linear model in which fund i's market betas are identical in up and down markets is a special case of the more general specification (15), the case where $\beta_i^+ = \beta_i^-$. However, the estimates reported in table 6.21 for the CSFB/Tremont hedge fund index returns show that beta asymmetries can be quite pronounced for certain hedge fund styles. For example, the Distressed index has an up-market beta of 0.04—seemingly market neutral—however, its down-market beta is 0.43! For the Managed Futures index, the asymmetries are even more pronounced: the coefficients are of opposite sign, with a beta of 0.05 in up markets and a beta of –0.41 in down markets. These asymmetries are to be expected for certain nonlinear investment strategies, particularly those that have option-like characteristics such as the short-put strategy of Capital Decimation Partners (see section 6.1.1). Such nonlinearities can yield even greater diversification benefits than more traditional asset classes—for example, Managed Futures seems to provide S&P 500 downside protection with little exposure on the upside—but investors must first be aware of the specific nonlinearities to take advantage of them.

In this section, we estimate risk models for each of the CSFB/Tremont hedge fund indexes as a "proof-of-concept" for developing more sophisticated risk analytics for hedge funds. With better risk models in hand, the systemic risk posed by hedge funds will be that much clearer. Of course, a more ambitious approach is to estimate risk models for each hedge fund and then aggregate risks accordingly, and for nonlinear risk models, a disaggregated approach may well yield additional insights not apparent from index-based risk models. However, this is beyond the scope of this study, and we focus our attention instead on the risk characteristics of the indexes.

We begin with a comprehensive set of risk factors that will be candidates for each of the risk models, covering stocks, bonds, currencies, commodities, and volatility. These factors are described in table 6.22, and their basic statistical properties have been summarized in table 6.4. Given the heterogeneity of investment strategies represented by the hedge-fund industry, the variables in table 6.22 are likely to be the smallest set of risk factors capable of spanning the risk exposures of most hedge funds.

Table 6.23 is a joint correlation matrix of the risk factors and the hedge fund indexes. Note that we have also included squared and cubed S&P 500

Table 6.21   Regressions of monthly CSFB/Tremont hedge fund index returns on the S&P 500 index return, and on positive and negative S&P 500 index returns, from January 1994 to August 2004

Category	α	$t(\alpha)$	β	$t(\beta)$	R^2 (%)	p-value (%)	α	$t(\alpha)$	β^+	$t(\beta^+)$	β^-	$t(\beta^-)$	R^2 (%)	p-value (%)
Hedge funds	0.74	3.60	0.24	5.48	21.0	0.0	1.14	3.22	0.14	1.58	0.34	3.95	22.4	0.0
Convertible arbitrage	0.83	6.31	0.03	1.17	1.2	23.8	1.00	4.37	-0.01	-0.18	0.08	1.36	1.9	33.2
Dedicated shortseller	0.70	2.12	-0.86	-12.26	57.2	0.0	0.23	0.41	-0.74	-5.33	-0.98	-7.01	57.6	0.0
Emerging markets	0.13	0.31	0.52	5.68	22.3	0.0	1.06	1.43	0.28	1.57	0.76	4.18	23.9	0.0
Equity-market neutral	0.80	10.23	0.08	4.57	15.6	0.0	0.67	4.95	0.11	3.34	0.04	1.26	16.7	0.0
Event driven	0.71	5.06	0.20	6.86	29.5	0.0	1.35	5.84	0.04	0.68	0.37	6.54	36.1	0.0
Distressed	0.84	5.16	0.23	6.72	28.6	0.0	1.58	5.86	0.04	0.65	0.43	6.42	35.2	0.0
Event driven multistrategy	0.64	4.09	0.19	5.59	21.7	0.0	1.25	4.76	0.03	0.46	0.34	5.34	27.0	0.0
Risk arbitrage	0.55	4.96	0.13	5.30	20.0	0.0	0.87	4.56	0.04	0.96	0.21	4.46	22.9	0.0
Fixed income arbitrage	0.59	5.57	0.00	-0.13	0.0	89.3	0.95	5.26	-0.10	-2.15	0.09	2.02	5.0	5.4
Global macro	1.14	3.53	0.16	2.27	4.4	2.4	1.48	2.64	0.07	0.50	0.25	1.78	4.8	5.9
Long/Short equity	0.67	2.66	0.39	7.40	32.7	0.0	0.92	2.12	0.33	3.11	0.46	4.32	33.0	0.0
Managed futures	0.80	2.40	-0.17	-2.47	5.1	1.4	-0.09	-0.15	0.05	0.38	-0.41	-2.90	8.1	0.8
Multistrategy	0.77	6.11	0.02	0.60	0.3	54.7	0.86	3.91	-0.01	-0.11	0.04	0.71	0.5	74.2

Table 6.22   **Correlation matrix for monthly returns of hedge fund risk factors from January 1994 to August 2004**

Correlation matrix	S&P 500	S&P 500^2	S&P 500^3	Banks	Libor	USD	Oil	Gold	Lehman bond	Large minus small cap	Value minus growth	Credit spread	Term spread	VIX
S&P 500	100.0													
S&P 500^2	−12.3	100.0												
S&P 500^3	77.1	−43.3	100.0											
Banks	55.8	−33.0	59.1	100.0										
LIBOR	3.5	−19.4	12.7	−16.9	100.0									
USD	7.3	−4.6	4.5	−1.2	8.9	100.0								
Oil	−1.6	−15.1	−1.7	−2.0	14.0	−13.4	100.0							
Gold	−7.2	−7.8	−2.6	6.1	−12.2	−35.2	20.1	100.0						
Lehman Bond	0.8	15.2	−8.9	7.5	−42.1	−55.6	7.0	25.7	100.0					
Large minus small cap	7.6	21.8	−0.6	−27.6	3.8	11.0	−19.7	−24.5	8.1	100.0				
Value minus growth	−48.9	14.4	−30.3	−5.4	−2.1	−4.0	−21.3	−3.9	10.9	32.7	100.0			
Credit spread	−30.6	30.1	−19.8	−16.0	−40.2	−13.0	−2.9	16.4	14.3	−7.2	16.5	100.0		
Term spread	−11.6	−6.1	−0.2	11.5	4.9	−21.5	7.0	20.4	−10.5	−13.7	2.6	38.7	100.0	
VIX	−67.3	26.2	−67.8	−49.6	−8.2	−9.2	−1.5	−3.4	15.3	9.7	38.5	3.1	−6.9	100.0
CSFB/Tremont indexes														
Hedge funds	45.9	−22.5	38.2	41.6	−0.2	22.0	7.9	8.9	3.6	−29.6	−41.0	−24.4	−8.1	−25.7
Convertible arbitrage	11.0	−19.1	29.4	29.8	−9.0	19.6	−4.3	2.1	2.2	−19.6	−6.2	−6.4	−15.2	−0.2
Dedicated shortseller	−75.6	20.1	−66.4	−52.1	4.0	−4.4	−9.2	−9.8	7.5	34.9	64.5	11.9	−10.5	57.2
Emerging markets	47.2	−24.6	50.1	43.8	5.6	19.4	0.7	7.7	−17.7	−27.2	−34.2	−9.9	16.2	−36.6
Equity-market neutral	39.6	3.2	34.5	30.9	−9.4	9.1	4.8	−6.8	7.3	1.4	−12.6	−12.6	−29.2	−17.1
Event driven	54.3	−44.8	67.8	65.4	−0.9	14.6	6.9	8.2	−7.6	−32.4	−30.7	−24.8	−3.6	−44.4
Distressed	53.5	−43.4	62.8	64.3	−10.7	9.7	5.2	13.5	−0.3	−26.7	−27.8	−21.6	−1.2	−43.9
Event driven multistrategy	46.6	−39.7	62.1	56.2	8.4	20.0	7.7	1.2	−14.6	−33.0	−29.9	−23.0	−3.4	−37.6
Risk arbitrage	44.7	−32.5	53.4	55.7	7.0	4.9	2.6	7.4	−6.4	−42.0	−22.0	−29.9	−20.5	−42.2
Fixed income arbitrage	−1.3	−29.2	5.9	18.8	6.9	18.5	9.4	0.9	2.0	−10.3	1.9	−17.6	3.5	16.9
Global macro	20.9	−10.8	14.4	28.5	−5.7	28.7	−4.0	−2.3	7.4	−8.8	−6.6	−11.2	−4.7	−5.3
Long/Short equity	57.2	−20.2	47.2	40.5	−4.3	−2.1	19.5	14.2	7.0	−48.9	−67.1	−22.9	−13.1	−36.2
Managed futures	−22.6	22.4	−32.2	−14.3	−13.0	−19.9	17.5	15.9	35.4	4.6	21.9	17.9	2.0	25.7
Multistrategy	5.6	−4.1	2.2	10.5	0.9	−13.3	5.6	−1.7	12.5	−8.8	−13.5	−18.9	−7.8	9.5

returns in the correlation matrix; they will be included as factors to capture nonlinear effects.[42] It is apparent from the lower left block of the correlation matrix that there are indeed nontrivial correlations between the risk factors and the hedge fund indexes. For example, there is a 67.8 percent correlation between the Event Driven index and the cubed S&P 500 return, implying skewness effects in this category of strategies. Also, the Long/Short Equity index has correlations of −48.9 percent and −67.1 with the

42. We have divided the squared and cubed S&P 500 return series by 10 and 100, respectively, so as to yield regression coefficients of comparable magnitudes to the other coefficients.

Hedge funds	Convertible arbitrage	Dedicated shortseller	Emerging markets	Equity-market neutral	Event driven	Distressed	Event driven multi-strategy	Risk arbitrage	Fixed income arbitrage	Global macro	Long/Short equity	Managed futures	Multi-strategy
100.0													
38.4	100.0												
−46.5	−21.7	100.0											
65.7	32.0	−57.0	100.0										
31.8	29.9	−34.9	24.2	100.0									
66.0	59.2	−63.1	66.6	39.8	100.0								
56.3	50.8	−62.7	57.7	36.2	93.6	100.0							
68.9	60.3	−53.9	67.2	37.6	93.0	74.8	100.0						
39.0	41.4	−49.1	44.2	31.9	70.1	58.4	66.9	100.0					
41.2	54.4	−5.3	28.2	7.0	37.4	28.1	43.4	14.1	100.0				
85.4	27.1	−10.6	41.6	19.1	36.8	29.3	42.6	12.4	41.8	100.0			
77.4	24.1	−71.8	58.8	33.9	65.0	56.9	63.6	51.0	17.2	40.3	100.0		
10.5	−21.5	24.5	−13.1	13.8	−23.4	−16.1	−26.8	−25.3	−6.9	26.6	−6.4	100.0	
15.0	33.5	−4.4	−3.9	20.1	14.9	10.0	18.8	4.2	27.5	10.8	13.4	−4.1	100.0

market-cap and equity-style factors, respectively, which is not surprising given the nature of this category.

Using a combination of statistical methods and empirical judgment, we use these factors to estimate risk models for each of the fourteen indexes, and the results are contained in table 6.24. The first row reports the sample size, the second contains the adjusted R^2, and the remaining rows contain regression coefficients and, in parentheses, t-statistics. The number of factors selected for each risk model varies from a minimum of four for Equity Market Neutral and Managed Futures to a maximum of thirteen for Event Driven, not including the constant term. This pattern is plausible because

Table 6.23   **Definitions of aggregate measures of market conditions and risk factors**

Variable	Definition
S&P 500	Monthly return of the S&P 500 index, including dividends
Banks	Monthly return of equal-weighted portfolio of bank stocks in CRSP (SIC codes 6000–6199 and 6710)
LIBOR	Monthly first-difference in U.S. dollar 6-month London interbank offer rate
USD	Monthly return on U.S. Dollar Spot Index
Oil	Monthly return on NYMEX crude oil front-month futures contract
Gold	Monthly return on gold spot price index
Lehman bond	Monthly return on Dow Jones/Lehman Bond Index
Large-cap minus small-cap	Monthly return difference between Dow Jones large-cap and small-cap indexes
Value minus growth	Monthly return difference between Dow Jones value and growth indexes
Credit spread	Beginning-of-month difference between KDP High Yield Daily Index and U.S. 10-year yield
Term spread	Beginning-of-month 10-year U.S. dollar swap rate minus 6-month U.S. dollar LIBOR
VIX	Monthly first-difference in the VIX implied volatility index

the Event Driven category includes a broad set of strategies; that is, various types of "events," hence a broader array of risk factors will be needed to capture the variation in this category versus Equity Market Neutral.

The statistical significance of squared and cubed S&P 500 returns highlights the presence of nonlinearities in a number of indexes as well as in the overall hedge fund index. Together with the S&P 500 return, these higher-order terms comprise a simple polynomial approximation to a nonlinear functional relation between certain hedge fund returns and the market. The squared term may be viewed as a proxy for volatility dependence, and the cubed term as a proxy for skewness dependence. These are, of course, very crude approximations for such phenomena, because the underlying strategies may not involve market exposure—a fixed-income arbitrage fund may well have nonlinear risk exposures but the nonlinearities are more likely to involve interest rate variables than equity market indexes. However, strategies such as Equity Market Neutral, Risk Arbitrage, and Long/Short Equity, which purposefully exploit tail risk in equity markets, do show significant exposure to higher-order S&P 500 terms as expected.

The last column of table 6.24 reports the number of times each risk factor is included in a particular risk model, and this provides an indication of systemic risk exposures in the hedge fund sector. In particular, if we discover a single factor that is included and significant in all hedge fund risk models, such a factor may be a bellwether for broad dislocation in the industry. But apart from the constant term, there is no such factor. Nevertheless, the first lag of the squared S&P 500 return and the cubed S&P 500

Table 6.24   Risk models for monthly CSFB/Tremont hedge fund index returns from January 1994 to August 2004

Regressor	Hedge funds	Convertible arbitrage	Dedicated shortseller	Emerging markets	Equity-market neutral	Event driven	Distressed	Event driven multistrategy	Risk arbitrage	Fixed income arbitrage	Global macro	Long/Short equity	Managed futures	Multi-strategy	Factor selection count
Sample size	118	118	118	118	118	118	118	118	118	118	118	118	118	117	
R^2 (%)	54.5	45.1	79.7	44.1	25.5	75.1	65.0	66.4	58.0	54.3	34.3	73.2	21.4	16.3	
Constant	0.30 (1.22)	0.08 (0.22)	1.90 (4.25)	−0.58 (−0.81)	0.98 (7.00)	0.29 (0.84)	0.94 (4.65)	0.75 (4.93)	1.14 (7.34)	0.06 (0.20)	0.31 (0.78)	1.09 (3.35)	0.19 (0.59)	0.58 (3.97)	14
SP500	0.23 (5.81)		−0.63 (−7.11)	0.44 (3.29)			0.13 (3.17)					0.28 (4.29)			5
SP500(Lag 1)						0.06 (2.39)	0.06 (1.82)								3
S&P500^2					0.07 (2.49)		−0.10 (−2.03)			−0.05 (−1.80)					3
SP500^2(Lag 1)	−0.12 (−2.12)		−0.14 (−1.60)	−0.30 (−2.44)		−0.12 (−3.70)	−0.09 (−2.09)	−0.10 (−2.68)	−0.06 (−1.89)	−0.06 (−2.08)	−0.16 (−1.76)	−0.09 (−1.74)		0.09 (2.07)	10
SP500^3		0.21 (5.92)	−0.24 (−2.49)	0.44 (2.82)	0.07 (2.80)	0.26 (8.22)	0.21 (3.63)	0.32 (12.00)	0.15 (5.57)			0.15 (2.10)	−0.26 (−3.15)		10
SP500^3(Lag 1)		0.15 (5.21)	−0.15 (−2.27)					0.08 (2.31)	0.05 (2.32)	0.19 (5.82)	0.15 (1.75)		−0.17 (−2.09)	0.08 (2.36)	7
SP500^3(Lag 2)	0.09 (1.74)	0.13 (4.34)								0.12 (4.79)	0.24 (3.43)			0.14 (4.39)	5
Banks					0.06 (2.47)	0.10 (2.94)		0.07 (2.19)	0.07 (2.65)	0.10 (3.76)					5
Banks(Lag 1)	0.08 (1.85)					0.07 (2.16)	0.08 (1.80)			−0.06 (−2.14)					5
Banks(Lag 2)	0.09 (1.71)					0.05 (1.98)	0.07 (2.05)			0.05 (1.78)	0.18 (2.04)	0.10 (2.33)			6

continued

Table 6.24   (continued)

Regressor	Hedge funds	Convertible arbitrage	Dedicated shortseller	Emerging markets	Equity-market neutral	Event driven	Distressed	Event driven multistrategy	Risk arbitrage	Fixed income arbitrage	Global macro	Long/Short equity	Managed futures	Multi-strategy	Factor selection count
USD	0.42 (4.86)	0.13 (2.21)		0.65 (3.74)		0.15 (3.00)	0.11 (2.06)	0.21 (3.95)		0.11 (2.97)	0.68 (4.85)			-0.15 (-2.78)	9
Gold	0.08 (1.62)			0.17 (1.50)		0.05 (2.14)	0.08 (2.33)							-0.05 (-1.39)	5
Lehman Bond	0.59 (3.77)	0.18 (1.56)				0.13 (1.32)		0.22 (2.16)		0.24 (3.17)	0.98 (3.69)	0.38 (2.82)	0.79 (3.08)		8
Large minus small cap	-0.19 (-4.30)	-0.07 (-2.98)	0.34 (5.55)	-0.40 (-4.35)		-0.10 (-3.98)	-0.11 (-3.89)	-0.17 (-6.69)	-0.13 (-6.24)			-0.36 (-8.38)			9
Value minus growth	-0.08 (-2.09)		0.23 (4.59)			-0.04 (-2.29)				-0.03 (-2.10)	-0.08 (-1.71)	-0.21 (-5.76)	0.08 (1.47)	-0.05 (-2.35)	8
LIBOR		-1.09 (-1.93)	2.26 (2.16)				-2.02 (-3.55)								3
Credit spread		0.20 (2.26)				0.14 (1.68)				0.09 (1.42)					3
Term spread		-0.20 (-1.99)	-0.65 (-3.26)	0.89 (2.66)	-0.24 (-3.86)	-0.20 (-2.14)			-0.31 (-4.51)			-0.38 (-2.69)			7
VIX		0.08 (2.37)		0.22 (1.69)						0.07 (2.80)		0.12 (2.11)			4
No. of factors selected	10	10	8	8	4	13	11	7	6	12	7	9	4	6	

return appear in ten out of fourteen risk models, implying that time-varying volatility, tail risk, and skewness are major risk factors across many different hedge fund styles. Close runners-up are the U.S. dollar index and the market-capitalization factors, appearing in nine of fourteen risk models. Liquidity exposure, as measured by either the lagged S&P 500 return (see Asness, Krail, and Liew 2001, and Getmansky, Lo, and Makarov 2004), or the credit spread factor, is significant for some indexes, such as Convertible Arbitrage, Event Driven, and Fixed-Income Arbitrage, but apparently does not affect other indexes.

The $\bar{R}^2$'s for these risk models vary, ranging from 16.3 percent for Fund of Funds to 79.7 percent for Dedicated Shortsellers. Given the relatively small sample of about ten years of monthly returns, the overall explanatory power of these risk models is encouraging. Of course, we must recognize that the process of variable selection has inevitably biased upward the $\bar{R}^2$s, hence these results should be viewed as useful summaries of risk exposures and correlations rather than structural factor models of hedge fund returns.

6.6.2 Hedge Funds and the Banking Sector

With the repeal in 1999 of the Glass-Steagall Act, many banks have now become broad-based financial institutions engaging in the full spectrum of financial services, including retail banking, underwriting, investment banking, brokerage services, asset management, venture capital, and proprietary trading. Accordingly, the risk exposures of such institutions have become considerably more complex and interdependent, especially in the face of globalization and the recent wave of consolidations in the banking and financial services sectors.

In particular, innovations in the banking industry have coincided with the rapid growth of hedge funds. Currently estimated at over $1 trillion in size, the hedge fund industry has a symbiotic relationship with the banking sector, providing an attractive outlet for bank capital, investment management services for banking clients, and fees for brokerage services, credit, and other banking functions. Moreover, many banks now operate proprietary trading units that are organized much like hedge funds. As a result, the risk exposures of the hedge fund industry may have a material impact on the banking sector, resulting in new sources of systemic risks. And although many hedge funds engage in *hedged* strategies—where market swings are partially or completely offset through strategically balanced long and short positions in various securities—such funds often have other risk exposures such as volatility risk, credit risk, and illiquidity risk. Moreover, a number of hedge funds and proprietary trading units are not hedged at all, and also use leverage to enhance their returns and, consequently, their risks.

To the extent that systemic risk also involves distress in the banking sector, we must examine the relation between the returns of publicly traded banks and hedge fund index returns. Using monthly total returns data from the University of Chicago's Center for Research in Security Prices database, we construct value-weighted portfolios of all stocks with SIC codes 6000–6199, and 6710, rebalanced monthly, and use the returns of these portfolios as proxies for the banking sector. Table 6.25 contains regressions of the equal-weighted bank index return on the S&P 500 and CSFB/Tremont hedge fund index returns, and table 6.26 contains the same regressions for the value-weighted bank index.

The interpretation of these regressions requires some further discussion because correlations between the return of bank stocks and hedge fund indexes do not necessarily imply any causal relations. For example, illiquidity in a bank stock need not be directly linked to illiquidity in the bank's underlying portfolio—for example, the equity of a small regional bank may be thinly traded—but this need not imply that the bank is engaged in illiquid hedge fund strategies. Nevertheless, if a bank does engage in such strategies—which is becoming more common as banks struggle to deal with increased competition and dwindling margins—then the regressions in table 6.25 and 6.26 should pick up significant factor exposures to certain hedge fund indexes.

The first column of table 6.25 is a regression of the equal-weighted bank index on the S&P 500 return and its first two lags. The fact that both contemporaneous and lagged S&P 500 returns are significant suggests that banks are exposed to market risk and also have some illiquidity exposure, much like serially correlated hedge fund returns in section 6.4 and the serially correlated asset returns in table 6.12.

The next fourteen columns contain regressions with both S&P 500 returns and two lags as well as each of the fourteen hedge fund index returns and two lags, respectively. A comparison of these regressions may provide some insight into links between certain hedge fund styles and the banking industry. These regressions have reasonable explanatory power, with $\overline{R}^2$s ranging from 54.6 percent for Managed Futures to 58.2 percent for Risk Arbitrage and Long/Short Equity. Among the fourteen indexes, the ones yielding the highest explanatory power are the event-related indexes: Event Driven, Distressed, Event-Driven Multi-Strategy, and Risk Arbitrage, with $\overline{R}^2$s of 48.4 percent, 47.3 percent, 42.4 percent, and 40.8 percent, respectively. The coefficients for the contemporaneous hedge fund indexes in each of these four regressions are also numerically comparable, suggesting that these four strategy groups have similar effects on the banking sector. The least significant hedge fund index for explaining the equal-weighted bank index is Managed Futures, with coefficients that are both statistically insignificant and numerically close to zero. Managed futures strategies are known to be relatively uncorrelated with most other asset classes, and the banking sector is apparently one of these asset classes.

Table 6.25   Regressions of monthly equal-weighted banking sector returns on the S&P 500 and various CSFB/Tremont hedge fund index returns from January 1994 to August 2004

Regression of equal-weighted bank index on S&P 500 and single hedge fund index

Regressors	Market model	Hedge funds	Convertible arbitrage	Dedicated shortseller	Emerging markets	Equity-market neutral	Event driven	Distressed	Event driven multi-strategy	Risk arbitrage	Fixed income arbitrage	Global macro	Long/Short equity	Managed futures	Multi-strategy	Multiple hedge fund indexes
Sample size	118	118	118	118	118	118	118	118	118	118	118	118	118	118	115	115
R^2 (%)	32.8	35.2	38.9	33.0	35.9	32.1	48.4	47.3	42.4	40.8	36.6	35.8	35.7	31.2	31.5	63.7
Constant	1.30	1.21	0.99	1.41	1.29	0.81	0.70	0.61	0.93	0.70	0.76	0.96	1.43	1.35	1.08	0.38
	(4.22)	(3.61)	(2.82)	(4.38)	(4.24)	(1.64)	(2.21)	(1.88)	(2.92)	(2.00)	(2.14)	(2.85)	(4.50)	(3.92)	(2.50)	(1.20)
SP500	0.47	0.37	0.42	0.34	0.37	0.45	0.22	0.25	0.31	0.34	0.47	0.44	0.39	0.47	0.46	0.24
	(7.42)	(5.19)	(6.76)	(3.40)	(4.89)	(6.32)	(3.06)	(3.56)	(4.32)	(5.14)	(7.58)	(6.83)	(5.02)	(7.15)	(7.14)	(3.21)
SP500(1)	0.13	0.14	0.09	0.11	0.17	0.11	0.05	0.04	0.08	0.04	0.12	0.14	0.19	0.12	0.12	0.10
	(2.05)	(1.92)	(1.41)	(1.08)	(2.28)	(1.52)	(0.67)	(0.57)	(1.13)	(0.54)	(1.84)	(2.15)	(2.46)	(1.83)	(1.88)	(1.56)
SP500(2)	−0.05	−0.08	−0.05	−0.03	−0.09	−0.06	−0.10	−0.12	−0.08	−0.08	−0.11	−0.11	0.01	−0.07	−0.06	
	(−0.86)	(−1.14)	(−0.82)	(−0.28)	(−1.25)	(−0.92)	(−1.48)	(−1.76)	(−1.24)	(−1.20)	(−1.64)	(−1.65)	(0.17)	(−0.98)	(−0.86)	
CSFBHEDGE		0.36														
		(2.61)														
CSFBHEDGE(1)		−0.11														
		(−0.85)														
CSFBHEDGE(2)		−0.03														−1.66
		(−0.24)														(−5.52)
CSFBCONVERT			0.89													
			(3.50)													
CSFBCONVERT(1)			−0.63													−0.39
			(−2.28)													(−1.67)
CSFBCONVERT(2)			0.20													
			(0.79)													
CSFBSHORT				−0.15												−0.10
				(−1.77)												(−1.32)
CSFBSHORT(1)				−0.02												
				(−0.19)												

continued

Table 6.25   (continued)

Regression of equal-weighted bank index on S&P 500 and single hedge fund index

Regressors	Market model	Hedge funds	Convertible arbitrage	Dedicated shortseller	Emerging markets	Equity-market neutral	Event driven	Distressed	Event driven multi-strategy	Risk arbitrage	Fixed income arbitrage	Global macro	Long/Short equity	Managed futures	Multi-strategy	Multiple hedge fund indexes
CSFBSHORT(2)				0.02 (0.25)												−0.15 (−2.27)
CSFBEMKTS					0.19 (2.70)											
CSFBEMKTS(1)					−0.11 (−1.39)											
CSFBEMKTS(2)					0.08 (1.21)											
CSFBEQMKTNEUT						0.32 (0.82)										
CSFBEQMKTNEUT(1)						0.23 (0.58)										
CSFBEQMKTNEUT(2)						0.08 (0.22)										
CSFBED							1.19 (5.85)									0.91 (3.83)
CSFBED(1)							−0.24 (−1.12)									−0.27 (−1.30)
CSFBED(2)							0.13 (0.67)									0.62 (2.60)
CSFBDST								0.93 (5.55)								
CSFBDST(1)								−0.04 (−0.26)								
CSFBDST(2)								0.12 (0.77)								
CSFBEDM									0.85 (4.41)							
CSFBEDM(1)									−0.25 (−1.24)							

Variable								
CSFBEDM(2)	0.14 (0.79)							
CSFBRISKARB		1.02 (4.11)						0.74 (3.05)
CSFBRISKARB(1)		0.11 (0.42)						
CSFBRISKARB(2)		0.08 (0.33)						
CSFBFIARB			0.68 (2.33)					
CSFBFIARB(1)			0.03 (0.10)					0.57 (2.23)
CSFBFIARB(2)			0.35 (1.27)					
CSFBGMACRO				0.22 (2.60)				
CSFBGMACRO(1)				0.01 (0.08)				
CSFBGMACRO(2)				0.10 (1.15)				0.99 (5.68)
CSFBLSE					0.19 (1.66)			−0.24 (−2.18)
CSFBLSE(1)					−0.16 (−1.45)			
CSFBLSE(2)					−0.19 (−1.75)			
CSFBMF						0.01 (0.11)		
CSFBMF(1)						−0.02 (−0.20)		
CSFBMF(2)						−0.05 (−0.57)		
CSFBMULT							0.27 (1.09)	
CSFBMULT(1)							−0.13 (−0.57)	
CSFBMULT(2)							0.14 (0.62)	

Table 6.26 Regressions of monthly value-weighted banking sector returns on the S&P 500 and various CSFB/Tremont hedge fund index returns from January 1994 to August 2004

Regression of value-weighted bank index on S&P 500 and single hedge fund index

Regressors	Market model	Hedge funds	Convertible arbitrage	Dedicated shortseller	Emerging markets	Equity-market neutral	Event driven	Distressed	Event driven multi-strategy	Risk arbitrage	Fixed income arbitrage	Global macro	Long/Short equity	Managed futures	Multi-strategy	Multiple hedge fund indexes
Sample size	118	118	118	118	118	118	118	118	118	118	118	118	118	118	115	115
R^2 (%)	55.7	55.8	55.6	57.1	54.9	55.0	56.1	55.6	55.5	58.2	54.7	55.1	58.2	54.6	55.5	64.2
Constant	0.73 (2.05)	1.02 (2.60)	0.60 (1.41)	0.57 (1.54)	0.76 (2.11)	0.30 (0.53)	0.69 (1.67)	0.67 (1.59)	0.72 (1.82)	0.48 (1.15)	0.71 (1.66)	0.80 (2.00)	1.04 (2.85)	0.75 (1.90)	0.65 (1.31)	0.47 (1.00)
SP500	0.89 (12.24)	0.91 (10.76)	0.87 (11.53)	1.10 (9.84)	0.89 (9.98)	0.87 (10.65)	0.81 (8.68)	0.83 (9.17)	0.84 (9.46)	0.81 (10.19)	0.90 (11.95)	0.87 (11.20)	0.99 (11.21)	0.90 (11.76)	0.90 (12.09)	1.09 (10.27)
SP500(1)	0.02 (0.31)	0.04 (0.47)	0.01 (0.08)	-0.03 (-0.23)	0.02 (0.19)	0.02 (0.22)	-0.06 (-0.60)	-0.03 (-0.34)	-0.04 (-0.40)	-0.08 (-0.93)	0.01 (0.15)	0.03 (0.43)	0.05 (0.53)	0.02 (0.25)	0.03 (0.46)	-0.02 (-0.34)
SP500(2)	-0.02 (-0.25)	0.06 (0.70)	-0.01 (-0.17)	0.01 (0.12)	0.02 (0.26)	-0.04 (-0.45)	0.02 (0.28)	0.01 (0.16)	0.01 (0.10)	0.00 (-0.05)	-0.03 (-0.36)	-0.02 (-0.32)	0.12 (1.40)	-0.03 (-0.38)	0.00 (-0.00)	
CSFBHEDGE		-0.12 (-0.72)														
CSFBHEDGE(1)		-0.07 (-0.47)														
CSFBHEDGE(2)		-0.24 (-1.53)														
CSFBCONVERT			0.45 (1.46)													0.83 (2.51)
CSFBCONVERT(1)			-0.38 (-1.14)													-0.59 (-1.79)
CSFBCONVERT(2)			0.12 (0.40)													
CSFBSHORT				0.24 (2.47)												0.28 (2.53)
CSFBSHORT(1)				-0.07 (-0.73)												
CSFBSHORT(2)				0.06 (0.60)												-0.14 (-1.58)

CSFBEMKTS	−0.01 (−0.11)						
CSFBEMKTS(1)	−0.01 (−0.07)						
CSFBEMKTS(2)	−0.07 (−0.89)						
CSFBEQMKTNEUT		0.33 (0.74)					
CSFBEQMKTNEUT(1)		−0.01 (−0.02)					
CSFBEQMKTNEUT(2)		0.23 (0.52)					
CSFBED			0.40 (1.51)				
CSFBED(1)			0.11 (0.41)				
CSFBED(2)			−0.34 (−1.36)				
CSFBDST				0.29 (1.32)			
CSFBDST(1)				0.07 (0.32)			
CSFBDST(2)				−0.22 (−1.05)			
CSFBEDM					0.29 (1.19)		
CSFBEDM(1)					0.08 (0.32)		
CSFBEDM(2)					−0.25 (−1.09)		
CSFBRISKARB						0.53 (1.79)	0.86 (2.69)
CSFBRISKARB(1)						0.53 (1.76)	
CSFBRISKARB(2)						−0.48 (−1.67)	
CSFBFIARB						0.06 (0.17)	

continued

Table 6.26 (continued)

Regression of value-weighted bank index on S&P 500 and single hedge fund index

Regressors	Market model	Hedge funds	Convertible arbitrage	Dedicated shortseller	Emerging markets	Equity-market neutral	Event driven	Distressed	Event driven multi-strategy	Risk arbitrage	Fixed income arbitrage	Global macro	Long/Short equity	Managed futures	Multi-strategy	Multiple hedge fund indexes
CSFBFIARB(1)											0.19 (0.52)					0.46 (1.32)
CSFBFIARB(2)											−0.18 (−0.55)					
CSFBGMACRO												0.09 (0.83)				
CSFBGMACRO(1)												−0.08 (−0.81)				
CSFBGMACRO(2)												−0.05 (−0.50)				
CSFBLSE													−0.28 (−2.13)			−0.23 (−1.56)
CSFBLSE(1)													0.00 (−0.01)			
CSFBLSE(2)													−0.28 (−2.17)			−0.34 (−2.38)
CSFBMF														0.03 (0.32)		
CSFBMF(1)														−0.03 (−0.28)		
CSFBMF(2)														−0.04 (−0.37)		
CSFBMULT															−0.33 (−1.18)	−0.49 (−1.73)
CSFBMULT(1)															0.00 (0.00)	
CSFBMULT(2)															0.35 (1.33)	

The last column reports a final regression that includes multiple hedge fund indexes as well as the S&P 500 return and its two lags. The hedge fund indexes were selected using a combination of statistical techniques and empirical judgment, and the $\overline{R}^2$ of 63.7 percent shows a significant increase in explanatory power with the additional hedge fund indexes. As before, this $\overline{R}^2$ is likely to be upward biased because of the variable-selection process. Unlike the single hedge fund index regressions where the coefficients on the contemporaneous hedge fund indexes were positive except for Dedicated Shortsellers (which is not surprising given that banks have positive market exposure), in this case several hedge fund indexes have negative exposures: the aggregate Hedge Fund, Convertible Arbitrage, Dedicated Shortsellers, and Long/Short Equity. However, the equal-weighted bank index has positive exposure to Event Driven, Risk Arbitrage, Fixed-Income Arbitrage, and Global Macro indexes.

Table 6.26 presents corresponding regression results for the value-weighted bank index, and some intriguing patterns emerge. For the contemporaneous and lagged S&P 500 return regression, the results are somewhat different than those of table 6.25—the contemporaneous coefficient is significant but the lagged coefficients are not, implying the presence of market exposure but little liquidity exposure. This is plausible given the fact that the value-weighted index consists mainly of the largest banks and bank holding-companies, whereas the equal-weighted index is tilted more toward smaller banking institutions.

The single hedge fund index regressions in the next fourteen columns also differ from those in table 6.25 in several respects. The explanatory power is uniformly higher in these regressions than in table 6.25, and also remarkably consistent across all fourteen regressions—the $\overline{R}^2$s range from 54.6 percent (Managed Futures) to 58.2 percent (Risk Arbitrage). However, this does not imply that larger banking institutions have more in common with all hedge fund investment strategies. In fact, it is the S&P 500 that seems to be providing most of the explanatory power (compare the first column with the next fourteen in table 6.26), and although some hedge fund indexes do have significant coefficients, the $\overline{R}^2$s change very little when hedge fund indexes are included one at a time. The multiple hedge fund index regression in the last column does yield somewhat higher explanatory power, an $\overline{R}^2$ of 64.2 percent, but in contrast to the negative coefficients in the equal-weighted bank index regression, in this case most of the coefficients are positive. In particular, Convertible Arbitrage, Dedicated Shortsellers, Risk Arbitrage, and Fixed-Income Arbitrage all have positive coefficients. One possible explanation is that the larger banking institutions are involved in similar investment activities through their proprietary trading desks. Another explanation is that large banks offer related fee-based services to such hedge funds (e.g., credit, prime brokerage, trading, structured products), and do well when their hedge fund clients do well.

In summary, it is apparent from the regressions in table 6.25 and 6.26 that the banking sector has significant exposure to certain hedge fund indexes, implying the presence of some common factors between hedge funds and banks, and raises the possibility that dislocation among the former can affect the latter. This provides yet another channel by which the hedge fund industry generates systemic risk exposures.

6.6.3   Regime-Switching Models

Our final hedge fund-based measure of systemic risk is motivated by the phase-locking example of section 6.1.2 where the return-generating process exhibits apparent changes in expected returns and volatility that are discrete and sudden. The Mexican peso crisis of 1994–1995, the Asian crisis of 1997, and the global flight to quality precipitated by the default of Russian GKO debt in August 1998 are all examples of such regime shifts. Linear models are generally incapable of capturing such discrete shifts, hence more sophisticated methods are required. In particular, we propose to model such shifts by a regime-switching process in which two states of the world are hypothesized, and the data are allowed to determine the parameters of these states and the likelihood of transitioning from one to the other. Regime-switching models have been used in a number of contexts, ranging from Hamilton's (1989) model of the business cycle to Ang and Bekaert's (2004) regime-switching asset allocation model, and we propose to apply it to the CSFB/Tremont indexes to obtain another measure of systemic risk—the possibility of switching from a normal to a distressed regime.

The return of a hedge fund index, R_t is normally distributed with mean (μ_i) and variance (σ_i^2). Denote by R_t the return of a hedge fund index in period t and suppose R_t satisfies the following:

(17a)
$$R_t = I_t \cdot R_{1t} + (1 - I_t) \cdot R_{2t}$$

(17b)
$$R_{it} \sim \mathcal{N}(\mu_i, \sigma_i^2)$$

(17c)
$$I_t = \begin{cases} 1 & \text{with probability } p_{11} \text{ if } I_{t-1} = 1 \\ 1 & \text{with probability } p_{21} \text{ if } I_{t-1} = 0 \\ 0 & \text{with probability } p_{12} \text{ if } I_{t-1} = 1 \\ 0 & \text{with probability } p_{22} \text{ if } I_{t-1} = 0 \end{cases}$$

This is the simplest specification for a two-state regime-switching process where I_t is an indicator that determines whether R_t is in state 1 or state 2, and R_{it} is the return in state i. Each state has its own mean and variance, and the regime-switching process I_t has two probabilities; hence there are a total of six parameters to be estimated. Despite the fact that the state I_t is unobservable, it can be estimated statistically (see, for example, Hamilton 1989, 1990) along with the parameters via maximum likelihood.

This specification is similar to the well-known "mixture of distributions" model. However, unlike standard mixture models, the regime-switching model is not independently distributed over time unless $p_{11} = p_{21}$. Once estimated, forecasts of changes in regime can be readily obtained, as well as forecasts of R_t itself. In particular, because the k-step transition matrix of a Markov chain is simply given by $\mathbf{P}^k$, the conditional probability of the regime I_{t+k} given date-t data $\mathfrak{R}_t \equiv (R_t, R_{t-1}, \ldots, R_1)$ takes on a particularly simple form:

(18a) $\text{Prob}(I_{t+k} = 1 \mid \mathfrak{R}_t) = \pi_1 + (p_{11} - p_{21})^k [\text{Prob}(I_t = 1 \mid \mathfrak{R}_t) - \pi_1]$

(18b) $$\pi_1 \equiv \frac{p_{21}}{p_{12} + p_{21}},$$

where $\text{Prob}(I_t = 1 \mid \mathfrak{R}_t)$ is the probability that the date-t regime is 1 given the historical data up to and including date t (this is a by-product of the maximum-likelihood estimation procedure). Using similar recursions of the Markov chain, the conditional expectation of R_{t+k} can be readily derived as:

(19a) $E(R_{t+k} \mid \mathfrak{R}_t) = \mathbf{a}_t' \mathbf{P}^k \boldsymbol{\mu}$

(19b) $\mathbf{a}_t = [\text{Prob}(I_t = 1 \mid \mathfrak{R}_t) \text{Prob}(I_t = 2 \mid \mathfrak{R}_t)]'$

(19c) $\boldsymbol{\mu} \equiv (\mu_1 \ \mu_2)'$

Table 6.27 reports the maximum-likelihood estimates of the means and standard deviations in each of two states for the fourteen CSFB/Tremont hedge fund indexes, as well as the transition probabilities for the two states. Note that two rows in table 6.27 are in boldface—Dedicated Shortselling and Managed Futures—because the maximum-likelihood estimation procedure did not converge properly for these two categories, implying that the regime-switching process may not be a good model of their returns. The remaining twelve series yielded well-defined parameter estimates, and by convention, we denote by state 1 the lower-volatility state.

Consider the second row, corresponding to the Convertible Arbitrage index. The parameter estimates indicate that in state 1, this index has an expected return of 16.1 percent with a volatility of 1.9 percent, but in state 2, the expected return is –1.6 percent with a volatility of 6.1 percent. The latter state is clearly a crisis state for convertible arbitrage, while the former is a more normal state. The other hedge fund indexes have similar parameter estimates—the low-volatility state is typically paired with higher means, and the high-volatility state is paired with lower means. While such pairings may seem natural for hedge funds, there are three exceptions to this

| Table 6.27 | | | | | Maximum likelihood parameter estimates of a two-state regime-switching model for CSFB/Tremont hedge fund indexes from January 1994 to August 2004 | | | | |

| Index | p_{11} (%) | p_{21} (%) | p_{12} (%) | p_{22} (%) | Annualized mean (%) | | Annualized standard deviation (%) | | Log(L) |
					State 1	State 2	State 1	State 2	
Hedge funds	100.0	1.2	0.0	98.8	6.8	12.4	2.9	9.9	323.6
Convertible arbitrage	89.9	17.9	10.1	82.1	16.1	−1.6	1.9	6.1	404.0
Dedicated shortseller	**23.5**	**12.6**	**76.5**	**87.4**	**−76.2**	**11.7**	**2.3**	**16.5**	**208.5**
Emerging markets	100.0	1.2	0.0	98.8	11.5	6.6	8.2	20.3	218.0
Equity market-neutral	95.0	2.4	5.0	97.6	4.4	13.8	2.1	3.1	435.1
Event driven	98.0	45.0	2.0	55.0	13.3	−47.0	3.8	14.0	377.0
Distressed	97.9	58.0	2.1	42.0	15.2	−57.5	4.8	15.6	349.4
Event driven multistrategy	98.7	38.4	1.3	61.6	12.0	−55.2	4.5	15.0	363.6
Risk arbitrage	89.4	25.6	10.6	74.4	9.6	3.1	2.7	6.9	391.8
Fixed income arbitrage	95.6	29.8	4.4	70.2	10.0	−12.2	1.9	6.6	442.3
Global macro	100.0	1.2	0.0	98.8	13.6	14.0	3.2	14.2	286.3
Long/Short equity	98.5	2.5	1.5	97.5	6.1	21.1	6.3	15.3	285.0
Managed futures	**32.0**	**22.2**	**68.0**	**77.8**	**−6.0**	**10.7**	**3.8**	**13.7**	**252.1**
Multistrategy	98.2	25.0	1.8	75.0	10.8	−7.6	3.2	9.2	387.9

rule; for equity market neutral, global macro, and long/short equity, the higher-volatility state has higher expected returns. This suggests that for these strategies, volatility may be a necessary ingredient for their expected returns.

From these parameter estimates, it is possible to estimate the probability of being in state 1 or 2 at each point in time for each hedge fund index. For example, in figure 6.10 we plot the estimated probabilities of being in state 2, the high-volatility state, for the Fixed-Income Arbitrage index for each month from January 1994 to August 2004. We see that this probability begins to increase in the months leading up to August 1998, and hits 100 percent in August and several months thereafter. However, this is not an isolated event, but occurs on several occasions both before and after August 1998.

To develop an aggregate measure of systemic risk based on this regime-switching model, we propose summing the state-2 probabilities across all hedge fund indexes every month to yield a time series that captures the likelihood of being in high-volatility periods. Of course, the summed probabilities—even if renormalized to lie in the unit interval—cannot be interpreted formally as a probability, because the regime-switching process was specified individually for each index, not jointly across all indexes. There-

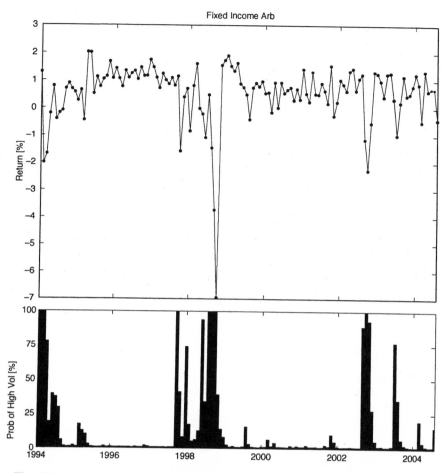

Fig. 6.10   Monthly returns and regime-switching model estimates of the probability of being in the high-volatility state for CSFB/Tremont Fixed-Income Arbitrage hedge-fund index, from January 1994 to August 2004

fore, the interpretation of "state 2" for convertible arbitrage may be quite different than the interpretation of "state 2" for equity market neutral. Nevertheless, as an aggregate measure of the state of the hedge fund industry, the summed probabilities may contain useful information about systemic risk exposures.

Figure 6.11 plots the monthly summed probabilities from January 1994 to August 2004, and we see that peak occurs around August 1998, with local maxima around the middle of 1994 and the middle of 2002, which corresponds roughly to our intuition of high-volatility periods for the hedge fund industry.

Alternatively, we can construct a similar aggregate measure by summing the probabilities of being in a low-mean state, which involves summing the

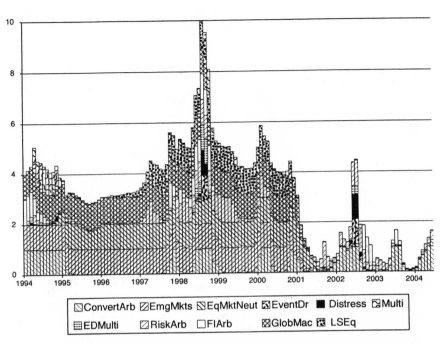

Fig. 6.11   Aggregate hedge-fund risk indicator: Sum of monthly regime-switching model estimates of the probability of being in the high-volatility state (p_2) for eleven CSFB/Tremont hedge-fund indexes from January 1994 to Autust 2004

Notes: Convertible Arbitrage; Emerging Markets; Equity Market Neutral; Event Driven; Distressed; Even-Driven Multi-Strategy; Risk Arbitrage; Fixed-Income Arbitrage; Global Macro; Long/Short Equity; and Multi-Strategy.

state-2 probabilities for those indexes where high volatility is paired with low mean with the state-1 probabilities for those indexes where low volatility is paired with low mean. Figure 6.12 contains this indicator, which differs significantly from figure 6.11. The low-mean indicator also has local maxima in 1994 and 1998 as expected, but now there is a stronger peak around 2002, largely due to equity market neutral, global macro, and long/short equity. This corresponds remarkably well to the common wisdom that over the past two years these three strategy classes have underperformed for a variety of reasons.[43] Therefore, this measure may capture more of the spirit of systemic risk than the high-volatility indicator in figure 6.11. The implications of figure 6.12 for systemic risk are clear: the probabilities of being in low-mean regimes have increased for a number of hedge fund indexes, which may foreshadow fund outflows in the coming

---

43. Large fund flows into these strategies and changes in equity markets such as decimalization, the rise of ECN's, automated trading, and Regulation FD are often cited as reasons for the decreased profitability of these strategies.

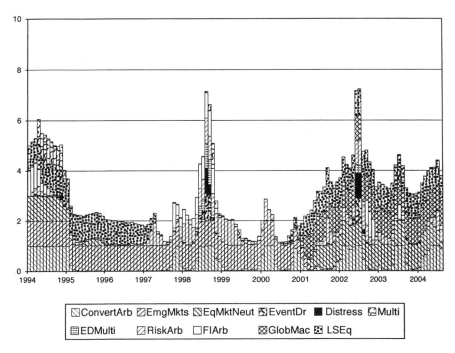

Fig. 6.12   Aggregate hedge-fund risk indicator: sum of monthly regime-switching model estimates of the probability of being in the low-mean state for eleven CSFB/ Tremont hedge-fund indexes, from January 1994 to August 2004
Note: See fig. 6.11.

months. To the extent that investors are disappointed with hedge fund returns, they may reallocate capital quickly, which places additional stress on the industry that can lead to further dislocation and instability.

6.7   The Current Outlook

A definitive assessment of the systemic risks posed by hedge funds requires certain data that is currently unavailable, and is unlikely to become available in the near future—that is, counter-party credit exposures, the net degree of leverage of hedge fund managers and investors, the gross amount of structured products involving hedge funds, and so forth. Therefore, we cannot determine the magnitude of current systemic risk exposures with any degree of accuracy. However, based on the analytics developed in this study, there are a few tentative inferences that we can draw.

1. The hedge fund industry has grown tremendously over the last few years, fueled by the demand for higher returns in the face of stock market declines and mounting pension-fund liabilities. These massive fund inflows

have had a material impact on hedge fund returns and risks in recent years, as evidenced by changes in correlations, reduced performance, and increased illiquidity as measured by the weighted autocorrelation ρ_i^*.

2. Mean and median liquidation probabilities for hedge funds have increased in 2004, based on logit estimates that link several factors to the liquidation probability of a given hedge fund, including past performance, assets under management, fund flows, and age. In particular, our estimates imply that the average liquidation probability for funds in 2004 is over 11 percent, which is higher than the historical unconditional attrition rate of 8.8 percent. A higher attrition rate is not surprising for a rapidly growing industry, but it may foreshadow potential instabilities that can be triggered by seemingly innocuous market events.

3. The banking sector is exposed to hedge fund risks, especially smaller institutions, but the largest banks are also exposed through proprietary trading activities, credit arrangements and structured products, and prime brokerage services.

4. The risks facing hedge funds are nonlinear and more complex than those facing traditional asset classes. Because of the dynamic nature of hedge fund investment strategies, and the impact of fund flows on leverage and performance, hedge fund risk models require more sophisticated analytics, and more sophisticated users.

5. The sum of our regime-switching models' high-volatility or low-mean state probabilities is one proxy for the aggregate level of distress in the hedge fund sector. Recent measurements suggest that we may be entering a challenging period. This, coupled with the recent uptrend in the weighted autocorrelation ρ_i^*, and the increased mean and median liquidation probabilities for hedge funds in 2004 from our logit model, implies that systemic risk is increasing.

We hasten to qualify our tentative conclusions by emphasizing the speculative nature of these inferences, and hope that our analysis spurs additional research and data collection to refine both the analytics and the empirical measurement of systemic risk in the hedge-fund industry. As with all risk management challenges, we should hope for the best, and prepare for the worst.

Appendix

The following is a list of category descriptions, taken directly from TASS documentation, that define the criteria used by TASS in assigning funds in their database to one of eleven possible categories:

Convertible Arbitrage   This strategy is identified by hedge investing in the convertible securities of a company. A typical investment is to be long the convertible bond and short the common stock of the same company. Positions are designed to generate profits from the fixed income security as well as the short sale of stock, while protecting principal from market moves.

Dedicated Shortseller   Dedicated short sellers were once a robust category of hedge funds before the long bull market rendered the strategy difficult to implement. A new category, short biased, has emerged. The strategy is to maintain net short as opposed to pure short exposure. Short-biased managers take short positions in mostly equities and derivatives. The short bias of a manager's portfolio must be constantly greater than zero to be classified in this category.

Emerging Markets   This strategy involves equity or fixed income investing in emerging markets around the world. Because many emerging markets do not allow short selling, nor offer viable futures or other derivative products with which to hedge, emerging market investing often employs a long-only strategy.

Equity Market Neutral   This investment strategy is designed to exploit equity market inefficiencies and usually involves being simultaneously long and short matched equity portfolios of the same size within a country. Market neutral portfolios are designed to be either beta or currency neutral, or both. Well-designed portfolios typically control for industry, sector, market capitalization, and other exposures. Leverage is often applied to enhance returns.

Event Driven   This strategy is defined as "special situations" investing designed to capture price movement generated by a significant pending corporate event such as a merger, corporate restructuring, liquidation, bankruptcy, or reorganization. There are three popular subcategories in event-driven strategies: risk (merger) arbitrage, distressed/high yield securities, and Regulation D.

Fixed-Income Arbitrage   The fixed-income arbitrageur aims to profit from price anomalies between related interest rate securities. Most managers trade globally with a goal of generating steady returns with low volatility. This category includes interest rate swap arbitrage, U.S. and non-U.S. government bond arbitrage, forward yield curve arbitrage, and mortgage-backed securities arbitrage. The mortgage-backed market is primarily U.S.-based, over-the-counter and particularly complex.

Global Macro   Global macro managers carry long and short positions in any of the world's major capital or derivative markets. These positions reflect their views on overall market direction as influenced by major economic trends and/or events. The portfolios of these funds can include stocks, bonds, currencies, and commodities in the form of cash or derivatives instruments. Most funds invest globally in both developed and emerging markets.

Long/Short Equity   This directional strategy involves equity-oriented investing on both the long and short sides of the market. The objective is not to be market neutral. Managers have the ability to shift from value to growth, from small to medium to large capitalization stocks, and from a net long position to a net short position. Managers may use futures and options to hedge. The focus may be regional, such as long/short U.S. or European equity, or sector specific, such as long and short technology or healthcare stocks. Long/short equity funds tend to build and hold portfolios that are substantially more concentrated than those of traditional stock funds.

Managed Futures   This strategy invests in listed financial and commodity futures markets and currency markets around the world. The managers are usually referred to as Commodity Trading Advisors, or CTAs. Trading disciplines are generally systematic or discretionary. Systematic traders tend to use price and market-specific information (often technical) to make trading decisions, while discretionary managers use a judgmental approach.

Multi-Strategy   The funds in this category are characterized by their ability to dynamically allocate capital among strategies falling within several traditional hedge fund disciplines. The use of many strategies, and the ability to reallocate capital between them in response to market opportunities, means that such funds are not easily assigned to any traditional category.

The Multi-Strategy category also includes funds employing unique strategies that do not fall under any of the other descriptions.

Fund of Funds   A "Multi-Manager" fund will employ the services of two or more trading advisors or Hedge Funds who will be allocated cash by the trading manager to trade on behalf of the fund.

References

Ackermann, C., R. McEnally, and D. Ravenscraft. 1999. The performance of hedge funds: Risk, return, and incentives. *Journal of Finance* 54:833–74.

Agarwal, A., N. Daniel, and N. Naik. 2004. Flows, performance and managerial incentives in hedge funds. Working Paper, Georgia State University, J. Mack Robinson College of Business.

Agarwal, V., and N. Naik. 2000a. Generalized style analysis of hedge funds. *Journal of Asset Management* 1:93–109.

Agarwal, V., and N. Naik. 2000b. Multi-period performance persistence analysis of hedge funds source. *Journal of Financial and Quantitative Analysis* 35:327–42.

Agarwal, V., and N. Naik. 2000c. On taking the 'alternative' route: The risks, rewards, and performance persistence of hedge funds. *Journal of Alternative Investments* 2:6–23.

Agarwal, V., and N. Naik. 2000d. Performance evaluation of hedge funds with buy-and-hold and option-based strategies. Hedge Fund Centre Working Paper no. HF-003, London Business School.

Amin, G., and H. Kat. 2003a. Hedge fund performance 1990–2000: DO the money machines really add value? *Journal of Financial and Quantitative Analysis* 38: 251–74.

Amin, G., and H. Kat. 2003b. Stocks, bonds, and hedge funds. *Journal of Portfolio Management* 29:113–19.

Amin, G., and H. Kat. 2003c. Welcome to the dark side: Hedge fund attrition and survivorship bias over the period 1994–2001. *Journal of Alternative Investments* 6:57–73.

Ang, A., and G. Bekaert. 2004. How regimes affect asset allocation. *Financial Analysts Journal* 60:86–99.

Asness, C., R. Krail, and J. Liew. 2001. Do hedge funds hedge? *The Journal of Portfolio Management* 28:6–19.

Baquero, G., J. Horst, and M. Verbeek. 2004. Forthcoming. Survival, look-ahead bias and the performance of hedge funds. *Journal of Financial and Quantitative Analysis.*

Bares, P., R. Gibson, and S. Gyger. 2003. Style consistency and survival probability in the hedge funds industry. Unpublished working paper, University of Zurich, Swiss Banking Institute.

Berk, J., and R. Green. 2004. Mutual fund flows and performance in rational markets. *Journal of Political Economy* 112:1269–95.

Bookstaber, R. 1999. A framework for understanding market crisis. In *Risk management: Principles and practices,* 7–19. Charlottesville, VA: Association for Investment Management and Research.

Bookstaber, R. 2000. Understanding and monitoring the liquidity crisis cycle. *Financial Analysts Journal* 17–22.

Boyson, N. 2002. How are hedge fund manager characteristics related to performance, volatility and survival? Unpublished working paper, Ohio State University, Fisher College of Business.

Brooks, C., and H. Kat. 2002. The statistical properties of hedge fund index returns and their implications for investors. *Journal of Alternative Investments* 5:25–44.

Brown, S., and W. Goetzmann. 2003. Hedge funds with style. *Journal of Portfolio Management* 29:101–12.

Brown, S., W. Goetzmann, and R. Ibbotson. 1999. Offshore hedge funds: Survival and performance 1989–1995. *Journal of Business* 72:91–118.

Brown, S., W. Goetzmann, R. Ibbotson, and S. Ross. 1992. Survivorship bias in performance studies. *Review of Financial Studies* 5:553–80.

Brown, S., W. Goetzmann, and J. Park. 2000. Hedge funds and the Asian currency crisis. *Journal of Portfolio Management* 26:95–101.

Brown, S., W. Goetzmann, and J. Park. 2001a. Careers and survival: Competition and risks in the hedge fund and CTA Industry. *Journal of Finance* 56:1869–86.

Brown, S., W. Goetzmann, and J. Park. 2001b. Conditions for survival: Changing risk and the performance of hedge fund managers and CTAs. Yale School of Management Working Paper no. F-59.

Campbell, J., A. Lo, and C. MacKinlay. 1997. *The econometrics of financial markets.* Princeton, NJ: Princeton University Press.

Carpenter, J., and A. Lynch. 1999. Survivorship bias and attrition effects in measures of performance persistence. *Journal of Financial Economics* 54:337–74.

Chandar, N., and R. Bricker. 2002. Incentives, discretion, and asset valuation in closed-end mutual funds. *Journal of Accounting Research* 40:1037–70.

Chevalier, J., and G. Ellison. 1997. Risk taking by mutual funds as a response to incentives. *Journal of Political Economy* 105:1167–1200.

Cox, D., and E. Snell. 1989. *The analysis of binary data,* 2nd ed. London: Chapman and Hall.

Edwards, F., and M. Caglayan. 2001. Hedge fund and commodity fund investments in bull and bear markets. *The Journal of Portfolio Management* 27:97–108.

Farmer, D., and A. Lo. 1999. Frontiers of finance: Evolution and efficient markets. *Proceedings of the National Academy of Sciences* 96:9991–2.

Feffer, S., and C. Kundro. 2003. Understanding and mitigating operational risk in hedge fund investments. Unpublished working paper, The Capital Markets Company Ltd.

Fung, W., and D. Hsieh. 1997a. Empirical characteristics of dynamic trading strategies: The case of hedge funds. *Review of Financial Studies* 10:275–302.

———. 1997b. Investment style and survivorship bias in the returns of CTAs: The information content of track records. *Journal of Portfolio Management* 24:30–41.

———. 1999. A primer on hedge funds. *Journal of Empirical Finance* 6:309–31.

———. 2000. Performance characteristics of hedge funds and commodity funds: Natural versus spurious biases. *Journal of Financial and Quantitative Analysis* 35:291–307.

———. 2001. The risk in hedge fund strategies: Theory and evidence from trend followers. *Review of Financial Studies* 14:313–41.

———. 2002a. Asset-based style factors for hedge funds. *Financial Analysts Journal* 58:16–27.

———. 2002b. Benchmarks of hedge fund performance: Information content and measurement biases. *Journal of Alternative Investments* 58:22–34.

Getmansky, M. 2004. The life cycle of hedge funds: Fund flows, size and performance. Unpublished working paper. Cambridge, MA: MIT Laboratory for Financial Engineering.

Getmansky, M., A. Lo, and I. Makarov. 2004. An econometric model of serial correlation and illiquidity in hedge fund returns. *Journal of Financial Economics* 74 (3): 529–610.

Getmansky, M., A. Lo, and S. Mei. 2004. Sifting through the wreckage: Lessons from recent hedge-fund liquidations. *Journal of Investment Management* 2:6–38.

Goetzmann, W., J. Ingersoll, and S. Ross. 2003. High water marks and hedge fund management contracts. *Journal of Finance* 58:1685–1718.

Goetzmann, W., and N. Peles. 1997. Cognitive dissonance and mutual fund investors. *Journal of Financial Research* 20:145–58.

Greenspan, A. 1998. Statement before the committee on banking and financial services, U.S. House of Representatives. *Federal Reserve Bulletin* 84:1046–50.

Gregoriou, G. 2002. Hedge fund survival lifetimes. *Journal of Asset Management* 3:237–52.

Granger, C. 1980. Long memory relations and the aggregation of dynamic models. *Journal of Econometrics* 14:227–38.

———. 1988. Aggregation of time series variables—A survey. Federal Reserve Bank of Minneapolis Institute for Empirical Macroeconomics, Discussion Paper 1.

Gruber, M. 1996. Another puzzle: The growth in actively managed mutual funds. *The Journal of Finance* 51:783–810.

Hamilton, J. 1989. A new approach to the economic analysis of nonstationary time series and the business cycle. *Econometrica* 57:357–84.

———. 1990. Analysis of time series subject to changes in regime. *Journal of Econometrics* 45:39–70.

Hendricks, D., J. Patel, and R. Zeckhauser. 1997. The J-shape of performance persistence given survivorship bias. *Review of Economics and Statistics* 79:161–70.

Horst, J., T. Nijman, and M. Verbeek. 2001. Eliminating look-ahead bias in evaluating persistence in mutual fund performance. *Journal of Empirical Finance* 8:345–73.

Howell, M. J. 2001. Fund age and performance. *Journal of Alternative Investments* 4:57–60.

Ineichen, A. 2001. The myth of hedge funds: Are hedge funds the fireflies ahead of the storm? *Journal of Global Financial Markets* 2:34–46.

Ippolito, R. 1992. Consumer reaction to measures of poor quality: Evidence from the mutual fund industry. *Journal of Law and Economics* 35:45–70.

Jen, P., C. Heasman, and K. Boyatt. 2001. Alternative asset strategies: Early performance in hedge fund managers. Internal document, Lazard Asset Management, London.

Kadlec, G., and D. Patterson. 1999. A transactions data analysis of nonsynchronous trading. *Review of Financial Studies* 12:609–30.

Kao, D. L. 2000. Estimating and pricing credit risk: An overview. *Financial Analysts Journal* 56 (4): 50–66.

Kao, D. L. 2002. Battle for alphas: Hedge funds versus long-only portfolios. *Financial Analysts Journal* 58:16–36.

Kaplan, S., and A. Schoar. 2004. Forthcoming. Private equity performance: Returns, persistence and capital flows. *Journal of Finance.*

Kendall, M., A. D. Stuart, and J. K. Ord. 1983. *The advanced theory of statistics, Vol. 3* (4th ed.). London: Griffin.

Kramer, D. 2001. Hedge fund disasters: Avoiding the next catastrophe. *Journal of Investment Management* 2 (4): 6–38.

Leamer, E. 1978. *Specification searches.* New York: Wiley.

Liang, B. 1999. On the performance of hedge funds. *Financial Analysts Journal* 55:72–85.

———. 2000. Hedge funds: The living and the dead. *Journal of Financial and Quantitative Analysis* 35:309–26.

———. 2001. Hedge fund performance: 1990–1999. *Financial Analysts Journal* 57: 11–18.

———. 2003. The accuracy of hedge fund returns. *Journal of Portfolio Management* 29:111–22.

Lo, A. 2001. Risk management for hedge funds: Introduction and overview. *Financial Analysts Journal* 57:16–33.

———. 2002. The statistics of Sharpe ratios. *Financial Analysts Journal* 58:36–50.

———. 2004. The adaptive markets hypothesis: Market efficiency from an evolutionary perspective. *Journal of Portfolio Management* 30:15–29.

Lo, A., and C. MacKinlay. 1988. Stock market prices do not follow random walks: Evidence from a simple specification test. *Review of Financial Studies* 1:41–66.

———. 1990. Data snooping biases in tests of financial asset pricing models. *Review of Financial Studies* 3:431–68.

Lochoff, R. 2002. Hedge funds and hope. *The Journal of Portfolio Management* 28:92–99.

Ljung, G., and G. Box. 1978. On a measure of lack of fit in time series models. *Biometrika* 67:297–303.

MacKenzie, P. 2003. Long-Term Capital Management and the sociology of arbitrage. *Economy and Society* 32:349–80.

Maddala, G. 1983. *Limited-dependent and qualitative variables in econometrics.* Cambridge: Cambridge University Press.

McDonough, W. 1998. Statement before the committee on banking and financial services, U.S. House of Representatives. *Federal Reserve Bulletin* 84:1050–54.

Mishkin, F. 1996/1997. Financial crises. *NBER Reporter,* 10–12.

Nagelkerke, N. 1991. A note on a general definition of the coefficient of determination. *Biometrika* 78:691–2.

Pérold, A. 1999. Long-Term Capital Management, LP. (A–D) Harvard Business School case study. Boston: Harvard Business School Press.

Pérold, A., and R. Salomon. 1991. The right amount of assets under management. *Financial Analysts Journal* (May–June): 31–39.

President's Working Group on Financial Markets. 1999. *Hedge funds, leverage, and the lessons of Long-Term Capital Management.*

Samuelson, P. 1965. Proof that properly anticipated prices fluctuate randomly. *Industrial Management Review* 6:41–49.

Schneeweis, T., and R. Spurgin. 1996. Survivor bias in commodity trading advisor performance. *Journal of Futures Markets* 16:757–72.

Sirri, E., and P. Tufano. 1998. Costly search and mutual fund flows. *The Journal of Finance* 53:1589–1622.

Strogatz, S. H. 1994. *Nonlinear dynamics and chaos: With applications to physics, biology, chemistry, and engineering.* Reading, MA: Perseus.

Watts, D. 1999. *Small worlds: The dynamics of networks between order and randomness.* Princeton, NJ: Princeton University Press.

Watts, D., and S. Strogatz. 1998. Collective dynamics of 'small-world' networks. *Nature* 393:440–42.

Zheng, L. 1999. Is money smart?—A study of mutual fund investors' fund selection ability. *Journal of Finance* 54:901–33.

Comment   David M. Modest

This is an ambitious research effort focused on the risks of hedge funds—both the risks that hedge funds face and the potential risks that hedge funds pose to the global financial system. It makes a significant and important contribution to the nascent and burgeoning research in this area. With over $1 trillion currently invested in over 8,000 hedge funds, and projections of that sum rising to over $2 trillion in the next decade, hedge funds have become an increasingly important part of the financial sector. They account for a substantial and rising share of trading volume on most major stock exchanges, account for a sizable and growing fraction of revenue and profit for global investment and commercial banks, are major risk intermediaries for a full range of publicly traded and private securities, and are a major source of brain drain for competitors ranging from banks to insurance companies to mutual funds to universities.

Two of the most important functions of capital markets are: (a) the pooling of capital that facilitates the undertaking of large-scale projects, and (b) the concomitant diversification of risk. The last fifty years have witnessed a dramatic increase in the scope and breadth of vehicles to transfer and share risk, including: stock and bond mutual funds, index funds, exchange-traded funds, futures, options, asset-backed securities (ABS), ABS tranches, catastrophe (CAT) bonds, credit derivatives, and hedge funds.

Alfred Winslow Jones is credited with launching the first hedge fund in the late 1940s—a long/short equity fund whose goal was to generate consistent returns regardless of the overall direction of the stock market. Jones received notoriety in an article Carol Loomis wrote for *Fortune* in April 1966 entitled: "The Jones Nobody Keeps Up With," in which she describes Jones as outperforming the best mutual fund by 44 percent over a five-year period and 87 percent over a ten-year period. That article helped spurn a boom in hedge funds that has led to an ever-widening scope of investing activities over the last forty years.

As figure 6.4 of the paper illustrates, most of the investment focus of the early hedge funds was concentrated on long/short equity, global macro, and event-driven strategies. Over time, that focus has branched out to include fixed income, convertible bond, and statistical equity arbitrage; long/short credit; distressed debt investing; long/short emerging market equity and debt; mezzanine lending; ABS strategies; pass-through and structured mortgage product-based investments; CDO structured trades, private investment in public equities (PIPES); and other private equity-type strategies typified by ESL's purchase of Kmart and subsequent takeover of Sears. Over time, hedge funds have thus taken a bigger part in bearing the less liquid financial risks of the economy. On the surface, the increased diversification of risks—across hedge funds and other investors—should make the financial markets more stable and less susceptible to cataclysmic shocks and systemic risks. The use of leverage by hedge funds, however, raises the specter of financial market contagion and leaves open the question of whether markets are more robust than in the past or whether increased hedge fund participation has elevated the potential for financial market calamity.

The strength of the paper is the breadth of focus on potential pitfalls and solutions to measuring hedge fund risks. As the paper argues, the risks of many hedge fund strategies are difficult, if not impossible, to detect empirically without an economic understanding of the structure of the trades and of the markets involved—especially given the rapid innovation of financial products and the rapid growth in their investment scope. The hypothetical strategy of Capital Decimation Partners L.P. (i.e., writing out of the money puts) displays the difficulty of capturing low frequency/high intensity tail risk using traditional mean-variance risk measures. And the phase-locking risk model of section 6.1.2 shows the difficulty of measuring correlations during crisis periods (i.e., systemic shocks) using unconditional moments. As mentioned at the outset of this paragraph, the strongest part of the paper is the development of new and better risk measures to measure the dynamic nature of hedge fund risks as illustrated in these two examples. The weakest part of the paper is the causal link between these risks and their impact on the global financial system.

The paper makes use of two main datasets: The CSFB/Tremont hedge fund strategy and aggregate hedge fund indices, and the TASS database for individual hedge fund returns. One of the most important and pervasive features of both the index and individual fund data is the persistent serial correlation of hedge fund returns—far in excess of the serial correlation apparent in the returns of traditional assets such as the returns on major equity benchmarks. The CSFB/Tremont convertible bond (CB) arbitrage index, for instance, has autocorrelation coefficients of 0.558, 0.411, and 0.144 at lags 1, 2, and 3—using monthly data over the January 1994–August 2004 period. Table 6.12 shows the mean first-order autocorrelation coefficient of individual convertible bond arbitrage funds ("combined" databases) was 0.314 over the February 1977–August 2004 period. It is of interest that the first order autocorrelation coefficient of 0.558 for the CB hedge fund index and 0.314 average for individual CB funds far exceeds the AR1 coefficient of 0.064 given in table 6.17 for the Merrill Lynch convertible index. The paper convincingly documents that the serial correlation is more prevalent in some strategies than others (e.g., 0.558 in convertible arbitrage and 0.058 in managed futures), that some pairs of strategies have very high cross-correlations (e.g., event and distressed have a correlation of 0.936 in table 6.8), that the correlations have very significant time variation (e.g., fig. 6.4), and that some strategies have significant correlations with lagged S&P 500 returns (e.g., fig. 6.3).

The authors note that "the degree of serial correlation in an asset's returns can be viewed as a proxy for the magnitude of the frictions, and illiquidity is one of the most common forms of such frictions." Although the authors note that there are many possible explanations for the serial correlation, they cite Getmansky, Lo, and Makarov (2004) as concluding that illiquidity and smoothed returns are "the most plausible explanation" for hedge funds. The authors distinguish between four distinct sources of serial correlation: (1) nonsynchronous trading, (2) linear extrapolation of past transaction prices for illiquid securities in determining marks, (3) use of dealer-average and potentially linearly extrapolated prices in marking positions, and (4) performance smoothing. A fifth source, and perhaps the most likely, is the pushing of marks in relatively illiquid securities—especially by larger funds and the collective effort of smaller hedge funds that often tend to be on the same side of trades. What is perhaps most striking about the results (and the underlying markets) is how many markets are plagued by evidence of illiquidity. A potentially rich vein for future research would be to try to link the serial correlation pattern of hedge fund returns (e.g., CB hedge funds) to the serial correlation pattern of the underlying instruments that they hold. In this paper, that link is asserted rather than investigated. It would also be interesting to try to link the serial correlation pattern of hedge fund returns to the serial correlation of flows into and out of different strategy groups.

Sections 6.4.2 and 6.4.3 of the paper formalize the econometric modeling of returns and presents the model introduced in Getmansky, Lo, and Makarov (2004). In this model, "true" hedge fund returns are described by a single factor linear model, and observed returns depend on a distributed lag of past true returns—with the restriction that the moving average (MA) coefficients lie between zero and one, and that the sum of the MA coefficients equals one. The authors argue that "(t)his is a sensible restriction" in that "Even the most illiquid securities will trade eventually, and when that occurs, all of the cumulative information affecting that security will be fully impounded into its transaction price." Although the restriction is sensible and the model is elegant, the problem with illiquid securities is that even when the assets trade, the price may not be one that would actually clear markets and hence may not "fully impound" all of the relevant information. Trade may occur (typically in very small size) when two "noise traders" meet, and the executed price may not reflect the price at which more informed traders would trade. Illiquid markets are typically characterized by very thin trading—often at dubious prices—but not necessarily by no trading. Informed traders often have an incentive not to trade—so as to leave prices and marks little changed. In illiquid markets, hedge funds often trade off the benefit of unloading relatively illiquid positions against the price impact it will have on the remaining positions on the book.

Section 6.5 of the paper contains a very interesting analysis of hedge fund liquidations—making use of TASS's Graveyard database. Table 6.19 contains a fascinating breakdown of the reasons funds reached the Graveyard. Of the 1,765 funds in the Graveyard database, the most common reason funds reached the Graveyard is because they were liquidated (913 funds). In principle the Graveyard database also includes funds that still exist, but are closed to new investment. The small number associated with this tag (7), however, strains credulity and raises the question of how closed funds are handled.

The authors present a very thorough analysis of the full range of reasons funds reached the Graveyard, the age distribution and assets under management (AUM) of Graveyard funds, attrition rates by year and by strategy as well as a thorough comparison of the risk and return differences between Graveyard and Live funds. For the strategies of convertible bond arbitrage, equity market neutral, and dedicated short sellers, the average return for Graveyard funds actually exceeds that for Live funds. It would be interesting to know whether this result also holds in excess return space—where the return of the fund is looked at relative to the return on the strategy index (for the sample period over which the fund data exists). As the strategies themselves show significant year-to-year return variation, this may explain part of the result. The median age for Graveyard funds is forty-five months and the median AUM of Graveyard funds is $6.3 million. At a 1.5 percent management fee, the management fee income for this size fund is only on the order of $100,000 (ignoring any incentive fees) and hence it is relatively uneconomic to keep a business of this size going for very long.

Section 6.5.1 of the paper analyzes the attrition rates of the aggregate hedge fund universe and the attrition rates broken down by strategy. The authors find substantial variation in attrition rates across strategies—with convertible bond arbitrage having the lowest attrition rate of 5.2 percent and managed futures having an attrition rate of 14.4 percent. The authors attribute this partly to risk, since convertible bond arbitrage has the second lowest volatility over the sample period and managed futures has the highest volatility. Returns may also be part of the story, however, as convertible bond arbitrage has the second highest Sharpe ratio over the period and managed futures has one of the lowest Sharpe ratios. Evidence suggests that many investors chase returns, so it would not be surprising to funds leaving underperforming hedge fund strategies (resulting in a certain amount of liquidations) and funds flowing into outperforming strategies.

The logit analysis of liquidations (section 6.5.2) is one of the more interesting and new parts of the paper. The authors examine the role of fund age, assets under management, returns, and fund flows in predicting the probability of liquidations. Fixed-effects models are also used to look for differences by year and by strategy (table 6.26). Not too surprisingly, age, assets, cumulative return, and inflows all lower the probability of fund liquidations. In future research, it would be interesting to see whether raw returns or excess returns (relative to an appropriate benchmark) have more explanatory power. Consider, for instance, an individual convertible bond hedge fund which returned 15 percent in 2000. This fund likely returned more than the average hedge fund in 2000, but perhaps underperformed the typical CB hedge fund by upward of 10 percent. It is of interest to know whether this fund was likely to be the recipient of inflows in 2001 for having outperformed the average fund, or be subject to withdrawals since it underperformed its peers. The results for Model 1, presented in table 6.27, show a substantial increase, relative to prior years, in the mean probabilities of liquidation. This is most likely a result of the explosion of new funds (which tend to have smaller AUM and obviously lower age) and the falling level of returns in the hedge fund industry. It would seem to be an open question whether this presages more systemic risk in the global financial system.

The serial correlation patterns of hedge fund returns and the dynamic and wide-ranging investment menu of hedge funds suggest the need in constructing hedge fund risk models for: (1) Scholes-Williams type estimation techniques that adjust for asynchronous prices, (2) estimation techniques consistent with time-varying parameters, and (3) a wide range of risk factors. The authors undertake this endeavor in section 6.6 by illustrating the importance of: (1) allowing different up-market and down-market betas (table 6.28)—especially for certain strategies, such as event-driven arbitrage, (2) incorporating Scholes-Williams types adjustment in estimating market exposures (table 6.31), higher-order moments (table 6.31) which, in part, capture time-varying coefficients, and (3) a wide range of prespecified factors, including the returns on gold, the Lehman bond index, large minus small capitalization stocks, value minus growth stocks, exchange rates, interest rates, credit spreads, term spreads, the volatility index (VIX), and the contemporaneous and lagged returns on a portfolio of bank stocks. As the authors note, "these results should be viewed as useful summaries of risk exposures and correlations rather than structural factor models of hedge fund returns"—as they reflect one sample period (January 1994–August 2004) and no attempt is made to examine the structural stability of the parameters.

In section 6.6, the authors also examine the statistical relationship between hedge funds and the banking sector. The analysis begins with regressions of bank indexes (equally weighted in table 6.32 and value-weighted in table 6.33) on contemporaneous and lagged S&P 500 returns and contemporaneous hedge fund strategy returns. The authors note: "The fact that both contemporaneous and lagged S&P 500 returns are significant suggests that banks are exposed to market risk and also have some illiquidity exposure, much like serially correlated hedge fund returns." This analogy, however, is not entirely appropriate. While the serial correlation properties of hedge fund returns (which reflect the sum of the net asset values of the underlying investments) are an indication of the illiquidity of the underlying assets, the autocorrelation apparent in the bank return data reflects the illiquidity in the bank stocks themselves and says nothing about the illiquidity of the underlying investments or exposures.

Tables 6.25 and 6.26 present data indicating significant contemporaneous and lagged correlations between portfolios of bank stocks and a variety of hedge fund strategies. The coefficient estimates appear relatively unstable—with the signs varying depending on whether the variables are included in univariate or multivariate form and whether the dependent variable is an equally weighted or value-weighted bank return index. While the regressions suggest there are important common factors affecting both banks and hedge funds, the structural link is unclear; the results would seem to offer little causal evidence on the impact that banks have on hedge fund returns or vice versa.

Finally, section 6.6.3 undertakes to implement a two-state regime-switching model to capture hedge fund risk, and is motivated by the phase-locking example given earlier in the paper. The model is estimated for fourteen CSFB/Tremont hedge fund indexes and, in general, the results show that "the low-volatility state is typically paired with higher means, and the high-volatility state is paired with lower means." The authors then aggregate (with a number of caveats) the probabilities of being in the high-volatility state (fig. 6.11) and low mean state (figure 6.12) in an attempt to shed some light on the current state of the hedge fund industry and how it compares to the past. The two figures tell a somewhat different story. Figure 6.11 suggests that, relative to the period since 1994, the probability of being in a high-volatility state is relatively low—although higher than in January 2004. On the other hand, figure 6.12 suggests that the probability of being in a low mean state is relatively high—based on estimated probabilities since 1994.

This seems to reflect that ultra-low volatility that has been apparent in most markets over the past few years—in part generated by the extremely low level of interest rates and the abundance of risk capital. Economic logic, based on the current pricing levels in most markets, where very little premium is being received ex ante for bearing risk, would seem to suggest that in fact the size of crisis shock could be quite large—although this doesn't speak to the probability of a crisis.

One of the most intriguing graphs is figure 6.7, which depicts a time series of the asset-weighted and median first-order autocorrelation coefficients of individual hedge funds. The authors use this graph to conclude in section 6.7:

(1) "These massive fund inflows have had a material impact on hedge fund returns and risks in recent years, as evidenced by . . . increased illiquidity as measured by the weighted autocorrelations" and

(2) "This, coupled with the recent uptrend in the weighted autocorrelation ρ_t^*, and increased mean and median liquidation probabilities for hedge funds in 2004 from our logit model implies, that systemic risk is increasing."

This line of reasoning seems to be the weakest in the paper. Systemic and contagion risk largely arise when there is mismatch between the maturity structure of the assets and the maturity structure of the liabilities. There is no doubt that on an aggregate basis hedge fund strategies have increasingly involved less liquid securities (e.g., high yield and distressed debt, private placements, control positions, thinly traded asset-backed securities, structured product tranches), but the authors fail to make the case that this increases systemic risk. This would require proving that these assets have moved from more stable hands to less stable hands. To the extent these investments are being made by firms like ESL and Eton Park—hedge funds with long lock-ups and proven investing and risk management skill—the move into less liquid securities may be prudent and risk-reducing for the financial system. The implicit assumption of the authors is that hedge fund investors are per se more fickle and that the growth of hedge funds inherently makes the system less stable—but the analyses shed little light on this implicit assertion.

In discussing systemic risk, it is also worth noting that most hedge funds have nowhere near the balance sheet leverage that fixed-income arbitrage funds typically have, which is on the order of 10:1–20:1. Long/short equity and event-driven funds, as illustrated in figures 6.2 and 6.5, account for close to 50 percent of the funds and assets under management, and usually have gross exposures (long plus short positions) on the order of 150 percent and net exposures that are less than 50 percent. Hence a repeat of October 19, 1987, would likely lead to a maximum loss of 12.5 percent for most of these funds—probably not a serious enough loss to generate hysteria and market contagion. A slow bleed, due to high fees and low alpha-generating ability, is much more likely to befall these funds than a cataclysmic crisis.

In sum, this is an interesting paper that covers a wide and disparate set of issues related to modeling hedge fund risk. The authors are very convincing in arguing for and implementing new models that more accurately capture the risk of hedge fund investments. Hedge funds' assets under management have grown significantly over the past few years, and the dearth of return possibilities in traditional hunting grounds had led many funds to seek opportunities in less liquid areas. It is unclear, however, whether this poses more systemic risk to the global financial system—a question left for future research.

Discussion Summary

Gary Gorton opened the general discussion, suggesting that the hedge-fund index data used by Chan et al. may be problematic because the details of index construction may amount to a choice of trading strategy that does not match the strategies the funds follow.

Much of the general discussion focused on the intuition and utility of the portion of the paper that uses serial correlation in hedge fund returns as an indicator of systemic liquidity risk. *Darrell Duffie* suggested that serial correlation may be different for positive and negative returns, and also may differ in high- and low-volatility environments even if the high-volatility periods are not characterized by the phase-locking that characterizes crises. *Philipp Hartmann* noted that some returns of some hedge funds appear to be negatively correlated with bank returns whereas others are positively correlated, so perhaps the hedge fund sector as a whole would not add to systemic risk. *Andrew Lo* responded that exposure to a given set of prices may be limited to a subset of fund styles, and that liquidity problems could affect funds with a wide range of styles.

Peter Garber suggested a different mechanism by which the growth of hedge funds may affect systemic risk. In previous decades, large dealer banks tended to be the main providers of liquidity in many markets, directly or indirectly, and they were able to collect rents from such liquidity provision. Hedge fund activity has been eroding such rents and thus liquidity from banks is less available in at least some markets. In a crisis, if hedge funds withdraw as liquidity providers, banks may no longer be prepared to step in.

III

Regulation

Systemic Risk and Regulation

Franklin Allen and Douglas Gale

7.1 Introduction

The experience of banking crises in the 1930s was severe. Before this, assuring financial stability was primarily the responsibility of central banks. The Bank of England had led the way. The last true panic in England was associated with the collapse of the Overend, Gurney, and Company in 1866. After that the Bank avoided crises by skillful manipulation of the discount rate and supply of liquidity to the market. Many other central banks followed suit, and by the end of the nineteenth century crises in Europe were rare. Although the Federal Reserve System was founded in 1914, its decentralized structure meant that it was not able to effectively prevent banking crises. The effect of the banking crises in the 1930s was so detrimental that in addition to reforming the Federal Reserve System the United States also imposed many types of banking regulation to prevent systemic risk. These included capital adequacy standards, asset restrictions, liquidity requirements, reserve requirements, interest rate ceilings on deposits, and restrictions on services and product lines. Over the years many of these regulations have been removed. However, capital adequacy requirements in the form of the Basel agreements remain.

We are grateful to our discussant Charles Calomiris and other participants at the NBER Conference on "The Risks of Financial Institutions" held in Woodstock, Vermont, October 22–23, 2004, our discussant Martin Hellwig and other participants at the Center for Financial Studies (CFS) Conference on "Risk Transfer between (Re-)Insurers, Banks, and Markets" held in Frankfurt, June 10–11, 2005, and our discussant Charles Kahn and other participants at the Bank of Portugal Conference on "Financial Fragility and Bank Regulation" held in Lisbon, June 24–25, 2005. Finally, we also thank the editors, Mark Carey and René Stulz, for their very helpful comments on an earlier version, and Florian Preis for pointing out an error in an earlier version.

If properly designed and implemented, capital regulations may reduce systemic risk. However, the growing importance of credit risk transfer has raised concerns about whether regulation as currently implemented does increase financial stability. The evidence reviewed subsequently suggests that there is a transfer of risk from the banks to insurance companies. One view is that this credit risk transfer is desirable because it allows diversification between different sectors of the financial system that cannot be achieved in other ways. On the other hand, if the transfer arises because of ill-designed regulations it may be undesirable. For example, regulatory arbitrage between the banking and insurance sectors could conceivably lead to an increase in risk in the insurance sector, which increases overall systemic risk. As Hellwig (1994, 1995, 1998) has repeatedly argued, attempts to shift risks can lead to a situation where these risks come back in the form of counterparty credit risk.

The purpose of this paper is to consider both arguments. We show first that diversification across sectors can lead to an optimal allocation of resources, and second that poorly designed and implemented capital regulation can lead to an increase in systemic risk.

Our analysis builds on our previous work on financial crises (see, e.g., Allen and Gale 1998, 2000a–c, 2003, 2004a–b, and Gale 2003, 2004). In Allen and Gale (2004b) we argued that financial regulation should be based on a careful analysis of the market failure that justifies government intervention. We developed a model of intermediaries and financial markets in which intermediaries could trade risk. It was shown that, provided financial markets and financial contracts are complete, the allocation is incentive efficient. When contracts are incomplete—for example, if the banks use deposit contracts with fixed promised payments—then the allocation is constrained efficient. In other words, there is no justification for regulation by the government. In order for regulation to be justified markets must be incomplete. As in standard theories of government regulation, it is first necessary to identify a market failure to analyze intervention. In Allen and Gale (2003) we suggested that the standard justification for capital regulation, namely that it controls moral hazard arising from deposit insurance, is not a good motivation. The two policies must be jointly justified and the literature does not do this.

There is a small but growing literature on credit risk transfer. The first part considers the impact of credit risk transfer on the allocation of resources when there is asymmetric information. Morrison (2005) shows that a market for credit derivatives can destroy the signalling role of bank debt and lead to an overall reduction in welfare as a result. He suggests that disclosure requirements for credit derivatives can help offset this effect. Nicolo and Pelizzon (2004) show that if there are banks with different abilities to screen borrowers, then good banks can signal their type using first-to-default basket contracts, which are often used in practice. These involve a payment to the protection buyer, if any, of a basket of assets defaults. Only protection sellers with very good screening abilities will be prepared to use such contracts. Chiesa (2004) considers a situation wherein banks have a comparative advantage in evaluating and monitoring risks but limited risk-bearing capacity. Credit risk transfer improves efficiency by allowing the monitored debt of large firms to be transferred to the market while banks can use their limited risk-bearing capacity for loans to small businesses. In contrast to these papers, our paper focuses on the situation where there is symmetric information, and shows how credit risk transfer can improve the allocation of resources through better risk sharing.

The second part of the literature focuses on the stability aspects of credit risk transfer. Wagner and Marsh (2004) consider the transfer of risk between banking and nonbanking sectors. They find that the transfer of risk out of a relatively fragile banking sector leads to an improvement in stability. Wagner (2005b) develops a model where credit risk transfer improves the liquidity of bank assets. However, this can increase the probability of crises by increasing the risks that banks are prepared to take. Wagner (2005a) shows that the increased portfolio diversification possibilities introduced by credit risk transfer can increase the probability of liquidity-based crises. The reason is that the increased diversification leads banks to reduce the amount of liquid assets they hold and increase the amount of risky assets. In contrast to these contributions, in our paper the focus is on the role of poorly designed regulation and its interaction with credit risk transfer in increasing systemic risk.

The rest of the paper proceeds as follows. We start in section 7.2 by considering the institutional background of credit risk transfer. We consider the evidence on how important risk transfers are quantitatively and which entities they occur between. Section 7.3 develops a model with a banking sector where consumers deposit their funds and firms borrow and repay these loans with some probability. There is also an insurance sector. Some firms have an asset that may be damaged. They require insurance to allow this asset to be repaired if it is damaged. The equilibrium with complete markets and contracts is characterized. In this case, complete markets allow full risk sharing. Section 7.4 develops an example with incomplete markets and contracts and shows how inefficient capital regulation can increase systemic risk. Finally, section 7.5 contains concluding remarks.

7.2   Institutional Background on Credit Risk Transfer

Credit risk has been transferred between parties for many years. Bank guarantees and credit insurance provided by insurance companies, for example, have a long history. Securitization of mortgages occurred in the 1970s. Bank loans were syndicated in the 1970s, and secondary markets for bank loans developed in the 1980s. In recent years a number of other methods of risk transfer have come to be widely used.

In table 7.1, Bank of International Settlements (BIS 2003) shows the

Table 7.1   **Size of credit risk transfer markets (in billions of U.S.$)**

Instrument	1995	1996	1997	1998	1999	2000	2001	2002
Loan trading (turnover)								
U.S. market	34	40	61	78	79	102	118	117[a]
(Loan Pricing Corporation)								
Credit Derivatives (outstanding)								
BIS triennial survey					108		693	
US OCC[b]					144	287	426	395	492[c]
British Bankers Association				180	350	586	893	1,189	1,952[d]
Risk magazine							810	1,398	
ISDA								919	1,600[d]
Asset-backed securities								
U.S. market (outstanding)	315	403	517	684	816	947	1,114	1,258[f]
(Bond Market Association)[e]								
European Market (issuance)								
(Moody's)[g]						68	80	134	50[h]
Australian market (outstanding)	7	10	15	19	27	33	38	54
(Australian Bureau of Statistics)								
Collateralized debt obligations								
U.S. market (outstanding)	1	1	19	48	85	125	167	232[f]
(Bond Market Association)								
European market (issuance)								
(Moody's)						42	71	114	70[h]
Total bank credit (outstanding)[j]								
IMF	23,424	23,576	23,309	26,018	26,904	27,221	27,442	29,435[i]
Corporate debt securities (outstanding)[k]								
BIS	3,241	3,373	3,444	4,042	4,584	4,939	5,233	5,505[i]

Source: BIS (2003).

[a] First three quarters of 2002, annualized.

[b] Holdings of U.S. commercial banks.

[c] Second quarter of 2002.

[d] Forecast for 2002.

[e] Excluding CBOs/CDOs.

[f] September 2002.

[g] ABSs and MBSs.

[h] First half of 2002.

[i] June 2002.

[j] Domestic and international credit to nonbank borrowers (United States, United Kingdom, Japan, Canada, Euro area).

[k] Debt securities issued in international and domestic markets, nonfinancial corporates.

size of credit risk transfer markets using various instruments from 1995–2002. Institutions transferring risk out are referred to as "risk shedders" while institutions taking on risk on are referred to as "risk buyers." One important class of instrument is credit derivatives. An example of these is credit default swaps. These are bilateral contracts where the risk shedder pays a fixed periodic fee in exchange for a payment contingent on an event such as default on a reference asset or assets. The contingent payment is provided by the risk buyer. With asset-backed securities, loans, bonds, or other receivables are transferred to a special purpose vehicle (SPV). The payoffs from these assets are then paid out to investors. The credit risk of the instruments in the SPV is borne by the investors. The underlying pool of assets in asset-backed securities is relatively homogeneous. Collateralized debt obligations also use an SPV but have more heterogeneous assets. Payouts are tranched, with claims on the pools separated into different degrees of seniority in bankruptcy and timing of default. The equity tranche is the residual claim and has the highest risk. The mezzanine tranche comes next in priority. The senior tranche has the highest priority and is often AAA rated.

It can be seen from table 7.1 that the use of all types of credit risk transfer has increased substantially. The growth has been particularly rapid in credit derivatives and collateralized debt obligations, however. Despite this rapid growth, a comparison of the outstanding amounts of credit risk transfer instruments with the total outstanding amounts of bank credit and corporate debt securities shows that they remain small in relative terms.

In table 7.2, British Bankers Association (BBA 2002) shows the buyers of credit protection in panel A and the sellers in panel B. From panel A it can be seen that the buyers are primarily banks. Securities houses also play

Table 7.2	Buyers and sellers of credit protection (percent of market)	
	End of 1999	End of 2001
A. Buyers of credit protection		
Banks	63	52
Securities houses	18	21
Hedge funds	3	12
Corporates	6	4
Insurance companies[a]	7	6
Mutual funds	1	2
Pension funds	1	1
Government/Export credit agencies	1	2
B. Sellers of credit protection		
Banks	47	39
Securities houses	16	16
Hedge funds	5	5
Corporates	3	2
Insurance companies[a]	23	33
Mutual funds	2	3
Pension funds	3	2
Government/Export credit agencies	1	0

Source: BBA Credit Derivatives Report 2001/2002.
[a]Includes monoline companies and reinsurers.

an important role. Hedge funds went from being fairly insignificant in 1999 to being significant in 2001. Corporates, insurance companies, and the other buyers do not constitute an important part of demand in the market. From panel B, it can be seen that banks are also important sellers of credit protection. In contrast to their involvement as buyers, the role of insurance companies as sellers is significant. Securities houses also sell significant amounts, while the remaining institutions play a fairly limited role. The results of a survey contained in Fitch (2003) are consistent with table 7.2. They found that the global insurance sector had a net seller position after deducting protection bought of $283 billion. The global banking industry purchased $97 billion of credit protection. A significant amount of risk is thus being transferred into the insurance industry from banks and other financial institutions. However, BIS (2005) reports that credit risk transfer investments made up only 1 percent of insurers' total investments, and that their financial strength is not threatened by their involvement in these types of investment.

As discussed in the introduction, these figures raise the important issue of why these transfers of risk are taking place. Is it the result of financial institutions seeking to diversify their risk? Alternatively, is it the result of regulatory arbitrage, and if so, can this arbitrage lead to a concentration of risk that increases the probability of systemic collapse?

We turn next to the role of credit risk transfer in allowing diversification between different sectors of the economy.

7.3   Diversification through Credit Risk Transfer

We use a simple Arrow-Debreu economy to illustrate the welfare properties of credit risk transfer when markets are complete. First we describe the primitives of the model, which will be used here and in following sections. Then we describe an equilibrium with complete markets. We note that the fundamental theorems of welfare economics imply that risk sharing is efficient and, hence, there is no role for government regulation in this setting. It is also worth noting that there is no role for capital. More precisely, the capital structure is irrelevant to the value of the firm, as claimed by Modigliani and Miller, and in particular there is no rationale for capital regulation. (This point has been made repeatedly by Gale 2003, 2004; Allen and Gale 2003; and Gale and Özgür 2005).

The model serves two purposes. First, it serves to show how credit risk transfers can promote efficient risk sharing if we interpret the markets for contingent securities in the Arrow-Debreu model as derivatives or insurance contracts. Secondly, it provides a benchmark for the discussion of incomplete markets that follows. By contrast with the Arrow-Debreu model, there is no reason to think that the equilibrium allocation of risk bearing is efficient when markets are incomplete. So, incompleteness of markets provides a potential role for regulation to improve risk sharing. However, as we shall see, a badly designed policy of capital regulation may lead to greater instability.

7.3.1 The Basic Model

There are three dates $t = 0, 1, 2$ and a single, all-purpose good that can be used for consumption or investment at each date. There are two securities, one *short* and one *long*. The short security is represented by a storage technology: one unit at date t produces one unit at date $t + 1$. The long security is represented by a constant-returns-to-scale investment technology that takes two periods to mature: one unit invested in the long security at date 0 produces $R > 1$ units of the good at date 2 (and nothing at date 1). This simple structure provides a tradeoff between liquidity and the rate of return (the yield curve). Banks would like to earn the higher return offered by the long asset, but that may cause problems, because the banks' liabilities (demand deposits) are liquid.

In addition to these securities, banks and insurance companies have distinct profitable investment opportunities. Banks can make loans to firms that succeed with probability β. More precisely, each firm borrows one unit at date 0 and invests in a risky venture that produces B_H units of the good at date 2 if successful and B_L if unsuccessful. There is assumed to be an infinite supply of such firms, so the banks take all the surplus. (In effect, these "firms" simply represent a constant-returns-to-scale investment technology for the banks.) Because we are only interested in nondiversifiable risks, we assume that the loans made by an individual bank are perfectly correlated: either they all pay off or none do. This is a gross simplification that does not essentially affect the points we want to make.

The bank's other customers are depositors, who have one unit of the good at date 0 and none at dates 1 and 2. Depositors are uncertain of their preferences: with probability λ they are *early consumers,* who only value the good at date 1 and with probability $1 - \lambda$ they are *late consumers,* who only value the good at date 2. The utility of consumption is represented by a utility function $U(c)$ with the usual properties. We normalize the number of consumers to 1. The form of the depositors' preferences provides a demand for liquidity and explains why the bank must offer a contract that allows the option of withdrawing either at date 1 or date 2.

The insurance companies have access to a large number of firms, whose measure is normalized to one. Each firm owns an asset that produces A units of the good at date 2. With probability α the asset suffers some damage at date 1. Unless this damage is repaired, at a cost of C, the asset becomes worthless and will produce nothing at date 2. The firms also have a unit endowment at date 0 which the insurance company invests in the short and long securities in order to pay the firms' damages at date 1. The risks to different firms are assumed to be independent, so the fraction of firms suffering damage in any state is equal to the probability α. More importantly, the risks faced by the insurance and banking sectors are not perfectly correlated, so there are some gains from sharing risks. This in turn provides the potential for gains from credit risk transfer.

Finally, we introduce a class of risk-neutral investors who provide capital to the insurance and banking sectors. Although investors are risk neutral, we assume that their consumption must be nonnegative at each date. This is a crucial assumption. Without it, the investors could absorb all risk and provide unlimited liquidity, and the problem of achieving efficient risk sharing would be trivial. The assumption of nonnegative consumption, on the other hand, implies that investors can only provide risk-sharing services to banks and/or insurance companies if they invest in real assets that provide future income streams. The investor's utility function is defined by

$$u(c_0, c_1, c_2) = \rho c_0 + c_1 + c_2,$$

where $c_t \geq 0$ denotes the investor's consumption at date $t = 0, 1, 2$. The constant $\rho > E(R)$ represents the investor's opportunity cost of funds. For example, the investors may have access to investments that yield a very high rate of return but are very risky and very illiquid. Markets are segmented, and other agents do not have access to these assets. Banks cannot include these assets in their portfolios, so they cannot earn as much on the capital invested in the bank as the investors could. This gap defines the economic cost of capital: in order to compensate the investors for the opportunity cost of the capital they invest, the depositors must take a smaller payout in order to subsidize the earnings of the investors.

We can assume without loss of generality that the role of investors is simply to provide capital to the intermediary through a contract $e = (e_0, e_1, e_2)$ where $e_0 \geq 0$ denotes the investor's supply of capital at date $t = 0$, and $e_t \geq 0$ denotes the investor's consumption at dates $t = 1, 2$. While it is feasible for the investors to invest in assets at date 0 and trade them at date 1, it can never be profitable for them to do so in equilibrium. More precisely, the no-arbitrage conditions ensure that profits from trading assets are zero or negative at any admissible prices, and the investor's preferences for consumption at date 0 imply that the investors will never want to invest in assets at date 0 and consume the returns at dates 1 and 2. An investor's endowment consists of a large (unbounded) amount of the good X_0 at date 0 and nothing at dates 1 and 2. This assumption has two important implications. First, since the investors have an unbounded endowment at date 0 there is free entry into the capital market, and the usual zero-profit condition implies that investors receive no surplus in equilibrium. Second, the fact that investors have no endowment (and nonnegative consumption) at dates 1 and 2 implies that their capital must be converted into assets in order to provide risk sharing at dates 1 and 2. We can then write the investors' utility in the form:

$$u(e_0, e_1, e_2) = \rho X_0 - \rho e_0 + e_1 + e_2.$$

The most plausible structure of uncertainty is one that allows for some diversification and some aggregate risk. This is achieved by assuming that the proportions of damaged firms for the insurance sector and failing firms for the banking sector equal the probabilities α and β, respectively, and that these probabilities are themselves random. For the purposes of illustration, suppose that α and β each take on two values, α_H and α_L and β_H and β_L. Nothing would change if we adopted a more general structure, but this is enough to make the essential points. Note that α and β are not perfectly correlated. We may observe any combination of values, (α_H, β_H), (α_L, β_H), (α_H, β_L), or (α_L, β_L). The uncertainty in the model is resolved at the beginning of date 1. Banks' depositors learn whether they are early or late consumers and banks learn whether the firms borrowing from them have failed. Insurance companies learn which firms' assets have suffered damage.

7.3.2 An Arrow-Debreu Equilibrium

In this section we provide a sketch of the definition of Arrow-Debreu equilibrium for the model outlined previously. (A more complete treatment of equilibrium can be found in Gale 2004.) We stress the market structure and its role in allowing economic agents to achieve an optimal allocation of risk and intertemporal consumption.

Contingent Securities

Aggregate uncertainty is determined by the four states of nature

$$s \in S = [(\alpha_H, \beta_H), (\alpha_L, \beta_H), (\alpha_H, \beta_L), (\alpha_L, \beta_L)].$$

We denote these four states HH, LH, HL, LL. Contingent securities are defined by the date of delivery and the state on which delivery is contingent. The true aggregate state s is unknown at date 0 and is revealed at date 1, so there are nine contingent securities, a single contingent security which promises one unit of the good at date 0 and a contingent security that promises delivery of one unit of the good at date t in state s for every $t = 1$, 2 and $s = S$. We denote the security delivering the good at date 0 by 0 and the security delivering the good at date t in state s by (t, s) for $t = 1$, 2 and $s \in S$.

The simplest way to represent complete markets is to assume there exists a separate market at date 0 for each of the previously defined contingent securities. Take security 0 to be the numeraire and let $q_t(s)$ denote the price, in terms of the numeraire, of one unit of security (t, s).

It is important to realize that the Arrow security markets only allow one to hedge aggregate risks. The idiosyncratic risks presented by the damage to individual firms insured by the insurance sector and the failure of individual firms borrowing from the banking sector cannot be hedged using these markets. However, because there are large numbers of firms in the respective sectors and the insurance companies and banks, respectively, can perfectly hedge these risks by pooling, markets for all risks, aggregate and idiosyncratic, are effectively complete once we take into account the role of the intermediaries as well as the Arrow securities. An alternative approach would have been to allow firms to enter markets for idiosyncratic risk. These markets would be competitive despite the presence of a single supplier, since the risks are effectively perfect substitutes in a world with perfect diversification.

No-Arbitrage Conditions

Because markets are complete, economic agents do not need to hold assets for the purpose of hedging risks or smoothing consumption. In fact, assets are redundant securities in the sense that they can be synthesized by trading contingent securities. Assets play an important role in equilibrium, however, because their existence places constraints on equilibrium prices and they are necessary to clear the goods market by altering the supply of contingent securities.

The short asset converts one unit of the good at date t into one unit of the good at date $t + 1$, independently of the state. Since the state is unknown at date 0, the storage technology converts one unit of the good at date 0 into one unit of the good at date 1, independently of the state. So investing one unit of the good in the storage technology at date 0 produces one unit of each of the contingent securities $(1, s)$ at date 1. If the cost of the inputs is less than the value of the outputs, there is a riskless arbitrage, so equilibrium requires

$$\sum_{s \in S} q_1(s) \le 1.$$

At date 1, the state is known, so it is possible to invest one unit in the short asset in state s and produce one unit of the contingent security $(2, s)$ at date 2. Then the no-arbitrage condition requires

$$q_2(s) \le q_1(s)$$

for each state s. To see why this condition must hold, consider the following example, which violates the condition:

$$q_1(s) = 0.2 < 0.3 = q_2(s).$$

A riskless arbitrage profit can be achieved as follows. At date 0, buy one unit of the $(1, s)$ contingent security and sell one unit of the $(2, s)$ security for a profit of $0.3 - 0.2 = 0.1$. At date 1, if state s occurs, the $(1, s)$ contingent security yields one unit of the good. Investing this unit of the good in the short asset produces one unit of the good at date 2 in state s, which can be used to redeem the unit of the $(2, s)$ contingent security issued at date 0.

Investment in the long asset is only possible at date 0, when the state is unknown, so the long asset only gives rise to one no-arbitrage condition. One unit of the good at date 0 yields R units of the good at date 2, independently of the state; in other words, R units of the contingent security $(2, s)$ for each state s. Then the no-arbitrage condition that the cost of the inputs is greater than or equal to the value of the outputs is

$$\sum_{s \in S} q_2(s)R \le 1.$$

These no-arbitrage conditions can also be thought of as zero-profit conditions. If the profit is negative, no one invests in the asset at that date and state; if someone does invest, the profit is zero. In either case, investments in the assets do not affect an economic agent's wealth (in the case of an individual) or market value (in the case of a firm). In the aggregate, some investment in these assets may be necessary in order to transform goods at one date into goods at a future date, but it is a matter of indifference which economic agent undertakes the investment activity. In particular, this implies a separation property that holds for every agent's decision problem: the optimal investment in the short and long asset is independent of the agent's optimal choice of other variables, such as consumption or loan and insurance contracts.

Banking

As in the standard Diamond and Dybvig (1983) model, banks provide liquidity insurance for consumers who are uncertain about the optimal timing of their consumption. Consumers deposit their endowments of one unit of the good with the bank at date 0 and are promised future consumption payments conditional on their types, early or late. An early consumer is promised $c_1(s)$ of the contingent security $(1, s)$ for each state s; a late consumer is promised $c_2(s)$ units of the contingent security $(2, s)$ for each state s. Thus, the contracts the banks offer are complete in the sense that they allow the payments made to vary across the aggregate states s. Free entry and competition in the banking sector force banks to offer contracts that maximize the expected utility of the typical depositor subject to the constraint that the bank break even on the deal. If a bank did not maximize the expected utility of depositors another bank would enter, offer a better contract and take away all its customers. The break-even condition is equivalent to a budget constraint that says that the value of promised consumption is less than or equal to the value of the deposits. The deposits are one unit per capita and the per capita demand for consumption is $\lambda c_1(s)$ at date 1 in state s and $(1 - \lambda)c_2(s)$ at date 2 in state s. The budget constraint can be written

$$\sum_{s \in S} [q_1(s)\lambda c_1(s) + q_2(s)(1 - \lambda)c_2(s)] \le 1.$$

Recall that we can ignore the bank's investments since they yield zero profits. The expected utility of the typical depositor can be constructed as follows. In each state s, the depositor has a probability λ of being an early consumer and $1 - \lambda$ of being a late consumer, so his expected utility conditional on s is $\lambda U[c_1(s)] + (1 - \lambda)U[c_2(s)]$. Then the expected utility at date 0, before the state is known, is obtained by taking expectations over states

$$E\{\lambda U[c_1(s)] + (1 - \lambda)U[c_2(s)]\}.$$

It is important to note that the depositors cannot trade directly in the markets for contingent securities or assets. As Cone (1983) and Jacklin (1986) have shown, it is not possible for depositors to obtain liquidity insurance from a bank if they can directly trade the securities the banks hold.

In addition to providing consumption smoothing for consumers, the banks can invest in loans to firms. Because we assume that entrepreneurs with projects are in perfectly elastic supply and banks have access to a limited amount of deposits, equilibrium requires that entrepreneurs earn zero profits. In other words, all the surplus goes to the banks. Since one unit of the good at date 0 produces B_H when the payoff is high and B_L when the payoff is low, the zero-profit condition requires that the face value of a loan of one unit to the firm is $D = B_H$. In the high-payoff state the firm can repay the loan, but in the low payoff-state it defaults and the bank seizes the remaining value of the firm B_L. Because entrepreneurs are indifferent between borrowing to fund a project and not undertaking the project at all, the number of projects undertaken is determined by the supply of loanable funds from the bank. Although banks are earning a positive return on each loan, they are indifferent about the number of loans they offer because they can replicate these loans through the markets for Arrow securities (after pooling the idiosyncratic risks).

Insurance

Insurance companies provide two services to firms. Note that these firms are different from the firms that borrow from banks. The insurance companies insure the firm's assets against damage (if it is efficient to do so) and they provide consumption smoothing to the owner of the firm. We make this assumption for convenience, but it is not necessary. The firms could provide the same consumption-smoothing services for themselves by trading contingent securities. Recall that in order for banks to provide insurance to their depositors it was necessary to exclude the depositors from the asset markets. By contrast, there is no need to limit the market participation of the insurance companies' customers. Since the damage to assets is observed by the insurance companies, there is no incentive constraint to worry about. We will allow firms to participate in markets when we consider the case of incomplete markets in the sequel.

It is efficient to repair the damage to the firm's asset if the cost of doing so is less than or equal to the value of the asset's output; that is, if $q_1(s)C \leq q_2(s)A$. An optimal insurance contract will make the decision to pay the damages contingent on the state. Contracts are again complete. The insurance company will also promise the firm owner consumption $a_2(s)$ at date 2 in state s. Free entry and competition in the insurance sector imply that the insurance companies offer firms a contract that maximizes the utility of the firm's owner subject to a break-even constraint. The break-even constraint is equivalent to the following budget constraint:

$$\sum_{s \in S} q_2(s)a_2(s) \leq 1 + \sum_{s \in S} \{\alpha(s)\max[q_2(s)A - q_1(s)C,0] + [1 - \alpha(s)]q_2(s)A\}.$$

The left-hand side is the value of consumption promised to the owner; the right-hand side is the value of the owner's endowment at date 0 plus the value of outputs from the firm's assets at date 2 net of damage payments at date 1. Note that we assume here that the insurance company can perfectly diversify across firms, so that exactly a fraction $\alpha(s)$ of its customers suffer damage in state s and $1 - \alpha(s)$ suffer no damage. Since the insurance companies are competitive, their objective is to maximize the firm owner's expected utility

$$E\{U[a_2(s)]\},$$

subject to the budget constraint above.

Investors

We can describe the investors' decision problem in a similar way, although it adds relatively little to our understanding of the model when markets are complete. Since there are a large number of investors with very large endowments, their consumption at date 0 is assumed to be positive. This implies that, unless they make zero profits by trading in markets for contingent securities, there will be an excess supply of investment. The only important implication for equilibrium takes the form of a no-arbitrage condition: any feasible consumption plan that requires the investor to sell e_0 units at date 0 and purchase $e_t(s) \geq 0$ units of the contingent security (t, s) that increases expected utility must also cost a positive amount. Formally, if there exists a trade $(e_0, e_t[s])$ such that

$$E[e_1(s) + e_2(s)] > \rho e_0,$$

then it must be the case that

$$\sum_{s \in S}[q_1(s)e_1(s) + q_2(s)e_2(s)] > e_0.$$

Conversely, if $(e_0, e_t[s])$ is a trade that occurs in equilibrium, then it must be the case that it leaves expected utility unchanged

$$E[e_1(s) + e_2(s)] = \rho e_0,$$

and it leaves the budget constraint unchanged.

$$\sum_{s \in S} [q_1(s)e_1(s) + q_2(s)e_2(s)] = e_0$$

Otherwise, the trade would violate the no-arbitrage condition. Again, the no-arbitrage condition constrains equilibrium prices but does not otherwise affect equilibrium.

Investors may share some of the risks born by consumers and firms, but they do so indirectly through the markets for contingent securities rather than through explicit risk-sharing contracts with individual consumers and firms. They perform this function by supplying e_0 at date 0, which can be invested in short or long assets or can be used to finance loans by the banks, and then take their earnings in states where consumers and owners have a high marginal utility of consumption. By doing this, they allow consumers and owners to reduce the variation in their consumption across states.

Welfare

The first theorem of welfare economics tells us that, under very weak assumptions about nonsatiation, every equilibrium of an Arrow-Debreu economy has a Pareto-efficient allocation of goods and services. So in the equilibrium sketched previously, it is impossible to make some economic agents better off without making others worse off. In particular, risk sharing is efficient and there is no scope for government intervention or regulation to increase efficiency.

Absence of Bank Runs, Bankruptcy, and Systemic Risk

One important thing to note about the case of complete markets and contracts is that there is no bankruptcy for banks or insurance companies. Since it is possible to trade contingent securities for every state and contract payments can be varied in every state, assets and liabilities can always be matched so bank runs and bankruptcy do not occur. Since bank runs and bankruptcy do not occur there is no systemic risk with complete markets. As we will see, when markets and contracts are incomplete this is no longer the case, and this has important implications for the characteristics of equilibrium.

7.3.3 The Modigliani-Miller Theorem for Risk Sharing

In an Arrow-Debreu world, risk sharing is mediated by markets. In particular, the capital is provided to the market and not to any specific individual financial institution. Similarly, there are no over-the-counter (OTC) derivatives traded between banks and insurance companies. Instead, they trade contingent securities with "the market." One could introduce specific capital contracts between investors and banks or insurers, but these would be redundant securities. In fact, we can establish a Modigliani-Miller theorem for banks and insurers along the lines of Gale (2004). For example, suppose that a bank wants to raise an amount of capital e_0. It will offer investors a contract (e_0, e_1, e_2) under which it promises to pay investors $e_t(s)$ in state s at date t in exchange for the contribution of e_0 at date 0. In order to be acceptable to the investors, the capital contract (e_0, e_1, e_2) will have to satisfy the participation constraint

$$E[-\rho e_0 + e_1(s) + e_2(s)] \geq 0.$$

The bank's objective function remains the same as before, but now the value of the capital contract is added to its budget constraint. Clearly, the bank will want to minimize the cost of the contract in order to maximize the market value of the bank. Thus, an optimal contract will minimize

$$E[-e_0 + q_1(s)e_1(s) + q_2(s)e_2(s)],$$

subject to the participation constraint above. This problem is the dual of the investor's decision problem in the preceding section. Because of the linearity of the problem, in equilibrium the market value of the contract is zero and the participation constraint is binding. In other words, the capital contract will have no effect on the bank's budget constraint and no effect on its objective function. Furthermore, the introduction of an explicit capital structure has no effect on the endogenous variables we care about (the allocation of consumption and investment in assets) because the trades implied by the contract are offset in the contingent security markets.

In an exactly similar way, we can show that any insurance contract between banks and insurance companies would be redundant. This does not mean that risk is not being shared between the insurance and banking sectors. To the extent that there is any scope for sharing risk between the two sectors (credit risk transfer), it is exploited fully and efficiently, using the markets for contingent securities.

7.3.4   Derivatives and Contracts

In practice, we do not observe markets for contingent securities as such. Instead, we observe markets for spot trading of assets, a variety of derivative securities whose purpose is to allow hedging of risk from the underlying securities, and a variety of risk-sharing contracts such as insurance contracts. Regardless of the form that risk sharing takes, similarly to Ross (1976), if there are enough derivatives and contracts, markets will effectively be complete and the allocation of risk will be the same as in the Arrow-Debreu equilibrium. This is the sense in which credit risk transfer is desirable. If the instruments that transfer risk allow markets to be effectively complete, then they ensure a Pareto-efficient allocation of resources is achieved. This is the first main result of the paper—that credit risk transfer is desirable when markets and contracts are effectively complete.

This argument assumes there is no capital regulation and indeed this is optimal. What happens if there is capital regulation? Suppose next we get rid of all contingent securities so markets are no longer complete but allow a spot market for assets at date 1 (equivalent to a forward market for consumption at date 2). If we still allow banks and insurers to write complete contracts, then markets are effectively complete, because there are only two representative agents (plus the risk-neutral investors who receive no surplus). However, in this case, the net effect of risk sharing between investors and the banks or insurance companies must be mediated by an explicit contract, and it is this contract that is controlled by capital-adequacy regulation. If the bank is required to increase e_0, this will have a real impact on its feasible set and on the value of its objective function. It cannot be offset by side trades, because we assume that all trades are governed by pairwise contracts, and those between the investors and banks are explicitly regulated. Markets are no longer effectively complete and the properties of equilibrium change significantly.

We next develop a simple numerical example to show that, when markets and contracts are incomplete, there can be an increase in systemic risk as a result of capital regulation that forces banks to hold too much capital.

7.4   Increased Systemic Risk from Capital Regulation

In this section we present simple numerical examples to illustrate our second result—that capital regulation can increase systemic risk when markets and contracts are incomplete. In contrast to the previous section, we assume there are no state-contingent securities. Whereas with complete markets it was possible to trade securities that paid off 1 unit of the consumption good in aggregate states HH, LH, HL, and LL at dates $t = 1, 2$, now this is not the case. There are only markets for the long and short assets. Contracts are also incomplete. Whereas before payoffs could be made explicitly contingent on states HH, LH, HL, and LL, this is no longer possible.

We start by considering the banking sector on its own and then go on to consider the insurance sector in isolation. Without capital regulation we show that in the example there is no incentive to have credit risk transfer between the two sectors. However, with capital regulation where capital can be reduced when there is credit risk transfer between the sectors, we show that the transfer will take place. Moreover, this credit risk transfer can increase systemic risk in the banking sector.

7.4.1   The Banking Sector

No Capital

To start with we consider what happens if there is no capital available for banks from investors.

Example 1. The return on the long asset is $R = 1.4$.

For depositors in the banks $\lambda = 0.5$; and $U(c) = \text{Ln}(c)$. In state β_H for banks, which occurs with probability 0.7, the loans pay off $B_H = 1.7$ with probability $\beta_H = 1$. The probability of state β_L is 0.3 and in this state the loans pay off $B_L = 0.9$ with probability $1 - \beta_L = 1$.

Banks' investment in the short asset is denoted x, their investment in the long asset is denoted y, and their loans to firms are denoted z. They receive an endowment of 1 from depositors, so $x + y + z = 1$.

The contract the banks use with their depositors are incomplete in the following sense. The banks cannot make the payment at date 1 contingent on the aggregate state. The aggregate state at date 1 is now observable but not verifiable, and hence contracts cannot be made contingent on it. Instead, the deposit contract banks use promises a fixed amount c_1 to any depositor wishing to withdraw. Since the banking industry is competitive, then as before each bank's objective is to maximize the expected utility of its depositors. If a bank did not do this then another bank would enter, offer a better contract, and take away all its customers. The implication of this is that the banks will pay out all their remaining funds to late consumers at date 2. The amount the late consumers will receive will depend on whether firms' loans are repaid in full. Hence there are two possible payouts, c_{2H} in state β_H, and c_{2L} in state β_L.

Banks are unable to distinguish between early and late consumers. If late consumers deduce that they will be better off withdrawing at date 1 then all depositors will attempt to withdraw. If a bank is unable to meet the demands of its depositors then it goes bankrupt, its assets are liquidated, and the proceeds are distributed to the depositors in proportion to their deposits. When markets and contracts were complete, assets and liabilities could be balanced state by state and bankruptcy never occurred. Now, however, bankruptcy may occur if late consumers have an incentive to pretend to be early consumers, so there is a run on the bank.

At date 0, the banks choose their portfolio, x, y, and z, and the deposit contract c_1, c_{2H}, and c_{2L}, to maximize the expected utility of the depositors. In equilibrium, x, y, and z must be nonnegative. We will suppose initially that there are no runs and check to see that this assumption is satisfied. Since in this case there is no uncertainty about the banks' needs for liquidity at date 1, they will use the short-term asset to provide consumption at date 1. The optimization problem of the banks is to choose x, y, and z to

$$\text{Max } 0.5U(c_1) + 0.5[0.7U(c_{2H}) + 0.3U(c_{2L})]$$

$$\text{subject to } x + y + z = 1,$$

$$c_1 = \frac{x}{0.5},$$

$$c_{2H} = \frac{yR + zB_H}{0.5},$$

$$c_{2L} = \frac{yR + zB_L}{0.5}.$$

The first constraint is the budget constraint at date 0. The second constraint gives the per capita consumption of the early consumers. Since there is 1 depositor and 0.5 of these are early consumers and 0.5 are late consumers, we need to divide the total consumption produced by the investment in the short asset at date 1 by 0.5 to get the per capita consumption. The third and fourth constraints give the per capita consumption of the late consumers in states β_H and β_L respectively. Clearly, $c_{2H} \geq c_{2L}$. In order for a run to be avoided, we also need $c_{2L} \geq c_1$; otherwise, late consumers will pretend to be early consumers and will withdraw their money at date 1.

Denoting the Lagrange multiplier for the constraint μ, the first order conditions are:

$$\frac{0.5}{x} - \mu \leq 0,$$

$$\frac{0.35R}{yR + zB_H} + \frac{0.15R}{yR + zB_L} - \mu \leq 0,$$

$$\frac{0.35B_H}{yR + zB_H} + \frac{0.15B_L}{yR + zB_L} - \mu \leq 0.$$

The solution for the equilibrium is

$$x = 0.5; y = 0.22; z = 0.28$$

$$c_1 = 1; c_{2H} = 1.568; c_{2L} = 1.12$$

$$EU = 0.1744$$

It can be seen directly that $c_{2L} > c_1$, so in state β_L late consumers will not have an incentive to withdraw their money and cause a run. As a result there will be no systemic risk in the banking industry.

The Role of Capital

Next consider what happens if there are investors who can make capital available to the banks.

For the investors providing equity capital, the opportunity cost is $\rho = 1.5$.

Since the investors are indifferent between consumption at date 1 and date 2, it is optimal to set $e_1 = 0$ and not invest any of the capital e_0 that is contributed at date 0 in the short asset. In state β_H, when depositors' marginal utility of consumption is the lowest, it is possible to make a payout e_2 to investors. The banks' optimization problem is the same as before except now the date 0 budget constraint is

$$x + y + z + e_0 = 1.$$

and

$$c_{2H} = \frac{yR + zB_H - e_2}{0.5}.$$

In order for the investors to be willing to supply the capital e_0 it is necessary that

$$e_0\rho = 0.7e_2$$

so

$$c_{2H} = \frac{yR + zB_H - e_0\rho/0.7}{0.5}.$$

The first-order conditions for x, y, z, and e_0 are now

$$\frac{0.5}{x} - \mu \leq 0,$$

$$\frac{0.35R}{yR + zB_H - e_0\rho/0.7} + \frac{0.15R}{yR + zB_L} - \mu \leq 0,$$

$$\frac{0.35B_H}{yR + zB_H - e_0\rho/0.7} + \frac{0.15B_L}{yR + zB_L} - \mu \leq 0,$$

$$-\frac{0.35\rho/0.7}{yR + zB_H - e_0\rho/0.7} + \mu \leq 0.$$

The solution for the equilibrium in this case is

$$x = 0.5; \ y = 0; \ z = 0.726; \ e_0 = 0.226$$

$$c_1 = 1; \ c_{2H} = 1.5; \ c_{2L} = 1.306$$

$$EU = 0.1820$$

Once again there is no danger of runs and hence no systemic risk, since $c_{2L} > c_1$.

Comparing the case without capital to the case with, it can be seen that expected utility is increased from 0.174 to 0.182. Capital allows the depositors to share risk with the investors. This improves welfare directly but it also allows the bank to invest more in loans and less in the long asset, which has a lower expected return (1.40) than the loans (1.46). This increases expected consumption for the late consumers from $0.7 \times 1.568 + 0.3 \times 1.12 = 1.434$ to $0.7 \times 1.5 + 0.3 \times 1.306 = 1.442$. In addition to this increase in expected consumption there is also clearly a reduction in the variability of consumption (1.568 and 1.12 before versus 1.5 and 1.306 now), because the repayment to investors occurs only in the good state. Risk is not eliminated from the depositors' consumption even though the investors providing the capital are risk neutral because capital is costly. The investors' opportunity cost of capital is $\rho = 1.5$ while the expected return on the loans is only 1.46 and on the long asset 1.4. It is only the increase in expected utility from smoothing consumption that makes it worthwhile using investors' capital, and only up to the point where the marginal benefit is equal to the marginal cost. This is why depositors continue to bear risk.

This is not the only kind of situation that can occur. In some cases the bank will not want to use capital at all. To see this consider the following example.

Example 2. This is exactly the same as Example 1 except that $R = 1.28$, $B_H = 1.6$, and $B_L = 0.8$, so $EB = 1.36$.

It can be shown that the equilibrium—whether capital is available or not—is the same.

$$x = 0.5; y = 0.333; z = 0.314; e_0 = 0$$

$$c_1 = 0.990; c_{2H} = 1.494; c_{2L} = 0.990$$

$$EU = 0.1341$$

There is no role for capital at all in this example. Any capital regulation that imposes a positive minimum requirement will lead to inefficiency.

We will use Example 2 when we consider the banking and insurance sectors together.

7.4.2   The Insurance Sector

We next turn to the insurance sector and consider it on its own. As explained earlier there are firms that own assets that produce A at $t = 2$ if they are undamaged. For our example, we assume that $A = 1.3$. The owners of these firms consume at date 2 and have $U = \text{Ln}(c)$.

With some probability $\alpha(s)$ a firm's asset is damaged at date $t = 1$. It costs

$C = 0.8$ to repair the asset, in which case it produces A at $t = 2$. Without repair the asset produces nothing. Insurance companies insure the firms and allow the risk to be pooled. As before, the firms that the insurance companies insure are different from the firms that the banks make loans to.

The parameters for Example 2 are used, so $R = 1.28$.

State α_H occurs with probability 0.9, and in this case $\alpha_H = 0.5$ firms have damaged machines. State α_L occurs with probability 0.1 and $\alpha_L = 1$ firms have damaged machines.

Similarly to the banking sector, the insurance companies cannot access complete markets with securities contingent on aggregate states. They can only buy the long and short assets. They also cannot write state-contingent contracts. They can promise to insure the firms' machines irrespective of state s. This means that an insurance company may go bankrupt. In this case its assets are liquidated and distributed to the firms it was insuring.

The costs of an insurance company liquidating long-term assets at date $t = 1$ if it goes bankrupt is such that the proceeds are zero. Grace, Klein, and Phillips (2003) have found that for a large sample of insurers that went bankrupt from 1986–1999 the average cost of insolvent firms accessing the guarantee funds was $1.10 per $1 of preinsolvency assets. By way of contrast, James (1991) found that the figure for banks for the late 1980s was $0.30.

Each firm has an endowment of 0.8 at date $t = 0$ that it can use to buy insurance or invest itself. As mentioned in the previous section, it will be assumed that the firms just buy insurance from the insurance companies. The firms can use the markets for the long and the short assets to smooth consumption for their owners.

No Capital

The insurance industry is competitive, so the companies do not earn any profits—all funds are paid out to the firms they insure. At date 0 the insurance companies' objective is to maximize the expected utility of the firms' owners. If they did not do this another insurance company would enter and take their business away. The insurance companies can offer partial or full insurance to firms. If they offer partial insurance they charge $0.5C = 0.4$ at date $t = 0$. Suppose the firms put the other 0.4 of their endowment in the long-term asset (it will be shown that this is optimal shortly). In order to have funds to allow firms' damaged assets to be repaired, the insurance companies must invest in the short asset so that they have liquidity at date $t = 1$. In state α_H, the funds they need for claims to repair the damaged assets are $\alpha_H C = 0.4$. They have funds of 0.4 and can pay all the claims to repair the damaged assets. The amount the owners of the firms obtain is therefore $A + 0.4R = 1.812$. In state α_L, the insurance companies receive claims of $\alpha_L C = 0.8$. They don't have sufficient funds to pay these so they go bankrupt. With partial insurance there is thus systemic risk in the insurance industry. When the insurance companies go bankrupt their assets are distributed equally among the claimants. The firms receive 0.4 from the insurance companies' liquidation of its short term assets. The firms can't repair their assets so these produce nothing. In state α_L, the amount the owners of the firm receive is therefore $0.4 + 0.4R = 0.912$. Their expected utility with partial insurance is

$$EU_{\text{partial}} = 0.9U(A + 0.4R) + 0.1U(0.4 + 0.4R) = 0.5258.$$

If the insurance company offered full insurance they would charge 0.8 at $t = 0$ and could meet all of their claims in both states. At $t = 1$ in state α_H they would have 0.4 left over. Since the industry is competitive, they would pay this out to the insured firms. In this case

$$EU_{\text{full}} = 0.9U(A - 0.4) + 0.1U(A) = 0.5038.$$

This is worse than partial insurance.

If the firms decide not to have insurance then they would invest their endowment in the long asset. Their expected utility would be

$$EU_{\text{none}} = 0.9[0.5U(0.8R) + 0.5U(A + 0.8R)] + 0.1U(0.8R) = 0.3925.$$

Finally, if they decided to self-insure and hold their endowment in the short asset so they could repair their machines when necessary they would obtain

$$EU_{\text{self}} = 0.9[0.5U(A) + 0.5U(A + 0.8)] + 0.1U(A) = 0.4782.$$

Thus the optimal scheme is for the insurance industry to partially insure firms and to charge 0.4 at $t = 0$. The firms put the remaining part of their endowment in the long asset.

The Role of Capital

In this case there is no role for capital in the insurance sector. Capital providers charge a premium. Their funds would have to be invested in the short asset. There are already potentially enough funds from customers to do this, but it is simply not worth it. If there is a premium to be paid for the capital it is even less worth it. Capital will not be used in the insurance industry if it is not regulated to do so.

7.4.3   Bringing Together the Banking and Insurance Sectors

Now consider what happens if we consider the two sectors together and look at possible interactions. We start with the situation where there is no regulation and then go on to consider what happens with regulation.

No Regulation

Without any regulation both sectors have the same equilibrium as when they are considered on their own. Given that markets and contracts are incomplete, there are no incentives for the insurance sector to insure the banking sector and have credit risk transfer. All the insurance sector could do is to hold the long-term asset and pay off when the loans default. But the banking sector can do this on its own. In fact, with insurance the systemic risk means that there would be a strict loss in this case. The value of the long-term assets held in the insurance companies would be lost.

There is also no gain for the banking sector to bear the risk of the insurance sector. They would have to hold the short-term asset, but the insurance sector can do this just as efficiently.

Of course, if markets and contracts were complete then there would be an incentive to share risk. The consumption at date 2 of the bank depositors and insured firms' owners are as follows.

	State			
	HH	*LH*	*HL*	*LL*
Bank depositors	1.494	1.494	0.990	0.990
Insured firm owners	1.812	0.912	1.812	0.912

By, for example, transferring consumption from the bank depositors to the insured firms' owners in state *LH* in the amount of 0.0386 and vice versa in state *HL* in the amount of 0.01 it is possible to make both groups better off. If the shocks to the two sectors are independent then the expected value of this transfer is

$$0.07 \times 0.0386 - 0.27 \times 0.01 = 0.$$

The expected utility of the bank depositors is improved from 0.1341 to 0.1394 and the expected utility of the insured firms' owners goes from 0.5258 to 0.5272. With complete markets and contracts optimal risk sharing would ensure that the ratios of marginal utilities of consumption of the bank depositors and the owners of the insured firms across states would be equated. This is clearly far from being the case here. The incomplete markets and contracts that are actually in place in this section prevent improved risk sharing of this type, and in fact there is no possibility of an improvement through credit risk transfer in the absence of capital regulation.

Equilibrium with Inefficient Capital Regulation in the Banking Sector

Now suppose that the government requires banks to have a certain minimum amount of capital. There is no role for capital regulation in our model, so it can have no benefit. It may be harmless if the required level is below the optimal level. The more interesting case is when it is set at too high a level.

Suppose in Example 2 that the government requires banks to have $e_0 = 0.2$ compared to the optimal level of 0. The solution to the banks' problem then becomes

$$e_0 = 0.2;\ e_1 = 0;\ e_2 = 0.429;$$

$$x = 0.494;\ y = 0;\ z = 0.706$$

$$c_1 = 0.988;\ c_{2H} = 1.401;\ c_{2L} = 1.129$$

$$EU = 0.1305$$

The capital improves risk sharing and allows more funds to be invested in loans, both from the extra capital and from the lower-return long asset. However, the high cost of capital means that this is inefficient; welfare is reduced from the case with no regulation.

Inefficient Capital Regulation in Banking and Credit Risk Transfer to the Insurance Sector

Next, consider what happens if we allow for the possibility of credit risk transfer from the banking sector to the insurance sector. It is supposed that the shocks to the two sectors are independent. The regulation is such that the existence of hedging of credit risk allows a reduction in the capital requirement. By purchasing an insurance contract with cost of $G = 0.02$ at date 0 and a payoff of $0.02 \times R = 0.026$ at date 2 when loans do not pay off it is possible for a bank to reduce its capital requirement to the optimal level of 0. The idea here is that the regulation does not work effectively, since under Basel II banks can use their own risk models. They can therefore construct their risk models to make it look as if the hedging instrument reduces risk the right amount so as to allow them to reduce capital to the optimal level. Notice that in order for this insurance contract to be such that the insurance companies break even, which is necessary because of competition, they will also provide a payment of 0.026 when the loans do pay off, if they are able to. The insurance companies use the initial payment from the banks at date 0 to buy the long-term asset and then pay out the proceeds when they are solvent. When they are not solvent the long-term asset is wasted because of the inefficient liquidation in the insurance sector. The only point of the credit risk transfer is to arbitrage the inefficient capital regulation in the banking sector. The key issue is whether the gain from this inefficient risk transfer outweighs the inefficiency of the capital regulation. It can be shown that in the example it does. The bank chooses its portfolio x, y, and z to maximize the depositors' expected utility, taking $G = 0.02$ and $e_0 = 0$ as given.

Max $EU = 0.5U(c_1) + 0.5\{0.7[0.9U(c_{2HH}) + 0.1U(c_{2LH})]$

$$+ 0.3[0.9U(c_{2HL}) + 0.1U(c_{2LL})]\}$$

subject to $1 + e_0 = x + y + z + G$.

$$c_1 = \frac{x}{0.5},$$

$$c_{2HH} = \frac{yR + zB_H - e_0\rho/0.7 + GR}{0.5},$$

$$c_{2LH} = \frac{yR + zB_H - e_0\rho/0.7}{0.5},$$

$$c_{2HL} = \frac{yR + zB_L + GR}{0.5},$$

$$c_{2LL} = \frac{yR + zB_L}{0.5}.$$

Solving this gives the following:

$$x = 0.5; y = 0.15; z = 0.33; e_0 = 0$$

$$c_1 = 1; c_{2HH} = 1.491; c_{2LH} = 1.440; c_{2HL} = 0.963; c_{2LL} = 0.912$$

$$EU = 0.1322$$

So the expected utility of the banks' depositors is improved relative to the case with no credit risk transfer ($EU = 0.1305$) but, of course, they are not as well off as in the case with no regulation ($EU = 0.1341$), because the credit risk transfer has costs associated with it. However, all this is beside the point, because the solution assumes there will be no runs—but in fact there will be runs in states HL and LL. In state HL, $c_{2HL} = 0.963 < c_1 = 1$, and in state LL, $c_{2LL} = 0.912 < c_1 = 1$. In both cases the late consumers as well as the early consumers will attempt to withdraw their funds. The banks will anticipate this and will optimize taking this into account.

A key issue is what happens if there is a run on the bank in terms of the liquidation value of the long asset and loans it holds. For simplicity, we assume the bank can liquidate its assets for their full value. As mentioned previously, James (1991) found that the cost of liquidating bank assets in the late 1980s was $0.30 per dollar of assets, which is much lower than the $1.10 per dollar cost of liquidating insurance assets that Grace, Klein, and Phillips (2003) found. We could allow for some small loss of asset value and all of these results would hold. The more inefficient the banking regulation, the greater this loss can be.

In the optimal solution, taking into account bankruptcy, the banks go bankrupt in state LL and both the early and late consumers receive the same amount

$$c_{1LL} = c_{2LL} = x + yR + zB_L.$$

The full solution is

$$x = 0.492; y = 0.188; z = 0.300; e_0 = 0$$

In states HH, LH, and HL the banks avoid bankruptcy:

$$c_1 = 0.984; c_{2HH} = 1.493; c_{2LH} = 1.441; c_{2HL} = 1.012$$

In state LL the banks go bankrupt:

$$c_{1LL} = c_{2LL} = 0.973$$

$$EU = 0.1318$$

We have thus shown the second result of the paper, namely that with inefficient banking regulation credit risk transfer can increase overall systemic risk. The insurance industry is hit by a large shock when it has high claims from the firms it insures. At the same time, the banking industry has low returns on its loans. Whereas without credit risk transfer the banks avoided bankruptcy, this is not optimal any longer. They go bankrupt and there is contagion from the insurance industry to the banking industry. The credit risk transfer has created links between the industries and this allows contagion.

7.5   Concluding Remarks

In this paper we have developed a model of a financial system with both banking and insurance sectors. Banks and insurance companies do different things. Banks provide liquidity insurance to depositors, whereas insurance companies pool risks. The first result was to show that with complete markets and contracts for aggregate risks intersectoral transfers are desirable. They allow risk to be shared efficiently between the different industries. The second result was to show that with incomplete markets and contracts for aggregate risks credit risk transfer can occur as the result of regulatory arbitrage and this can increase overall systemic risk.

The key question going forward, of course, is which view of credit risk transfer is empirically relevant. As documented in section 7.2, the amount of credit risk transfer between the two industries is currently relatively small. Even if one were to take the view that this credit risk transfer is the result of regulatory arbitrage then the systemic risk may be slight. However, going forward, transfers between sectors may increase, and if they are the result of regulatory arbitrage, they may lead to an increase in systemic risk.

Perhaps more importantly, although the model can be interpreted literally as being about banking and insurance, it can also be viewed more generally. The other group of institutions that in recent years has been playing an increasingly important role in the transfer of credit and the repackaging of risk in general has been hedge funds (BIS 2005). If markets function well in the sense that risk-sharing opportunities are complete, then these transfers of risk around the economy are desirable. However, if they are the result of inefficient regulation and regulatory arbitrage, they may not be. Since hedge funds are unregulated while a large part of the financial services industry is regulated, much of this activity may well be the result of regulatory arbitrage. More empirical work analyzing the nature of risk reallocation in the economy is required to understand the full consequences on systemic risk.

In the model presented, systemic risk was not particularly damaging. Assets could be liquidated in the banking system for the full amount of their value. In practice, systemic risk can be extremely damaging. Augmenting the model to allow for endogenous liquidation values and spillovers to the real economy means that the kind of effect modeled here with incomplete markets may be quite damaging.

References

Allen, F., and D. Gale. 1998. Optimal financial crises. *Journal of Finance* 53:1245–84.
———. 2000a. *Comparing financial systems.* Cambridge, MA: MIT Press.
———. 2000b. Financial contagion. *Journal of Political Economy* 108:1–33.
———. 2000c. Optimal currency crises. *Carnegie-Rochester Conference Series on Public Policy* 53:177–230.
———. 2003. Capital adequacy regulation: In search of a rationale. In *Economics for an imperfect world: Essays in honor of Joseph Stiglitz,* ed. R. Arnott, B. Greenwald, R. Kanbur, and B. Nalebuff, 83–109. Cambridge, MA: MIT Press.
———. 2004a. Financial fragility, liquidity, and asset prices. *Journal of the European Economic Association* 2:1015–48.
———. 2004b. Financial intermediaries and markets. *Econometrica* 72:1023–61.
British Bankers Association (BBA). 2002. *Credit Derivatives Report.* London: British Bankers Association.
Bank for International Settlements (BIS). 2003. Committee on the Global Financial System. *Credit Risk Transfer.* Basel, Switzerland: Bank for International Settlements.
———. 2005. Basel Committee on Banking Supevision. *Credit Risk Transfer.* Basel, Switzerland: Bank for International Settlements.
Chiesa, G. 2004. Risk transfer, lending capacity and real investment activity. Working paper, Department of Economics, University of Bologna.
Cone, K. 1983. Regulation of depository institutions. PhD diss., Stanford University.
Diamond, D., and P. Dybvig. 1983. Bank runs, deposit insurance, and liquidity. *Journal of Political Economy* 91:401–19.

Fitch Ratings. 2003. *Global credit derivatives: Risk management or risk?* Retrieved March 10, 2003. www.fitchratings.com.

Gale, D. 2003. Financial regulation in a changing environment. In *Framing financial structure in an information environment,* ed. T. Courchene and E. Neave, 15–36. Kingston, Ontario: John Deutsch Institute for the Study of Economic Policy, Queen's University.

———. 2004. Notes on optimal capital regulation. In *The evolving financial system and public policy,* ed. P. St-Amant and C. Wilkins, 225–53. Ottawa: Bank of Canada.

Gale, D., and O. Özgür. 2005. Are bank capital ratios too high or too low: Risk aversion, incomplete markets, and optimal capital structures. *Journal of the European Economic Association* 3:690–700.

Grace, M., R. Klein, and R. Phillips. 2003. Insurance company failures: Why do they cost so much? Working paper, Georgia State University, Department of Management and Insurance.

Hellwig, M. 1994. Liquidity provision, banking, and the allocation of interest rate risk. *European Economic Review* 38:1363–89.

———. 1995. Systemic aspects of risk management in banking and finance. *Schweizerische Zeitschrift für Volkswirtschaft und Statistik* 131:723–37.

———. 1998. Banks, markets, and the allocation of risks. *Journal of Institutional and Theoretical Economics* 154:328–51.

Jacklin, C. 1986. Demand deposits, trading restrictions, and risk sharing. In *Contractual arrangements for intertemporal trade,* ed. E. Prescott and N. Wallace, 26–47. Minneapolis: University of Minnesota Press.

James, C. 1991. The losses realized in bank failures. *Journal of Finance* 46:1223–42.

Morrison, A. 2005. Credit derivatives, disintermediation and investment decisions. *Journal of Business* 78:621–47.

Nicolo, A., and L. Pelizzon. 2004. Credit derivatives: Capital requirements and strategic contracting. Working paper, Department of Economics, University of Padua.

Ross, S. 1976. Options and efficiency. *Quarterly Journal of Economics* 90:75–89.

Wagner, W. 2005a. Interbank diversification, liquidity shortages and banking crises. Working paper. Cambridge Endowment for Research in Finance, University of Cambridge.

———. 2005b. The liquidity of bank assets and banking stability. Working paper. Cambridge Endowment for Research in Finance, University of Cambridge.

Wagner, W., and I. Marsh. 2004. Credit risk transfer and financial sector stability. Working paper. Cambridge Endowment for Research in Finance, University of Cambridge.

Comment   Charles W. Calomiris

The Allen-Gale paper is motivated in part by the observation that substantial credit risk has been transferred from bank portfolios to insurance company portfolios in recent years through credit risk derivatives. The authors ask whether this risk transfer reflects, in part, a form of regulatory capital arbitrage, as risk migrates toward a more favorable (lenient) set of risk-based regulatory capital requirements for insurance companies. Their model shows that, under those circumstances, such a risk transfer can have the undesirable effect of making the financial system as a whole more fragile by reducing the amount of capital relative to risk for the financial system as a whole.

In a recent study, Minton, Stulz, and Williamson (2005) quantified the use of credit risk derivatives and found that, as of 2003, only nineteen of 345 large U.S. bank holding companies in their sample actually use credit derivatives, but the assets of these nineteen bank holding companies account for roughly two-thirds of total bank holding company assets. They also find that banks that are more likely to buy protection in the credit derivatives market are also more likely to be asset securitizers, and that those banks also tend to have low capital ratios. Those facts provide some evidence that at least is consistent with the notion that regulatory capital arbitrage could be a factor in bank decisions to use credit derivatives to hedge loans.

But there are reasons to think that (a) regulatory capital arbitrage may not be all bad, and (b) minimum regulatory capital requirements for insurance companies or banks may not be binding constraints on the amount of capital that is allocated to absorb default risk. With respect to the possible desirability of regulatory capital arbitrage, it is important to remember that it is possible for regulatory requirements to be set too high as well as too low. Suppose that, absent any regulatory limits, and based solely on the preferences of market participants (including the stockholders and debtholders of banks and insurance companies), the equilibrium capital ratios of banks would be lower than the minimum regulatory requirements set by regulators. In that case, it is possible that regulatory capital arbitrage can be socially beneficial, since it allows the financial system to make full use of scarce equity capital. That is particularly true if private market discipline substitutes for regulatory discipline by ensuring that capital is maintained by arbitraging financial institutions so that its quantity varies positively with asset risk.

Calomiris and Mason (2004) make precisely these arguments about credit card–securitizing banks. While they recognize that an important part of the motivation for credit card securitization is regulatory capital arbitrage, they conclude that credit card issuers choose equilibrium capital ratios above the regulatory minimum that those institutions could have chosen. They interpret that evidence as suggesting that market discipline is the binding constraint determining the capital requirements for card issuers (relative to total, on– and off–balance sheet risk). Furthermore, Calomiris and Mason (2004) argue that part of the reason that regulators, ratings agencies, and market participants may permit arbitrage, as well as some other questionable accounting practices that securitization entails, is that they recognize that the one-size-fits-all, "risk-based" capital standard applied to banks probably results in a disproportionately large ratio of bank capital relative to risk (compared to other banks) for credit card banks that would keep credit card receivables entirely on their balance sheets. Thus, in the case of credit card receivables, it may be that markets, not regulators, are constraining capital-risk choices of banks, and that regulatory capital arbitrage makes financial intermediation more efficient by avoiding the waste of idle equity capital.

With respect to credit risk derivatives, the analogous question is whether insurance companies face market discipline that constrains their choices of risk in ways that limit the systemic vulnerability that Allen and Gale posit. Surely, policyholders in insurance companies, or guaranteed investment contract (GIC) holders, wish to avoid loss, and to the extent that they are not perfectly protected by governments, might react to unwarranted choices of risk relative to capital by moving their business to other insurance companies. Indeed, there is a substantial body of evidence suggesting that market discipline can constrain the risk choices of financial institutions, including banks and insurance companies, so long as they are not protected too much from market discipline by the government safety net (Brewer, Mondschean, and Strahan 1992, Brewer and Mondschean 1993, Calomiris and Powell 2001, Calomiris and Mason 2003, Calomiris and Wilson 2004, Barth, Caprio, and Levine 2004).

Indeed, in historical banking systems that lacked both deposit insurance and minimum capital ratio requirements (the former having been created in the United States in 1934, the latter dating from the 1980s), bank capital ratios tended to be higher than for today's banks. The same is true for uninsured financial institutions today. For example, finance companies, which rely primarily on very short-term commercial paper for their funding, maintain capital ratios that vary positively with their asset risk (Calomiris and Mason 1998). Calomiris and Mason also show that, as of 1996, book equity capital relative to assets differed substantially across types of financial intermediaries, and that, on average, categories of intermediaries with higher asset risk (measured by the standard deviation of asset returns, inferred from equity returns and leverage ratios) maintained higher book equity capital, as shown in table 7C.1.

Thus, from the perspective of the literature on the market discipline of financial institutions, regulatory capital arbitrage, per se, may not pose a significant systemic risk; rather, the greater threat to systemic risk likely comes from the *joint imposition* of government protection and government prudential regulation and supervision (including the setting and enforcing of capital ratios) in ways that remove market incentives to limit bank risk and maintain adequate capital. Part of that risk relates to the failure of regulators to properly set minimum risk-based capital requirements; part of that systemic risk relates to the failure of supervisors to enforce regulatory limits that have been set (e.g., by properly accounting for bank losses). In short, it may be that regulatory arbitrage is mainly a problem in the finan-

Table 7C.1   Equity ratios and asset risks for various financial intermediaries

	N	BE/A	Sigma of assets
Bank holding companies	378	0.09138	0.25553
Investment banks	55	0.29358	0.91031
Life insurance companies	51	0.12796	0.27275
Property and casualty	108	0.28110	0.52845
Finance companies	95	0.25442	0.96147

Source: Calomiris and Mason (1998).
Note: BE/A = book equity/assets.

cial system when government puts itself in charge of managing risk by removing any private incentive to do so, and then fails to provide an adequate regulatory substitute for private market discipline.

Of course, that is not the end of the story. There is no guarantee, even in a well-functioning financial system with private market discipline, that the aggregate amount of capital chosen by financial institutions will be the socially optimal level. Liquidity crises, after all, probably entail significant economic externalities. The loss of bank capital in the aggregate can prevent the financial system from maintaining its proper role in providing new credit to the nonfinancial sector, resulting in endogenous declines in asset prices, bank loan quality, and macroeconomic activity, which feed on one another. Externalities arise because the failure of one firm, sector, or intermediary can have consequences for others. For example, in the fall of 1998, Russia's financial collapse put pressure on global hedge funds to cut their risks in order to maintain low default probabilities on their debts, in the wake of losses from their Russian positions. Other emerging market securities that trade in international markets declined in price, putting pressure on many other financial institutions and issuers that had no direct connection to Russia's problems.

It would be desirable to construct a realistic model that would capture such effects and help us to gauge whether macroeconomic externalities are large enough to motivate minimum capital requirements in excess of the privately chosen optimum. Such a model should consider how private market discipline works (that is, solve for the privately determined risk-based capital ratios of intermediaries in the absence of regulation), and should model the causal links from an initial loss of capital to a subsequent contraction of credit supply by banks seeking to meet private market discipline, which would entail further declines in firms' asset values, leading in turn to further loan losses for banks and further market discipline (see, for example, Von Peter 2004). And such a model should also recognize the social costs of raising capital requirements (since equity capital is costly to raise, and a scarcity of equity capital can limit the supply of credit).

Many models of banking, including the one in this chapter, are not likely to get us very far toward addressing the question of whether, and by how much, externalities motivate higher capital requirements. Allen and Gale's model conceives of banks as a consumption inventory technology (i.e., following the Diamond and Dybvig 1983 model), not a risk-control/credit-supply technology. We are not going to get very far down the road toward modeling macroeconomic externalities and capital requirements for banks without considering (1) how private market discipline would constrain capital and risk choices in the absence of capital requirements, (2) how costly it is to raise equity capital, (3) how those costs of raising capital vary over the business cycle, or (4) how to model dynamic linkages among bank credit, asset prices, loan quality, and bank capital ratios.

If it could be shown that macroeconomic externalities motivate an increase in minimum capital requirements, the next step would be to ask how those capital requirements (in excess of what is demanded by the market) might be credibly enforced. Experience has taught that one cannot simply take for granted that such requirements will be enforced, since the rule throughout the world has been that enforcement is lax when it is most needed. Much recent work has argued that market signals could be harnessed by regulators to improve the credible enforcement of capital requirements, and this seems to be a promising approach, especially for constraining supervisory and regulatory forbearance (see, for example, Shadow Financial Regulatory Committee 2000, Calomiris and Powell 2001). The current regulatory approach favored by the Group of Seven (G7), however, is quite different, relying on complex formulas constructed by regulators, and internal bank risk modeling subject to regulatory scrutiny. That approach may work, but it has not been tested yet and I am very skeptical. The biggest problem of capital standards enforcement is the tendency of supervisors and regulators to relax standards when times get rough. Complex formulas and internal modeling oversight unfortunately are ideally suited to granting regulators the discretion they need to decide not to do their jobs when that becomes politically expedient.

As part of the discussion of capital requirements, it is also important for economists and regulators to recognize the prevalence and the shortcomings of ex post policies that are often used to deal with financial collapses, which often result from maintaining inadequate bank capital. Those include various kinds of loss-sharing arrangements between banks and taxpayers (including bank bailouts, debt forgiveness, forbearance of regulatory enforcement, and taxpayer-subsidized preferred stock injections into banks in reaction to loan losses). The lessons of recent experience strongly suggest that such ex post policy responses are extremely costly and often result from inadequate ex ante incentives to manage risk properly (for a review, see Calomiris, Laeven, and Klingebiel 2005). The recognition that generous safety net protections encourage excessive risk taking, and that this often results in extremely socially costly ex post interventions into the financial sector, offers a reason to set capital requirements higher ex ante than they would need to be in a truly laissez faire world.

The twin goals of (a) determining the right level of risk-based capital for the economy, and (b) finding a way to enforce capital standards if the amounts of capital chosen by private market discipline are inadequate, remain elusive, especially in the presence of generous government safety nets. The hardest challenge for financial economists is to devise models of the linkages among financial system credit, financial intermediaries' capital, financial intermediaries' risks, nonfinancial firms' asset prices, and macroeconomic activity that would be realistic enough to help us gauge the optimal risk-based capital ratio for the economy. The hardest challenge for policymakers is to find a way to enforce such policies credibly, while remaining flexible enough to permit activities with relatively low fundamental risks to avoid being penalized by the capital budgeting mandates of one-size-fits-all rules.

References

Barth, James, Gerard Caprio, and Ross Levine. 2004. Bank regulation and supervision: What works best. *Journal of Financial Intermediation* 13:205–48.

Brewer, Elijah, III, and Thomas H. Mondschean. 1993. Junk bond holdings, premium tax offsets, and risk exposure at life insurance companies. Federal Reserve Bank of Chicago Working Paper no. 93-3. Chicago: Federal Reserve Bank of Chicago.

Brewer, Elijah, III, Thomas H. Mondschean, and Philip E. Strahan. 1992. The effects of capital on portfolio risk at life insurance companies. Federal Reserve Bank of Chicago Working Paper no. 92-29. Chicago: Federal Reserve Bank of Chicago.

Calomiris, Charles W., Luc Laeven, and Daniela Klingebiel. 2005. Financial crisis policies and resolution mechanisms: A taxonomy from cross-country experience. In *Systematic financial crises: Containment and resolution,* ed. P. Hanohan and L. Laeven, 25–75. Cambridge: Cambridge University Press.

Calomiris, Charles W., and Joseph R. Mason. 1998. Comparing bank holding companies' risk-based capital to other financial intermediaries. Unpublished manuscript.

———. 2003. Fundamentals, panics, and bank distress during the depression. *American Economic Review* (December): 1615–47.

———. 2004. Credit card securitization and regulatory arbitrage. *Journal of Financial Services Research* (August): 5–28.

Calomiris, Charles W., and Andrew Powell. 2001. Can emerging market bank regulators establish credible discipline? The case of Argentina, 1992–99. In *Prudential Supervision: What Works and What Doesn't,* ed. F. S. Mishkin, 147–96. Chicago: University of Chicago Press.

Calomiris, Charles W., and Berry Wilson. 2004. Bank capital and portfolio management: The 1930s 'capital crunch' and the scramble to shed risk. *Journal of Business* (July): 421–55.

Diamond, Douglas W., and Phillip H. Dybvig. 1983. Bank runs, deposit insurance, and liquidity. *Journal of Political Economy* (June): 401–19.

Minton, Bernadette A., René M. Stulz, and Rohan Williamson. 2005. How much do banks use credit derivatives to reduce risk? NBER Working Paper no. 11579. Cambridge, MA: National Bureau of Economic Research, August.

Shadow Financial Regulatory Committee. 2000. *Reforming bank capital regulation.* Washington, DC: AEI Press.

Von Peter, Goetz. 2004. Asset prices and banking distress: A macroeconomic approach. BIS Working Paper no. 167. Basel, Switzerland: Bank for International Settlements.

Discussion Summary

Gary Gorton began the general discussion by questioning whether the amount of risk transferred from banks to insurance companies is as large as some statistics imply. Although credit derivative contracts may transfer risk, many securitizations receive implicit support from sponsors. He also questioned whether capital requirements can be binding in the long run, because banking business can move to nonbank financial institutions.

Martin Feldstein observed that economic capital considerations drive large-bank decision making, not regulatory capital requirements.

Anthony Saunders noted that the behavior of insurance companies (and other nonbank institutions) in bad states of the world is important to understanding systemic risk. Defaults by nonbanks, in addition to disrupting nonbank markets, could affect bank solvency. *Peter Garber* noted that U.S. insurance companies are subject to capital regulations, which are complicated, and that in bad states of the world insurance companies may gamble for redemption just like banks. *Martin Feldstein* observed that the guarantee funds that protect U.S. policyholders may strengthen moral hazard incentives of weak insurers. Surviving insurance companies must make up the losses imposed by those that fail.

When discussion turned to the experience of European insurance companies, *Paul Kupiec* noted that their losses in recent years were mainly driven by losses on their equity investments, which are much larger as a proportion of assets than at U.S. insurance companies. *Philipp Hartmann* agreed that equity losses were the first and primary source of loss, but noted that losses on credit derivatives were a material second leg of the double whammy they suffered.

Hayne Leland argued that credit derivatives might cause systemic problems for reasons other than those mentioned in Allen and Gale's paper. If dynamic hedging is used by protection sellers to hedge their credit derivative portfolios, increases in default rates may have knock-on effects in equity and bond markets, amplifying the price declines that are in any case likely to be associated with increased credit risk. *Peter Garber* agreed that such dynamic hedging is common in practice.

In the course of the discussion, several participants mentioned the common wisdom that (a) many risk-transfer transactions by banks (securitizations, credit derivatives, and others) are "capital arbitrage" (intended primarily to reduce regulatory capital requirements), and (b) losses suffered by insurance companies on their investments in credit derivative contracts were due to insurance companies' lack of expertise in pricing credit risk. *Richard Cantor* noted that, at least in the United States, it is not clear that credit protection sellers lost money on the whole in the long run. Although their portfolios may have suffered mark-to-market losses during 2001–2003, when credit spreads were high, over the longer term the premiums they earn may more than compensate for payouts. *Ken Abbott* commented that concerns about the precision of credit risk pricing should be more general. He does not have great confidence in the credit risk pricing models he has seen used in practice. Most of the risk-transfer transactions he has seen have economic motivations and are not capital arbitrage. *David Modest* observed that at the time of the conference, the cyclical pendulum appeared to have swung to an excess of supply by protection sellers, forcing spreads down to unreasonable levels.

Commenting on some of the assumptions of the Allen and Gale model, *Casper de Vries* wondered if results would be different if capital regulation was useful rather than having no role in enhancing welfare. The assumption that regulation is binding in equilibrium may not be necessary for it to affect the equilibrium, as it might affect the value of off-equilibrium-path alternatives even if not binding.

Pillar 1 versus Pillar 2 under Risk Management

Loriana Pelizzon and Stephen Schaefer

8.1   Introduction

Under the New Basel Accord, bank capital adequacy rules (Pillar 1) are substantially revised—but the introduction of two new dimensions to the regulatory framework is, perhaps, of even greater significance. Pillar 2 increases the number of instruments available to the regulator: (1) intensifying monitoring, (2) restricting the payment of dividends, (3) requiring the preparation and implementation of a satisfactory capital-adequacy restoration plan, and (4) requiring the bank to raise additional capital immediately. Pillar 3 enhances disclosure (that is, publicly available information). This paper investigates the consequences of adding Pillar 2 alongside Pillar 1 in terms of bank risk taking and the scale of bank lending. The results suggest that Pillar 2 should more properly be seen as a substitute for, rather than a complement to, Pillar 1, and that, in particular, Pillar 2 affects bank risk taking only when Pillar 1 rules cannot be effectively enforced.

If regulators are able to enforce a risk-based capital requirements rule at all times, then both failure and, consequently, calls on the deposit insurance fund can be effectively eliminated. In this case, the details of the rule are of little importance because as soon as capital reaches some lower threshold[1] the regulator simply has to force the bank to invest entirely in

We gratefully acknowledge conversations with Mark Carey, Mark Flannery, Patricia Jackson, Ed Krane, Daniel Nuxoll, James O'Brien, Jack Reidhill, Marc Saidenberg, René Stulz, and seminar audiences at National Bureau of Economic Research (NBER) workshops in Boston, 2004, and Woodstock, 2004. All errors are our own. Financial support by NBER is gratefully acknowledged.

1. The conclusion that continuous monitoring and perfect liquidity would eliminate the possibility of default rests on the assumption of asset price continuity, that is, the absence of jumps. In the context of a single obligor this assumption is indeed critical but, for banks with

riskless assets. Under these conditions additional regulatory instruments such as Pillars 2 and 3 would have no role.[2] Thus, the design of capital requirements is a significant problem only in the case when the regulator is either unable to observe the bank's portfolio perfectly or lacks the authority to force changes in its composition. In this event, and if they are able to change their portfolio composition over time—that is, engage in *risk management*[3]—banks may deliberately deviate from compliance with capital adequacy rules, in other words, they may cheat. Under these circumstances, instruments such as Pillar 2 and Pillar 3 may not be redundant. Our paper focuses on the interaction between Pillar 1 and Pillar 2 when banks are able to use risk management to cheat in relation to capital requirements.

We construct a model of bank behavior in which banks manage their portfolios in the interests of their shareholders subject to the constraints imposed by regulation. These regulatory constraints include not only capital requirements but actions on closure and recapitalization taken by the regulator under the new Pillar 2.

Our model has three main innovations. First, the model includes both costly recapitalization and dynamic portfolio management. The latter means that banks are concerned about survival as well as exploiting deposit insurance. Second, we consider explicitly a regime in which banks' compliance with capital requirements is imperfect; that is, a world where banks can cheat. In our analysis we consider two cases. In the first, the implementation of capital requirements is relatively effective and banks are constrained to be quite close to compliance at all points in time. In the second, the implementation of capital requirements is less effective, allowing banks to deviate substantially from the ideal of compliance at all points in time. Thus, in the first of these cases there is extensive cheating and, in the second, only limited cheating. Third, we model Pillar 2 as a threshold level such that, if a bank's capital falls below this level at the time of an audit, it must either recapitalize or face closure. This view of Pillar 2 is similar to the concept of Prompt Corrective Action (PCA) promulgated by the FDIC. This additional constraint on the bank's capital position gives the regulator an extra degree of freedom. In this sense it is therefore a simple

---

large, well-diversified portfolios, the conclusion is much more robust—in the sense that a jump in the value of a claim on a single counterpart would have only a small effect on the value of the portfolio as a whole.

2. A similar point is made by Berlin, Saunders, and Udell (1991, p. 740), who point out that, with perfect observability, even capital requirements are redundant and could be replaced by a simple closure rule: "A credible net-worth closure rule for banks relegates depositor discipline to a minor role. Indeed, a totally credible and error- and forbearance free closure rule removes any need for depositors to monitor bank risk at all since they would never lose on closure."

3. We use the term risk management to include any action that (deliberately) changes the risk of the bank's position over time.

constraint on leverage. We also consider the case when a bank that recapitalizes at the Pillar 2 threshold level incurs a fixed cost. This cost may be thought of as an increase in compliance costs brought about by more intensive scrutiny on the part of the regulator, the frictional cost of recapitalization or, simply, as a fine.

Our analysis addresses the trade-off between the costs and benefits of the regulatory framework. Thus we need to consider not only measures of the negative externalities associated with bank failure but also some measure of the cost of regulation imposed by constraining bank activity. Therefore we include the probability of bank closure and the value of deposit insurance liabilities (PVDIL) as measures of the negative externalities of bank risk taking, and the average investment in risky assets and capital utilization as, respectively, measures of bank activity, to reflect the negative externality of reduced activity induced by regulation, and the private costs associated with high capital levels.

Our paper focuses on two main questions: (1) what is the effect of risk-based capital regulation (RBCR) on the trade-off between the costs and benefits of banking activity (a) when the bank manages its portfolio dynamically; (b) when, at the time of an audit, the bank's capital is below a certain threshold level, the bank must either recapitalize or it will be closed and (c) when banks' compliance with RBCR is imperfect? and (2) how does the answer to the first question change when the regulator imposes a Pillar 2/PCA leverage constraint in addition to RBCR?

In our results we distinguish between a regime where there is only limited cheating and where there is extensive cheating. In the first case, RBCR are still effective in that they reduce the cost of failure as measured by the probability of closure and the PVDIL. Importantly, when there is limited cheating, we find that the level of investment in risky assets is relatively unaffected by the level of RBCR. On the other hand, when there is extensive cheating, we find that increasing capital requirements reduces banks' investment in risky assets and increases the probability of failure.

In relation to question (2), we ask whether an intervention rule in the spirit of Pillar 2/PCA and based simply on leverage rather than portfolio risk is effective in conjunction with RBCR. We show that Pillar 2/PCA is indeed effective in reducing PVDIL: substantially when there is extensive cheating, and more modestly when there is limited cheating. When there is only limited cheating, Pillar 2/PCA increases the probability of bank closure and decreases the amount invested in risky assets. In the latter case, and especially taking into account the costs of more frequent recapitalization, it is possible that the net benefits of Pillar 2/PCA may be negative.

The paper is organized as follows. Sections 8.2 and 8.3 describe the New Basel Accord and its main advantages and drawbacks. Section 8.4 describes the model and characterizes the bank's optimal investment decisions. Section 8.5 introduces the costs of recapitalization and examines their effect on dynamic portfolio management. Section 8.6 extends the analysis introducing risk-based capital requirements (Pillar 1). Section 8.7 presents the results of the interaction between Pillar 1 and Pillar 2, and section 8.8 concludes.

8.2   The New Basel Accord: A Brief Description

In the early 1980s, as concern about the financial health of international banks mounted and complaints of unfair competition increased, the Basel Committee on Banking Supervision initiated a discussion on the revision of capital standards. An agreement was reached in July 1988, under which new rules would be phased in by January 1993 (Basel Committee 1988). The Basel Accord of 1988 explicitly considered only credit risk, and the scheme was based entirely on capital requirements. These requirements, still in force, comprise four elements: (1) the definition of regulatory capital, (2) the definition of the assets subject to risk weighting, (3) the risk weighting system, and (4) the minimum ratio of 8 percent.[4]

When the Accord was introduced in 1988, its design was criticized as being too crude and for its one-size-fits-all approach.[5] Given these shortcomings, together with the experience accumulated since the Accord was introduced, the Basel Committee is considering revising the current accord (Basel Committee 1999, 2001, 2003, 2005).

The proposed new accord differs from the old one in two major respects. First, it allows the use of internal models by banks to assess the riskiness of their portfolios and to determine their required capital cushion. This applies to credit risk as well as to operational risk, and delegates to a significant extent the determination of regulatory capital-adequacy requirements. This regime is available to banks if they choose this option and if

4. Following its introduction, the accord has been fine-tuned to accommodate financial innovation and some of the risks not initially considered. For example, it was amended in 1995 and 1996 to require banks to set aside capital in order to cover the risk of losses arising from movements in market prices. In 1995, the required capital charge was based on the "standard approach" similar to that applied to credit risk. The standard approach defines the risk charges associated with each position and specifies how any risk position has to be aggregated into the overall market risk capital charge. The amendment of 1996 allows banks to use, as an alternative to the standard approach, their internal models to determine the required capital charge for market risk. The internal model approach allows a bank to use its model to estimate the Value-at-Risk (VaR) in its trading account; that is, the maximum loss that the portfolio is likely to experience over a given holding period with a certain probability. The market risk capital requirement is then set based on the VaR estimate. The main novelty of this approach is that it accounts for risk reduction in the portfolio resulting from hedging and diversification.

5. The main criticisms were, among other things, (1) the capital ratio appeared to lack economic foundation, (2) the risk weights did not reflect accurately the risk of the obligor, and (3) it did not account for the benefits from diversification. One of the main problems with the existing accord is the ability of banks to arbitrage their regulatory capital requirements (see Jones 2000) and exploit divergences between true economic risk and risk measured under the accord.

their internal model is validated by the regulatory authority. Second, by adding two additional pillars alongside the traditional focus on minimum bank capital, the new accord acknowledges the importance of complementary mechanisms to safeguard against bank failure. Thus, the new capital adequacy scheme is based on three pillars: (1) capital adequacy requirements (Pillar 1), (2) supervisory review (Pillar 2), and (3) market discipline (Pillar 3).

With regard to the first pillar, the Committee proposes two approaches. The first, so-called "standardized" approach, adopts external ratings, such as those provided by rating agencies, export credit agencies, and other qualified institutions. The second approach, called the "Internal rating-based approach," allows the use of internal rating systems developed by banks (subject to their meeting specific criteria yet to be defined), and validation by the relevant national supervisory authority. The internal ratings approach is also divided in two broad approaches: the "advanced" and the "foundation." The former gives some discretion to banks in choosing the parameters that determine risk weights, and consequently, in determining their capital requirements. The foundation approach, in contrast, provides little discretion.[6]

As far as the second pillar is concerned, the proposals of the Basel Committee underline the importance of supervisory activity such as reports and inspections. These are carried out by individual national authorities who are authorized to impose, through moral suasion, higher capital requirements than the minimum under the capital adequacy rules. In particular, Pillar 2 emphasizes the importance of the supervisory review process as an essential element of the new Accord (see Santos 2001). Pillar 2 encourages banks to develop internal economic capital assessments, appropriate to their own risk profiles, for identifying, measuring, and controlling risks. The emphasis on internal assessments of capital adequacy recognizes that any rules-based approach will inevitably lag behind the changing risk profiles of complex banking organizations. Banks' internal assessments should give explicit recognition to the quality of the risk management and control processes and to risks not fully addressed in Pillar 1. Importantly, Pillar 2 provides the basis for supervisory intervention and allows regulators to consider a range of options if they become concerned that banks are not meeting the requirements. These actions may include more intense monitoring of the bank; restricting the payment of dividends; requiring the bank to prepare and implement a satisfactory capital-adequacy restoration plan; and requiring the bank to raise additional capital immediately. Supervisors should have the discretion to use the tools best suited to the

---

6. In addition to revising the criteria for the determination of the minimum capital associated to the credit risk of individual exposures, the reform proposals advanced by the committee introduce a capital requirement for operational risks, which is in turn determined using three different approaches presenting a growing degree of sophistication.

circumstances of the bank and its operating environment (New Accord: Principle 4: 717).

Finally, the third pillar is intended to encourage banks to disclose information in order to enhance the role of the market in monitoring banks. To that end, the Committee is proposing that banks disclose information on, among other things, the composition of their regulatory capital, risk exposures, and risk-based capital ratios computed in accordance with the Accord's methodology.

In the light of these objectives, the Basel Committee has articulated four principles: (1) Each bank should assess its internal capital adequacy in light of its risk profile, (2) Supervisors should review internal assessments, (3) Banks should hold capital above regulatory minimums, and (4) Supervisors should intervene at an early stage.

The descriptions of the second and third pillars by the Basel Committee are not as extensive or detailed as that of the first. Nevertheless, it is significant that for the first time in international capital regulation, supervision and market discipline are placed at the same point of the hierarchy as the regulatory minimum. In discussing the second pillar the proposal states that: "The supervisory review process should not be viewed as a discretionary pillar but, rather, as a critical complement to both the minimum regulatory capital requirement and market discipline" (Basel Committee 1999, p. 53).

In this paper we analyze the effects of Pillar 2 intervention and, in particular, the interaction between Pillar 2 and Pillar 1. We characterize Pillar 2 as a threshold level of leverage such that a bank with higher leverage than this threshold at the time of an audit is required either to recapitalize or to close. If a bank recapitalizes it incurs a cost. This characterization is therefore firmly in the spirit of both PCA and Basel II.

We show first that Pillar 2 intervention has a significant impact on the frequency of bank closure and the value of deposit insurance liabilities only when regulators are unable to force banks to comply with Pillar 1 risk-based capital requirements at all times. This may arise, for example, as the result of monitoring costs. If banks always comply with risk-based capital requirements then both failure rates and the present value of deposit insurance liability go to zero.[7]

However, if banks do not always comply with Pillar 1 capital requirements, Pillar 2 may have a role, by inducing banks to manage their portfolios so as to reduce the likelihood of incurring recapitalization costs. A central issue that we explore in the paper is the interaction between the level of risk-based capital requirements (Pillar 1), the threshold leverage level (Pillar 2) and the degree of noncompliance with Pillar 1 rules. More particularly, we investigate whether, as the regulators hope, Pillar 2 does indeed act

---

7. Unless there are jumps in the value of the portfolio of bank assets.

as complement to Pillar 1—in the sense that it increases the effectiveness of Pillar 1—or whether it is simply a substitute, a second line of defense.

8.3 Advantages and Main Drawbacks of the New Accord

The Basel Committee's proposals can be seen as an attempt to address some of the drawbacks of the previous capital adequacy scheme. In particular, the new accord represents an advance in three main areas. First, with the objective of making capital requirements more risk sensitive, it introduces a more accurate framework for the assessment of risk, in particular credit risk. Although the new proposals have undoubtedly raised the level of the analysis of credit risk from the first accord, there remain some important questions about some aspects; for example, how the correlation of credit exposures is treated. Moreover, for the first time the rules explicitly include operational risk as one of the determinants of required capital (Pillar 1). The new rules will also enhance the role of banks' internal assessments of risk as the basis for capital requirements. Second, the new accord represents an attempt on the part of regulators to lower the impact of capital regulation as a source of competitive inequality by reducing the opportunity for regulatory arbitrage. Third, the new accord enhances the role for regulatory review and intervention (Pillar 2) and market discipline (Pillar 3).

In introducing an extension to the current accord that concentrates only on capital requirements, Basel II is more consistent with the consensus of the literature on asymmetries of information; that, in general, it is advantageous to consider a menu-based approach rather than a uniform one-size-fits-all rule.[8] The limitations of a simple capital-adequacy approach in our paper arise when bank portfolios are imperfectly observable by the auditor and banks are able to engage in dynamic portfolio management.

Nonetheless, it appears that the new accord does have some significant weaknesses and, among these, we draw particular attention to the following.

A major problem—long present in the literature—in assessing developments in banking regulation, and financial regulation in general, is that there is little discussion, and certainly no consensus, on the objectives that the regulator should pursue (Dewatripont and Tirole 1994). The two most-commonly cited justifications for bank regulation, and capital regulation in particular, are (1) the mitigation of systemic risks (see Goodhart et al. 1998, and Benston and Kaufman 1996 among others) and (2) the need to control the value of deposit insurance liabilities (see Merton 1997, Genotte

---

8. See Kane (1990) and Goodhart et al. (1998) for a discussion of the principal-agent problems that can arise between regulators and regulated, and Hauswald and Senbet (1999) for the design of optimal banking regulation in the presence of incentive conflicts between regulators and society. For other analysis of the interplay between capital regulation and monitoring of the bank by a regulator, see Campbell, Chan, and Marino (1992) and Milne and Whalley (2001).

and Pyle 1991, Buser, Chen, and Kane 1981, Chan, Greenbaum, and Thakor 1992, and Diamond and Dybvig 1986, among others). Indeed, the authors of the Basel II proposals refer to their "fundamental objective . . . to develop a framework that would further enhance the soundness and stability of the international banking system."

Thus it might seem curious to an outsider that the new Basel II accord is so little concerned with the problem of systemic risk, which has for so long been seen as central to the design of bank regulation. Nonetheless we find this nonsystemic same view expressed repeatedly by the regulators in describing the goals of the new accord. For example, the following quotation, which comes from the Bank for International Settlements (BIS) itself, addresses what we would regard as some of the central questions in bank regulation, and does so without any reference to systemic costs:

Why are banks subject to capital requirements?
Nearly all jurisdictions with active banking markets require banking organizations to maintain at least a minimum level of capital. Capital serves as a foundation for a bank's future growth and as a cushion against its unexpected losses. Adequately capitalized banks that are well managed are better able to withstand losses and to provide credit to consumers and businesses alike throughout the business cycle, including during downturns. Adequate levels of capital thereby help to promote public confidence in the banking system.

Why is a new capital standard necessary today?
Advances in risk management practices, technology, and banking markets have made the 1988 Accord's simple approach to measuring capital less meaningful for many banking organizations.

What is the goal for the Basel II Framework and how will it be accomplished?
The overarching goal for the Basel II Framework is to promote the adequate capitalization of banks and to encourage improvements in risk management, thereby strengthening the stability of the financial system. This goal will be accomplished through the introduction of "three pillars" that reinforce each other and that create incentives for banks to enhance the quality of their control processes. (BIS 2004)

The connection between the objective of enhancing the "soundness and stability" of the banking system and the specifics of the proposal, particularly in relation to systemic risk, are unclear. More broadly, the Basel II Accord is almost silent on the presence of externalities such as systemic failure and contagion, which would be regarded by many as the principal justification for regulatory intervention (Berlin, Saunders, and Uddell 1991, Allen and Gale 2003). Without externalities, decisions—for example, on capital structure—that are optimal from the private perspective of bank owners would also be socially optimal and, in this case, there would be no need for regulation.

The "externality-free" view of regulation that Basel II appears to espouse is also reflected in Pillar 3. This seeks to "encourage market discipline by developing a set of disclosure requirements that allow market participants to assess key information about a bank's risk profile and level of capitalization" (Basel Committee 2005, p. 184). However, it is unclear what impact greater transparency would have. If capital requirements are set without reference to the social costs of failure—that is, regulatory capital requirements coincide with privately optimal levels of capital—then banks are, in any case, incentivized to maintain these levels, and greater transparency would have little effect. If capital requirements do reflect the social costs of failure—that is, are higher than those banks would choose privately—then it is not clear how disclosing to a private counterparty a deficit against regulatory capital requirements would give the bank any incentive to increase capital.

When systemic costs are taken into account, optimal regulatory design involves trading off the social benefits of, for example, a lower frequency of failure with the private costs of achieving this. But when systemic issues are excluded from the analysis, there is no trade-off, because the interests of private owners and social welfare coincide. In this case the prescriptions of the regulator are those that the bank would optimally choose for itself and the regulator becomes a sort of "super consultant" helping to promote good practice and sound analysis. These are worthy objectives, but it is unclear why they need to be promoted within a legal framework such as Basel II. For example, the Basel Committee states that it "believes that the revised framework will promote the adoption of stronger risk management practices by the banking industry" (Basel Committee 2005, p. 2). While undoubtedly desirable, it is not clear how improving management practice in the area of risk management addresses the broad objectives of soundness and stability or, indeed, that banks themselves are not in a better position to decide on the appropriate level of investment in risk management.

The absence in the Basel Accord of any substantial discussion of costs is a major omission.[9] For example, if the costs imposed by capital requirements were small while the social costs of failure were significant, required capital should be set to sufficiently high levels that the incidence of bank failure would be minimal. The fact that no bank regulator proposes such a regime suggests that regulators at least consider that the costs imposed by capital regulation are significant. Certainly the U.S. House of Representa-

---

9. References to the cost of capital requirements by the Basel Committee are rare. Among the small number of examples, the following quotation makes an implicit reference to cost when it refers to the possibility that capital level might be "too high": "The technical challenge for both banks and supervisors has been to determine how much capital is necessary to serve as a sufficient buffer against unexpected losses. If capital levels are too low, banks may be unable to absorb high levels of losses. Excessively low levels of capital increase the risk of bank failures which, in turn, may put depositors' funds at risk. If capital levels are too high, banks may not be able to make the most efficient use of their resources, which may constrain their ability to make credit available" (BIS, 2004, p. 1).

tives Committee on Financial Services (USHRCFS) has reservations about the costs imposed by capital requirements: "We are concerned that the bank capital charges created by Basel II, if implemented, could be overly onerous and may discourage banks from engaging in activities which promote economic developments."[10]

In our analysis we reflect the trade-off between, on one hand, the public and private costs of failure and, on the other, the costs imposed by regulation. Ideally, alternative designs for Basel II would find the best trade-off between these costs using a general equilibrium approach.[11] In the absence of such a model, we focus on four outcome variables that are plausible candidates for the arguments of the welfare function that might be derived from an equilibrium model.

The first is the PVDIL: the cost of insuring deposits. The second is the frequency of bank closure, which we regard as an index of the systemic cost of failure. All else equal, a low frequency of failure would promote confidence in the banking system and enhance the efficiency of the payments mechanism (see Diamond and Dybvig 1986).

Third, there is a widely held—if imperfectly articulated—view, reflected in the concerns expressed by the USHRCFS, that high levels of capital impose a cost on banks. In our analysis we use the average level of bank capital as a measure of this cost.

Finally, we wish to capture the positive externalities that may arise from banking activity, for example, bank lending. Clearly, a capital requirements regime that was so onerous as to substantially eliminate banking activity would also reduce both the frequency of failure and the PVDIL to zero. A former chairman of the London Stock Exchange once referred to this approach as the "regulation of the graveyard." The previous quotation from the USHRCFS suggests that they share these concerns and so we also report the average level of risky assets held as a proxy for banks' contribution to economic activity through lending.

The Basel Committee has attempted to assess the potential impact of the new accord on capital requirements for different types of banks in a variety of countries by carrying out Quantitative Impact Studies (QIS). These entail each bank recalculating capital requirements for its current portfolio under the new accord. However, the QIS calculations were conducted under ceteris paribus assumptions and did not attempt to take into account any behavioral response on the part of banks to the new accord. One of the aims of this paper is to provide a framework within which the behavioral response of banks to changes in regulation might be studied.

---

10. U.S. House of Representatives Committee on Financial Services letter to the chairmen of the Federal Reserve and the FDIC, the Comptroller of the Currency and the Director of the Office of Thrift Supervision, November 3, 2003, p. 2.

11. See, for example, Suarez and Repullo (2004). However, defining an appropriate social welfare function is always problematical.

Pillars 2 and 3 are major innovations in the new accord and represent an explicit recognition that capital supervision involves more than capital requirements. Pillar 2, in particular, adds an important instrument to the bank regulator's armory and allows for some discretion over important elements such as closure, dividend payments, and recapitalization. Pillar 3, by encouraging transparency, attempts to capture the benefits of market discipline. However, two important issues remain. First, as other authors (see Saidenberg and Schuermann 2003 and von Thadden 2003) have pointed out, there is a substantial imbalance in the detail provided by the committee between Pillar 1, on one hand, and Pillars 2 and 3 on the other. The focus of the committee's attention seems clear. Second, and more important, there is no discussion of the interaction between capital rules and market discipline and the rules governing closure, dividend payments, and recapitalization.

The main aim of this paper is to try to provide a framework within which to analyze the relations between capital requirements and closure, dividend payments, and recapitalization. Descamps, Rochet, and Roger (2003) have also drawn attention to the importance of this issue.

Finally, one aspect of the objectives of Basel II is to ensure that "capital adequacy regulation will not be a significant source of competitive inequality among internationally active banks" (Basel Committee 2005, p. 2). However, trying to make regulation neutral with respect to competition (the level playing field) is a more demanding objective. First, regulation almost inevitably affects competition because it affects bank costs. Second, if the regulator attempts to design capital requirements, say, by finding the optimal trade-off between private and social costs, then capital rules will almost inevitably vary across banks unless they are all identical in terms of their social costs (e.g., of failure). Differentiation of this kind—for example, between large banks and small banks—is not found in the Basel II rules or, indeed, in other capital adequacy regimes. It appears that the pressure on regulators for equal treatment among banks dominates a more fine-tuned approach to regulatory design.

8.4   The Model

8.4.1   Timing and Assumptions

In our model a bank is an institution that holds financial assets and is financed by equity and deposits.

Bank Shareholders and Depositors

Shareholders are risk neutral, enjoy limited liability, and are initially granted a banking charter. The charter permits the bank to continue in business indefinitely under the control of its shareholders unless, at the time of an audit, the regulator finds the bank is in violation of regulations such as capital requirements. In this case the charter is not renewed, the shareholders lose control of the bank, and the value of their equity is zero.

If the bank is solvent at time $t - 1$, it raises deposits[12] D_{t-1} and capital kD_{t-1}, $k > 0$ so that total assets invested are

(1) $$A_{t-1} = (1 + k)D_{t-1}.$$

The deposits are one-period term deposits paying a total rate of return of r^d. Thus, at maturity the amount due to depositors is

(2) $$D_t = D_{t-1}(1 + r^d).$$

At this point, if the bank is solvent, the accrued interest, $r^d D_{t-1}$, is paid to depositors and deposits are rolled over at the same interest rate.

Regulators and Audit Frequency

We assume that audits take place at fixed times $t = 1, 2, \ldots$. The government guarantees the deposits and charges the bank a fixed premium per dollar of insured deposits that is the same for all banks.[13] This premium is included in the deposit rate r^d.[14]

Portfolio Revisions and Investment Choice

Between successive audit dates there are n equally spaced times at which the portfolio may be revised. Setting $\Delta t \equiv 1/n$, the portfolio revision dates, between audit dates t and $t + 1$, are therefore

(3) $$t, t + \Delta t, t + 2\Delta t, \ldots , t + (n - 1)\Delta t, t + 1.$$

For simplicity we assume that the bank may choose between two assets: a risk-free bond with maturity $1/n$, yielding a constant net return $\hat{r}$ per period of length $1/n$ (r per period of length 1) and a risky asset yielding a gross random return $R_{t+j\Delta t}$ over the period $(t + [j - 1]\Delta t)$ to $(t + j\Delta t)$.[15] Returns on the risky asset are independently distributed over time and have a constant expected gross return of $E(R_{t+j\Delta t}) \equiv (1 + \hat{a})$, where $\hat{a}$ is the net expected return per period of length $1/n$ (a per period of length 1). Notice that we assume that, at each portfolio revision date, the bank is allowed either to increase or decrease its investment in the risky asset; that is, the risky asset is marketable.

In our model we assume that the only source of bank rent is deposit insurance—that is, $r^d = r = a$. This may appear to be a very pessimistic view

12. We take the volume of a bank's deposits as exogenous.
13. This means that the deposit insurance premium is not risk dependent and is therefore not actuarially fair.
14. Equivalently, we may interpret this arrangement as one where the depositors pay the deposit insurance premium and receive a net interest rate of r^d.
15. This means that we do not address the issues related to portfolio diversification as in Boot and Thakor (1991).

of banking, as in this case a bank's only objective is to try to exploit deposit insurance. However, we know that when banks have other sources of rents this acts as a natural curb on excessive risk taking and capital requirements will be less necessary. In our framework the banks that are most likely to default are those without other significant sources of rents, who will try to hold as little capital as possible.

In making these assumptions we have in mind a competitive market where the surplus associated with the projects financed by loans is captured entirely by the borrowers. The presence of a borrower surplus means, as we have mentioned earlier, that lending is, on average, improving welfare. For this reason, again as mentioned earlier, we use the volume of risky assets held by the bank as one argument of a measure of welfare.

Portfolio Choice

Let $w_{t+j\Delta t}$ denote the percentage of the portfolio held in the risky asset at time $t + j\Delta t$, with the remainder invested in the "safe" security. We limit the leverage that the bank can take on by imposing a no-short selling constraint ($0 \leq w_{t+j\Delta t} \leq 1$) on both the risky and safe assets:[16]

(4) $$0 \leq w_{t+j\Delta t} \leq 1 \; \forall \, t \in (0, \infty), \forall \, j \in (0, n - 1)$$

The bank's portfolio management strategy is represented as a sequence of variables $\Theta = (\theta_0, \theta_1, \ldots, \theta_t, \ldots, \theta_\infty)$, with

(5) $\theta_t = (w_t, w_{t+\Delta t}, \ldots, w_{t+j\Delta t}, \ldots, w_{t+j\Delta t}, \ldots, w_{t+(n-1)\Delta t})$ for all $0 \leq t \leq \infty$.

and $0 \leq j \leq n - 1$, where θ_t represents the strategy between audit dates t and $t + 1$ and Θ the collection of these substrategies for audit dates $1, 2, \ldots, t, \ldots \infty$.

Intertemporal Budget Constraint

The intertemporal budget constraint is given by

(6) $$A_{t+(j+1)\Delta t} = [w_{t+j\Delta t} R_{t+j\Delta t} + (1 - w_{t+j\Delta t})(1 + \hat{r})] A_{t+j\Delta t},$$

and so the bank's asset value at the audit time $t + 1$ is

(7) $$A_{t+1} = \prod_{j=0}^{n-1} [w_{t+j\Delta t} R_{t+j\Delta t} + (1 - w_{t+j\Delta t})(1 + \hat{r})] A_t.$$

Bank Closure Rule (Transfer of Control from Shareholders to Supervisor)

Most of the previous literature has assumed a closure rule under which banking authorities deny the renewal of the banking license and close the

---

16. It may not be immediately apparent that a nonnegativity constraint on the risky asset would ever be binding. However, under the assumptions that we introduce (limited liability) we show that the bank will be risk preferring in some regions and would short the risky asset if it could.

bank if its net worth (asset value minus deposits) is negative at the end of a period—that is, if the asset value is lower than the threshold point represented by the deposit value (Marcus 1984, Keeley 1990, Hellman, Murdock, and Stiglitz 2000, and Pelizzon and Schaefer 2003). This closure rule induces the bank to be prudent when the bank has a sufficiently high rent from deposit insurance, interest ceilings, or monopoly power in the deposit or asset market. Such a closure policy serves as a mechanism that both manages bank distress ex post and may also have a disciplinary effect on ex ante actions. A major drawback of this approach, however, is that shareholders who wish to provide capital to reestablish solvency are prevented from doing so. Among the problems raised by this assumption is the question of whether, by refusing to allow recapitalization, the government would be illegally expropriating the property of bank shareholders.

Thus, in this paper we consider the case where the banking authorities, instead of closing the bank or intervening and assuming control (for equityholders this is the same as closing the bank), allow recapitalization by shareholders[17] and renewal of the license if, after recapitalization, the volume of capital meets a given minimum threshold level, $\bar{k}$.[18] In the papers cited in the previous paragraph, $\bar{k}$ is a small quantity of capital that guarantees solvency. Later in the paper, where we introduce Pillar 2/PCA, this threshold will be higher.

Under this rule, equityholders have an option to retain the banking license. They will exercise this option when there is an amount of capital, k^* $\geq \bar{k}$, such that the volume of capital the bank shareholders need to raise, $k^*D + D_t - A_t$, is lower than the value of equity, S, after recapitalization.

More formally, let the indicator variable I_t represent whether the bank is open ($I_t = 1$) or closed ($I_t = 0$) at time t,

$$
(8) \qquad I_t = \begin{cases} 0 \text{ if } \prod_{s=0}^{t-1} I_s = 0 \\ 0 \text{ if } \prod_{s=0}^{t-1} I_s = 1 \text{ and } S < k^*D + D_t - A_t, \\ 1 \text{ if } \prod_{s=0}^{t-1} I_s = 1 \text{ and } S > k^*D + D_t - A_t \end{cases}
$$

with $I_0 = 1$.

17. Other authors consider this option. See Suarez (1994), Fries, Barral, and Perraudin (1997), and Pages and Santos (2003), among others.

18. A typical situation is when bank losses are covered by bank mergers and acquisitions. In our framework, it is the same if capital is replenished by old or new shareholders; the key point is that old shareholders do not lose 100 percent of the franchise value. Dewatripont and Tirole (1994) state that this closure policy is very common in the United States (73.8 percent).

Another rescue policy documented by Dewatripont and Tirole (1994) is the "open bank assistance" policy, also called "bail-out." In a bail-out the bank liquidates the defaulted assets, the government covers the shortfall to the depositors whose claims are in default, and the bank is not closed. This rescue policy is assimilable to our closure rule if shareholders still maintain a proportional claim on the bank franchise value. It is also assimilable to the government takeover when the bank is completely nationalized.

Dividend Policy and Capital Replenishment

With this new feature, the shareholder cash flow (a dividend, if positive, or equity issue amount, if negative) is

(9)
$$d_t = \begin{cases} A_t - D_t - k^*D \text{ if } S \geq D_t + k^*D - A_t \\ 0 \quad \text{otherwise.} \end{cases}$$

8.4.2 The Problem

The bank chooses its investment policy θ_t^*, (i.e., the percentage $w_{t+j\Delta t}^*$ invested in the risky asset at each time $t + j\Delta t$) and the level of capital after recapitalization, k^*. The value of equity is given by the present value of future dividends:

(10)
$$S_0 = \sum_{t=1}^{\infty} (1 + r)^{-t} E[d_t(\theta_t, k_t)]$$

The problem faced by the bank is to choose the policy (θ_t^*, k_t^*) that maximizes the value to shareholders, subject to equation (4), $k_t > \bar{k}$, and where dividends, d_t, are defined in equation (9).

This problem is time invariant for any audit time because, if the bank is solvent at audit time t, then, since the distribution of future dividends at $t + 1$ is identical for all t, the portfolio problem faced by the bank is also identical at each audit time when the bank is solvent. This means that the value of equity at time t, conditional on solvency, is given by[19]

(11) $$S_t = \begin{cases} \sum_{t+1}^{\infty}(1 + r)^{-(s-t)}E(d_s) = (1 + r)[E(d_{t+1}) + S_{t+1}] \text{ if } I_{t+1} = 1. \\ 0 \text{ of } I_{t+1} = 0 \end{cases}$$

This quantity is constant at each audit time when the bank is solvent and can be written as[20]

(12)
$$S(\theta^*, k^*) = \frac{E[d(\theta^*, k^*)]}{r + \pi(\theta^*, k^*)},$$

where $\pi(\theta^*, k^*)$ is the probability of default at the next audit. Thus, the value of equity is equal to the expected dividend divided by the sum of risk-free rate and the probability of default. In other words, the value of equity has a character of perpetuity where the discount rate is adjusted for default.[21]

---

19. Note that d_{t+1} and S_{t+1} are functions of the portfolio strategy, θ_t, and the level of capital, k_t, but, for sake of notational clarity, we suppress this dependence.
20. For details see Pelizzon and Schaefer (2003).
21. A similar relation obtained in a number of models of defaultable bonds (see Lando 1997 and Duffie and Singleton 1999).

The bank's portfolio and capital problem may also be defined as the maximization of the franchise value, defined as the difference between the value of equity and the amount of capital, k^*, provided by shareholders:

$$(13) \qquad F = S(\theta^*, k^*) - k^*D.$$

8.4.3 Welfare Function Variables

To evaluate the performance of Pillar 1 and Pillar 2 we need some measures of the welfare outcomes to which these rules give rise. In the absence of a formal welfare function, and as described earlier, we employ the following four measures: (1) the probability of bank closure, (2) the value of deposit insurance liabilities (PVDIL) as measures of the negative externalities of bank risk taking, (3) the average investment in risky assets and the capital utilization as, respectively, measures of bank activity, to reflect the positive externalities of bank lending, and (4) the private costs associated with high capital levels.

The first measure, the probability of bank closure, π, has already been described above. Using equations (9), (11), and (12), it is straightforward to show that the PVDIL of the bank can be written as

$$(14) \qquad \frac{E(\text{Put})}{r + \pi(\theta^*, k^*)} = \text{PVDIL},$$

where "Put" represents the payoff on a one-period option held by the bank on the deposit insurance scheme—that is,

$$(15) \qquad E_{t-1}(\text{Put}) = \int_0^{D_t - F} (D_t - A_t)f(A_t)dA_t \equiv E(\text{Put}).$$

The average investment in the risky asset, $\overline{Aw}$, is defined as

$$(16) \qquad \overline{Aw} = E_{\{\omega\}}\left[\frac{1}{n-1}\sum_{j=0}^{n-1} w^*_{t+j\Delta t}(\omega)A_{t+j\Delta t}(\omega)\right],$$

where the expectation of the term in square brackets is taken over paths for the asset value, $A_{t+j\Delta t}$, and portfolio proportion, $w^*_{t+j\Delta t}$, and where ω denotes the path.

Finally, the capital utilization is the optimal amount of capital that shareholders decide to provide at time zero and at each audit date—that is, k^*.

8.4.4 Bank's Optimal Policy

In this section we show that the disciplinary effect of the franchise value vanishes when closure rules allow costless recapitalization. The feedback effect of alternative closure policies on the incentives of bank owners to avoid financial distress warrants closer attention, a point emphasized by the wide range of such policies that regulators actually employ.[22] This result is summarized in the following lemma.

LEMMA 1: *When recapitalization is allowed (and F < D), the optimal policy for the bank is the riskiest policy, irrespective of the source of the franchise value.*

PROOF.

Assuming that the risky asset distribution is lognormal and constant portfolio proportion imply that

$$S = (1 + r)^{-1} \int_{D_t + kD - S}^{\infty} (A_t - D_t - kD - S) f(A_t) dA_t.$$

Clearly this is the value of a call option; increasing the investment in the risky asset the bank rises the volatility of the asset A_t and so the value of equity (i.e., the value of the call option).

Q.E.D.

This result (already proved by Suarez 1994 for the case with deposit rents only and Pelizzon 2001 for different sources of rents) is driven by the form of the payoffs associated with one-period decisions. Under the simple rule described earlier, when closure takes place when the asset value is lower than the threshold point represented by the deposit value, the payoff to shareholders at the time of an audit, when the bank continues, is given by the sum of the dividend cash flow, d (which is negative in the case of recapitalization) and the value of the equity in continuation, S. If, at the time of an audit, the bank is closed when $A_t < D_t$ the payoff to equityholders is zero. This is illustrated in figure 8.1.

In contrast, when recapitalization is allowed, even when the value of assets is below that of liabilities, shareholders' total payoff is given by the sum of value of equity S and the dividend cash flow d when the value of equity after recapitalization is higher than the amount of capital contributed ($S > A_t - D_t + k^*D$), and zero otherwise. Figure 8.2 shows the total payoff in this case.

Figures 8.1 with 8.2 differ for asset values between $D_t + k^*D - S$ and D_t. The nonconvexity of the total payoff as a function of the asset value in the first case explains shareholders' aversion to risk when F is sufficiently high.

---

22. See Dewatripont and Tirole (1994) for a comparison of rescue policies employed in the developed economies of the United States, Japan, and European Nordic countries. Legislation in general calls for increasingly strict sanctions against banks as their capital levels deteriorate (see, for example, the Prompt Corrective Action) but still permits some regulators discretion concerning the closure of banks. See also Gupta and Misra (1999) for a review of failure and failure resolution in the U.S. thrift and banking industries.

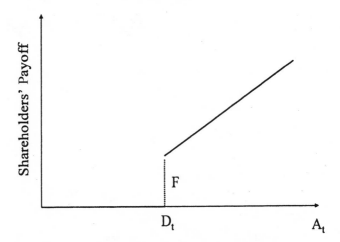

Fig. 8.1   Shareholders' payoff without the option to recapitalize

Note: This figure shows the shareholders' payoff at the next audit time under the threshold closure rule.

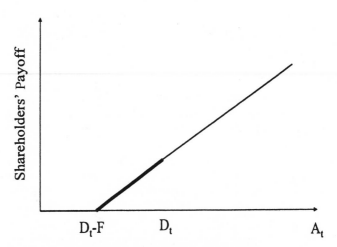

Fig. 8.2.   Shareholders' payoff *with* the option to recapitalize

Note: This figure shows the shareholders' payoff at the next audit time under the option to recapitalize closure rule and no costs of recapitalization.

Conversely, the convexity of the total payoff in the second case induces risk loving.

As Lemma 1 states, in the case of a convex payoff function, the optimal portfolio strategy for bank is always to invest entirely in the risky asset. The option to recapitalize in this case not only induces the bank to choose the most risky strategy but also affects the probability of default and the value of deposit insurance liabilities (Pelizzon 2001).

8.5 Costs of Recapitalization

Thus, the case of a convex payoff function analyzed by Suarez (1994) allows recapitalization but leads to the prediction that banks always seek to maximize risk. As a characterization of actual bank behavior this approach probably has limited descriptive power. As mentioned previously, the approach taken in earlier literature induced prudence on the part of banks, but only by expropriating the positive franchise value that insolvent banks ($A < D$) would have had if allowed to recapitalize.

In this paper we follow Suarez (1994) in allowing recapitalization for all values of A, but with a frictional cost, v. In this case equation (9) that defines the dividend becomes

$$
(17) \ d_t = \begin{cases} A_t - D_t - k^*D \text{ if } A_t \geq D_t + k^*D \\ (A_t - D_t - k^*D)(1 + v) \text{ if } S \geq D_t + k^*D - A_t \text{ and } A_t < D_t + k^*D \\ 0 \quad \text{otherwise.} \end{cases}
$$

The presence of these costs reintroduces concavity into the bank's payoff function and, depending on the parameters, this is sufficient to induce prudence on the part of the bank. Figure 8.3 shows the payoff to shareholders as a function of the asset value where the bank incurs a variable cost of replenishing the bank's capital[23] to a level k^*.

There is a second cost that banks incur when they recapitalize. This is a fixed cost, C, that is related to the Pillar 2/PCA intervention threshold $\hat{k}$ and, in this case, the formula defining the dividend is

$$
(18) \qquad d_t = \begin{cases} A_t - D_t - k^*D \text{ if } A_t \geq D_t + k^*D \\ (A_t - D_t - k^*D)(1 + v) - C \text{ if } S \geq D_t + k^*D - A_t \\ \text{and } A_t < D_t + k^*D \\ 0 \quad \text{otherwise.} \end{cases}
$$

Our interpretation of this cost is as an increase in the direct and indirect costs of compliance that come about as a result of the regulator increasing its intensity of monitoring. This may be viewed in terms of increased direct compliance costs, diversion of management time, restrictions on new business activities, and so on. This situation is illustrated in figure 8.4 where, for simplicity, we suppress the variable cost of recapitalization that was illustrated in figure 8.3.

23. Our model does not explain why equity is relatively expensive. This can be because of tax rules, agency costs of equity, and in the case of banks, a comparative advantage in the collection of deposit funds (Taggart and Greenbaum 1978). For other motivations of expensive bank costs of capital see Boot (2001).

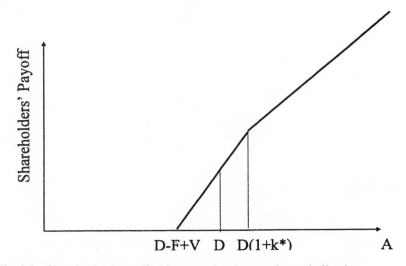

Fig. 8.3   Shareholders' payoff with proportional costs of recapitalization

Note: This figure shows the shareholders' payoff at the next audit time under the option to re-capitalize closure rule and proportional costs of recapitalization.

Note that in our analysis the impact of the threshold $\hat{k}$ on the shareholders' payoff comes entirely from the cost imposed on the bank rather than the specifics of the action taken by the regulator (inspections, detailed auditing, etc.).

The shape of this objective function is almost identical to the one presented in Pelizzon and Schaefer (2003) and provides the bank with an incentive to manage its portfolio dynamically. The optimal strategy is characterized by a U-shaped relation between the amount invested in the risky asset and the value of bank assets. This relation has a strong discontinuity. When the bank is solvent it follows a portfolio insurance strategy, which means that the amount invested in the risky asset falls toward zero as the bank's net worth falls to zero. However, when the bank becomes insolvent by even a small amount the amount invested in the risky asset jumps to the maximum possible.

As shown in Pelizzon and Schaefer (2003), this strategy has a strong effect on the distribution of the bank's asset value at an audit time. Moreover, as shown in Pelizzon and Schaefer (2003), under risk management the one-to-one relation between π and PVDIL is no longer guaranteed. Indeed, with portfolio revision the asset risk is, in some states, lower than the maximum, and so the average risk is also lower. We might expect, therefore, that both π and PVDIL would be lower in the latter case. In fact, while the probability of default is indeed lower, the PVDIL is higher. This occurs because the shape of the distribution in these two cases is different. The rents

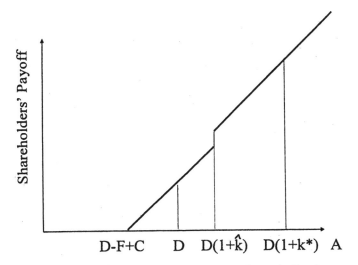

Fig. 8.4   Shareholders' payoff with fix costs of recapitalization

Note: This figure shows the shareholders' payoff at the next audit time under the option to recapitalize closure rule and Pillar 2/PCA fixed costs of recapitalization.

earned by the bank are generated by exploiting the deposit insurance and so, to exploit this source of rents to the maximum, the bank uses risk management to increase the expected loss in those cases where the bank does default, while simultaneously increasing the probability of survival and therefore the length of time the shareholders expect to receive dividends before closure.

A consequence of our analysis is that the value of deposit insurance is different when banks have the ability to engage in risk management. Ignoring this feature is likely to lead to an understatement of the cost of deposit insurance and unreliable conclusions about the consequences of bank capital regulation. These two points are central to the analysis performed in the remainder of this paper.

8.6   Risk-Based Capital Requirements (Pillar 1)

Under the 1988 Accord a bank's required capital was a linear function of the amount invested in risky assets. More recent rules rely on the VaR (value-at-risk) framework. In our model there is only one risky asset and therefore, under both the 1988 Accord and the Basel II (i.e., the VaR rule), required capital depends only on w_j, the fraction of assets invested in the risky asset.

We assume a risk-based capital rule in which the required level of capital is proportional to the amount invested in the risky asset:

$$(19) \qquad k_R = \lambda w_j \frac{A_j}{D_j},$$

where k_R is the required amount of capital expressed as a percentage of deposits and λ is the required capital per unit of investment in the risky asset. In the case with constant portfolio positions and normally distributed asset values, for example, λ is the product of (1) the number of standard deviations defining the confidence level, (2) the volatility of the rate of return on risky assets, and (3) a scaling factor.

Under this rule, which we apply in the paper, the bank's investment in the risky asset at each portfolio revision date, w_j, is constrained according to

$$(20) \qquad w_j \leq k_j \frac{D_j}{A_j} \frac{1}{\lambda} \equiv \overline{w}\left(k_j, \frac{D_j}{A_j}, \lambda\right),$$

where $\overline{w}$ represents the maximum permissible investment in the risky asset for a given ratio of deposits to assets and to a percentage of capital k_j, defined as

$$(21) \qquad k_j = \frac{A_j - D(1 + r)^{1/n}}{D}.$$

One of the main objectives of our paper is to analyze the effects of capital regulation on bank risk taking. However, our analysis to this point assumes an environment that is entirely unregulated except for the periodic audits when, if the percentage of capital is lower than $\overline{k}$, the bank must either recapitalize or is closed. Between audits, however, we have assumed that the bank has complete freedom to choose the risk of its portfolio, even if insolvent.

In practice, banks are required to observe capital requirements continuously through time and face censure or worse, if they are discovered, even ex post, to have violated the rules. However, if (1) asset prices are continuous, (2) capital rules are applied continuously through time, and (3) capital rules force banks to eliminate risk from their portfolio when their capital falls below a given (nonnegative) level, a bank's probability of default becomes zero.[24]

With continuous portfolio revision the only way to avoid this unrealistic conclusion is to assume—perhaps not unrealistically—that banks are able to continue to operate, and to invest in risky assets, even when in violation of either, or both, the leverage constraint ($\overline{k}$) and the risk-based capital requirements (RBCR). Without some assumption of this kind the analysis of the effect of capital requirements in a dynamic context is without content. However, in order to say something about the effects of capital require-

---

24. As mentioned earlier, in this setting, the relevant assumption is the absence of jumps in the value of the entire portfolio, a much less stringent constraint than the absence of jumps for any single claim in the portfolio.

ments in this case, we must also say something about the extent to which banks are able to deviate from regulatory constraints on leverage and exposure to risky assets. In other words, we have to make assumptions about the extent to which banks are able to cheat.

We consider two different levels of cheating:

1. Extensive Cheating (Ext-Cheat). Here, capital requirements are binding only when there is an audit; at all other times the bank faces no constraints on its portfolio. Moreover, irrespective of its portfolio composition prior to audit, any solvent bank may reorganize its portfolio to meet capital requirements but is then constrained to hold this portfolio up to the next portfolio revision date. In all other periods the portfolio is unconstrained, so the bank satisfies the RBCR audit simply by window dressing its portfolio for the audit date. In this highly ineffective capital-requirements regime, a regulator is able to monitor and control the activities of banks only at the time of an audit.

$$(22) \qquad 0 < w_t \le k \frac{D}{A} \frac{1}{\lambda} \text{ and } 0 < w_{t+j\Delta t} \le 1$$

2. Limited Cheating (Lim-Cheat). Between two audit dates, the maximum exposure of the bank to the risky asset is the greater of (1) the level determined by its capital at the earlier audit date and (2) the exposure based on its actual capital at the time. Here, the capital requirements regime is much more effective than under the Ext-Cheat rule. Its main deficiency is that banks are able to conceal any decrease in capital from the level observed by the regulator at the previous audit date and are therefore able to invest in the risky asset up to an amount determined either by this amount or their actual capital, whichever is higher.

$$(23) \qquad w_j \le \max \left(k_j \frac{D_j}{A_j} \frac{1}{\lambda}; k \frac{D}{A} \frac{1}{\lambda} \right) \equiv \overline{w}_m$$

Two points are worth noting here. First, these rules are different only when banks are able to engage in risk management, since otherwise banks choose their portfolios only on the audit date, when, under both regimes, they comply with capital requirements. Second, since in our model a bank is always able to liquidate its holding of risky assets and invest the proceeds in the riskless asset (at which point the risk-based required capital is zero), a bank will never be closed as a result of a violation of RBCR.

8.6.1   Effect of RBCR on Welfare Function Variables

We now ask how changes in risk-based capital requirements affect risk taking when banks are able to engage in risk management and when capital requirements are imperfectly enforced.

In our model at each audit date the bank chooses its level of capital, taking into account the constraints that RBCR place on its decisions. The endogeneity of the bank's capital decision, together with the opportunity for insolvent banks to recapitalize,[25] are critical determinants of behavior and differentiate our approach from much of the previous literature on RBCR (see Rochet 1992, Marshal and Venkatarman 1999, and Dangl and Lehar 2004).

The four panels of figure 8.5 show the effect of changing λ, the required capital per unit of investment in the risky asset, on the four welfare function variables: the bank's choice of capital, k^*, the PVDIL, the probability of default, π, and the average investment in the risky asset, Aw.

In our model and under both compliance regimes, a bank must be compliant with RBCR at the time of an audit. It is important to stress that the capital decision of the bank at this time is made jointly with its dynamic portfolio policy. Thus the capital decision will take into account the opportunity that the bank will have to invest in the risky asset both (1) at the audit date and (2) between audit dates, where the latter depends on the compliance regime.

Panel A shows the level of capital, k^*, under Lim-Cheat (dotted line) and Ext-Cheat (solid line). With limited cheating, the banks' choice of capital, k^*, increases monotonically with the value of λ. In this case, the initial capital decision establishes a lower bound on the maximum exposure to the risky asset up to the next audit date. For the parameters used in our calculations (see fig. 8.5), it is optimal for the bank to hold an amount of capital, approximately[26] equal to λ, that allows it to hold the maximum amount of the risky asset. This result is robust for quite a wide range of parameter values. The only parameter that has a significant effect on the result is the proportional cost of recapitalization, v, and when this is high it leads the shareholders to decide initially not to open the bank rather than to hold a lower level of capital.

With extensive cheating, the capital decision is different. When λ is below a value of approximately 4 percent, that is, when RBCR are relatively unburdensome, it is again optimal for the bank to comply.

This occurs because our example considers only a limited number of

---

25. Surprisedly, little research on banking either the level of capital or the franchise value as endogenous, and little research takes into account either the dynamic risk management or the options to recapitalize or close. An analysis of endogenous capital closely related to our own is Froot and Stein (1998). They assume convex costs of capital issue and examine the implications for bank risk management, capital structure, and capital budgeting. But they do not allow for bank regulation or deposit insurance and, since theirs is a static model, they are unable to explore the potential implications of an endogenous franchise value. Another is Milne and Whalley (2001), but they do not consider risk-based capital requirements.

26. The relationship between λ and k^* is not one-to-one, because the former is the required capital per unit invested in the risky asset and the latter is the amount of capital expressed as a fraction of deposits. If 100 percent of the assets is invested in risky assets, the relation between the two is: $k = \lambda/(1-\lambda)$.

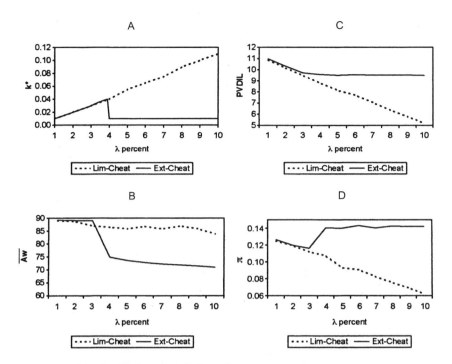

Fig. 8.5   Pillar 1–risk-based capital requirements

Notes: The figure plots the effect of changing the required capital per unit of investment in the risky asset λ on the four welfare function variables: capital utilization k^*, Present Value of Deposit Insurance Liabilities (PVDIL), probability of default π, and the average investment in risky asset $\overline{Aw}$. The parameters used are: $D = 100$, $\hat{k} = 1$ percent, $n = 4$, $r = 5$ percent, $\sigma = 10$ percent, $\upsilon = 5$ percent.

portfolio revision opportunities between audit dates and, in order to invest as much as possible in the risky asset on the audit date (when the bank must comply), the bank chooses a high level of capital. Clearly, if the frequency of portfolio revision were higher (or if recapitalization costs were high), the bank would reduce its level of initial capital.

When λ is above 4 percent, the bank's optimal strategy changes and it now chooses a low level of capital and a lower investment in the risky asset on the audit date. At first sight the result that an *increase* in capital requirements results in *both* lower levels of capital *and* less investment in the risky asset may be surprising. We might expect that increasing capital requirements would lead *either* to higher levels of capital and a maintained level of investment in the risky asset *or* a maintained level of capital and a lower investment in the risky asset.

This counterintuitive result comes about for the following reason. The amount of capital, k, affects the franchise value through the value of the deposit insurance put, the probability of default, and the expected cost of recapitalization. Increasing k allows the bank to increase its holding of the risky asset but also increases the "strike" of the deposit insurance put and, for this reason, an increase in k may either increase or decrease the value of the deposit insurance put, the probability of default, and the expected cost of recapitalization. Therefore, the effect of increasing k on the franchise value may be either positive or negative.

In our example, increasing k leads to increases in the franchise value for values of λ below around 4 percent but decreases for values above this level. The threshold level where the bank's policy changes—around 4 percent in this case—is strongly related to the volatility of the risky asset, the frequency of portfolio revision, and the cost of recapitalization.

The effect of changing the capital requirements parameter λ, on the other three welfare variables can be easily understood in terms of its effect on k^*.

With Lim-cheat, because (as the regulator would hope), higher RBCR induce the bank to increase capital, the average investment in the risky asset $(\overline{Aw})$ remains almost unchanged, the PVDIL and the probability of default decreases monotonically with λ (as shown in panels B, C, and D). In this case, we also find that the average investment in the risky asset is little affected by changes in λ.

With Ext-cheat, the results follow those for k^* and fall into two regimes. For low values of λ they mirror those for the Lim-cheat case since, in this case, the bank chooses to comply. For higher values of λ, however, the bank chooses a low level of capital. In this case, the average investment in the risky asset first decreases and then remains unaffected by λ. Because both PVDIL and the probability of default are insensitive to increases in λ, RBCR in this case remain ineffective.

Our results emphasize that allowing for the behavioral response on the part of banks in terms of capital and portfolio management is critical to a proper evaluation of the effects of changes in regulation (λ). In the QIS carried out by the Basel Committee, the behavioral response was ignored. Our results also show that the behavioral response itself depends on the way the formal rules actually work in practice; that is, the scope they give for banks to cheat.

8.7   Pillar 1 and Pillar 2 (PCA)

The results on RBCR in the previous section are presented to provide a benchmark against which to assess the role of Pillar 2/PCA when applied in conjunction with Pillar 1. We investigate this issue for the two cheating regimes described and analyzed earlier.

Recall that, in our framework, Pillar 2/PCA acts as a minimum capital requirement ($\hat{k}$) at the time of an audit, where $\hat{k} > \overline{k}$—that is, Pillar 2/PCA maximum leverage is a more binding constraint on capital than the simple solvency constraint $\bar{k}$. Because it is independent of the composition of the bank's portfolio it therefore acts simply as a constraint on leverage. If a bank violates the Pillar 2/PCA constraint[27] at audit and chooses to recapitalize, it incurs a fixed cost, C, in addition to the variable cost, v, described earlier. In our calculations, $\hat{k}$, the maximum capital level, is set at 4 percent.

Figure 8.6 shows the effect on the four output variables from changing the required capital per unit of risky asset, λ, when Pillar 2/PCA is applied in conjunction with RBCR.

When the level of compliance with RBCR is good (Lim-cheat)—see panels A–D—Pillar 2/PCA has relatively little effect. For values of λ above the threshold level $\hat{k}$ the value of k^* is driven by RBCR and is effectively unchanged from the result with Pillar 1 alone. The same applies to PVDIL and the average investment in the risky asset. The frequency of default, however, increases, because the fixed cost of recapitalization means that banks will more often choose to close rather than recapitalize. Therefore, when the level of compliance with RBCR is good, Pillar 2/PCA may actually reduce welfare when it increases both banks' costs (recapitalization) and the probability of default.

For values of λ below the threshold level $\hat{k}$ the latter becomes the effective minimum value of k^*. This is because when λ is below $\hat{k}$, and even if the bank were to invest entirely in the risky asset, its required capital under RBCR would be lower than $\hat{k}$. This is reflected in the behavior of k^* (panel A), PVDIL (panel B) and π (panel C) of figure 8.6.

However, Pillar 2/PCA plays a potentially important role when compliance with RBCR is poor (Ext-cheat). However, as we show, in this case it acts more as a substitute for, rather than a complement to RBCR.

The solid line in panel E of figure 8.6 shows the value of k^* under RBCR from the earlier analysis. The minimum value of capital under Pillar 2/PCA is $\hat{k}$ and the dotted line in panel E shows that, in our example, this is also the value of k^* for all values of λ.[28]

Panel (E) shows that Pillar 2/PCA is successful in increasing the level of

27. The prompt corrective action scheme has been in effect in the United States since the passage in 1991 of the Federal Deposit Insurance Improvement Act. The scheme defines a series of trigger points based on a bank's capitalization and a set of mandatory actions for supervisors to implement at each point. The series of actions that FDIC must implement is detailed in the Risk Management Manual of Examination Policies. If a trigger point is violated the first action given in the manual is to require the bank to propose a capital restoration plan. Our closure rule is designed to conform to the spirit of this requirement.

28. Two points related to $\hat{k}$ in panel (E) of figure 8.6 should be noted. First, in our example, the threshold level of around 4 percent for λ that induced a shift in portfolio composition under RBCR happens in this case to be close to the value we have chosen for $\hat{k}$. This means that in panel E of figure 8.6 the two lines coincide for a value of λ close to 4 percent. Second, for values of $\hat{k}$ that are sufficiently low so that it is not a binding constraint for all values of λ, the value of k^* may differ from the value obtained with Pillar 1 alone. The reason is that, although for some value of λ, $\hat{k}$ may not be a currently binding constraint, the fact that it may be a binding constraint in some future state of the world may induce a different capital decision now.

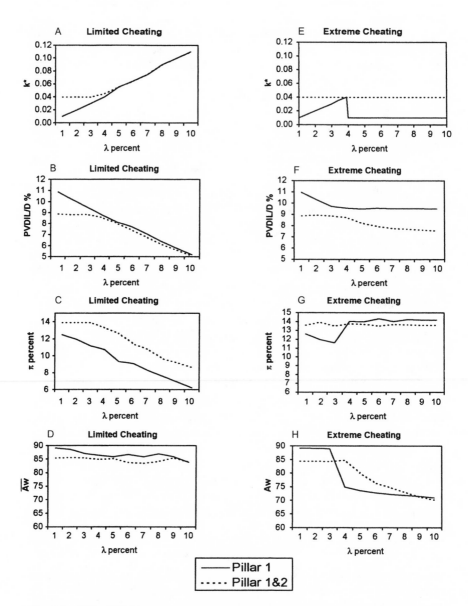

Fig. 8.6   Pillar 2/PCA

Notes: Under Pillar 2/PCA, the figure plots the effect of changing the required capital per unit of investment in the risky asset λ on the four output variables: capital utilization k^*, Present Value of Deposit Insurance Liabilities (PVDIL), probability of default π, and the average investment in risky asset $\overline{Aw}$. The parameters used are: $D = 100$, $\hat{k} = 4$ percent, $n = 4$, $r = 5$ percent, $\sigma = 10$ percent, $\upsilon = 5$ percent, $C = 1$.

capital that banks hold: in our example, k^* is higher for all value of λ except 4 percent, where it is the same. However, as panel E also shows, with poor compliance Pillar 2/PCA does not succeed in reestablishing the link between actual bank capital and RBCR. In other words, it does not correct the ineffectiveness of RBCR that a poor compliance regime produces. Panel E shows that the amount of capital that the bank holds is the same when $\lambda = 10$ percent as it is when $\lambda = 1$ percent, even though the average risky asset holding in the two cases differs by only about 20 percent. Thus Pillar 2/PCA does not complement RBCR in the sense of increasing the sensitivity of bank capital to λ.

Panel F of figure 8.6 shows that Pillar 2/PCA does indeed reduce the PVDIL but, as with the level of capital, does so in a way that is almost independent of λ. Comparing panels F and G shows that this reduction in PVDIL is not brought about by a reduction in the frequency of default (π), but as a result of the higher level of capital that banks hold. This reduces the average liability of the deposit insurer compared with the case without Pillar 2. As just mentioned, panel G shows that there is little effect on the probability of default (except for low values of λ) even though capital levels are higher; this is a result of the fixed cost of recapitalization that leads banks to default more often. For low values of λ, particularly for values just lower than the threshold value of 4 percent, banks hold more capital than without Pillar 2/PCA and, again as a result of the fixed cost of recapitalization, now default more often.

Finally, panel H shows that because it forces banks to hold more capital, for λ greater than around 4 percent. Pillar 2/PCA allows them to increase the amount they hold in the risky asset. For low values of λ the risky-asset holding is actually lower, because the higher threshold level for recapitalization under Pillar 2/PCA means that when asset prices fall the bank reduces its holding in the risky asset (i.e., initiates a portfolio insurance policy) sooner.

8.8 Conclusion

This paper investigates the interaction between Pillar 1 (risk-based capital requirements) and Pillar 2/PCA and, in particular, the role of closure rules with costly recapitalization and where banks are able to manage their portfolios dynamically.

In our analysis we make the perhaps extreme assumption that the only source of rents in the banking system is deposit insurance. In a static setting, we know from Merton's (1977) model that banks will choose the portfolio with the maximum risk. However, in a multiperiod setting, taking into account the possibility of costly recapitalization, banks have an incentive to manage their portfolios dynamically. As a consequence, the cost of deposit insurance is affected by the cost of recapitalization and its effect on banks' incentive to engage in risk management. In particular, the presence of costs of recapitalization reduce the cost of deposit insurance but increase the probability of default.

A feature of our approach is to consider the costs as well as the benefits of capital regulation and to do so in a way that accommodates the behavioral response of banks in terms of their portfolio strategy and capital structure decisions and, further, the extent to which capital rules are effective—that is, the extent to which banks can cheat.

We measure the effects of capital regulation, for both Pillars 1 and 2, in terms of four output variables that we use as proxies for the costs and benefits—both private and social—of capital regulation.

Without cheating, the problem of bank capital adequacy is relatively minor and is related largely to discontinuity in asset prices, which would lead to difficulties in implementing a stopping policy. However, the regulator faces a much more difficult problem when banks are able to deviate significantly from capital adequacy. Thus, the extent of banks' ability to cheat is fundamental to the analysis of capital requirements. For this reason in our analysis we consider two cases, one with extensive cheating and the other with only limited cheating.

Our results fall into two parts. First, in order to establish a benchmark for assessing the effect of Pillar 2/PCA, we analyze the effect of RBCR in our model with imperfect compliance but without Pillar 2/PCA intervention. In the second part, we introduce Pillar 2/PCA.

Without Pillar 2/PCA, we find that even when banks' compliance is relatively good (limited cheating) RBCR may nonetheless be effective in the sense that, for higher levels of RBCR, banks do indeed hold higher amounts of capital. As result, (1) the PVDIL is lower and (2) the probability of default is also lower. Moreover, we also find that in this case, an increase in RBCR does not reduce the volume of risky assets that a bank is willing to hold (and therefore there does not appear to be a significant negative externality from reduced bank activity).

However, when compliance is poor (extensive cheating), RBCR are ineffective in the sense that for higher levels of RBCR banks do not increase their volume of capital. Consequently, increasing RBCR decreases neither (1) the PVDIL nor (2) the probability of default. Moreover, we find that, in this case, the volume of risky assets held by banks decreases the RBCR increase because banks choose to increase their leverage rather than hold higher volumes of both capital and risky assets.

The degree of compliance with RBCR is similarly crucial in assessing the role of Pillar 2/PCA. If banks were to comply with RBCR continuously Pillar 2/PCA would be redundant. Only where there is the possibility of at least some noncompliance does this type of intervention have a potential role.

We investigate this issue for the two cheating regimes considered in the paper. With limited cheat Pillar 2/PCA has little effect on the level of capital that banks choose, the PVDIL or the average investment in the risky asset. The frequency of default, however, increases. The potential role that PVCA/Pillar 2 may play is as a complement to RBCR, not as a substitute. When the level of compliance with RBCR is good, Pillar 2/PCA may actually reduce welfare because it increases both banks' costs (recapitalization) and the probability of default.

However, Pillar 2/PCA plays a potentially important role with extensive cheating, although the results are complex. Introducing Pillar 2/PCA increases the amount of capital that banks hold but does not result in a more effective RBCR regime in the sense that, even with Pillar 2/PCA, increasing RBCR does not result in higher levels of capital. The same result applies to the probability of default, the PVDIL, and the average investment in the risky asset. Introducing Pillar 2/PCA lowers PVDIL but, as before, increasing RBCR does not further strongly reduce PVDIL. For the probability of default the results are mixed but, once again, introducing Pillar 2/PCA does not make the probability of default sensitive to the level of RBCR. The results on the average investment in the risky asset are similarly mixed, but the striking result is that, for higher levels of RBCR, the bank's investment in the risky asset decreases. In general, when extensive cheating is possible, Pillar 2/PCA does not complement RBCR in the sense of making them more effective; rather, they act as a separate, substitute form of regulatory control.

Because we find that Pillar 2/PCA is most effective in reducing the cost of deposit insurance when compliance is relatively poor, we might infer from the fact that (1) in the United States, the FDIC has chosen to introduce PCA after Basel I and (2) the Basel Committee has included Pillar 2, that all these regulators perceive the degree of compliance—for at least some banks—to be relatively poor.

In making this observation it is important to bear in mind that our analysis suggests that, when the level of compliance is high, there may be few benefits to offset the costs of Pillar 2/PCA (the frictional costs of recapitalization).

Both these points suggest that future work in the area of RBCR should pay more attention to compliance rather than simply the design of the rules.

References

Allen, F., and D. Gale. 2003. Capital adequacy regulation: In search of a rationale. In *Economic for an imperfect world: Essays in honor of Joseph Stiglitz,* ed. R. Arnott, B. Greenwald, R. Kanbur, and B. Nalebuff, 83–109. Cambridge, MA: MIT Press.

Bank for International Settlements. Press release. "G10 central bank governors and heads of supervision endorse the publication of the revised capital framework." June 26, 2004. Available at: http://www.bis.org/press/p040626.htm.

Basel Committee. 1988. *International convergence of capital measurement and capital standards.* Basel, Switzerland: Bank for International Settlements.

———. 1999. A new capital adequacy framework. Consultative paper. Basel, Switzerland: Bank for International Settlements.

———. 2001. *The new Basel accord: Consultative package.* Basel, Switzerland: Bank for International Settlements.

———. 2003. *The new Basel capital accord: Consultative package.* Basel, Switzerland: Bank for International Settlements.

———. 2005. *Basel II: International convergence of capital measurement and capital standards: A revised framework.* Basel, Switzerland: Bank for International Settlements.

Benston, G. L., & G. G. Kaufman. 1996. The approximate role of bank regulation. *Economic Journal* 106:688–97.

Berlin, M., A. Saunders, and G. Udell. 1991. Deposit insurance reform: What are the issues and what needs to be fixed? *Journal of Banking and Finance* 15:735–52.

Boot, A. 2001. Regulation and banks' incentives to control risk. *Sveriges Riksbank Economic Review* 2:14–24.

Boot, A., and A. Thakor. 1991. Off-balance sheet liabilities, deposit insurance and capital regulation. *Journal of Banking and Finance* 15:825–46.

Buser, S. A., A. H. Chen, and E. J. Kane. 1981. Federal deposit insurance, regulatory policy, and optimal bank capital. *Journal of Finance* 35:51–60.

Campbell, T. S., Y. S. Chan, and A. M. Marino. 1992. An incentive-based theory of bank regulation. *Journal of Financial Intermediation* 2:255–76.

Chan, Y. S., S. I. Greenbaum, and A. V. Thakor. 1992. Is fairly priced deposit insurance possible? *Journal of Finance* 47:227–45.

Dangl, T., and A. Lehar. 2004. Value-at-risk vs. building block regulation in banking. *Journal of Financial Intermediation* 13:96–131.

Descamps, J., J. Rochet, and B. Roger. 2003. The 3 Pillars of Basel II: Optimizing the mix. *Journal of Financial Intermediation* 13:132–44.

Dewatripont, M., and J. Tirole. 1994. *The prudential regulation of banks.* Cambridge, MA: MIT Press.

Diamond, D. W., and P. H. Dybvig. 1986. Banking theory, deposit insurance, and bank regulation. *Journal of Business* 59:53–68.

Duffie, D., and K. J. Singleton. 1999. Modelling term structures of defaultable bonds. *Review of Financial Studies* (12) 4: 687–720.

Fries, S., P. M. Barral, and W. Perraudin. 1997. Optimal bank reorganization and the fair pricing of deposit guarantees. *Journal of Banking and Finance* 21:441–68.

Froot, K., and J. Stein. 1998. Risk management, capital budgeting and capital structure policy for financial institutions: An integrated approach. *Journal of Financial Economics* 47:55–82.

Genotte, G., and D. Pyle. 1991. Capital controls and bank risk. *Journal of Banking and Finance* 15:805–24.

Goodhart, C., P. Hartmann, D. Llewellyn, L. Rojas-Suarez, and S. Weisbrod. 1998. *Financial regulation: Why, how, and where now?* New York: Routledge.

Gupta, A., and L. Misra. 1999. Failure and failure resolution in the US thrift and banking industries. *Financial Management* 28 (4): 87–105.

Hauswald, R. B., and L. W. Senbet. 1999. Public and private agency conflict in banking regulation. Kelley School of Business, Indiana University. Mimeograph.

Hellman, T., K. Murdock, and J. Stiglitz. 2000. Liberalization, moral hazard in banking, and prudential regulation: Are capital requirements enough? *American Economic Review* (March): 147–65.

Jones, D. 2000. Emerging problems with the Basel Capital Accord: Regulatory capital arbitrage and related issues. *Journal of Banking and Finance* 24:35–58.

Kane, E. J. 1990. Principal-agent problems in SL salvage. *Journal of Finance* 45 (3): 755–64.

Keeley, M. 1990. Deposit insurance, risk and market power in banking. *The American Economic Review* (December): 1183–1200.

Lando, D. 1997. Modelling bonds and derivatives with default risk. In *Mathematics of derivatives securities,* ed. M. Demptster and S. Pliska, 369–93. Cambridge: Cambridge University Press.

Marcus, A. 1984. Deregulation and bank financial policy. *Journal of Banking and Finance* 8:557–65.

Marshall, D., and S. Venkataraman. 1999. Bank capital standards for market risk: A welfare analysis. *European Finance Review* 2:125–57.

Merton, R. 1997. An analytic derivation of the cost of deposit insurance and loan guarantees. *Journal of Banking and Finance* 1:3–11.

Milne, A., and Whalley, E. 2001. Bank capital and incentives for risk taking. Unpublished manuscript. London: City University Business School.

Pages, H., and J. Santos. 2003. Optimal supervisory policies and depositor-preference laws. BIS Working Paper no. 131. Basel, Switzerland: Bank for International Settlements.

Pelizzon, L. 2001. Franchise value in a model of bank portfolio management. London Business School. www.ssrn.com. Mimeograph.

Pelizzon, L., and S. Schaefer. 2003. Do bank risk management and capital requirements reduce risk in banking? IFA Working Paper no. 381.

Rochet, J. 1992. Capital requirements and the behavior of commercial banks. *European Economic Review* 36:1137–78.

Saidenberg, M., and T. Schuermann. 2003. The new Basel Capital Accord and questions for research. Wharton FIC 03-14.

Suarez, J. 1994. Closure rules, market power and risk-taking in a dynamic model of bank behavior. LSE Discussion Paper no. 196. London: London School of Economics.

Suarez, J., and R. Repullo. 2004. Loan pricing under Basel capital requirements. *Journal of Financial Intermediation* 13:496–521.

Taggart, R., and S. Greenbaum. 1978. Bank capital and public regulation. *Journal of Money Credit and Banking* 10:158–69.

VonThadden, E. 2004. Bank capital adequacy regulation under the new Basel Accord. *Journal of Financial Intermediation* 13 (2): 90–95.

Comment   Marc Saidenberg

Pelizzon and Schaefer's paper takes another step in their research program, which examines the implications for regulation of bank portfolio choice in a dynamic setting. The current paper examines the effects of capital requirements under various assumptions about regulators' ability to detect and punish undercapitalization. Some of the paper's ideas have been in the academic literature for many years. For example, the idea that capital re-

The views expressed in this article are those of the author and do not necessarily reflect the position of Merrill Lynch & Co., of the Federal Reserve Bank of New York, or the Federal Reserves System.

quirements, regulators' bank closure practices, and deposit insurance pricing are intimately related, with any one of them serving as a sufficient restraint on bank risk taking in simple setups, has been around at least since the early 1990s (for example, Acharya and Dreyfus 1989, Davies and McManus 1991, and Levonian 1991 analyzed closure rules). Pelizzaon and Schaeffer's result, that capital requirements might increase bank risk-taking as well as reduce it, was a result in Koehn and Santomero (1980) as well. Another example of a precursor is Ritchken, Thomson, DeGennaro, and Li (1995), which presents a dynamic model in which banks' ability to alter their risk postures between regulatory audits leads to a richer description of risk taking than in one-period models.[1]

Pelizzon and Schaefer's work represents an important contribution because it brings together many ideas about an important subject in a nice modeling framework. In the richest version of their model, banks choose their risk posture not only at the time regulators examine solvency, but also at points in between such audits (so the regulatory closure rule is not perfectly effective at maintaining solvency). Importantly, banks can completely change their risk posture, without transaction costs, from one moment to the next. Banks face two kinds of capital requirements: a simple leverage ratio and a risk-based capital requirement. The risk-based measure is a perfect indicator of risk posture, and the regulator can observe compliance perfectly at the time of an audit. However, the regulator can observe compliance in between audits imperfectly or not at all. Another important innovation of the setup is that a bank in violation of capital requirements has a (costly) right to recapitalize. Deposit insurance is flat rate and serves only to make the depositors insensitive to risk; that is, the implications of risk-sensitive deposit insurance in combination with rich closure rules and capital requirements are not analyzed, which is a reasonable simplification. The model is nice because many things of interest are endogenous: bank risk posture, capital level, dividend payouts, and the bank's decision whether to recapitalize.

Some of the terminology is a bit different than that used in many other papers. "Risk management" means the bank is able to change its risk posture between audits. In other papers and in the practitioner community, the phrase often refers to the systems and activities that help financial institutions (and other firms) measure, optimize, and control their risk posture. Banks have long been able to change their risk postures in between the annual (or less frequent) examinations that are common in the United States, but modern quantitative risk management systems are a relatively recent innovation.

In Pelizzon and Schaefer's model, "Pillar 2" is the existence of a leverage

---

1. Berger, Herring, and Szegö's (1995) survey on capital, and Berlin, Saunders, and Udell's (1991) survey on deposit insurance include many references to other related papers.

ratio capital requirement (alongside a risk-based capital requirement), with violations of the leverage requirement leading to seizure by regulators in the event the bank does not recapitalize, or increased regulatory costs if it does recapitalize. In common parlance, "Pillar 2" is a term introduced by the Basel Committee on Banking Supervision, and refers to a broad array of regulatory responsibilities and actions.

Although the paper's formal definition of Pillar 2 is narrow, the title of the paper is apt, because the paper's most interesting results flow from varying the assumption about the effectiveness of regulatory monitoring of capital adequacy, and Pillar 2 is all about the effectiveness of regulatory monitoring. As the minimum required capital ratio varies, so do average levels of bank capital, the value of the deposit insurance put option, bank failure rates, and loan volume, but the behavior of such variables of interest is much different when regulatory monitoring is effective than when it is not. Behavior is also different with a leverage ratio capital requirement and a risk-based capital requirement than with a risk-based capital requirement alone.

In drawing conclusions about the efficacy of "Pillar 2," the authors choose to emphasize differences in outcomes between the with-leverage-ratio and no-leverage-ratio cases, whereas I prefer to focus on differences when regulatory enforcement of capital requirements is less versus more effective. The authors emphasize that "Pillar 2" should be applied with care, because imposition of leverage-ratio capital requirements on top of relatively effectively enforced risk-based capital requirements can be undesirable (bank failure rates increase, and risk taking that perhaps is socially desirable by banks decreases). I prefer to emphasize their finding that good enforcement of capital requirements is better than weak enforcement. Pretty much regardless of whether a leverage-ratio capital requirement is imposed or not, variables of interest behave sensibly (and, in my opinion, desirably) as the risk-based capital requirement is varied when enforcement is good. When enforcement is weak, varying capital requirements often has little effect on outcomes and sometimes has perverse effects. That is, Pelizzon and Schaefer's results imply that Pillar 2 in the Basel Committee's meaning of the term is a good thing.[2]

The subtitle of the Pillar 2 section of the new Basel Accord is "supervisory review process." I can offer a practicing supervisor's perspective of how supervisory review is related to formal capital regulation at very large

---

2. I prefer to emphasize the enforcement results in part because, in Pelizzon and Schaefer's setup, a bank can costlessly remedy violations of risk-based capital requirements, whereas leverage-ratio violations must be fixed by costly recapitalizations. I suspect the difference in costs is at least in part responsible for the apparently undesirable effects of leverage-ratio requirements on bank failure rates and investment policies. Moreover, leverage ratios and associated PCA mechanisms are present only in a subset of nations, most notably the United States, whereas some form if Pillar 2 (whether weak or strong) is widespread.

banks. Although supervisory reviews are concerned with many things other than capital adequacy, I will focus only on capital. And I emphasize again that these are my views, not those of the Federal Reserve, and that I focus on large banks.

A paraphrasing of the four principles that appear in the Accord's Pillar 2 section is helpful.

- Each bank should assess internal capital adequacy in light of its risk profile.
- Supervisors should review internal assessments and take action as appropriate.
- Banks should hold capital above regulatory minimums.
- Supervisors should intervene at an early stage to prevent capital from falling below levels appropriate to the risk characteristics of the bank.

Notice that regulatory minimums are mentioned only once, and then with the implication that de facto minimums flowing from banks' internal assessments should usually be the ones that are binding.

Ideally, the real capital requirements flow from Pillar 2. Pillar 1 requirements are an important part of the setup because they represent a framework for relating risk and capital that can help organize the discussion between the bank and supervisor.[3] But for large banks, which are complex and often at the forefront of financial innovation, the risk measurement schemes embedded in Pillar 1 regulations will always be an incomplete approximation for any given bank.

How would it work in the ideal case? A large bank would have a series of formal risk exposure and capital allocation models, each dealing with different kinds of risks, and a way of aggregating the risk levels and capital requirements the models estimate. For risks that are not formally modeled, the bank would have ad hoc procedures for judging the exposure and adding appropriate capital to the aggregate. Suppose the whole exercise is done monthly, with reporting to senior management (in reality, for risks that can change rapidly, the exercise is done at much higher frequency). Supervisors would review the reports and make their own assessment of capital adequacy relative to risk. To do so, supervisors must understand the nature of the risks the bank takes and the models the bank uses, and this in turn requires a nearly continuous dialog with relevant bank personnel.

Obviously, in such a setup, supervisors would be aware as quickly as the bank itself of major changes in risk posture and capital adequacy. This puts them in a position to intervene early in the sense of suggesting that risk be

---

3. And, in the event of a disagreement, formal capital regulations provide a set of legally verifiable standards that make it easier for the supervisor to address challenges to its authority.

shed or capital be raised. But this is neither the most common nor the most important form of supervisory early intervention, because at a well-functioning bank, the management would act anyway upon receiving information that capital adequacy or risk has changed. More important is a kind of intervention in the bank's internal procedures. Most of all, supervisors want to be comfortable that the bank understands the risks it is taking and that it has reasonably robust procedures for maintaining capital adequacy. Supervisors are usually reluctant to dictate details of formal models or of procedures. But supervisors are in a good position to notice that a bank may be entirely ignoring a material class of risk, or that its models or procedures are seriously flawed, because supervisors are able to observe the inner workings of many banks.

As large banks have become ever larger and more complex institutions, supervisors have put increasing emphasis on the Pillar 2 processes I have just sketched. It is comforting that Pelizzon and Schaefer's results imply that the improved maintenance of capital adequacy that such processes foster leads to better economic outcomes than situations where supervisory evaluations are infrequent and less effective. Of course, the optimal design of Pillar 2 processes is itself an important research question, and I hope that future work will shed more light on it.

References

Acharya, Sankarshan, and Jean-Francois Dreyfus. 1989. Optimal bank reorganization policies and the pricing of federal deposit insurance. *Journal of Finance* 44 (5): 1313–33.

Berger, Allen N., Richard J. Herring, and Giorgio P. Szego. 1995. The role of capital in financial institutions. *Journal of Banking and Finance* 19:393–430.

Berlin, Mitchell, Anthony Saunders, and Gregory F. Udell. 1991. Deposit insurance reform: What are the issues and what needs to be fixed? *Journal of Banking and Finance* 15:735–521.

Davies, Sally M., and Douglas A. McManus. 1991. The effects of closure policies on bank risk-taking. *Journal of Banking and Finance* 15:917–38.

Koehn, M., and Anthony M. Santomero. 1980. Regulation of bank capital and portfolio risk. *Journal of Finance* 35:1235–50.

Levonian, Mark. 1991. What happens if banks are closed early. Federal Reserve Bank of Chicago. *Proceedings of the 27th annual conference on bank structure and competition,* 273–95.

Ritchken, Peter, James Thomson, Ramon DeGennaro, and Anlong Li. 1995. *Research in Finance* 13:219–36.

Discussion Summary

Charles Calomiris opened the general discussion with two observations: (1) Pillar 2 cannot be assumed to work, so market discipline is important as well, and (2) during times of stress (meaning reduced solvency), asset substitution by banks is toward risks that often are not socially productive (gambling for redemption), so both regulatory and market monitoring of banks is especially important in crisis situations.

Ross Levine suggested an additional motivation for the tradeoff between failure risk and productive investment that the authors emphasize. Especially outside the industrialized countries, stronger supervisory powers are often used by bank regulators to direct lending to politically favored constituencies, and such loans are often not economically productive.

Patricia Jackson defended the importance of Pillar 2, noting that even the relatively sophisticated formulas of the Basel II Pillar-1 regime will not reflect all the risks faced by banks. With regard to the claim that Pillar 1 was already conservative, it targeted a credit value-at-risk (VaR) percentile, which is the equivalent of a rating riskier than single-A. However, large banks that are systemically important are not likely to be viable if rated riskier than A-minus because many counterparties would refuse to deal with them. Prompt corrective actions triggered by changes in Pillar-1 regulatory capital adequacy almost surely would come too late in such cases. *Martin Feldstein* added that what amounted to Pillar 2 actions by U.S. bank supervisors seemed to work to prevent a systemic crisis in the late 1980s and early 1990s. *Richard Evans* noted that many managers of large banks have been concerned that Pillar 2 will be applied inconsistently across nations, but that the recent formation by regulators of a "college of supervisors" offers hope that inconsistencies may be modest. Such cooperation among supervisors may also reduce systemic risk by promoting good cooperation among supervisors internationally in a crisis.

To shed light on whether capital requirements are binding, Martin Feldstein asked for evidence that Basel I increased regulatory capital requirements. *Mark Carey* recalled that book-capital ratios of U.S. banks reached a trough in the late 1980s and increased substantially after implementation of Basel I, and that recent papers by Mark Flannery and Kasturi Rangan offer evidence that market-price-based measures of bank leverage also imply an increase since the 1980s. Richard Evans observed that large dealer banks strive to choose their leverage based on economic considerations, balancing the need for a buffer stock of capital to support capturing rapidly developing market opportunities with a desire to maximize shareholder value, which sometimes is best done by dividend payouts or share repurchases. However, Basel I requirements have been a constraint at times, and do seem to affect the decision making of some banks.

Responding to the authors' remarks about the absence of clear discussions in regulatory documents of the market failure that capital requirements are meant to address, Mark Carey observed that such ambiguity arises because regulators have too many hypotheses about the nature of such market failures, not no hypotheses at all, and moreover that intuition suggests that the weight placed on different possible market failures is likely to be different over time, across nations, and in the case of large and small banks. Thus, it is difficult for regulators to produce a concise treatment. But he agreed that research on the nature of such market failures could produce large benefits.

IV New Frontiers in Risk Measurement

Global Business Cycles
and Credit Risk

M. Hashem Pesaran, Til Schuermann, and
Björn-Jakob Treutler

9.1 Introduction

In theory, the potential for credit risk diversification for banks can be considerable. Insofar as different industries or sectors are more or less procyclical, banks can alter their lending policy and capital allocation across those sectors. Similarly, internationally active banks are able to apply analogous changes across countries. In addition to such *passive* credit portfolio management, financial engineering—using instruments such as credit derivatives—enables banks (and other financial institutions) to engage in *active* credit portfolio management by buying and selling credit risk (or credit protection) across sectors and countries. Credit exposure to the U.S. chemical industry, for example, can be traded for credit exposure to the Korean steel sector. One may, therefore, think of a global market for credit exposures wherein credit risk can be exported and imported.

Within such a global context, default probabilities are driven primarily by how firms are tied to fundamental risk factors, both domestic and foreign, and how those factors are linked across countries. In order to implement such a global approach in the analysis of credit risk, we have developed in Pesaran, Schuermann, and Weiner (2004; hereafter PSW) a global vector autoregressive macroeconometric model (GVAR) for a set of twenty-five countries accounting for about 80 percent of world output.

We would like to thank the National Bureau of Economic Research (NBER) Conference on Risk of Financial Institutions participants, the editors Mark Carey and René Stulz, and our discussant Richard Cantor for helpful and insightful comments. We would also like to thank Yue Chen and Sam Hanson for their excellent research assistance.

Any views expressed represent those of the authors only, and not necessarily those of the Federal Reserve Bank of New York, the Federal Reserve System, or Mercer Oliver Wyman.

Importantly, the foreign variables in the GVAR are tailored to match the international trade pattern of the country under consideration.

Pesaran, Schuermann, Treutler, and Weiner (2005; hereafter PSTW) relate asset returns for a portfolio of 119 firms to the global macroeconometric model, thus isolating macro effects from idiosyncratic shocks as they relate to default (and hence loss). The GVAR effectively serves as the macroeconomic engine capturing the economic environment faced by an internationally active global bank. Domestic and foreign macroeconomic variables are allowed to impact each firm differently. In this way we are able to account for firm-specific heterogeneity in an explicitly interdependent global context. Developing such a conditional modeling framework is particularly important for the analysis of the effects of different types of shock scenarios on credit risk, an important feature we exploit here.

In this paper we extend the analysis of PSTW along four dimensions. First, we provide some analytical results on the limits of credit risk diversification. Second, we illustrate the impact of two different identification restrictions regarding the default condition on the resulting loss distributions. Third, we use this framework to understand the degree of diversification, with five models that differ in their degree of parameter heterogeneity, from fully homogeneous to allowing for industry and regional heterogeneity but homogeneous factor sensitivities. Fourth, we have more than doubled the number of firms in the portfolio, from 119 and 243 firms, providing for more robust results and allowing us to explore the importance of exposure granularity. We go on to explore the impact of shocks to real equity prices, interest rates, and real output on the resulting loss distribution as implied by the different model specifications.

Such conditional analysis using shock scenarios from observable risk factors is not possible in the most commonly used model in the credit risk literature, namely the Vasicek (1987, 1991, 2002) adaptation of the Merton (1974) default model. In addition to being driven by a single and *unob*served risk factor, this model also assumes that risk factor sensitivities, analogous to capital asset pricing model (CAPM)–style betas, are the same across all firms in all regions and industries, yielding a fully homogeneous model. This single-factor model also underlies the risk-based capital standards in the New Basel Accord (BCBS 2004), as shown in Gordy (2003).

We find that firm-level parameter heterogeneity and information about credit ratings matter a great deal for capturing differences in the loss distributions. In line with theoretical and empirical results in Hanson, Pesaran, and Schuermann (2005; hereafter HPS), we show that neglected heterogeneity leads to *under*estimation of expected losses, and once those are controlled for, to *over*estimation of unexpected losses. Wrongly imposing homogeneity results in excessively skewed and fat-tailed loss distributions. In the process of allowing for firm heterogeneity, credit rating information turns out to be particularly important, since default correlation and credit ratings are closely related even if return correlations across firms are kept constant. These differences become more pronounced in the presence of systematic risk factor shocks: increased parameter heterogeneity greatly reduces shock sensitivity. For example, an adverse 2.33σ shock to U.S. equity prices increases loss volatility by about 31 percent for the fully heterogeneous model, but by 73 percent for the homogeneous pooled model. These differences become even more pronounced as shocks become more extreme: for an adverse 5σ shock to U.S. equity prices, loss volatility increases by about 85 percent for the heterogeneous model, but by more than 240 percent for the restricted model.

We further find that symmetric shocks result in asymmetric and non-proportional loss outcomes due to the nonlinearity of the default model. Loss increases arising from adverse shocks are larger than corresponding loss decreases from benign (but equiprobable) shocks. Here too there are important differences in the loss distributions depending on the degree of underlying model heterogeneity. While all models exhibit this asymmetry for expected losses and loss volatility, only the fully heterogeneous model exhibits this particular asymmetric response in the tail of the loss distribution. For the restricted models the opposite is true: the reduction in tail risk arising from the benign shock is larger than the corresponding increase due to the adverse shock. By imposing homogeneity, not only are the relative loss responses exaggerated (most of the percentage increases and all of the decreases are larger for the restricted than for the unrestricted model), but perceived reduction of risk in the tail of the loss distribution tends to be overly optimistic. Failing to properly account for parameter heterogeneity could therefore result in too much implied risk capital.

Both the baseline and shock-conditional loss distributions seem to change noticeably with the addition of heterogeneous factor loadings. Allowing for regional heterogeneity appears to be more important than allowing for industry or sector heterogeneity. However, the biggest marginal change arises when allowing for full heterogeneity.

The apparently innocuous choice of identifying restriction—same default threshold versus same unconditional probability of default (or distance to default), by credit rating—appears to make a material difference. Under the same threshold (by rating) restriction, conditioning on risk factor forecasts changes firm default probabilities only somewhat: unconditional and conditional probabilities of default are highly correlated (96 percent). By contrast, such conditioning has a significant impact under the same distance to default (by rating) restriction. The conditional default probabilities disperse, resulting in a lower correlation with unconditional default probabilities (79 percent).

We find that the loss distributions are relatively insensitive to typical business cycle shocks arising from changes in interest rates or real output. Furthermore, these results seem to be reasonably robust to the choice of firm-specific return regressions, and if true are likely to have important policy implications, particularly given the intense debate surrounding the possible procyclicality of the New Basel Accord (Carpenter, Whitesell, and Zakrajšek 2001, Altman, Bharath, and Saunders 2002, Carey 2002, Allen and Saunders 2004).

Finally, we are able to assess the impact of granularity or portfolio size on the risk of the portfolio for a simplified version of the model where analytic solutions for unexpected loss (UL) are available. The lower the average correlation across firm returns, the greater is the potential for diversification. But to achieve the theoretical (asymptotic) lower bound to the UL, a relatively large N is required when return correlations are low. A common rule of thumb for return diversification of a portfolio of equities is around 50. Default correlations are, of course, much lower than return correlations, and we show that to come within 3 percent of the asymptotic UL values, more than 5,000 firms are needed. Thus credit portfolios or credit derivatives such as CDOs, which contain rather fewer numbers of firms, most likely would still retain a significant degree of idiosyncratic risk. In the case, for instance, of our more modestly sized portfolio of 243 firms, the UL is some 44 percent above its asymptotic value.

The plan for the remainder of the paper is as follows: section 9.2 provides a model of firm value and default. Section 9.3 covers some useful analytical results for the loss distribution of a credit portfolio. Section 9.4 presents the framework for conditional credit risk modeling including a brief overview of the global macroeconometric model. In section 9.5 we introduce the credit portfolio and present the results from the multifactor return regressions that link firm returns to the observable systematic risk factors from the macroeconomic engine. We present results for five models, ranging from the homogeneous pooled model to one allowing for full heterogeneity, with intermediate specifications that allow for industry and geography effects. In section 9.6 we consider how those models impact the resulting loss distributions under a variety of macroeconomic shock scenarios. In this section we also consider the impact of portfolio size and granularity on the resulting loss distribution. Some concluding remarks are provided in section 9.7.

9.2   Firm Value and Default

Most credit default models have two basic components: (1) a model of the firm value, and (2) conditions under which default occurs.[1] In this section we set out such a model by adapting the option theoretic default model (Merton 1974) to our global macroeconometric specification of the systematic factors. Merton recognized that a lender is effectively writing a put

---

1. This section follows the approach introduced in PSTW.

option on the assets of the borrowing firm; owners and owner-managers (i.e., shareholders) hold the call option. If the value of the firm falls below a certain threshold, the owners will put the firm to the debtholders. Thus a firm is expected to default when the value of its assets falls below a threshold value determined by its liabilities. In this way default risk is expected to vary across firms due to differences in leverage or volatility. While the latter is typically estimated using market data, the former is often measured using balance sheet data, which is noisy and prone to manipulation.

The problem of modeling firm default is that it inherits all the asymmetric information and agency problems between borrower and lender, well known in the banking literature. The argument is roughly as follows. A firm, particularly if it is young and privately held, knows more about its health, quality, and prospects than outsiders—for example, lenders. Banks are particularly well suited to help overcome these informational asymmetries through relationship lending; learning by lending. Moreover, managers and owners of firms have an incentive to substitute higher risk for lower risk investments as they are able to receive upside gains (they hold a call option on the firm's assets) while lenders are not (they hold a put option). See the survey by James and Smith (2000) for a more extensive discussion, as well as Garbade (2001). If the firm is public, we have other sources of information, such as quarterly and annual reports which, though accounting based, are then digested and interpreted by the market. Stock and bond prices serve as summary statistics of that information.

The scope for credit risk diversification thus can manifest itself through two channels: how firm value reacts to changes in the systematic risk factors, and through differentiated default thresholds. Both channels need to be modeled. Since we shall be concerned with possibilities of diversification along the dimensions of geography and industry (or sector), we will consider firms $j, j = 1, \ldots, N$, in country or region $i, i = 1, \ldots, M$, and sector $s, s = 1, \ldots, S$, and denote the firm's asset value at the end of period t by $V_{jis,t}$, and its outstanding stock of debt by $D_{jis,t}$. According to Merton's model, default occurs at the maturity date of the debt, $t + H$, when the firm's assets, $V_{jis,t+H}$, are less than the face value of the debt at that time, $D_{jis,t+H}$. This is in contrast with the first-passage model, where default would occur the first time that $V_{jis,t}$ falls below a default boundary (or threshold) over the period t to $t + H$.[2] Under both models the default probabilities are computed with respect to the probability distribution of asset values at the terminal date—$t + H$ in the case of the original Merton model—and over the period from t to $t + H$ in the case of the first-passage

2. See Black and Cox (1976). More recent modeling approaches include direct strategic default considerations (e.g., Mella-Barral and Perraudin [1997]). Leland and Toft (1996) develop a model wherein default is determined endogenously rather than by the imposition of a positive net worth condition. For a review of these models, see, for example, Lando (2004, chapter 3).

models. Although our approach can be adapted to the first-passage model, for simplicity we follow the Merton approach here.

We follow the approach developed in detail in PSTW, where default is said to occur if the value of equity, $E_{jis,t+H}$, falls below a possibly small but positive threshold value, $C_{jis,t+H}$,

$$(1) \qquad E_{jis,t+H} < C_{jis,t+H}.$$

This is reasonable since technical default definitions used by banks and bondholders are typically weaker than outright bankruptcy. Moreover, because bankruptcies are costly and violations to the absolute priority rule in bankruptcy proceedings are so common, in practice the debtholders have an incentive to put the firm into receivership even before the equity value of the firm hits the zero value. The default point could vary over time and with the firm's particular characteristics (region and sector being two of them, of course). It is, however, difficult to measure, since observable accounting-based factors are at best noisy and at worst reported with bias, highlighting the information asymmetry between managers (agents) and shareholders and debtholders (principals).[3]

To overcome these measurement difficulties and information asymmetries, we make use of a firm's credit rating $R \in \mathcal{R} = \mathcal{AAA}, \mathcal{AA}, \ldots.$[4] This will help us specifically in nailing down the default threshold, details of which are given in section 9.2.1. Naturally, rating agencies have access to, and presumably make use of, private information about the firm to arrive at their firm-specific credit rating, in addition to incorporating public information such as, for instance, financial statements and equity returns.

To simplify the exposition here we adopt the standard practice and assume that asset values follow a Gaussian geometric random walk with a fixed drift.

$$\ln(E_{jis,t+1}/E_{jist}) = r_{jis,t+1} = \mu_{jis} + \sigma_{jis}\varepsilon_{jis,t+1},$$

where $\varepsilon_{jis,t+1} \sim N(0, 1)$, distributed independently across t (but not necessarily across firms, σ_{jis} is the return innovation volatility and μ_{jis} the drift of the one-period holding return, $r_{jis,t+1}$). This specification is "unconditional" in the sense that it does not allow for the effects of business cycle and monetary policy variables on returns (and hence defaults). We shall return to conditional asset return specifications that allow for such effects in section 9.2.2. The distribution of the H-period ahead holding period return associated with the previous specification is then given by

$$(2) \qquad r_{jis}(t, t + H) = \sum_{\tau=1}^{H} r_{jis,t+\tau} \sim N(H\mu_{jis}, \sqrt{H}\,\sigma_{jis}),$$

3. Duffie and Lando (2001), with this in mind, allow for imperfect information about the firm's assets and default threshold in the context of a first-passage model.

4. For an overview of the rating industry, see Cantor and Packer (1995). For no reason other than convenience, we shall be using the ratings nomenclature used by Standard & Poor's and Fitch.

where the notation $(t, t + H)$ is used throughout to mean over the period "from $t + 1$ to $t + H$."

Default then occurs at the end of H periods if the H-period change in firm value (or return) falls below the log threshold-equity ratio, or return default threshold, as in

$$\ln\left(\frac{E_{jis,t+H}}{E_{jis,t}}\right) < \ln\left(\frac{C_{jis,t+H}}{E_{jis,t}}\right),$$

or

$$r_{jis}(t, t + H) < \lambda_{jis}(t, t + H).$$

Therefore, using equation (2), the firm's probability of default (PD) at the terminal date $t + H$ is given by

(3)
$$\pi_{jis}(t, t + H) = \Phi\left(\frac{\lambda_{jis}(t, t + H) - H\mu_{jis}}{\sigma_{jis}\sqrt{H}}\right),$$

where $\Phi(\cdot)$ is the distribution function of the standard normal variate. The argument of $\Phi(\cdot)$ in equation (3) is sometimes called the distance to default (DD). We may rewrite the H-period forward return default threshold as

$$\lambda_{jis}(t, t + H) = H\mu_{jis} + \Phi^{-1}[\pi_{jis}(t, t + H)]\sigma_{jis}\sqrt{H}.$$

where $\Phi^{-1}(\pi_{jis}[t, t + H])$ is the quantile associated with the default probability $\pi_{jis}(t, t + H)$. The firm defaults if its H-period return, $r_{jis}(t, t + H)$, falls below its expected H-period return, less a multiple of its H-period volatility.[5]

9.2.1 Identification of the Default Threshold

In this section we provide a brief discussion of the problem of identifying the default threshold for each firm. Details can be found in Hanson, Pesaran, and Schuermann (2005). In what follows we shall be suppressing the country and sector subscript for simplicity. Suppose now that at time t we have a portfolio of size N_t of firms, or credit exposures to those firms, and denote the exposure share or weight for the jth firm a $w_{jt} \geq 0$ such that $\sum_{j=1}^{N_t} w_{jt} = 1$.[6] At time t the expected portfolio default rate at the end of H-periods from now (e.g., one year) is then given by

(4)
$$\pi(t, t + H) = \sum_{j=1}^{N_t} w_{jt}\Phi\left[\frac{\lambda_j(t, t + H) - H\mu_j}{\sigma_j\sqrt{H}}\right].$$

Relation (4) may be thought of as a moment estimator for the unknown thresholds $\lambda_j(t, t + H)$, since μ_j and σ_j and $\pi(t, t + H)$ can be estimated

---

5. Note that $\Phi^{-1})\pi_{jis}[t, t + H])$ is negative for $\pi_{jis}(t, t + H) < 0.5$, which covers the default probability values typically considered in the literature.
6. Note that we are disallowing short positions, which is not very restrictive for credit assets.

from past observed returns and realized defaults. With one moment condition and N_t unknown thresholds, one needs to impose $N_t - 1$ identifying restrictions; for example, one could impose the same threshold for every firm in the portfolio. The number of required identifying restrictions could be reduced if further information can be used. One such type of information is provided by credit rating-specific default information.

Although firm-specific default probabilities, $\pi_j(t, t + H)$, are not observable, the default rate by rating, $\pi_R(t, t + H)$, can be estimated by pooling historical observations of firms' defaults in a particular rating class, using a sample spanning $t = 1, \ldots, T$. In this case the number of identifying restrictions can be reduced to $N_T - k$, where k denotes the number of rating categories, and N_T the number of firms in the portfolio at time T. There are two simple ways that identification can be achieved. One could, for example, impose the same distance to default on all firms in the same rating category, namely

$$(5) \qquad \frac{\hat{\lambda}_j(T, T + H) - H\overline{\mu}_j}{\overline{\sigma}_j\sqrt{H}} = \mathrm{DD}_R(T, T + H) \quad \forall j \in R,$$

where $\hat{\lambda}_j(T, T + H)$ is the default threshold estimated on the basis of information available at time T, and $\overline{\mu}_j$ and $\overline{\sigma}_j$ are sample estimates of (unconditional) mean and standard deviations of one-period holding returns obtained over the period $t = 1, 2, \ldots, T$. Then, with estimates of default frequencies by rating in hand, namely $\hat{\pi}_R(T, T + H)$, we are able to obtain an estimate of $\mathrm{DD}_R(T, T + H)$ given by[7]

$$(6) \qquad \widehat{\mathrm{DD}}_R(T, T + H) = \Phi^{-1}[\hat{\pi}_R(T, T + H)],$$

and hence the firm-specific default thresholds

$$(7) \qquad \hat{\lambda}_j(T, T + H) = \overline{\sigma}_j\sqrt{H}\Phi^{-1}[\hat{\pi}_R(T, T + H)] + H\overline{\mu}_j.$$

Note that imposing the same DD by rating as in (5) imposes the same unconditional PD for each R-rated firm, as in (6), but allows for variation in the estimated default thresholds $\hat{\lambda}_j(T, T + H)$ across firms within a rating because of different unconditional means and standard deviations of returns, as in (7). Note also that each element on the right-hand side of (7) is horizon dependent, making the default threshold horizon dependent.

Alternatively, one could impose the restriction that the default threshold $\hat{\lambda}_j(T, T + H)$ is the same across firms in the same rating category:

$$(8) \qquad \tilde{\lambda}_j(T, T + H) = \hat{\lambda}_R(T, T + H) \quad \forall j \in R,$$

which, when substituted into equation (4), now yields

7. Condition (5) implies that all firms with rating R have the same unconditional distance to default and hence the same unconditional default probability, as in equation (6).

$$(9) \qquad \hat{\pi}_R(T, T + H) = \sum_{j \in R} w_{j,T} \Phi \left[\frac{\hat{\lambda}_R(T, T + H) - H\overline{\mu}_j}{\overline{\sigma}_j \sqrt{H}} \right].$$

This is a nonlinear equation that needs to be solved numerically for $\hat{\lambda}_R(T, T + H)$. Condition (9) implies that DD, and hence unconditional PDs, will vary across firms within a rating, since $\hat{\lambda}_R(T, T + H)$ is chosen such that *on average* the PD by firm with rating R is equal to $\hat{\pi}_R(T, T + H)$.

9.2.2   Firm-Specific Conditional Defaults

For the credit risk analysis of different shock scenarios it is important to distinguish between *conditional* and *unconditional* default probabilities. For the conditional analysis we assume that conditional on the information available at time t, Ω_t, and as before the return of firm j in region i and sector s over the period t to $t + H$, $r_{jis}(t, t + H) = \ln(E_{jis,t+H}/E_{jis,t})$, can be decomposed as

$$(10) \qquad r_{jis}(t, t + H) = \mu_{jis}(t, t + H) + \xi_{jis}(t, t + H),$$

where $\mu_{jis}(t, t + H)$ is the (forecastable) conditional mean (H-step ahead), and $\xi_{jis}(t, t + H)$ is the (nonforecastable) component of the return process over the period t to $t + H$. It may contain firm-specific idiosyncratic as well as systematic risk factor innovations. We shall assume that

$$(11) \qquad \xi_{jis}(t, t + H) \sim N[0, \sigma_{jis}^2(t, t + H)].$$

We can now characterize the separation between a default and a nondefault state with an indicator variable $z_{jis}(t, t + H)$,

$$(12) \qquad z_{jis}(t, t + H) = I[r_{jis}(t, t + H) < \lambda_{jis}(t, t + H)],$$

such that,

$$(13) \quad z_{jis}(t, t + H) = 1 \text{ if } r_{jis}(t, t + H) < \lambda_{jis}(t, t + H) \Rightarrow \text{Default},$$

$$z_{jis}(t, t + H) = 0 \text{ if } r_{jis}(t, t + H) \geq \lambda_{jis}(t, t + H) \Rightarrow \text{No Default}.$$

Using the same approach, the H-period ahead *conditional* default probability for firm j is given by

$$(14) \qquad \pi_{jis}(t, t + H) = \Phi \left[\frac{\lambda_{jis}(t, t + H) - \mu_{jis}(t, t + H)}{\sigma_{jis}(t, t + H)} \right].$$

We can estimate $\mu_{jis}(t, t + H)$ and $\sigma_{jis}(t, t + H)$ using the firm-specific multifactor regressions using a sample ending in period T. In what follows we denote these estimates by $\hat{\mu}_{jis}(T, T + H)$ and $\hat{\sigma}_{jis}(T, T + H)$, respectively. The default thresholds, $\lambda_{jis}(T, T + H)$, can be estimated, following the discussion in section 9.2.1, by imposing either the same distance to default by rating, $DD_R(T, T + H)$, as in equation (5), or the same default threshold by rating, as in equation (8). Specifically, under the same DD by rating, the firm-specific conditional *PD* will be given by

(15) $\hat{\pi}_{jis}(T, T + H) =$

$$\Phi\left\{\frac{\overline{\sigma}_{jis}\sqrt{H}\Phi^{-1}[\hat{\pi}_R(T, T + H)] + H\overline{\mu}_{jis} - \hat{\mu}_{jis}(T, T + H)}{\hat{\sigma}_{jis}(T, T, + H)}\right\}.$$

Under the same default threshold by rating we have

(16) $\hat{\pi}_{jis}(T, T + H) = \Phi\left[\dfrac{\hat{\lambda}_R(T, T + H) - \hat{\mu}_{jis}(T, T + H)}{\hat{\sigma}_{\xi jis}(T, T + H)}\right],$

where $\hat{\lambda}_R(T, T + H)$ is determined by (9).

Similarly, in the case of the same DD by rating, the empirical default condition for firm j with credit rating R can now be written as

(17) $I[r_{jis}(T, T + H) < \hat{\lambda}_{jis}(T, T + H)] = 1$ if $r_{jis}(T, T + H)$

$$< \overline{\sigma}_{jis}\sqrt{H}\Phi^{-1}[\hat{\pi}_R(T, T + H)] + H\overline{\mu}_{jis},$$

and in the case of the same default threshold by rating the default condition will be

(18) $I[r_{jis}(T, T + H) < \hat{\lambda}_R(T, T + H)] = 1$ if $r_{jis}(T, T + H) < \hat{\lambda}_R(T, T + H),$

where, as before, $\hat{\lambda}_R(T, T + H)$ is given as the solution to equation (9). Note that in the case of (18) there are only as many default thresholds as there are credit ratings, whereas in the case of equation (17) each default threshold is firm specific (through $\overline{\mu}_{jis}$ and $\overline{\sigma}_{jis}$).

Mappings from credit ratings to default probabilities are typically obtained using corporate bond rating histories over many years, often twenty years or more, and thus represent averages across business cycles. The reason for such long samples is simple: default events for investment grade firms are quite rare; for example, the annual default probability even for an $\mathcal{A}$-rated firm is approximately one basis point for both Moody's and S&P-rated firms (see, for example, Jafry and Schuermann 2004). Accordingly, we will make the further identifying assumption that credit ratings are "cycle-neutral," in the sense that ratings are assigned only on the basis of firm-specific information and not on systematic or macroeconomic information. On this interpretation of credit ratings see also Saunders and Allen (2002) and Amato and Furfine (2004).

Given sufficient data for a particular region or country i (the United States comes to mind) or sector s, one could in principle consider default probabilities that vary over those dimensions as well. However, since a particular firm j's default is only observable once, multiple (serial) bankruptcies notwithstanding, it makes less sense to allow π to vary across j.[8] Em-

---

8. To be sure, one is not strictly prevented from obtaining firm-specific default probabilities estimates at a given point in time. The bankruptcy models of Altman (1968), Lennox (1999) and Shumway (2001) are such examples, as is the industry model by KMV (Kealhofer and

pirically, then, we abstract from possible variation in default rates across regions and sectors, so that probabilities of default vary only across credit ratings and over time.

Finally, another important source of heterogeneity that could be of particular concern for out multicountry analysis is the differences that prevail in bankruptcy laws and regulations across countries. However, by using rating agency default data, which, broadly speaking, are based on homogeneous definition of default, we expect our analysis to be reasonably robust to such heterogeneities.

9.3   Credit Loss Distribution

The complicated relationship between return correlations and defaults manifests itself at the portfolio level.[9] Consider a credit portfolio composed of N different credit assets such as loans at date t, and for simplicity assume that loss given default (LGD) is 100 percent, meaning that no recovery is made in the event of default. Then we may define loss as a fraction of total exposure by

$$(19) \qquad \ell_{N,t+1} = \sum_{j=1}^{N} w_j z_{j,t+1},$$

where w_j is the exposure share, where $w_j \geq 0$ and $\sum_{j=1}^{N} w_j = 1$, and $z_{j,t+1} = I(r_{j,t+1} < \lambda_{jt})$, with λ_{jt} assumed as given.[10] Under the Vasicek model

$$\mathrm{Var}(\ell_{N,t+1}) = \pi(1-\pi)\left(\sum_{j=1}^{N} w_j^2\right) + \pi(1-\pi)\rho^*\left(\sum_{j\neq j'} w_j w_{j'}\right),$$

where $\pi = E(z_{j,t+1})$, which is the same for all firms, and ρ^* is the default correlation,

$$(20) \qquad \rho^*(\pi, \rho) = \frac{E\left\{\left[\Phi\left(\frac{\Phi^{-1}(\pi)}{\sqrt{1-\rho}} - \sqrt{\frac{\rho}{1-\rho}}f_{t+1}\right)\right]^2\right\} - \pi^2}{\pi(1-\pi)},$$

where expectations are taken with respect to the distribution of f_{t+1}, assumed here to be $N(0, 1)$.[11] For example, for $\pi = 0.01$, and $\rho = 0.30$, we have $\rho^* = 0.05$. Since $\sum_{j=1}^{N} w_j = 1$, it is easily seen that

Kurbat 2002). However, all of these studies focus on just one country at a time (the United States and United Kingdom in this list) and do not address the formidable challenges of point-in-time bankruptcy forecasting with a multicountry portfolio.

9. This section presents a synopsis of results developed in detail in Hanson, Pesaran, and Schuermann (2005).

10. To simplify the notations and without loss of generality, in this section we assume N and the exposure weights are time invariant.

11. For a derivation of equation (20), see Hanson, Pesaran, and Schuermann (2005).

$$\sum_{j=1}^{N} w_j^2 + \sum_{j \neq j'}^{N} w_j w_{j'} = 1,$$

and hence

(21) $$\mathrm{Var}(\ell_{N,t+1}) = \pi(1 - \pi) \left[\rho^* + (1 - \rho^*) \sum_{j=1}^{N} w_j^2 \right].$$

Under

(22) $$\sum_{j=1}^{N} w_j^2 \to 0, \text{ as } N \to \infty,$$

which is often referred to as the granularity condition; the second term in brackets in equation (21) becomes negligible as N becomes very large, and $\mathrm{Var}(\ell_{N,t+1})$ converges to the first term, which will be nonzero for $\rho^* \neq 0$. Hence, in the limit the unexpected loss is bounded by $\sqrt{\pi(1 - \pi)}\rho^*$. For a finite value of N, the unexpected loss is minimized by adopting an equal weighted portfolio, with $w_j = 1/N$. Full diversification is possible only in the extreme case where $\rho^* = 0$ (which is implied by $\rho = 1$), and assuming that the granularity condition is satisfied.

The loss distribution associated with this homogeneous model is derived in Vasicek (1991, 2002) and Gordy (2000). Not surprisingly, Vasicek's limiting (as $N \to \infty$) distribution is also fully determined in terms of π and ρ. The former parameter sets the expected loss of the portfolio, while the latter controls the shape of the loss distribution. In effect one parameter, ρ, controls all aspects of the loss distribution: its volatility, skewness, and kurtosis. It would not be possible to calibrate two Vasicek loss distributions with the same expected and unexpected losses, but with different degrees of fat-tailedness, for example.[12]

Further, Vasicek's distribution does not depend on the portfolio weights so long as equation (22) is satisfied. Therefore, for sufficiently large portfolios that satisfy the granularity condition, equation (22), there is no further scope for credit risk diversification if attention is confined to the homogeneous return model that underlies Vasicek's loss distribution. Also, Vasicek's setup does not allow conditional risk modeling where the effects of macroeconomic shocks on credit loss distribution might be of interest. With these considerations in mind, we allow for systematic factors and heterogeneity along several dimensions. These are: (1) multiple and observable factors, (2) firm fixed effects, (3) differentiated default thresholds, and (4) differentiated factor sensitivities (analogous to firm betas) by region, sector, or even firm-specific. If the Vasicek model lies at the fully homogeneous end of the spectrum, the model laid out in section 9.2 describes the

---

12. The literature on modeling correlated defaults has been growing enormously. For a recent survey, see Lando (2004, chapter 9).

fully heterogeneous end. How much does accounting for heterogeneity matter for credit risk? The outcomes we are interested in exploring are different measures of credit risk, be it means or volatilities of credit losses (expected and unexpected losses in the argot of risk management), as well as quantiles in the tails or value-at-risk (VaR). Before we are able to answer some of these questions we first need to introduce the macroeconomic or systematic risk model that we plan to utilize in our empirical analysis.

9.4   Conditional Credit Modeling

9.4.1   The Macroeconomic Engine: Global Vector Autoregression (GVAR)

The conditional loss distribution of a given credit portfolio can be derived by linking up the return processes of individual firms, initially presented in equation (10), explicitly to the macro and global variables in the GVAR model. The macroeconomic engine driving the credit risk model is described in detail in PSW. We only provide a very brief, nontechnical overview here. The GVAR is a global quarterly model estimated over the period 1979Q1–1999Q1 comprising a total of twenty-five countries, which are grouped into eleven regions (shown in bold in table 9.1 from PSTW, reproduced here for convenience). The advantage of the GVAR is that it allows for a true multicountry setting; however, it can become computationally demanding very quickly. For that reason we model the seven key economies of the United States, Japan, China, Germany, United Kingdom, France, and Italy as regions of their own while grouping the other eighteen countries into four regions.[13] The output from these countries comprises around 80 percent of world GDP (in 1999).

In contrast to existing modeling approaches, in the GVAR the use of cointegration is not confined to a single country or region. By estimating a cointegrating model for each country/region separately, the model also allows for endowment and institutional heterogeneities that exist across the different countries. Accordingly, specific vector error-correcting models (VECM) are estimated for individual countries (or regions) by relating domestic macroeconomic variables such as GDP, inflation, equity prices, money supply, exchange rates, and interest rates to corresponding, and therefore country-specific, foreign variables constructed exclusively to match the international trade pattern of the country/region under consideration. By making use of specific exogeneity assumptions regarding the "rest of the world" with respect to a given domestic or regional economy, the GVAR makes efficient use of limited amounts of data and presents a

---

13. See PSW, section 9.8, for details on cross-country aggregation into regions.

Table 9.1   Countries/Regions in the GVAR model

United Kingdom	Germany	Italy	France
Western Europe	Southeast Asia	Latin America	Middle East
Belgium	Indonesia	Argentina	Kuwait
Netherlands	Korea	Brazil	Saudi Arabia
Spain	Malaysia	Chile	Turkey
Switzerland	Philippines	Mexico	
	Singapore	Peru	
	Thailand		
United States	Japan	China	

consistently estimated global model for use in portfolio applications and beyond.[14]

The GVAR allows for interactions to take place between factors and economies through three distinct but interrelated channels:

- Contemporaneous dependence of domestic on foreign variables and their lagged values
- Dependence of country-specific variables on observed common global effects such as oil prices
- Weak cross-sectional dependence of the idiosyncratic shocks

The individual models are estimated allowing for unit roots and co-integration assuming that region-specific foreign variables are weakly exogenous, with the exception of the model for the U.S. economy, which is treated as a closed-economy model. The U.S. model is linked to the outside world through exchange rates, which in turn are themselves determined by the rest of the region-specific models. PSW show that the careful construction of the global variables as weighted averages of the other regional variables leads to a simultaneous system of regional equations that may be solved to form a global system. They also provide theoretical arguments as well as empirical evidence in support of the weak exogeneity assumption that allows the region-specific models to be estimated consistently.

The conditional loss distribution of a given credit portfolio can now be derived by linking up the return processes of individual firms, initially presented in equation (10), explicitly to the macro and global variables in the GVAR model. We provide a synopsis of the model developed in full detail in PSTW.

---

14. For a more updated version of the GVAR model that covers a longer period and a larger number of countries see Dees, di Mauro, Pesaran, and Smith (2005). This version also provides a theoretical framework wherein the GVAR is derived as an approximation to a global, unobserved common-factor model.

9.4.2 Firm Returns Based on Observed Common Factors Linked to GVAR

Here we extend the firm return model by incorporating the full dynamic structure of the systematic risk factors captured by the GVAR. We present a notationally simplified version of the model outlined in detail in PSTW. Accordingly, a firm's return is assumed to be a function of changes in the underlying macroeconomic factors (domestic and foreign), the exogenous global variables (in our application, oil prices) and the firm-specific idiosyncratic shocks $\eta_{jis,t+\tau}$:

$$(23) \qquad r_{jis,t+\tau} = \alpha_{jis} + \gamma'_{jis}\mathbf{f}_{t+\tau} + \sigma_{jis,t+\tau}, \quad t = 1, 2, \ldots, T,$$

where $\eta_{jis,t+\tau} \sim$ i.i.d. $N(0, 1), \tau = 1, 2, \ldots, H, r_{jis,t+\tau}$ is the equity return of firm $j\, (j = 1, \ldots, nc_i)$ in region i and sector s, α_{jis} is a regression constant (or firm alpha), γ_{jis} are the factor loadings (firm "betas"), and $\mathbf{f}_{t+\tau}$ collects all the *observed* macroeconomic variables plus oil prices in the global model (totaling sixty-four in PSW). To be sure, these return regressions are not prediction equations per se, as they depend on contemporaneous variables.

The GVAR model provides forecasts of all the global variables that directly or indirectly affect the returns. As a result, default correlation enters through the shared set of common factors, $\mathbf{f}_{t+\tau}$, and the factor loadings, γ_{jis}. If the model captures all systematic risk, the idiosyncratic risk components of any two companies in the model would be uncorrelated; namely, the idiosyncratic risks ought to be cross-sectionally uncorrelated. In practice, of course, it will be hard to absorb all of the cross-section correlation with the systematic risk factors modeled by the GVAR.

Note that we started by decomposing firm returns into forecastable and nonforecastable components in equation (10), namely $r_{jis}(t, t + H) = \mu_{jis}(t, t + H) + \xi_{jis}(t, t + H)$. In the case of the previous specification we have

$$r_{jis}(t, t + H) = H\alpha_{jis} + \gamma'_{jis}\sum_{\tau=1}^{H}\mathbf{f}_{t+\tau} + \sigma_{jis}\sum_{\tau=1}^{H}\eta_{jis,t+\tau},$$

and as an illustration assuming a first-order vector autoregression for the common factors:

$$\mathbf{f}_{t+\tau} = \Lambda\mathbf{f}_{t+\tau-1} + \mathbf{v}_{t+\tau},$$

we have[15]

$$(25) \qquad \mu_{jis}(t, t + H) = H\alpha_{jis} + \gamma'_{jis}\left(\sum_{\tau=1}^{H}\Lambda^{\tau}\right)\mathbf{f}_{t},$$

---

15. Note that for a pure random walk, $\Lambda = \mathbf{0}$, and conditional and unconditional returns processes are identical.

and

$$(26) \qquad \xi_{jis}(t, t + H) = \gamma'_{jis}\left(\sum_{\tau=1}^{H} \boldsymbol{\Psi}_{H-\tau}\mathbf{v}_{t+\tau}\right) + \sigma_{jis}\sum_{\tau=1}^{H} \eta_{jis,t+\tau},$$

where

$$\boldsymbol{\Psi}_{H-\tau} = \mathbf{I} + \boldsymbol{\Lambda} + \ldots + \boldsymbol{\Lambda}^{H-\tau}.$$

The composite innovation $\xi_{jis}(t, t + H)$ contains the idiosyncratic innovation $\eta_{jis,t+\tau}$, and common macro innovations from the GVAR, here represented by $\mathbf{v}_{t+\tau}$, for $\tau = 1, 2, \ldots, H$. The predictable component is likely to be weak and will depend on the size of the factor loadings, γ_{jis}, and the extent to which the underlying global variables are cointegrating. In the absence of any cointegrating relations in the global model, none of the asset returns are predictable. As it happens, the econometric evidence presented in PSW strongly supports the existence of thirty-six cointegrating relations in the sixty-three-equation global model and is, therefore, compatible with some degree of predictability in asset returns, at least at the quarterly horizon modeled here. The extent to which asset returns are predicted could reflect time-varying risk premia and does not necessarily imply market inefficiencies. Our modeling approach provides an operational procedure for relating excess returns of individual firms to all the observable macrofactors in the global economy.

9.4.3   Expected Loss Due to Default

Given the value change process for firm j, defined by (23), with $\mu_{jis}(T, T + H)$ and $\xi_{jis}(T, T + H)$ by (25) and (26), and the return default threshold, $\hat{\lambda}_R(T, T + H)$, obtainable from an initial credit rating (see section 9.2), we are now in a position to compute (conditional) expected loss. Suppose we have data for firms and systematic factors in the GVAR for a sample period $t = 1, \ldots, T$. We need to define the expected loss to firm j at time $T + H$, given information available to the lender (e.g., a bank) at time T, which we assume is given by Ω_T. Default occurs when the firm's return falls below the return default threshold $\hat{\lambda}_{jis}(T, T + H)$ or $\tilde{\lambda}_{jis}(T, T + H)$ defined by (7) and (8), depending on the scheme used to identify the thresholds. Expected loss at time T (and realized at $T + H$), $E_T(L_{jis,T+H}) = E(L_{jis,T+H} \mid \Omega_T)$, is given by (using $\tilde{\lambda}_{jis}[T, T + H] = \hat{\lambda}_R[T, T + H]$, for $j \in R$, for example) and

$$(27) \quad E_T(L_{jis,T+H}) = \Pr[\xi_{jis}(T, T + H) < \tilde{\lambda}_{jis}(T, T + H)$$
$$- \mu_{jis}(T, T + H) \mid \Omega_T] \times A_{jis,T} \times E_T(\varphi_{jis,T+H}),$$

where $A_{jis,T}$ is the exposure assuming no recoveries (typically the face value of the loan) and is known at time T, and $\varphi_{jis,T+H}$ is the percentage of exposure which cannot be recovered in the event of default or loss given default

(*LGD*). Typically $\varphi_{jis,T+H}$ is not known at time of default and is therefore treated as a random variable over the unit interval. In what follows we make the simplifying assumption that *LGD* is 100 percent.

Substituting equation (23) into equation (27) we obtain:

$$(28) \qquad E_T(L_{jis,T+H}) = \pi_{jis}(T, T + H) \times A_{jis,T},$$

where

$$\pi_{jis}(T, T + H) = \Pr[\xi_{jis}(T, T + H) < \tilde{\lambda}_{jis}(T, T + H) - \mu_{jis}(T, T + H) \,|\, \Omega_T].$$

is the conditional default probability over the period T to $T + H$, formed at time T. Under the assumption that the macro and the idiosyncratic shocks are normally distributed and that the parameter estimates are given, we have the following expression for the probability of default over $T + T + H$ formed at T[16]

$$(29) \qquad \pi_{jis}(T, T + H) = \Phi\left[\frac{\tilde{\lambda}_{jis}(T, T + H) - \mu_{jis}(T, T + H)}{\sigma_{\xi\,jis}(T, T + H)}\right],$$

where $\sigma_{\xi jis}(T, T + H) = \sqrt{\mathrm{Var}[\xi_{jis}(T, T + H) \,|\, \Omega_T]}$. Exact expressions for $\mu_{jis}(t, t + H)$ and $\sigma_{\xi\,jis}(t, t + H)$ will depend on the nature of the global model used to identify the macro innovations. In the case of the illustrative example given in equation (29), we have

$$Var[\xi_{jis}(T, T + H) \,|\, \Omega_T] = \gamma'_{jis}\left(\sum_{\tau=1}^{H} \Psi_{H-\tau}\Omega_v\Psi'_{H-\tau}\right)\gamma_{jis} + H\sigma^2_{jis},$$

where Ω_v is the covariance matrix of the common shocks, v_t. The relevant expressions for $\mu_{jis}(T, T + H)$ and $\sigma_{\xi jis}(T, T + H)$ in the case of the GVAR model are provided in the supplement to PSTW.

The expected loss due to default of a loan (credit) portfolio can now be computed by aggregating the expected losses across the different loans. Denoting the loss of a loan portfolio over the period T to $T + H$ by L_{T+H} we have

$$(30) \qquad E_T(L_{T+H}) = \sum_{i=1}^{N} \sum_{j=1}^{nc_i} \pi_{jis}(T, T + H) \times A_{jis,T},$$

where nc_i is the number of obligors (which could be zero) in the bank's loan portfolio resident in country/region i.

Finally, note that $\mu_{jis,T}$ is the explained or expected component of firm j's return, obtained from the multiperiod GVAR forecasts, which in general could depend on macroeconomic shocks worldwide. Thus, although indi-

---

16. Joint normality is sufficient but not necessary for $\xi_{jis}(T, T + H)$ to be approximately normally distributed. This is because $\xi_{jis}(T, T + H)$ is a linear function of a larger number of weakly correlated shocks (63 in our particular application).

vidual firms operate in a particular country/region i, their probability of default can be affected by global macroeconomic conditions.

9.4.4   Simulation of the Loss Distribution

The expected loss as well as the entire loss distribution can be computed once the GVAR model parameters, the return process parameters in equation (23), and the thresholds using either equations (7) or (8) have been estimated for a sample of observations $t = 1, 2, \ldots, T$. We do this by stochastic simulation, using draws from the joint distribution of the shocks, $\xi_{jis}(T, T + H)$, which is assumed to have a conditional normal distribution with variance $\sigma^2_{\xi jis}(T, T + H)$.

Denote the *bth* draw of this vector by $\xi^{(b)}_{jis}(T, T + H)$, and compute the H-period firm-specific return, $r^{(b)}_{ijs}(T, T + H)$, noting that

$$(31) \qquad r^{(b)}_{ijs}(T, T + H) = \mu_{jis}(T, T + H) + \xi^{(b)}_{jis}(T, T + H),$$

where $\mu_{jis}(T, T + H)$ is derived from the GVAR forecasts (along the lines of equation [25]), and

$$(32) \qquad \xi^{(b)}_{jis}(T, T + H) = \psi_{jis,H} Z^{(b)}_0 + \sigma_{jis}\sqrt{H}Z^{(b)}_{jis}$$

is the composite innovation, where $Z^{(b)}_0$ and $Z^{(b)}_{jis}$ are independent draws from $N(0, 1)$. The loading coefficients $\psi_{jis,H}$ and $\sigma_{jis}\sqrt{H}$ are determined by the parameters of the GVAR and the coefficients of the asset return regressions, equation (23). In the case of the GVAR model, the relevant expressions for the simulation of the multiperiod returns are provided in section B of the supplement to PSTW.

Note that $Z^{(b)}_0$ is shared by all firms for a given draw b. Details on the derivation of $\psi_{jis,H}$ for the GVAR model can be found in PSTW. The idiosyncratic portion of the innovation is composed of the firm-specific volatility, σ_{jis}, estimated using a sample ending in periods T, and a firm-specific standard normal draw, $Z^{(b)}_{jis}$. One may then simulate the loss at the end of period $T + H$ using (known) loan face values, $A_{jis,T}$, as exposures:

$$(33) \qquad L^{(b)}_{T+H} = \sum_{i=0}^{N} \sum_{j=1}^{nc_i} I[r^{(b)}_{ijs}(T, T + H) < \tilde{\lambda}_{jis}(T, T + H)]A_{jis,T}.$$

The simulated expected loss due to default is given by (using B replications)

$$(34) \qquad \overline{L}_{B,T+H} = \frac{1}{B}\sum_{b=1}^{B} L^{(b)}_{T+H} \overset{p}{\to} E_T(L_{T+H}), \text{ as } B \to \infty.$$

The simulated loss distribution is given by ordered values of $L^{(b)}_{T+H}$, for $b = 1, 2, \ldots, B$. For desired percentile, for example the 99 percent, and a given number of replications, say $B = 100,000$, credit value at risk is given as the 1000th highest loss.

9.5   An Empirical Application

9.5.1   The Credit Portfolio

To analyze the effects of different model specifications, parameter homogeneity versus heterogeneity, we construct a fictitious large-corporate loan portfolio. This portfolio is an extended version of that used in PSTW and is summarized in table 9.2. It contains a total of 243 companies, resident in twenty-one countries across ten of the eleven regions in the GVAR model. In order for a firm to enter our sample, several criteria had to be met. We restricted ourselves to major, publicly traded firms with a credit rating from either Moody's or S&P. Thus, for example, Chinese companies were not included for lack of a credit rating. The firms should be represented within the major equity index for that country. We favored firms for which equity return data was available for the entire sample period, that is, going back to 1979. Typically this would exclude large firms such as telephone operators, which in many instances have been privatized only recently, even though they may represent a significant share in their country's dominant equity index today. The data source is Datastream, and we took their Total Return Index variable, which is a cum dividend return measure.

The third column in table 9.2 indicates the inception of the equity series

Table 9.2   **The composition of the sample portfolio by regions**

Region	No. of obligors	Equity series[a] quarterly	Credit rating[b] range	Portfolio exposure (%)
United States	63	1979Q1–99Q1	$\mathcal{AAA}$ to $\mathcal{BBB}-$	20
United Kingdom	24	1979Q1–99Q1	$\mathcal{AA}$ to $\mathcal{BBB}+$	8
Germany	21	1979Q1–99Q1	$\mathcal{AAA}$ to $\mathcal{BBB}-$	10
France	15	1979Q1–99Q1	$\mathcal{AA}$ to $\mathcal{BBB}$	8
Italy	10	1979Q1–99Q1	$\mathcal{A}$ to $\mathcal{BBB}-$	8
Western Europe	24	1979Q1–99Q1	$\mathcal{AAA}$ to $\mathcal{BBB}+$	11
Middle East	4	1990Q3–99Q1	$\mathcal{B}-$	2
Southeast Asia	34	1989Q3–99Q1	$\mathcal{A}$ to $\mathcal{B}$	14
Japan	35	1979Q1–99Q1	$\mathcal{AAA}$ to $\mathcal{B}+$	14
Latin America	14	1989Q3–99Q1	$\mathcal{A}$ to $\mathcal{B}-$	5
Total	243			100

[a]Equity prices of companies in emerging markets are not available over the full sample period used for the estimation horizon of the GVAR. We have a complete series for all firms only for the United States, United Kingdom, Germany, and Japan. For France, Italy, and Western Europe, although some of the series go back through 1979Q1, data are available for all firms from 1987Q4 (France), 1987Q4 (Italy), 1989Q3 (Western Europe). For these regions the estimation of the multifactor regressions are based on the available samples. For Latin America we have observations for all firms from 1990Q2.

[b]The sample contains a mix of Moody's and S&P ratings, although S&P rating nomenclature is used for convenience.

available for the multifactor regressions. We allocated exposure roughly by share of output of the region (in our "world" of twenty-five countries). Within a region, loan exposure is randomly assigned. Loss given default is assumed to be 100 percent for simplicity. Table 9.3 provides summary information of the number of firms in the portfolio by industry.

In order to obtain estimates for the rating-specific default frequencies ($\hat{\pi}_{R,T+H\,|\,T}$), we make use of the rating histories from Standard & Poor's, spanning 1981–1999, roughly the same sample period as is covered by our GVAR model. The results are presented in table 9.4 for the range of ratings that are represented in our portfolio of firms, namely $\mathcal{AAA}$ to $\mathcal{B}$. Empirical default probabilities, $\hat{\pi}_{R,T+\tau}$, for $\tau = 1, 2, \ldots, H$ are obtained using default intensity-based estimates detailed in Lando and Skødeberg (2002) and computed for different horizons, under the assumption that the credit migrations are governed by a Markov process (in our application, $H = 4$ quarters). This assumption is reasonable for moderate horizons, up to about two years; see Bangia et al. (2002). Since S&P rates only a subset of firms (in 1981 S&P rated 1,378 firms of which about 98 percent were U.S.-domiciled; by early 1999 this had risen to 4,910, about 68 percent in the United States), it is reasonable to assign a nonzero (albeit very small) prob-

Table 9.3   **Portfolio breakdown by industry**

	Percentage of firms
Agriculture, mining, and construction	24 (9.9)
Communication, electric, and gas	45 (18.4)
Durable manufacturing	30 (12.3)
Finance, insurance, and real estate	71 (29.2)
Nondurable manufacturing	27 (11.1)
Service	6 (2.5)
Wholesale and retail trade	40 (16.4)
Total	243 (100)

Table 9.4   **Unconditional default probabilities by rating**

S&P rating	Exposure share (%)	$\hat{\pi}_{\mathcal{R}}(T, T+4)$
$\mathcal{AAA}$	4.8	0.100 (0.005)
$\mathcal{AA}$	17.6	0.372 (0.066)
$\mathcal{A}$	32.5	0.721 (0.234)
$\mathcal{BBB}$	27.7	10.69 (2.97)
$\mathcal{BB}$	11.6	49.54 (5.72)
$\mathcal{B}$	5.8	353.61 (20.42)
Portfolio	100	29.42

Note: Exposure share and one-year-ahead probability of default (in basis points), exposure weighted in parentheses, by credit rating. Based on ratings histories from S&P, 1981Q1–1999Q1.

ability of default, even if the empirical estimate is zero. This is particularly relevant if we wish to infer default behavior for a much broader set of firms than is covered by the rating agencies. With this in mind, we impose a lower bound on the quarterly default frequency of 0.025 basis points per quarter or 0.1 basis points per annum. As can be seen in table 9.4, this constraint is binding only for the $\mathcal{AAA}$ rating. In this table we also show in parentheses the exposure share by rating and the resulting expected loss (EL). Based on the exposures in our portfolio, the (unconditional) expected default (or loss under the maintained assumption of no recovery) over one year is 0.294 percent, or 29.4bp (basis points), bolded in the table.

9.5.2   Multifactor Return Regressions: Specification, Estimation, and Selection

With the GVAR framework serving as the global economic engine, multifactor return regressions are specified in terms of the observed macrofactors in the GVAR model. A general form of these return regressions is given by equation (23). Given the diverse nature of the firms in our portfolio, one is tempted to include all the domestic, foreign, and global factors (i.e., oil price changes) in the multifactor regressions. Such a general specification may be particularly important in the case where a multinational is resident in one country, but the bulk of its operations takes place in the global arena. However, because there is likely to be a high degree of correlation between some of the domestic and foreign variables (in particular the domestic and foreign real equity prices), it is by no means obvious that a general-to-specific model selection process would be appropriate, particularly considering the short time series data available relative to the number of different factors in the GVAR.

An alternative model selection strategy, which we adopted in PSTW and follow in this paper, is to view the 243 multifactor regressions as forming a panel data model with heterogeneous coefficients. Such panels have been studied by Pesaran and Smith (1995) and Pesaran, Smith, and Im (1996) where it is shown that instead of considering firm-specific estimates one could base the analysis on the means of the estimated coefficients, referred to as the mean group estimates (MGE). This approach assumes that the variations of factor loadings across firms in different regions are approximately randomly distributed around fixed means. This is the standard random coefficient model introduced into the panel literature by Swamy (1970) and used extensively in the empirical literature.[17] The choice of the factors in the multifactor regressions can now be based on the statistical significance of the (population) mean coefficients by using the MGE to select a slimmed-down regressor set.[18]

---

17. A recent review of the random coefficient models is provided by Hsiao and Pesaran (2004).

18. The appropriate test statistics for this purpose are given in PSTW, section 6.

This factor selection procedure, applied to the panel of 243 firms, led to the following set of factors: changes in domestic or foreign real equity prices, which we denote by $\Delta\tilde{q}_{i,t+1}$, domestic interest rate ($\Delta\rho_{i,t+1}$), and oil price changes (Δp^0_{t+1}). We ran two sets of multifactor regressions (including the interest rate and oil price variables); one with $\Delta q_{i,t+1}$ (the domestic aggregate equity return variable), and another with Δq^*_{it} (the foreign country-specific equity return variable), and selected the regression with the higher $\overline{R}^2$. For three-quarters of the portfolio (183 firms) the domestic equity market return was chosen. This fully heterogeneous return equation (to be denoted as model M_0) is given by

$$(35) \qquad r_{jis,t+1} = \alpha_{jis} + \beta_{1,jis}\Delta\tilde{q}_{i,t+1} + \beta_{2,jis}\Delta\rho_{i,t+1} + \beta_{3,jis}\Delta p^0_{t+1} + \varepsilon_{jis,t+1},$$

where the idiosyncratic errors, $\varepsilon_{jis,t+1}$, are assumed to be i.i.d. $N(0, \sigma^2_{jis})$. As credit rating information is used, default thresholds are computed using equations (7) and (8), depending on whether we fix DD or λ by rating.

The summary of the final set of multifactor regressions of equation (35) and the associated mean group (MG) estimates are given in table 9.5. In this specification, changes in equity prices, interest rates, and oil prices remain the key driving factors in the multifactor regressions.

As is to be expected, the portfolio equity beta is highly significant, but somewhat below unity at 0.918. An increase in the rate of interest results in a decline in firm returns, whereas the overall effect of the oil price changes is positive. This seems a reasonable outcome for energy and petrochemical companies and for some of the banks, although one would not expect this result to be universal. In fact, we do observe considerable variations in the individual estimates of the coefficients of oil price changes across different firms in our portfolio. In the final regressions, of the 243 firm regressions, the coefficient on oil price changes was positive for 144 firms (about 59 percent of the total), and negative for the remaining firms. The MGE for each

Table 9.5   **Mean group estimates (MGE) of factor loadings, heterogeneous model (M_0)**

Factors	MGE $\hat{\beta}$	Standard error of MGE SE($\hat{\beta}$)	t-ratios
Constant	0.022	0.002	10.495
$\Delta\tilde{q}_{i,t+1}$	0.918	0.026	34.862
$\Delta\rho_{i,t+1}$	−2.990	0.528	−5.663
Δp^o_{t+1}	0.145	0.042	3.456
Average R^2	0.238		
Average $\overline{R}^2$	0.201		
No. of firm quarters	17,114		

Notes: $\Delta\tilde{q}_{i,t+1}$ is equal to $\Delta q_{i,t+1}$ (domestic equity return) or $\Delta q^*_{i,t+1}$ (foreign equity return), depending on which yields a better in-sample fit. $\Delta\rho_{i,t+1}$ is the change in the domestic interest rate; $\Delta p^o_{i,t+1}$ is the change in oil prices.

subset was also significant. A pooled estimate would, of course, impose the same factor loadings, in this case positive, on *all* firms.[19]

The lack of other observable systematic risk factors entering the return model confirms that most information relevant for firm returns is contained in the contemporaneous market return. Only interest rates and oil price changes provided marginal explanatory power. To be sure, when forecasting the macroeconomic variables, and when conducting scenario analyses, the dynamics of *all* the variables modeled in the GVAR (all sixty-three of them, plus oil prices) can still affect returns through their possible impacts on equity returns and interest rates. A direct presence in the firm-return equation is not necessary for real output, for example, to influence returns. Output shocks influence returns and credit losses to the extent that real output, interest rates, and stock market returns are contemporaneously correlated.

In addition, to this fully heterogeneous specification, we also consider a number of specifications with differing degrees of slope and error variance heterogeneity, but based on the same three systematic factors ($\Delta\tilde{q}_{i,t+1}$, $\Delta\rho_{i,t+1}$, Δp^0_{t+1}). We consider the following additional models.

M_1 *(Fully Homogeneous Model)*

Pooled return equations with the same alpha and beta across all 243 firms in the portfolio:

$$(36) \qquad r_{jis,t+1} = \alpha + \beta_1\Delta\tilde{q}_{i,t+1} + \beta_2\Delta\rho_{i,t+1} + \beta_3\Delta p^0_{t+1} + \varepsilon_{jis,t+1},$$

where the error variances are assumed to be the same for all firms, i.e., $\sigma^2_{jis} = \sigma^2_\varepsilon \; \forall \; jis.$[20]

M_2 *(Firm Fixed Effects)*

This is the standard fixed effects specification:

$$(37) \qquad r_{jis,t+1} = \alpha_{jis} + \beta_1\Delta\tilde{q}_{i,t+1} + \beta_2\Delta\rho_{i,t+1} + \beta_3\Delta p^0_{t+1} + \varepsilon_{jis,t+1},$$

where the error variances are assumed to be the same for all firms, as in the model M_1.

M_3 *(Industry/Sector Fixed and Marginal Effects)*

This model imposes the same intercept (alphas) and slopes (betas) within an industry/sector but allows those parameters to vary across industries:

$$(38) \qquad r_{jis,t+1} = \sum_{s=1}^{S}\alpha_{3s}SD_s + \sum_{s=1}^{S}\beta_{1s}SD_s\Delta\tilde{q}_{i,t+1} + \sum_{s=1}^{S}\beta_{2s}SD_s\Delta\rho_{i,t+1}$$

$$+ \sum_{s=1}^{S}\beta_{3s}SD_s\Delta p^0_{t+1} + \varepsilon_{jis,t+1},$$

19. Similarly for $\Delta\rho_{i,t+1}$, 38 percent of firms actually have a positive coefficient.
20. The parameters α and β'_i are estimated by pooled OLS.

where SD_s is a sector dummy variable that takes the value of 1 for sector s and 0 otherwise, for all t, i, and j. All firms within a given sector have the same error variance, but those variances are allowed to vary across industries.

M_4 (Region Fixed and Marginal Effects)

In this model we impose the same intercept (alpha) and slope (beta) within a region but allow those parameters to vary across regions:

$$(39) \quad r_{jis,t+1} = \sum_{i=1}^{M} \alpha_i RD_i + \sum_{i=1}^{M} \beta_{1i} RD_i \Delta \tilde{q}_{i,t+1} + \sum_{i=1}^{M} \beta_{2i} RD_i \Delta \rho_{i,t+1}$$
$$+ \sum_{i=1}^{M} \beta_{3i} RD_i \Delta p_{t+1}^0 + \xi_{jis,t+1},$$

where RD_i is a dummy variable that takes the value of 1 for region i and 0 otherwise, for all t, s, and j. All firms within a given region have the same error variance, but those variances are allowed to vary across regions.

Model M_2 is arguably the simplest complication beyond a fully homogeneous model in that it allows firm fixed effects (firm alphas) but still imposes the same error variance on all firms. Models M_3 and M_4 explore the impact of parameter (mean and variance) heterogeneity by industry and region, respectively.

Table 9.6 summarizes the regression results for the remaining models, M_1 to M_4. The equity factor loading is highly statistically significant (1 percent or better) across all models, and for the pooled models, with or without a firm fixed effect, M_2 (0.869) and M_1 (0.865) respectively, the coefficient is close to the MG estimate for the heterogeneous model, M_0 (0.918). There is, however, considerable variation across industries (M_3) and regions (M_4). For the industry model, the equity beta is lowest for communication, electric and gas, and nondurable manufacturing, both 0.752, and highest for finance, insurance, and real estate (FIRE), 0.909. The sector equity beta closest to the pooled model is agriculture, mining, and construction, 0.889.

There is even more variation in the equity beta across regions, ranging from a low of 0.622 for Latin America to a high of 1.926 for the Middle East, represented in our portfolio simply by four Turkish firms, and so should not be taken as typical.[21] The second-lowest beta was estimated for Italy, 0.663, and the second-highest for neighboring Germany, 1.165. Evidently geographic proximity does not translate to similarity in equity betas, at least not for our portfolio. Southeast Asia is closest to the pooled beta at 0.842.

Turning now to interest rate sensitivity, recall that the MGE of the

---

21. The Middle East region did not include a domestic equity variable, so all return equations for the Turkish firms include the foreign equity return variable, $\Delta q_{i,t+1}^*$, for i = Turkey.

Table 9.6   **Return regression results for models M₁–M₄**

	M₁: Pooled	M₂: Pooled + firm FE	M₃: Industry fixed and marginal effects						
			Communication, electric, and gas	Agriculture, mining, and construction	Durable manufacturing	FIRE	Nondurable manufacturing	Service	Wholesale and retail trade
Constant	0.020***		0.022***	0.014***	0.015***	0.023***	0.030***	0.028***	0.015***
	(0.001)		(0.003)	(0.004)	(0.004)	(0.003)	(0.004)	(0.008)	(0.003)
Equity	0.869***	0.865***	0.752***	0.889***	0.834***	0.909***	0.752***	0.775***	0.944***
	(0.016)	(0.016)	(0.081)	(0.051)	(0.044)	(0.028)	(0.055)	(0.122)	(0.045)
Interest rate	0.018	0.031	−0.020	0.115	0.124	−5.590***	3.402**	−2.717	−3.711***
	(0.050)	(0.050)	(0.081)	(0.106)	(0.082)	(0.573)	(1.515)	(3.480)	(1.316)
Oil price	0.063***	0.064***	0.113**	0.067	0.059	0.175***	0.012	0.058	−0.006
	(0.021)	(0.020)	(0.049)	(0.065)	(0.057)	(0.040)	(0.059)	(0.124)	(0.048)
R^2	0.144	0.160				0.152			
$\bar{R}^2$	0.144	0.148				0.151			
No. of firm quarters	17,114	17,114	2,989	1,689	2,178	4,546	2,099	474	3,139

	M₄: Region fixed and marginal effects									
	United States	United Kingdom	Germany	France	Italy	Western Europe	Middle East (Turkey only)	Southeast Asia	Japan	Latin America
Constant	0.015***	0.032***	0.006	0.020***	0.027***	0.026***	0.156***	0.012***	0.008***	0.076***
	(0.003)	(0.004)	(0.004)	(0.005)	(0.006)	(0.004)	(0.014)	(0.004)	(0.003)	(0.007)
Equity	0.916***	0.801***	1.165***	1.097***	0.663***	0.808***	1.926***	0.842***	0.904***	0.622***
	(0.039)	(0.065)	(0.064)	(0.067)	(0.059)	(0.056)	(0.242)	(0.036)	(0.044)	(0.045)

continued

Table 9.6 (continued)

						M_4: Region fixed and marginal effects					
	United States	United Kingdom	Germany	France	Italy	Western Europe	Middle East (Turkey only)	Southeast Asia	Japan	Latin America
Interest rate	-5.974***	0.669	0.699	-1.016	-0.576	-2.493	-6.676***	-5.454***	-0.885	0.111**
	(0.907)	(1.366)	(3.061)	(2.414)	(2.961)	(2.288)	(0.840)	(0.824)	(2.072)	(0.050)
Oil price	0.076**	0.058	0.230***	0.023	-0.004	-0.117	2.341***	0.047	0.009	1.035***
	(0.038)	(0.061)	(0.067)	(0.085)	(0.104)	(0.067)	(0.241)	(0.066)	(0.053)	(0.0125)
R^2						0.173				
$\bar{R}^2$						0.171				
No. of firm quarters	4,977	1,896	1,622	1,030	674	1,634	156	1,799	2,765	561

Note: Numbers in parentheses indicate the standard error of the parameter estimate. Firm return regressions using quarterly returns for 243 firms from twenty-one countries grouped into ten regions. More detail on the equity return data series by region is contained in table 9.2. Systematic risk factors are market equity return, "Equity," the change in the domestic (short) interest rate, "Interest rate," and the change in the (global) price of oil, "Oil price." The factor selection process and details on the return specifications for models M_1 to M_4 are given in section 9.5.2.

***Indicates significance at the 1 percent level.

**Indicates significance at the 5 percent level.

interest rate variable for the heterogeneous model is −2.990, meaning an increase in interest rates has an adverse effect on firm returns. This coefficient is not significant for either of the pooled models, M_1 and M_2, and it has the wrong sign. Allowing for variation across sectors, M_3, results in significant and negative coefficients for FIRE, −5.590, and wholesale and retail trade, −3.711. Just one of the positive coefficients is significant: 3.402 for nondurable manufacturing. Similar results are obtained in the case of Model M_4, where the interest rate variable is statistically significant with a correct sign only in case of U.S. firms (−5.974), the Turkish firms in the Middle Eastern region (−6.676), and Southeast Asia (−5.454). Only one of the positive estimates is statistically significant, although it is small, and that is for Latin America, 0.111.

The coefficient on oil price changes is significant and positive for both pooled models, M_1 (0.063) and M_2 (0.064), echoing the MGE for the heterogeneous model M_0 (0.145). Recall, however, that the MGE of the subgroups with positive and negative coefficients were also significant, suggesting that firm-level heterogeneity for this factor loading may be particularly important. When grouping by industry or region, however, only the positive coefficients are significant. Indeed, in the industry/sector model, the coefficient of the oil price variable is significant only for communication, Electric and Gas, at 0.113. In the regional model it is significant for several regions, including the United States (0.076), Germany (0.230), Middle East (2.341), which is not surprising, and Latin America (1.035), although the oil exporter Venezuela is not part of our Latin American region.

From a model fit perspective, as measured by $\overline{R}^2$, regional heterogeneity is more important than industry heterogeneity: $\overline{R}^2 = 0.171$ for the former and 0.151 for the latter. Both are preferred to just adding firm fixed effects to the pooled model: the $\overline{R}^2$ for M_2 is 0.148. By comparison, the average $\overline{R}^2$ for the heterogeneous model M_0 is 0.201; see table 9.5.

Finally, we computed the average pairwise cross-sectional return correlation across all firms in our portfolio as well as of the residuals for each of the return specifications, M_0 through M_4. The average pairwise cross-sectional return correlation turns out to be about 11.2 percent. While this may seem low for equity returns, note first that returns are measured at relatively low frequency—quarterly, and second that our portfolio is quite well diversified, with firms from twenty-one countries grouped into ten regions, and across all major industry groups. The three factors used in the five model specifications are able to absorb a significant amount of the cross-firm dependence: the average residual correlation ranges from 3.7 percent to 4 percent across the models.

Another consideration in our comparative analysis is the extent to which the five alternative parametric specifications affect cross-section correlations of the simulated returns. Since all of the five models are based on the same set of observed factors, cross-section correlations of the simulated returns will be affected significantly by parameter heterogeneity only if the differences of parameters across firms are systematic. In the case of pure random differences across slopes, it is easily seen that all specifications would imply similar degrees of error cross-correlations, and this is in fact true in the present application.

9.6   Simulated Credit Loss Distributions

9.6.1   Unconditional and Conditional Loss

With the estimated GVAR model serving as the macroeconomic scenario generator and the fitted multifactor regressions as the linkage between firms and the global economy, we simulated loss distributions one year ahead. We do this by first forecasting, out of sample, the evolution of the sixty-four GVAR risk factors, using those forecasts and the risk factor loadings or return regression coefficients to compute firm-return forecasts, and then seeing if that return forecast falls below the default threshold. A one-year horizon is typical for credit risk management and thus of particular interest. We carried out 200,000 replications for each scenario, baseline as well as shock scenarios, using Gaussian innovations.

The estimation period ends in 1999Q1, and we generate the loss distribution out of samples over one year to the end of 2000Q1. The year over which the loss distribution is simulated turned out to have been relatively benign for the firms in our portfolio when compared to the sample period, which we use to compute unconditional parameters such as expected returns and return volatilities. The unconditional one-year portfolio return (i.e., the exposure-weighted average return of all firms in the portfolio) is 14.67 percent, while using the specification for the fully heterogeneous model M_0, the conditional portfolio return projected for the forecast year is 37.78 percent. This is reflected in the difference between conditional and unconditional portfolio default (the same as expected loss under the maintained assumption of no loss recovery). Recall from table 9.4 that unconditional EL is 0.294 percent, but conditional EL under the default threshold (λ) identifying assumption (8) is 0.096 percent, and under the same distance to default (DD) assumption (5) is 0.089 percent.[22] When we compare the analytical to the simulated conditional portfolio default or expected loss, they are very close: 0.096 percent for same λ and 0.087 percent for same DD.

Fixing DD to be the same across firms by rating also fixes the unconditional default probability; the two are isomorphic. Conditioning on return

---

22. The differences between the latter two estimates are due to rounding error arising from the inverse normal transform on very small probabilities.

forecasts updates those probabilities. Fixing the default threshold λ by rating, however, allows for heterogeneity in the unconditional default probabilities; they just need to be the same on average (see the discussion in section 9.2.2). Those, in turn, may be updated over time as conditioning information is incorporated. This firm-level heterogeneity in unconditional probabilities of default (PD) can make a big difference empirically, as is seen in figure 9.1, which displays a scatter plot of unconditional (horizontal axis) and conditional (vertical axis) one-year PDs for the 243 firms in the portfolio. The top panel is for the same default threshold (λ) by credit rating for all firms, while the bottom panel is for the same DD by credit rating for all firms. The axes on both charts are scaled to be directly comparable. We see immediately in the top panel that conditional and unconditional PDs are not only widely dispersed, reflective of the underlying firm-level heterogeneity, but also highly correlated ($\rho = 0.961$). By contrast, the same DD by rating chart (bottom panel) has both the unconditional and conditional PDs tightly clustered in a narrow range. As there are six credit ratings represented in this study, so we see six vertical lines, where the vertical scatter represents the variation in conditional PD by rating (all having the same unconditional PD, of course) resulting in a lower correlation between unconditional and conditional PDs ($\rho = 0.790$). In contrast to same λ, the PDs implied by same DD change dramatically through conditioning (or updating). These differences will become more explicit and pronounced in the loss distributions across the model specifications, an issue we address next.

9.6.2   Model Heterogeneity and Baseline Losses

In moving from the most homogeneous model M_1 to M_2, we add heterogeneity in the conditional mean by allowing for firm fixed effects, as well as heterogeneity in the unconditional probability of default, namely by introducing credit rating information. To isolate the effects of these relaxations of the homogeneity restrictions, we add an intermediate model, which augments model M_1 with credit rating information. Consequently we denote M_{1a} to be the homogeneous model without the use of rating information, and M_{1b} the homogeneous model that allows for credit ratings in determination of the default thresholds.

HPS provide theoretical results and empirical support showing that neglecting parameter heterogeneity can lead to underestimation of expected losses. But once EL is controlled for, neglecting parameter heterogeneity can lead to overestimation of unexpected losses or risk. Their results are not sensitive to the choice of identification restrictions.

Table 9.7 gives summary statistics for the baseline (i.e., no risk factor shocks) loss distribution for all models, with the top panel imposing the same threshold, λ, identifying restriction, and the bottom panel the same distance to default, DD, restriction. We show the first four moments as well

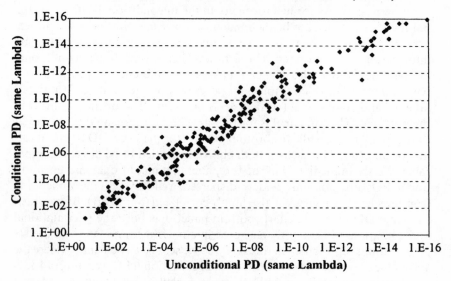

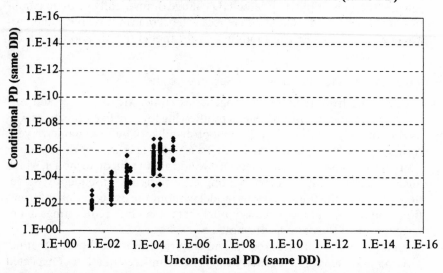

Fig. 9.1   Scatter plot of unconditional (horizontal axis) and conditional (vertical axis) one-year probabilities of default (PD) for 243 firms in portfolio

Notes: Top panel: same default threshold (λ) by credit rating for all firms. Bottom panel: same distance to default (DD) by credit rating for all firms.

Table 9.7 Baseline scenario statistics of simulated losses for models M_0–M_4, one year ahead

Model	Specifications	EL (%)	UL (%)	UL/EL	Skewness	Kurtosis	VaR/EL (%) 99.0	99.5	99.9
Same λ									
M_{1a}	Homogeneous—no rating	0.001	0.030	20.8	29.4	1200	0 (0)	0 (0)	0.56 (382)
M_{1b}	Homogeneous—w/ rating	0.002	0.035	17.1	22.1	633	0 (0)	0 (0)	0.62 (305)
M_2	Firm fixed effects (σ^2)	0.002	0.030	19.4	23.9	691	0 (0)	0 (0)	0.59 (3.77)
M_3	Industry (σ_s^2)	0.006	0.062	10.7	12.9	194	0.15 (26)	0.53 (92)	0.88 (153)
M_4	Regional (σ_i^2)	0.023	0.120	5.2	6.5	56	0.63 (27)	0.85 (37)	1.25 (54)
M_0	Heterogeneous (σ_{jis}^2)	0.094	0.239	2.5	3.6	24	1.06 (11)	1.33 (14)	1.93 (21)
Same DD									
M_{1a}	Homogeneous—no rating	0.644	0.905	1.4	2.9	19	4.1 (6)	5.07 (8)	7.31 (11)
M_{1b}	Homogeneous—w/ rating	0.150	0.363	2.4	4.3	36	1.63 (11)	2.08 (14)	3.27 (22)
M_2	Firm fixed effects (σ^2)	0.131	0.324	2.5	4.3	36	1.47 (11)	1.84 (14)	2.91 (22)
M_3	Industry (σ_s^2)	0.146	0.358	2.5	4.2	34	1.63 (11)	2.06 (14)	3.16 (22)
M_4	Regional (σ_i^2)	0.152	0.358	2.4	3.8	27	1.62 (11)	2.01 (13)	2.96 (19)
M_0	Heterogeneous (σ_{jis}^2)	0.086	0.259	3.0	5.4	58	1.18 (14)	1.52 (18)	2.43 (28)

Note: Simulated one year ahead loss distributions for all return model specifications using 200,000 simulations. Details on the return specifications for models M_0 to M_4 are given in section 9.5.2. Table compares two alternative identification restrictions: top panel imposes the same return default threshold, λ, by rating when rating information is used (this is the case for all models except M_{1a}), while bottom panel imposes the same distance to default, DD, by rating when rating information is used. EL = expected loss; UL = unexpected loss.

as three tail quartiles or values-at-risk (VaR): 99.0 percent, 99.5 percent and 99.9 percent, corresponding to levels commonly used by risk managers, and in the last case, the risk tolerance level of the New Basel Capital Accord (BCBS 2004).

Looking first at the top panel, EL and UL vary significantly across the different specifications, both increasing as we increase model heterogeneity. However, as shown in HPS, it is important that the differences in ELs across the different portfolios are taken into account before implications of heterogeneity for unexpected losses can be evaluated. There is no obvious way that this can be done. Here we normalize risk, whether measured by unexpected loss (UL) or VaR, by EL. We shall refer to these as EL multiples.

The results in table 9.7 show that it takes about 21 EL multiples to obtain one standard deviation of losses for the most homogeneous model M_{1a}, just eleven for the industry model M_3, and only 2.5 for the fully heterogeneous model M_0. The third and fourth moments, skewness and kurtosis respectively, also decline when more heterogeneity is allowed for. Imposing homogeneity results in overly skewed and fat-tailed loss distributions. This point becomes quite clear when looking at the 99.9 percent VaR: model M_{1a} and M_{1b} have EL multiples in excess of 300, while the regional model M_4 has a multiple of only 54 and the fully heterogeneous model M_0 only 21, less than one-tenth of the most homogeneous model.

An important source of heterogeneity turns out to be the credit rating, which influences, among other things, the default threshold. Adding credit ratings to the homogeneous specification, model M_{1b}, results in a noticeable drop in EL multiples: UL/EL drops from 20.8 to 17.1, and 99.9 percent VaR from 382 to 305. Adding firm-fixed effects, model M_2 does not help; in fact, risk seems to increase slightly, although this could be due to simulation errors. We need to allow for variation in factor loadings, either by industry (model M_3), or region (model M_4), before EL multiples decline further. These findings are in line with the results reported in HPS: the factor that changes the shape of the loss density the most is the use of information on credit ratings in the construction of the loss distribution. Considering that the New Basel Capital Accord is centered around more careful modeling of credit ratings, either internal or external, this emphasis seems well placed indeed. A similar pattern holds when looking at Value at Risk. In this regard, regional heterogeneity seems to play a more important role than industry heterogeneity, perhaps not surprising given the international nature of this portfolio.[23]

Turning to the bottom panel, where the loss distributions are simulated under the same DD-identifying restriction, differences across model spec-

23. We tried a different industry specification using ten instead of six groups to match the number of parameters in the regional model (there are ten regions). This did not change our conclusions.

ifications are much more muted. The results for the heterogeneous model M_0 are broadly in line with its same λ counterpart in the top panel (EL, UL, and VaR are similar). However, EL decreases as we increase the degree of parameter heterogeneity. Moreover, there is little difference in EL multiples, whether looking at loss volatility (UL) or VaR. In fact, the results would suggest that increased heterogeneity actually increases risk: UL/EL for M_{1a} is 1.4 and for M_0 is 3.0. Further, 99.9 percent VaR, normalized by EL, is 11 for M_{1a} and 28 for M_0.

These results differ both from those under the same threshold-identifying restriction and from those reported in HPS for the same DD restrictions. Under the same DD assumption, the actual default threshold used in the simulations is firm-specific, and is computed using firm-specific estimates for unconditional expected returns and their standard deviations. Since the sample period is short for several firms, we may have rather poor estimates of the unconditional moments. The same λ assumption implies varying DDs (and hence unconditional PDs) across firms within a rating category, although, importantly, they average out to match the rating-specific unconditional PD. In the absence of reliable estimates of unconditional means and volatilities of firm returns, the resulting firm-specific default thresholds are likely to be rather noisy. In light of these results, and the previous discussion of unconditional and conditional PDs, in the remaining analysis we focus on the same threshold (λ)-identify restrictions.

Before proceeding to the shock scenarios, it may be of interest to compare the simulated UL to that implied by the Vasicek model, as discussed in section 9.3. This asymptotic expression, given in equation (21), is driven by the average default rate across the portfolio, π, and the default correlation, ρ^*, itself a function of π and the average return correlation of the firms in the portfolio, ρ, which is 11.2 percent for our portfolio; see equation (20) in section 9.3. Thus, using the unconditional portfolio default rate from table 9.4, $\pi = 0.294$ percent; this yields a default correlation of $\rho^* = 0.470$ percent and an asymptotic UL $= \sqrt{\pi(1-\pi)\rho^*} = 0.371$ percent, which is above the simulated UL of all models. However, those simulated ULs are conditional, not unconditional, and if we substitute the simulated (conditional) EL (which, under the maintained assumption of no loss recovery, is identical to π), all asymptotic UL values are below their simulated counterparts, as they should be, assuming that the average return correlation ρ remains unchanged. For example, in the case of model M_0, $\pi = 0.094$ percent, so that $\rho^* = 0.208$ percent. In that case, asymptotic UL $= 0.140$ percent, which is below the simulated UL of 0.239 percent. The difference is clearly due to granularity, an issue we pick up in Section 6.5.

In figure 9.2 we compare the simulated loss distributions across model specifications. The top panel displays the 20 percent tail (80th percentile and beyond) and the bottom panel focuses on the 5 percent tail. The tail of that loss distribution rises earlier and more gradually for the most

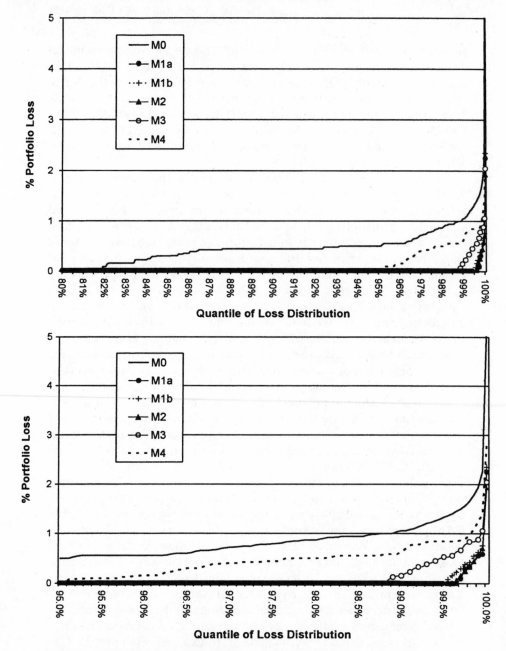

Fig. 9.2 Comparing the tail of the baseline loss distributions across models, same λ identifying restriction by rating when rating information is used, 200,000 simulations

Notes: Top panel: 20 percent tail (losses beyond the 80th percentile). Bottom panel: 5 percent tail (losses beyond the 95th percentile). Model M_0 is fully heterogeneous model, M_{1a} is homogenous (no rating information), M_{1b} is homogenous (with rating information), M_2 is firm fixed effects, M_3 is industry fixed and marginal effects, and M_4 is regional fixed and marginal effects.

heterogeneous model, M_0, and late and suddenly for the more homogeneous models. We see that the fully heterogeneous model in particular accumulates losses much earlier in the distribution, already by about the 82nd percentile, than the other models. Significant losses are not seen until about the 95th percentile for the regional model M_4, not until after the 97th percentile for the industry model M_3, and well beyond the 99th percentile for all other models.

9.6.3   Model Heterogeneity and Risk Factor Shocks

One of the main advantages of our conditional modeling approach is that it allows us to consider the impact of different macroeconomic or risk factor shock scenarios. The ability to conduct shock scenario analysis with observable risk factors is clearly important for policy analysis, be it business or public policy.

Recall that the risk factors in the firm-return models are equity returns, interest rates, and oil prices. In addition, we shall explore the impact of business cycle heterogeneity across different countries by considering shocks to real output, which (as noted earlier) can influence the loss distributions indirectly through their contemporaneous correlations with equity returns and interest rates. Accordingly, we examine the following equiprobable scenarios, though others, of course, are possible.[24]

- a $\pm 2.33\sigma$ shock to real U.S. equity, corresponding to a quarterly change of ± 14.28 percent from the baseline forecast[25]
- a $\pm 2.33\sigma$ shock to the German short-term interest rate, corresponding to a quarterly rise of 0.33 percent
- a -2.33σ shock to real U.S. output, corresponding to a quarterly drop of 1.85 percent

In order to learn more about the tail properties of the various loss distributions, we also consider an extreme stress scenario for the U.S. equity market, as reported in PSTW, namely an adverse shock of 8.02σ. This corresponds to a quarterly drop of 49 percent, which is the largest quarterly drop in the S&P 500 index since 1928, which occurred over the three months of March to May of 1932. Finally, we include an intermediate negative equity shock of -5σ, which corresponds to a quarterly decline of 30.64 percent. Details of how the macroeconomic shocks are generated and how they feed through firm returns to the loss distribution can be found in PSTW.

We start the discussion with a $\pm 2.33\sigma$ shock to real U.S. equity under the same threshold, λ, restriction, summarized in table 9.8. For each model we

---

24. 2.33σ corresponds, in the Gaussian case, to the 99 percent VaR, a typical benchmark in risk management.

25. Relative to historic averages, this shock corresponds to a rise (drop) of 17.95 percent (11.35 percent), computed as $\exp(2.23 \text{ percent} \pm 14.28 \text{ percent}) - 1$.

Table 9.8 ±2.33σ shock to U.S. real equity returns: Statistics of simulated losses for models M_0–M_4, one year ahead, same λ

Model	Specification	EL (%)	Percentage of EL to baseline	UL (%)	Percentage of UL to baseline	Skewness	Kurtosis	Value-at-Risk (%) 99.0	99.5	99.9 (%Δ to baseline)
M_{1a}	Homogeneous—No rating									
−2.33 σ		0.004	172	0.052	73	19.4	537	0.0	0.38	0.74 (33)
Baseline		0.001		0.030		29.4	1,200	0.0	0.0	0.56
+2.33 σ		0.0005	−67	0.016	−48	38.0	1,652	0.0	0.0	0.12 (−78)
M_{1b}	Homogeneous—w/rating									
−2.33 σ		0.007	221	0.066	88	13.9	279	0.25	0.56	0.88 (41)
Baseline		0.002		0.035		22.1	633	0.0	0.0	0.635
+2.33 σ		0.0007	−68	0.019	−45	36.7	1,673	0.0	0.0	0.30 (−52)
M_2	Firm fixed effects (σ^2)									
−2.33 σ		0.005	228	0.056	87	14.3	259	0.15	0.44	0.83 (41)
Baseline		0.002		0.030		23.9	691	0.0	0.0	0.59
+2.33 σ		0.0005	−69	0.016	−46	39.0	1,704	0.0	0.0	0.16 (−73)
M_3	Industry (σ_s^2)									
−2.33 σ		0.014	151	0.102	65	9.0	108	0.62	0.83	1.08 (23)
Baseline		0.006		0.062		12.9	194	0.0	0.53	0.88
+2.33 σ		0.002	−61	0.037	−40	19.0	400	0.0	0.0	0.67 (−24)
M_4	Regional (σ_i^2)									
−2.33 σ		0.043	88	0.171	42	5.1	37	0.85	1.00	1.50 (20)
Baseline		0.023		0.120		6.5	56	0.63	0.85	1.25
+2.33 σ		0.012	−46	0.085	−29	8.4	86	0.50	0.59	0.87 (−30)
M_0	Heterogeneous (σ_{jis}^2)									
−2.33 σ		0.142	51	0.314	31	3.4	21	1.41	1.73	2.55 (32)
Baseline		0.094		0.239		3.6	24	1.06	1.33	1.94
+2.33 σ		0.065	−31	0.189	−21	3.9	26	0.89	1.00	1.52 (−21)

Notes: Simulated one-year-ahead loss distributions for all return model specifications imposing symmetric shocks to U.S. market equity returns. Two hundred thousand simulations are used, and the same return default threshold, λ, by rating when rating information is used (this is the case for all models except M_{1a}). EL = expected loss; UL = unexpected loss.

repeat the baseline results for ease of comparison and display the percentage increase (decrease) from that baseline of EL, UL, and 99.9 percent VaR. For each model, the percentage increase in EL and UL arising from the adverse shock is always larger than the corresponding decline in losses due to a benign shock. Consider model M_{1a}: EL (UL) increases by 172 percent (73 percent) under the adverse shock and decreases by 67 percent (48 percent) under the benign shock. The size of those impact declines as we allow for more heterogeneity. The regional model M_4, for instance, shows an increase in EL (UL) of 88 percent (42 percent) from the adverse shock, against a decline of 46 percent (29 percent) from the benign shock. The smallest impact can be seen from the most heterogeneous model, M_0: the adverse shock increases EL (UL) by 51 percent (31 percent), and the benign shock decreases EL (UL) by 31 percent (21 percent).

This asymmetric and nonproportional response of credit losses to symmetric shocks is due to the nonlinearity of the credit risk model. When focusing on the tails of the loss distribution, however, only the fully heterogeneous model M_0 exhibits this particular asymmetric response; namely, that risk reductions are proportionately less than risk increases due to an adverse and benign shock, respectively. For all other model specifications the opposite seems to be true: the reduction in 99.9 percent VaR arising from the benign shock is larger than the corresponding increase in 99.9 percent VaR due to the adverse shock. Thus, by imposing homogeneity, not only are the relative loss responses exaggerated (all the percentage increases and decreases are larger for the restricted than for the unrestricted model), but perceived reduction in risk in the tail of the loss distribution tends to be overly optimistic.

Finally, note that an adverse shock results in less skewed and fat-tailed loss distributions, relative to their respective baselines, across all models; conversely, a benign shock renders them more extreme. The advise (benign) shock results in more (fewer) firms defaulting systematically due to the displacement of expected (i.e., forecast) returns, before any additional idiosyncratic risk is accounted for. As a result, an adverse (benign) shock shifts probability mass of the loss distribution closer to (further from) the mean. The effects of the shocks on the shape of the loss distribution is quite large for relatively homogeneous models, and much more modest for heterogeneous ones. For instance, the skewness (kurtosis) for M_{1a} decreases to 19.4 (537) under the adverse shock compared to the baseline, 29.4 (1200), but increases to 38.0 (1652) under the benign shock. By contrast, the skewness and kurtosis decrease to 5.1 and 37.0, respectively, for the regional model, M_4, under the adverse shock scenario, as compared to the baseline values of 6.5 and 56, but increases to 8.4 and 86.0 under the benign shock scenario, respectively. The relative impact is, of course, even smaller for the fully heterogeneous model, M_0.

The evidence thus far suggests that heterogeneity is important in controlling risk, both under a baseline forecast and under shock scenarios. Allowing for regional heterogeneity appears to be more important than allowing for industry or sector heterogeneity. Both the baseline and shock-conditional loss distributions seem to change noticeably with the addition of heterogeneous factor loadings, that is, starting with model M_3. However, the biggest marginal change arises when allowing for full heterogeneity with model M_0.

Next we consider an adverse shock to German interest rates. Naturally, we could have shocked interest rates of other countries, for example, the United States, but since we already have other U.S.-based shock scenarios, we wanted to broaden the discussion by considering shocks to other countries' macroeconomic factors. Interest rate shocks are of particular interest in our modeling context because the corresponding factor loading is positive, but insignificant, for the pooled models M_1 and M_2, on average negative and significant for the heterogeneous model M_0, and rather mixed for the industry and regional models, M_3 and M_4.

The loss simulation results are summarized in table 9.9. Compared with adverse U.S. equity shocks, the impact on credit losses due to an equiprobable adverse shock to German interest rates is more modest. EL increases on average by only about 24 percent, UL by only 12 percent, and 99.9 percent VaR by around 5 percent. Here too we see a similar model ranking as before, with the most homogeneous model M_{1a} being the most shock sensitive, at least when measured by EL and UL impact, and the most heterogeneous model M_0 the least shock sensitive. The impact on 99.9 percent VaR is modest, and given parameter uncertainty, broadly similar across the different model specifications.

Even though the factor loading on interest rates is positive, albeit small and not significant, for the pooled models M_{1a}, M_{1b}, and M_2, losses still increase in reaction to an adverse interest rate shock. Because of the complicated interdependencies that exist in the GVAR model, shocking one of the factors will potentially impact all the other sixty-two factors. As a result, the overall effect of the shock on the loss distribution need not have the same sign as the coefficient of the factor in the return equation. Consequently, an adverse interest rate shock may have the counterintuitive, benign direct effect on firm returns in the pooled return regressions, but the intuitive adverse indirect effects through the equity return factor.

With this in mind we consider the effects of an adverse shock to real U.S. output. Recall that output does not enter the firm-return regressions; however, shocks in output may enter indirectly through other variables, such as interest rates and equity prices. We summarize those results in table 9.10 and notice immediately that the changes from the baseline are of the "wrong" sign, but quite small, and are unlikely to be statistically significant. One year after the shock, credit losses are projected to actually decline somewhat. Average decline in EL across models is about 5 percent,

Table 9.9 **+2.33σ shock to German interest rates—Quarterly increase of 0.33 percent: Statistics of simulated losses for models M_0–M_4, one year ahead, same λ**

Model	Specification	EL (%)	Percentage Δ EL to baseline	UL (%)	Percentage Δ UL to baseline	Skewness	Kurtosis	Value-at-Risk (%) 99.0	99.5	99.9 (%Δ to baseline)
M_{1a}	Homogeneous—no rating	0.002	39	0.036	20	26.2	980	0.0	0.0	0.58 (5)
M_{1b}	Homogeneous—w/ rating	0.003	32	0.041	16	19.7	511	0.0	0.180	0.65 (4)
M_2	Firm fixed effects (σ^2)	0.002	28	0.034	13	20.8	520	0.0	0.0	0.59 (1)
M_3	Industry (σ_s^2)	0.007	22	0.068	10	11.7	164	0.33	0.56	0.88 (<1)
M_4	Regional (σ_i^2)	0.026	15	0.130	8	6.2	51	0.77	0.85	1.34 (7)
M_0	Heterogeneous (σ_{jis}^2)	0.10	8	0.25	5	3.6	23	1.11	1.40	2.04 (5)

Note: Simulated one-year-ahead loss distributions for all return model specifications imposing an adverse shock to the German short maturity interest rate. Two hundred thousand simulations are used, and the same return default threshold, λ, by rating when rating information is used (this is the case for all models except M_{1a}). EL = expected loss; UL = unexpected loss.

Table 9.10   **−2.33σ shock to U.S. real output—Quarterly decline of 1.85 percent: Statistics of simulated losses for models M_0–M_4, one year ahead, same λ**

Model	Specification	EL (%)	Percentage ΔEL to baseline	UL (%)	Percentage ΔUL to baseline	Skewness	Kurtosis	Value-at-Risk (%)		99.9 (%Δ to baseline)
								99.0	99.5	
M_{1a}	Homogeneous—no rating	0.001	−13	0.028	−6	31.8	1,405	0.0	0.0	0.53 (−4)
M_{1b}	Homogeneous—w/ rating	0.002	−2	0.035	0	22.2	619	0.0	0.0	0.63 (<1)
M_2	Firm fixed effects ($\sigma^2 0$)	0.001	−4	0.030	−2	24.3	703	0.0	0.0	0.59 (<1)
M_3	Industry (σ_s^2)	0.006	−2	0.062	0	12.9	192	0.15	0.53	0.88 (<1)
M_4	Regional (σ_i^2)	0.022	−6	0.117	−3	6.7	59	0.59	0.85	1.23 (−2)
M_0	Heterogeneous (σ_{jis}^2)	0.088	−7	0.230	−4	3.7	24	1.00	1.28	1.86 (−4)

Notes: Simulated one-year-ahead loss distributions for all return model specifications imposing an adverse shock to U.S. real output growth. Two hundred thousand simulations are used, and the same return default threshold, λ, by rating when rating information is used (this is the case for all models except M_{1a}). EL = expected loss; UL = unexpected loss.

the decline in UL is about 3 percent, and the decline in 99.9 percent VaR is about 2 percent relative to the baseline loss distribution. In section 9.6.4 we explore whether including output directly in the firm-specific return regressions makes any difference.

Finally, we consider the effect of extreme risk factor shocks on the resulting distribution of credit losses under different model specifications. Table 9.11 presents results from two different U.S. real-equity shock scenarios: -5.00σ in panel A, and -8.02σ in panel B, the latter matching the largest quarterly drop in the S&P 500 index since 1928. To be sure, a shock as extreme as -8.02σ is, of course, outside the bounds of the estimated model. It would be unreasonable to believe that such a large shock would not result in changes to the underlying parameters. However, it is still instructive to examine the impact of an extreme shock, as one way that one might stress a credit risk model. Moreover, 5σ events are more common at higher frequencies than the quarterly data we have available to us indicates, and because of this our results will likely underestimate the true loss outcomes.

Under the -5σ shock scenario, shown in panel A, increases in expected losses across models range from eleven-fold (1035 percent); M_2 to ninefold (794 percent; M_{1a}) to just 154 percent (M_0). UL increases for the same models are about three-and-a-half-fold for M_{1a} (244 percent) and M_2 (266 percent), and not quite double for M_0 (85 percent). Differences in the tail impact at the 99.9 percent level are not as extreme: 150 percent for M_{1a}, 107 percent for M_2, and 83 percent for M_0. As the shock becomes more extreme and takes the value of -8.02σ, the different shock sensitivities of the models, as measured, for instance, by 99.9 percent VaR, become even more apparent (see panel B in table 9.11). Increases in VaR values relative to baseline losses are less than 200 percent for models M_0 and M_4, and nearly 400 percent for model M_{1a}. The broad pattern observed so far holds: the more restrictive (homogeneous) the model, the more sensitively it reacts to shock scenarios.

As the shock becomes more extreme to -8.02σ, the resulting loss distribution for all models becomes less skewed and fat-tailed, as measured by kurtosis. To see this graphically we generated density plots for model M_0, presented in figure 9.3, where we display the simulated loss densities for the baseline, the symmetric $\pm 2.33\sigma$ shocks, and the two severe adverse shocks to U.S. real equity prices. The ordering of the shocks is clearly seen in the plot around the 1 percent portfolio loss point: from benign and lowest density to most adverse and highest density.

9.6.4   Business Cycle Shocks: An Alternative Model Specification

The return regressions used in the previous simulation exercises do not select the growth rate of real output as a risk factor. As noted earlier, this might not be that surprising, as the effects of business cycle fluctuations on

Table 9.11 Extreme shocks to real U.S. equity returns Statistics of simulated losses for models M_0–M_4, one year ahead, same λ

Model	Specification	EL (%)	Percentage ΔEL to baseline	UL (%)	Percentage ΔUL to baseline	Skewness	Kurtosis	Value-at-Risk (%)		
								99.0	99.5	99.9 (%Δ to baseline)
				A. −5σ, Quarterly decline of 30.6 percent						
M_{1a}	Homogeneous—no rating	0.01	794	0.10	244	12.7	241	0.53	0.64	1.39 (150)
M_{1b}	Homogeneous—w/ rating	0.02	963	0.13	265	8.8	116	0.64	0.88	1.47 (135)
M_2	Firm fixed effects (σ^2)	0.02	1035	0.11	266	8.8	113	0.62	0.76	1.22 (107)
M_3	Industry (σ_v^2)	0.04	588	0.18	192	6.3	59	0.88	1.08	1.77 (101)
M_4	Regional (σ_l^2)	0.09	275	0.26	113	4.1	2.7	1.20	1.43	2.15 (72)
M_0	Heterogeneous (σ_{jls}^2)	0.24	154	0.44	85	3.1	19	1.98	2.42	3.53 (83)
				B. −8.02σ, Quarterly decline of 49 percent						
M_{1a}	Homogeneous—no rating	0.05	3363	0.23	674	8.5	119	1.17	1.54	2.72 (390)
M_{1b}	Homogeneous—w/ rating	0.08	3914	0.28	689	5.7	57	1.29	1.67	2.79 (347)
M_2	Firm fixed effects (σ^2)	0.07	4203	0.24	687	5.7	55	1.08	1.44	2.36 (302)
M_3	Industry (σ_v^2)	0.12	1974	0.35	460	4.4	32	1.63	1.98	3.07 (249)
M_4	Regional (σ_l^2)	0.19	714	0.41	242	3.4	20	1.86	2.24	3.32 (165)
M_0	Heterogeneous (σ_{jls}^2)	0.45	382	0.69	187	2.9	19	3.09	3.74	5.44 (181)

Notes: Simulated one-year-ahead loss distributions for all return model specifications imposing two more extreme adverse shocks to U.S. market equity returns. Two hundred thousand simulations are used, and the same return default threshold, λ, by rating when rating information is used (this is the case for all models except M_{1a}). EL = expected loss; UL = unexpected loss.

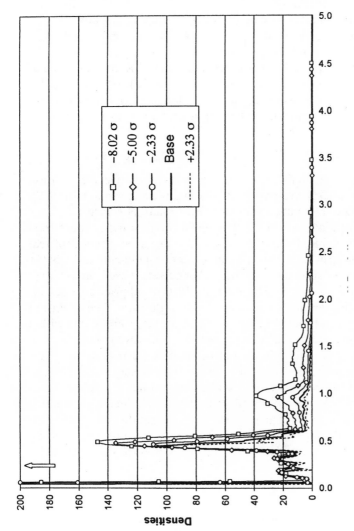

Fig. 9.3   Comparing simulated loss densities across different shocks to U.S. real equity prices, fully heterogeneous model M_0 imposing the same default threshold λ identifying condition, 200,000 simulations

Notes: All densities are estimated with an Epanechnikov kernel using Silverman's (1986) optimal bandwidth. The vertical axis is cropped at the top (hence the up arrow) to allow for better visualization of the different densities; most of the loss density is at or very near the origin. The ordering of the shocks is clearly seen in the plot around the 1 percent portfolio loss point: from benign and lowest density to most adverse and highest density.

firm returns could have already been incorporated indirectly through market returns. It is, however, possible that the factor selection and the subsequent model estimation could have been biased due to the use of country-specific asset return variables, particularly in the case of countries with relatively small asset markets.[26]

With this in mind, and following the work of Kapetanios and Pesaran (2004), we proceed to estimate an alternative version of the fully heterogeneous model, which includes a global equity return, $\Delta \overline{q}_{t+1}$, defined as the cross-sectional average of all equity indexes in the GVAR model instead of the country-specific market returns, $\Delta \tilde{q}_{i,t+1}$, used in (35). We then run this version of the return regression augmented with real output growth for region i, denoted by $\Delta y_{i,t+1}$, and the other variables, namely changes in interest rates ($\Delta \rho_{i,t+1}$) and oil prices (Δp^0_{t+1}).[27]

$$(40) \quad r_{jis,t+1} = \alpha_{jis} + \beta_{1,jis}\Delta \overline{q}_{t+1} + \beta_{2,jis}\Delta \rho_{i,t+1} + \beta_{3,jis}\Delta p^0_{t+1} + \beta_{4,jis}\Delta y_{i,t+1} + \xi_{jis,t+1}$$

The mean group estimate (MGE) results for the alternative specification (40) using purchasing-power-parity (PPP) weights are given in table 9.12. These new estimates attribute a smaller effect to market returns, with the average market beta falling from 0.918 to 0.780 and the interest rate effects rising (in absolute value) from –2.99 to –4.236. The average effect of real output growth on firm returns is also statistically significant and has the correct sign, which contrasts with the earlier results, based on country-specific equity market returns. The average effects of oil price changes, although still positive, are no longer statistically significant. The change in the estimates as a result of using $\Delta \overline{q}_{t+1}$ instead of $\Delta \tilde{q}_{i,t+1}$ are in line with a priori expectations and could be explained by a positive correlation between the country-specific market returns and the errors in the firm-specific return regressions. This is also reflected in the estimates of the in-sample fit of the return regressions where the average $\overline{R}^2$ declines from 0.201 and 0.103 as we move from $\Delta \tilde{q}_{i,t+1}$ to $\Delta \overline{q}_{t+1}$. The decline in the fit is quite substantial and could be an important consideration in the choice between the alternative specifications, although any simultaneity arising from inclusion of $\Delta \tilde{q}_{i,t+1}$ could in itself result in an upward bias in the average $\overline{R}^2$.

Bearing in mind the uncertainty associated with these alternative speci-

---

26. Recall that the estimates of the output effects are obtained by regression of firm-specific returns on the market returns, output growth, and other variables, such as changes in the interest rates and oil prices. Since market returns are in effect weighted averages of the firm-specific returns, the return regressions could yield biased estimates if the market return happens to be based on a relatively few firms.

27. This cross-sectional average may be either equal weighted or PPP weighted. We experimented with both. In the latter case we used PPP weights from 1996, the same weights used in the GVAR to construct regions from countries. There were little differences in the result, and in what follows we focus on the estimates based on the PPP-weighted global real equity index.

Table 9.12   **Mean group estimates (MGE) of factor loadings, heterogeneous model (M$_0$): Alternative specification**

Factors ratios	MGE $\hat{\beta}$	Standard error of MGE SE($\hat{\beta}$)	t-
Constant	0.010	0.003	3.075
$\Delta \bar{q}_{t+1}$	0.780	0.031	24.874
$\Delta \rho_{i,t+1}$	−4.326	0.520	−6.923
Δp^o_{t+1}	0.041	0.038	1.064
$\Delta y_{i,t+1}$	0.700	0.260	2.695
Average R^2	0.157		
Average $\bar{R}^2$	0.103		
No. of firm quarters	17,114		

Notes: $\Delta \bar{q}_{t+1}$ is the cross-sectional average of all equity indexes in the GVAR model using 1996 PPP weights. $\Delta \rho_{i,t+1}$ is the change in the domestic interest rate; Δp^o_{t+1} is the change in oil prices; $\Delta y_{i,t+1}$ is the change in domestic real GDP.

fications, the loss simulations based on the new return regressions for the baseline scenario as well as for the 2.33σ shock scenarios are summarized in table 9.13. These simulations can be viewed as providing a check on the robustness of the loss-simulation results obtained so far. Baseline loss behavior is only somewhat different from M$_0$ (see last row of table 9.7, top panel), but, importantly, it is closer than any of the other restricted models, even though their in-sample goodness of fit was higher. When we examine the impact of shocks, even though real output now directly enters the firm return regressions, the impact of an adverse shock to real U.S. output growth is very similar to the previous specification: it is both small and of the wrong sign. Meanwhile, the impact of the other shocks is similar in this as in the original specification.

Although the average loading on output is positive, statistically significant, and large at 0.7, it turns out that about half (45 percent) of the firms actually have a negative coefficient (loading) on output. Indeed, when we look at the MGE of the positive and negative subsets, they are both significant. Hence it is not surprising that for our portfolio the net impact of an adverse shock to output is about zero. Of course, if the portfolio were composed only of firms with a positive loading, credit losses would likely increase in the event of an adverse output shock.

As far as loss distributions are concerned, our overall conclusions seem to be robust to the choice of the firm-specific return regressions.

9.6.5   Idiosyncratic Risk and Granularity

Portfolio-level results of credit risk models such as those discussed in Vasicek (1987, 2002) assume that the portfolio is sufficiently large that all idiosyncratic risk has been diversified away. More generally, we consider a

Table 9.13   Impact of various 2.33σ shocks on alternative model: Statistics of simulated losses, one year ahead, Same λ

Scenario	EL (%)	Percentage Δ EL to baseline	UL (%)	Percentage Δ UL to baseline	Skewness	Kurtosis	Value-at-Risk (%) 99.0	99.5	99.9 (%Δ to baseline)
Baseline	0.091		0.208		2.7	12	0.92	1.00	1.43
−2.33σ shock to U.S. real output growth	0.090	−1	0.205	−2	2.6	11	0.91	0.97	1.39 (−3)
+2.33σ shock to German interest rates	0.097	6	0.215	4	2.7	12	0.94	1.07	1.52 (6)
−2.33σ shock to U.S. equity returns	0.137	51	0.259	25	2.3	10	1.08	1.26	1.74 (22)
+2.33σ shock to U.S. equity returns	0.066	−28	0.176	−15	3.1	15	0.79	0.94	1.28 (−11)

Notes: Simulated one-year-ahead loss distributions using the alternative specification of the fully heterogeneous model M_0, described in section 9.6.4. Comparing loss distributions for the baseline scenario, adverse shocks to U.S. real output growth and German short maturity interest rates, and symmetric shocks to U.S. equity returns. For all scenarios, 200,000 simulations are used, and the same return default threshold, λ, by rating when rating information is used (this is the case for all models except M_{1a}). EL = expected loss; UL = unexpected loss.

credit portfolio composed of N different credit assets, such as loans, each with exposures or weights w_i, for $i = 1, 2, \ldots, N$, such that the granularity condition (22) holds. Recall that a sufficient condition for equation (22) to hold is given by $w_i = O(N^{-1})$.[28] The lower the average firm return correlation, the greater the potential for diversification, but a larger N is required to attain that limit if correlations are lower. A common rule of thumb for return diversification of a portfolio of equities is $N \approx 50$. But as seen in section 9.6.2, default correlations are much lower than return correlations, meaning that more firms are needed to reach the diversification limits of credit risk.

Thus it seems reasonable to ask if a portfolio of $N = 243$ is large enough to diversify away the idiosyncratic risk. To answer this question we used an empirical version of the one-factor Vasicek model (described in section 9.3) and analyzed the impact of increasing N on simulated compared to analytic (asymptotic) unexpected loss (UL). For simulation purposes, Vasicek's model takes the following form:

$$(41) \qquad r_{j,t+1} = \bar{r} + \sigma_f f_{t+1} + \sigma_\varepsilon \varepsilon_{j,t+1},$$

where $\bar{r} = \sum_{t=1}^{T} \sum_{j=1}^{N} r_{jt}/NT$,

$$\begin{pmatrix} \varepsilon_{j,t+1} \\ f_{t+1} \end{pmatrix} \sim \text{i.i.d.} N(\mathbf{0}, \mathbf{I}_2),$$

$\mathbf{I}_2$ is a 2-dimensional identity matrix, $\rho = \sigma_f^2/(\sigma_f^2 + \sigma_\varepsilon^2)$, and σ_f^2 is the variance of the market return. These parameters can be estimated as

$$(42) \qquad \hat{\sigma}_f^2 = \frac{\sum_{t=1}^{T} (\bar{r}_t - r)^2}{T - 1}, \bar{r}_t = \sum_{j=1}^{N} r_{jt}/N,$$

and

$$(43) \qquad \hat{\sigma}_\varepsilon^2 = \frac{\sum_{t=1}^{T} \sum_{j=1}^{N} (r_{jt} - r_t)^2}{NT - 2}.$$

Loss is given by (19) with the return default threshold given by

$$(44) \qquad \lambda = \bar{r} + \sqrt{\sigma_f^2 + \sigma_\varepsilon^2} \Phi^{-1}(\pi).$$

For our portfolio, for the one-year horizon we have the following parameter values: $\bar{r} = 13.356$ percent, $\hat{\sigma}_f = 11.230$ percent, $\hat{\sigma}_\varepsilon = 34.856$ percent, $\hat{\pi} = 0.294$ percent, so that the implied average return correlation $\rho = 9.404$ percent, with an associated default correlation of $\rho^* = 0.369$ percent.[29] Substituting these values in (44) obtains a one-year return default thresh-

---

28. Condition (22) on the portfolio weights was in fact embodied in the initial proposal of the New Basel Accord in the form of the Granularity Adjustments, which was designed to mitigate the effects of significant single-borrower concentrations on the credit loss distribution. See Basel Committee (2001, chapter 8).

29. The relationship between ρ and ρ^* is given by equation (20).

Table 9.14   **Impact of granularity using Vasicek model**

	Number of loans in portfolio (N)				
	119	243	1,000	5,000	10,000
Deviation from asymptotic lower bound (%)	80	44	12	3	2

old of –87.51 percent, meaning that any firm that experiences a one-year return worse than –87.51 percent would default.

Calibrating Vasicek's model to these parameters we simulated losses assuming different portfolio granularity, ranging from 119 to 10,000 firms. To be sure, all firms share the same draw of the systematic factor f and the same default threshold lambda, while each firm carries idiosyncratic risk (reflected by firm-specific draws from $\varepsilon_{j,t+1} \sim N(0, 1)$. Idiosyncratic risk should diversify away, with the simulated UL approaching the analytic UL as the number of firms increases.

The results are summarized in table 9.14. The result for $N = 119$ relates to the number of firms in the PSTW portfolio. By more than doubling N we cut idiosyncratic risk nearly in half. But to come within 3 percent of the asymptotic UL of the portfolio, more than 5,000 firms are needed! Thus credit portfolios or credit derivatives such as CDOs, which contain rather fewer number of firms, will likely still retain a significant degree of idiosyncratic risk, an observation also made by Amato and Remolona (2004).

9.7   Concluding Remarks

In this paper we have made use of a conditional credit risk model with observable risk factors, developed in Pesaran, Schuermann, Treutler, and Weiner (2005), to explore several dimensions of credit risk diversification: across industries (sectors) and across different countries or regions, either in a relatively restrictive fixed effects return specification, or by allowing for full firm-level heterogeneity. Specifically, we fix the number of risk factors—there are three: market equity returns and changes in domestic interest rates and oil prices—and only vary the degree of parameter heterogeneity across models. We find that full firm-level parameter heterogeneity matters a great deal for capturing differences in simulated credit loss distributions. Expected loss increases as more heterogeneity is allowed for. However, unexpected losses, normalized by EL, decline dramatically. Moreover, imposing homogeneity results in overly skewed and fat-tailed loss distributions.

These differences become more pronounced in the presence of shocks to systematic risk factors. The most restricted model, which imposes the same factor sensitivities across all firms, is overly sensitive to such shocks, and thus failing to properly account for parameter heterogeneity could result in too much implied risk capital. Allowing for regional parameter heterogeneity seems to better approximate the loss distributions generated by the fully heterogeneous model than just allowing for industry heterogeneity.

Our findings have a number of implications for both public and private (or business) policy. For example, in the case of a bank's risk management practices, neglected heterogeneity resulting in underestimation of expected losses would cause a bank to underprovision for (expected) losses. Furthermore, the resulting overestimation of unexpected losses would cause a bank to hold too much capital. Another example is the structuring and pricing of collateralized debt obligations (CDOs). These increasingly popular and widespread credit instruments are structured, and priced, by segmenting the loss distribution into risk tranches. We have shown that the shape of the loss distribution is affected significantly under neglected heterogeneity, in which case the resulting pricing and risk assessment would in turn be significantly affected. Related, our analysis shows that the size of the portfolio needed to eliminate most of the idiosyncratic risk, and thus fully exploit the diversification potential that exists in credit portfolios, may be in the thousands. This is sobering, considering that most CDOs rarely contain more than 100 names. Finally, the relative insensitivity of credit risk to business cycle shocks under alternative model specifications could be important in the current debate over the procyclicality of the New Basel Accord.

The results raise a number of questions and issues that merit further exploration. Our portfolio, by virtue of being allocated across twenty-one countries in ten regions, is already quite diversified, as evidenced by an average cross-sectional pairwise return correlation of 11.2 percent. Concentrating all of the nominal exposure into just one region or one industry would undoubtedly have a significant impact on the resulting loss distribution, in addition to yielding differences across models. A difficulty one would quickly encounter in exploring this problem is the rating or default probability differences across these dimensions. The average rating in the United Kingdom, for instance, is much higher than for the Latin American obligors, especially if one follows the rule that an obligor rating cannot exceed the sovereign rating.[30]

It is also worth exploring the impact of fat-tailed innovations on the resulting loss distributions. The current application is limited to the double-Gaussian assumption (both idiosyncratic and systematic innovations are normal), but it seems reasonable to relax this assumption by considering, for example, draws from Student-t distributions with low degrees of freedom.

---

30. This rule seems quite reasonable when one considers debt denominated in, say, USD (or euros), but perhaps less so if the debt is exclusively in the local currency.

References

Allen, Linda, and Anthony Saunders. 2004. Incorporating systemic influences into risk measurements: A survey of the literature. *Journal of Financial Services Research* 26:161–91.

Altman, Edward I. 1968. Financial ratios, discriminant analysis and the prediction of corporate bankruptcy. *Journal of Finance* 20:589–609.

Altman, Edward I., Sreedhar Bharath, and Anthony Saunders. 2002. Credit ratings and the BIS capital adequacy reform agenda. *Journal of Banking and Finance* 26:909–21.

Amato, Jeffrey D., and Craig H. Furfine. 2004. Are credit ratings procyclical? *Journal of Banking and Finance* 28:2641–77.

Amato, Jeffrey D., and Eli Remolona. 2004. The pricing of unexpected losses. Paper presented at the Workshop on the Pricing of Credit Risk, Bank for International Settlements, September 2004.

Bangia, Anil, Francis X. Diebold, André Kronimus, Christian Schagen and Til Schuermann. 2002. Ratings migration and the business cycle, with applications to credit portfolio stress testing. *Journal of Banking and Finance* 26:235–64.

Basel Committee on Banking Supervision. 2001. The New Basel Capital Accord. Retrieved January, 2001, at http://www.bis.org/publ/bcbsca03.pdf.

Basel Committee on Banking Supervision (BCBS). 2004. International convergence of capital measurement and capital standards: A revised framework. Retrieved June, 2004, at http://www.bis.org/publ/bcbs107.htm.

Black, Fischer, and John C. Cox. 1976. Valuing corporate securities: Some effects of bond indenture provisions. *Journal of Finance* 31:351–67.

Cantor, Richard, and Frank Packer. 1995. The credit rating industry. *Journal of Fixed Income* (December): 10–34.

Carey, Mark. 2002. A guide to choosing absolute bank capital requirements. *Journal of Banking and Finance* 26:929–51.

Carpenter, Seth B., William Whitesell, and Egon Zakrajšek. 2001. Capital requirements, business loans and business cycles: An empirical analysis of the standardized approach in the New Basel Accord. Federal Reserve Board, Finance and Economics Discussion Series no. 2001-48. Washington, DC: Federal Reserve Board.

Dees, S., F. di Mauro, M. H. Pesaran, and L. V. Smith. 2006. Forthcoming. Exploring the international linkages of the euro area: A global VaR analysis. *Journal of Applied Econometrics*.

Duffie, Darrell, and David Lando. 2001. Term structures of credit spreads with incomplete accounting information. *Econometrica* 69:633–64.

Garbade, Kenneth. 2001. *Pricing Corporate Securities as Contingent Claims*. Cambridge, MA: MIT Press.

Gordy, Michael B. 2000. A comparative anatomy of credit risk models. *Journal of Banking and Finance* 24 (1–2): 119–49.

———. 2003. A risk-factor model foundation for ratings-based bank capital rules. *Journal of Financial Intermediation* 12:199–232.

Hanson, Samuel G., M. Hashem Pesaran, and Til Schuermann. 2005. Firm heterogeneity and credit risk diversification. Wharton Financial Institutions Center Working Paper no. 05-05.

Hsiao, C., and M. Hashem Pesaran. 2004. Random coefficient panel data models. CESifo Working Paper Series no. 1233; IZA Discussion Paper No. 1236, Institute for the Study of Labor.

Jafry, Yusuf, and Til Schuermann. 2004. Measuring, estimating and comparing credit migration matrices. *Journal of Banking and Finance* 28:2603–39.

James, Christopher, and David C. Smith. 2000. Are banks still special? New evidence on their role in the corporate capital-raising process. *Journal of Applied Corporate Finance* 13:52–63.

Kapetanios, George, and M. Hashem Pesaran. 2004. Alternative approaches to estimation and inference in large multifactor panels: Small sample results with an application to modelling of asset returns. CESifo Working Paper no. 1416; available at http://www.econ.cam.ac.uk/faculty/pesaran/.

Kealhofer, S., and M. Kurbat. 2002. Predictive merton models. *Risk* (February): 67–71.

Lando, David. 2004. *Credit risk modeling: Theory and applications.* Princeton, NJ: Princeton University Press.

Lando, David, and Torben Skødeberg. 2002. Analyzing ratings transitions and rating drift with continuous observations. *Journal of Banking and Finance* 26 (2–3): 423–44.

Leland, Hayne E., and Klaus Bjerre Toft. 1996. Optimal capital structure, endogenous bankruptcy, and the term structure of credit spreads. *Journal of Finance* 51:987–1019.

Lennox, Clive. 1999. Identifying failing companies: A re-evaluation of the logit, probit and DA approaches. *Journal of Economics and Business* 51:347–64.

Mella-Barral, Pierre, and William Perraudin. 1997. Strategic debt service. *Journal of Finance* 52 (2): 531–56.

Merton, Robert C. 1974. On the pricing of corporate debt: The risk structure of interest rates. *Journal of Finance* 29:449–70.

Psaran, M. Hashem, Til Schuermann, Björn-Jakob Treutler, and Scott M. Weiner. 2005. Macroeconomics and credit risk: A global perspective. *Journal of Money, Credit and Banking.* Available as Wharton Financial Institutions Center Working Paper no. 03-13B.

Pesaran, M. Hashem, Til Schuermann, and Scott M. Weiner. 2004. Modeling regional interdependencies using a global error-correcting macroeconometric model. *Journal of Business and Economic Statistics* 22:129–62 and 175–81.

Pesaran, M. Hashem, and Ron P. Smith. 1995. Long-run relationships from dynamic heterogeneous panels. *Journal of Econometrics* 68:79–113.

Pesaran, M. Hashem, Ron P. Smith, and Kyung S. Him. 1996. Dynamic linear models for heterogeneous panels. In *The Econometrics of Panel Data,* ed. L. Mátyás and P. Sevestre, 145–95. Dordrecht, The Netherlands: Kluwer Academic.

Saunders, Anthony, and Linda Allen. 2002. *Credit risk measurement: New approaches to value at risk and other paradigms,* 2nd ed. New York: Wiley.

Shumway, Tyler. 2001. Forecasting bankruptcy more accurately: A simple hazard model. *Journal of Business* 74:101–24.

Silverman, Bernard W. 1986. *Density estimation for statistics and data analysis.* New York: Chapman and Hall.

Swamy, P. A. V. B. 1970. Efficient inference in a random coefficient regression model. *Econometrica* 38:311–23.

Vasicek, Oldrich. 1987. Probability of loss on loan portfolio. Moody's KMV Corp., San Francisco. Available at www.kmv.com.

———. 1991. Limiting loan loss distribution. Moody's KMV Corp., San Francisco. Available at www.kmv.com.

———. 2002. Loan portfolio value. *Risk* 15:160–62.

Comment   Richard Cantor

At the most fundamental level, the authors' work is motivated by the recognition that we know very little about what constitutes a good portfolio credit risk model. Our models rely on highly imperfect estimates of obligation-specific default probabilities and default correlations. However, our ability to test the performance of estimated default probabilities is limited, and we have virtually no ability to test the out-of-sample performance of default correlation models.[1]

In the absence of a good test of model accuracy, other factors necessarily play important roles in determining which portfolio risk models we use. These factors may include ease of application, the ability to undertake scenario analysis, and transparency of results and interpretations.

One key aspect of any portfolio risk model that affects its ease of use is the parameter heterogeneity it permits across firms. At one extreme, a purely homogeneous portfolio risk model is commonly used to price (or at least quote) synthetic collateralized debt obligation (CDO) tranches. This copula model assumes that all firms share the same default intensity and their default intensities share the same sensitivity to a single common macroeconomic factor. At the other extreme, one can simulate (if not solve) a completely heterogeneous model in which firms have different default intensities and different intensity sensitivities to a wide array of systematic risk factors. Allowing for such heterogeneity, however, not only complicates the model, it potentially introduces considerable parameter estimation error and reduces model transparency.

Pesaran, Schuermann, and Treutler address two major questions:

- What are the effects on tail risk in a portfolio credit risk model of firm heterogeneity with respect to firm-level default probabilities and default sensitivities to global macroeconomic, regional, and industry risk factors?
- How does the influence of forecasts of the systematic risk variables and shock variables on the conditional risk distribution vary with the amount of firm heterogeneity incorporated into the model?

To answer these questions, the authors develop a portfolio credit risk model, using real-world data with three components:

- A vector autoregression of the joint distribution of sixty-four global macroeconomic variables for a set of twenty-five countries, accounting for about 80 percent of world output

---

1. See Cantor and Falkenstein (2001) and Cantor and Mann (2003) and Lopez and Saidenberg (2000). One can, of course, test whether correlation models effectively predict asset prices, but it seems highly unlikely that there will ever be enough panel default data to test whether our models correctly parameterize physical default correlations.

- A model of firm-level equity returns for 243 firms as functions of global macroeconomic variables and region and industry effects
- A structural model of default, in which a firm defaults whenever its stock price falls by an amount that depends upon the firm's credit rating.

Increased Parameter Heterogeneity and Tail Risk

Does tail risk increase or decrease with increased heterogeneity in firm-level PDs or firm-level sensitivities to systematic factors? According to the paper's model the answer depends on which of two methods is used to identify each firm's default equity threshold (table 9.6). The first method ("the same λ method"), which assumes the default threshold depends only on credit ratings, leads to the conclusion that tail risk declines as parameter heterogeneity increases. The second method ("the same DD method"), which assumes that a firm's credit rating identifies its equity-volatility and drift-adjusted distance-to-default, leads to the opposite conclusion—increased heterogeneity leads to greater tail risk.

Intuitively, I think heterogeneity should lead to smaller tail risk, since the likelihood of all firms defaulting at the same time ought to decline as they become more heterogeneous. I find the paper's ambiguous finding particularly puzzling because I find the rationale behind the same-DD method more compelling than the rationale supporting the same-λ method. Yet the DD method seems to imply that increased heterogeneity somehow increases tail risk.

Why? The answer probably lies in the fact that when the authors change the degree of parameter heterogeneity they do not hold everything else constant. In particular, when they increase heterogeneity, they do not keep the portfolio's expected loss rate constant. As modeled, increased heterogeneity sharply increases the portfolio's expected loss rate under the same-λ assumption and sharply reduces it under the same-DD assumption (table 9.6). If the authors had managed to isolate an increase in heterogeneity without changing expected loss rates, I suspect they would have unambiguously concluded that increased heterogeneity does reduce tail risk.[2]

If homogeneous models do systematically understate tail risk, then some degree of model heterogeneity is likely worth the effort. For example, the simple copula models generally used to price synthetic CDO tranches are likely to underprice senior tranches and overprice junior tranches.

Increased Parameter Heterogeneity and Sensitivity to Systematic Risk Factor Shocks

When discussing the sensitivity of the conditional portfolio risk distribution to systematic shocks, the authors limit their analysis to the results

---

2. This view appears to be confirmed in a recent theoretical paper by two of the same authors of this paper, along with another author. See Samuel Hanson, M. Hashem Pesaran, and Til Schuermann (2005).

that pertain to the same-λ default threshold identification method, which does imply that greater heterogeneity reduces tail risk. In general, they find that conditional tail risk is less sensitive to systematic shocks under more heterogeneous models. This finding is consistent with the intuition mentioned earlier. More heterogeneous portfolios are less likely to experience nearly all firms defaulting at the same time. Similarly, adverse shifts in systematic risk variables are less likely to have a big impact on tail risk when firm-default sensitivities to those risk factors are heterogeneous.

Other Results

In the course of developing these models, the authors derive at least two other significant results that may be of broad interest.

First, they find that a greater portion of the correlation across firm stock returns can be explained by common regional factors than by common industry factors. Considerable effort in modeling can perhaps be saved if, indeed, industry factors can be safely ignored in modeling firm-equity correlations. One should recognize, however, that the seven industry definitions used in the paper are very broad. Many of the historically important industry concentrations—such as energy, telecom, casinos and hotels, real estate, and retail—are not separately modeled.

Second, the authors find that firm stock returns are strongly influenced by regional and global stock market factors, oil prices, and (to a lesser extent) interest rates, but national gross domestic product (GDP) growth is not important. GDP and other macroeconomic variables have some modest impacts through their influence on broader equity market indexes, but they do not have strong direct effects on firm-level stock returns or firm default rates.

However, like other structural portfolio models that rely on fluctuations in equity prices to induce firm defaults, these models may underestimate the effects of macroeconomic risk factors on portfolio risk. In less restrictive models, the estimated effects of GDP growth and other macroeconomic variables on realized default rates tend to be more substantial.[3]

Model Structure Extremely Useful

Most credit risk portfolio models currently used in industry are not particularly well suited for scenario analysis and the calculation of conditional risk distributions. Their underlying default correlations are usually derived from asset correlations, equity correlations, or rating change correlations, without direct reference to the underlying systematic risks driving those

---

3. Carty (2000) finds in a hazard-rate model based on firm credit ratings, GDP growth, S&P 500 growth rates, and other variables, that GDP growth has a power effect on default rates. Duffie and Wang (2004), in a single-country (United States) model, also find in a hazard-rate model with a Merton-type distance-to-default risk measure, personal income growth, and other variables, that personal income growth is highly significant.

correlations. In contrast, Pesaran, Schuermann, and Treutler have developed a three-module framework—with a macroeconomic VaR, an equity return model, and an equity-price-based default model—that permits a transparent separation of the distribution of systematic risk variables from a credit portfolio's conditional risk distribution. Other researchers and market practitioners should find this framework very useful.

References

Cantor, R., and E. Falkenstein. 2001. Testing the consistency in annual default rates. *Journal of Fixed Income,* September, 36–51.

Cantor, R., and C. Mann. 2003. Measuring the performance of corporate bond ratings. *Special Comment, Moody's Investor Services,* April.

Carty, L. 2000. Corporate credit-risk dynamics. *Financial analysts Journal 56* (4): 67–81.

Duffie, D., and K. Wang. 2004. Multi-period corporate failure prediction with stochastic covariates, NBER Working Paper no. 10743. Cambridge, MA: National Bureau of Economic Research, September.

Hanson, S., M. H. Pesaran, and T. Schuermann. 2005. Firm heterogeneity and credit risk diversification. Working Paper. Wharton Financial Institutions Center.

Lopez, J. A., and M. Saidenberg. 2000. Evaluating credit risk models. *Journal of Banking & Finance* 24:151–67.

Discussion Summary

Darrell Duffie liked the idea of examining the impact of changes in model assumptions on tail behavior, having previously observed that our understanding of tails of credit loss distributions is too limited. He suggested that the model might be used to examine the impact of correlated measurement error: if errors in estimation of individual-firm solvency or asset volatility are correlated, actual tails will be much fatter than the tails measured by currently popular portfolio credit risk models.

Much of the discussion revolved around technical issues. There was considerable discussion of the authors' methods of estimating rating transition matrices, with *Til Schuermann* responding that their modification of Lando's method addresses the concerns. *Torben Andersen* suggested that recent upgrades and downgrades are informative and might be incorporated into estimation, and *Schuermann* agreed.

Implications of Alternative Operational Risk Modeling Techniques

Patrick de Fontnouvelle, Eric S. Rosengren, and
John S. Jordan

10.1 Introduction

Large operational losses as a result of accounting scandals, insider fraud, and rogue trading, to name just a few, have received increasing attention from the press, the public, and policymakers. The frequency of severe losses, with more than 100 instances of losses at financial institutions exceeding $100 million, has caused many financial institutions to try to explicitly model operational risk to determine their own economic capital. As financial institutions have begun to comprehensively collect loss data and use it to manage operational risk, bank regulators have increased their expectations for measuring and modeling operational risk. Under the current U.S. rules proposal for implementing the Basle Accord, large, internationally active banks will be expected to use internal models to estimate capital for unexpected operational losses. A criticism of this proposal has been that the tools for modeling operational risk are in their infancy, making estimating capital problematic.

This paper uses data supplied by six large, internationally active banks to determine if the regularities in the loss data will make consistent modeling of operational losses possible. We find that there are similarities in the results of models of operational loss across institutions, and that our results are consistent with publicly reported operational risk capital estimates produced by banks' internal economic capital models.

This paper was prepared for the NBER Project on the Risks of Financial Institutions. It was substantially completed while John Jordan was with the Federal Reserve Bank of Boston. We thank our colleagues in the Federal Reserve System and in the Risk Management Group of the Basel Committee for the many fruitful interactions that have contributed to this work. However, the views expressed in this paper do not necessarily reflect their views, those of the Federal Reserve Bank of Boston, or those of the Federal Reserve System.

We begin the analysis by considering tail plots of each bank's loss data by business line and event type. Three findings clearly emerge from this descriptive analysis.[1] First, loss data for most business lines and event types may be well modeled by a Pareto-type distribution, as most of the tail plots are linear when viewed on a log-log scale. Second, the severity ranking of event types is consistent across institutions. Clients, products, and business practices is the highest severity event type, while external fraud and employment practices are the lowest severity event types. Third, the tail plots suggest that losses for certain business lines and event types are very heavy tailed. This last finding highlights that while basic measurement approaches such as the tail plot are easy to implement and are intuitively appealing, overly simplistic approaches may yield implausible estimates of economic capital. A main contribution of this paper is to show how quantitative modeling can result in more plausible conclusions regarding tail thickness and economic capital.

We next attempt to model the distribution of loss amounts using a "full-data" approach, whereby one fits all of the available loss data with a parametric severity distribution. We consider nine commonly used distributions, four of which are light-tailed and five of which are heavy-tailed. We fit each of these distributions by business line and event type at each of the six institutions considered. The heavy-tailed distributions provide consistently good fits to the loss data, which confirms our findings based on visual inspection of the tail plots. The light-tailed distributions do not generally provide good fits. However, we find that some parameter estimates for the heavy-tailed distributions can have implausible implications for both tail thickness and economic capital.

Extreme Value Theory (EVT) is an alternative to the full-data approach that is increasingly being explored by researchers, by financial institutions, and by their regulators. However, it is well-known that EVT techniques yield upward-biased tail estimates in small samples. Huisman, Koedijk, Kool, and Palm (2001) have proposed a regression-based EVT technique that corrects for small-sample bias in the tail parameter estimate. Applying their technique (hereafter HKKP) to the six banks in our sample, we obtain estimates that are both plausible and consistent with earlier estimates using purely external data (de Fontnouvelle et al., 2003).

It is important to stress that the statistical analysis of operational loss data is a new field, and that this paper's results should be viewed as preliminary. This is particularly true given that we only have data for one year from each bank. The paper also raises several technical issues that should be addressed in future research as a longer time series becomes available.

---

1. Suppose one has a series of observations (x_i) with a cumulative empirical distribution function denoted by $F(x)$. A tail plot is obtained by plotting $\log(1 - F[x_i])$ on the vertical axis against $\log(x_i)$ on the horizontal axis.

The most significant such issue is that even though the data appear to be heavy-tailed, we cannot formally reject the hypothesis that they are drawn from a light-tailed distribution, such as the lognormal. To investigate this possibility, we propose a threshold analysis of the lognormal distribution that, to our knowledge, is new to this subject. This technique also provides a reasonable characterization of the tail behavior of operational losses.

We also examine the frequency of operational losses. We consider both the Poisson distribution and the Negative Binomial distribution as potential models for the number of losses that a bank could incur over the course of one year. Using Monte Carlo simulation to combine the frequency and severity distributions, we obtain an estimate for the distribution of total annual operational losses. The quantiles of this aggregate loss distribution are interpreted as economic capital estimates for operational risk. These estimates should be viewed with several significant cautions. First, we are assuming that the data are complete: however, banks have moved to more comprehensive data collection platforms, which may improve the loss capture. Second, we are only using internal data for one year, and banks will be required to have three years of comprehensive data. Third, analysis of internal loss data will not be the sole determinant of capital for operational risk; banks will also be required to demonstrate that their risk estimates reflect exposures that are not captured in internal loss data.[2] Given these qualifications, the estimates should be viewed as a preliminary indication (and most probably a lower bound) for the amount of capital needed.

Despite these caveats, the estimates implied by the modeling of the internal loss data are consistent with capital estimates using purely external data (de Fontnouvelle et al., 2003). The results imply that for a variety of plausible assumptions regarding the frequency and severity of operational losses, the level of capital needed for operational risk for the typical (median) bank in our sample would be equivalent to 5–9 percent of the bank's current minimum regulatory capital requirement. This range also seems consistent with the 12–15 percent of minimum regulatory capital that most banks are currently allocating to operational risk, given that the banks' models tend to have a broader set of model inputs than those used in this analysis, including external data, scenarios, and qualitative risk assessments.[3] Our results thus confirm that operational risk is a material risk faced by financial institutions.

The remainder of the paper is organized as follows. The next section

2. The proposed Basel Accord requires banks to measure losses to which they are exposed, but that have not actually occurred (via analysis of scenarios and external data). Banks would also be required to measure exposures that have arisen since the data collection period (via analysis of business environment and control factors).

3. See page 26 of Basel Committee on Banking Supervision (2001). Given the uncertainties in evaluating the relative merits of different techniques and estimators using only limited data, we would consider results to be consistent if they are within an order of magnitude of each other.

(10.2) provides a description of the data. Section 10.3 reviews related literature on the measurement of operational risk in financial institutions. Section 10.4 discusses some commonly used continuous distributions, and discusses their potential relevance to modeling the severity of operational losses. Section 10.5 presents visual analyses of the loss data, and draws preliminary conclusions regarding which distributions may be appropriate for modeling loss severity. Section 10.6 explores full-data approaches to modeling operational losses, and formally compares the alternative severity distributions. Section 10.7 explores EVT-based approaches to modeling the loss data. Section 10.8 compares alternative frequency distributions. Section 10.9 provides the implied capital numbers from estimating different loss distributions using Monte Carlo simulations. The final section provides conclusions on using these techniques for quantifying operational risk.

10.2   Data

The 2002 Operational Risk Loss Data Collection Exercise (LDCE) was initiated by the Risk Management Group (RMG) of the Basel Committee on Banking Supervision in June 2002. The LDCE asked participating banks to provide information on individual operational losses exceeding €10,000 during 2001, among various other data items. Banks were also asked to indicate whether their loss data were complete. The LDCE data include 47,269 operational loss events reported by eighty-nine banks from nineteen countries in Europe, North and South America, Asia, and Australasia. For additional information and summary statistics regarding the LDCE, readers can refer to Risk Management Group (2003).

Based on the information provided in the LDCE, and on our knowledge of the banks involved, we identified a list of institutions whose data submissions seem relatively complete. Due to practical considerations, we limit our sample to loss data from six of these banks. This paper presents results for these six banks on a bank-by-bank basis (with the exception of the operational risk exposure figures reported in table 10.5). However, the results are presented in a way that makes it impossible to identify the individual banks. Focusing on a cross-sectional study of banks enables us to determine whether the same statistical techniques and distributions apply across institutions that may have very different business mixes and risk exposures.

The LDCE categorizes losses into eight business lines and seven event types. To protect the confidentiality of banks participating in the LDCE, we present results only for those business lines and event types when three or more banks reported sufficient data to support analysis. The business lines presented are: trading and sales, retail banking, payment and settlement, and asset management. The loss types presented are: internal fraud, external fraud, employment practices and workplace safety, clients, products, and business practices, and execution, delivery, and process management.[4]

10.3   Related Literature

Moscadelli (2003) also analyzes data from the 2002 LDCE, and performs a thorough comparison of traditional full-data analyses and extreme value methods for estimating the operational loss severity distribution. He finds that extreme value theory outperforms the traditional methods in all eight Basel Business Lines. He also finds that the severity distribution is very heavy-tailed, and that there is a substantial difference in loss severity across business lines.

There are several differences between the current paper and Moscadelli (2003). First, Moscadelli (2003) aggregates the data across all banks in the LDCE sample. In this paper, we analyze data at the individual bank level in order to determine whether the same quantitative techniques work for a variety of banks with different business mixes, control infrastructures, and geographic exposures. We believe that doing so provides a useful test of the techniques under consideration, and also yields an indication of their ultimate applicability at individual banks. Second, the current paper explores the newly developed technique of Huisman et al. (2001) to correct for potential bias in the tail parameter estimate. Third, we explore several models of the loss frequency distribution, which allows us to obtain indicative estimates of economic capital for operational risk.

10.4   Distributions for Operational Loss Data

We begin our empirical analysis by exploring which of various empirical approaches best fits the data. In principle, we are willing to consider any distribution with positive support as an acceptable candidate for modeling operational loss severity. To keep the size of our tables within reason, however, we will focus on nine commonly used distributions. This section discusses the salient features of each. In section 10.6, we consider how well these distributions describe the statistical behavior of losses in our database.

Table 10.1 lists each distribution we consider, together with its density function and its maximal moment (discussed at the end of this section). We begin our discussion with the exponential distribution, which is one of the simplest statistical distributions—both analytically and computationally. The exponential distribution is frequently used to analyze duration data

---

4. The following business lines were omitted: corporate finance, commercial banking, agency services, and retail brokerage. The following event types were omitted: damage to physical assets, business disruption, and system failure. To preserve confidentiality, we do not report the cutoff that was used for inclusion of business lines and event types.

Table 10.1   **Parametric distributions used for modeling operational loss severity**

Distribution name	Density, $f(x)$	Maximal moment
Exponential	$(1/b)\exp(-x/b)$	∞
Weibull	$(\beta x^{\beta-1}/\eta^{\beta})\exp(-(x/\eta)^{\beta})$	∞
Gamma	$(x/b)^{c-1}[\exp(-x/b)]/[b\Gamma(c)]$	∞
LogGamma	$[\log(x)/b]^{c-1}x^{-1/b-1}/[b\Gamma(c)]$	$1/b$
Pareto	$\xi^{-1}x^{-1/\xi-1}$	$1/\xi$
GPD	$\beta^{-1}(1 + \xi x/\beta)^{-1/\xi-1}$	$1/\xi$
Burr	$(\tau/\beta)x^{\tau-1}(1 + \xi x^{\tau}/\beta)^{-1/\xi-1}$	τ/ξ
Lognormal	$(2\pi x^2\sigma^2)^{-1/2}\exp\{-[\log(x) - \mu]^2/(2\sigma^2)\}$	∞
LogLogistic	$\alpha x^{1/b-1}/[b(1 + \alpha x^{1/b})^2]$	$1/b$

(e.g., time to failure of a machine part), and is the only continuous distribution characterized by a "lack of memory." In the duration context, lack of memory means that the time until the occurrence of an event (failure) does not depend on the length of time that has already elapsed (time since installation). In the operational loss context, lack of memory implies that the distribution of excess losses over a threshold does not depend on the value of the threshold. So if half of all losses exceeding $1 are less than $10, then half of all losses exceeding $1 million will be less than $1,000,010 ($1,000,000 + $10). Such a result does not seem plausible. However, the exponential distribution arises in the context of EVT as a possible limiting distribution for excess losses above high thresholds. For this reason (and also because it can be transformed into other interesting distributions), we include it in our analysis.

The Weibull distribution is a two-parameter generalization of the exponential that allows the time-until-event occurrence to depend on the amount of time that has already elapsed. Thus, the Weibull can capture phenomena such as "burn in," in which the failure rate is initially high but decreases over time. In the context of operational risk, the Weibull may be appropriate for modeling a business line exposed to many small losses but only a few large losses. The gamma distribution is another two-parameter generalization of the exponential. A gamma-distributed random variable arises as the sum of n exponentially distributed random variables. Thus, a machine's failure time is gamma distributed if the machine fails whenever n components fail, and if each component's failure time is exponentially distributed. Like the Weibull distribution, the gamma also allows the time until event occurrence to depend on the amount of time that has already elapsed.

Another generalization of the exponential distribution can be obtained by exponentiating an exponentially distributed random variable. The resulting distribution is called a Type I Pareto, and can also be referred to as a log-exponential or power-law distribution. The lack of memory of the exponential distribution manifests itself as scale invariance in the Pareto distribution. Roughly speaking, scale invariance means that data "look the same" no matter what the unit of measure (e.g., hundreds of dollars versus millions of dollars). So in the earlier example, where half of all losses exceeding $1 were less than $10, half of all losses over $1 million would be less than $10 million. Power-law behavior has been observed in phenomena as disparate as city sizes, income distributions, and insurance claim amounts, and has been an important research topic for those interested in the behavior of complex systems (i.e., systems consisting of agents linked via a decentralized network rather than via a market or social planner).[5] A variation of the Pareto distribution can be obtained by exponentiating a gamma-distributed random variable instead of an exponentially distributed random variable. The result is referred to as the Loggamma distribution.

The Pareto distribution also arises in EVT as another limiting distribution of excesses over a high threshold. In this case, the limiting distribution is given by a two-parameter variant of the Pareto, which is known as the Generalized Pareto Distribution (GPD). One commonly used transformation of the GPD is obtained by raising a GPD-distributed variable to a power. The result is called the Burr distribution.

Another distribution that we consider is the Lognormal, which is so widely used that little discussion is required here. However, it is worth noting that the normal distribution is appropriate for modeling variables that arise as the sum of many different components. It is also a worthwhile exercise to consider which types of operational losses may be characterized in this manner. Consider, for example, losses arising from workplace safety lapses. One could argue that the severity of these losses may be approximated by the lognormal distribution, as it is influenced by many factors, including weather, overall health of the injured party, physical layout of the workplace, and the type of activity involved. The final distribution that we consider is the loglogistic, which is obtained by exponentiating a logistic-distributed random variable. The Loglogistic is similar to the Lognormal, but may be more appropriate for modeling operational loss data because it has a slightly heavier tail.

We conclude this section by classifying the distributions discussed previously according to their tail thickness. This will facilitate interpretation of the estimation results, as the relevance of a particular distribution to modeling operational losses will be suggestive of the relevance of other distributions with similar tail thickness. There is no commonly agreed-upon definition of what constitutes a heavy-tailed distribution. However, one

---

5. See Embrechts, Klüppelberg, and Mikosch (1997), Gabaix (1999), and references therein.

such definition can be based on a distribution's maximal moment, which is defined as $\sup(r : E[x'] < \infty)$. Maximal moments for the distributions under consideration are reported in table 10.1. In this paper, we will call a distribution light tailed if it has finite moments of all orders, and heavy tailed otherwise. Under this definition, four of the distributions being considered are light tailed (exponential, Weibull, gamma, and lognormal), and the remaining five distributions are heavy tailed (loggamma, Pareto, GPD, Burr, and loglogistic).

10.5   Descriptive Analysis

This section considers several tools that provide a visual characterization of the loss data. Suppose one has a series of observations (x_i) with a cumulative empirical distribution function denoted by $F(x)$. A tail plot is obtained by plotting $\log(1 - F[x_i])$ on the vertical axis against $\log(x_i)$ on the horizontal axis. Figures 10.1 and 10.2 present tail plots of the six banks' loss data by Basel event type and Basel business line, respectively.

Many of the tail plots show linear behavior. This is quite interesting, as a linear tail plot implies that the data are drawn from a power-law distribution. Furthermore, the slope of the plot provides a heuristic estimate of the tail parameter, as $\log(1 - F[x_i]) = -a \log(x_i) + c$, where c denotes a constant.

Another feature of these plots is that the slopes associated with the seven Basel event types preserve roughly the same ordering across banks. For example, client's products and business practices is one of the heaviest-tailed event types for all of the banks where it is plotted separately. Employment practices and workplace safety is always one of the thinnest-tailed event types. While the tail plots by business line also suggest power-law tail behavior, there is no evident consistent cross-bank ordering of business lines. We interpret this as initial evidence that risk may be better ordered by event type, but will revisit this issue later in the paper.

Each of the tail plots also indicates a reference line with slope of –1. Many of the plots lie near or above this line, thus implying heuristic tail-parameter estimates of 1 or higher. These estimates highlight the shortcomings of using an overly simplistic approach to measuring operational risk: tail parameters exceeding 1 suggest that the expected loss is infinite for many business lines and event types, and that the capital required for operational risk alone could exceed the amount of capital that large banks are currently allocating to all risks.[6] We will argue in this paper that the distribution of operational losses is not as heavy tailed as it first appears, and

6. The LDCE data suggest that a $100 billion bank could experience 500 operational losses (exceeding $10,000) per year. If these follow a Pareto distribution with a tail parameter equal to 1, then Monte Carlo simulation of the aggregate loss distribution indicates capital of $5 billion at the 99.9 percent soundness level. Tail parameters of greater than 1 would imply capital levels several times larger than this figure.

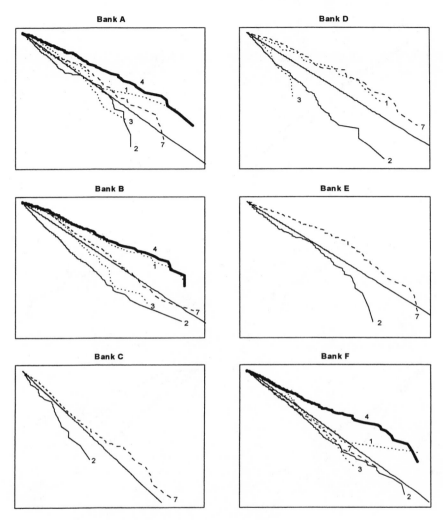

Fig. 10.1   Tail plots of loss data by Basel Event Type

Notes: Event Types are labeled as follows. 1—Internal Fraud. 2—External Fraud. 3—Employment Practices and Workplace Safety. 4—Clients, Products, and Business Practices. 7—Execution, Delivery, and Process Management.

that it is possible to obtain more plausible estimates of regulatory capital for operational risk.

Another useful diagnostic tool is the mean excess plot. The mean excess for a given threshold is defined as the average of all losses exceeding the threshold, minus the threshold value. The mean excess plot reports the mean excess as a function of the threshold value. The shape of the mean excess plot varies according to the type of distribution underlying the data.

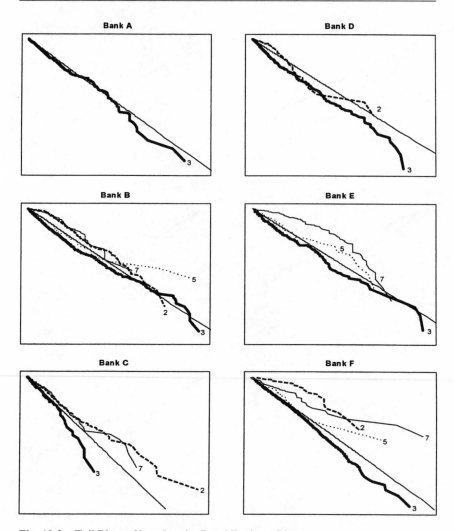

Fig. 10.2   Tail Plots of loss data by Basel Business Line

Notes: Business lines are labels as follows. 2—Trading and Sales. 3—Retail Banking. 5—Payment and Settlement. 7—Asset Management.

For example, a Pareto distribution implies a linear, upward-sloping mean excess plot; an exponential distribution implies a horizontal linear mean excess plot, and a lognormal distribution implies a concave, upward-sloping mean excess plot.

Figures 10.3 and 10.4 present mean excess plots for loss data by event type and business line, respectively. (Each curve has been rescaled in order to display the different business lines and event types together on one plot. Thus, these plots cannot be used to risk-rank business lines or event types.)

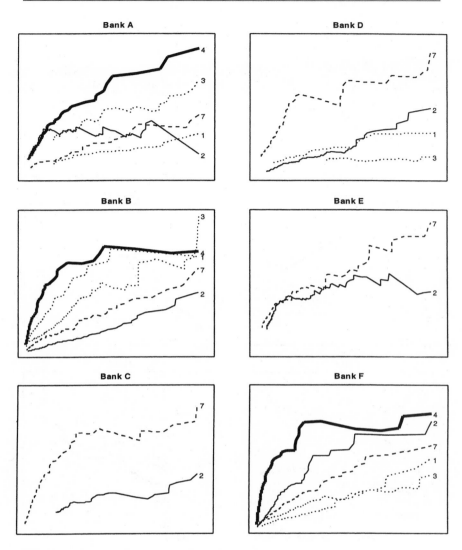

Fig. 10.3   Mean excess plots by Basel Event Type
Note: See fig. 10.1.

Nearly all of the plots slope upward, which indicates tails that are heavier than exponential. Some of the plots are linear (e.g., event type 7 for bank B), which suggests a Pareto-like distribution. Some are concave, which suggests a lognormal or Weibull-like distribution. It is also difficult to establish a consistent pattern across either business line or event type. Potentially, this issue would be less severe with more data.

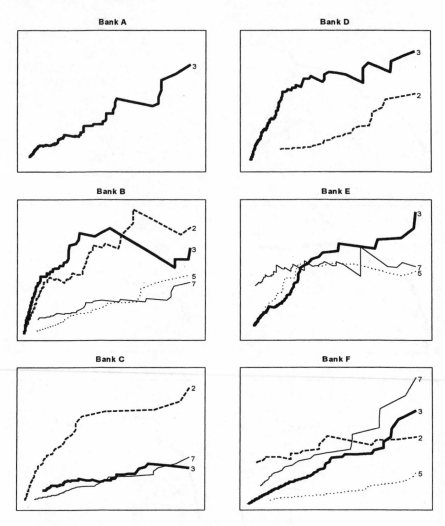

Fig. 10.4   Mean excess plots by Basel Business Line
Note: See fig. 10.2.

10.6   Fitting the Distributions

In this section, we fit each of the distributions listed in table 10.1 to the LDCE data via maximum likelihood. Results are reported separately for each bank under consideration, and are also broken down by business line and event type.

Table 10.2 reports probability values for Pearson's χ^2 goodness-of-fit

Table 10.2   **Goodness of fit across Basel Business Lines and Event Types (%)**

Distribution	Bank A	Bank B	Bank C	Bank D	Bank E	Bank F
			All observations			
Burr	0.0	6.4	72.0	23.3	13.6	0.1
Exponential	0.0	0.0	0.0	0.0	0.0	0.0
Gamma	0.0	0.0	0.0	0.0	1.5	0.0
LogGamma	0.0	1.5	64.1	33.9	1.4	0.7
LogLogistic	0.0	6.4	79.4	23.8	2.1	0.7
Lognormal	0.0	0.2	51.8	0.0	3.5	0.2
GPD	0.0	4.5	75.8	25.7	1.6	0.8
Weibull	0.0	0.0	0.0	0.0	54.7	0.0
			Event type 1—Internal fraud			
Burr	31.7	86.1		99.1		13.0
Exponential	0.0	0.0		0.1		0.0
Gamma	12.2	0.0		73.4		0.0
LogGamma	32.7	85.6		98.1		18.9
LogLogistic	31.8	87.4		98.1		13.6
Lognormal	35.0	86.4		98.4		13.7
GPD	33.1	87.6		95.1		13.3
Weibull	74.9	0.4		40.9		0.0
			Event type 2—External fraud			
Burr	0.0	10.8	6.4	13.2	1.7	0.0
Exponential	0.0	0.0	0.1	0.0	0.0	0.0
Gamma	0.0	0.0	0.7	0.0	1.8	0.0
LogGamma	0.3	6.5	7.6	7.3	2.8	0.0
LogLogistic	0.0	5.1	5.8	9.3	2.7	0.0
Lognormal	0.0	0.0	6.6	4.8	3.0	0.0
GPD	0.0	10.5	6.1	13.9	1.7	0.1
Weibull	0.0	0.0	5.9	0.1	9.9	0.0
			Event type 3—Employment practices and workplace safety			
Burr	87.2	36.7		85.0		23.0
Exponential	1.0	0.0		29.0		0.0
Gamma	66.5	0.0		86.9		0.2
LogGamma	88.1	7.8		74.7		0.2
LogLogistic	91.7	59.5		92.0		24.5
Lognormal	95.5	57.1		86.7		24.8
GPD	92.9	64.4		82.0		35.2
Weibull	87.0	0.2		85.8		7.6
			Event type 4—Clients, products, and business practices			
Burr	98.9	58.0				37.0
Exponential	0.0	0.0				0.0
Gamma	0.6	0.0				0.0
LogGamma	80.1	77.2				42.2
LogLogistic	80.8	58.6				39.0
Lognormal	81.4	36.5				40.3
GPD	76.7	57.4				34.7
Weibull	50.1	0.0				0.0

Table 10.2 (continued)

Distribution	Bank A	Bank B	Bank C	Bank D	Bank E	Bank F
Event type 7—Execution, delivery, and process management						
Burr	3.0	1.1	78.9	24.7	78.1	72.6
Exponential	0.0	0.0	0.0	0.0	0.0	0.0
Gamma	0.2	0.0	0.0	0.0	19.8	0.0
LogGamma	0.8	0.4	54.7	22.3	26.6	67.1
LogLogistic	0.1	0.0	76.8	47.7	89.4	77.3
Lognormal	0.1	0.0	51.7	52.1	68.7	0.0
GPD	2.6	0.0	77.6	39.8	83.6	89.6
Weibull	12.0	0.0	0.0	0.6	47.1	7.1
Business line 2—Trading and sales						
Burr		1.6	68.6	88.1		58.4
Exponential		0.0	0.0	1.7		12.4
Gamma		0.0	0.0	1.1		27.4
LogGamma		0.0	65.1	70.6		42.1
LogLogistic		0.0	69.7	65.3		91.8
Lognormal		0.0	67.0	18.8		86.9
GPD		0.0	70.6	25.1		58.0
Weibull		0.0	0.0	2.3		18.3
Business line 3—Retail banking						
Burr	0.1	12.5	32.3	8.5	0.9	1.7
Exponential	0.0	0.0	0.3	0.0	0.0	0.0
Gamma	0.0	0.0	8.1	0.0	0.1	0.0
LogGamma	0.0	0.2	43.0	1.3	5.8	2.4
LogLogistic	0.0	0.0	35.2	0.2	5.6	3.7
Lognormal	0.0	0.0	46.9	0.0	5.5	3.8
GPD	0.1	12.5	32.2	9.0	2.4	4.7
Weibull	0.0	0.0	15.5	0.0	14.7	0.0
Business line 5—Payment and settlement						
Burr		48.5			11.0	69.2
Exponential		0.0			0.0	0.0
Gamma		0.0			7.2	1.7
LogGamma		66.7			40.2	62.0
LogLogistic		49.4			22.7	
Lognormal		63.0			38.5	63.4
GPD		45.3			11.1	66.8
Weibull		0.3			13.3	52.4
Business line 7—Asset management						
Burr		64.9	84.4		30.1	20.2
Exponential		6.4	0.0		3.6	0.0
Gamma		32.3	0.0		43.4	0.0
LogGamma		31.3	79.9		15.9	17.6
LogLogistic		63.1	63.6		44.9	17.4
Lognormal		45.9	62.6		69.8	18.2
GPD		67.5	64.2		61.1	20.8
Weibull		25.7	4.5		44.8	2.3

Notes: This table reports goodness of fit for each of the distributions under consideration. The test was based on a standard chisquare procedure, except for the rounding adjustment discussed in section 10.6. The reported figures are probability values, so that a value of 5 percent or less indicates a poor fit.

statistic.[7] In general, the heavy-tailed distributions (Burr, loggamma, log-logistic, and Pareto) seem to fit the data quite well. The reported probability values exceed 5 percent for many business lines and event types, which suggests that we cannot reject the null that data are in fact drawn from the distribution under consideration. Conversely, most of the light-tailed distributions rarely provide an adequate fit to the data. This is not surprising, as the tail plots suggested that most of the data are heavy tailed. What is somewhat surprising is the degree to which the lognormal distribution fits the data. In fact, this light-tailed distribution fits the loss data for roughly as many business lines and event types as many of the heavier-tailed distributions.

Table 10.3 presents parameter estimation results for the GPD and lognormal distributions. To preserve bank confidentiality, we present only the estimate of the tail parameter ξ for the GPD and only the value of $\mu + \sigma^2/2$ for the lognormal distribution. While the χ^2 statistics presented in table 10.2 suggested that these two distributions provide a reasonable fit to the data, the parameter estimates generally suggest the opposite. Panel A reports estimates of the GPD tail parameter ξ. The parameter estimates are at or above 1 for many business lines and event types, and also above 1 when data is pooled across business lines and event types. Note that a tail parameter of 1 or higher has implausible implications for both expected losses and regulatory capital. Panel B of table 10.3 reports the estimated value of $\mu + \sigma^2/2$ for the lognormal distribution, which enables one to calculate the average loss severity via the formula $\exp(\mu + \sigma^2/2)$. While estimates of the average loss vary by business line and event type, one can see that it is less than $\exp(0)$ dollars for multiple business lines and event types. Thus, neither the Pareto nor the lognormal distribution consistently yields plausible parameter estimates.

Because of space considerations, we do not provide parameter estimates for the other distributions that were estimated. However, the GPD is of special interest because of its role in EVT and the lognormal is of special interest because it is the only light-tailed distribution that seems to fit the data (according to the χ^2 test). Parameter estimates for other heavy-tailed distributions were qualitatively similar to those of the GPD, in that they had implausible implications for tail thickness of the aggregate loss distribution.

10.6.1   For Which Business Lines and Event Types Can Full Data be Fit?

In this subsection, we ask whether there seem to be particular event types for which the full-data approach might work. Losses due to employment practices and workplace safety (event type 3) are well fit by most of

---

7. We calculated χ^2 goodness-of-fit tests because tests based on the empirical distribution function can be sensitive to data rounding, which is prevalent in the LDCE data. One can accommodate rounding within the χ^2 test by choosing bin values appropriately.

Table 10.3   **Parameter estimates for the Generalized Pareto and lognormal distributions**

	Bank A	Bank B	Bank C	Bank D	Bank E	Bank F
	A. Estimates of the tail parameter ξ for the GPD					
All BL & ET	1.28 (0.08)	0.87 (0.03)	0.99 (0.08)	0.92 (0.07)	0.97 (0.11)	1.01 (0.03)
ET1-IntFrd	1.24 (0.36)	1.31 (0.18)		1.10 (0.38)		1.02 (0.14)
ET2-ExtFrd	1.17 (0.12)	0.79 (0.05)	0.63 (0.19)	0.69 (0.07)	0.86 (0.14)	0.93 (0.03)
ET3-EP&WS	0.50 (0.16)	0.42 (0.05)		−0.15 (0.22)		0.50 (0.06)
ET4-CPBP	1.36 (0.21)	1.25 (0.15)				1.46 (0.13)
ET7-EDPM	1.42 (0.16)	0.71 (0.05)	0.94 (0.08)	1.00 (0.18)	0.96 (0.17)	0.93 (0.09)
BL2-T&S		0.68 (0.06)	1.18 (0.13)	0.49 (0.18)		0.42 (0.28)
BL3-RetBnk	1.15 (0.10)	1.09 (0.05)	0.55 (0.17)	0.94 (0.07)	0.99 (0.14)	0.93 (0.03)
BL5-P&S		1.06 (0.23)			1.07 (0.35)	1.03 (0.29)
BL7-AsstMgt		0.49 (0.20)	0.96 (0.21)		0.37 (0.18)	1.64 (0.40)
	B. Estimates of $\mu + \sigma^2/2$ for the lognormal distribution					
All BL & ET	−6.08	>0	>0	−21.27	>0	−9.23
ET-IntFrd	−9.85	>0		>0		−6.49
ET2-ExtFrd	−8.35	−22.68	>0	−5.84	>0	−22.31
ET3-EP&WS	>0	>0		>0		>0
ET4-CPBP	>0	>0				−5.85
ET7-EDPM	−9.64	>0	>0	>0	>0	−21.51
BL2-T&S		>0	−3.73	>0		>0
BL3-RetBnk	−13.32	−7.45	>0	−5.24	−11.77	−9.61
BL5-P&S		−12.09			>0	−2.01
BL7-AsstMgt		>0	>0		>0	−2.12

the heavy-tailed distributions as well as the lognormal. Furthermore, the parameter estimates for both the GPD and lognormal are plausible. There are two event types (internal fraud, and clients, products, and business practices) where several banks' data are well fit by multiple distributions, but where the resulting parameter estimates are not plausible. External fraud losses are not consistently well fit by any distribution on a cross-bank basis. Results for execution, delivery, and process management are less consistent across banks, with two institutions failing the goodness-of-fit tests, but the others having good fits and (perhaps) plausible parameter estimates.

The results are broadly similar in the case of estimation by business line. There are two business lines (agency services, and asset management) that pass the goodness-of-fit tests, and yield plausible parameter estimates for several banks. Another business line (retail banking) fails the fit tests at most banks, and the final business line (payment and settlement) yields implausible parameter estimates.

10.6.2   What Might Individual Banks Do?

Our discussion to this point has searched for features of operational loss data that hold across all of the six banks in our sample. However, the measurement of operational risk will ultimately take place at individual banks, who may not have the luxury of seeing whether their choices and assumptions are also valid at other institutions. We begin our discussion by focusing on bank F. Bank staff might begin by fitting one statistical distribution across all business lines and event types, but poor goodness-of-fit statistics would quickly lead them to alternate approaches. They might consider fitting a separate loss-severity distribution to each of the seven event types. However, they would find that losses from the most frequent event type (external fraud) were not well modeled by any of the distributions. The next most frequent event type (clients, products, and business practices) is modeled quite well by several heavy-tailed distributions. However, they would be quite surprised to find tail-parameter estimates exceeding 1, and might conclude that this was not a reasonable way to model operational risk. If they next attempted to fit separate loss-severity distributions for each business line, they would discover that loss data for the most common business line (retail banking) were not well-modeled by any of the distributions considered.

Bank F was chosen at random for discussion. If presented with their bank's results from tables 10.2 and 10.3, risk management staff from the other five institutions might reach similar conclusions. They would discover that for many of the important business lines and event types, none of the statistical distributions considered adequately captured the behavior of operational losses. They would also discover that some business lines and event types were well modeled by heavy-tailed distributions, but that the resulting parameter estimates had implausible implications for their overall operational risk exposure.

10.7   Threshold Analysis of Loss Data

The previous section's results suggest that it may be difficult to fit parametric loss-severity distributions over the entire range of loss amounts, even if separate analyses are conducted for each business line and event type. In this section, we focus on the largest losses, as these are most relevant for determining a bank's operational risk exposure. The main theoretical result underlying this "Peaks Over Threshold" (POT) approach is that if the distribution of excess losses converges to a limiting distribution as the threshold increases, then this limiting distribution is either the exponential distribution or the generalized Pareto distribution.

Implementation of the POT approach begins with choosing an estimator for the tail index parameter ξ, the most common being the Hill estimator. The appeal of this estimator derives from its conceptual and computational simplicity. For a set of losses exceeding a given threshold, the Hill estimator equals the average of the log of the losses minus the log of the threshold. If the underlying loss distribution is a Type I Pareto, then the Hill estimator is the maximum likelihood estimate of the tail thickness parameter. This property is quite useful, as it enables one to conduct likelihood ratio tests of various hypotheses.

Let k denote the number of observations exceeding a given threshold value. The quantity k is often referred to as the number of *exceedances*. Figure 10.5 presents plots of the Hill estimator for the six banks under consideration. The solid black line represents the Hill estimator calculated across all business lines and all event types for various values of k between 1 and 200. Traditionally, the final estimate of the tail index parameter has depended heavily on the choice of k. However, Huisman, Koedijk, Kool, and Palm (2001; hereafter HKKP) have recently proposed a regression-based enhancement to the Hill estimator that minimizes the role of threshold selection. HKKP note that the Hill estimator is biased in small samples, and that the bias is approximately linear in k, so that

(1) $$E(\gamma(k)) = \xi + ck,$$

where $\gamma(k)$ denotes the Hill estimator calculated using k exceedances, and ξ denotes the true value of the tail index parameter. HKKP use equation (1) to motivate the following regression

(2) $$\gamma(k) = \beta_0 + \beta_1 k + \varepsilon(k),$$

which is estimated for k in $(1, \ldots, K)$. The estimate of β_0 is interpreted as a bias-corrected estimate of ξ. This method also requires the researcher to choose the number of exceedances to include in the analysis. However, HKKP conclude that the estimate of β_0 is robust to the choice of k.

We apply the HKKP technique to the six Hill plots presented in figure 10.5. The results are presented in table 10.4.

The second column reports the number of exceedances (K) that were used to estimate the above regression. HKKP suggest setting K equal to half the sample size N, and also note that the function $\gamma(k)$ should be approximately linear over the range $k = (1, \ldots, K)$. In results not reported, we found that setting $K = N/2$ would not be appropriate, as none of the six Hill plots were linear over such a wide range.[8] However, each of the plots in figure 10.5 do indicate a range of k over which $\gamma(k)$ is approximately linear. We have chosen K accordingly.

The third column of table 10.4 reports the estimate of β_0 that was obtained using the optimal K. The estimates vary between 0.50 and 0.86, which implies that the maximal moment $\alpha = 1/\xi$ varies between 1.16 and 2.00. These findings confirm the intuition that operational losses have a heavy-tailed severity distribution. The parameter estimates in the third column of table 10.4 are used in simulations of the aggregate loss distribution reported in section 10.9, table 10.5.

---

8. To preserve the banks' confidentiality, we do not report Hill plots using either N or $N/2$ exceedances, as doing so would reveal the number of losses at each bank.

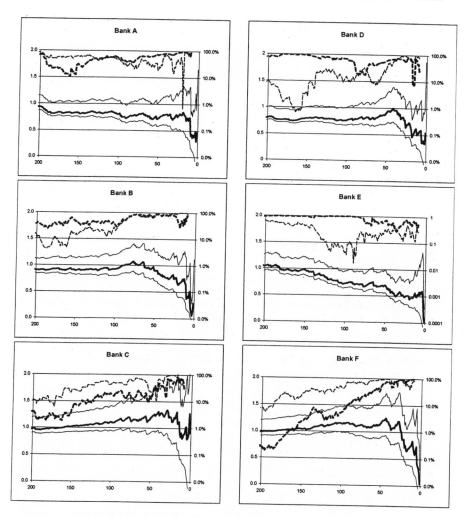

Fig. 10.5   Hill plots of the tail index parameter

Notes: The following are Hill plots of the tail index parameter for the six banks under construction. The thick dark line indicates the point estimates of the tail parameter as the number of exceedances varies between 1 and 200. The thin dark lines indicate 95 percent confidence intervals for the point estimates. The thick, medium gray (light gray) line indicates *P*-values for the Likelihood Ratio test of the hypothesis that the tail parameter is constant across business lines (event types).

The last row of the table reports results obtained for a sample consisting of all six banks. Interestingly, the resulting parameter estimate of 0.68 is consistent with the results of de Fontnouvelle et al. (2003), who reported tail-parameter estimates of about 0.65. This consistency is remarkable, given that de Fontnouvelle et al. (2003) used external, publicly reported

Table 10.4   **Tail parameter estimates based on the HKKP method**

		No. of exceedances used in estimation			
Bank ID	Optimal K	K	$0.75K$	$0.5K$	$0.25K$
A	180	0.823	0.794	0.817	0.717
		(0.016)	(0.020)	(0.030)	(0.042)
B	80	0.628	0.591	0.565	0.313
		(0.020)	(0.022)	(0.029)	(0.016)
C	30	0.859	0.824	0.952	1.032
		(0.085)	(0.097)	(0.182)	(0.353)
D	50	0.498	0.405	0.456	0.415
		(0.019)	(0.015)	(0.028)	(0.039)
E	200	0.552	0.534	0.558	0.488
		(0.003)	(0.008)	(0.013)	(0.018)
F	50	0.633	0.538	0.536	0.342
		(0.030)	(0.019)	(0.038)	(0.026)
All	140	0.681	0.554	0.419	0.305
		(0.014)	(0.012)	(0.008)	(0.015)

Notes: This table reports tail index estimates calculated under the HKKP regression algorithm. The optimal number of exceedances (K) is chosen to correspond to the linear portion of the Hill plot. Standard errors are reported in parentheses.

loss data (rather than internal data), as well as substantially different empirical techniques than the current paper.

The final three columns of table 10.4 report tail-index estimates obtained using different numbers of exceedances in the regression procedure of HKKP. For all six banks, the results do not change materially when the number of exceedances is reduced from K to $0.75K$ or $0.5K$. The results change more when $0.25K$ exceedances are used. Overall, table 10.4 confirms that the estimation results are not highly sensitive to the choice of K.

10.7.1   Estimation by Business Line and Event Type

Our Hill plot analyses have thus far taken place at the "top of the house" level, where data are aggregated across both business line and event type. However, one might ask whether this approach is appropriate, or whether the tail behavior of the loss-severity distribution might vary by business line and event type. To investigate this issue, we calculated for each value of k (the number of exceedances) separate Hill estimators for each business line and event type. For each k, we then calculated likelihood ratio test statistics for the hypothesis that the tail index is constant across business lines and that it is constant across event types. The probability values for these statistics are reported graphically in figure 10.5. The results indicate that both hypotheses can sometimes be rejected at the 10 percent level when k is near 200. However, neither hypothesis can be rejected at the 10 percent level for values of k where the Hill estimator is constant (banks A, C, and

E) or decreasing (banks B, D, and F). Because choosing a small k provides a less biased value of the Hill estimator, segregating the analysis by business line or event type does not seem to be called for. This finding does not mean that tail behavior of operational losses is constant across business lines and event types. Rather, the ability of statistical estimation techniques to meaningfully differentiate tail behavior across business lines is hindered by a lack of data on large losses using only internal data for one year, and by the concentration of these data in one or two business lines and event types.

10.7.2   On the Possibility of Thin-Tailed Severity Distributions

The results presented in table 10.4 suggest that loss-severity distributions at the six banks under consideration have tail indexes ranging between 0.50 and 0.86. The reported standard errors also seem to exclude the possibility that $\xi = 0$, which would indicate a thin-tailed loss distribution. However, the Hill estimator is designed for situations where $\xi > 0$. Thus, it cannot be used to reject the hypothesis of a thin-tailed loss distribution. This is an interesting hypothesis, because thin-tailed distributions, such as the lognormal, could have significantly different implications for capital than fatter-tailed distributions, such as the Pareto.

Dekkers, Einmahl, and de Haan (1989) show how to extend the Hill estimator so that it is valid for any ξ in $\mathfrak{R}$. The graph of this estimator as k varies is commonly referred to as a DEdH plot. Figure 10.6 reports DEdH plots for the six banks under consideration. These plots indicate that for the low values of k for which the Hill estimator was constant or decreasing, we cannot reject the null of a thin-tailed severity distribution at any of the six banks. This is problematic. The choice of fat versus thin tailed loss severity distribution will have significant impact on the capital calculation, yet based on limited data for only one year, available statistical techniques provide little guidance on which choice is more appropriate. We expect that as banks accumulate more data on large losses, the DEdH plots will either be able to reject the null of $\xi = 0$ or will indicate tail estimates close enough to zero that the choice does not matter so much. For now, we explore the empirical consequences of assuming a thin-tailed loss severity distribution.

Extreme value theory suggests that the exponential distribution is an appropriate choice for modeling loss severity under the thin-tailed assumption. Thus, we wish to construct a threshold plot showing how the exponential parameter varies as the threshold increases (k decreases). Because the maximum likelihood estimate of this parameter is given by the mean excess, these threshold plots would be identical to the mean excess plots already presented in figures 10.3 and 10.4. As discussed earlier, the mean excess plots suggest that the exponential distribution does not provide an accurate description of the tail behavior of operational losses. All six banks' excess plots are concave and increasing, whereas exponentially distributed data imply a linear and horizontal excess plot.

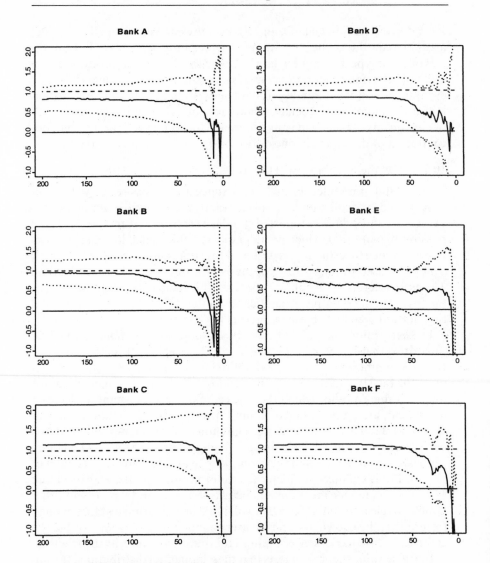

Fig. 10.6   DEdH plots of the tail index parameter

Notes: The following are DEdH plots of the tail index parameter for the six banks under consideration. The solid line indicates the point estimates of the tail parameter as the number of exceedances varies between 1 and 500. The dotted lines indicate 95 percent confidence intervals for the point estimates.

Since the DEdH plots do suggest that tail behavior of operational losses might be modeled with a light-tailed distribution, we consider whether some other such distribution provides a better fit to the data than the exponential. Because the log-normal was the one light-tailed distribution investigated in section 10.6 that provided a good fit across multiple banks, business lines, and event types, we investigate whether it might also provide a useful description of the tail behavior of operational losses.

Figures 10.7 and 10.8 present threshold plots for the six banks, under the assumption that losses above high thresholds follow a (truncated) lognormal distribution. For each value of k (the number of exceedances), estimates

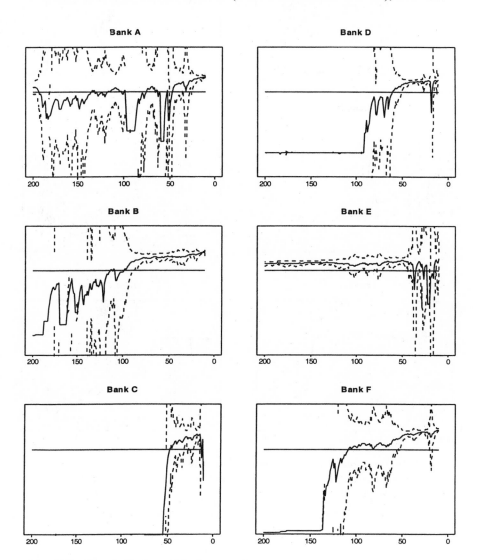

Fig. 10.7   Threshold plots of the lognormal parameter μ

Notes: The following are threshold plots of the lognormal parameter μ for the six banks under consideration. The solid line indicates the point estimates of μ as the number of exceedances varies between 10 and 200. The dotted lines indicate 95 percent confidence intervals for the point estimates. Labels are omitted from the vertical axis to preserve confidentiality.

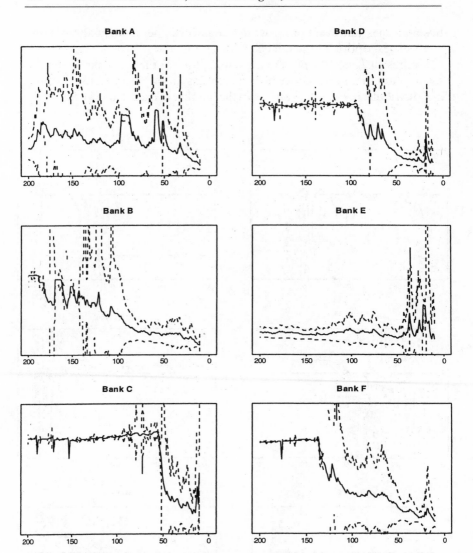

Fig. 10.8   Threshold plots of the lognormal parameter σ

Notes: The following are threshold plots of the lognormal parameter σ for the six banks under consideration. The solid line indicates the point estimates of σ as the number of exceedances varies between 10 and 200. The dotted lines indicate 95 percent confidence intervals for the point estimates. Labels are omitted from the vertical axis to preserve confidentiality.

of the lognormal parameters were obtained via maximum likelihood. (Vertical axis scales have been omitted to protect data confidentiality. However, a reference line in figure 10.7 indicates the location of μ = 0.) One can discern a common pattern in the estimates of μ and σ across all six banks. For example, consider the plots for bank B. Both suggest that the lognormal is not a good fit for more than 100 exceedances, in that the estimates are unstable as k varies and the point estimate for μ is less than 0. We have already argued that this is not a reasonable characterization of operational loss data. However, parameter estimates are both stable and reasonable when thirty to seventy exceedances are used for estimation. The μ estimate lies between 4 and 8, while the σ estimate lies between 0 and 2.[9] Three of the other banks display a similar pattern, with stable (and reasonable) parameter estimates emerging over high thresholds. The two remaining banks' (C and E) POT plots become unstable for small numbers of exceedances.

In results not reported, we chose a specific number of exceedances K for each of the six banks reported in figures 7 and 8, such that the estimates of μ and σ are stable for $k \leq K$.[10] (This procedure follows the traditional analysis of the Hill plot as discussed in Embrechts, Klüppelburg, and Mikosch, 1997). The resulting estimates of μ and σ are used in simulations of the aggregate loss distribution reported in section 10.9, table 10.5.

10.8 The Operational Loss Frequency Distribution

We have thus far focused on the loss severity distribution, which describes the potential size of an operational loss, given that the loss has occurred. Operational risk capital will also depend on the loss frequency distribution, which describes how many losses might actually occur over a given time period. The Poisson distribution is a natural starting point for modeling loss frequency because it arises whenever the loss occurrence rate is constant over time. We thus begin by modeling frequency at bank i by the following:

$$(3) \qquad\qquad n_i \sim \text{Po}(\lambda_i)$$

That the Poisson distribution has only one parameter makes it particularly attractive in the current context. The LDCE does not provide information regarding the date of an event, beyond the knowledge that all losses occurred sometime during the year 2001. Thus, we have enough information to estimate the Poisson parameter, but not enough to estimate multiparameter frequency distributions. Maximum likelihood estimates of the parameter λ are given by the annual number of loss events.[11]

An interesting property of a Poisson variable is that the mean and variance are equal. So if a LDCE bank were to report 10,000 loss events for the year 2001, we would expect (with 95 percent probability) it to report between 9,800 and 10,200 events the following year. On an intuitive level, this

---

9. The actual range of variation is significantly narrower, but has not been reported, so as to protect data confidentiality.

10. These results were not reported because estimates of μ and σ would reveal confidential information regarding the loss-severity distribution at individual institutions.

11. To preserve confidentiality, we have not reported the number of loss events.

seems like a very narrow range, and one might ask whether frequency should be modeled via a distribution permitting more variability than the Poisson. One such distribution is the negative binomial, which is a commonly used generalization of the Poisson.

As was discussed earlier, the LDCE data do not support estimation of two-parameter frequency distributions at the individual bank level. In order to model excess dispersion in the loss frequency distribution, we take a cross-sectional approach. That is, we estimate the following regression:

$$(4) \qquad\qquad n_i \sim F(X_i, \mathbf{b}),$$

where $F(\cdot)$ is a discrete nonnegative-valued distribution, X_i is an observable characteristic of bank i (e.g., asset size), and $\mathbf{b}$ is a parameter vector. Because our data set is purely cross-sectional (i.e., there is no time series element), we cannot estimate any fixed effects. Fixed effects represent bank-specific variation in the frequency of operational losses, which could arise from factors such as the quality of an individual bank's risk control environment. However, it is worth nothing that equation (3) can be interpreted as a fixed effects model. Seen in this light, equations (3) and (4) are different but complementary ways of treating the fixed effects issue. Under the latter, the expected number of events is purely a function of a bank's observable characteristics, whereas under the former, the expected number of events is purely bank specific.

We begin by estimating equation (4) under the assumption that $F(\cdot)$ is the Poisson distribution, so that $n_i \sim \mathrm{PO}(\text{mean} = bX_i)$. Setting each X_i as bank i's total assets as of year-end 2001, we obtain an estimate of 8.2 for the parameter b. This indicates that banks in our sample reported on average 8.2 operational events for every billion dollars in assets. Next, we estimate equation (4) under the assumption that $F(\cdot)$ is the negative binomial distribution, so that $n_i \sim \mathrm{NB}(\text{mean} = b_1 X_i, \text{dispersion} = b_2)$. We obtain an estimate of 7.4 for b_1 and 0.43 for b_2.

10.9   The Aggregate Loss Distribution

In this section, we combine the severity results of section 10.7 with the frequency results of section 10.8 in order to estimate economic capital for operational risk, which is specified as the 99.9th percentile of the aggregate loss distribution. We explore two alternate assumptions regarding the loss frequency distribution: the Poisson and negative binomial distributions, as estimated in section 10.8. We also explore three different assumptions regarding the tail of the loss-severity distribution: the Pareto as estimated in section 10.7 (table 10.4), the lognormal as estimated in section 10.7b, and the empirical distribution.

We use Monte Carlo simulation to derive an estimate of the aggregate loss distribution as follows. In the case of the empirical severity distribution, the number of loss events in year i is drawn at random from the frequency distribution, and is denoted N_i. Then, N_i individual losses $(l[1], \ldots, l[N_i])$ are drawn from the empirical distribution. The N_i losses are summed to obtain the aggregate loss for year i. This process is repeated for one million simulated years in order to obtain the aggregate loss distribution.

Monte Carlo simulation for the Pareto (lognormal) severity distribution proceeds similarly, except that losses in $(l[1], \ldots, l[N_i])$ greater than or equal to the relevant threshold value are replaced with random draws from the Pareto (lognormal) distribution estimated in section 10.6.[12] The N_i losses are then summed to obtain the aggregate loss for year i, and the process is repeated for one million simulated years in order to obtain the aggregate loss distribution. The use of Monte Carlo techniques in the current context has already been extensively documented, and we refer readers interested in further details to Klugman, Panjer, and Wilmot (1998) and Embrechts, Kaufmann, and Samorodnitsky (2002), and to their references.

10.9.1   Simulations Based on a Poisson Frequency Distribution

In this subsection, we assume that the frequency of operational losses follows a Poisson distribution with a fixed effects specification, as in equation (3). We make three different assumptions for loss severity: the Pareto, the lognormal, and the empirical distribution. Results are presented in panel A of table 10.5. To preserve the confidentiality of the banks in the sample, we scaled each percentile for each bank by that bank's assets. The cross-bank median for each percentile is then reported.

In 2001, the Basel Committee conducted a quantitative impact study covering 140 banks in twenty-four countries. The committee reported that the median (mean) ratio of reported operational risk capital to minimum regulatory capital was 12.8 percent (15.3 percent), and concluded that "a reasonable level of the overall operational risk capital charge would be about 12 percent of minimum regulatory capital."[13] If one estimates minimum regulatory capital to be 5 percent of a bank's assets, then a reasonable benchmark value for operational risk capital would be 0.6 percent of assets. The median value of 0.468 percent reported in Panel A (for the 99.9th percentile) seems roughly consistent with this benchmark. It is also worth noting that our estimation is based solely on internal loss data for one year, providing limited data to estimate high-severity losses. Banks are also using external loss data and scenario analysis to provide additional information on the tail where they have insufficient high-severity losses in

---

12. For the lognormal distribution, the relevant threshold is the same as that used for estimation of the tail parameter. For the Pareto distribution, the relevant threshold is the largest observed loss value. This is because by construction, the HKKP tail-parameter estimate β_0 corresponds to zero exceedances.

13. See page 26 of Basel Committee on Banking Supervision (2001).

Table 10.5   **Quantiles of the simulated aggregate loss distribution**

	Percentiles of the aggregate loss distribution (%)		
Severity distribution	95	99	99.9
A. Poisson frequency distribution—fixed effects model			
Pareto	0.066	0.117	0.468
Lognormal	0.047	0.056	0.070
Empirical	0.047	0.053	0.058
B. Poisson frequency distribution—cross-sectional model			
Pareto	0.106	0.148	0.362
Lognormal	0.089	0.101	0.121
Empirical	0.086	0.093	0.102
C. Negative binomial frequency distribution—cross-sectional model			
Pareto	0.166	0.237	0.400
Lognormal	0.143	0.198	0.273
Empirical	0.146	0.202	0.273

Notes: This table reports quantiles of the simulated aggregate loss distribution. To preserve the confidentiality of the banks in the sample, we scale each percentile for each bank by that bank's assets. The cross-bank median for each percentile is then reported. Panel A presents results under the assumption that loss frequency follows a Poisson distribution whose parameter is estimated separately for each bank (fixed-effects model). Panel B presents results under the assumption that loss frequency follows a Poisson distribution whose parameter is a linear function of each bank's asset size (cross-sectional model). Panel C presents results under the assumption that loss frequency follows a negative binomial distribution whose parameter is a linear function of each bank's asset size (cross-sectional model).

a particular business line. Thus, we would view the figure of 0.468 percent as a lower bound on the banks' true operational risk exposure.

The next set of simulations is conducted under the assumption that the severity of operational losses follows a lognormal distribution. The results suggest that cross-bank median of the 99.9th percentile is 0.07 percent of assets. This figure seems small in comparison with both that obtained in the Pareto-based simulations and with the 0.6 percent benchmark discussed previously.

We conducted the final set of simulations by drawing the number of loss events from a Poisson distribution and the loss amounts from the empirical severity distribution. One may think of the resulting 99.9th percentiles as a lower bound on the true capital requirement. Alternatively, one may think of these percentiles as representing the portion of capital that derives from banks' actual loss experience, rather than from their exposure—as measured by a fitted distribution function, which would also include information from external data and scenario analysis. Because the lognormal is a thin-tailed distribution, the 99.9th percentile based on the lognormal severity distribution exceeds that based on the empirical distribution by about 20 percent. Because the Pareto is a heavy-tailed distribution, the 99.9th percentile based on the Pareto severity distribution exceeds that based on the empirical distribution by a factor of eight.

10.9.2   Simulations Based on a Negative Binomial
Frequency Distribution

In the previous section, we assumed that the frequency of operational losses followed a Poisson distribution. We found that assuming a Pareto severity distribution yielded capital estimates that were broadly consistent with the Basel Committee's expectation that operational risk accounts for 12 percent of minimum regulatory capital. Assuming a lognormal severity distribution yielded markedly lower capital estimates. In this section, we investigate how these results change under the assumption that the frequency of operational losses follows a negative binomial distribution, as was discussed in section 10.8.

Panels B and C of table 10.5 report quantiles of aggregate loss distributions that were simulated using cross-sectional frequency models based on the Poisson and negative binomial distributions, respectively. (Note that the cross-sectional Poisson model is included because it is not informative to directly compare the cross-sectional negative binomial results with the fixed-effects Poisson results, as differences could be due to either differences in the handling of effects or to differences in the assumed frequency distribution.) The negative binomial specification implies significantly more variability in the number of operational losses than does the Poisson specification. Thus, intuition suggests that the aggregate loss distribution should have a heavier tail under the negative binomial specification. This intuition proves correct in the case of the lognormal severity distribution. The median 99.9th percentile is about twice as large under the negative binomial as under the cross-sectional Poisson specification. However, intuition proves incorrect in the case of the Pareto distribution, for which the median 99.9th percentile is not materially different under the negative binomial than under the Poisson.[14]

Under the negative binomial specification of loss frequency, it is difficult to decide whether the Pareto or the lognormal provides the more useful characterization of the loss-severity distribution. The difference between the two sets of results is within an order of magnitude that may be considered close given the preliminary nature of the data and techniques.

10.10   Conclusion

This paper examines operational risk modeling using only internal operational loss data. By focusing on internal data, it captures the potential modeling issues faced by banking organizations that have only recently started to collect comprehensive loss data. The analysis indicates that the

---

14. It has been argued that intuition can be misleading if risks follow very heavy-tailed Pareto-type distributions (e.g., Embrechts, McNeill, and Straumann 2002, Rootzen and Klüppelberg 1999).

data do show statistical regularities, and that the severity ranking of event types is similar across banks. The analysis also shows that the data is reasonably fit by heavy-tailed distributions (such as the Pareto), and illustrates that certain statistical methods yield plausible tail-parameter estimates for these heavy-tailed distributions. In fact, the tail-parameter estimates for the severity distribution are quite close to the estimates based on publicly available time series of high-severity losses (de Fontnouvelle et al. 2003).

It is important to qualify our results by noting that they are based on only one year of loss data. This limited data makes it difficult to distinguish between different distributional assumptions, though some thin-tailed distributions do appear inconsistent with the data. At this point, we would conclude that a variety of threshold-based techniques seem to yield results that are consistently plausible across banks. However, we may need to await the arrival of better data before making more definitive conclusions. As banks obtain three or more years of good operational loss data, the ability to differentiate across alternative distributional assumptions should improve.

References

Basel Committee on Banking Supervision. 2001. Working Paper on the regulatory treatment of operational risk. Basel, Switzerland: Bank for International Settlements.

De Fontnouvelle, Patrick, Virginia Dejesus-Rueff, John Jordan, and Eric Rosengren. 2006. Forthcoming. Capital and risk: New evidence on implications of large operational losses. *Journal of Money, Credit and Banking.*

Dekkers, A., J. Einmahl, and L. de Haan. 1989. A moment estimator for the index of an extreme-value distribution. *Annals of Statistics* 17:1833–55.

Embrechts, Paul, Roger Kaufmann, and Gennady Samorodnitsky. 2002. Ruin theory revisited: Stochastic models for operational risk. In *Risk management for central bank foreign reserves,* ed. C. Bernadell, P. Cardon, J. Coche, F. Diebold, and S. Manganelli, 143–61. Frankfurt: European Central Bank.

Embrechts, Paul, Claudia Klüppelberg, and Thomas Mikosch. 1997. *Modelling external events for insurance and finance.* New York: Springer-Verlag.

Embrechts, Paul, Alexander McNeil, and Daniel Straumann. 2002. Correlation and dependence in risk management: Properties and pitfalls. In *Risk management: Value-at-Risk and beyond,* ed. M. A. H. Dempster, 176–223. Cambridge: Cambridge University Press.

Gabaix, Xavier. 1999. Zipf's Law for cities: An explanation. *Quarterly Journal of Economics* 114:739–67.

Huisman, Ronald, Kees Koedijk, Clemens Kool, and Franz Palm. 2001. Tail-index estimates in small samples. *Journal of Business and Economic Statistics* 19:208–16.

Klugman, Stuart, Harry Panjer, and Gordon Willmot. 1998. *Loss models.* New York: Wiley.

Moscadelli, Marco. 2004. The modeling of operational risk: The experience from the analysis of the data collected by the Risk Management Group of the Basel Committee, Working paper no. 517, Bank of Italy.

Risk Management Group. 2003. *The 2002 Loss Data Collection Exercise for Operational Risk: Summary of the data collected.* Report to the Basel Committee on Banking Supervision. Basel, Switzerland: Bank for International Settlements.

Rootzen, Holger, and Claudia Klüppelberg. 1999. A single number can't hedge against economic catastrophes. *Ambio* 28 (6): 550–55.

Comment   Andrew Kuritzkes

Until recently, operational risk was hard enough to define, let alone quantify. One of the undoubted benefits of the New Basel Capital Accord (Basel II) for international bank capital regulation is that it has standardized the definition of operational risk, at least for the banking industry.[1] Basel II requires banks around the world to collect internal data on operational losses—defined to include losses resulting from the failure of "internal processes, people, or systems" or from external events—and classify losses into one of seven categories.[2] As a result of this mandatory data collection effort, it is now becoming increasingly possible to analyze the behavior of operational losses systematically, within a commonly accepted definitional framework.

Once we are in a position to define operational risk, the next question becomes whether we can measure it. The ability to quantify operational risk has important policy implications, because Basel II bases a new regulatory capital charge for operational risk on banks' internal modeling of operational losses. Under Basel II's "Advanced Measurement Approach," internationally active banks will be required to estimate their exposure to operational losses over a one-year time horizon at the 99.9th percentile level. The regulatory capital charge for operational risk will then be set equivalent to a bank's internal estimate of the tail risk at the 99.9th percentile, or a one-in-one-thousand-year outcome. Overall, the Basel Committee responsible for developing the new bank capital rules expects that this bottom-up calculation of operational risk capital will comprise about 12 percent of total bank regulatory capital. By comparison, the expected operational risk capital requirement is more than five times the regulatory capital charge for market risk that was introduced for banks in the mid-1990s.[3]

I would like to thank Mark Ames of Mercer Oliver Wyman for his help in preparing this comment. Any errors or omissions are my responsibility.

1. See Kuritzkes (2002) for a discussion of the difficulties of defining operational risk, and implications for quantification.

2. See Basel Committee on Banking Supervision (2001).

3. According to a recent study by Beverly Hirtle of the Federal Reserve Bank of New York, the median market risk capital charge for nineteen U.S. bank holding companies subject to Basel's market risk amendment ranged from 1.0 percent to 2.3 percent of required regulatory capital on a quarterly basis from 1998 through 2001. See Hirtle 2005.

Within this context, de Fontnouvelle, Rosengren, and Jordan, working together at the Federal Reserve Bank of Boston, seek to assess how bank operational losses can be modeled from internal data sets. Narrowly, their focus is on whether the techniques of Extreme Value Theory (EVT) can be successfully applied to estimate operational risk distributions for individual banks using internal loss data. The analysis follows from a previous study by the same authors and another colleague (de Fontnouvelle et al. 2003) that applied an EVT approach to two external databases of publicly reported operational losses for the banking industry. That study concluded that a generalized Pareto distribution appeared to fit an aggregate operational loss distribution well.

Significantly, in this paper, the authors extend their analysis to a confidential set of bank-level data collected by the Federal Reserve as part of Basel II's second Quantitative Impact Study (QIS 2). Through QIS 2, the authors are able to analyze the internal loss distributions of six large, internationally active banks that were deemed to have comprehensive data sets for 2001, the year of the impact study. Given confidentiality restrictions, de Fontnouvelle et al. need to protect the anonymity of the six banks in their sample, and they take care in reporting results not to reveal information that could be used to identify the institutions.

The authors make excellent use of their access to the regulatory dataset to provide a unique window on estimation techniques for modeling operational risk. Specifically, they are concerned with three main questions:

1. Are operational losses best characterized by a thin-tailed (e.g., log-normal), or fat-tailed (e.g., Pareto) distribution?

2. Are the shapes of these distributions consistent across individual banks?

3. Do the results provide a reasonable basis for allocating regulatory capital?

Affirmative answers to the first two questions lead to a tentative yes to the third: to the extent that operational losses are fat tailed and can be modeled by a Pareto distribution, then tail estimates of operational risk at the 99.9 percent level are more likely to fall within the expected range for regulatory capital. And to the extent that the same modeling approach can be shown to generate consistent results across the six banks in the sample, the more confident we can be that reliance on internal models will not lead to random differences in capital requirements for similar institutions.

In addressing these questions, de Fontnouvelle et al. need to overcome two challenges.

First, since operational risk capital is defined at a point in the tail of the loss distribution, by definition there will be a paucity of data on extreme losses (99.9 percent events) within any one institution. This is particularly true when looking at a one-year time horizon (although the problem per-

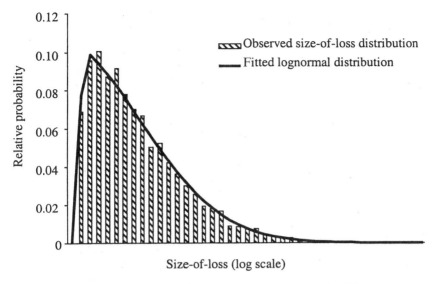

Fig. 10C.1   Lognormal versus empirical fit for a large international bank
Note: Based on five years of internal operational loss data.

sists even if the measurement period is extended to three or more years, as has been the case with many of the large banks preparing for Basel II implementation). If a bank experiences an extreme loss within the measurement period, is this a sign that it is intrinsically more prone to control breakdowns and operational failures, or has the bank just been unlucky? The measurement problem is most acute in the tail—the region of relevance for setting operational risk capital.

Second, observable operational losses are characterized by a large mode of high-frequency, low-severity events, and they appear to fit a lognormal distribution well. This is evident in Figure 10C.1, which shows a fitted lognormal distribution plotted against empirically observed losses for a large international bank, based on five years of the bank's operational loss history. (Like the authors, I cannot reveal the identity of this bank for confidentiality reasons.) A quick visual check reveals that the fit is quite good. Similarly, the authors' own data show how close a lognormal distribution comes to the empirically observed data across the six banks in their study. As summarized in table 10C.1, the lognormal estimates of severity under three different frequency-estimation techniques fall within 9 percent of the observed empirical values at the 99th percentile.

Yet if operational risk is appropriately characterized by a lognormal distribution, the resulting capital estimates will be too "low" to be reasonable. To see this, I have, in table 10C.2, normalized the authors' estimate of the 99.9 percent loss from the lognormal distribution under each of their

Table 10C.1   Lognormal severity versus empirical observations: Aggregate loss distribution across six banks (%)

Frequency estimation approach	99th percentile, empirical fit	99th percentile, lognormal estimate
Poisson fixed effects	.053	.056
Poisson cross-sectional	.093	.101
Negative binomial	.202	.198

Source: De Fontnouvelle et al., table 5.
Note: Scaled as a percentage of bank assets.

Table 10C.2   Lognormal estimates at 99.9 percent

Frequency estimation approach	99.9th percentile (as percent of regulatory capital)
Poisson fixed effects	1.40
Poisson cross-sectional	2.42
Negative binomial	5.46

Source: De Fontnouvelle et al., Table 5.
Note: Scaled relative to 5 percent total regulatory capital to assets.

frequency-estimation approaches (which the authors report as a percentage of total assets) to the 5 percent Basel II regulatory capital-to-asset ratio suggested by the authors.[4] On this basis, the implied regulatory capital charge for operational risk would range from 1.40 percent to 5.46 percent of total Basel II regulatory capital—significantly lower than the Basel Committee's expectation that operational risk capital would account for roughly 12 percent of total regulatory capital.

De Fontnouvelle et al. marshal an impressive array of counterevidence to demonstrate that operational losses should be modeled with a fat-tailed distribution. Their argument follows five main steps.

1. For capital purposes, we are not concerned with the mode of the distribution, but with the tail at the 99.9 percent level.

2. Extreme Value Theory and experience in modeling risks that are similar to operational losses, such as catastrophe risks in insurance, suggests that tails can behave very differently from the body of the distribution.

---

4. It would be more convenient if the authors reported the results scaled by risk-weighted assets rather than by total bank assets, since total Basel II regulatory capital is defined as a fixed percentage (8 percent) of risk-weighted assets. For consistency, I have adopted the authors' suggestion that total regulatory capital is around 5 percent of total assets in normalizing the results.

3. Profiling of operational loss data for each of the six banks in their sample by tail plots, average excess plots, and chi-square tests indicates that fat-tailed distributions generally outperform thin-tailed distributions.

4. Using the EVT-based peaks-over-threshold approach developed by Huisman, Koedijk, Kool, and Palm (HKKP 2001), a Pareto distribution appears to provide a strong fit in the tail for all six banks.

5. The results are consistent with the previous paper by de Fontnouvelle and colleagues on publicly reported operational losses.

Taken together, the evidence is persuasive that operational losses are indeed fat tailed. For practitioners interested in the behavior of the distribution at around the 99.9 percent level—in particular, bank risk managers and regulators—modeling the operational risk tail using a peaks-over-threshold approach and a generalized Pareto distribution offers a promising solution.

Turning to the paper's second question, do the estimates across individual banks converge? Here we are hampered by the aggregation of results necessary to protect the anonymity of the six banks studied. The authors are not able to report the regulatory capital estimate at the 99.9 percent level for each of the six banks in the study without risking disclosure of confidential information, so instead they report the median result across the six banks (after scaling each bank's results by total assets). This is the basis on which they conclude that "the median value of .468 percent (of assets, equivalent to 9.36 percent of total regulatory capital) reported (see the author's table 10.5) for the 99.9th percentile seems reasonable" in comparison to regulatory expectations.

But while the authors do not report individual loss estimates for the six banks, they do report the shape parameter, ξ, for the generalized Pareto distribution for each bank under the HKKP estimation. The ξ's range from a low of .498 to a high of .859, with a combined aggregate value for the six banks of .681. The difference in shape parameters actually implies a very wide range in tail estimates at the individual bank level.

To illustrate the effect of differences in the shape parameter, my colleague, Mark Ames, and I calculated regulatory capital at the 99.9 percent level across the six values of ξ for hypothetical banks whose exposures were otherwise identical. For each bank we assumed twenty operational loss exceedances per year above a $1 MM threshold, and a value of $0.75 MM for the GPD beta. The threshold and beta values were chosen to be broadly consistent with de Fontnouvelle and colleagues' work in their previous study (de Fontnouvelle et al. 2003). The results are reported in table 10C.3.

Differences in the shape parameter appear to have a significant impact on an individual bank's tail risk. The estimates for our hypothetical bank show that for twenty exceedances above $1 MM, if the shape parameter

Table 10C.3   **Regulatory capital as a function of tail density**

Sample	Value of shape parameter ξ	Regulatory capital estimate at 99.9 percent in $MMs
Bank D	0.498	208
Bank E	0.552	321
Bank B	0.628	600
Bank F	0.633	625
Combined	0.681	935
Bank A	0.823	3,157
Bank C	0.859	4,320

Source: De Fontnouvelle et al., table 4.
Note: HKKP estimates of GPD shape parameter ξ for six banks.

were as low as .498 the 99.9th percentile loss estimate would be $200 MM. If the shape parameter were as high as .859 the 99.9th percentile loss estimate would be $4.3 billion. This twenty-to-one range is consistent with the findings of de Fontnouvelle and colleagues' previous study (de Fontnouvelle et al. 2003) based on externally reported operational losses. From a regulatory perspective, the key question is how confident can we be in each bank's own estimate—based solely on internal data—of its shape parameter. Do such apparently large differences in the shapes of the tail reflect true differences in banks' vulnerability to operational losses, or are they artifacts of measurement?

An order-of-magnitude range may not be that surprising for an attempt to estimate the one-in-one-thousand-year tail risk of operational loss, given that the authors were only able to work with a single year's worth of data for each of the six banks. More generally, the range in magnitude is a reflection of the early stage of development of operational risk measurement. No doubt future research across more banks and on longer datasets will help narrow the range.

In light of the differences in the shape parameter, can we say that the results provide a reasonable basis for allocating capital to individual banks? In my view, the answer is that it is too early to tell. Until we know more about the behavior of tail estimates at the individual bank level, we will not know whether differences in operational risk capital calculations across banks reflect true differences in their loss experience and control environment, or the limitations of using sparse data to forecast extreme events.

References

Basel Committee on Banking Supervision. 2001. Regulatory treatment of operational risk. Bank for International Settlements (BIS) Working Paper no. 8. Available at: www.bis.org/publ/bcbs_wp8.pdf.

de Fontnouvelle, Patrick, Virginia DeJesus-Rueff, John Jordan, and Eric Rosengren. 2003. Using loss data to quantify operational risk. Federal Reserve Bank of Boston Working Paper. Available at: www.bos.frb.org/bankinfo/oprisk/articles .htm.

Hirtle, Beverly. 2005. What market risk capital tells us about bank risk. Forthcoming. *Federal Reserve Bank of New York Economic Policy Review.*

Huisman, Ronald, Kees Koedjik, Clemens Kool, and Franz Palm. 2001. Tail-index estimates in small samples. *Journal of Business and Economic Studies* 19:208–16.

Kuritzkes, Andrew. 2002. Operational risk capital: A problem of definition. *Journal of Risk Finance* 4 (1): 47–56.

Discussion Summary

Part of the discussion revolved around the paucity of observations in the tails of loss distributions, both currently and going forward. *Eric Rosengren* noted that the tail is more populated for some banks than others and that such variation may be a source of the variation in estimated tail-index values that the authors observe. He also noted that under Basel II's advanced-measurement approach, banks are not limited to internal data, but also may use external data and scenario analysis. *Patricia Jackson* wondered whether Basel II's loss-size cutoff for data collection might be raised to reduce costs, but *Ken Abbott* observed that, in his experience, small losses may be indicative of process problems that might result in very large losses under other circumstances. Thus, there should be a role for judgment in internal reporting of small losses.

Darrell Duffie suggested that the authors might take a Bayesian approach to dealing with a potential censorship problem in their data: losses are capped at the level of a firm's capital, because only surviving firms contribute observations to operational risk-loss databases. *Casper de Vries* suggested that the authors could use bootstrap methods in determining the optimal number of observations to use in tail estimation, that they use the empirical distribution in estimating losses occurring in the body of the distribution rather than the lognormal, and that variation in constant terms may account for the variation in tail-index estimates that they observe.

Practical Volatility and Correlation Modeling for Financial Market Risk Management

Torben G. Andersen, Tim Bollerslev,
Peter F. Christoffersen, and Francis X. Diebold

11.1 Introduction

It is now widely agreed that financial asset return volatilities and correlations (henceforth "volatilities") are time varying, with persistent dynamics. This is true across assets, asset classes, time periods, and countries. Moreover, asset return volatilities are central to finance, whether in asset pricing, portfolio allocation, or market risk measurement. Hence the field of financial econometrics devotes considerable attention to time-varying volatility and associated tools for its measurement, modeling, and forecasting.

In this chapter we suggest practical applications of recent developments in financial econometrics dealing with time-varying volatility to the measurement and management of market risk, stressing parsimonious models that are easily estimated. Our ultimate goal is to stimulate dialog between the academic and practitioner communities, advancing best-practice market risk measurement and management technologies by drawing upon the best of both worlds. Three themes appear repeatedly, and so we highlight them here.

The first is the issue of aggregation level. We consider both aggregated (portfolio-level) and disaggregated (asset-level) modeling, emphasizing the related distinction between risk *measurement* and risk *management,* because risk measurement generally requires only a portfolio-level model, whereas

For helpful comments we would like to thank Ken Abbott, Casper de Vries, Philipp Hartmann, Patricia Jackson, Jim O'Brien, Hashem Pesaran, and Pedro Santa-Clara. For research support, Andersen, Bollerslev, and Diebold thank the U.S. National Science Foundation, and Christoffersen thanks Fonds Québécois de la Recherche sur la Société et la Culture (FQRSC), Social Sciences and Humanities Research Council of Canada (SSHRC), and Institut de Finance Mathématique de Montréal (IFM2).

risk management requires an asset-level model. At the asset level, the issue of dimensionality and dimensionality reduction arises repeatedly, and we devote considerable attention to methods for tractable modeling of the very high-dimensional covariance matrices of practical relevance.

The second theme concerns the use of low-frequency versus high-frequency data, and the associated issue of parametric versus nonparametric volatility measurement. We treat all cases, but we emphasize the appeal of volatility *measurement* using nonparametric methods in conjunction with high-frequency data, followed by *modeling* that is intentionally parametric.

The third theme relates to the issue of unconditional versus conditional risk measurement. We argue that, for most financial risk management purposes, the *conditional* perspective is exclusively relevant, notwithstanding, for example, the fact that popular approaches based on historical simulation and extreme-value theory typically adopt an unconditional perspective. We advocate, moreover, moving beyond a conditional *volatility* perspective to a full conditional *density* perspective, and we discuss methods for constructing and evaluating full conditional density forecasts.

We proceed systematically in several steps. In section 11.2, we consider portfolio-level analysis, directly modeling portfolio volatility using historical simulation, exponential smoothing, and generalized autoregressive conditional heteroskedastic (GARCH) methods. In section 11.3, we consider asset-level analysis, modeling asset covariance matrices using exponential smoothing and multivariate GARCH methods, paying special attention to dimensionality-reduction methods. In section 11.4, we explore the use of high-frequency data for improved covariance matrix measurement and modeling, treating realized variance and covariance, and again discussing procedures for dimensionality reduction. In section 11.5 we treat the construction of complete conditional density forecasts via simulation methods. We conclude in section 11.6.

11.2   Portfolio Level Analysis: Modeling Portfolio Volatility

Portfolio risk measurement requires only a univariate portfolio-level model (e.g., Benson and Zangari 1997). In this section, we discuss such univariate portfolio methods. In contrast, active portfolio risk management, including value-at-risk (VaR) minimization and sensitivity analysis, requires a multivariate model, as we discuss subsequently in section 11.3.

In particular, portfolio level analysis is rarely done other than via historical simulation (defined subsequently). But we will argue that there is no reason why one cannot estimate a parsimonious dynamic model for portfolio-level returns. If interest centers on the distribution of the portfolio returns, then this distribution can be modeled directly rather than via aggregation based on a larger and almost inevitably less-well-specified multivariate model.

Berkowitz and O'Brien (2002) find evidence that existing bank risk models perform poorly and are easily outperformed by a simple univariate GARCH model (defined subsequently). Their result is remarkable in that they estimate a GARCH model fit to the time series of actual historical portfolio returns where the underlying asset weights are changing over time. Berkowitz and O'Brien find that banks' reported ex ante VaR forecasts are exceeded by the ex post profits and losses (P/Ls) on less than the predicted 1 percent of days. This apparent finding of risk underestimation could, however, simply be due to the reported P/Ls being "dirty" in that they contain nonrisky income from fees, commissions, and intraday trading profits.[1] More seriously, though, Berkowitz and O'Brien find that the VaR violations which do occur tend to cluster in time. Episodes such as the fall 1998 Russia default and Long-term Capital Management (LTCM) debacle set off a dramatic and persistent increase in market volatility which bank models appear to largely ignore, or at least react to with considerable delay. Such VaR violation clustering is evidence of a lack of conditionality in bank VaR systems, which in turn is a key theme in our discussion that follows.[2]

We first discuss the construction of historical portfolio values, which is a necessary precursor to any portfolio-level VaR analysis. We then discuss direct computation of portfolio VaR via historical simulation, exponential smoothing, and GARCH modeling.[3]

11.2.1   Constructing Historical Pseudo-Portfolio Values

In principle it is easy to construct a time series of historical portfolio returns using current portfolio holdings and historical asset returns:

$$(1) \qquad r_{w,t} = \sum_{i=1}^{N} w_{i,T} r_{i,t} \equiv W_T' R_t, \quad t = 1, 2, \ldots, T.$$

In practice, however, historical prices for the assets held today may not be available. Examples of such difficulties include derivatives, individual bonds with various maturities, private equity, new public companies, merger companies, and so on. For these cases, "pseudo historical" prices must be constructed using either pricing models, factor models, or some ad hoc considerations. The current assets without historical prices can, for example, be matched to similar assets by capitalization, industry, leverage, and duration. Historical pseudo asset prices and returns can then be constructed using the historical prices on these substitute assets.

---

1. Although the Basel Accord calls for banks to report 1 percent VaRs, for various reasons most banks tend to actually report more conservative VaRs. Rather than simply scaling up a 1 percent VaR based on some arbitrary multiplication factor, the procedures that we subsequently discuss are readily adapted to achieve any desired, more conservative, VaR.

2. See also Jackson, Maude, and Perraudin (1997).

3. Duffie and Pan (1997) provide an earlier incisive discussion of related VaR procedures and corresponding practical empirical problems.

11.2.2 Volatility via Historical Simulation

Banks often rely on VaRs from historical simulations (HS-VaR). In this case, the VaR is calculated as the $100p$'th percentile or the $(T + 1)p$'th order statistic of the set of pseudo returns calculated in (1). We can write

$$(2) \qquad HS\text{-}VaR^p_{T+1\,|\,T} \equiv r_w([T + 1]p),$$

where $r_w([T + 1]p)$ is taken from the set of ordered pseudo returns $(r_w[1], r_w[2], \ldots, r_w[T])$. If $[T + 1]p$ is not an integer value then the two adjacent observations can be interpolated to calculate the VaR.

Historical simulation has some serious problems, which have been well documented. Perhaps most importantly, it does not properly incorporate conditionality into the VaR forecast. The only source of dynamics in the HS-VaR is the fact that the sample window in equation (1) is updated over time. However, this source of conditionality is minor in practice.[4]

Figure 11.1 illustrates the hidden dangers of HS as discussed by Pritsker (2001). We plot the daily percentage loss on an S&P 500 portfolio along with the 1 percent HS-VaR calculated from a 250-day moving window. The crash on October 19, 1987, dramatically increased market volatility; however, the HS-VaR barely moved. Only after the second large drop, which occurred on October 26, does the HS-VaR increase noticeably.

This admittedly extreme example illustrates a key problem with the HS-VaR. Mechanically, from equation (2) we see that HS-VaR changes significantly only if the observations around the order statistic $r_w([T + 1]p)$ change significantly. When using a 250-day moving window for a 1 percent HS-VaR, only the second and third smallest returns will matter for the calculation. Including a crash in the sample, which now becomes the smallest return, may therefore not change the HS-VaR very much if the new second smallest return is similar to the previous one.

Moreover, the lack of a properly defined conditional model in the HS methodology implies that it does not allow for the construction of a term structure of VaR. Calculating a 1 percent one-day HS-VaR may be possible on a window of 250 observations, but calculating a ten-day 1 percent VaR on 250 daily returns is not. Often the one-day VaR is simply scaled by the square root of 10, but this extrapolation is only valid under the assumption of i.i.d. normal daily returns. A redeeming feature of the daily HS-VaR is exactly that it does not rely on an assumption of normal returns, and the square root scaling therefore seems curious at best.

In order to further illustrate the lack of conditionality in the HS-VaR method, consider figure 11.2. We first simulate daily portfolio returns from

---

4. Bodoukh, Richardson, and Whitelaw (1998) introduce updating into the historical simulation method. Note, however, the concerns in Pritsker (2001).

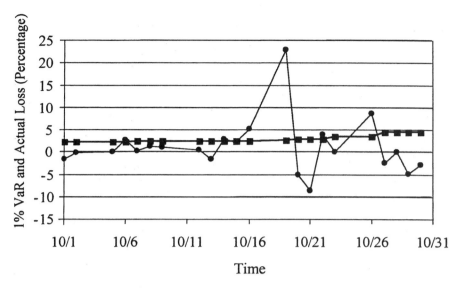

Fig. 11.1   October 1987: Daily S&P 500 Loss and 1 percent HS-VaR

Notes: The thin line with dots shows the daily percentage loss on an S&P 500 portfolio during October 1987. The thick line with squares shows the daily 1 percent VaR from historical simulation using a 250-day window.

a mean-reverting volatility model and then calculate the nominal 1 percent HS-VaR on these returns using a moving window of 250 observations. As the true portfolio return distribution is known, the true daily coverage of the nominal 1 percent HS-VaR can be calculated using the return-generating model. Figure 11.2 shows the conditional coverage probability of the 1 percent HS-VaR over time. Notice from the figure how an HS-VaR with a nominal coverage probability of 1 percent can have a true *conditional* probability as high as 10 percent, even though the *unconditional* coverage is correctly calibrated at 1 percent. On any given day the risk manager thinks that there is a 1 percent chance of getting a return worse than the HS-VaR, but in actuality there may be as much as a 10 percent chance of exceeding the VaR. Figure 11.2 highlights the potential benefit of conditional density modeling: the HS-VaR computes an essentially unconditional VaR, which on any given day can be terribly wrong. A conditional density model will generate a dynamic VaR in an attempt to keep the conditional coverage rate at 1 percent on any given day, thus creating a horizontal line in figure 11.2.

The preceding discussion also hints at a problem with the VaR risk measures itself. It does not say anything about how large the expected loss will be on the days where the VaR is exceeded. Other measures, such as expected shortfall, do, but VaR has emerged as the industry risk measurement standard and we will focus on it here. The methods we will suggest

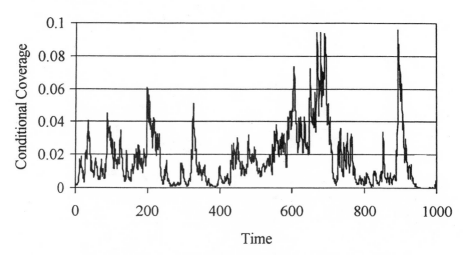

Fig. 11.2 True conditional coverage of 1 percent VaR from historical simulation

Notes: We simulate returns from a GARCH model with normal innovations, after which we compute the 1 percent HS-VaR using a rolling window of 250 observations, and then we plot the *true* conditional coverage probability of the HS-VaR, which we calculate using the GARCH structure. The true conditional coverage probability plotted thus denotes the likelihood each day of getting a VaR violation when using a misspecified 1 percent HS-VaR when the returns are simulated using GARCH.

can, however, equally well be used to calculate expected shortfall and other related risk measures.

11.2.3 Volatility via Exponential Smoothing

Although the HS-VaR methodology discussed previously makes no explicit assumptions about the distributional model generating the returns, the RiskMetrics (RM) filter/model instead assumes a very tight parametric specification. One can begin to incorporate conditionality via univariate portfolio-level exponential smoothing of squared portfolio returns, in precise parallel to the exponential smoothing of individual return squares and cross products that underlies RM.

Still taking the portfolio-level pseudo returns from (1) as the data series of interest, we can define the portfolio-level RM variance as

$$(3) \qquad \sigma_t^2 = \lambda \sigma_{t-1}^2 + (1 - \lambda) r_{w,t-1}^2,$$

where the variance forecast for day t is constructed at the end of day $t - 1$ using the square of the return observed at the end of day $t - 1$ as well as the variance on day $t - 1$. In practice, this recursion can be initialized by setting the initial σ_0^2 equal to the unconditional sample standard deviation, for example, $\hat{\sigma}^2$.

Note that back substitution in equation (3) yields an expression for the current smoothed value as an exponentially weighted moving average of past squared returns:

$$\sigma_t^2 = \sum_{j=0}^{\infty} \varphi_j r_{w,t-1-j}^2,$$

where $\varphi_j = (1 - \lambda)/\lambda^j$. Hence the name "exponential smoothing."

Following RM, the VaR is simply calculated as

(4) $$RM\text{-}VaR_{T+1\,|\,T}^p \equiv \sigma_{T+1} \Phi_p^{-1},$$

where Φ_p^{-1} denotes the pth quantile in the standard normal distribution. Although the smoothing parameter λ may in principle be calibrated to best fit the specific historical returns at hand, following RM it is often simply fixed at 0.94 with daily returns. The implicit assumption of zero mean and standard normal innovations therefore implies that no parameters need to be estimated.

The conditional variance for the k-day aggregate return in RM is simply

(5) $$\text{Var}(r_{w,t+k} + r_{w,t+k-1} + \ldots + r_{w,t+1} \,|\, \mathcal{F}_t) \equiv \sigma_{t:t+k\,|\,t}^2 = k\sigma_{t+1}^2.$$

The RM model can thus be thought of as a random-walk model in variance. The lack of mean-reversion in the RM variance model implies that the term structure of volatility is flat. Figure 11.3 illustrates the difference between the volatility term structure for the random-walk RM model versus a mean-reverting volatility model. Assuming a low current volatility,

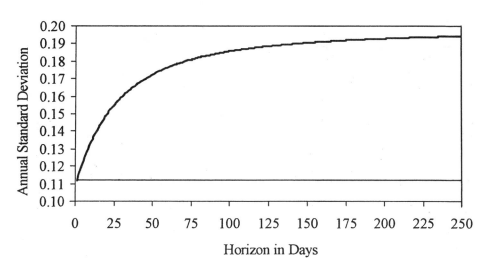

Fig. 11.3   Term Structure of Variance in GARCH and RiskMetrics Models

Notes: We plot the term structure of variance from a mean-reverting GARCH model (thick line) as well as the term structure from a RiskMetrics model (thin line). The current variance is assumed to be identical across models.

which is identical across models, the mean-reverting model will display an upward sloping term structure of volatility, whereas the RM model will extrapolate the low current volatility across all horizons. When taken this literally, the RM model does not appear to be a prudent approach to volatility modeling. The dangers of scaling the daily variance by k, as done in equation (5), are discussed further in Diebold, Hickman, Inoue, and Schuermann (1998).

11.2.4   Volatility via GARCH

The implausible temporal aggregation properties of the RM model, which we discussed earlier, motivates us to introduce the general class of GARCH models, which imply mean-reversion and which contain the RM model as a special case.

First we specify the general univariate portfolio return process

$$(6) \qquad r_{w,t} = \mu_t + \sigma_t z_t \quad z_t \sim \text{i.i.d.} \quad E(z_t) = 0 \quad \text{Var}(z_t) = 1.$$

In the following, we will assume that the mean is zero, which is common in risk management, at least when short horizons are considered. Although difficult to estimate with much accuracy in practice, mean-dynamics could in principle easily be incorporated into the models discussed in the following.

The simple symmetric GARCH(1,1) model introduced by Bollerslev (1986) is written as

$$(7) \qquad \sigma_t^2 = \omega + \alpha r_{w,t-1}^2 + \beta \sigma_{t-1}^2.$$

Extensions to higher-order models are straightforward, but for notational simplicity we will concentrate on the (1,1) case here and throughout the chapter. Repeated substitution in (7) readily yields

$$\sigma_t^2 = \frac{\omega}{1 - \beta} + \alpha \sum \beta^{j-1} r_{t-j}^2,$$

so that the GARCH(1,1) process implies that current volatility is an exponentially weighted moving average of past squared returns. Hence the GARCH(1,1) volatility measurement is seemingly very similar to RM volatility measurement. There are crucial differences, however.

First, GARCH parameters, and hence ultimately GARCH volatility, are estimated using rigorous statistical methods that facilitate probabilistic inference, in contrast to exponential smoothing, in which the parameter is set in an ad hoc fashion. Typically we estimate the vector of GARCH parameters θ by maximizing the log likelihood function,

$$(8) \qquad \log L(\theta; r_{w,T}, \dots, r_{w,1}) \propto - \sum_{t=1}^{T} [\log \sigma_t^2(\theta) - \sigma_t^{-2}(\theta) r_{w,t}^2].$$

Note that the assumption of conditional normality underlying the (quasi) likelihood function in equation (8) is merely a matter of convenience. The conditional return distribution will generally be nonnormal, but it does not need to be: quasi maximum likelihood estimation still produces consistent and asymptotically normal parameter estimates. The log-likelihood optimization in equation (9) can only be done numerically. However, GARCH models are parsimonious and specified directly in terms of univariate portfolio returns, so that only a single numerical optimization needs to be performed.[5]

Second, the covariance stationary GARCH(1,1) process has dynamics that eventually produce reversion in volatility to a constant long-run value, which enables interesting and realistic forecasts. This contrasts sharply with the RM exponential smoothing approach. As is well-known (e.g., Nerlove and Wage 1964, Theil and Wage 1964), exponential smoothing is optimal if and only if squared returns follow a "random walk plus noise" model (a "local level" model in the terminology of Harvey 1989), in which case the minimum mean squared error forecast at any horizon is simply the current smoothed value. The historical records of volatilities of numerous assets (not to mention the fact that volatilities are bounded below by zero) suggest, however, that volatilities are unlikely to follow random walks, and hence that the flat forecast function associated with exponential smoothing is unrealistic and undesirable for volatility forecasting purposes.

Let us elaborate. We can rewrite the GARCH(1,1) model in equation (7) as

$$(9) \qquad \sigma_t^2 = (1 - \alpha - \beta)\sigma^2 + \alpha r_{w,t-1}^2 + \beta \sigma_{t-1}^2,$$

where $\sigma^2 \equiv \omega/(1 - \alpha - \beta)$ denotes the long-run, or unconditional daily variance. This representation shows that the GARCH forecast is constructed as an average of three elements. Equivalently, we can also write the model as

$$(10) \qquad \sigma_t^2 = \sigma^2 + \alpha(r_{w,t-1}^2 - \sigma^2) + \beta(\sigma_{t-1}^2 - \sigma^2),$$

which explicitly shows how the GARCH(1,1) model forecasts by making adjustments to the current variance and the influence of the squared return around the long-run, or unconditional variance. Finally, we can also write

$$\sigma_t^2 = \sigma^2 + (\alpha + \beta)(\sigma_{t-1}^2 - \sigma^2) + \alpha\sigma_{t-1}^2(z_{t-1}^2 - 1),$$

where the last term on the right-hand side, on average, is equal to zero. Hence, this shows how the GARCH(1,1) forecasts by making adjustments around the long-run variance, with variance persistence governed by (α + β) and the (contemporaneous) volatility-of-volatility linked to the level of volatility as well as the size of α.

The mean-reverting property of GARCH volatility forecasts has impor-

---

5. This optimization can be performed in a matter of seconds on a standard desktop computer using standard software such as Excel, as discussed by Christoffersen (2003). For further discussion of inference in GARCH models, see also Andersen, Bollerslev, Christoffersen, and Diebold (2005).

tant implications for the volatility term structure. To construct the volatility term structure corresponding to a GARCH(1,1) model, we need the k-day ahead variance forecast, which is

$$(11) \qquad \sigma^2_{t+k|t} = \sigma^2 + (\alpha + \beta)^{k-1}(\sigma^2_{t+1} - \sigma^2).$$

Assuming that the daily returns are serially uncorrelated, the variance of the k-day cumulative returns, which we use to calculate the volatility term structure, is then

$$(12) \qquad \sigma^2_{t:t+k|t} = k\sigma^2 + (\sigma^2_{t+1} - \sigma^2)[1 - (\alpha + \beta)^k](1 - \alpha - \beta)^{-1}.$$

Compare this mean-reverting expression with the RM forecast in equation (5). In particular, note that the speed of mean reversion in the GARCH(1,1) model is governed by $\alpha + \beta$. The mean-reverting line in figure 11.3 is calculated from equation (12), normalizing by k and taking the square root to display the graph in daily standard deviation units.

Third, the dynamics associated with the GARCH(1,1) model afford rich and intuitive interpretations, and they are readily generalized to even richer specifications. To take one important example, note that the dynamics may be enriched via higher-ordered specifications, such as GARCH(2,2). Indeed, Engle and Lee (1999) show that the GARCH(2,2) is of particular interest, because under certain parameter restrictions it implies a component structure obtained by allowing for time variation in the long-run variance in (10),

$$(13) \qquad \sigma^2_t = q_t + \alpha(r^2_{w,t-1} - q_{t-1}) + \beta(\sigma^2_{t-1} - q_{t-1}),$$

with the long-run component, q_t, modeled as a separate autoregressive process,

$$(14) \qquad q_t = \omega + \rho q_{t-1} + \phi(r^2_{w,t-1} - \sigma^2_{t-1}).$$

Many authors, including Gallant, Hsu, and Tauchen (1999) and Alizadeh, Brandt, and Diebold (2002) have found evidence of component structure in volatility, suitable generalizations of which can be shown to approximate long memory (e.g., Andersen and Bollerslev 1997, and Barndorff-Nielsen and Shephard 2001), which is routinely found in asset return volatilities (e.g., Bollerslev and Mikkelsen 1999).

To take a second example of the extensibility of GARCH models, note that all models considered thus far imply symmetric response to positive versus negative return shocks. However, equity markets, and particularly equity indexes, often seem to display a strong asymmetry, whereby a negative return boosts volatility by more than a positive return of the same absolute magnitude. The GARCH model is readily generalized to capture this effect. In particular, the asymmetric GJR GARCH(1,1) model of Glosten, Jagannathan, and Runkle (1993) is simply defined by

(15) $\sigma_t^2 = \omega + \alpha r_{w,t-1}^2 + \gamma r_{w,t-1}^2 \mathbf{1}(r_{w,t-1} < 0) + \beta\sigma_{t-1}^2.$

Asymmetric response in the conventional direction thus occurs when $\gamma > 0.$[6]

11.3   Asset Level Analysis: Modeling Asset Return Covariance Matrices

The preceding discussion focused on the specification of dynamic volatility models for the aggregate portfolio return. These methods are well suited to providing forecasts of portfolio-level risk measures such as aggregate VaR. However they are less well suited for providing input into the active risk management process. If, for example, the risk manager wants to know the sensitivity of the portfolio VaR to increases in stock market volatility and asset correlations, which typically occur in times of market stress, then a multivariate model is needed. Active risk management such as portfolio VaR minimization also requires a multivariate model, which provides a forecast for the entire covariance matrix.[7]

Multivariate models are also better suited for calculating sensitivity risk measures to answer questions such as: "If I add an additional 1,000 shares of IBM to my portfolio, how much will my VaR increase?" Moreover, bank-wide VaR is made up of many desks with multiple traders on each desk, and any subportfolio analysis is not possible with the aggregate portfolio-based approach.[8]

In this section we therefore consider the specification of models for the full N-dimensional conditional distribution of asset returns. Generalizing the expression in equation (6), we write the multivariate model as

(16) $R_t = \Omega_t^{1/2} Z_t \quad Z_t \sim \text{i.i.d.} \quad E(Z_t) = 0 \quad \text{Var}(Z_t) = I,$

where we have again set the mean to zero and where I denotes the identity matrix. The $N \times N$ $\Omega_t^{1/2}$ matrix can be thought of as the square root, or Cholesky decomposition, of the covariance matrix Ω_t. This section will focus on specifying a dynamic model for this matrix, whereas section 11.5 will suggest methods for specifying the distribution of the innovation vector Z_t.

Constructing positive semidefinite (psd) covariance matrix forecasts, which ensures that the portfolio variance is always nonnegative, subsequently presents a key challenge. The covariance matrix will have $(1/2)N(N + 1)$ distinct elements, but structure needs to be imposed to guarantee psd.

---

6. Engle (2001, 2004) demonstrates empirically that allowing for asymmetries in the conditional variance can materially affect GARCH-based VaR calculations.

7. Brandt, Santa-Clara, and Valkanov (2004) provide an alternative and intriguing new approach for dimension reduction by explicitly parameterizing the portfolio weights as a function of observable state variables, thereby sidestepping the need to estimate the full covariance matrix. See also Pesaran and Zaffaroni (2004).

8. See Manganelli (2004) for an interesting new low-dimensional approach to this problem.

The practical issues involved in estimating the parameters guarding the dynamics for the $(1/2)N(N + 1)$ elements are related and equally important. Although much of the academic literature focuses on relatively small multivariate examples, in this section we will confine our attention to methods that are applicable even with N (relatively) large.

11.3.1   Covariance Matrices via Exponential Smoothing

The natural analogue to the RM variance dynamics in (3) assumes that the covariance matrix dynamics are driven by the single parameter λ for all variances and covariance in Ω_t:

$$(17) \qquad \Omega_t = \lambda\Omega_{t-1} + (1 - \lambda)R_{t-1}R'_{t-1}.$$

The covariance matrix recursion may again be initialized by setting Ω_0 equal to the sample average coverage matrix.

The RM approach is clearly very restrictive, imposing the same degree of smoothness on all elements of the estimated covariance matrix. Moreover, covariance matrix forecasts generated by RM are in general suboptimal, for precisely the same reason as with the univariate RM variance forecasts discussed earlier. If the multivariate RM approach has costs, it also has benefits. In particular, the simple structure in (17) immediately guarantees that the estimated covariance matrices are psd, as the outer product of the return vector must be psd unless some assets are trivial linear combinations of others. Moreover, as long as the initial covariance matrix is psd (which will necessarily be the case when we set Ω_0 equal to the sample average coverage matrix as suggested earlier, so long as the sample size T is larger than the number of assets N), RM covariance matrix forecasts will also be psd, because a sum of psd matrices is itself psd.

11.3.2   Covariance Matrices via Multivariate GARCH

Although easily implemented, the RM approach (17) may be much too restrictive in many cases. Hence we now consider multivariate GARCH models. The most general multivariate GARCH(1,1) model is

$$(18) \qquad \text{vech}(\Omega_t) = \text{vech}(C) + B\,\text{vech}(\Omega_{t-1}) + A\,\text{vech}(R_{t-1}R'_{t-1}),$$

where the vech ("vector half") operator converts the unique upper triangular elements of a symmetric matrix into a $(1/2)N(N + 1) \times 1$ column vector, and A and B are $(1/2)N(N + 1) \times (1/2)N(N + 1)$ matrices. Notice that in this general specification, each element of Ω_{t-1} may potentially affect each element of Ω_t, and similarly for the outer product of past returns, producing a serious "curse-of-dimensionality" problem. In its most general form, the GARCH(1,1) model (18) has a total of $(1/2)N^4 + N^{3+} N^2 + (1/2)N = O(N^4)$ parameters. Hence, for example, for $N = 100$ the model has 51,010,050 parameters! Estimating this many free parameters is obviously infeasible. Note also that without specifying more structure on the model there is no guarantee of positive definiteness of the fitted or forecasted co-variance matrices.

The dimensionality problem can be alleviated somewhat by replacing the constant term via "variance targeting," as suggested by Engle and Mezrich (1996). Variance targeting forces the model-implied unconditional covariance matrix to equal a precalculated estimate from the simple sample average. This, in turn, avoids the cumbersome nonlinear estimation of the matrix of constant terms, which instead is computed from the other parameters as follows:

$$(19) \qquad \text{vech}(C) = (I - A - B)\text{vech}\left(\frac{1}{T}\sum_{t=1}^{T} R_t R_t'\right).$$

This is also very useful from a forecasting perspective, as small perturbations in A and B sometimes result in large changes in the implied unconditional variance to which the long-run forecasts converge. However, there are still too many parameters to be estimated simultaneously in A and B in the general multivariate model when N is large.

More severe (and hence less palatable) restrictions may be imposed to achieve additional parsimony, as, for example, with the "diagonal GARCH" parameterization proposed by Bollerslev, Engle, and Wooldridge (1988). In a diagonal GARCH model, the matrices A and B have zeros in all off-diagonal elements, which in turn implies that each element of the covariance matrix follows a simple dynamic with univariate flavor: conditional variances depend only on their own lags and own lagged squared returns, and conditional covariances depend only on their own lags and own lagged cross products of returns. Even the diagonal GARCH framework, however, results in $O(N^2)$ parameters to be jointly estimated, which is computationally infeasible in systems of medium and large size.

One approach is to move to the most draconian version of the diagonal GARCH model, in which the matrices B and A are simply scalar matrices. Specifically,

$$(20) \qquad \Omega_t = C + \beta\Omega_{t-1} + \alpha(R_{t-1}R_{t-1}'),$$

where the value of each diagonal element of B is β, and each diagonal element of A is α. Rearrangement yields

$$\Omega_t = \Omega + \beta(\Omega_{t-1} - \Omega) + \alpha(R_{t-1}R_{t-1}' - \Omega),$$

which is closely related to the multivariate RM approach, with the important difference that it introduces a nondegenerate long-run covariance matrix Ω, to which Ω_t reverts (provided that $\alpha + \beta < 1$). Notice also, though, that all variances and covariances are assumed to have the same speed of mean reversion, because of common α and β parameters, which may be overly restrictive.

11.3.3   Dimensionality Reduction I: Covariance Matrices via Flex-GARCH

Ledoit, Santa-Clara, and Wolf (2003) suggest an attractive Flex-GARCH method for reducing the computational burden in the estimation of the diagonal GARCH model without moving to the scalar version. Intuitively, Flex-GARCH decentralizes the estimation procedure by estimating $N(N + 1)/2$ bivariate GARCH models with certain parameter constraints, and then pasting them together to form the matrices A, B, and C in equation (18). Specific transformations of the parameter matrices from the bivariate models ensure that the resulting conditional covariance matrix forecast is psd. Flex-GARCH appears to be a viable modeling approach when N is larger than, say, 5, where estimation of the general diagonal GARCH model becomes intractable. However, when N is of the order of 30 and above, which is often the case in practical risk management applications, it becomes cumbersome to estimate $N(N + 1)/2$ bivariate models, and alternative dimensionality reduction methods are necessary. One such method is the dynamic conditional correlation framework, to which we now turn.

11.3.4   Dimensionality Reduction II: Covariance Matrices via Dynamic Conditional Correlation

Recall the simple but useful decomposition of the covariance matrix into the correlation matrix pre- and post-multiplied by the diagonal standard deviation matrix,

$$(21) \qquad \Omega_t \equiv D_t \Gamma_t D_t.$$

Bollerslev (1990) uses this decomposition, along with an assumption of constant conditional correlations ($\Gamma_t = \Gamma$) to develop his Constant Conditional Correlation (CCC) GARCH model. The assumption of constant conditional correlation, however, is arguably too restrictive over long time periods.

Engle (2002) generalizes Bollerslev's (1990) CCC model to obtain a Dynamic Conditional Correlation (DCC) model. Crucially, he also provides a decentralized estimation procedure. First, one fits to each asset return an appropriate univariate GARCH model (the models can differ from asset to asset) and then standardizes the returns by the estimated GARCH conditional standard deviations. Then one uses the standardized return vector, say $e_t \equiv R_t \hat{D}_t^{-1}$, to model the correlation dynamics. For instance, a simple scalar diagonal GARCH(1,1) correlation dynamic would be

$$(22) \qquad Q_t = C + \beta Q_{t-1} + \alpha(e_{t-1} e'_{t-1}),$$

with the individual correlations in the Γ_t matrix defined by the corresponding normalized elements of Q_t,

$$(23) \qquad \rho_{i,j,t} = q_{i,j,t}/(\sqrt{q_{i,i,t}}\sqrt{q_{j,j,t}}).$$

The normalization in (23) ensures that all correlation forecasts fall in the $[-1; 1]$ interval, while the simple scalar structure for the dynamics of Q_t in equation (22) ensures that Γ_t is psd.

If C is preestimated by correlation targeting, as discussed earlier, only two parameters need to be estimated in equation (22). Estimating variance dynamics asset by asset and then assuming a simple structure for the correlation dynamics thus ensures that the DCC model can be implemented in large systems: $N + 1$ numerical optimizations must be performed, but each involves only a few parameters, regardless of the size of N.

Although the DCC model offers a promising framework for exploring correlation dynamics in large systems, the simple dynamic structure in (22) may be too restrictive for many applications. For example, volatility and correlation responses may be asymmetric in the signs of past shocks.[9] Researchers are therefore currently working to extend the DCC model to more general dynamic correlation specifications. Relevant work includes Franses and Hafner (2003), Pelletier (2004), and Cappiello, Engle, and Sheppard (2004).

To convey a feel for the importance of allowing for time-varying conditional correlation, we show in figure 11.4 the bond return correlation between Germany and Japan estimated using a DCC model allowing for asymmetric correlation responses to positive versus negative returns, reproduced from Cappiello, Engle, and Sheppard (2004). The conditional correlation clearly varies a great deal. Note in particular the dramatic change in the conditional correlation around the time of the euro's introduction in 1999. Such large movements in conditional correlation are not rare, and they underscore the desirability of allowing for different dynamics in volatility versus correlation.[10]

11.4   Exploiting High-Frequency Return Data for Improved Covariance Matrix Measurement

Thus far our discussion has implicitly focused on models tailored to capturing the dynamics in returns by relying only on daily return information. For many assets, however, high-frequency price data are available and should be useful for the estimation of asset return variances and covari-

---

9. A related example is the often-found positive relationship between volatility changes and correlation changes. If present but ignored, this effect can have serious consequences for portfolio hedging effectiveness.

10. As another example, cross-market stock-bond return correlations are often found to be close to zero or slightly positive during bad economic times (recessions), but negative in good economic times (expansions); see, for example, the discussion in Andersen, Bollerslev, Diebold, and Vega (2004).

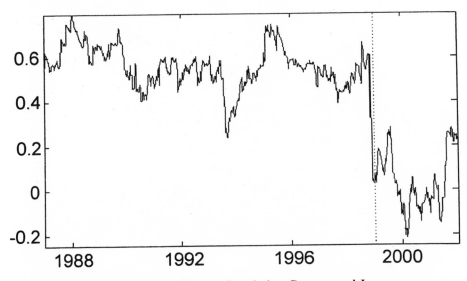

Fig. 11.4   Time-Varying Bond Return Correlation: Germany and Japan

Notes: We reconstruct this figure from Capiello, Engle, and Sheppard (2004), plotting the correlation between Germany and Japanese government bond returns calculated from a DCC model allowing for asymmetric correlation responses to positive and negative returns. The vertical dashed line denotes the euro's introduction in 1999.

ances. Here we review recent work in this area and speculate on its usefulness for constructing large-scale models of market risk.

11.4.1   Realized Variances

Following Andersen, Bollerslev, Diebold, and Labys (2003; henceforth ABDL), define the realized variance (RV) on day t using returns constructed at the Δ intraday frequency as

$$(24) \qquad \sigma_{t,\Delta}^2 \equiv \sum_{j=1}^{1/\Delta} r_{t-1+j\Delta,\Delta}^2,$$

where $1/\Delta$ is, for example, 48 for thirty-minute returns in twenty-four-hour markets. Theoretically, letting Δ go to zero, which implies sampling continuously, we approach the true *integrated* volatility of the underlying continuous time process on day t.[11]

In practice, market microstructure noise will affect the RV estimate when Δ gets too small. Prices sampled at fifteen to thirty minute intervals, depending on the market, are therefore often used. Notice also that, in markets that are not open twenty-four hours per day, the potential jump from the closing price on day $t - 1$ to the opening price on day t must be ac-

---

11. For a full treatment, see Andersen, Bollerslev, and Diebold (forthcoming).

counted for. This can be done using the method in Hansen and Lunde (2005). As is the case for the daily GARCH models considered earlier, corrections may also have to be made for the fact that days following weekends and holidays tend to have higher-than-average volatility.

Although the daily realized variance is just an estimate of the underlying integrated variance and is likely measured with some error, it presents an intriguing opportunity: it is potentially highly accurate, and indeed accurate enough such that we might take the realized daily variance as an observation of the true daily variance, modeling and forecasting it using standard autoregressive moving average (ARMA) time series tools. Allowing for certain kinds of measurement error can also easily be done in this framework. The upshot is that if the fundamental frequency of interest is daily, then using sufficiently high-quality intraday price data enables the risk manager to treat volatility as essentially observed. This is vastly different from the GARCH style models discussed earlier, in which the daily variance is constructed recursively from past daily returns.

As an example of the direct modeling of realized volatility, one can specify a simple first-order autoregressive model for the log realized volatility,

$$(25) \qquad \log(\sigma_{t,\Delta}) \equiv c + \beta \log(\sigma_{t-1,\Delta}) + v_t,$$

which can be estimated using simple ordinary least squares (OLS). The log specification guarantees positivity of forecasted volatilities and induces (approximate) normality, as demonstrated empirically in Andersen, Bollerslev, Diebold, and Labys (2000, 2001). ABDL show the superior forecasting properties of RV-based forecasts compared with GARCH forecasts. Rather than relying on a simple short-memory ARMA model as in equation (25), they specify a fractionally integrated model to better account for the apparent long-memory routinely found in volatility dynamics.

Along these lines, figure 11.5 shows clear evidence of long-memory in foreign exchange RVs as evidenced by the sample autocorrelation function for lags of 1 through 100 days. We first construct the daily RVs from thirty-minute FX returns and then calculate the corresponding daily sample autocorrelations of the RVs. Note that the RV autocorrelations are significantly positive for all 100 lags when compared with the conventional 95 percent Bartlett confidence bands.

The RV forecasts may also be integrated into the standard GARCH modeling framework, as explored in Engle and Gallo (2004).[12] Similarly, rather than relying on GARCH variance models to standardize returns in the first step of the DCC model, RVs can be used instead. Doing so would result in a more accurate standardization and would require only a single

---

12. Intriguing new procedures for combining high-frequency data and RV-type measures with lower-frequency daily returns in volatility forecasting models have also recently been developed by Ghysels, Santa-Clara, and Valkanov (2005).

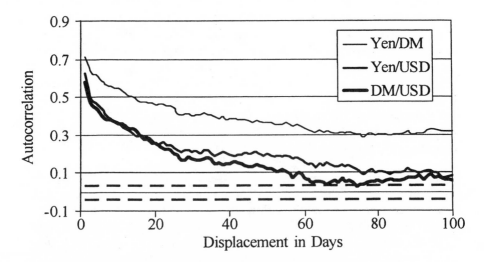

Fig. 11.5   Sample autocorrelations of realized volatility: Three currencies

Notes: We plot the sample autocorrelations of daily realized log standard deviations for three FX rates, together with Bartlett's ±2 standard error bands for the sample autocorrelations of white noise. We construct the underlying daily realized variances using thirty-minute returns from December 1, 1986, through December 1, 1996.

numerical optimization step—estimation of correlation dynamics—thereby rendering the computational burden in DCC nearly negligible.

We next discuss how realized variances and their natural multivariate counterparts, realized covariances, can be used in a more systematic fashion in risk management.

11.4.2   Realized Covariances

Generalizing the realized variance idea to the multivariate case, we can define the daily realized covariance matrix as

$$(26) \qquad \Omega_{t,\Delta} \equiv \sum_{j=1}^{1/\Delta} R_{t-1+j\Delta,\Delta} R'_{t-1+j\Delta,\Delta}.$$

The upshot again is that variances and covariances no longer have to be extracted from a nonlinear model estimated via treacherous maximum-likelihood procedures, as was the case for the preceding GARCH models. Using intraday price observations, we essentially observe the daily covariances and can model them as if they were observed. ABDL show that, as long as the asset returns are linearly independent and the number of assets, N, is less than $1/\Delta$, the realized covariance matrix will be positive definite. However, for a sampling interval of, for example, thirty minutes in twenty-four-hour markets, $1/\Delta$ is 48, so in large portfolios the condition is likely to be violated. We return to this important issue at the end of this section.

Microstructure noise may plague realized covariances, just as it may plague realized variances. Nonsynchronous trading, however, creates additional complications in the multivariate case. These are similar, but potentially more severe, than the nonsynchronous trading issues that arise in the estimation of, say, monthly covariances and CAPM betas with nonsynchronous daily data. A possible fix involves the inclusion of additional lead and lag terms in the realized covariance measure (26), along the lines of the Scholes and Williams (1977) beta-correction technique. Work on this is still in its infancy, and we will not discuss it any further here, but an important recent contribution is Martens (2004).

We now consider various strategies for modeling and forecasting realized covariances, treating them as directly observable vector time series. These all are quite speculative, as little work has been done to date in terms of actually assessing the economic value of using realized covariances for practical risk measurement and management problems.[13]

Paralleling the tradition of the scalar diagonal GARCH model, directly suggests the following model

$$(27) \qquad \text{vech}(\Omega_{t,\Delta}) = \text{vech}(C) + \beta\,\text{vech}(\Omega_{t-1,\Delta}) + v_t,$$

which requires nothing but simple OLS to implement, while guaranteeing positive definiteness of the corresponding covariance matrix forecasts for any positive definite matrix C and positive values of β. This does again, however, impose a common mean-reversion parameter across variances and covariances, which may be overly restrictive. Realized covariance versions of the nonscalar diagonal GARCH model could be developed in a similar manner, keeping in mind the restrictions required for positive definiteness.

Positive definiteness may also be imposed by modeling the Cholesky decomposition of the realized covariance matrix rather than the matrix itself, as suggested by ABDL. We have

$$(28) \qquad\qquad\qquad \Omega_{t,\Delta} \equiv P_{t,\Delta}P'_{t,\Delta},$$

where $P_{t,\Delta}$ is a unique lower triangular matrix. The data vector is then $\text{vech}(P_{t,\Delta})$, and we substitute the forecast of $\text{vech}(P_{t+k,\Delta})$ back into equation (28) to construct a forecast of $\Omega_{t+k,\Delta}$.

Alternatively, in the tradition of Ledoit and Wolf (2003), one may induce positive definiteness of high-dimensional realized covariance matrices by shrinking toward the covariance matrix implied by a single-factor structure, in which the optimal shrinkage parameter is estimated directly from the data.

---

13. One notable exception is the work of Fleming, Kirby, and Oestdiek (2003), which suggests dramatic improvements vis-à-vis the RM and multivariate GARCH frameworks for standard mean-variance efficient asset allocation problems.

We can also use a DCC-type framework for realized correlation modeling. In parallel to equation (21) we write

$$(29) \qquad \Omega_{t,\Delta} \equiv D_{t,\Delta}\,\Gamma_{t,\Delta}D_{t,\Delta},$$

where the typical element in the diagonal matrix $D_{t,\Delta}$ is the realized standard deviation, and the typical element in $\Gamma_{t,\Delta}$ is constructed from the elements in $\Omega_{t,\Delta}$ as

$$(30) \qquad \rho_{i,j,t,\Delta} \equiv \sigma_{i,j,t,\Delta}/(\sigma_{i,i,t,\Delta}\sigma_{j,j,t,\Delta}).$$

Following the DCC idea, we model the standard deviations asset by asset in the first step, and the correlations in a second step. Keeping a simple structure, as in equation (22), we have

$$(31) \qquad \text{vech}(Q_{t,\Delta}) = \text{vech}(C) + \beta\,\text{vech}(Q_{t-1,\Delta}) + v_t,$$

where simple OLS again is all that is required for estimation. Once again, a normalization is needed to ensure that the correlation forecasts fall in the $[-1;1]$ interval. Specifically,

$$(32) \qquad \hat{\rho}_{i,j,t,\Delta} = \hat{q}_{i,j,t,\Delta}/(\sqrt{\hat{q}_{i,i,t,\Delta}}\sqrt{\hat{q}_{j,j,t,\Delta}}).$$

The advantages of this approach are twofold: first, high-frequency information is used to obtain more precise forecasts of variances and correlations. Second, numerical optimization is not needed at all. Long-memory dynamics or regime switching could, of course, be incorporated as well.

Although there appear to be several avenues for exploiting intraday price information in daily risk management, two key problems remain. First, many assets in typical portfolios are not liquid enough for intraday information to be available and useful. Second, even in highly liquid environments, when N is very large the positive definiteness problem remains. We now explore a potential solution to these problems.

11.4.3   Dimensionality Reduction III: (Realized) Covariance Matrices via Mapping to Liquid Base Assets

Multivariate market risk management systems for portfolios of thousands of assets in many cases work from a set of, say, thirty observed base assets believed to be key drivers of risk. Such a base asset factor structure is, of course, more justified for a relatively specialized application such as a U.S. equity portfolio than for a large diversified entity such as a major international bank. The choice of factors depends on the portfolio at hand but can, for example, consist of equity market indexes, FX rates, benchmark interest rates, and so on, which are believed to capture the main sources of uncertainty in the portfolio. The assumptions made on the multivariate distribution of base assets are naturally of crucial importance for the accuracy of the risk management system.

Note that base assets typically correspond to the most liquid assets in the market. The upshot here is that we *can* credibly rely on realized volatility and covariances in this case. Using the result from ABDL, a base asset system of dimension $N_F < 1/\Delta$ will ensure that the realized covariance matrix is psd and therefore useful for forecasting.

The mapping from base assets to the full set of assets is discussed in Jorion (2000). In particular, the factor model is naturally expressed as[14]

$$(33) \qquad R_t = BR_{F,t} + v_t,$$

where v_t denotes the idiosyncratic risk. The factor loadings in the $N \times N_F$ matrix B may be obtained from regression (if data exists), or via pricing model sensitivities (if a pricing model exists). Otherwise the loadings may be determined by ad hoc considerations, such as matching a security without a well-defined factor loading to another similar security which has a well-defined factor loading.

We now need a multivariate model for the N_F base assets. However, assuming that

$$(34) \qquad R_{F,t} = \Omega_{F,t}^{1/2} Z_{F,t} \quad Z_{F,t} \sim \text{i.i.d.} \quad E(Z_{F,t}) = 0 \quad \text{Var}(Z_{F,t}) = I,$$

we can use the modeling strategies discussed earlier to construct the $N_F \times N_F$ realized factor covariance matrix $\Omega_{F,t}$ and the resulting systematic covariance matrix measurements and forecast.

11.5   Modeling Entire Conditional Return Distributions

Best-practice risk measurement and management often requires knowing the entire distribution of asset or base asset returns, not just the second moments. Conventional risk measures such as VaR and expected shortfall, however, capture only limited aspects of the distribution. They collapse a two-dimensional object, the return distribution function, into a one-dimensional object, the risk measure. Clearly information is lost in this dimension reduction in all but certain counterfactual special cases such as the normal distribution with a zero mean, which only depends on one parameter (the variance).

In this section we explore various approaches to complete the model. Notice that in equation (34) we deliberately left the distributional assumption on the standardized returns unspecified. We simply assumed that the standardized returns were i.i.d. We will keep the assumption of i.i.d. standardized returns and focus on ways to estimate the constant conditional density. This is, of course, with some loss of generality, as dynamics in moments beyond second order could be operative. The empirical evidence for

---

14. Diebold and Nerlove (1989) construct a multivariate ARCH factor model in which the latent time-varying volatility factors can be viewed as the base assets.

such higher-ordered conditional moment dynamics is, however, much less conclusive at this stage.

The evidence that daily standardized returns are not normally distributed is, however, quite conclusive. Although GARCH and other dynamic volatility models do remove some of the nonnormality in the unconditional returns, conditional returns still exhibit nonnormal features. Interestingly, these features vary systematically from market to market. For example, mature FX market returns are generally strongly conditionally kurtotic, but approximately symmetric. Meanwhile, most aggregate index equity returns appear to be both conditionally skewed and fat tailed.

As an example of the latter, we show in figure 11.6 the daily quantile-quantile (QQ) plot for S&P 500 returns from January 2, 1990, to December 31, 2002, standardized using the (constant) average daily volatility across the sample. That is, we plot quantiles of standardized returns against quantiles of the standard normal distribution. Clearly the daily returns are not unconditionally normally distributed.

Consider now figure 11.7, in which the daily returns are instead stan-

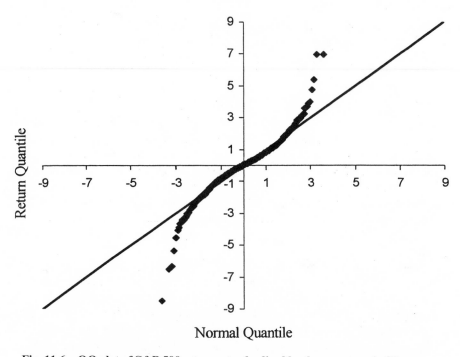

Fig. 11.6   **QQ plot of S&P 500 returns standardized by the average volatility**

Notes: We show quantiles of daily S&P 500 returns from January 2, 1990, to December 31, 2002, standardized by the average daily volatility during the sample, against the corresponding quantiles from a standard normal distribution.

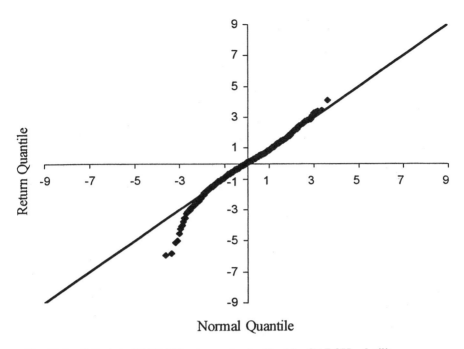

Normal Quantile

Fig. 11.7   QQ plot of S&P 500 returns standardized by GARCH volatility

Notes: We show quantiles of daily S&P 500 returns from January 2, 1990, to December 31, 2002, standardized by volatility from an estimated asymmetric GJR GARCH(1,1) model, against the corresponding quantiles from a standard normal distribution. The units on each axis are standard deviations.

dardized by the time-varying volatilities from an asymmetric GJR GARCH(1,1) model. The QQ plot in figure 11.7 makes clear that although the GARCH innovations conform more closely to the normal distribution than do the raw returns, the left tail of the S&P 500 returns conforms much less well to the normal distribution than does the right tail: there are more large innovations than one would expect under normality.

As the VaR itself is a quantile, the QQ plot also gives an assessment of the accuracy of the normal-GARCH VaR for different coverage rates. Figure 11.7 suggests that a normal-GARCH VaR would work well for any coverage rate for a portfolio which is short the S&P 500. It may also work well for a long portfolio, but only if the coverage rate is relatively large, say in excess of 5 percent.

Consider now instead the distribution of returns standardized by realized volatility. In contrast to the poor fit in the left tail evident in figure 11.7, the distribution in figure 11.8 is strikingly close to normal, as first noticed by Zhou (1996) and Andersen, Bollerslev, Diebold, and Labys (2000). Figures 11.7 and 11.8 rely on the same series of daily S&P 500 returns but

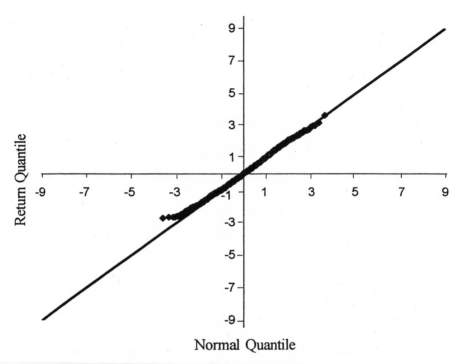

Fig. 11.8   QQ plot of S&P 500 returns standardized by realized volatility

Notes: We show quantiles of daily S&P 500 returns from January 2, 1990, to December 31, 2002, standardized by realized volatility calculated from five-minute futures returns, against the corresponding quantiles from a standard normal distribution. The units on each axis are standard deviations.

simply use two different volatility measures to standardize the raw returns. The conditional nonnormality of daily returns has been a key stylized fact in market risk management. Finding a volatility measure that can generate standardized returns that are close to normal is therefore surprising and noteworthy.

Figure 11.8 and the frequently found lognormality of realized volatility itself suggest that a good approximation to the distribution of returns may be obtained using a normal/lognormal mixture model. In this model, the standardized return is normal and the distribution of realized volatility at time t conditional on time $t - 1$ information is lognormal. This idea is explored empirically in ABDL, who find that a lognormal/normal mixture VaR model performs very well in an application to foreign exchange returns.

The recent empirical results in Andersen, Bollerslev, and Diebold (2006) suggest that even better results may be obtained by separately measuring and modeling the part of the realized volatility attributable to jumps in the price process through so-called realized bipower variation measures, as formally developed by Barndorff-Nielsen and Shephard (2004). These results have great potential for application in financial risk management, and their practical implications are topics of current research.

Although realized volatility measures may be available for highly liquid assets, it is often not possible to construct realized volatility-based portfolio risk measures. We therefore now survey some of the more conventional methods, first for univariate and then for multivariate models.

11.5.1 Portfolio Level: Univariate Analytic Methods

Although the normal assumption works well in certain cases, we want to consider alternatives that allow for fat tails and asymmetry in the conditional distribution, as depicted in figure 11.7. In the case of VaR we are looking for ways to calculate the cutoff z_p^{-1} in

$$(35) \qquad VaR_{T+1\,|\,T}^p \equiv \sigma_{T+1} z_p^{-1}.$$

Perhaps the most obvious approach is simply to look for a parametric distribution more flexible than the normal while still tightly parameterized. One such example is the (standardized) Student's t distribution suggested by Bollerslev (1987), which relies on only one additional parameter in generating symmetric fat tails. Recently, generalizations of the Student's t that allow for asymmetry have also been suggested, as in Fernandez and Steel (1998) and Hansen (1994).

Rather than assuming a particular parametric density, one can approximate the quantiles of nonnormal distributions via Cornish-Fisher approximations. Baillie and Bollerslev (1992) first advocated this approach in the context of GARCH modeling and forecasting. The only inputs needed are the sample estimates of skewness and kurtosis of the standardized returns. Extreme value theory provides another approximation alternative, in which the tail(s) of the conditional distribution is estimated using only the extreme observations, as suggested in Diebold, Schuermann, and Stroughair (1998), Longin (2000), and McNeil and Frey (2000).

A common problem with most GARCH models, regardless of the innovation distribution, is that the conditional distribution of returns is not preserved under temporal aggregation. Hence even if the standardized daily returns from a GARCH(1,1) model were normal, the implied weekly returns will not be. This in turn implies that the term structure of VaR or expected shortfall needs to be calculated via Monte Carlo simulation, as in, for example, Guidolin and Timmermann (2004). But Monte Carlo simulation requires a properly specified probability distribution, which would rule out the Cornish-Fisher and extreme-value-theory approximations.

Heston and Nandi (2000) suggest a specific affine GARCH-normal model, which may work well for certain portfolios, and which, combined with the methods of Albanese, Jackson, and Wiberg (2004), allows for relatively easy calculation of the term structure of VaRs. In general, however, simulation methods are needed; we now discuss a viable approach that combines a parametric volatility model with a data-driven conditional distribution.

11.5.2   Portfolio Level: Univariate Simulation Methods

Bootstrapping, or Filtered Historical Simulation (FHS) assumes a parametric model for the second-moment dynamics but bootstraps from standardized returns to construct the distribution. At the portfolio level this is easy to do. Calculate the standardized pseudo portfolio returns as

$$(36) \qquad \hat{z}_{w,t} = r_{w,t}/\hat{\sigma}_t, \quad \text{for } t = 1, 2, \ldots, T,$$

using one of the variance models from section 11.2. For the one-day-ahead VaR, we then simply use the order statistic for the standardized returns combined with the volatility forecast to construct

$$(37) \qquad FHS\text{-}VaR^p_{T+1} \equiv \sigma_{T+1}\hat{z}_w([T + 1]p).$$

Multiday VaR requires simulating paths from the volatility model using the standardized returns sampled with replacement as innovations. This approach has been suggested by Diebold, Schuermann, and Stroughair (1998), Hull and White (1998), and Barone-Adesi, Bourgoin, and Giannopoulos (1998), who coined the term FHS. Pritsker (2001) also provides evidence on its effectiveness.

11.5.3   Asset Level: Multivariate Analytic Methods

Just as a fully specified univariate distribution is needed for risk measurement, so too is a fully specified multivariate distribution often needed for risk management. For example, a fully specified multivariate distribution allows for the computation of VaR sensitivities and VaR-minimizing portfolio weights. The cost, of course, is that we must make an assumption about the multivariate (but constant) distribution of Z_t in (16).

The results of Andersen, Bollerslev, Diebold, and Labys (2000) suggest that, at least in the FX market, the multivariate distribution of returns standardized by the realized covariance matrix is again closely approximated by a normal distribution. As long as the realized volatilities are available, a multivariate version of the lognormal mixture model discussed in connection with figure 11.8 could therefore be developed.

As noted earlier, however, construction and use of realized covariance matrices may be problematic in situations when liquidity is not high, in which case traditional parametric models may be used. As in the univariate case, however, the multivariate normal distribution, coupled with multivariate standardization using covariance matrices estimated from traditional parametric models, although obviously convenient, does not generally provide an accurate picture of tail risk.[15]

A few analytic alternatives to the multivariate normal paradigm do exist, such as the multivariate Student's t distribution first considered by Harvey, Ruiz, and Sentana (1992), along with the more recent related work by Glasserman, Heidelberger, and Shahbuddin (2002). Recently much attention has also been focused on the construction of multivariate densities from the marginal densities via copulas, as in Jondeau and Rockinger (2004) and Patton (2002), although the viability of the methods in very high-dimensional systems remains to be established.

Multivariate extreme value theory offers a tool for exploring cross-asset tail dependencies, which are not captured by standard correlation measures. For example, Longin and Solnik (2001) define and compute extreme correlations between monthly U.S. index returns and a number of foreign country indexes. In the case of the bivariate normal distribution, correlations between extremes taper off to zero as the thresholds defining the extremes get larger in absolute value. The actual equity data, however, behave quite differently. The correlation between negative extremes is much larger than the normal distribution would suggest.[16] Such strong correlation between negative extremes is clearly a key risk management concern. Poon, Rockinger, and Tawn (2004) explore the portfolio risk management implications of extremal dependencies, while Hartmann, Straetmans, and de Vries (chapter 4, this volume) consider their effect on banking system stability. Once again, however, it is not yet clear whether such methods will be operational in large-dimensional systems.

Issues of scalability, as well as cross-sectional and temporal aggregation problems in parametric approaches, thus once again lead us to consider simulation-based solutions.

11.5.4   Asset Level: Multivariate Simulation Methods

In the general multivariate case, we can in principle use FHS with dynamic correlations, but a multivariate standardization is needed. Using the Cholesky decomposition, we first create vectors of standardized returns from (16). We write the standardized returns from an estimated multivariate dynamic covariance matrix as

$$(38) \qquad \hat{Z}_t = \hat{\Omega}_t^{-1/2} R_t, \text{ for } t = 1, 2, \ldots, T,$$

where we calculate $\hat{\Omega}_t^{-1/2}$ from the Cholesky decomposition of the inverse covariance matrix $\hat{\Omega}_t^{-1}$. Now, resampling with replacement vectorwise from the standardized returns will ensure that the marginal distributions as well

---

15. In the multivariate case the normal distribution is even more tempting to use, because it implies that the aggregate portfolio distribution itself is also normally distributed.

16. In contrast, and interestingly, the correlations of positive extremes appear to approach zero in accordance with the normal distribution.

as particular features of the multivariate distribution, as for example, the cross-sectional dependencies suggested by Longin and Solnik (2001), will be preserved in the simulated data.

The dimensionality of the system in equation (38) may render the necessary multivariate standardization practically infeasible. However, the same FHS approach can be applied with the base asset setup in equation (34), resampling from the factor innovations calculated as

$$(39) \qquad \hat{Z}_{F,t} = \hat{\Omega}_{F,t}^{-1/2} R_{F,t} \text{ for } t = 1, 2, \ldots, T,$$

where we again use the Cholesky decomposition to build up the distribution of the factor returns. From equation (33) we can then construct the corresponding idiosyncratic asset innovations as

$$(40) \qquad \hat{v}_t = R_t - \hat{B} R_{F,t} \text{ for } t = 1, 2, \ldots, T,$$

in turn resampling from $\hat{Z}_t$ and $\hat{v}_t$ to build up the required distribution of the individual asset returns in the base asset model.

Alternatively, if one is willing to assume constant conditional correlations, then the standardization can simply be done on an individual asset-by-asset basis using the univariate GARCH volatilities. Resampling vectorwise from the standardized returns will preserve the cross-sectional dependencies in the historical data.

11.6   Summary and Directions for Future Research

We have attempted to demonstrate the power and potential of dynamic financial econometric methods for practical financial risk management, surveying the large literature on high-frequency volatility measurement and modeling, interpreting and unifying the most important and intriguing results for practical risk management. The paper complements the more general and technical survey of volatility and covariance forecasting in Andersen, Bollerslev, Christoffersen, and Diebold (2005).

Our discussion has many implications for practical financial risk management; some point toward desirable extensions of existing approaches, and some suggest new directions. Key points include:

1. Standard model-free methods, such as historical simulation, rely on false assumptions of independent returns. Reliable risk measurement requires a *conditional* density model that allows for time-varying volatility.

2. For the purpose of risk *measurement,* specifying a univariate density model directly on the portfolio return is likely to be most accurate. Risk-Metrics offers one possible approach, but the temporal aggregation properties—including the volatility term structure—of RiskMetrics appear to be counterfactual.

3. GARCH volatility models offer a convenient and parsimonious

framework for modeling key dynamic features of returns, including volatility mean-reversion, long-memory, and asymmetries.

4. Although risk measurement can be done from a univariate model for a given set of portfolio weights, risk *management* requires a fully specified multivariate density model. Unfortunately, standard multivariate GARCH models are too heavily parameterized to be useful in realistic large-scale problems.

5. Recent advances in multivariate GARCH modeling are likely to be useful for medium-scale models, but very large scale modeling requires decoupling variance and correlation dynamics, as in the dynamic conditional correlation model.

6. Volatility measures based on high-frequency return data hold great promise for practical risk management. Realized volatility and correlation measures give more accurate forecasts of future realizations than their conventional competitors. Because high-frequency information is only available for highly liquid assets, we suggest a base-asset factor approach.

7. Risk management requires fully specified conditional *density* models, not just conditional covariance models. Resampling returns standardized by the conditional covariance matrix presents an attractive strategy for accommodating conditionally nonnormal returns.

8. The near lognormality of realized volatility, together with the near normality of returns standardized by realized volatility, holds promise for relatively simple-to-implement lognormal/normal mixture models in financial risk management.

References

Albanese, C., K. Jackson, and P. Wiberg. 2004. A new Fourier transform algorithm for Value-at-Risk. *Quantitative Finance* 4:328–38.

Alizadeh, S., M. Brandt, and F. X. Diebold. 2002. Range-based estimation of stochastic volatility models. *Journal of Finance* 57:1047–91.

Andersen, T. G., and T. Bollerslev. 1997. Heterogeneous information arrivals and return volatility dynamics: Uncovering the long run in high frequency returns. *Journal of Finance* 52:975–1005.

Andersen, T. G., Bollerslev, P. Christoffersen, and F. X. Diebold. 2006. Volatility forecasting. In *Handbook of economic forecasting,* ed. G. Elliott, C. Granger, and A. Timmermann, 778–878. Amsterdam: North-Holland.

Andersen, T. G., T. Bollerslev, and F. X. Diebold. Forthcoming. Parametric and nonparametric volatility measurement. In *Handbook of financial econometrics,* ed. L. P. Hansen and Y. Ait-Sahalia, Amsterdam: North-Holland.

———. 2006. Forthcoming. Roughing it up: Including jump components in the measurement, modeling and forecasting of return volatility. *Review of Economics and Statistics.*

Andersen, T. G., T. Bollerslev, F. X. Diebold, and H. Ebens. 2001. The distribution of realized stock return volatility. *Journal of Financial Economics* 61:43–76.

Andersen, T. G., T. Bollerslev, F. X. Diebold, and P. Labys. 2000. Exchange rate returns standardized by realized volatility are (nearly) Gaussian. *Multinational Finance Journal* 4:159–79.

———. 2001. The distribution of realized exchange rate volatility. *Journal of the American Statistical Association* 96:42–55.

———. 2003. Modeling and forecasting realized volatility. *Econometrica* 71:529–626.

Andersen, T. G., T. Bollerslev, F. X. Diebold, and C. Vega. 2004. Real-time price discovery in stock, bond, and foreign exchange markets. Unpublished manuscript. Northwestern University, Duke University, University of Pennsylvania, and University of Rochester.

Baillie, R. T., and T. Bollerslev. 1992. Prediction in dynamic models with time-dependent conditional variances. *Journal of Econometrics* 51:91–113.

Barndorff-Nielsen, O. E., and N. Shephard. 2001. Non-Gaussian Ornstein-Uhlenbeck-based models and some of their uses in financial economics (with discussion). *Journal of the Royal Statistical Society, B* 63:167–241.

———. 2004. Power and bipower variation with stochastic volatility and jumps. *Journal of Financial Econometrics* 2:1–48.

Barone-Adesi, G., F. Bourgoin, and K. Giannopoulos. 1998. Don't look back. *Risk* 11:100–104.

Benson, P., and P. Zangari. 1997. A general approach to calculating VaR without volatilities and correlations. *RiskMetrics Monitor* (Summer): 19–23.

Berkowitz, J., and J. O'Brien. 2002. How accurate are Value-at-Risk models at commercial banks? *Journal of Finance* 57:1093–1112.

Bodoukh, J., M. Richardson, and R. Whitelaw. 1998. The best of both worlds. *Risk* 11:64–67.

Bollerslev, T. 1986. Generalized autoregressive conditional heteroskedasticity. *Journal of Econometrics* 31:307–27.

———. 1987. A conditionally heteroskedastic time series model for speculative prices and rates of return. *Review of Economics and Statistics* 69:542–47.

Bollerslev, T., R. F. Engle, and J. Wooldridge. 1988. A capital asset pricing model with time-varying covariances. *Journal of Political Economy* 96:116–31.

Bollerslev, T., and H. O. Mikkelsen. 1999. Long-term equity anticipation securities and stock market volatility dynamics. *Journal of Econometrics* 92:75–99.

Brandt, M., P. Santa-Clara, and R. Valkanov. 2004. Optimal portfolios with parametric weights. Unpublished manuscript, Duke University and University of California (Los Angeles).

Cappiello, L., R. F. Engle, and K. Sheppard. 2004. Asymmetric dynamics in the correlations of global equity and bond returns. Unpublished manuscript, New York University.

Christoffersen, P. 2003. *Elements of financial risk management.* San Diego: Academic Press.

Christoffersen, P., and K. Jacobs. 2004. Which GARCH model for option valuation? *Management Science* 50:1204–21.

Diebold, F. X., A. Hickman, A. Inoue, and T. Schuermann. 1998. Converting 1-day volatility to h-day volatility: Scaling by root-h is worse than you think. Wharton Financial Institutions Center, Working Paper no. 97-34. Philadelphia: Wharton School of Finance.

Diebold, F. X., and M. Nerlove. 1989. The dynamics of exchange rate volatility: A multivariate latent-factor ARCH model. *Journal of Applied Econometrics* 4:1–22.

Diebold, F. X., T. Schuermann, and J. Stroughair. 1998. Pitfalls and opportunities in the use of extreme value theory in risk management. In *Decision technologies for computational finance,* ed. A.-P. N. Refenes, A. N. Burgess, and J. D. Moody, 3–12. Amsterdam: Kluwer Academic.

Duffie, D., and J. Pan. 1997. An overview of Value at Risk. *Journal of Derivatives* (Spring): 7–49.

Engle, R. F. 2001. GARCH 101: The use of ARCH/GARCH models in applied econometrics. *Journal of Economic Perspectives* 15:157–68.

———. 2002. Dynamic conditional correlation: A simple class of multivariate generalized autoregressive conditional heteroskedasticity models. *Journal of Business and Economic Statistics* 20:339–50.

———. 2004. Risk and volatility: Econometric models and financial practice. *American Economic Review* 94:405–20.

Engle, R. F., and G. M. Gallo. 2004. A multiple indicators model for volatility using intra-daily data. Unpublished manuscript. New York University and University of Firenze.

Engle, R. F., and G. G. J. Lee. 1999. A permanent and transitory component model of stock return volatility. In *Cointegration, causality, and forecasting: A Festschrift in honor of Clive W. J. Granger,* ed. R. F. Engle and H. White, 475–97. Oxford, UK: Oxford University Press.

Engle, R. F., and J. Mezrich. 1996. GARCH for groups. *Risk* 8:36–40.

Fernandez, C., and M. F. J. Steel. 1998. On Bayesian modeling of fat tails and skewness. *Journal of the American Statistical Association* 93:359–71.

Fleming, J., C. Kirby, and B. Ostdiek. 2003. The economic value of volatility timing using realized volatility. *Journal of Financial Economics* 67:473–509.

Franses, P. H., and C. Hafner. 2003. A generalized dynamic conditional correlation model for many asset returns. Manuscript. Erasmus University Rotterdam.

Gallant, A. R., C. T. Hsu, and G. E. Tauchen. 1999. Using daily range data to calibrate volatility diffusions and extract the forward integrated variance. *Review of Economics and Statistics* 81:617–31.

Ghysels, E., P. Santa-Clara, and R. Valkanov. 2006. Predicting volatility: Getting the most out of return data sampled at different frequencies. *Journal of Econometrics* 131:59–95.

Glasserman, P., P. Heidelberger, and P. Shahbuddin. 2002. Portfolio Value-at-Risk with heavy-tailed risk factors. *Mathematical Finance* 12 (3): 239–69.

Glosten, L. R., R. Jagannathan, and D. Runkle. 1993. On the relation between the expected value and the volatility of the nominal excess return on stocks. *Journal of Finance* 48:1779–1801.

Guidolin, M., and A. Timmermann. 2006. Term structure of risk alternative econometric specifications. *Journal of Econometrics* 131:285–308.

Hansen, B. 1994. Autoregressive conditional density estimation. *International Economic Review* 35:705–30.

Hansen, P. R., and A. Lunde. 2005. A realized variance for the whole day based on intermittent high-frequency data. *Journal of Financial Econometrics* 3:525–54.

Harvey, A. C. 1989. *Forecasting structural time series models and the Kalman filter.* Cambridge: Cambridge University Press.

Harvey, A. C., E. Ruiz, and E. Sentana. 1992. Unobserved component time series models with ARCH disturbances. *Journal of Econometrics* 52:129–57.

Heston, S., and S. Nandi. 2000. A closed-form GARCH option pricing model. *Review of Financial Studies* 13:585–626.

Hull, J., and A. White. 1998. Incorporating volatility updating into the historical simulation method for VaR. *Journal of Risk* 1:5–19.

Jackson, P., D. Maude, and W. Perraudin. 1997. Bank capital and Value at Risk. *Journal of Derivtives* 4:73–89.

Jondeau, E., and M. Rockinger. 2004. Forthcoming. The copula-GARCH model of conditional dependence: An international stock market application. *Journal of International Money and Finance.*

Jorion, P. 2000. *Value-at-Risk.* New York: McGraw-Hill.

Ledoit, O., P. Santa-Clara, and M. Wolf. 2003. Flexible multivariate GARCH modeling with an application to international stock markets. *Review of Economics and Statistics* 85:735–47.

Ledoit, O., and M. Wolf. 2003. Improved estimation of the covariance matrix of stock returns with an application to portfolio selection. *Journal of Empirical Finance* 10:603–21.

Longin, F. 2000. From VaR to stress testing: The extreme value approach. *Journal of Banking and Finance* 24:1097–1130.

Longin, F., and B. Solnik. 2001. Extreme correlation of international equity markets. *Journal of Finance* 56:649–76.

Manganelli, S. 2004. Asset allocation by variance sensitivity analysis. *Journal of Financial Econometrics* 2:370–89.

Martens, M. 2004. Estimating unbiased and precise realized covariances. Unpublished manuscript. Erasmus University, Rotterdam.

McNeil, A. J., and R. Frey. 2000. Estimation of tail-related risk measures for heteroskedastic financial time series: An extreme value approach. *Journal of Empirical Finance* 7:271–300.

Nerlove, M., and S. Wage. 1964. On the optimality of adaptive forecasting. *Management Science* 10:207–29.

Patton, A. J. 2005. Modeling asymmetric exchange rate dependence. Forthcoming. *International Economic Review.*

Pelletier, D. 2006. Regime switching for dynamic correlations. *Journal of Econometrics* 131:445–73.

Pesaran, H., and P. Zaffaroni. 2004. Model averaging and Value-at-Risk based evaluation of large-multi asset volatility models for risk management. Unpublished manuscript, University of Cambridge.

Poon, S.-H., M. Rockinger, and J. Tawn. 2004. Extreme value dependence in financial markets: Diagnostics, models and financial implications. *Review of Financial Studies* 17:581–610.

Pritsker, M. 2001. The hidden dangers of historical simulation. Unpublished manuscript. Washington, DC: Federal Reserve Board.

Scholes, M., and J. T. Williams. 1977. Estimating betas from nonsynchronous data. *Journal of Financial Economics* 5:309–27.

Theil, H., and S. Wage. 1964. Some observations on adaptive forecasting. *Management Science* 10:198–206.

Zhou, B. 1996. High-frequency data and volatility in foreign-exchange rates. *Journal of Business and Economic Statistics* 14:45–52.

Comment   Pedro Santa-Clara

Andersen, Bollerslev, Christoffersen, and Diebold (henceforth ABCD) provide a comprehensive overview of financial risk management from the point of view of both Wall Street and the ivory tower. Most usefully, ABCD discuss a number of recent developments in the econometrics of time-varying risk that hold vast promise for risk management applications: the dynamic conditional correlation model of Engle (2002), which permits large-scale, flexible modeling of conditional covariance matrices, the use of high-frequency data to measure realized variances and covariances that has been developed largely by the authors, and the modeling of the full distribution of conditional returns. In this discussion I will just offer a couple of comments and extensions to ABCD's very well-organized survey.

Unconditional Versus Conditional Risk

ABCD discuss extensively the pros and cons of both unconditional and conditional (dynamic) measures of risk. There is, however, an additional source of risk dynamics that is ignored in the paper and that, in fact, has not been studied much in the literature. Most financial assets are managed over time, and it is therefore more important to study the risks of dynamic investment strategies rather than the risks of static portfolios. Especially for supervision and regulation purposes, it matters more to forecast the risk of a portfolio taking into account the likely variation in its weights than to forecast the risk of the current positions that are unlikely to remain in place for long.

Assume that there exist some state variables that forecast both risk and return. A trader that adjusts the portfolio according to those state variables, for instance to maximize the conditional Sharpe ratio, will produce a portfolio with time-varying risk. Many authors have shown that the level of interest rates, the term spread, and the default spread have forecasting power for both first and second moments of returns of stocks and bonds. Brandt and Santa-Clara (2005) show that the optimal asset allocation for a mean-variance investor that recognizes the forecasting power of these state variables displays considerable time variation in portfolio weights and conditional moments.

As another example, investment strategies are typically conditioned on the level of risk in the markets. Either formally, through Value-at-Risk (VaR) constraints, or informally, according to the trader's feelings, the level of exposure is adjusted when risks change. Consider a trader with a VaR limit that manages the exposure of the portfolio to always be at that limit. When market risk is high, the exposure is reduced, and when risk is low, the exposure is increased. Interestingly, the result of this dynamic strategy is a series of returns that have constant conditional VaR. That is, in this case, a dynamic strategy produces a series of returns with static risk.

This example explains why the realized risk of a managed portfolio may not display GARCH characteristics even though the assets in the portfolio have them. Ex ante, if the portfolio were to remain constant, its risk would be changing. Ex post, given that the portfolio changes with the ex ante risk assessment, the realized risk is not time varying. This distinction between ex ante and ex post risk of an investment strategy has been the basis of much confusion relating to the need of unconditional versus conditional risk models. It justifies the use of unconditional VaR by regulators, since they care only about ex post risk. On the other hand, traders need the more sophisticated models of conditional risk to be able to manage the exposures in a timely manner.

Modeling the Entire Distribution of Returns

ABCD explain that the common use of summary statistics such as volatility, VaR, or expected shortfall is likely to give a partial view of the true risk of a portfolio. Only the full (conditional) distribution of returns, including skewness and fat tails, will correctly capture the likelihood of different levels of losses.

Santa-Clara and Schwartz (2005) offer a simple alternative that captures the impact of the full distribution of returns on the risk of a portfolio. Their approach can be summarized briefly. The idea is that the investor (or the regulator) analyzes the distribution of returns through the lens of a utility function of returns that is concave (reflecting risk aversion). A simple example is the well-known power utility function, $u(t) = (1 + r)^{1-\gamma}/(1 - \gamma)$, with relative risk aversion γ.

Given portfolio weights w, simulate the history of portfolio returns:

$$r_{p,t+1} = \sum_{i=1}^{N} w_i r_{i,t+1} \text{ for } t = 1, \ldots, T - 1,$$

and evaluate the corresponding time series of realized utilities of the portfolio $u(r_{p,t+1})$. Then, regress the realized utilities on state variables z that condition the joint return distribution:[1]

$$u(r_{p,t+1}) = \phi z_t + \varepsilon_{t+1}.$$

The fitted values of this regression are estimates of the conditional expected utility $E_t(u[r_{p,t+1}])$. At the current time T, the regression is estimated with historic data, and the fitted value $E_T(u[r_{p,T+1}]) = \phi z_T$ is a forecast of the risk of the portfolio in the next period $T + 1$. Actually, a more easily interpreted measure of risk is the conditional certainty equivalent $c_t = u^{-1}(E_t[u\{r_{p,t+1}\}])$, which is expressed in units of returns.

We can run similar regressions for the partial derivatives of the expected utility relative to portfolio weights. These derivatives can be used for risk management as they quantify how much the utility (or certainty equivalent) changes when the weight of each asset changes marginally.

Santa-Clara and Schwartz's measure of risk takes into account the full

---

1. The variable z may contain basis functions of a more fundamental set of state variables y. In this way the specification can accommodate a nonlinear relation between y and the expected utility. Also, the returns may be demeaned prior to running the regression in order to concentrate on risk and discard the effect of the average return on the investor's utility.

distribution of returns. The investor cares about the expected value of the utility, which in turn depends on all the moments of the distribution of the portfolio returns:

$$E_t[u(r_{p,t+1})] \approx u[E_t(r_{p,t+1})] + u''[E_t(r_{p,t+1})]\mathrm{Var}_t(r_{p,t+1})/2$$
$$+ u'''[E_t(r_{p,t+1})]\mathrm{Skew}_t(r_{p,t+1})/6 + \dots,$$

which depend implicitly on the full joint distribution of the assets' returns. We have therefore a measure of risk that combines all the features of the distribution of returns weighted in an optimal manner according to the risk preferences of the investor.

Finally, this approach can easily accommodate dynamic investment strategies. Simply model the portfolio weights as a function of state variables x_t (which may or may not be different from z_t):

$$r_{p,t+1} = \sum_{t=1}^{N_t} w_{i,t} r_{i,t+1} = \sum_{i=1}^{N} (\theta x_t) r_{i,t+1},$$

compute the realized utilities, and perform the above regression. Going a step further, the coefficients of the portfolio policy can be optimized to maximize the conditional expected utility of the portfolio along the lines of Brandt and Santa-Clara (2005) and Brandt, Santa-Clara, and Valkanov (2005):

$$\max_{\theta} \frac{1}{T} \sum_{t=1}^{T} u(r_{p,t+1}) = \frac{1}{T} \sum_{t=1}^{T} u\left[\sum_{i=1}^{N} (\theta x_t) r_{i,t+1} \right]$$

Conclusion

The econometrics of risk is an exciting area right now. ABCD's paper is a precious guide to recent developments and points to interesting directions for future research.

References

Brandt, Michael, and Pedro Santa-Clara. 2005. Forthcoming. Dynamic portfolio selection by augmenting the asset space. *Journal of Finance.*

Brandt, Michael, Pedro Santa-Clara, and Rossen Valkanov. 2005. Parametric portfolio policies: Exploiting characteristics in the cross section of equity returns. UCLA Working Paper. Los Angeles: University of California.

Engle, Robert F. 2002. Dynamic conditional correlation: A simple class of multivariate generalized autoregressive conditional heteroskedasticity models. *Journal of Business and Economic Statistics* 20:339–50.

Santa-Clara, Pedro, and Eduardo Schwartz. 2005. Certainty equivalent Value at Risk. UCLA Working Paper. Los Angeles: University of California.

Discussion Summary

Ken Abbott opened the general discussion by suggesting that the methods suggested by the authors may be more applicable to modeling of credit risk, where correlation skew is a concern and copula methods are coming into favor, than in traditional market-risk applications. In his experience, historical simulation methods work well in practice and are relatively easy for bank staff and management to understand. The dynamic issues raised by the authors, which are particularly dramatic in cases like the 1987 crash, are handled in practice by stress-test exercises, which are done along with VaR modeling.

Patricia Jackson observed that the use to which a VaR model is put is a key consideration in its design. Where the purpose is estimating the capital required by the financial institution, including dynamic volatility is undesirable because volatility falls during safe periods and thus implied capital requirements fall. The change to the high volatility characteristic of periods of stress may occur quickly, leaving the institution with little time to increase its capital. Historical simulation methods are less subject to this problem. However, the methods suggested by the authors may be preferable for other uses.

On the other hand, *Jim O'Brien* noted that although historical simulation may tend to give the "correct" number of violations of a VaR quantile, violations tend to be bunched in time, which appears to be a sign of worrisome historical dependence.

The discussion turned to technical considerations; *Philipp Hartmann* noted that some of the methods suggested by the authors implicitly use linear measures in the tails of the return distribution, but tail events tend to occur during crisis periods and may require a more complex specification. *Hayne Leland* noted that bid-ask bounce and infrequent-trading problems can be an issue in the high-frequency data that the authors suggest be used for volatility estimation, and *Hashem Pesaran* noted that such data also are often rather dirty. *Peter Christoffersen* agreed that such problems exist, but suggested that they might be relatively easy to overcome for instruments traded in very liquid markets.

Special Purpose Vehicles and Securitization

Gary B. Gorton and Nicholas S. Souleles

12.1 Introduction

This paper analyzes securitization and, more generally, "special purpose vehicles" (SPVs), which are now pervasive in corporate finance.[1] What is the source of value to organizing corporate activity using SPVs? We argue that SPVs exist in large part to reduce bankruptcy costs, and we find evidence consistent with this view, using unique data on credit card securitizations. The way in which the reduction in costs is accomplished sheds some light on how bank risk should be assessed.

By financing the firm in pieces, some on–balance sheet and some off–balance sheet, control rights to business decisions are separated from financing decisions. The SPV-sponsoring firm maintains control over business decisions, whereas the financing is done in SPVs, which are passive; they cannot make business decisions. Furthermore, the SPVs are not subject to bankruptcy costs because they cannot in practice go bankrupt, as a matter of design. Bankruptcy is a process of transferring control rights over corporate assets. Securitization reduces the amount of assets that are subject to this expensive and lengthy process. We argue that the existence

Thanks to Moody's Investors Service, Sunita Ganapati of Lehman Brothers, and Andrew Silver of Moody's for assistance with data. Thanks to Charles Calomiris, Richard Cantor, Mark Carey, Darrell Duffie, Loretta Mester, Mitch Petersen, Jeremy Stein, René Stulz, Peter Tufano, and seminar participants at the Philadelphia Federal Reserve Bank, Moody's Investors Service, and the NBER Conference on the Risks of Financial Institutions for comments and suggestions. Souleles acknowledges financial support from the Rodney L. White Center for Financial Research, through the New York Stock Exchange (NYSE) and Merrill Lynch Research Fellowships.

1. In the following we present evidence on the use of SPVs in the cases where such data exist. As explained subsequently, these are "qualified" SPVs. Data on other types of SPVs are not systematically collected.

of SPVs depends on implicit contractual arrangements that avoid accounting and regulatory impediments to reducing bankruptcy costs. We develop a model of off–balance sheet financing and test the implications of the model.

An SPV, or a special purpose entity (SPE), is a legal entity created by a firm (known as the sponsor or originator) by transferring assets to the SPV, to carry out some specific purpose or circumscribed activity, or a series of such transactions. SPVs have no purpose other than the transaction(s) for which they were created, and they can make no substantive decisions; the rules governing them are set down in advance and carefully circumscribe their activities. Indeed, no one works at an SPV and it has no physical location.

The legal form for an SPV may be a limited partnership, a limited liability company, a trust, or a corporation.[2] Typically, off–balance sheet SPVs have the following characteristics:

- They are thinly capitalized.
- They have no independent management or employees.
- Their administrative functions are performed by a trustee who follows prespecified rules with regard to the receipt and distribution of cash; there are no other decisions.
- Assets held by the SPV are serviced via a servicing arrangement.
- They are structured so that, as a practical matter, they cannot become bankrupt.

In short, SPVs are essentially robot firms that have no employees, make no substantive economic decisions, have no physical location, and cannot go bankrupt. Off–balance sheet financing arrangements can take the form of research and development limited partnerships, leasing transactions, or asset securitizations, to name the most prominent.[3] And less visible are tax arbitrage-related transactions. In this paper we address the question of why SPVs exist.

The existence of SPVs raises important issues for the theory of the firm: what is a firm and what are its boundaries? Does a "firm" include the SPVs that it sponsors? (From an accounting or tax point of view, this is the issue of consolidation.) What is the relationship between a sponsoring firm and its SPV? In what sense does the sponsor control the SPV? Are investors indifferent between investing in SPV securities and the sponsor's securities?

---

2. There are also a number of vehicles that owe their existence to special legislation. These include real estate mortgage investment conduits (REMICs), financial asset securitization investment trusts (FASITs), regulated investment companies (RICs), and real estate investment trusts (REITs). In particular, their tax status is subject to specific tax code provisions. See Kramer (2003).

3. On research and development limited partnerships see, for example, Shevlin (1987) and Beatty, Berger, and Magliolo (1995); on leasing see, for example, Hodge (1996, 1998), and Weidner (2000). Securitization is later discussed in detail.

To make headway on these questions we first theoretically investigate the question of the existence of SPVs. Then we test some implications of the theory, using unique data on credit card securitizations.

One argument for why SPVs are used is that sponsors may benefit from a lower cost of capital, because sponsors can remove debt from the balance sheet, so balance sheet leverage is reduced. Enron, which created over 3,000 off–balance sheet SPVs, is the leading example of this (see Klee and Butler 2002). But Enron was able to keep their off–balance sheet debt from being observed by investors, and so obtained a lower cost of capital. If market participants are aware of the off–balance sheet vehicles, and assuming that these vehicles truly satisfy the legal and accounting requirements to be off–balance sheet, then it is not immediately obvious how this lowers the cost of capital for the sponsor. In the context of operating leases Lim, Mann, and Mihov (2003) find that bond yields reflect off–balance sheet debt.[4]

The key issue concerns why otherwise equivalent debt issued by the SPV is priced or valued differently than on–balance sheet debt by investors. The difference between on– and off–balance sheet debt turns on the question of what is meant by the phrase "truly satisfy the legal and accounting requirements to be off–balance sheet." In this paper we argue that "off–balance sheet" is not a completely accurate description of what is going on. The difficulty lies in the distinction between formal contracts (which are subject to accounting and regulatory rules) and relational or implicit contracts. Relational contracts are arrangements that circumvent the difficulties of formally contracting (that is, entering into an arrangement that can be enforced by the legal system).[5]

While there are formal requirements, reviewed subsequently, for determining the relationships between sponsors and their SPVs, including when the SPVs are not consolidated and when the SPVs' debts are off–balance sheet, this is not the whole story. There are other, implicit, contractual relations. The relational contract we focus on concerns sponsors' support of their SPVs in certain states of the world, and investors' reliance on this support, even though sponsors are not legally bound to support their SPVs—and in fact, under accounting and regulatory rules, are not supposed to provide support.

---

4. There are other accounting motivations for setting up off–balance sheet SPVs. For example, Shakespeare (2001, 2003) argues, in the context of securitization, that managers use the gains from securitization to meet earnings targets and analysts' earnings forecasts. This is based on the discretionary element of how the "gain on sale" is booked. Calomiris and Mason (2004) consider regulatory capital arbitrage as a motivation for securitization, but conclude in favor of the "efficient contracting view," by which they mean that "banks use securitization with recourse to permit them to set capital relative to risk in a manner consistent with market, rather than regulatory, capital requirements and to permit them to overcome problems of asymmetric information" (p. 26).

5. On relational contracts in the context of the theory of the firm see Baker, Gibbons, and Murphy (2002) and the references cited therein.

The possibility of this implicit support, "implicit recourse," or "moral recourse" has been noted by regulators, rating agencies, and academic researchers. U.S. bank regulators define implicit recourse or moral recourse as the "provision of credit support, beyond contractual obligations . . ." See Office of the Comptroller of the Currency et al. (2002, p. 1). The OCC goes on to offer guidance as to how bank examiners are to detect this problem. An example of the rating agency view is that of FitchIBCA (1999): "Although not legally required, issuers [sponsors] may feel compelled to support a securitization and absorb credit risk beyond the residual exposure. In effect, there is moral recourse since failure to support the securitization may impair future access to the capital markets" (p. 4). Gorton and Pennacchi (1989, 1995) first discussed the issue of implicit recourse in financial markets in the context of the bank loan sales market; they also provide some empirical evidence for its existence.

Nonetheless, there are many unanswered questions. Why are SPVs valuable? Are they equally valuable to all firms? Why do sponsors offer recourse? How is the implicit arrangement self-enforcing? The details of how the arrangement works and, in particular, how it is a source of value have never been explained. We show that the value of the relational contract, in terms of cost of capital for the sponsor, is related to the details of the legal and accounting structure, which we subsequently explain. To briefly foreshadow the arguments to come, the key point is that SPVs cannot in practice go bankrupt. In the United States it is not possible to waive the right to have access to the government's bankruptcy procedure, but it is possible to structure an SPV so that there cannot be "an event of default" that would throw the SPV into bankruptcy. This means that debt issued by the SPV should not include a premium reflecting expected bankruptcy costs, as there never will be any such costs.[6] So, one benefit to sponsors is that the off–balance sheet debt should be cheaper, ceteris paribus. However, there are potential costs to off–balance sheet debt. One is the fixed cost of setting up the SPV. Another is that there is no tax advantage of off–balance sheet debt to the SPV sponsor. Depending on the structure of the SPV, the interest expense of off–balance sheet debt may not be tax deductible.

After reviewing the institutional detail, which is particularly important for this subject, we develop these ideas in the context of a simple model, and then test some implications of the model using data on credit card securitizations. The model analysis unfolds in steps. First, we determine a benchmark corresponding to the value of the stand-alone firm, which issues debt to investors in the capital markets. For concreteness we refer to this firm as a bank. The bank makes an effort choice to create assets of types that are unobservable to the outside investors. Step two considers the

---

6. However, as we discuss subsequently, the debt may be repaid early due to early amortization. This is a kind of prepayment risk from the point of view of the investors.

situation where the assets can be allocated between on– and off–balance sheet financing, but the allocation of the assets occurs *before* the quality of individual assets has been determined. From the point of view of investors in the SPV's debt, there is a moral hazard problem in that the bank may not make an effort to create high-value assets. The sponsoring bank's decision problem depends on bankruptcy costs, taxes, and other considerations. We provide conditions under which it is optimal for the sponsoring bank to use an SPV.

The third step allows the bank to allocate assets *after* it has determined the qualities of its individual assets. In other words, investors in the debt issued by the SPV face an additional problem. In addition to the moral hazard associated with the effort choice, there is an adverse selection problem with regard to which projects are allocated to the SPV. We call this problem the "strategic adverse selection problem." In the case without commitment, investors will not buy the debt of the SPV because they cannot overcome the strategic adverse selection problem. However, we show that if the sponsor can commit to subsidize the SPV in states of the world where the SPV's assets are low quality and the sponsor's on–balance sheet assets are high quality, then the SPV is viable. In particular, if the bank can commit to subsidize the SPV in certain states of the world, then the profitability of the bank is the same as it would be when projects were allocated between the bank and the SPV prior to their realization, that is, when there was no strategic adverse selection.

But how does the commitment happen? Sponsors cannot verifiably commit to state-contingent subsidies. Even if they could verifiably commit to such strategies, legal considerations would make this undesirable because the courts view such recourse as meaning that the assets were never sold to the SPV in the first place. In this case, the SPV is not bankruptcy remote, meaning that creditors of the sponsoring firm could "claw back" the SPV's assets in a bankruptcy proceeding. As Klee and Butler (2002) write:

> The presence of recourse is the most important aspect of risk allocation because it suggests that the parties intended a loan and not a sale. If the parties had intended a sale, then the buyer would have retained the risk of default, not the seller. The greater the recourse the SPV has against the Originator, through for example chargebacks or adjustments to the purchase price, the more the transfer resembles a disguised loan rather than a sale. Courts differ on the weight they attach to the presence of recourse provisions. Some courts view the presence of such a provision as nearly conclusive of the parties' intent to create a security interest, while others view recourse as only one of a number of factors. (p. 52)

This means that, as a practical matter, the recourse must not be explicit, cannot be formalized, and must be subtle and rare.

The final step in the analysis is to show that in a repeated context it is possible to implement a form of commitment. This result is based on the familiar use of trigger strategies (e.g., Friedman 1971, and Green and Porter 1984), which create an incentive for the sponsor to follow the implicit arrangement. Previous applications of such strategies involve settings of oligopolistic competition, where firms want to collude but cannot observe strategic price or quantity choices of rivals. Intertemporal incentives to collude are maintained via punishment periods triggered by deviations from the implicit collusive arrangements. Our application is quite different. Here, firms sponsoring SPVs "collude" with the investors in the SPVs by agreeing to the state-contingent subsidization of the SPV—recourse that is prohibited by accounting and regulatory rules. In this sense SPVs are a kind of regulatory arbitrage.

Two empirically testable implications follow from the theoretical analysis. First, because the value in using SPVs derives in large part from avoiding bankruptcy costs, riskier firms should be more likely to engage in off–balance sheet financing. Mills and Newberry (2004) find that riskier firms use more off–balance sheet debt. Also, see Moody's (1997a and 1997b).

Second, following Gorton and Pennacchi (1989, 1995), implicit recourse implies that investors in the debt of the SPV incorporate expectations about the risk of the sponsor. This is because the sponsor must exist in order to subsidize the SPV in some states of the world. As Moody's (1997b) puts it: "Part of the reason for the favorable pricing of the [SPVs'] securities is the perception on the part of many investors that originators (i.e., the 'sponsors' of the securitizations) will voluntarily support—beyond that for which they are contractually obligated—transactions in which asset performance deteriorates significantly in the future. Many originators have, in fact, taken such actions in the past" (p. 40).

We test these two implications using unique data on credit card securitizations. We focus on securitization, a key form of off–balance sheet financing, because of data availability. Credit cards are a particularly interesting asset class because they involve revolving credits that are repeatedly sold into SPVs. Moreover, they represent the largest category within non-mortgage securitizations.

We find that, even controlling for the quality of the underlying assets and other factors, investors do require significantly higher yields for credit card asset-backed securities (ABS) issued by riskier sponsors, as measured by the sponsors' credit ratings. Also, riskier firms generally securitize more, ceteris paribus. These results are consistent with our model.

The paper proceeds as follows. In section 12.2 we provide some background information on off–balance sheet vehicles in general. Then, in section 12.3 we focus more narrowly on some of the details of how securitization vehicles in particular work. Section 12.4 presents and analyzes a model of off–balance sheet financing. In section 12.5 we explain and review the datasets used in the empirical work. The first hypothesis, concerning the existence of implicit recourse, is tested in section 12.6. The second hypothesis, that riskier firms securitize more, is tested in section 12.7. Finally, section 12.8 concludes, and is followed by a mathematical appendix.

12.2   Background on SPVs

In this section we briefly review some of the important institutional background for understanding SPVs and their relation to their sponsor.

12.2.1   Legal Form of the SPV

A special purpose vehicle or special purpose entity is a legal entity that has been set up for a specific, limited purpose by another entity, the sponsoring firm. An SPV can take the form of a corporation, trust, partnership, or a limited liability company. The SPV may be a subsidiary of the sponsoring firm, or it may be an orphan SPV, one that is not consolidated with the sponsoring firm for tax, accounting, or legal purposes (or may be consolidated for some purposes but not others).

In securitization, the SPV most commonly takes the legal form of a trust. A trust is a legal construct in which a fiduciary relationship is created with respect to some property. A trustee then has duties to perform for the benefit of third party beneficiaries. See Restatement (Third) of Trusts. Often the SPV is a charitable or purpose trust. These traditional trusts have been transformed into a vehicle with a different economic substance than what was perhaps contemplated by the law. These transformed trusts—commercial trusts—are very different from the traditional trusts (see Schwarcz 2003a, Langbein 1997, and Sitkoff 2003).

A purpose trust (called a STAR trust in the Cayman Islands) is a trust set up to fulfill specific purposes rather than for beneficiaries. A charitable trust has charities as the beneficiaries. For many transactions there are benefits if the SPV is domiciled offshore, usually in Bermuda, the Cayman Islands, or the British Virgin Islands.

12.2.2   Accounting

A key question for an SPV (from the point of view of SPV sponsors, if not economists) is whether the SPV is off–balance sheet or not with respect to some other entity. This is an accounting issue, which turns on the question of whether the transfer of receivables from the sponsor to the SPV is treated as a sale or a loan for accounting purposes.[7] The requirements for the transfer to be treated as a sale, and hence receive off–balance sheet treatment, are set out in Financial Accounting Standard No. 140 (FAS 140), "Accounting for Transfers and Servicing of Financial Assets and Extinguishment of Liabilities," promulgated in September 2000.[8] FAS 140 es-

7. If the conditions of a sale are met, then the transferor must recognize a gain or loss on the sale.

8. Prior to FAS 140 the issue was addressed by FAS 125. FAS 140 was intended to clarify several outstanding questions left ambiguous in FAS 125.

sentially has two broad requirements for a "true sale." First, the SPV must be a qualifying SPV, and second, the sponsor must surrender control of the receivables.

In response to Enron's demise, the Financial Accounting Standard Board (FASB) adopted FASB Interpretation No. 46 (FIN 46; revised December 2003), "Consolidation of Variable Interest Entities, an Interpretation of Accounting Research Bulletin (ARB) No. 51," which has the aim of improving financial reporting and disclosure by companies with variable interest entities (VIEs).[9] Basically, FASB's view is that the then-current accounting rules that determined whether an SPV should be consolidated were inadequate. Because FASB had difficulty defining an SPV, it created the VIE concept. FIN 46 sets forth a new measure of financial control, one based not on majority of voting interests, but instead on who holds the majority of the residual risk and obtains the majority of the benefits, or both—independent of voting power.

A "qualifying" SPV (QSPV) is an SPV that meets the requirements set forth in FAS 140; otherwise, it is treated as a VIE in accordance with FIN 46. FIN 46 does not apply to QSPVs. To be a qualifying SPV means that the vehicle: (1) is "demonstrably distinct" from the sponsor, (2) is significantly limited in its permitted activities, and these activities are entirely specified by the legal documents defining its existence, (3) holds only "passive" receivables—that is, there are no decisions to be made, and (4) has the right, if any, to sell or otherwise dispose of noncash receivables only in "automatic response" to the occurrence of certain events. The term "demonstrably distinct," means that the sponsor cannot have the ability to unilaterally dissolve the SPV, and that at least 10 percent of the fair value (of its beneficial interests) must be held by unrelated third parties.

On the second requirement of FAS 140, the important aspect of surrendering control is that the sponsor cannot retain effective control over the transferred assets through an ability to unilaterally cause the SPV to return specific assets (other than through a cleanup call or, to some extent, removal of accounts provisions).

FAS 140 states that the sponsor need not include the debt of a qualifying SPV subsidiary in the sponsor's consolidated financial statements.

A QSPV must be a separate and distinct legal entity—separate and distinct, that is, from the sponsor (the sponsor does not consolidate the SPV for accounting reasons). It must be an automaton in the sense that there are no substantive decisions for it to ever make, simply rules that must be followed; it must be bankruptcy remote, meaning that the bankruptcy of the

---

9. VIEs are defined by FASB to be entities that do not have sufficient equity to finance their activities without additional subordinated support. It also includes entities where the equity holders do not have voting or other rights to make decisions about the equity, are not effectively residual claimants, and do not have the right to expected residual returns.

sponsor has no implications for the SPV, and the SPV itself must (as a practical matter) never be able to become bankrupt.

12.2.3   Bankruptcy

An essential feature of an SPV is that it be bankruptcy remote. This means that should the sponsoring firm enter a bankruptcy procedure, the firm's creditors cannot seize the assets of the SPV. It also means that the SPV itself can never become legally bankrupt. The most straightforward way to achieve this would be for the SPV to waive its right to file a voluntary bankruptcy petition, but this is legally unenforceable (see Klee and Butler 2002, p. 33 ff.). The only way to completely eliminate the risk of either voluntary or involuntary bankruptcy is to create the SPV in a legal form that is ineligible to be a debtor under the U.S. Bankruptcy Code. The SPV can be structured to achieve this result. As described by Klee and Butler: "The use of SPVs is simply a disguised form of bankruptcy waiver" (p. 34).

To make the SPV as bankruptcy remote as possible, its activities can be restricted. For instance, it can be restricted from issuing debt beyond a stated limit. Standard and Poor's (2002) lists the following traditional characteristics for a bankrupt-remote SPV:

- Restrictions on objects, powers, and purposes
- Limitations on ability to incur indebtedness
- Restrictions or prohibitions on merger, consolidation, dissolution, liquidation, winding up, asset sales, transfers of equity interests, and amendments to the organizational documents relating to "separateness"
- Incorporation of separateness covenants restricting dealings with parents and affiliates
- "Nonpetition" language (i.e., a covenant not to file the SPE into involuntary bankruptcy)
- Security interests over assets
- An independent director (or functional equivalent) whose consent is required for the filing of a voluntary bankruptcy petition

The SPV can also obtain agreements from its creditors that they will not file involuntary petitions for bankruptcy. Depending on the legal form of the SPV, it may require more structure to ensure effective bankruptcy remoteness. For example, if the SPV is a corporation, where the power to file a voluntary bankruptcy petition lies with the board of directors, then the charter or by-laws can be structured to require unanimity. Sometimes charters or by-laws have provisions that negate the board's discretion unless certain other criteria are met.

An involuntary bankruptcy occurs under certain circumstances (see Section 303[b] of the Bankruptcy Code). Chief among the criteria is nonpayment of debts as they become due. Perhaps most important for securi-

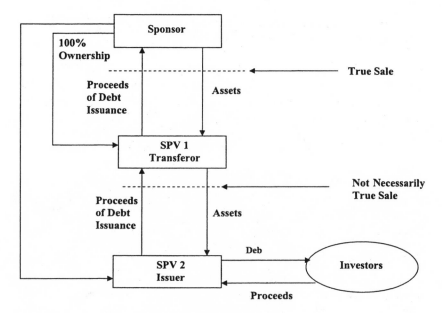

Fig. 12.1   A two-tiered bankruptcy remote structure
Source: Moody's (August 30, 2002).

tization vehicles, shortfalls of cash leading to an inability to make promised coupon payments can lead to early amortization rather than an event of default on the debt. This is subsequently discussed further.

There is also the risk that if the sponsor of the SPV goes bankrupt, the bankruptcy judge will recharacterize the "true sale" of assets to the SPV as a secured financing, which would bring the assets back onto the bankrupt sponsor's balance sheet. Or the court may consolidate the assets of the sponsor and the SPV. As a result of this risk, most structured financings have a two-tiered structure involving two SPVs. The sponsor often retains a residual interest in the SPV that provides a form of credit enhancement, but the residual interest may preclude a true sale. Consequently, the residual interest is held by another SPV, not the sponsor. The true sale occurs with respect to this second vehicle. This is shown in figure 12.1, which is taken from Moody's (2002a).

12.2.4   Taxes

There are two tax issues.[10] First, how is the SPV taxed? Second, what are the tax implications of the SPV's debt for the sponsoring firm? We briefly summarize the answers to these questions.

---

10. This subsection is based on Kramer (2003), Peaslee and Nirenberg (2001), and Humphreys and Kreistman (1995).

The first question is easier to answer. SPVs are usually structured to be tax neutral, that is, so that their profits are not taxed. The failure to achieve tax neutrality would usually result in taxes being imposed once on the income of the sponsor and once again on the distributions from the SPV. This "double tax" would most likely make SPVs unprofitable for the sponsor. There are a number of ways to design an SPV to achieve tax neutrality. We briefly review some of them.

Many SPVs are incorporated in a tax haven jurisdiction, such as the Cayman Islands, where they are treated as "exempted companies." See Ashman (2000). An exempted company is not permitted to conduct business in, for example, the Cayman Islands, and in return is awarded a total tax holiday for twenty years, with the possibility of a ten-year extension. Because such entities are not organized or created in the United States, they are not subject to U.S. federal income tax, except to the extent that their income arises from doing business in the United States. However, the organizational documents for the SPV will limit it so that for purposes of the U.S. Internal Revenue Code of 1986, it can be construed as not being "engaged in U.S. trade or business."

An investment trust that issues pass-through certificates is tax neutral; that is, the trust is ignored for tax purposes—there is no taxation at the trust level—and the certificate owners are subject to tax. Pass-through certificates represent pro rata interests in the underlying pool. To maintain this tax-neutral status, it is important that the SPV not be reclassified as a corporation. To avoid such reclassification, the trustee must have no power to vary the investments in the asset pool, and its activities must be limited to conserving and protecting the assets for the benefit of the beneficiaries of the trust. See Kramer (2003).

More common than pass-through structures are pay-through structures. Pay-through bonds are issued by SPVs that are corporations or owner trusts. In these structures, the SPVs issue bonds, but this requires that there be a party that holds the residual risk, an equity holder. If the SPV is a corporation, then the pay-through bonds have minimal tax at the corporate level because the SPV's taxable income or loss is the difference between the yields on its assets and the coupons on its pay-through bonds. Typically these are matched as closely as possible.

The second question is more complicated. Some SPVs achieve off–balance sheet status for accounting purposes but not for tax purposes. Securitizations can fit into this category because they can be treated as secured financing for tax purposes.

12.2.5   Credit Enhancement

Because the SPV's business activities are constrained and its ability to incur debt is limited, it faces the risk of a shortfall of cash below what it is obligated to pay investors. This chance is minimized via credit enhancement.

The most important form of credit enhancement occurs via tranching of the risk of loss due to default of the underlying borrowers. Tranching takes the form of a capital structure for the SPV, with some senior-rated tranches sold to investors in the capital markets (called A notes and B notes), a junior security (called a C note) which is typically privately placed, and various forms of equity-like claims. Credit enhancement takes a variety of other forms as well, including over-collateralization, securities backed by a letter of credit, or a surety bond, or a tranche may be guaranteed by a monoline insurance company. There may also be internal reserve funds that build-up and diminish based on various criteria. We will review this in more detail later with respect to credit card securitization in particular.

12.2.6   The Use of Off–Balance Sheet Financing

Off–balance sheet financing is, by definition, excluded from the sponsor's financial statement balance sheet, and so it is not systematically reported. Consequently, it is hard to say how extensive the use of SPVs has become. Qualified off–balance sheet SPVs that are used for asset securitization usually issue publicly rated debt, so there is more data about these vehicles. This data is presented and discussed in the following. SPVs that are not qualified, however, are hidden, as was revealed by the demise of Enron. Enron led to assertions that the use of off–balance sheet SPVs is extreme.[11] But, in fact, the extent of the use of SPVs is unknown.

12.3   Securitization

Securitization is one of the more visible forms of the use of off–balance sheet SPVs because securitization uses qualified SPVs and involves selling registered, rated securities in the capital markets. Consequently, there is data available. Our empirical work will concentrate on credit card receivables securitization. In this section we briefly review the important features of securitization SPVs.

12.3.1   Overview of Securitization

Securitization involves the following steps: (1) a sponsor or originator of receivables sets up the bankruptcy-remote SPV, pools the receivables, and transfers them to the SPV as a true sale; (2) the cash flows are tranched into asset-backed securities, the most senior of which are rated and issued in the market; (3) the proceeds are used to purchase the receivables from the sponsor; (4) the pool revolves, in that over a period of time the principal received on the underlying receivables is used to purchase new receivables;

---

11. For example, Henry et al. (2002, p. 36): "Hundreds of respected U.S. companies are ferreting away trillions of dollars in debt in off–balance sheet subsidiaries, partnerships, and assorted obligations."

and (5) there is a final amortization period, during which all payments received from the receivables are used to pay down tranche principal amounts. Credit card receivables are different from other pools of underlying loans because the underlying loan to the consumer is a revolving credit; it has no natural maturity, unlike an automobile loan, for example. Consequently, the maturity of the SPV debt is determined arbitrarily by stating that receivable payments after a certain date are "principal" payments.

Figure 12.2 shows a schematic drawing of a typical securitization transaction. The diagram shows the two key steps in the securitization process: pooling and tranching. Pooling and tranching correspond to different types of risk. Pooling minimizes the potential adverse selection problem associated with the selection of the assets to be sold to the SPV. Conditional on selection of the assets, tranching divides the risk of loss due to default based on seniority. Since tranching is based on seniority, the risk of loss due to default of the underlying assets is stratified, with the residual risks borne by the sponsor.

Securitization is a significant and growing phenomenon. Figure 12.3 and table 12.1 provide some information on nonmortgage QSPV outstanding amounts. The figure shows that the liabilities of nonmortgage vehicles grew rapidly since the late 1990s, and by 2004 amounted to almost $1.8 trillion. Table 12.1 shows the breakdown by type of receivable. Note that credit card receivables are the largest component of (nonmortgage) asset-backed securities. See Kendall and Fishman (1996) and Johnson (2002) for earlier discussions of securitization in the United States, and Moody's (2003) on the growth of securitization internationally.

Closely related to securitization is asset-backed commercial paper (ABCP). Asset-backed commercial paper SPVs are called "conduits."

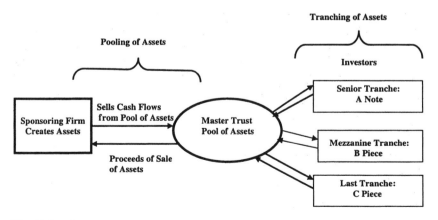

Fig. 12.2   Schematic of a securitization transaction

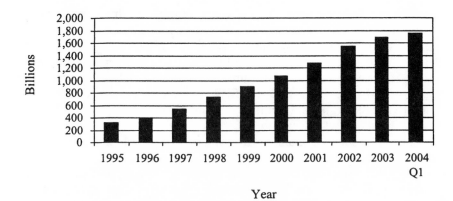

Fig. 12.3   Total non-mortgage ABS/CDO outstandings
Source: Bond Market Association.

Table 12.1   Asset-backed securities outstanding amounts

	Cars	Credit cards	Home equity	Manufactured housing	Student loans	Equipment leases	CBO/CDO	Other
1995	59.5	153.1	33.1	11.2	3.7	10.6	1.2	43.9
1996	71.4	180.7	51.6	14.6	10.1	23.7	1.4	50.9
1997	77	214.5	90.2	19.1	18.3	35.2	19.	62.5
1998	86.9	236.7	124.2	25	25	41.1	47.6	144.7
1999	114.1	257.9	141.9	33.8	36.4	51.4	84.6	180.7
2000	133.1	306.3	151.5	36.9	41.1	58.8	124.5	219.6
2001	187.9	361.9	185.1	42.7	60.2	70.2	167.1	206.1
2002	221.7	397.9	286.5	44.5	74.4	68.3	234.5	215.4
2003	234.5	401.9	346	44.3	99.2	70.1	250.9	246.8
2004 Q1	238.3	406.5	385.1	43.9	102.4	68.7	253.3	250.4

Source: Bond Market Association.

ABCP conduits are bankruptcy-remote SPVs that finance the purchase of receivables primarily through issuing commercial paper. ABCP conduits are also very large. The U.S. commercial paper market, as of August 2004, stood at $1.3 trillion, having grown from $570 billion in January 1991. Figure 12.4 shows the ratio of ABCP to total outstanding commercial paper over the last twelve years. Over half of the total now consists of ABCP.[12]

12. ABCP conduits are an interesting topic in the own right. See Moody's (1993), FitchIBCA (2001), Elmer (1999), Croke (2003), and Standard and Poor's (2002). ABCP conduits can be multiseller, meaning that the receivables in the conduit have been originated by different institutions.

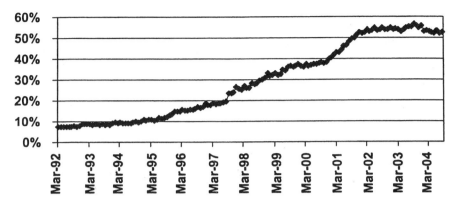

Fig. 12.4   Asset-backed commercial paper conduits

Source: Board of Governors of the Federal Reserve System (http://www.federalreserve.gov/
releases/cp/histouts.txt).

12.3.2   The Structure of Securitization Vehicles

Some of the details of the structure of credit-card securitization SPVs
are important for the subsequent empirical work. These details are briefly
reviewed in this section.

Trusts—Master Trusts

Securitization SPVs are invariably trusts. The sponsor transfers receivables to the trust for the benefit of the certificate holders, that is, the investors in the SPV. Most trusts are Master Trusts, which allow for repeated
transfers of new receivables, whenever the sponsor chooses.[13] At each such
instance, the trust issues a series of securities (trust certificates) to investors
in the capital markets. Each series has an undivided interest in the assets
and an allocable interest in the collections of the receivables in the master
trust, based on the size of each series. Trust assets that have not been allocated to a series are called the "seller's interest," discussed in the following
section. See Schwarcz (2003b).

Master trusts can be "socialized" or "nonsocialized," two categories
that generally refer to how the SPV waterfall works; that is, how the receivables' cash flows are internally allocated. In nonsocialized trusts there
is no reallocation of excess cash flow until each series is paid its full
amount. Socialized trusts pay the trust's expenses, including the monthly
interest to investors, based on the needs of individualized series. Generally,
the socialized excess spread is socialized across all SPV notes issued by the
trust. This means that should there be an early amortization event (dis-

13. A "discrete trust" is an SPV used for a single initial transfer of assets.

cussed subsequently), then all the notes go into early amortization. In a nonsocialized trust, the notes have their own separate excess spreads. See Standard and Poor's (n.d.) for details.

Seller's Interest

The "seller's interest" refers to the sponsor's ownership of trust assets that have not been allocated to any series of securities issued by the trust. The size of the seller's interest varies through time as the amounts of securities issued by the SPV changes and as the balance of principal receivables in the trust assets changes. The seller's interest is usually initially set at 7 percent.

Excess Spread and Early Amortization

A general feature of asset-backed securities is that they involve "excess spread." The yield on the underlying loans that is paid into the trust should be high enough to cover the payment of interest on the ABS tranches in addition to the servicing fees. Excess spread is generally defined as finance charges collections (i.e., the gross yield on the underlying receivables) minus certificate interest (paid to the holders of the SPV debt), servicing fees (paid to the servicer of the receivables, usually the sponsor), and charge-offs (due to default by the underlying borrowers) allocated to the series. For example:

Gross yield on portfolio	18%
Investors' weighted average coupon	–7%
Servicing expense	–2%
Charge-offs	–5%
Excess spread	4%

Depending on the structure of the SPV, available excess spread may be shared with other series in the Master Trust, used to pay credit enhancers, deposited into a reserve account to be used to cover charge-offs, or released to the sponsor.

Practitioners view the excess spread as providing a rough indication of the financial health of a transaction. Excess spread is in fact highly persistent and consequently can be used as a way to monitor a transaction.

All credit card structures have a series of early amortization triggers, which, if hit, cause the payments to investors to be defined as principal, so that the SPVs' liabilities are paid off early—that is, before the scheduled payment date. Early amortization events include insolvency of the originator of the receivables, breaches of representations or warranties, a service default, failure to add receivables as required, and others. Most importantly, however, a transaction will amortize early if the monthly excess spread falls to zero or below for three consecutive months.

Credit Enhancement

In the most common securitization structure the SPV issues tranches of securities to the capital markets based on seniority. There are senior notes, called A notes, and junior or mezzanine notes, called B notes. A common form of credit enhancement to the more senior classes, A notes and B notes, is a subordinated interest known as the collateral invested amount (CIA). The most subordinated interest is referred to by a number of different names, including the C class, C note, or collateral interest.[14] As mentioned, C notes are typically privately placed. This is partly because they are riskier, but also because they do not qualify as debt for tax purposes, making them ERISA-ineligible. Because they are privately placed, they are not rated, and much less information is available about them. See Moody's (November 11, 1994) on C notes.

Credit enhancement for the CIA is a reserve account, which grows depending on the level of the excess spread. If the excess spread is low, then excess spread is trapped inside the SPV and is used to build up the reserve account to a specified level. Reserve account structures vary, with different structures having different amounts of excess spread trapped inside the trust, depending on different contingencies. If the excess spread is negative, the reserve account is drawn down to make up the shortfall.

12.3.3   Implicit Recourse

There are examples of recourse in credit card securitizations that are known publicly. Moody's (January 1997) gives fourteen examples of "notable instances" of voluntary support. The earliest example is from May 1989 and the latest is from November 1996. Higgins and Mason (2004) study a sample of seventeen implicit recourse events involving ten banks during the period 1987 to 2001.[15] They document that firms that engage in subsidization of their SPVs face long delays before returning to market.

12.4   A Theoretical Analysis of SPVs

In this section we analyze a simple model of off–balance sheet financing, a game played between a representative firm (the sponsor of the SPV) and a large number of investors. The goal is to understand the source of value in the use of SPVs.

For concreteness we call the sponsoring firm a bank, by which we mean

---

14. Prior to the development and widespread use of CIAs, credit card transactions employed letters of credit (LOCs) from highly rated institutions to protect investors against default. CIAs became prevalent as a way to avoid dependency on the LOC issuer's credit quality.

15. Higgins and Mason (2004) report two instances of early amortization during 1987–2001, both associated with the failure of the sponsoring institution, namely, Republic Bank and Southeast Bank.

any financial intermediary or, indeed, any firm. We proceed by first setting out a model of the bank financing a portfolio of two projects in a one-period setting. The bank's efforts determine the quality of the projects, unbeknownst to the lenders to the bank. Project quality is implicitly determined by various activities of banks, including information production, screening, and monitoring, but for simplicity it is modeled as an "effort" choice by the bank.[16] This provides a benchmark against which we can determine the value of securitization in the one-period setting.

We will subsequently allow for the possibility of securitization, where one project may be financed off–balance sheet in an SPV. The timing is as follows: projects are allocated to be financed on– or off–balance sheet, and then the bank makes a single effort choice that determines the quality of both the on– and off–balance sheet projects (though, ex post, their realized qualities can differ). To emphasize, projects are allocated first, and then project quality is realized. So, the focus at this point is on the moral hazard problem involving effort choice, rather than on the strategic allocation of projects after their qualities are known (i.e., the adverse selection problem). By comparing the value of the bank when securitization is allowed to the benchmark bank value when there is no securitization, we determine the factors causing securitization to be valuable.

Finally, we will allow for strategic allocation of the two projects; that is, projects are allocated between the balance sheet of the bank and the balance sheet of the SPV *after* their qualities are known. The possibility of strategic allocation of projects adds an additional problem that investors must be concerned about. In this setting, the bank cannot commit to allocate a high-type project to the SPV. In the credit card case there are some constraints on the lemons problem because accounts to be sold to the trust are supposed to be chosen randomly. In this case, the adverse selection may have more to do with the timing of the addition of accounts, depending on the state of the on–balance sheet assets, or perhaps with the removal of accounts.[17]

Without the ability to commit to transfer a high-quality project to the SPV, we show that no lender will lend to the SPV. Off–balance sheet financing, or securitization, in this setting is not possible. This sets the stage for the repeated SPV game, analyzed briefly in the final part of this section. The point there is that repetition of the stage game between the bank and the outside investors can create equilibria in which an implicit contractual arrangement involving bailouts of the SPV by the sponsoring bank can be enforced. By "bailouts" we mean extracontractual support for the SPV, as will become clear later.

---

16. See Gorton and Winton (2003) for a review of the literature on banks' information production, screening, and monitoring activities.

17. Also, sometimes sponsors add "high quality" accounts to improve the overall quality of the receivables pool.

12.4.1   Model Set-Up

A competitive bank seeks to finance two one-period nondivisible projects. Each project requires \$1 of investment. The bank has an amount \$$E < 2$ available to finance the two projects. Since $E < 2$, the bank must borrow $D = 2 - E$, promising to repay F at the end of the period. Debt, however, is tax advantaged, so only $(1 - \tau)F$ needs to be repaid, where τ is the relevant tax rate. The interest rate in the economy, r, is assumed to be zero for simplicity.

We analyze a representative bank and a unit interval of investors. All agents, that is, the banks and the investors, are risk-neutral. Consumption occurs at the end of the period.

The bank determines the quality of its projects by expending "effort," $e \in (e_H, e_L)$, where $e_H > e_L$, and such that a project returns y^H with probability e and y^L with probability $(1 - e)$, where $y^H > y^L$. The single effort choice determines the qualities of both projects, but project realizations are independent. Thus, there are four possible outcomes or states of the world at the end of the period: (y^H, y^H), (y^H, y^L), (y^L, y^H), and (y^L, y^L). The single effort costs $h(e)$. "Effort" is to be interpreted as the resources necessary to produce information about a project and to monitor it. Effort is not contractible.

Projects satisfy the following assumptions:

A1. $2(e_H y^H + [1 - e_H]y^L) - h(e_H) > D$; that is, a project is a positive net present value investment when a high effort level is chosen, such that $e = e_H$.

A2. $2(e_L y^H + [1 - e_L]y^L) - h(e_L) < D$; that is, a project is a negative net present value investment when a low effort level is chosen, such that $e = e_L$.

A3. $2y^L - h(e) < F$, for $e \in (e_H, e_L)$; that is, default is certain if each project returns y^L (state $[y^L, y^L]$).

A4. $2y^H - h(e) > y^H + y^L - h(e) > F$, for $e \in (e_H, e_L)$; that is, default does not occur in the other states.

Assumption A1 ensures that investors will only invest if they are sure that the bank will make a high-effort choice. A project is not worth undertaking otherwise. Below, the incentive compatibility constraints ensure that banks will make the high-effort choice. Assumptions A3 and A4 are stated in terms of the face value of the debt, F, which is an endogenous variable. Nevertheless, the point of A3 and A4 is to determine the states of the world when default occurs. Default occurs only in the state (y^L, y^L). We will subsequently solve for the equilibrium F under this assumption and then verify that this value of F is consistent with assumptions A3 and A4 when F is eliminated through substitution; the assumptions can then be stated entirely in terms of primitives.

Corporations face a proportional bankruptcy cost, proportional to the realized output. In other words, larger firms have higher bankruptcy costs. This cost is borne by the creditors. Making the bankruptcy cost proportional, rather than lump sum, is both realistic and also simplifies the model, as will become clear subsequently. The bankruptcy cost is $c \in (0,1)$ per unit of output. A fixed bankruptcy cost could be added to this, though with binomial outcomes it has no additional content. The bankruptcy cost is subsequently discussed further.

On–balance sheet debt has a tax advantage. Off–balance sheet debt usually does not have this advantage. Here the cost of using off–balance sheet debt is the loss of the tax shield to the sponsoring firm. The sponsor may structure the SPV so that this cost does not exist. In that case, we would point to other costs. In general, some limit to how much can be financed off–balance sheet is needed for there to be an interior solution. However, recent whole-firm securitizations suggest that there may be few limits (see Pfister 2000).

12.4.2   Discussion of the Model

The model provides a role for the bank; it has the unique ability to find high-quality projects by making an effort. However, this value production is not observable to outside investors, since they cannot confirm the effort level chosen by the bank. This is essentially the usual model of bank activity. We assume that the bank issues debt to outside investors, and do not explain why debt is the security of choice. Any firm transferring assets off–balance sheet has created assets of a certain value, which may not be known to outside investors, so the "bank" need not literally be interpreted to exclude nonfinancial firms.

12.4.3   The Benchmark Case of No Securitization

We begin with the benchmark problem of the bank when there is no off–blaance securitization. In that case, the bank's problem is to choose F and $e \in (e_H, e_L)$ to maximize the expected value of its projects:

$$\text{max:} \quad V = e^2[2y^H - h(e) - (1 - \tau)F]$$
$$+ 2e(1 - e)[y^H + y^L - h(e) - (1 - \tau)F] \quad \text{(Problem [1])}$$

subject to: (1) $E(F) \geq D$ (Participation of Investors)

(2) $V(e = e_H; e_0 = e_H) \geq V(e = e_L; e_0 = e_H)$

(Incentive Compatibility)

The first constraint says that the expected pay-off to the investors who purchase the bank debt, $E(F)$, must be at least what was lent (D)—otherwise, the risk-neutral investors will not lend to the bank (since the interest rate is zero). The second constraint says that if investors lend to the bank believing that the bank will choose effort level e_H, where e_0 is the belief of the lenders regarding the bank's effort choice, then the bank behaves consistently with these beliefs, choosing $e = e_H$.

The optimization problem is written assuming that the bank defaults only in state (y^L, y^L), as assumed by A3 and A4.

Note that the Participation Constraint can be written as follows, since investors get only the remaining cash flows net of the bankruptcy and effort costs:

$$[e^2 + 2e(1 - e)]F + (1 - e)^2[2y^L(1 - c) - h(e)] \geq D$$

Suppose investors' beliefs about the bank's effort choice are $e = e_0$. Then the lowest promised repayment amount that lenders will accept, in order to lend, is

$$F_0 = \frac{D - (1 - e_0)^2[2y^L(1 - c) - h(e_0)]}{e_0(2 - e_0)}.$$

Substituting this into the bank's problem, the bank's problem is now to choose $e \in (e_H, e_L)$ to:

$$\max V = 2ey^H + 2e(1 - e)y^L - e(2 - e)h(e) - (1 - \tau)e(2 - e)$$

$$\times \left\{ \frac{D - (1 - e_0)^2[2y^L(1 - c) - h(e_0)]}{e_0(2 - e_0)} \right\}$$

subject to: (ii) $V(e = e_H; e_0 = e_H) \geq V(e = e_L; e_0 = e_H)$

(Incentive Compatibility)

Incentive compatibility requires that the bank's choice of $e \in (e_H, e_L)$ be the same as what the lenders believe it will be, namely e_0. Suppose that beliefs are consistent; that is, that $e = e_0 = e_H$. Then, indicating bank value by V^H, we have:

(1)
$$V^H = 2e_H y^H + 2e_H(1 - e_H)y^L - e_H(2 - e_H)h(e_H)$$
$$- (1 - \tau)\{D - (1 - e_H)^2[2y^L(1 - c) - h(e_H)]\}$$

If beliefs were inconsistent, that is, if lenders' beliefs were $e_0 = e_H$ but the bank chose $e = e_L$, then the value of the bank would be given by:

$$V(e = e_L; e_0 = e_H) = 2e_L y^H + 2e_L(1 - e_L)y^L - e_L(2 - e_L)h(e_L)$$

$$- (1 - \tau)e_L(2 - e_L)\left[\frac{D - (1 - e_H)^2[2y^L(1 - c) - h(e_H)]}{e_H(2 - e_H)} \right]$$

LEMMA 1: If

$$2y^H(e_H - e_L) + 2y^L[e_H(1 - e_H) - e_L(1 - e_L)] - h(e_H)e_H(2 - e_H) + h(e_L)e_L(2 - e_L)$$

$$- (1 - \tau)\{D - (1 - e_H)^2[2y^L(1 - c) - h(e_H)]\}\left[1 - \frac{e_L(2 - e_L)}{e_H(2 - e_H)}\right] > 0,$$

then at the optimum, investors believe $e_0 = e_H$ and the bank chooses $e = e_H$. The value of the bank is given by equation (1).

PROOF: The incentive compatibility constraint, $V(e = e_H; e_0 = e_H) \geq V(e = e_L; e_0 = e_H)$, is satisfied if the condition in the lemma holds. It remains to verify that the equilibrium F derived under A3 and A4 is consistent, that is, to state A3 and A4 in terms of primitives. That is left to the appendix.

In what follows we will refer to V^H as the value of the bank when there is no securitization. This will be the benchmark value against which the value of the bank with securitization will be compared.

12.4.4   Special Purpose Vehicles and Securitization

Now, suppose the bank sets up an SPV to finance one of the projects. One project will be financed on–balance sheet, and one will be financed off–balance sheet.[18] The SPV has no bankruptcy costs, as discussed previously, and its debt has no tax advantage. As before, the effort choice is made at the bank level and determines the qualities of both projects, though the outcomes are independent.[19] To be clear, the projects are first allocated to be on– or off–balance sheet, and then the bank makes its effort choice.

On–balance sheet, the bank will borrow $0.5D$, promising to repay F^B at the end of the period. Off–balance sheet, the SPV will borrow $0.5D$, promising to repay F^S at the end of the period.[20] The bank then has two assets on–balance sheet: its own project and an equity claim on the SPV—that is, if y is the realization of the SPV's project, then the bank's equity claim on the SPV at the end of the period is max($y - F^S$, 0).[21]

---

18. This assumption is made for simplicity. The model does not determine the scale of the SPV.

19. Note that no effort choice can be made by the SPV, as it is passive. If the effort choice could be made at that level, the entity would be a subsidiary of the bank, rather than an SPV.

20. For simplicity, other financing choices are assumed to not be available. While we do not model tranching, it is not inconsistent with the model to allow for additional motivations for securitization beyond those we consider, such as clientele effects (e.g., perhaps due to eligibility requirements of the Employee Retirement Income Security Act [ERISA]).

21. Strictly speaking there is an intermediate step, because the bank funds both projects initially on–balance sheet and then transfers one, in a true sale, to the SPV. We assume that the proceeds from selling the project to the SPV are used to pay down on–balance sheet debt. For simplicity, this step is omitted.

Assumptions analogous to A3 and A4 define the bankruptcy states:

A3a. $2y^L - h(e) < F^B + F^S$, for $e \in (e_H, e_L)$; that is, default of both the bank and the SPV occurs if the realized state of the world is (y^L, y^L).

A4a. $2y^H - h(e) > y^H + y^L - h(e) > F^B + F^S$, for $e \in (e_H, e_L)$; that is, there need not be default of either entity in the other states.

As before, assumptions A3a and A4a are stated in terms of F^B and F^S, endogenous variables. Assumption A3a determines the states of the world when default definitely will occur, namely, in state (y^L, y^L). Assumption A4a states that the two projects generate sufficient payoffs in the other states to avoid bankruptcy, though whether that is the outcome will depend on the relationship between the bank and the SPV. We will subsequently solve for the equilibrium F^B and F^S under these assumptions and then verify that those values of F^B and F^S are consistent with assumptions A3a and A4a when F is eliminated through substitution; the assumptions can then be stated entirely in terms of primitives.

We also now assume:

A5. $(1 - e_H)^2 y^L (1 - c) < 0.5D$; that is, the expected return for the bank, from the on–balance sheet project in the bankruptcy state (y^L, y^L), which occurs with probability $[1 - e_H]^2$, is insufficient to pay $0.5D$, the amount borrowed.

At the end of the period, by A3a and A4a, the possible outcomes are as follows, where the first element is the on–balance sheet project state realization and the second element is the off–balance sheet project state realization:

- (y^H, y^H): Both projects realize y^H, this occurs with probability e^2, $e \in (e_H, e_L)$. In this event, both on– and off–balance sheet debts can be repaid in full.
- (y^H, y^L): The on–balance sheet project realizes y^H, and the SPV's project is worth y^L. This occurs with probability $e(1 - e)$, $e \in (e_H, e_L)$. The bank is solvent, but the SPV defaults on its debt.
- (y^L, y^H): The off–balance sheet project realizes y^H, but the bank's project is worth y^L. This occurs with probability $e(1 - e)$, $e \in (e_H, e_L)$. The SPV can honor its debt, and so can the bank, because the bank is the equity holder of the SPV.
- (y^L, y^L): Both projects realize y^L; this occurs with probability $(1 - e)^2$, $e \in (e_H, e_L)$. Neither the bank nor the SPV can honor their debt.

Note that with or without securitization, the bank fails only if the realized state is (y^L, y^L). Consequently, with only two states a lump-sum bankruptcy cost would always be borne in this, and only this, state. This is due to the simplicity of the model. However, the proportional bankruptcy cost will be affected by securitization, since the on–balance sheet assets have been reduced to one project. In a more complicated model, with a continuous range of project realizations, a fixed bankruptcy cost could be borne as a function of the bank's leverage, which could be chosen endogenously. Here, the simplicity of the model dictates use of a proportional bankruptcy cost. But clearly this is not essential for the main point.

The bank's problem is to choose F^B, F^S, and $e \in (e_H, e_L)$ to:

$$\max V^S = e^2[2y^H - h(e) - (1 - \tau)F^B - F^S]$$
$$+ e(1 - e)[y^L + y^H - h(e) - (1 - \tau)F^B - F^S]$$
$$+ e(1 - e)[y^H - h(e) - (1 - \tau)F^B) \quad \text{(Problem [II])}$$

subject to (i) $E(F^B) \geq 0.5D$ (Participation of Investors in the Bank)

(ii) $E(F^S) \geq 0.5D$ (Participation of Investors in the SPV)

(iii) $V^S(e = e_H; e_0 = e_H) \geq V^S(e = e_L; e_0 = e_H)$

(Incentive Compatibility)

The solution method for Problem (II) is analogous to that for Problem (I), and so is left to the appendix, including a lemma (Lemma 2) that is analogous to Lemma 1. We refer to V^S as the resulting value of the bank with securitization. We now state:

PROPOSITION 1 *(Feasibility of Securitization): If* $(1 - e_H)^2 y^L c - \tau(0.5D - [1 - e_H]^2 y^L[1 - c]) > 0$, *then it is optimal for the bank to use the SPV to finance one project.*

PROOF: The condition in the proposition is a simplification of $V^S - V^H > 0$.

The factors that effect the profitability of securitization are taxes (τ), the bankruptcy cost (c), and risk, as measured by $(1 - e_H)^2$, that is, the chance of bankruptcy occurring. Taxes matter, to the extent that bankruptcy does not occur, because debt issued by the SPV is not tax advantaged (by assumption). The bankruptcy cost matters because expected bankruptcy costs are reduced to the extent that projects are financed off–balance sheet. This is due to the legal structure of the SPV. Finally, the risk of bankruptcy, $(1 - e_H)^2$, makes the chance of incurring the bankruptcy cost higher.

COROLLARY 1: *The profitability of off–balance sheet financing is increasing in the bankruptcy cost,* c, *decreasing in the tax rate,* τ, *and increasing in the riskiness of the project (i.e., the chance of bankruptcy),* $(1 - e_H)^2$.

PROOF: The derivatives of $V^S - V^H$ with respect to c, τ, and $(1 - e_H)^2$, respectively, are:

$$\frac{\partial(V^S - V^H)}{\partial \tau} = -[0.5D - (1 - e_H)^2 y^L (1 - c)] < 0, \text{ by A5.}$$

$$\frac{\partial(V^S - V^H)}{\partial c} = (1 - e_H)^2 y^L (1 - \tau) > 0.$$

$$\frac{\partial(V^S - V^H)}{\partial(1 - e_H)^2} = (1 - \tau)cy^L + \tau y^L > 0.$$

Corollary 1 identifies the basic drivers of SPV value, under the assumption that the projects are allocated to on– or off–balance sheet before their quality is known, that is, there is no adverse selection.

12.4.5   Securitization with Moral Hazard and Strategic Adverse Selection

Now, suppose that the bank makes an effort choice, that is, $e \in (e_H, e_L)$, but then *after* observing the realized project qualities, one of the projects is allocated to the SPV. Recall that project quality is not verifiable. This means that investors in the debt issued by the SPV face an additional problem. In addition to the moral hazard associated with the effort choice, there is an adverse selection problem with regard to which project is allocated to the SPV—the strategic adverse selection problem.

For this subsection we will also assume:

A6. $e_H^2 y^H + (1 - e_H^2)y^L < 0.5D$

The meaning of A6 will become clear shortly.

With the possibility of strategic adverse selection, at the end of the period the possible outcomes (following A3a and A4a) are as follows.

- (y^H, y^H): Both projects realize y^H; this occurs with probability e^2. The bank allocates one of the y^H projects to the SPV and retains the other one on–balance sheet. Both on– and off–balance sheet debts can be repaid in full.
- (y^H, y^L) and (y^L, y^H): The realization of projects is: one y^H and one y^L. This occurs with probability $2e(1-e)$. In both of these states of the world, the bank keeps the y^H project on–balance sheet and allocates the y^L project to the SPV. The bank is solvent, but the SPV defaults on its debt.
- (y^L, y^L): Both projects realize y^L; this occurs with probability $(1 - e)^2$. One of the y^L projects is allocated to the SPV and the bank retains the other on–balance sheet. Neither the bank nor the SPV can honor its debt.

In the previous subsection the SPV failed in two states of the world, the two situations where it realized y^L. Now, the SPV fails in three states of the world, due to the strategic adverse selection problem. Only if (y^H, y^H) is realized will the SPV be solvent. So, the expected income of the SPV is: $e^2 y^H + (2e[1 - e] + [1 - e]^2)y^L = e^2 y^H + (1 - e^2)y^L$. But this is less than $0.5D$, by A6. Consequently, no investor will lend to the SPV. Recognizing this problem, the bank would like to commit to not engage in strategic adverse selection; the bank would like to commit to allocate projects prior to the realization of the project outcome. But there is no way to do this, because project quality is not verifiable.

Imagine for a moment that the bank could commit to subsidize the SPV in the event that the SPV realized y^L and the bank realized y^H. Shortly, we will make clear what "subsidize" means. Let F^{SC} be the face value of the debt issued by the SPV under such commitment, and F^C the corresponding face value of the debt issued by the bank. Then at the end of the period, the possible outcomes would be as follows:

- (y^H, y^H): Both projects realize y^H; this occurs with probability e^2. Both on– and off–balance sheet debts can be repaid in full. The expected profit to the bank in this case is

$$e^2[2y^H - h(e) - (1 - \tau)F^C - F^{SC}].$$

- (y^H, y^L): The bank's project is worth y^H and the SPV's is worth y^L. This occurs with probability $e(1 - e)$. The bank is solvent and subsidizes the SPV, so that neither defaults on its debt. "Subsidize" means that the bank assumes responsibility for the debt of the SPV. The bank's expected profit in this state of the world is

$$e(1 - e)[y^H + y^L - h(e) - (1 - \tau)F^C - F^{SC}].$$

- (y^L, y^H): The bank's project is worth y^L and the SPV's is worth y^H. This occurs with probability $e(1 - e)$. The SPV is solvent. Without the return on its SPV equity the bank would be insolvent. But the SPV has done well, so that neither defaults on its debt. The expected profit in this case is the same as in the previous case, though the interpretation is different:

$$e(1 - e)[y^H + y^L - h(e) - (1 - \tau)F^C - F^{SC}].$$

- (y^L, y^L): Both projects realize y^L; this occurs with probability $(1 - e)^2$. Neither the bank nor the SPV can honor its debt. The bank earns zero.

With this commitment, the bank's problem is to choose F^C, F^{SC}, and $e \in (e_H, e_L)$ to

$$\max V^C = e^2[2y^H - h(e) - (1 - \tau)F^C - F^{SC}]$$
$$+ 2e(1 - e)[y^H + y^L - h(e) - (1 - \tau)F^C - F^{SC}] \quad \text{(Problem [III])}$$

subject to (i) $E(F^C) \geq 0.5D$ (Participation of Bank Investors)

(ii) $E(F^{SC}) \geq 0.5D$ (Participation of SPV Investors)

(iii) $V^C(e = e_H; e_0 = e_H) \geq V^C(e = e_L; e_0 = e_H)$

(Incentive Compatibility)

Constraints (i) and (ii) can be rewritten, respectively, as

$$e(2 - e)F^C + (1 - e)^2[y^L(1 - c) - h(e)] \geq 0.5D,$$

and

$$e(2 - e)F^{SC} + (1 - e)^2 y^L \geq 0.5D.$$

The solution to Problem (III) is contained in the appendix, including a lemma (Lemma 3) that is analogous to Lemma 1. We refer to V^C as the resulting value of the bank with commitment. We now state:

PROPOSITION 2 *(Equivalence of Problems II and III): If the bank can commit to subsidize the SPV, then the profitability of the bank is the same as it would be when projects were allocated between the bank and the SPV prior to their realizations, that is, when there was no strategic adverse selection.*

PROOF: It may be verified that $V^S = V^C$.

Intuitively, while the debt is repriced to reflect the subsidy from the bank in the state (y^H, y^L), there are no effects involving the bankruptcy cost or taxes. Consequently, the bank's value is the same as in Problem II, when projects were allocated between the bank and the SPV prior to their realizations.

Proposition 2 states that securitization would be feasible; that is, investors would lend to the SPV, and that would be profitable for the bank (under the conditions stated in Proposition 1), if it were possible to overcome the problem of strategic adverse selection by the bank committing to subsidize the SPV. However, accounting and regulatory rules prohibit such a commitment, even if it were possible. That is, a formal contract, which can be upheld in court and which is consistent with accounting and regulatory rules, effectively would not be consistent with the SPV being a QSPV, and hence the debt would not be off–balance sheet. The bankruptcy costs would not be minimized. We now turn to the issue of whether a commitment is implicitly possible in a repeated context.

12.4.6   The Repeated SPV Game: The Implicit Recourse Equilibrium

In any single period, the bank cannot securitize a project because lenders will not lend to the SPV due to the strategic adverse selection problem. We now consider an infinite repetition of the one-period problem, where for simplicity we assume that the bank has exactly \$E available every period to finance the two projects.[22] The one-shot-game outcome of no securitization can be infinitely repeated, so this is an equilibrium of the repeated game. However, the idea that repetition can expand the set of equilibria, when commitment is possible, is familiar from the work of Friedman (1971), Green and Porter (1984), and Rotemberg and Saloner (1986), among others. The usual context is oligopolistic competition, where the competing firms are incompletely informed about their rivals' decisions. The firms want to collude to maintain oligopolistic profits, but cannot formally commit to do so. Here the context is somewhat different. The sponsoring bank and the investors in the SPV collude in adopting a contractual mechanism that cannot be written down because of accounting and regulatory rules. In a sense the two parties are colluding against the accountants and regulators. We will call such an equilibrium an "Implicit Recourse Equilibrium."

For this section we will suppose that the interest rate, r, is positive and constant. This means that everywhere there was a "D" above, it must be replaced by $(1 + r)D$, as the risk-neutral investors require that they earn an expected rate of return of r.

The basic idea of repeating the SPV game is as follows. Suppose investors believe that the bank will subsidize the SPV in the state (y^H, y^L), when the SPV would otherwise default. That is, investors have priced the debt as F^C and F^{SC}, as previously given, and their beliefs are $e_0 = e_H$. Now, suppose that the state (y^H, y^L) occurs, that is, the state of the world where the bank is supposed to subsidize the SPV. The realized bank profit is supposed to be

$$y^H + y^L - h(e_H) - (1 - \tau)F^C - F^{SC}.$$

But, suppose the bank reneges and leaves the SPV bankrupt with $y^L - F^{SC} < 0$, that is, there is no subsidy. The SPV then defaults on its debt. In that case, on–balance sheet the bank realizes

$$y^H - h(e_H) - (1 - \tau)F^C.$$

So, the one-shot gain from reneging on the implicit contract is $F^{SC} - y^L > 0$. Since this is positive, the bank has an incentive to renege. But, in a repeated setting, investors can punish the bank by not investing in the bank's SPV in the future, say for N periods. If the bank cannot securitize again for N periods, it loses (from Proposition 1):

---

22. In other words, we assume that if the bank does well it pays a dividend such that E remains as the equity in the bank. If the bank does poorly, we assume that the bank can obtain more equity so that again there is E. Obviously, this omits some interesting dynamics about the bank's capital ratio and begs the question of the coexistence of outside equity and debt. These issues are beyond the scope of this paper.

$$\sum_{t=1}^{N} \delta^t (V^S - V^H) =$$

$$\sum_{t=1}^{N} \delta^t \{(1 - e_H)^2 y^L c - \tau c (1 - e_H)^2 y^L - \tau[0.5D - (1 - e_H)^2 y^L]\},$$

where δ is the discount rate. Obviously, the bank will not renege on subsidizing the SPV if the expected present value of the loss is greater than the one-shot gain to deviating. There are combinations of N and δ that will support the Implicit Recourse Equilibrium. While this is the intuition for Implicit Recourse Equilibrium, it clearly depends on the beliefs of the investors and the bank. There may be many such equilibria, with very complicated, history-dependent, punishment strategies.

The idea is for the investors in the SPV to enforce support when needed by the threat of refusing to invest in SPV debt in the future if the sponsoring firm deviates from the implicit contract. This means that there is a punishment period in which investors refuse to invest in SPV debt if the sponsor has not supported the SPV in the past. In general, strategies can be path dependent in complicated ways (see Abreu 1988). However, a simple approach is to restrict attention to punishments involving playing the no-SPV stage game equilibrium for some period of time, starting the period after a deviation has been detected. We adopt this approach and assume investor and bank beliefs are consistent with this.

For simplicity we will construct a simple example of an Implicit Recourse Equilibrium. Assume that all agents discount at the rate r, and consider the case where $N = \infty$. This corresponds to a punishment period of forever.[23] At the start of each period the game proceeds as follows:

1. The bank and the SPV offer debt in the capital markets to investors with face values of F^C and F^{SC}, respectively.
2. Investors choose which type of debt, and how much, to buy.

If investors purchase the SPV debt, then off–balance sheet financing proceeds. Otherwise, the bank finances both projects on–balance sheet.

At the end of a period, the state of the world is observed, but cannot be verified. If the state of the world is (y^H, y^L); that is, the on–balance sheet project returns y^H while the off–balance sheet project returns y^L, then the bank is supposed to subsidize the SPV, as previously described. At the start of any period, both the banks and investors know all the previous outcomes.

Consider the following trigger strategy based on investor and bank beliefs: if the bank ever does not subsidize the SPV when the state of the world is (y^H, y^L), then investors never again invest in the SPV, because they believe that the sponsor will not support it and hence the promised interest

---

23. We do not claim that this is the optimal punishment period.

rate, corresponding to F^{SC}, is too low. The bank believes that if it deviates investors will never again buy its SPV's debt in the market. Then a subgame perfect Nash equilibrium exists under certain conditions:

PROPOSITION 3 *(Existence of the Implicit Recourse Equilibrium): If there exists an interest rate, $0 \le r \le 1$, such that the following quadratic inequality is satisfied,*

$$0.5Dr^2 + r\{0.5D[1 - \tau e_H(2 - e_H)] + (1 - e_H)^2 h(e_H) + y^L B\}$$

$$- 0.5D \tau e_H(2 - e_H) + y^L A > 0$$

where $A \equiv [(1 - e_H)^2[c + \tau(1 - c)]e_H(2 - e_H) - \tau(1 - e_H)^2 ce_H(2 - e_H)\}$

and $B \equiv [(1 - e_H)^2(1 - c) - e_H(2 - e_H)]$,

then securitization is feasible and optimal for any bank that would choose securitization were it able to commit to the policy of subsidization.

PROOF: See appendix.

Obviously, other equilibria could exist. But, the point is that there can exist equilibria where the costs of bankruptcy are avoided by using off–balance sheet financing.

12.4.7   Summary and Empirical Implications

The conclusion of the previous analysis is that the value of SPVs lies in their ability to minimize expected bankruptcy costs—securitization arises to avoid bankruptcy costs. By financing the firm in pieces, control rights to the business decisions are separated from the financing decisions. The sponsor maintains control over the business while the financing is done via SPVs that are passive; that is, there are no control rights associated with the SPVs' assets. Bankruptcy is a process of transferring control rights over corporate assets. Off–balance sheet financing reduces the amount of assets that are subject to this expensive and lengthy process.

We have argued that the ability to finance off–balance sheet via the debt of SPVs is critically dependent on a relational, or implicit, contract between the SPV sponsor and investors. The relational contract depends upon repeated use of off–balance sheet financing. We showed that this repetition can lead to an equilibrium with implicit recourse. Such an equilibrium implements the outcome of the equilibrium with formal commitments (Problem III), were such contracts possible. The comparative static properties of the Implicit Recourse Equilibrium are based on the result that the equilibrium outcomes of the Implicit Recourse Equilibrium are the same as the commitment equilibrium.

The idea of a relational contract supporting the feasibility of SPVs leads to our first set of empirical tests; namely, that the trigger strategy can only provide intertemporal incentives for the sponsor insofar as the sponsor exists. If the sponsor is so risky that there is a chance the sponsor will fail and be unable to support the SPV, then investors will not purchase the SPV debt. We examine this idea by testing the hypothesis that investors, in pricing the debt of the SPV, care about the risk of the sponsor defaulting, above and beyond the risks of the SPV's assets.

The second hypothesis that we empirically investigate is suggested by Corollary 1. Because the Implicit Recourse Equilibrium implements the outcome with formal commitment, Corollary 1 also describes the repeated equilibrium with implicit recourse. Corollary 1 says that the profitability of off–balance sheet financing is increasing in the bankruptcy cost, c, and increasing in the riskiness of the project (i.e., the chance of bankruptcy), $(1 - e_H)$. In other words, riskier sponsors should securitize more, ceteris paribus. Bankruptcy costs are not observable, but the riskiness of the firm can be proxied for by its firm bond rating.

12.5   Data

The rest of the paper empirically examines these two hypotheses. Our analysis suggests that the risk of a sponsoring firm should, because of implicit recourse, affect the risk of the ABS that are issued by its SPVs. We measure the sponsor's risk by its bond rating, and focus on two ways that this risk might be manifested. As mentioned earlier, we first consider whether investors care about the strength of the sponsoring firm, above and beyond the characteristics of the ABS themselves. Second, we consider whether riskier firms are more likely to securitize in the first place. To these ends we utilize a number of datasets.

To investigate our first topic, investors' sensitivity to the sponsor's strength, we obtained from Moody's a unique dataset describing every credit card ABS issued between June 1988 and May 1990 that Moody's tracked. This covers essentially all credit card ABS through mid 1999. The dataset includes a detailed summary of the structure of each ABS, including the size and maturity of each ABS tranche. It summarizes the credit enhancements behind each tranche, such as the existence of any letters of credit, cash collateral accounts, and reserve accounts. Moody's also calculated the amount of direct subordination behind each A and B tranche.[24]

---

24. The amount of subordination behind the A note is calculated as (BalB + BalC)/(BalA + BalB + BalC), where BalX is the size (the balance) of tranche X when it exists. The dataset provided the current amount of subordination using current balances. For our following analysis, we want the original amount of subordination at the time of issuance. We were able to estimate this given the original balance sizes of the A and B notes, as well as an estimate of the size of any C note. The size of C notes is not directly publicly available, but we backed out their current size from the reported current amount of subordination behind the B notes. We used this to estimate the original amount of subordination behind the A and B notes.

These variables contain the information about the ABS structure that investors observed at the time of issuance. Further, the dataset includes some information about the asset collateral underlying each ABS, such as the age distribution of the credit card accounts. Also included is the month-by-month ex post performance of each note, in particular the excess spread and its components like the chargeoff rate. The following sample includes only the A and B tranches, that is, the tranches that were sold publicly.

Although it is difficult to find pricing information on credit card ABS, we obtained from Lehman Brothers a dataset containing the initial yields on a large subset of these bonds that were issued in 1997–1999, for both the A and B notes. We obtained similar data from *Asset Sales Reports* for bonds that were issued before 1997. We computed the initial spread as the initial yield minus one month London Interbank Offered Rate (LIBOR) at the time of issuance. We also collected Moody's ratings from Bloomberg for the sponsors of each ABS in the Moody's dataset, which are typically banks. We use the bank's senior unsecured bond rating at issuance.[25]

To investigate our second topic, an analysis of which banks securitize, we use the bank entity-level *Call Report* panel data that comes from the regulatory filings that banks file each quarter, from September 1991 to June 2000. Before 1996 we use only the third quarter (September) data, since credit card securitizations were reported only in the third quarter during that period. We also obtained from Moody's a large dataset of all of their ratings of banks' long-term senior obligations, including an identification (ID) variable that allowed us to match this data to the *Call Report* ID variables. Accordingly, our sample includes all the banks in the *Call Report* dataset for which we have a matching rating.[26] This yields a sample of almost 400 banks and over 5000 bank-quarters, which is large relative to the samples analyzed in previous related literature.

12.6   Empirical Tests: Are There Implicit Recourse Commitments?

In this section we analyze the determinants of the spread on the notes issued by the SPVs to the capital markets. Borgman and Flannery (1997) also analyze asset-backed security spreads, over the period 1990–1995. They find that credit card ABS require a lower market spread if the sponsoring firm is a bank or if the sponsor includes guarantees as a form of credit enhancement.

The unit of observation is a transaction, that is, a note issuance: either the A note or the B note. We examine the cross-sectional determinants of

---

25. We use the rating of the current owner of the ABS trust, accounting for any mergers and acquisitions.

26. Since small banks are less likely to be rated, matches are most common for the larger banks.

the spreads. The spreads provide us with investors' assessment of the risk factors behind each note. All the A notes were on issuance rated AAA by Moody's.[27] If these ratings are sufficient statistics for default, then the probability of default should be the same for all the A notes, and in the simplest case (e.g., if there is no implicit recourse) presumably investors would pay the same initial price for them. Even if there are differences across notes in the quality of the underlying assets or in other factors, the securitizations should be structured to offset these differences and yield the same probability of default. As discussed previously, to test for the existence of a relational contract allowing for recourse, we examine other factors affect the initial prices of the notes, in particular whether the strength of the sponsor matters, as estimated by its senior unsecured credit rating at the time of issuance. Specifically, we examine equations of the following form:

$$(2) \quad \text{Spread}_{i,j,k,t} = \beta_0'\text{Time}_t + \beta_1'\text{Structure}_i + \beta_2'\text{Assets}_i + \beta_3'\text{Trust}_j$$
$$+ \beta_4'\text{Rating}_{k,t} + \varepsilon_{i,j,k,t},$$

where $\text{Spread}_{i,j,k,t}$ is the initial spread (net of one month LIBOR) on note i from trust j and sponsor k at the time t of issuance. **Time** is a vector of year dummies that control for time-varying risk premia as well as all other macroeconomic factors, including the tremendous growth in the ABS market over the sample period. **Structure**$_i$ represents the structure of tranche i at the time of issuance, such as the degree of subordination and other credit enhancements supporting it, and **Assets**$_i$ represents the quality of the credit card assets underlying the tranche at that time. **Trust**$_j$ is a vector of trust dummies. $\text{Rating}_{k,t}$ is the senior unsecured bond rating of the sponsor k of the notes' trust at the time of issuance. The trust dummies control for all trust fixed effects. Since many sponsors have multiple trusts, the dummies also essentially control for sponsor fixed effects.[28] Given this, the ratings variable will essentially capture the effect of changes in a sponsor's rating over time.[29]

Our initial sample includes only the A notes, but later we add the B notes, with **Structure** then including an indicator for the B notes (Junior). Table 12.2 presents summary statistics for the key variables used in the analysis, for the sample of A notes. The sample runs from 1988–1999. Over that time the average A-note spread was just under 50 basis points (b.p.), with a relatively large standard deviation of 68 b.p. About half of the sponsors have

27. All but two of the B notes were initially rated A; the two exceptions were rated AA. By distinguishing the A and B notes, the analysis implicitly controls for any clientele effects.
28. Though a given trust can also have multiple owners over time, for example, after a merger or acquisition.
29. As evidenced by the significant results that follow, there is substantial within-trust variation in both the spreads and ratings over time, with over 30 percent of trusts exhibiting some change in rating over the sample period.

Table 12.2   Sponsor ratings and initial spreads on A notes: Summary statistics

	Mean	Standard deviation
Spread	0.48	0.68
RatingAA	0.25	0.44
RatingA	0.49	0.50
RatingB	0.26	0.44
LowSub	0.25	0.44
Maturity	5.70	2.25
SellersInt	6.38	1.21
FixedRt	0.35	0.48
I_CCA	0.43	0.50
I_LOC	0.03	0.17
I_RES	0.01	0.08
I_Other	0.02	0.15
Seasoned	0.43	0.50
Chargeoff	5.35	1.86

Notes: $N = 167$. The sample is that for A notes in table 12.3, column (5), averaging over 1988–99.

ratings of single A (RatingA) on their senior unsecured debt, with the rest being about equally likely to have ratings of AA (RatingAA) or ratings of Baa and Ba (RatingB).

12.6.1   Analysis of the A-Note Spreads

Table 12.3 shows the results for the A notes. Column (1) includes only the year dummies (omitting 1988[30]) and the sponsor ratings (as well as the trust fixed effects). Nonetheless, the adjusted R^2 is already relatively large. The year dummies are significant, with spreads peaking in the early 1990s, perhaps due to the recession. The sponsor ratings at the bottom of the table are of primary interest. Relative to the omitted AA-rated sponsors, the effects of riskier sponsor ratings are positive and monotonic. The coefficient on RatingB for the riskiest (Baa and Ba) sponsors is statistically significant. Thus investors do indeed require higher yields for bonds issued by the trusts of riskier sponsors. That is, even though the A notes all have the same bond ratings, the strength of the sponsor also matters, consistent with our model. This effect is also economically significant. The riskiest sponsors must pay an *additional* 46 b.p. on average, which is about the same size as the average A-note spread, and sizable relative to the standard deviation of spreads in table 12.2. This is a relatively strong result given the trust dummies, which control for all average and time-invariant effects. The variation in a sponsor's rating over time is sufficient to cause significant changes over time in the yields paid by its ABS.

30. Because of missing values in some of the covariates, some of the time dummies drop out of the regressions.

Table 12.3   Sponsor ratings and initial spreads on A notes

	(1)		(2)		(3)		(4)		(5)	
	Coef.	t	Coef.	t	Coef.	t	Coef.	t	Coef.	t
Yr89	-0.565	-0.92								
Yr90										
Yr91	0.915	2.79	1.263	2.13	0.339	0.73	1.360	2.82	0.671	1.34
Yr92	0.886	1.72								
Yr93	0.275	0.77	1.456	3.96	-0.804	-3.26	1.037	3.13	0.491	1.29
Yr94	-0.004	-0.01	0.069	0.24	-1.155	-4.81	0.216	0.85	0.034	0.11
Yr95	-0.771	-2.32	-0.150	-0.56	-1.091	-4.44	-0.137	-0.57	-0.409	-1.44
Yr96	-0.903	-2.78	-0.196	-0.74	-1.091	-4.44	-0.080	-0.34	-0.456	-1.70
Yr97	-0.819	-2.52	-0.132	-0.54	-1.126	-4.77	-0.106	-0.48	-0.519	-2.07
Yr98	-0.940	-2.84	-0.302	-1.33	-1.274	-5.44	-0.262	-1.26	-0.502	-2.27
Yr99	-0.659	-1.60			-1.019	-3.52				
LowSub			0.398	2.81	0.147	1.29	0.136	1.14	0.173	1.57
Maturity					0.050	3.20	0.049	3.10	0.039	2.56
SellersInt					-0.030	-0.39	-0.027	-0.33	0.004	0.06
FixedRt					0.713	8.67	0.722	8.09	0.726	9.05
I_CCA							-0.066	-0.39		
I_LOC							-0.107	-0.28		
I_RES							-0.228	-0.46		
I_Other							0.014	0.06		
Seasoned									-0.331	-2.92
Chargeoff									0.098	2.48
RatingA	0.235	1.29	0.266	1.49	0.324	2.31	0.321	2.25	0.363	2.60
RatingB	0.463	2.33	0.414	2.06	0.455	2.90	0.450	2.80	0.514	3.34
No. of observations	229		172		171		171		167	
Adjusted R^2	0.59		0.47		0.69		0.68		0.70	

Notes: The dependent variable is the initial spread on the A notes. Estimation is by ordinary least squares. The omitted year is 1988. The omitted rating (of the sponsor) is AA; Rating B signifies Baa and Ba ratings. All regressions include trust dummies. For variable definitions, see the text.

This result could be interpreted as suggesting that, even if the rating agencies place some weight on the risk of a sponsor in assessing the risk of their ABS notes, they do not do so fully. But the bond ratings are discretized, not continuous-valued, so there can be some differences in risk even among bonds with the same ratings. Also, investors' views of the risk might not completely coincide with the views of the ratings agencies. Hence we also directly control for the potential risk factors observable by investors. The next columns start by adding controls for the structure of the A notes. Of course, this structure is endogenous (but predetermined by the time of issuance) and should itself reflect the rating agencies' view of the notes' risk. Recall that the trust dummies already controlled for all time-invariant trust effects. These dummies are always jointly significant (unreported). For instance, some trusts might get locked into an older trust-structure technology that is considered riskier.

Column (2) explicitly controls for the amount of direct subordination behind each A note. LowSub is a dummy variable representing the quartile of notes with the smallest amount of subordination (i.e., the riskiest notes as measured by the relative size of their "buffer," ceteris paribus). It has a significant positive coefficient. Thus, the notes with less enhancement have to offer investors higher yields to compensate. Nonetheless, the coefficients on the ratings variables change very little.[31] Column (3) adds as a control the expected maturity of the notes (Maturity). It also adds the size of the sellers' interest (SellersInt) and a dummy variable for whether the note is fixed rate or not (FixedRt). The results indicate that longer maturity and fixed-rate notes pay significantly higher spreads.[32] Given these controls, the subordination measure (LowSub) becomes insignificant. This could mean that the size of the subordination might be a function of, among other things, maturity and whether the deal is fixed rate. Despite these effects, again the coefficients on the ratings do not change much. Column (4) controls for additional credit enhancement features, specifically dummy variables for the presence of a cash collateral account (I_CCA), a letter of credit (I_LOC), an internal reserve fund (I_RES), or other enhancement (I_Other). Given the other covariates, these additional enhancements are individually and jointly insignificant, though as indicated in table 12.2, only CCAs are frequently used. But the sponsor ratings remain significant.

Finally, column (5) includes measures of the riskiness of the underlying portfolio of credit card receivables. Again, these are variables that the rating agencies take into account when approving the bond structure with a given rating, so their effects could already have been taken into account. The variable "Seasoned" is an indicator for older portfolios, with an aver-

31. Since LowSub is often missing, the sample size is smaller than in column (1). Nonetheless our subsequent conclusions persist under the larger sample available if we do not control for LowSub.
32. Moody's (1995) noted a similar effect of maturity on spreads through 1993.

age account age above twenty-four months. Since older accounts tend to have lower probabilities of default, this should reflect a safer portfolio.[33] Chargeoff is the initial (ex post) chargeoff rate in the portfolio.[34] Both variables are statistically significant, with the intuitive signs. Riskier portfolios, whether unseasoned or with higher chargeoff rates, must pay higher spreads. While Chargeoff is an ex post chargeoff rate, the conclusions are the same on instrumenting for it using the balance-weighted average chargeoff rate in the trust from the month before the issuance of each note in the sample. Even with these controls, the sponsor's rating remains significant.[35]

12.6.2   Analysis of the A-Note and B-Note Spreads

Table 12.4 repeats this analysis using both the A and B notes. All regressions now include an indicator variable (Junior) for the B notes. In column (1), this indicator is significantly positive, as expected given the greater risk of the B notes. They must pay on average 29 b.p. more than the A notes. The coefficient on the riskiest sponsors, RatingB, remains significant and large at 42 b.p. Thus the extra yield that must be paid by risky sponsors is even larger than the extra yield that must be paid by B notes. In column (2), LowSub indicates the A notes with the lowest quartile of subordination, and LowSubJr indicates the B notes with the lowest quartile of subordination. The latter variable is significant (and drives out the direct effect of the Junior indicator), implying that B notes with less enhancement must pay higher yields. The rest of the analysis is analogous to that in table 12.3, and the conclusions are the same.

Overall, the estimated effects of the sponsors' ratings appear to be robust. Even controlling for the ABS structure and underlying assets, the ratings of the sponsors remain significant, both statistically and economically. This supports our theoretical conclusion that the strength of the sponsor

---

33. For an account-level analysis of the determinants of default probabilities, see Gross and Souleles (2002). For a portfolio-level analysis, see Musto and Souleles (2004). The original age data reflect the age of the accounts across the entire trust as of a given time. To estimate the age distribution of accounts underlying a given note at the time of issuance, we subtracted the time since closing. This assumes that the composition of the assets did not change too much between the time of closing and the time of reporting.

34. We take it from month three after issuance, since the excess spread components are sometimes missing in months one and two.

35. We also tried various extensions. For instance, we controlled for the importance of (on–balance sheet) credit card balances and other consumer receivables relative to total assets (CC/Assets). (When available from "Moody's Credit Opinions," CC/Assets is consumer receivables relative to assets. Otherwise, it is credit card balances relative to total assets from the *Call Report* data. In the latter case, in any given year CC/Assets is taken from the September quarter, and for 1988–90, it is taken from September 1991.) CC/Assets had a significant negative effect on spreads, but did not change the results regarding the ratings. This suggests that the latter effect might not reflect just a correlation between the assets in the trust and the assets on–balance sheet, since presumably the credit card assets in the trust are more highly correlated with the credit card assets on–balance sheet, compared to other on–balance sheet assets.

Table 12.4 Sponsor ratings and initial spreads on A and B notes

	(1)		(2)		(3)		(4)		(5)	
	Coef.	t	Coef.	t	Coef.	t	Coef.	t	Coef.	t
Yr89	-0.565	-0.92								
Yr90										
Yr91	0.940	3.22	0.112	0.25	0.570	1.62	0.525	1.49	0.831	2.14
Yr92	0.922	2.39	0.937	1.16	1.303	2.06	1.292	2.04	1.251	1.88
Yr93	0.341	1.08							0.318	1.06
Yr94	0.264	0.89	-0.628	-2.68	-0.183	-0.99	-0.247	-1.31	0.472	1.94
Yr95	-0.770	-2.59	-1.382	-5.99	-0.965	-5.23	-1.024	-5.43	-0.356	-1.60
Yr96	-0.893	-3.04	-1.503	-6.49	-0.875	-4.68	-0.952	-4.92	-0.329	-1.57
Yr97	-0.891	-3.04	-1.508	-6.69	-0.946	-5.24	-1.010	-5.38	-0.406	-2.06
Yr98	-0.996	-3.35	-1.637	-7.24	-1.113	-6.20	-1.192	-6.38	-0.395	-2.29
Yr99	-0.727	-2.12	-1.411	-4.97	-0.919	-4.13	-1.000	-4.04		
LowSub			0.203	1.77	0.010	0.11	-0.023	-0.25	0.010	0.11
LowSubJr			0.350	2.66	0.096	0.92	0.066	0.62	0.116	1.10
Maturity					0.044	3.98	0.042	3.75	0.038	3.44
SellersInt					-0.032	-0.53	-0.022	-0.35	-0.010	-0.17
FixedRt					0.858	13.22	0.878	13.05	0.889	13.70
I_CCA							-0.208	-1.65		
I_LOC							-0.250	-0.88		
I_RES							-0.271	-0.74		
I_Other							0.005	0.03		
Seasoned									-0.348	-3.86
Chargeoff									0.070	2.25
Junior	0.286	4.95	0.039	0.35	0.261	2.92	0.291	3.19	0.259	2.95
RatingA	0.154	1.15	0.215	1.56	0.285	2.66	0.274	2.54	0.331	3.01
RatingB	0.420	2.86	0.457	2.94	0.465	3.83	0.454	3.69	0.522	4.26
No. of observations	411		329		328		328		320	
Adjusted R^2	0.63		0.52		0.72		0.72		0.72	

Note: See table 12.3.

matters because of the possibility of implicit recourse commitment. To reiterate, the trigger strategy at the root of the relational contract concerning recourse requires that the sponsor exist—that is, has not defaulted. The results are consistent with the investors in the ABS markets pricing the risk that the sponsor disappears and cannot support its SPVs.

12.7   Empirical Tests: Which Firms Securitize?

In this section we turn to testing whether riskier firms securitize more than others. Since our model is, of course, highly stylized, we analyze more generally the determinants of securitization. We estimate equations of the following form, using the *Call Report* panel data from quarters 1991 (September)–2000 (June)

(3) $\text{Securitize}_{i,t} = \beta_0'\text{Time}_t + \beta_1'\text{Bank}_i + \beta_2'\mathbf{X}_{i,t} + \beta_3'\text{Rating}_{i,t} + u_{i,t},$

where $\text{Securitize}_{i,t}$ reflects the extent of credit card securitization by bank i at time t, measured in one of three ways: (1) We start with logit models of the probability that bank i has securitized, with dependent variable I_Sec being an indicator for whether the bank has any securitized credit card loans outstanding at time t (the extensive margin). (2) We also estimate Tobit models wherein the dependent variable Sec/Assets measures the amount of these securitizations normalized by total bank assets (including the securitized loans).[36] (3) To distinguish the intensive margin component in (2) from the extensive margin in (1), we also estimate conditional ordinary least square (OLS) models of Sec/Assets conditional on Sec/Assets > 0.[37]

The dependent variables again include a full set of time dummies, this time quarter dummies. $\mathbf{X}_{i,t}$ controls for various bank characteristics over time. In particular, it includes cubic polynomials in bank i's total assets, Assets$_{i,t}$, and in its share of credit card balances in total assets, CC/Assets$_{i,t}$. These control for scale effects, including costs that might arise in setting up and maintaining securitization trusts. We also control for the bank's capital ratio (equity capital divided by assets), CapRatio$_{i,t}$, again using a cubic polynomial.[38] Some specifications also control for all average and time-invariant bank effects (**Bank**$_i$), using the corresponding fixed effects esti-

---

36. We include the securitized loans in assets in the denominator for convenience in interpreting Sec/Assets as a fraction ≤ 1. The denominator can also be interpreted as managed assets, although we do not have information on the full extent of off–balance sheet assets (including non-credit card assets) under management. Our conclusions are similar on not including the securitized loans in the denominator.

37. We would also like to estimate selection models, but we lack persuasive omitted instruments.

38. We did not include the securitized loans (Sec) in assets in the denominator of CC/Assets or CapRatio, in order to avoid creating spurious correlations between these variables and the dependent variables (I_Sec and Sec/Assets). Calomiris and Mason (2004) discuss the relation between securitization and capital ratios.

Table 12.5   Sponsor ratings and the propensity to securitize: Summary statistics

	1991–2000		2000	
	Mean	Standard deviation	Mean	Standard deviation
I_Sec	0.113	0.317	0.146	0.317
Sec/Assets	0.033	0.124	0.041	0.124
RatingAA	0.462	0.499	0.474	0.499
RatingA	0.446	0.497	0.397	0.497
RatingB	0.092	0.289	0.129	0.289
Assets (mil $)	16.0	39.1	25.4	39.1
CC/Assets	0.050	0.178	0.038	0.178
CapRatio	0.086	0.036	0.086	0.034
No. of observations	5,012		363	

Notes: The first sample is that for table 12.6, columns (1) and (2), averaging over Call Report Data quarters September 1991–June 2000. The second sample averages over only March 2000 and June 2000. See table 12.6 and text for variable definitions.

mator. $Rating_{i,t}$ is the Moody's rating of a bank's long-term senior obligations. Given the bank effects, the ratings variable will capture only within-bank variation—that is, the effect of changes in a bank's rating over time on its propensity to securitize.[39]

Table 12.5 presents summary statistics for the key variables, for the entire sample period 1991–2000. To highlight the changes in the credit card ABS market over time, the second panel shows the same statistics for the end of the sample period (the first half of 2000). Comparing the panels shows the large growth in the market over the period. The fraction of banks that securitized (I_Sec) increased from about 8 percent in the early- to mid-1990s to 15 percent at the end of the sample period, averaging about 11 percent overall during the period. The magnitude of securitizations relative to assets (Sec/Assets) increased from about 1.6 percent to 4.1 percent over the sample period, averaging 3.3 percent. The average bank rating declined over the sample period, though this happened for both the banks that securitized and those that did not.

Further, at any given time there is substantial cross-sectional variation across banks in the incidence and amount of securitization and in their ratings. The raw data suggest potential scale effects, with the big securitizers often being the bigger banks. These include highly rated securitizers, such

39. The sample drops the few bank observations (about 10 banks) rated C and single B. Most of these were small banks in the early 1990s that did not securitize (only one of these banks securitized). As a result, they tended to be automatically dropped from the fixed-effects estimation (or otherwise, their effect was imprecisely estimated due to their small sample size).

as Citibank NV with an AA rating and Sec/Assets averaging about 71 percent. By contrast firms like Advanta (Sec/Assets = 70 percent), Capital One (= 57 percent), and Colonial (= 65 percent) have lower ratings (RatingB). Given the potential problem of unobserved heterogeneity, our fixed-effects estimators forego exploiting the purely cross-sectional average difference across banks; instead they set a high standard by relying on the more limited, but still substantial, within-bank variation over time in the incidence and amount of securitization and in the ratings. For instance, many banks were downgraded or upgraded at various times. Also, some banks securitized in only a few years (perhaps just trying it out), whereas others securitized frequently but in varying amounts over time.

The main results are in table 12.6. Column (1) begins with a logit model of the probability of securitizing (I_Sec), without bank effects. The effects of total assets (Assets), the importance of credit card assets (CC/Assets), and the capital ratio (CapRatio) are each jointly significant. Given the other covariates, in this specification the probability of securitizing is not monotonic in Assets; after initially increasing with Assets, it later declines. The probability of securitizing generally increases with CC/Assets (though declines a bit as CC/Assets gets very large). This could mean that having a large portfolio of credit cards provides economies of scale in securitizing. Also, the probability of securitizing is not monotonic in CapRatio (but increases for large CapRatio).

Of primary interest, listed at the bottom of the table, in this first specification the banks' ratings have a statistically significant, though nonmonotonic, effect. Relative to the omitted AA ratings, the middle (RatingA) banks are somewhat less likely to securitize. Nonetheless, the riskiest (RatingB) are indeed much more likely to securitize.

Column (2) estimates a Tobit model of the amount of securitization (Sec/Assets). The conclusions are similar to those in the previous column. In both of these specifications, and those that follow, the pseudo and adjusted R^2 statistics are relatively large.

The remaining columns control for bank fixed effects. Column (3) uses the fixed effects logit estimator. Note that as a result the sample size significantly declines, since this estimator drops banks for which I_Sec does not vary over time. Now the effect of Assets is monotonically increasing, though CC/Assets is less monotonic and CapRatio becomes insignificant. More importantly, both RatingA and RatingB have significant positive effects, with a larger effect for the latter. Thus these results suggest that the probability of securitizing does indeed increase monotonically with banks' riskiness, consistent with our model. Column (4) focuses instead on the intensive margin, estimating a conditional OLS model of the fraction of securitized assets conditional on Sec/Assets > 0. CapRatio now has a monotonically increasing effect, though Assets has a negative effect on the

Table 12.6   **Sponsor ratings and the use of securitization**

	(1)		(2)		(3)		(4)	
	Coef.	Standard error	Coef.	Standard error	Coef.	Standard error	Coef.	Standard error
Assets	0.031	0.004**	0.006	0.001**	0.235	0.039**	-0.006	0.001**
Assets2	-1.3E-04	2.5E-05**	-2.8E-05	4.7E-06**	-1.3E-03	2.7E-04**	2.7E-05	6.3E-06**
Assets3	1.4E-07	3.5E-08**	3.1E-08	6.7E-09**	2.4E-06	5.4E-07**	-4.1E-08	1.2E-08**
CC/Assets	5.092	2.393**	0.891	0.411**	53.172	11.598**	0.095	0.203
CC/Assets2	7.580	7.006	2.730	1.152**	-110.737	29.739**	0.736	0.507
CC/Assets3	-9.369	5.049*	-3.037	0.811**	61.963	19.573**	-0.926	0.338**
CapRatio	21.53	7.46**	5.46	1.35**	18.82	31.39	2.99	1.39**
CapRatio2	-91.93	36.87**	-19.46	6.79**	-142.06	133.26	-10.94	8.73
CapRatio3	77.47	44.05*	14.64	8.77*	137.38	125.64	14.21	16.16
RatingA	-0.552	0.120**	-0.103	0.020**	3.376	0.703**	0.009	0.014
RatingB	0.934	0.153**	0.220	0.027**	5.442	1.441**	0.034	0.018*
Bank effects?	no		no		yes		yes	
No. of observations	5,012		5,012		730		568	
Pseudo Adjusted R^2	0.23		0.34				0.95	
Log-likelihood	-1,369.0		-1,083.5		-195.2			

Notes: In columns (1) and (3), the dependent variable is the indicator I_Sec for whether the firm is currently securitizing (i.e., whether it has any securitized credit card loans currently outstanding). In column (2), it is the amount securitized normalized by assets (including the securitized loans), Sec/Assets. Column (3) uses the fixed effects logit estimator. In column (4), the dependent variable is Sec/Assets conditional on Sec/Assets > 0. CC/Assets is credit card balances divided by assets. CapRatio is equity capital divided by assets. The omitted firm rating is AA. The sample includes the September 1991–June 2000 Call Report Data, and all specifications include a complete set of quarter dummies.

intensive margin, and CC/Assets is not monotonic. While RatingA is positive but insignificant, RatingB has a larger positive coefficient, significant at the 6 percent level. Relative to banks with AA ratings, those with B ratings have about a 3.4 percentage point (p.p.) larger securitization fraction, on average. This is an economically significant effect, given that it is comparable in magnitude to the average Sec/Assets fraction of about 3.3 p.p.

Overall, we conclude that there is some evidence that riskier firms are more likely to securitize—consistent with our model—though the effect is not always monotonic, depending on the specification. The effects of Assets, CC/Assets, and CapRatio are more sensitive to the specification.[40]

12.7.1 Summary

The empirical results are consistent with the proposed theory, namely that an implicit contractual relationship between SPV sponsors and capital markets investors reduces bankruptcy costs. Consistent with the prediction that in the Implicit Recourse Equilibrium investors would price the risk of the sponsor defaulting, and hence being unable to subsidize the SPV, we found that the risk of the sponsor (as measured by the sponsor's bond rating) was consistently significant. The prediction of the model that firms with high expected bankruptcy costs would be the largest users of off–balance sheet financing was also generally confirmed.

12.8   Conclusion

Off–balance sheet financing is a pervasive phenomenon. It allows sponsoring firms to finance themselves by separating control rights over assets from financing. The operating entity, that is, the sponsoring firm, maintains control rights over the assets that generate cash flows. The assets (projects) can be financed by selling the cash flows to an SPV that has no need for control rights, because the cash flows have already been contracted for. We have argued that this arrangement is efficient because there is no need to absorb dead-weight bankruptcy costs with respect to cash flows that have already been contracted for. Off–balance sheet financing is about financing new projects by using cash flows promised under prior contracts as collateral. We showed that the efficient use of off–balance sheet financing is facilitated by an implicit arrangement, or contractual relations, between sponsoring firms and investors. The empirical tests, uti-

---

40. We also tried various extensions. For instance, to see whether the ratings in turn might reflect the amount of securitization, we tried instrumenting for the ratings using lagged ratings. However, it is not clear how long a lag would be best. At the extreme, we used the ratings from June 1991, the quarter before the sample period starts. Given how small the credit card ABS market was at the time, it is unlikely that those ratings were significantly affected by securitization. The results were generally insignificant. This is not surprising, however, given the smaller sample size (since the 1991 ratings are not always available) and reduced amount of variation.

lizing credit card asset-backed securitization as a testing ground, confirmed this interpretation of the SPV phenomenon.

Appendix

Proofs

Lemma 1 Completion

It remains to verify that the equilibrium F derived under assumptions A3 and A4 is consistent. That is, we now restate assumptions A3 and A4 in terms of primitives. Recall A3 was stated as: $2y^L - h(e) < F$. The equilibrium F is given by

$$F = \frac{D - (1 - e_H)^2[2y^L(1 - c) - h(e_H)]}{e_H(2 - e_H)}.$$

Substituting the expression for F into A3 and simplifying gives

$$2y^L[1 - c(1 - e_H)^2] - h(e_H) < D,$$

which is A3 stated in terms of primitives and consistent with the equilibrium.

Recall A4 was stated as: $2y^H - h(e) > y^H + y^L - h(e) > F$. Substitute the equilibrium value of F into $y^H + y^L - h(e) > F$, and simplify to obtain

$$(e_H - 1)^2 y^L(1 - 2c) - h(e_H) > D.$$

Solution to Problem (II)

Note that constraint (i) of Problem (II) in the main text can be written as

$$e(2 - e)F^B + (1 - e)^2[y^L(1 - c) - h(e)] \geq 0.5D.$$

Similarly, constraint (ii) of Problem (II) can be written as

$$eF^S + (1 - e)y^L \geq 0.5D.$$

As before, suppose lenders' beliefs are e_0. Then investors in the bank and SPV, respectively, will participate if the promised repayments are at least

$$F_0^B = \frac{0.5D - (1 - e_0)^2[y^L(1 - c) - h(e_0)]}{e_0(2 - e_0)},$$

and

$$F_0^S = \frac{0.5D - (1 - e_0)y^L}{e_0}.$$

Substitute these into the bank's problem. Then the bank's problem is to choose $e \in (e_H, e_L)$ to

$$\max V^S = 2ey^H + e(1 - e)y^L - e(2 - e)h(e) - (1 - \tau)e(2 - e)$$

$$\times \left\{ \frac{0.5D - (1 - e_0)^2[y^L(1 - c) - h(e_0)]}{e_0(2 - e_0)} \right\} - e \left[\frac{0.5D - (1 - e_0)y^L}{e_0} \right]$$

subject to (iii) $V^S(e = e_H; e_0 = e_H) \geq V^S(e = e_L; e_0 = e_H)$

(Incentive Compatibility).

Suppose that beliefs are consistent, that is, that $e = e_0 = e_H$. Then

(4)
$$V^S = 2e_H y^H + e_H(1 - e_H)y^L - e_H(2 - e_H)h(e_H)$$
$$- (1 - \tau)\{0.5D - (1 - e_H)^2[y^L(1 - c) - h(e_H)]\}$$
$$- [0.5D - (1 - e_H)y^L].$$

LEMMA 2: *If*

$$2y^H(e_H - e_L) + y^L[e_H(1 - e_H) - e_L(1 - e_L)] - h(e_H)e_H(2 - e_H)$$
$$+ h(e_L)e_L(2 - e_L) - (1 - \tau)\{0.5D - (1 - e_H)^2[y^L(1 - c) - h(e_H)]\}$$

$$\times \left[1 - \frac{e_L(2 - e_L)}{e_H(2 - e_H)} \right] > 0,$$

then at the optimum, lenders believe $e_0 = e_H$ and the bank chooses $e = e_H$. The value of the bank V^S is given by equation (4).

PROOF: The incentive compatibility constraint, $V^S(e = e_H; e_0 = e_H) \geq V^S(e = e_L; e_0 = e_H)$, is satisfied if the condition in the lemma holds. It remains to verify that the equilibrium F^B and F^S derived under A3a and A4a are consistent, that is, to state A3a and A4a in terms of primitives. Recall A3a: $2y^L - h(e) < F^B + F^S$. The equilibrium F^B and F^S are given by:

$$F^B = \frac{0.5D - (1 - e_H)^2[y^L(1 - c) - h(e_H)]}{e_H(2 - e_H)},$$

and

$$F^S = \frac{0.5D - (1 - e_H)y^L}{e_H}.$$

Substituting the expression for F^B and F^S into A3a and simplifying gives

$$y^L(3 - e_H) - h(e_H) + c(1 - e_H)^2 y^L < 0.5D(3 - e_H),$$

which is A3a stated in terms of primitives and consistent with the equilibrium.

Recall A4a: $2y^H - h(e) > y^H + y^L - h(e) > F^B + F^S$. Substitute the equilibrium values of F^B and F^S into $y^H + y^L - h(e) > F$, and simplify to obtain

$$y^H e_H(2 - e_H) + y^L(3 - 3e_H + e_H^2) - h(e_H) - cy^L(1 - e_H)^2 > 0.5D(3 - e_H),$$

which is A4a stated in terms of primitives and consistent with the equilibrium.

Solution to Problem (III)

In solving Problem (III) we proceed as before and suppose lenders' beliefs are e_0. Then lenders will participate in lending to the bank and the SPV, respectively, if the promised repayments are at least

$$F_0^C = \frac{0.5D - (1 - e_0)^2[y^L(1 - c) - h(e_0)]}{e_0(2 - e_0)}$$

and

$$F_0^{SC} = \frac{0.5D - (1 - e_0)^2 y^L}{e_0(2 - e_0)}.$$

Suppose that beliefs are consistent, that is, $e = e_0 = e_H$. Then

(5)
$$V^C = 2e_H y^H + 2e_H(1 - e_H)y^L - e_H(2 - e_H)h(e_H)$$
$$- (1 - \tau)\{0.5D - (1 - e_H)^2[y^L(1 - c) - h(e_H)]\}$$
$$- [0.5D - (1 - e_H)^2 y^L]$$

LEMMA 3: *If*

$$2y^H(e_H - e_L) + 2y^L[e_H(1 - e_H) - e_L(1 - e_L)] - h(e_H)e_H(2 - e_H) + h(e_L)e_L(2 - e_L)$$

$$- (1 - \tau)\{0.5D - (1 - e_H)^2[y^L(1 - c) - h(e_H)]\}\left[1 - \frac{e_L(2 - e_L)}{e_H(2 - e_H)}\right]$$

$$- [0.5D - (1 - e_H)^2 y^L]\left[1 - \frac{e_L(2 - e_L)}{e_H(2 - e_H)}\right] > 0,$$

then at the optimum, lenders believe $e_0 = e_H$ and the bank chooses $e = e_H$. The value of the bank is given by equation (5).

PROOF: The incentive compatibility constraint, $V^C(e = e_H; e_0 = e_H) \geq V^C(e = e_L; e_0 = e_H)$, is satisfied if the condition in the lemma holds.

Proof of Proposition 3

Consider a bank that would choose securitization were it able to commit to subsidize its SPV in the state (y^H, y^L), as in Problem (III). Also, consider a date at which the bank has always subsidized its SPV in the past. Over the next period the bank is worth V^C if it securitizes one project off–balance sheet and retains the other on–balance sheet. If both projects are financed on–balance sheet, the bank is worth V^H. By Propositions 1 and 2, $V^C > V^H$. The present value of this difference is the benefit to the bank of being able to utilize off–balance sheet financing, assuming that it continues to subsidize its SPV in the state (y^H, y^L). Over the infinite horizon this annuity value is: $(V^C - V^H)/r$. (Recall that agents discount at rate r.)

At the end of the period, suppose that the state of the world is, in fact, (y^H, y^L). Consider a one-shot deviation by the bank. That is, the bank decides not to subsidize the SPV, when investors expect the bank to subsidize it. From the expressions given above, the benefit to the bank of such a deviation is

$$y^H - h(e_H) - (1 - \tau)F^C > y^H + y^L - h(e_H) - (1 - c)F^C - F^{SC}$$

which reduces to: $F^{SC} - y^L$.

To decide whether to deviate or not the bank compares the costs and benefits of deviation and chooses to subsidize the SPV as long as

$$\frac{(V^C - V^H)}{r} > F^{SC} - y^L.$$

Substituting in this equation for V^C, V^H, and F^{SC} and simplifying gives the quadratic inequality in the proposition.

References

Abreu, Dilip. 1988. On the theory of infinitely repeated games with discounting. *Econometrica* 56:383–96.

American Law Institute. 2003. *Restatement of the Law Third, Trusts.* Volumes 1 and 2. St. Paul, MN: American Law Institute.

Ashman, Ian. 2000. Using Cayman Islands special purpose vehicles. *International Financial Law Review* (April): 32–34.

Baker, George, Robert Gibbons, and Kevin Murphy. 2002. Relational contracts and the theory of the firm. *Quarterly Journal of Economics* 117:39–83.

Beatty, Anne, Philip Berger, and Joseph Magliolo. 1995. Motives for forming research and development financing organizations. *Journal of Accounting and Economics* 19:411–42.

Borgman, Richard, and Mark Flannery. 1997. Loan securitization and agency: The value of originator-provided credit enhancement. University of Florida, School of Business. Working Paper.

Calomiris, Charles, and Joseph Mason. 2004. Credit card securitization and regulatory arbitrage. *Journal of Financial Services Research* 26:5–28.

Croke, Jim. 2003. New developments in asset-backed commercial paper. Unpublished Manuscript, Cadwalader, Wickersham, and Taft.

Elmer, Peter. 1999. Conduits: Their structure and risk. *FDIC Banking Review* 12:27–40.

Fitch IBCA. 1999. Implications of securitization for finance companies. Financial Services Special Report. November.

Fitch IBCA. 2001. Asset-backed commercial paper explained. Structured Finance Special Report. November.

Friedman, James W. 1971. A non-cooperative equilibrium for supergames. *Review of Economic Studies* 38:1–12.

Gorton, Gary, and George Pennacchi. 1989. Are loan sales really off-balance sheet? *Journal of Accounting, Auditing and Finance* 4 (2): 125–45.

———. 1995. Banks and loan sales: Marketing non-marketable assets. *Journal of Monetary Economics* 35 (3): 389–411.

Gorton, Gary, and Andrew Winton. 2003. Financial intermediation. In *The Handbook of the Economics of Finance: Corporate Finance,* ed. George Constantinides, Milton Harris, and René Stulz, 431–552. Elsevier Science.

Green, Edward, and Robert H. Porter. 1984. Noncooperative collusion under imperfect price information. *Econometrica* 52:87–100.

Gross, David, and Nicholas S. Souleles. 2002. An empirical analysis of personal bankruptcy and delinquency. *Review of Financial Studies* 15 (1): 319–47.

Henry, David, Heather Timmons, Steve Rosenbush, and Michael Arndt. 2002. Who else is hiding debt? *Business Week* (January 28): 36–37.

Higgins, Eric, and Joseph Mason. 2004. What is the value of recourse to asset backed securities? A study of credit card bank ABS rescues. *Journal of Banking and Finance* 28:857–74.

Hodge, J. B. 1996. The use of synthetic leases to finance build-to-suit transactions. *Real Estate Finance Journal* 11:17–21.

———. 1998. The synthetic lease: Off-balance-sheet financing of the acquisition of real property. *Real Estate Finance Journal* 14:159–76.

Humphreys, Thomas, and R. M. Kreistman. 1995. *Mortgage-backed securities including REMICs and other investment vehicles.* New York: Little, Brown.

Johnson, Kathleen. 2002. Consumer loan securitization. In *The Impact of Public Policy on Consumer Credit,* ed. T. A. Durkin and M. E. Staten, 287–306.

Kendall, Leon T., and Michael J. Fishman. 1996. *A primer on securitization.* Cambridge, MA: MIT Press.

Klee, Kenneth, and Brendt Butler. 2002. Asset-backed securitization, special purpose vehicles and other securitization issues. *Uniform Commercial Code Law Journal* 35:23–67.

Kramer, Andrea. 2003. *Financial products: Taxation, regulation and design.* New York: Aspen.

Langbein, John H. 1997. The secret life of the trust: The trust as an instrument of commerce. *Yale Law Journal* 107:165–89.

Lim, Steve, Steve Mann, and Vassil Mihov. 2003. Market evaluation of off-balance sheet financing: You can run but you can't hide. Texas Christian University. Working Paper.

Mills, Lillian, and Kaye Newberry. 2004. Firms' off-balance sheet financing: Evidence from their book-tax reporting differences. University of Arizona. Working Paper.

Moody's Investors Service. 1993. Asset-backed commercial paper: Understanding the risks. Special report. April.

———. 1994. The 'C' tranches of credit card-backed securities: Credit risks for investors vary. Special report. November.

———. 1995. Spread thin: An empirical investigation of yields on credit card asset-backed securities. Special report. May.

————. 1997a. Alternative financial ratios for the effects of securitization. In Moody's perspective 1987–2002: Securitization and its effect on the credit strength of companies. Special comments. September.

————. 1997b. The costs and benefits of supporting 'troubled' asset-backed securities: Has the balance shifted? In Moody's perspective 1987–2002: Securitization and its effect on the credit strength of companies. Special comments. January.

————. 2002. Bullet proof structures revisited: Bankruptcies and a market hangover test securitizations' mettle. Special report. August.

————. 2003. Securitization in new markets: Moody's perspective: Europe, Africa and the Middle East. International Structured Finance, Special report. May.

Musto, David, and Nicholas S. Souleles. 2006. A portfolio view of consumer credit. *Journal of Monetary Economics* 53:59–84.

Office of the Comptroller of the Currency, Federal Deposit Insurance Corporation, Board of Governors of the Federal Reserve System, and Office of Thrift Supervision. 2002. Interagency guidance on implicit recourse in asset securitizations. Washington, DC: OCC.

Peaslee, J., and D. Nirenberg. 2001. *Federal income taxation of securitization transactions,* 3rd ed. New Hope, PA: Frank J. Fabozzi Associates.

Pfister, Benedicte. 2000. Whole business securitizations: A unique opportunity for UK assets. Moody's Investors Service: International structured finance special report. October.

Rotemberg, Julio, and Garth Saloner. 1986. A supergame-theoretic model of price wars during booms. *American Economic Review* 76:390–407.

Schwarcz, Steven. 2003a. Commercial trusts as business organizations: Unraveling the mystery. *The Business Lawyer* 58 (February): 559–85.

————. 2003b. *Structured finance.* 3rd ed. New York: Practicing Law Institute.

Shakespeare, Catherine. 2001. Accounting for asset securitizations: Complex fair values and earnings management. University of Michigan, School of Business. Working Paper.

————. 2003. Do managers use securitization volume and fair value estimates to hit earnings targets? University of Michigan, School of Business. Working Paper.

Shevlin, Terrence. 1987. Taxes and off-balance sheet financing: Research and development limited partnerships. *The Accounting Review* 52:480–509.

Sitkoff, Robert H. 2003. Trust law, corporate law, and capital market efficiency. University of Michigan Law School, John M. Olin Center for Law and Economics. Working Paper no. 20.

Standard and Poor's. n.d. *Structured finance: Credit card criteria.* New York: Standard and Poor's.

Standard and Poor's. 2002. *U.S. legal criteria for "recycled" special purpose entities.* New York: Standard and Poor's.

Weidner, Donald. 2000. Synthetic leases: Structure finance, financial accounting and tax ownership. Florida State University, College of Law. Working Paper no. 06.

Comment   Peter Tufano

Gorton and Souleles' chapter on "Special Purpose Vehicles and Securitization" sheds light on an important element of the financial services world and highlights the gap between risk transfer on paper and in practice.

As the chapter makes clear, securitization is an important phenomenon. The authors report that nonmortgage securitizations had liabilities of almost $1.8 trillion in early 2004, with underlying assets including auto loans, credit card loans, home equity lines, and collateralized bond obligation/collateralized debt obligation (CBO/CDO) structures, among others. In addition, asset-backed commercial paper is perhaps another $0.6 trillion. The Federal Reserve Flow of Funds data provides even larger estimates. Liabilities of agency- and government-sponsored entity pools totaled over $3.5 billion in Q12004, and other asset-backed liabilities added another $2.5 trillion. (Federal Reserve Board, 2005, pp. 78–79). By any measure, it is apparent that securitization, special purpose vehicles (SPVs), and asset-backed financing are a material part of the financial world. To give a sense of scale for these numbers, total on–balance sheet commercial banking liabilities (including all deposits) were about $8 trillion.

The chapter has three related and useful sections. The first section provides a readable and concise introduction to securitization and SPVs. While there are many legal treatises on this topic, this chapter provides an efficient summary for novices, touching upon the legal forms of SPVs, accounting rules, treatment under bankruptcy, tax provisions, and credit enhancement. The authors go on to describe securitization, providing an introduction to trusts, the concept of seller's interest, excess spreads, and early amortization. While this section is extremely valuable, there may have been a missed opportunity to sharpen the piece by helping the reader understand key economic dimensions along which various securitization vehicles differ. For example, pools vary depending on whether there is a single contributor of assets or multiple contributors to the pool; whether the assets in the pool are relatively standard versus less well understood; or whether the pool is marketed to a handful of well-informed investors versus sold broadly in the market. These functional dimensions could influence the propensity of the sponsor to bail out an SPV that becomes insolvent.

The second section of the paper provides a model for the existence of SPVs. The ultimate version of the model recognizes that the sponsor (the bank) can affect the quality of the assets after the investor buys securities issued by the SPV. This corresponds to the situation in which a credit card issuer essentially "reloads" the receivables in an asset-backed credit card securitization routinely. There might be incentives for the bank to stuff low-quality assets into the pool or to expend less effort, both of which affect the quality of on–balance sheet and off–balance sheet projects.

The model produces a variety of insights. At one level, it advances one explanation why banks would choose to securitize in the first place. The costs of securitization are the cost of setting up the SPV and the loss of tax advantages to debt, because debt issued by the SPV does not generate tax benefits to the sponsor. The benefit of securitization is a reduction in bankruptcy costs, because the SPV is bankruptcy remote. These costs are proportional to the value of the assets of the bankrupt firm (or SPV). (If the costs of distress were related to the type of asset contributed to the pool, this might produce different results. This might be the case if the sponsor were to select assets for inclusion in the pool based on the extent to which they might deteriorate in value in financial distress.) Since the SPV cannot go bankrupt, financing in this way reduces the costs of financial distress and in turn reduces the cost of debt financing.

While the reduction of financial distress may be one reason why firms choose to securitize, it may not be the only—or most important—rationale for the practice. Securitization and SPVs can be used to get more attractive accounting treatment, to be more tax efficient, to avoid regulations (such as capital requirements), to tap new pools of capital through changing the risk characteristics of an asset, or to form more transparent funding vehicles and in turn reduce deadweight costs due to information asymmetries. While these other rationales for SPVs and securitization may not be inconsistent with the simple tradeoff presented by Gorton and Souleles, they could lead to a richer understanding of the phenomena than provided in their model. Put another way, it is hard to tell if the model is evaluating a first-order factor or a secondary explanation for securitization.

The series of models produces a second insight, which is probably more broadly applicable than the first. Were the sponsor to succumb to the moral hazard of expending less effort on projects or the strategic adverse selection of stuffing poor projects into the pool, it might completely disrupt the equilibrium in which it chooses to issue the asset-backed securities (ABS) and investors choose to purchase the ABS. But, if the bank can commit to subsidize the SPV, that is, bail it out if its assets fall short of its liabilities, then it can return to the mutually beneficial equilibrium. But because the sponsor cannot explicitly commit to the bailout without jeopardizing its off–balance sheet treatment, it must implicitly do so. Gorton and Souleles model this in equilibrium using a repeated SPV game, in which if the sponsor fails to support a failing SPV, it is precluded from raising funds again in this way for some "punishment period."

In essence, this model describes a "wink-wink-wink" equilibrium, where issuer, investor—and regulator—willingly turn a blind eye to the sponsor providing credit support. In this equilibrium, even lenders to the firm are fully informed and do not object to the credit support. To the contrary, all parties acknowledge that the bank might choose to voluntarily support the SPV in all but the most dire circumstances, when it could not support itself first. In the same way that parents of healthy adult sons and daughters are under no legal responsibility to continue to house and feed them, sponsors voluntarily choose to take care of the liabilities of their progeny—the SPVs.

Higgins and Mason (2004) have a related paper that demonstrates that this type of credit support indeed occurs. They study nineteen credit card securitizations that entered early amortization (a sign of distress) in the period 1987 through 2001, and found that in seventeen of the cases, the sponsor provided some form of recourse. Most of these sponsors were large, strong institutions, including Citibank, BancOne, AT&T, Sears Roebuck, and others. Only two sponsors chose not to provide recourse, and both subsequently failed. Apparently regulators did not object to this credit support—indeed, one can imagine that regulators would like to avoid situations in which large institutions had affiliated financing vehicles in distress. An inspection of the names—and clustered timing of the early amortizations—makes one less confident that this is a story about either moral hazard or adverse selection, but rather about downturns in the economy that affected strong and weak institutions alike. While this would not take away from the overall model, it would question the way it was set up.

Higgins and Mason find that the banks providing support enjoy positive short-term returns, positive long-run returns, and positive long-term operating performance. While there is some abnormal delay in issuance cycles, the largest institutions suffered none. In effect, it appears that the market responded positively to these institutions' willingness and ability to protect investors in their ABS.

Gorton and Souleles' empirical work complements these findings. They find, perhaps not surprisingly, that the spreads demanded by investors in credit card securitizations are a function of the rating of the sponsor, even though technically the investors in the asset-backed securities have no legal recourse against the sponsor. This result persists after controlling for various deal structure characteristics, aggregate measures of asset quality, and year fixed effects. The biggest worry—which they address as best as they can, but not convincingly—is that there is a common factor that affects both the riskiness of the firm and of the assets it puts into the ABS. For example, a subprime lender may have borrowers who are financially weak, and both their loans and their credit cards may reflect this weakness. If the credit card loans are securitized, but the loans held on–balance sheet, their positive correlation between the institution's bond rating and the spread on its ABS notes could simply reflect this common risk factor.

Nevertheless, the evidence is strongly suggestive that investors in credit card ABS look to the sponsor for potential credit support. (This would suggest a result not given in the paper; that the ratings effect of the sponsor should be greater when the ABS assets themselves are otherwise weaker, predicting an interaction effect between ratings and variables capturing asset quality.) To put the analogy back into familial terms, it suggests that investors are demanding a lower premium when lending to the children of rich parents, even if the parents do not formally cosign the loan. The economic effect of parent financial strength is material: ABS issued by the riskiest (B-rated) sponsors pay 46 basis points more than those issued by AA sponsors. In addition, Gorton and Souleles find that riskier banks are more likely to use ssecuritization although this result is not nearly as robust as the former result.

It is important to step back from this solid work and ask: What does this mean for executives in banks? Investors in banks? Regulators of the financial services sector? Ratings agencies? Recognition of material noncontractual implicit support, or "moral recourse," reminds us that firms and businesses are more than nexuses of written contracts. A host of unwritten and legally unsupportable agreements define business, as elsewhere in life. Whether they are enforced by threat of retributions—or by a sense of fair dealing—is hard to say.

The evidence in the chapter suggests that the market (at least the ABS market) is aware of the implicit relationships between sponsor and SPV and sets prices accordingly. Whether "accordingly" is correct is an interesting question: Do ABS investors properly estimate the conditional likelihood of moral recourse? If not, in what circumstances do they get it wrong? Going further, the problems with this unwritten deal may be more of a problem for risk managers, security holders of the sponsor, regulators, and the general business public.

First, from the perspective of risk managers, failure to take into account implicit support can possibly underestimate economic pressure on the sponsor in certain circumstances. There may be instances when the parent faces greater cash flow demands by virtue of its unwritten support promises; however, the voluntary nature of the payments suggests that simple models might be inappropriate to capture the effects. "Left tail" outcomes for the SPV contribute to the sponsor only if the sponsor itself is not experiencing one. Second, from the perspective of security holders of the sponsor, we have no evidence whether the implicit promises are factored into their pricing of the parent's securities. This is probably more of an issue for equity holders, because as residual claimants they would experience the economic brunt of the payments to support SPVs. Third, from the perspective of regulators, failure to take this support into account might give a misleading picture of true bank financial health, and could also give a false impression about the interrelationships that lead to systemic risk. However, given the voluntary nature of the payments, it may be less important in understanding potential calamity. However, were the ABS markets to close down because of a sudden shock and round of defaults, this could give rise to liquidity pressures that could have material business consequences.

Finally, while it seems reassuring that implicit contracts and trust exist even in the world of SPVs and ABS, to a nonlawyer there seems to be a certain disingenuousness when rules seem to say one thing (at least to a layperson), yet are interpreted in another way. Confidence in the financial system, or the legal system, or the regulatory system seems compromised somehow, in ways that go far beyond this paper.

References

Eric J. Higgins and Joseph R. Mason. 2004. What is the value of recourse to asset-backed securities? A clinical study of credit card banks. *Journal of Banking and Finance* 28:875–99.
Board of Governors of the Federal Reserve System. 2005. Flows of funds accounts of the United States. Washington, DC.

Discussion Summary

Charles Calomiris opened the general discussion by expressing a bit of skepticism that bankruptcy costs are the sole driver of the large-scale securitization that we see. An additional possibility is that adverse selection problems are mitigated by learning about asset quality, which takes place when assets are transferred to a special purpose vehicle. Both rating agencies and at least some investors closely scrutinize disclosure about the nature of such assets, and such disclosures would not occur if the assets remained on the balance sheet of the sponsor.

Patricia Jackson suggested, and *Richard Evans* agreed, that segmentation of funding markets is an additional motivation for securitization. Because many tranches of securitizations are typically bought by nonbank investors, a commercial bank may be able to attract buyers for paper on better terms than it could in the interbank or commercial-paper markets, where investors' single-name exposure limits may begin to bind as scale increases. *Hayne Leland* suggested that a financial institution may be able to lever up more by securitizing with implicit support.

A spirited debate about the role of regulatory capital arbitrage in securitization was opened by *Martin Feldstein*'s suggestion that it is material. *Michel Crouhy* agreed, noting that regulatory capital requirements are typically reduced by a securitization even though most or all risk is retained, and *Mark Saidenberg* suggested that banks have fought too hard recently to retain regulatory permissions for the contractual features that set up implicit support for regulatory-capital considerations to be immaterial. But *Richard Cantor* noted that securitization continues, even though regulatory sanctions have recently increased in cases where support occurs, and *Charles Calomiris* noted that securitization is a common tool of unregulated institutions like finance companies. *Nicholas Souleles* closed the discussion by agreeing that regulatory capital considerations may have some role. Their paper is intended to focus on other considerations that also have a role in securitization decisions.

Default Risk Sharing between Banks and Markets: The Contribution of Collateralized Debt Obligations

Günter Franke and Jan Pieter Krahnen

13.1 Introduction

In recent years the securitization of loan and bond portfolios became more and more popular among banks. The volume of collateralized loan obligations (CLOs) and collateralized bond obligations (CBOs) strongly increased in the United States and in Europe. This development raises several issues at the micro and the macro level. This paper will address some issues on the micro level, in particular the impact of CLO-transactions on the banks' risk taking.

In a CLO-transaction the bank transfers default risks of the underlying loans to other market participants, the investors. Since the bank usually has inside information about its borrowers, it has to offer some credit enhancements in a CLO-transaction to protect the investors against poten-

We are indebted to Dennis Hänsel, Thomas Weber, and Christian Wilde for their excellent computational assistance and their comments, which greatly helped us to improve the paper. Furthermore, we owe a debt to Mark Carey and René Stulz for their detailed and very helpful comments on earlier versions of this paper. We also gratefully acknowledge financial support by Deutsche Forschungsgemeinschaft and by the Center for Financial Studies at Frankfurt's Goethe University. In addition, we thank Andreas Jobst for helping us to set up the database and to discuss the intricacies of ABS markets, and Ralf Elsas for helpful comments. We are also indebted to market experts from major banks and agencies for their support and comments, in particular M. Hermann (Hong Kong and Shanghai Banking Corporation [HSBC]), T. Weinelt (Commerzbank), S. Nicolaus and R. Froitzheim (Deutsche Bank), T. Althaus (Standard & Poor's [S&P]), S. Bund (Fitch), C. Benkert (JPMorgan), T. Klotz (Moody's), J. Wasmund (DWS Investment), C.-R. Wagenknecht and B. Specht (Dresdner Kleinwort Wasserstein [DrKW]). Furthermore, we have received numerous helpful suggestions during the 2004 NBER Conference on Risk in Financial Institutions in Woodstock, Vermont. We are particularly indebted to our discussant, Patricia Jackson, and to Gary Gorton, Phillipe Jorion, Hashem Pesaran, and Til Schuermann for their valuable comments and suggestions.

tial effects of asymmetric information. For that purpose the bank usually takes a first-loss position in the default risks of the underlying loan portfolio. This raises the question about the effective extent of the risk transfer in a CLO-transaction. The first purpose of this paper is to look into this issue.

Our results show, first, that contrary to what many observers believe, the default losses of the securitized portfolio largely remain on the books of the issuing bank. Second, in a fully funded transaction, the risk of extreme unexpected losses—that is, the bad tail risk—is transferred from the bank to investors. We argue that the combined effect of retaining the first-loss piece and selling senior tranches to investors achieves an efficient risk allocation, reducing the bank's exposure to extreme risks that might endanger the bank's solvency. Thus, securitization should have a positive impact on the bank's solvency.

This direct effect of securitization on the bank's default risk is derived from simulations of the loss-rate distribution of the underlying loan portfolio. This distribution and the first-loss position jointly determine the eventual risk transfer to investors. The loss-rate distribution depends not only on the average quality of the underlying loans, but also on the correlation of defaults among these loans. Therefore, the correlation impact is also analyzed in the simulations.

Banks usually securitize loan portfolios not only for their direct effect, but also to enlarge their investment opportunity set. In a fully funded transaction, the bank can use the proceeds from issuing securities in various ways. The most conservative use would be to reinvest the proceeds in risk-free assets or to repay some of its own debt. In this case, securitization would reduce the overall risk of the bank. Alternatively, the bank could expand its loan business by granting new loans to new customers. Then the bank would retain the default risk of the first-loss position and, in addition, take the default risks of the new loans. Even though the total loan portfolio of the bank is now better diversified, the overall risk of the bank is likely to be higher than before securitization. We also simulate the effects of this reinvestment policy, assuming different correlations among the loan defaults. The simulation results indicate that the standard deviation of the bank's loan loss rate increases after securitization. Thus, it would be naive to assume that securitization generally reduces the bank's risks.

The nature of the bank's reinvestment policy is an empirical matter. Therefore, we try to obtain some insight into this question by analyzing the stock market reaction to securitization. This is the second main purpose of the paper. The underlying approach is based on the capital asset pricing model (CAPM). In an event study we look at the abnormal stock returns of a bank around the announcement date of a securitization, to find out whether the stockholders consider securitization as value enhancing. We also look at the bank's beta change around the securitization and try to infer from this change the nature of the bank's reinvestment policy. Obviously, such an approach is based on several assumptions. Therefore, the conclusions are preliminary, at best. A more careful analysis needs to look at the details of the bank's balance sheets. But this is beyond the scope of this paper.

We find no significant abnormal stock returns around the announcement dates. But we find significant increases in the banks' stock betas. We interpret this as evidence that most banks use securitization to take more systematic risks. Suppose, for example, that banks use the proceeds from securitization in a fully funded transaction to grant new loans to new customers. Then the granularity of the bank's total loan portfolio should increase, so that the correlation between the bank's default losses and the macrofactor of default losses should increase as well. Assuming a strong correlation between the macrofactor of default losses and the stock market return and a strong correlation between the bank's default losses and its stock return, the correlation between the bank's stock return and the market return should increase. In addition, this reinvestment policy is likely to raise the standard deviation of the bank's default losses and, thus, the standard deviation of the bank's stock return so that the bank's beta should increase.

The finding that, on average, the banks' betas increase with securitization announcements could be explained not only by taking more systematic risks, but also by secular increases of the banks' betas over the sampling period. However, we control for this possibility. Therefore, we regard our finding as preliminary empirical evidence about the banks' reinvestment policies.

These findings on the micro level can have important consequences on the macro level, in particular, on the stability of financial markets. We will comment on these potential effects only briefly in the conclusion.

The paper is organized as follows. In section 13.2, we first provide some institutional background and then analyze the securitization impact on the default risk of the bank's loan book. In section 13.3, we look at the stock market reaction to securitization announcements, including the beta effects. Section 13.4 concludes.

13.2 Tranching and the Allocation of Risk

In section 13.2.1, the typical securitization contracts are briefly described. Moreover, based on a European sample of collateralized debt obligations (CDOs), some evidence on first-loss pieces and tranching is presented. In section 13.2.2, we describe our method to simulate the default loss distribution for a given loan portfolio. Section 13.2.3 presents some European evidence on loss allocation to tranches in CDO-transactions. Section 13.2.4 then analyzes the effects on the bank's default losses of securitization and reinvestment policies.

13.2.1   Basics of Contract Design

There are basically two types of CDO transactions: fully funded asset-backed securities (ABS) and synthetic transactions. For a detailed description of contract types see Fabozzi et al. (chapters 24 and 25) and Das (2000; part one). In an ABS transaction the bank sells part of its loan portfolio to a special purpose vehicle (SPV), which refinances itself through the issue of bonds. Usually the bank has to take a first-loss position; that is, the bank agrees to absorb default losses up to a specified limit. To achieve this, the bank can buy the nonrated tranche (equity tranche), which absorbs all default losses up to its par value, before other tranches have to bear any further losses. In addition, or alternatively, the SPV can set up a reserve account that builds up over time from excess interest payments, received from the SPV after it has serviced other investors. The reserve account absorbs default losses in a similar way. In these transactions, the bank can use the proceeds from the sale of its loans to generate new business.

In a synthetic CLN (credit linked note) transaction, the bank retains the loans, but buys protection through a credit default swap with an SPV as the counterparty. Again, the bank usually takes a first-loss position by arranging the swap so that nothing is paid unless losses on the underlying loan portfolio exceed a threshold. Moreover, the maximum amount paid by the swap is often much smaller than the face value of the underlying loan portfolio. The bank thus retains both a first-loss position and the risk associated with very large losses. The bank may buy protection for these risks through a senior credit default swap with a different counterparty. A synthetic CLN arrangement differs from an ordinary credit default swap arrangement because the SPV's assets protect the bank against counterparty risk, may provide more regulatory capital relief, and may permit a wider-than-usual class of investors to act as protection sellers.

The first-loss position is motivated by information asymmetries. These asymmetries are a major obstacle to trading debt claims, in particular claims against small obligors about whom little is known publicly (Greenbaum and Thakor 1987). Adverse selection and moral hazard of the bank create problems similar to those in the insurance business. Therefore, suitable mechanisms of protection are also applied in CDO transactions. The main instruments are first-loss positions (deductibles in the case of insurance contracts) and risk-sharing arrangements (coinsurance in the case of insurance contracts). First-loss positions have been shown to be optimal arrangements in a number of papers, including Arrow (1971), Townsend (1979), and Gale and Hellwig (1985). Riddiough (1997) shows that splitting (tranching) the portfolio payoff into a risk-free security, which is not subject to asymmetric information problems and sold to outside investors, and a risky asset, which may be retained by the bank, is better than having one type of security only, which is partially sold to outside investors. De-

Marzo (2005) generalizes this idea, so that the tranches sold may also be risky. In a study on U.S. credit card securitizations, Calomiris and Mason (2004) argue that even in the absence of a first-loss piece retention, implicit recourse through early amortization may serve the same economic function, thereby circumventing minimum capital regulation.

Gorton and Pennacchi (1995) propose a partial loan sale to mitigate moral hazard problems. This is observed in credit card securitizations, for example, but not in CLO transactions. The reason may be that the originator is likely to earn a higher fraction of expected monitoring benefits if he takes a high first-loss position instead of retaining a moderate fraction of all tranches. Thus, investors may believe that a first-loss position (FLP) provides stronger monitoring incentives.

The first-loss piece reduces problems of asymmetric information faced by investors if it is held by the originating bank. In principle, the bank can transfer the default losses of a first-loss piece by buying a credit default swap or, in the case of an equity tranche, by selling this tranche. Usually banks do not publish information on this issue. An investigation of the Deutsche Bundesbank (2004) covering the ten major German banks securitizing loan portfolios revealed that, on average, they retain not only the first-loss piece, amounting to 2.1 percent of the transaction volume, but in addition also the lowest-rated tranches, amounting to another 4.9 percent of the transaction volume. Thus, it appears that the originating banks usually retain the first-loss piece. This would be in line with economic reasoning, since we would expect very high credit spreads required by investors for taking the default losses of the first-loss piece due to asymmetric information.

The optimal size of the first-loss position depends not only on problems of asymmetric information, but also on various other considerations. A larger first-loss piece reduces the default loss transfer and absorbs more regulatory as well as economic equity capital, leaving less room for new activities of the originating bank. Given the strong skewness of a typical loan portfolio's default loss distributions, as illustrated in the next section, we would expect the first-loss piece to clearly exceed the mean default loss.

The importance of default risk for the size of the FLP can be seen from a sample of forty-three European CLO transactions for which we could get a standardized measure of portfolio default risk.

This is done by converting Moody's weighted average rating factor or, if it is not available, the weighted average quality of the underlying loans into a weighted average default probability (wadp). We then regress the nominal size of the first-loss piece on the weighted average default probability, the issue date, and Moody's diversity score (ds). The latter statistic captures the diversification of the underlying asset portfolio. Its score is increasing if portfolio loans are spread more evenly within and across industries.

$$FLP = c + \beta \cdot wadp + \gamma \cdot ds + \delta \cdot date + \varepsilon$$

The regression result finds β to be positive and highly significant ($p = 0.00$), while γ is negative and weakly significant ($p = 0.07$); the adjusted R-squared is 0.73. The issue date is insignificant. Thus, the weighted average default probability is a strong determinant of the size of the FLP, confirming our conjecture that the first loss position increases with the expected default loss of the underlying portfolio. The protective role of the FLP will become more apparent when, in the next section, we simulate the loss distribution of the underlying portfolio, and estimate the share of expected default losses covered by the FLP.

The shape of the loss distribution is essential for understanding the relevance of the diversity score for the size of the FLP. A large diversity score is indicative of a steep loss distribution, with loss observations being more heavily concentrated around the mode.

A common feature of asset securitizations is the allocation of portfolio risk to several layers of claims. These layered claims, or tranches, obey the principle of strict subordination. Losses up to the par value of the lowest tranche are completely absorbed by the holders of this tranche. If accumulated losses of the underlying asset portfolio exceed the par value of the lowest tranche, which is the detachment point of the tranche and the attachment point of the next senior tranche, the latter will absorb the remaining losses, up to its detachment point, and so on for the remaining tranches. In this way, tranches that are more senior will only be affected if default losses reach their attachment point, after having wiped out all junior tranches.[1]

According to the model in Franke and Krahnen (2004), optimal securitization design aims at a structure that facilitates funding of relationship-specific assets by less informed (remote) investors. Senior tranches are suited for these investors since, by construction, they are largely free of default risk; see Riddiough (1997) and DeMarzo (2005). Therefore, holders of senior tranches are rarely exposed to the moral hazard component of the underlying lending relationships. Investors need not spend resources on monitoring the underlying lending relationships, thus lowering the required tranche rate of return in equilibrium.[2] Issuing mezzanine tranches to relatively more sophisticated investors supports the reduction in delegation costs even further. These investors have an expertise in risk assessment and monitoring, providing a buffer between the first-loss piece held by the issuer and the senior piece held by remote investors.

The number of distinct mezzanine tranches should therefore depend on

---

1. The strict seniority can be weakened by early amortization provisions. If, for example, a AAA-tranche and a A-tranche get repaid annually, then the latter tranche may receive substantial repayments in the early years, which, in the end, may reduce the final repayments on the AAA-tranche.

2. See Ongena and Smith (2000) and Elsas and Krahnen (2004) for a review of relationship lending and its role in a bank-oriented financial system.

the shape of the loss rate distribution. How does the number of tranches of a given transaction relate to the degree of diversification and the default probability of the underlying loan portfolio? An empirical estimate follows from regressing the number of tranches on Moody's diversity score and on the weighted average default probability:

$$\text{No. of tranches} = c + \beta \cdot \text{wadp} + \gamma \cdot \text{ds} + u$$

In a simple ordinary least squares (OLS) regression using the same forty-three European CLO transactions as before, we find that the diversity score has a positive and significant coefficient ($p = 0.00$), while wadp is insignificant. The adjusted R-squared is 0.2. Thus, after controlling for the default probability, a steeper loss rate distribution is associated with a higher number of mezzanine layers. Inclusion of the first-loss piece and the issue date do not change the regression results.

The implications of Franke and Krahnen (2004) relate to the risk allocation achieved by tranching the underlying collateral portfolio. By acquiring the senior tranche, remote investors essentially take on macroeconomic risk. To be more precise, the payoff from holding a senior tranche is effectively indexed to systemwide macroeconomic shocks. Define the macrofactor of default risks as the average default rate on the aggregate portfolio of debt claims. This factor is random and, by definition, ranges in the [0,1] interval. Then a well-diversified loan portfolio of average initial quality will only incur average default rates beyond, say, 10 percent if the macrofactor is in the same range. Hence the senior tranches will only incur default losses if the macrofactor turns out to be very bad.

This is not to say that in a similar situation there is no moral hazard of the bank. It may well be that in a severe downturn situation banks do not care much about their loans anymore. Moral hazard behavior may then be difficult to detect, so that reputational costs are low. Yet the senior tranches are only impaired if the macrofactor turns out to be bad. If the macrofactor turns out to be good, then even strong moral hazard behavior is very unlikely to affect the senior tranches at all.

Thus, the structural aspects characterizing collateralized debt obligations are devised to solve the inherent tension that exists between the originator, who has private information, and a diversified investor base without this information. Due to the informational disparity, the originator's claim is highly illiquid, and a direct sale of the asset would create a large discount relative to the going concern value of the asset; see Gorton and Pennacchi (1995) and Diamond and Rajan (2001).

In section 13.2.3 we will characterize the properties of junior and senior tranches, building on the information provided in the offering circulars of a large number of European CDO-transactions. This characterization requires knowledge of the loss rate distributions of the underlying portfolios, in particular the allocation of default losses to the various tranches. Whether the size of the first-loss piece appears sufficient to mitigate problems of asymmetric information depends on the shape of the loss distribution.

13.2.2   Estimating the Loss Distribution

To estimate the loss distribution of the underlying portfolio and the implied loss allocation to the various tranches, we proceed as follows. First, we use the information in the offering circular[3] on the quality of the underlying loans and their initial portfolio weights, as indicated by a rating agency. If this information is not available, we use the average initial loan quality as indicated by a rating agency. Then we use Standard and Poor's (S&P) transition matrix for different loan qualities to estimate the default probabilities for particular loans over the lifetime of the transaction: we use Monte Carlo simulation to generate a distribution of rating migration paths, assuming a 47.5 percent recovery rate throughout. Absent better data on loss given default, these assumptions are standard in the literature.

Multiyear asset value migration tables are derived from the one-year table through repeated multiplication. The migration matrix is then mapped into a matrix of standard normal threshold values. For each asset, a random draw from the standard normal distribution yields a migration from the beginning of the year to the end of the year rating notch. To arrive at a portfolio return, the correlations between loan migrations need to be taken into account. This is done by a Cholesky transformation.

For assets in the same industry (in different industries), the correlation coefficient is initially set at 0.3 (0.0), following common practice (Standard & Poor's 2002). Alterations of the assumptions on asset correlations will be used later on to analyze the impact of systematic risk on loss correlations between tranches.

The generation of final portfolio cash flows and their allocation to the tranches that constitute the issue is achieved in a last step. The cash flows of each period t are transformed in a realized final (compound) value, RFV_t, using a flat term structure of interest rates (4 percent). If a credit event is recorded (default), then the assumed recovery is accounted for, and all further cash flows from this asset are set equal to zero. All final cash flows are allocated to tranches according to the cashflow waterfall principle, as defined in the offering circular. Finally, for each tranche, the nominal claims of each period, NV_t, are transformed into a final value as well, NFV_t. The sum of these final values over all tranches defines the final value of all claims. The ratio of these two final values defines the portfolio loss rate, $\text{PLR}_T = 1 - \Sigma_t \, \text{RFV}_t / \Sigma_t \, \text{NFV}_t$. Using 50,000 observations, a loss dis-

---

3. Offering Circulars (OC) are official documents describing the issue's collateral composition, among many other contractual and legal details of the arrangement. OCs are public information to be posted at the issue date. In addition, most issues are accompanied by presale reports, published by rating agencies.

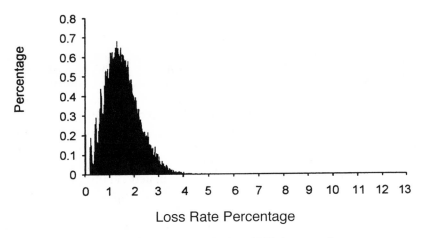

Fig. 13.1   Loss rate distribution of London Wall 2002-2 transaction, 50,000 iterations

Notes: This figure displays the loss rate distribution of London Wall, as it was simulated using the information contained in the offering circular. A loss rate distribution for the entire portfolio is generated that takes into account the correlation within and between industries and the credit migration risks referencing Standard and Poor's tables. The chart shows on the vertical axis the frequency of observations, and on the horizontal axis the associated loss rate, truncated at 13 percent. There was no observation surpassing this threshold.

tribution is generated that reflects the loss cascading inherent in the tranche structure.[4]

Figure 13.1 shows the loss rate distribution of the London Wall 2002-2 transaction, issued by Deutsche Bank in 2002, which appears to be a typical example of a CDO-transaction. Here we assume an intraindustry correlation of 0.3, and a zero interindustry correlation. The graph shows a pronounced skewness. The expected loss is 150 bp (1.5 percent) with an FLP of 246 bp. By retaining the FLP, the originator bears all losses within the 91 percent-quantile of the loss rate distribution. Hence, a large fraction of losses is not transferred to investors, which serves as a strong barrier to adverse selection and moral hazard.

13.2.3   Loss Allocation in CDO Transactions

How is the risk of an underlying portfolio allocated to tranches? In particular, to what extent are losses, given the estimated probability distribution of loss rates, absorbed by the various tranches? In a typical issue, the first-loss piece comprises between 2 percent and 10 percent of the issue volume, while the senior AAA-rated tranche comprises as much as 80–95 percent. Further evidence is derived from looking at a sample of forty Euro-

---

4. There are a few simplifying assumptions: (1) there is no rating upgrade once an asset has reached default status, (2) a defaulted asset immediately returns the recovery rate multiplied by the nominal amount, and (3) every asset has a bullet structure—there is no prepayment.

pean CDO-transactions with close to 150 tranches (see the list in table 13.1). This sample has some overlap with the CLO-sample used for the regressions in section 13.2.1.

In calculating the loss distributions for this European CDO sample, we rely on our own loss estimator, introduced in the last section. Given the loss distribution, we then take the ratings of the tranches from the offering circular and determine their attachment points. For this exercise we use S&P's table, which indicates the estimated default probability of a claim for a given rating and a given maturity. This exercise starts with the most senior tranche, and ends with the lowest-rated tranche. An AAA claim with maturity of ten years, for example, has an estimated default probability of about 1 percent. Then the attachment point of this tranche is the (100 − 1)-percent quantile of the loss distribution. By the same procedure, the attachment points of the other rated tranches are derived. The unrated first-loss piece is thus determined by the attachment point of the lowest-rated tranche.

Table 13.2 summarizes the results of this mapping exercise.[5] The table presents average values by type of asset. We consider three asset classes: collateralized loan obligations (CLO) with large loans and bonds, CLOs with small corporate loans (SME-CLO), and the rest (other, including CBOs and portfolios of CDO tranches). These asset classes differ with respect to diversification and relationship intensity. First, the degree of diversification is low for CBOs and high for SME-CLO issues, while CLOs are somewhat in between, as evidenced by the average diversity scores. Second, the relationship character of the underlying lending relationship is probably highest in the case of the SME loans, and lowest in the case of CBOs, which typically comprise bonds issued by large caps.

Table 13.2 uses a broad classification of forty European transactions issued between January 1999 and July 2002.[6] It is instructive to compare the second column with the fourth, SME-CLOs and CBOs, because the underlying assets differ. The former consists of bank loans extended to small and mid-sized companies, while the latter refers to bonds issued by large corporates. The average quality of the loans is below that of the bonds. Not only is the average issue size of SME portfolios about 80 percent higher than that of the average CBO portfolio, but also the number of loans exceeds by far the number of bonds, suggesting that SME-CLOs are more granular, that is, more diversified than CBOs. The table also shows that while the average size of the first-loss piece is similar for both issue types,[7]

5. The size of the senior tranche reported in the last line of table 13.2 may therefore differ somewhat from the value reported in the offering circulars. However, this method allows us to estimate the loss quantiles allocated to tranches, an information not available in the offering circulars.

6. All issues were selected for which we could get the offering circular.

7. The size of the first-loss piece is measured in percent of the underlying portfolio volume.

Table 13.1   List of European CDO issues used for loss rate estimation

Name	CBO/CLO	Maturity	Volume (bn €)	No. of rated tranches	No. of loans	Average rating	Dividend score
Dutch Care 2001-1	CLO	8	1.300	3	169	A1	12.4
Hesperic No. 1 pk	CLO	6	1.400	5	104	Baa1	31
IKB Credit Linked Notes 2000-1	CLO	10	0.534	3	61	Ba2	33
Leverage Finance Europe Capital I.B.V.	CLO	10	0.315	4	30	B1	26
London Wall 2002-1 PLC	CLO	6	3.000	5	330	Baa2	70
London Wall 2002-2 PLC	CLO	6	1.800	5	224	Baa2	70
ARCH ONE FINANCE LIMITED	other	4	0.490	2	70	Baa1	47
ARGON CAPITAL PLC— SERIES 1	other	7	1.382	5	53	Baa1	30
Brooklands Euro Ref. Linked Notes 2001-1	other	10	1.000	3	100	Baa1	50
Cathedral Limited	other	5	0.466	3	52	Baa1/Baa2	36
CDO Master Investment 2 SA	other	5	3.750	3	112	Baa1	66
CDO Master Investment 3 SA	other	5	2.500	3	86	Baa1	60
CDO Master Investment SA	other	5	1.625	3	100	Baa1	49
CIDNEO FINANCE Pk	other	10	0.250	3	57	Baa2	34
CLASSIC FINANCE B.V. (Petra III)	other	5	2.320	5	232	A3	103
Credico Funding S r.1	other	6	0.890	1	117	Ba1	30
Deutsche Bank—United Global Inv. Gr. CDO I	other	5	1.436	3	148	Baa1	60
DYNASO 2002-1 LTD	other	5	1.000	3	100	A3	55
Eirles Two Limited Series	other	7	0.626	3	74	A3	40.8
European Dream 2001-1	other	7	1.069	3	59	Aa1	26
Helix Capital (Netherlands) B.V. 2001-1	other	5	0.800	2	80	A3	50
Lusitano Global CDO No. 1, Pk	other	4	1.145	3	218	Baa3	35
Marche Asset Portfolio S r.1	other	3	0.168	3	59	Baa1	12
Redwood CBO	other	10	0.300	3	100	B2	45
Spices Finance Limited Peas	other	5	0.950	2	100	Baa2	56
Vintage Capital S.A.	other	10	0.360	1	76	Baa2	36
CAST 1999-1 Ltd.	SME CLO	7	2.900	4	4389	Baa3	70
CAST 2000-1 Ltd.	SME CLO	7	4.500	4	1991	Baa3	70
CAST 2000-2 Ltd.	SME CLO	7	2.500	4	5178	Baa3	95
HAT (Helvetic Asset Trust) AG	SME CLO	5	2.500	3	650	Ba2	100
HAT (Helvetic Asset Trust) II Limited	SME CLO	5	2.500	4	1455	Ba2	110
PROMISE-A-2000-1 pk	SME CLO	8	1.000	5	1097	Ba1	90
PROMISE-A-2002-1 pk	SME CLO	8	1.618	6	1277	Ba1	124
Promise-C-2002-1	SME CLO	6	1.500	5	4578	Baa3	90
Promise-Color-2003-1	SME CLO	5	1.130	5	1512	Ba2	80
Promise-G-2001-1	SME CLO	7	0.650	4	100	Ba1	85
Promise-I-2000-1	SME CLO	8	2.500	5	2267	Baa3	80
Promise-I-2002-1	SME CLO	7	3.650	5	4172	Baa3	80
Promise-K-2001-1	SME CLO	5	1.000	5	2916	Ba1/Ba2	100
Promise-Z-2001-1	SME CLO	8	1.000	5	658	Ba1	85

Note: This table summarizes descriptive statistics of the issues that have been used to calculate the loss rate distribution for the sample of European CDOs.

Table 13.2   Loss rate distribution of European CDOs: Descriptive statistics

	SME-CLO	Non-SME-CLO	CBO
Total volume (bn euros)	2.068	1.392	1.126
No. of claims	2,303	153	100
Portfolio rating (median)	Ba1	Baa2	Baa1
Most junior rated tranche (median)	Ba2	Ba1	A3
Size FLP (%)	6.7	8.61	5.93
FLP/E(L)	1.34	1.74	3.36
FLP quantile (cdf)	0.87	0.87	0.96
Number of tranches	4.57	4.17	2.85
Size senior tranche (%)	91.11	87.79	92.89

Notes: This table summarizes basic characteristics of the CDO sample, with forty European transactions used in the estimation of expected and unexpected loss. SME-CLOs are collateralized loan obligations where underlyings comprise loans to small- and medium-size firms, CBOs are collateralized bond obligations, with large firm corporate bonds as underlyings, and non-SME-CLOs are a mixture of the two asset classes, comprising corporate bonds and loans to large firms. The numbers in the table are averages across the transactions listed in the column. Total volume is the amount, in bn euros, of the portfolio underlying the transaction, and the number of tranches is the number of issued tranches, excluding the FLP. Size FLP is the nominal value of a tranche relative to the nominal amount of the issue in fully funded and synthetic transactions. Size senior tranche is the nominal value of the senior tranche relative to the nominal amount of the issue. FLP/E(L) is the size of the FLP tranche relative to expected loss E(L) of the underlying portfolio. The FLP quantile is the cumulative density of losses not exceeding the size of the first-loss piece. All tranche-related statistics rely on our own estimation of the loss rate distribution.

it covers a much wider portion of the loss rate distribution in case of CBOs. The size of their FLPs is on average 3.36 times the expected loss of the underlying portfolio, and it is 1.34 times the loss in the case of SME-CLOs, although the difference in rating quality of the underlying portfolios is small. Due to the difference in FLPs, the median rating of the most junior-rated tranche of the CBO transactions is several notches higher than its counterpart among SME-CLO transactions. CBO first-loss pieces cover 0.96 of the cumulative density of the underlying portfolio's loss rate distribution, on average. The remaining risk to be allocated to investors is relatively small, allowing for only 2.85 additional tranches to be issued for CBOs. This number is significantly lower than in the case of SME-CLOs, where it reaches 4.57.

In all asset classes, the first-loss piece covers more than 100 percent of the mean loss. Variations are sizeable, but there is no clear picture across asset classes. The average size of the first-loss piece is 7.1 percent, with a significant variation between non-SME-CLOs and CBOs. As a consequence, FLPs take over most of the losses, and the losses allocated to the senior tranche are restricted to extreme, systematic events. Their expected value is very low—0.01 percent of the senior tranche volume, on average—as is their default probability (0.5 percent).

13.2.4   Securitization Effects on the Bank's Overall Default Risk

Whereas the previous section analyzes the allocation of default losses to different tranches, this section looks at the impact of securitizations on the bank's overall default risk. This is also essential for the stock return analysis in section 13.3. Assuming a true sale, with all tranches being sold to outside investors, except the first-loss piece, what are the consequences for the risk exposure of the bank? The answer depends on several aspects: first, what other assets does the bank have on its book and how are their cash flows and default risks correlated with those of the securitized loans? Second, what would be the effect of securitizing all default risks? Third, how does securitization change the bank's loan policy?

So far, there is little evidence on the impact of securitization on bank policy. Cebenoyan and Strahan (2004) find mixed evidence on whether banks' risks increase with securitization. Regressing the banks' return volatility on securitization, they find positive (insignificant) and negative (significant) coefficients, depending on which other variables are included in the regression.

In order to improve our understanding, we consider a bank with a portfolio of fifty identical loans extended equally to obligors in five different industries, one year to maturity, and the same quality. The latter is set equal to a B rating, implying a 8.5 percent default rate (Moody's Investor Service 2002). The bank can either keep the loans in its books or securitize them. For the securitized portfolio, the bank retains a nonrated tranche of 10.11 percent, that is, a first-loss position. The bank then reinvests the proceeds, amounting to $(100 - 10.11)$ percent in new loans, to obligors with the same quality characteristics as those in the initial loan book. Hence the on–balance sheet loan book of the bank, including the retained first-loss piece, has the same size as before securitization. But the new loans are not perfect substitutes for the old loans because the new loans are granted to new obligors, so that the granularity of the total loan portfolio increases.

This assumption of reinvestment represents a polar case of bank policy. The other polar case would be that the bank reinvests the proceeds from securitization in risk-free assets. In this case, the bank would retain the risks of the first-loss piece, but not incur new risks. For a highly rated bank, the effects would be very similar to those of an early repayment of debt. In reality, banks are likely to follow some route between these polar cases, so that some new risks are added to the bank's portfolio.

Table 13.3 shows the first four moments of the distribution of loss rates (1) for the original loan portfolio without securitization and (2) for the new portfolio, whose default losses are composed of those from the FLP of the securitized portfolio plus all default losses from the newly granted loans. The moments depend on the assumed intra- and interindustry correlations; therefore, we report different correlation scenarios. In the first, the

Table 13.3   **Reinvestment of securitization proceeds: Simulation results for the loss rate distributions**

	A. Assumptions regarding correlations		
Within industries	0.3	0.5	0.7
Between industries	0.0	0.0	0.3

	B. Moments					
	Original portfolio	New portfolio	Original portfolio	New portfolio	Original portfolio	New portfolio
Mean (%)	5.67	10.51	5.70	10.30	5.64	9.52
Standard deviation (%)	3.52	5.43	4.29	6.61	7.63	11.26
Skewness	0.81	0.44	1.00	0.52	2.03	1.34
Excess kurtosis	0.68	−0.32	1.04	−0.46	4.76	1.13

Notes: This table summarizes the results of a simulation exercise. The original portfolio consists of 50 B-rated loans of equal par value with one year to maturity, split evenly across five industries. The new portfolio is obtained by securitizing the original portfolio, retaining a first-loss piece of 10.11 percent and reinvesting the par value of the original position minus the first-loss piece in another portfolio that has the same characteristics. The loss given default is assumed to be 52.5 percent. There are three scenarios in the table, which differ by their correlation assumptions. The lower panel shows the first four moments of the resulting loss rate distribution for the bank's loan book, including the retained first-loss tranches, for the three scenarios. The first column (original portfolio) describes the loan book before securitization, the second (new portfolio) describes the loan book after the securitization transaction.

base case, intraindustry dependence is set at 0.3, while interindustry correlation is zero. The other scenarios assume a stronger dependency, suggesting the existence of a common systematic factor. Higher correlations reflect a stronger macrofactor of default risks.

First, consider the effect of securitization and reinvestment in the correlation base case. Figure 13.2 plots the difference between the default rate distribution of the new and that of the original portfolio. The graph indicates that securitization and reinvestment lower the default probabilities in the range of 0–18 percent, and raise them in the range of 18–46 percent. Therefore, the mean loss rate of the new portfolio is higher than the respective rate of the original portfolio. The ratio of the mean of the new portfolio over that of the original portfolio is not just $(1 + [1 - 0.1011]) = 1.8989$, but clearly lower. The reason is that in the new portfolio the loss of the securitized portfolio is restricted to the FLP.

More difficult to grasp are the effects on the second, third, and fourth moments of the loss rate distribution. First, consider the standard deviation. In table 13.3, the standard deviation of the new portfolio exceeds that of the original portfolio. Intuitively, this is explained by scaling up losses through securitization and reinvestment. But this is not true in general. Let the par value of the original portfolio be 1\$. If the bank securitizes this portfolio, taking an FLP of 0.1\$, it grants new loans for 0.9\$. Let σ_{op} de-

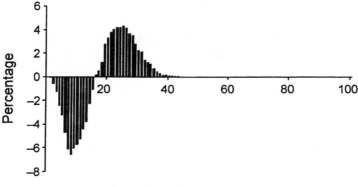

Loss Rate Percentage

Fig. 13.2   Securitization and reinvestment: Impact on loss rate distribution, 10,000 iterations

Notes: This figure displays the differential loss rate distribution of a simulated loan portfolio with securitization followed by reinvestment and without reinvestment. The original portfolio consists of fifty B-rated loans of equal par value with one year to maturity, split evenly across five industries. The new portfolio is obtained by securitizing the original portfolio, retaining a first-loss piece of 10.11 percent, and reinvesting the par value of the original position, minus the first-loss piece, in another portfolio that has the same characteristics. The loss given default is assumed to be 52.5 percent. The pairwise within-industry correlations are 0.3, while pairwise between-industry correlations are assumed to equal 0.0. The resulting differential loss rate distribution is displayed in the figure.

note the standard deviation of the loss of the original portfolio, σ_{FLP}, the standard deviation of the loss on the FLP, and ρ, the correlation coefficient between losses. Then the variance of the new portfolio equals

$$\sigma_{FLP}^2 + 2 \cdot 1 \cdot 0.9 \cdot \rho \cdot \sigma_{op} \cdot \sigma_{FLP} + 0.9^2 \cdot \sigma_{op}^2,$$

while the variance of the original portfolio equals σ_{op}^2. Obviously, the variance of the new portfolio is *smaller* than that of the original portfolio if the FLP is small relative to expected loss, so that it will be exhausted by losses with high probability. In the limit, σ_{FLP} tends to zero, implying the variance of the new portfolio roughly to equal 81 percent of the variance of the original portfolio. Therefore it is not obvious whether the bank's standard deviation of default losses will increase or decline through securitization and reinvestment.

In table 13.3, skewness and excess kurtosis of the new portfolio decrease relative to the original portfolio. From figure 13.2, this is not surprising, given a shift of the probability mass from the lower tail to the center. This effect is more dramatic for the kurtosis than for the skewness, since the kurtosis raises the differences to the mean to the fourth instead of the third power.

These effects can also be seen by looking at the cumulative loss distributions in figure 13.3. These distributions show that the change in the loss

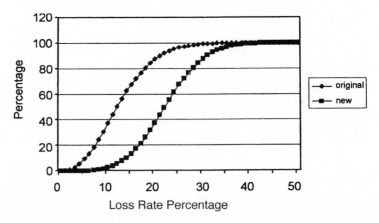

Fig. 13.3   Securitization and reinvestment: Impact on cumulative loss distribution, 10,000 iterations

Notes: This figure displays the cumulative loss rate distributions of a simulated loan portfolio with securitization and reinvestment (new) and without reinvestment (original). The same data as in figure 13.2 are used.

rate distribution caused by securitization and reinvestment is not merely a shift, but also a spreading out of the distribution.

Second, we look at the effects of correlations on these results. Of course, correlations have no effect on the average default rate of the original portfolio. This is always the same (around 5.67 percent), even though the simulation produces slight differences. Figure 13.4 displays the difference between two frequency distributions of default losses of the original portfolio, the first being determined by correlations (0.7; 0.3), the second by (0.3; 0.0), with the first number being the intraindustry correlation and the second the interindustry correlation. Raising the correlations shifts probability mass from the range (6–24 percent) to both tails. Therefore, the standard deviation, the skewness, and the excess kurtosis of the default rate of the original portfolio increase with correlations.

More complex is the effect of correlations on the default rate distribution of the new portfolio. Figure 13.4 indicates that a FLP of about 10 percent has to bear small losses (1–5 percent) with higher probabilities, and high losses (6–10 percent) with lower probabilities. Hence, in this example, higher correlations imply a lower average loss for the FLP. This also explains in table 13.3 why the ratio of average losses of the new over the original portfolio declines with higher correlations.

Table 13.3 also indicates, for our example, that standard deviation and skewness of the new portfolio increase with correlations, while this is not always true of the kurtosis. The relative increase in standard deviation (new over original portfolio) tends to slightly decline with higher correlations. The relative changes in skewness and excess kurtosis do not display such regular patterns.

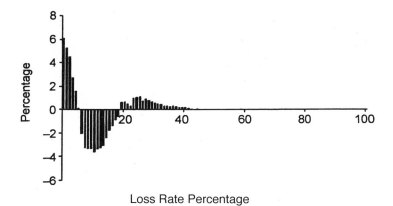

Fig. 13.4   Increase in correlation and loss rate distribution, 10,000 iterations

Notes: This figure displays the differential loss rate distribution of a simulated loan portfolio with a low and a high level of correlation. In the underlying collateral portfolios there are 100 assets each, all BB rated, two industries, the pairwise within-industry correlations increase from 0.3 to 0.7, while pairwise between-industry correlations increase from 0.0 to 0.3. The resulting differential loss rate distribution is displayed in the figure.

The simulation exercise begs the question whether securitization and reinvestment will have an impact on the systematic risk of the bank, as measured by the sensitivity of the bank's default losses to a macrofactor of default losses. If the bank retains the first-loss piece and reinvests the proceeds from securitization in loans to new obligors, then tranching and reinvestment raise the granularity of the total loan book, which in turn raises the bank's systematic cash flow risk. As a result, the bank's stock market beta may be affected as well. We will look into this matter in the next section.

13.3   Share Price Reactions to the Issue of Collateralized Debt Obligations

In this section we want to analyze how the securitization of loan assets affects the equity valuation of the bank. In accordance with the last section, emphasis will be on effects that are due to tranching and reinvestment. Earlier studies, including the event studies (Lockwood, Rutherford, and Herrera 1996, and Thomas 2001), have neglected the important risk-repackaging aspect of loan securitization.

13.3.1   Hypotheses and Test Design

Our main hypothesis relates the effects of securitization to the systematic stock market risk of the bank as measured by its beta. The change in beta depends on the change in the standard deviation of the bank's stock return and the change in the correlation between the bank's stock return and the market return. In order to derive hypotheses about these changes, we assume, first, that a higher standard deviation of the default losses incurred by the bank translates into a higher standard deviation of its stock return. Second, we assume that an increase in the granularity of the bank's loan portfolio translates into a higher correlation between the bank's stock return and the market return. This is motivated by the empirical observation that the credit spread of a corporate bond is negatively related to the corporation's stock return (see, for example, Blanco, Brennan, and Marsh 2005, and Collin-Dufresne, Goldstein, and Martin 2001). Hence the market value of a loan portfolio should be positively correlated with the market value of a portfolio of the stocks of the underlying corporations, which, in turn, are positively correlated with the market return. The more granular the loan portfolio, the better diversified it will be, and the stronger should be the correlation of its market value with the market return. Given the immediate impact of the market value of the bank's loan portfolio on its own market value, a more granular loan portfolio should translate into a higher correlation between the bank's stock return and the market return.

In the following we consider a bank that in a securitization retains the first-loss piece and sells or swaps the other tranches to investors. As shown before, the securitization impact on the bank's risk depends strongly on the bank's reinvestment policy. We consider again the two polar cases discussed before.

If the bank securitizes the loan portfolio in a true sale transaction, but takes no new risks, then the standard deviation of the bank's default losses should decline, because the bad tail risks of the loss distribution are transferred to investors. This is likely to reduce the standard deviation of the bank's stock return, holding the liability side of its balance sheet constant. Similarly, if the bank repays some of its debt, holding the equity capital constant, then this should also reduce the standard deviation of the bank's stock return. Regarding the correlation between the bank's stock return and the market return, we expect a slight decline, because the transfer of the bad tail risks to investors immunizes the bank to very bad outcomes of macro factors. Hence, overall we expect a slight decline of the bank's beta after a securitization, given a risk-free reinvestment policy.

Now consider the other polar case, in which the bank reinvests the proceeds from securitization in new loans of comparable quality. As shown before, the standard deviation of the bank's default losses is likely to increase, which should also raise the standard deviation of the bank's stock return. Since the reinvestment raises the granularity of the bank's loan portfolio, this should raise the correlation between the bank's stock return and the market return. Therefore, given this reinvestment policy, the bank's beta should increase. This effect should be stronger for banks that engage in repeated securitizations and thus, over time, increase the share of equity tranches among its assets. This motivates our first hypothesis.

HYPOTHESIS 1. *CDO-transactions will raise (reduce) the bank's beta if the proceeds of the securitization are reinvested in new loans to new obligors (risk-free assets). The effect will be stronger for repeated CDO-transactions.*

Hypothesis 1 addresses the two polar cases. Banks may well choose policies in between. Since we do not have detailed data on the banks' behavior, we cannot find out what they actually do. We can only try to find out whether the banks' betas increase or not. This is, at best, indirect evidence of the banks' policies. A more rigorous test would use figures from their quarterly reports. Even using such figures, it would be difficult to separate investment and capital structure decisions associated with securitizations from other decisions.

Similarly, one might argue that we should look at the banks' unlevered betas; that is, the beta defined by the joint stock and bond return of the bank and that of the market. This would require daily data on the bank's debt, a large part of which is not securitized. Since we do not have these data, we look at conventional betas. Given the small size of issues, 1.3 percent of the balance sheet on average (see table 13.4), the relative effects on equity beta and on asset beta are likely to be quite similar.

Hypothesis 1 refers to beta changes at the time securitizations are announced, presuming that such announcements are a surprise. In some countries, especially the United States, some banks engage in securitization programs. Although the timing of individual securitizations in a pro-

Table 13.4   European collateralized debt obligation (CDO) dataset: Descriptive statistics

Year	Number of issues	Size (collateral assets, € bn)	Number of tranches	Share of balance sheet assets (%)	Equity (book value, € bn)
		A. European dataset (n = 73)			
1999	10	1.682	6.40	0.54	12.531
2000	17	2.586	5.53	1.42	11.725
2001	20	2.629	5.60	2.08	14.692
2002	26	1.940	6.30	0.95	15.048
		B. Subsample of nonrepeat issues (n = 51)			
1999	7	1.674	5.43	0.66	10.341
2000	14	2.640	5.36	1.52	10.758
2001	15	2.850	5.67	2.66	12.440
2002	15	1.912	6.60	1.48	9.617

Note: This table presents descriptive statistics of the CDO data set. The numbers (except no. of issues) are averages across transactions. Panel A uses information on seventy-three issues underlying the estimations in section 13.3, collected from Datastream. Panel B represents a subsample of fifty-one, comprising only those issues that did not experience a repeat issue by the same issuer within five months after the first transaction. "Size" is the euro volume of collateral assets underlying the issue. "Number of tranches" is taken from the offering circulars. All tranches, including nonrated tranches, are considered. "Share of balance sheet assets" divides size by total assets of the bank. "Equity (book value)" is the issuing bank's sum of equity and open reserves, according to Datastream.

gram may not be perfectly anticipated by the market, the long-run effects on bank cash flows may be anticipated rather well, in which case we would expect little effect of announcements of individual securitizations. But at least during our sample period, European banks did not announce programs, apart from mortgage-backed master trust securitizations, which are absent from our data. Thus, the number, size, and timing of securitizations by European banks are difficult to predict. To the extent that the market is nevertheless able to make predictions, it would tend to weaken our ability to find any impact of securitization on returns and betas.

We now turn to the stock price reaction triggered by the announcement of the securitization, as captured by the abnormal return in a typical event study. The abnormal return is determined by the expectation of investors, given the information contained in the issue announcement.[8] If stockholders interpret the securitization as a pure change in the bank's financing strategy, then in a perfect market there should be no stock price effect, unless the change in the financing strategy redistributes wealth from the stockholders to the bondholders, or vice versa. Since the stockholders hold the equity piece and the bondholders hold the senior tranche of the bank's assets, securitization without risky reinvestment should typically reduce the expected default losses of the bank's bondholders and, thus, enrich them at the expense of the stockholders. This would argue in favor of a negative stock price reaction. Securitization with risky reinvestment might have the opposite effect.

Similarly, if the bank uses a true sale transaction to obtain new funding, then stockholders may interpret the transaction as unfavorable information about the bank's funding needs and react by a stock price decline. This, however, would not be true for a synthetic transaction, because then the bank does not receive funding. Finally, the transaction cost of securitization is nonnegligible, adding to a negative stock price impact.

On the other side, securitization enables the bank to expand its loan or other business. This may be considered by the stockholders as a valuable real option of the bank, so that the stock price should increase. Similarly, to the extent that securitization protects the bank against major default losses, it may reduce the costs of financial distress. This would also be good news for the stockholders.

Summarizing, the net impact of securitization on the bank's stock price is hard to predict. It is an empirical matter as to which effects dominate. Across the entire sample, we do not expect to find significant stock price reactions to the announcement of securitizations.

We will provide evidence, first, by looking at all transactions, and sec-

---

8. From conversations with practitioners we know that the valuation of CDO mezzanine tranches is typically preceded by a bookbuilding period resembling an English auction, as modeled in Plantin (2003).

ond, by looking at different subsets of transactions to find out whether the hypothesis holds equally well for all these subsets.

There are a number of characteristics that may be cross-sectionally relevant. Among these characteristics is the synthetic nature of a deal, because synthetic deals eliminate the funding component in an issue and, therefore, synthetic issues should have a smaller impact on the bank's asset composition, relative to a fully funded transaction.

A second characteristic of securitization transactions that may be relevant for cross-sectional differences is the nature of the issue as static or dynamic. Static issues maintain the original asset composition of the collateral portfolio throughout the life of the transaction. This typically implies a gradual redemption of the outstanding issue, in accordance with repayment of the underlying loans. Dynamic issues, in contrast, tend to maintain their original volume throughout the entire term of the issue. If loans in the collateral portfolio are redeemed, the issuer replaces them by new loans, safeguarding certain quality standards. While replenishment standards vary between issues, a general implication is that banks are required to assign new loans to the collateral portfolio in a systematic, nonrandom manner.

Since both properties—synthetic/true sale and static/dynamic—exert an influence on the asset composition of the bank, we expect both characteristics to be consequential for the value effect of the issue announcement.

13.3.2 Data and Results of the Event Study

In compiling our data set we initially looked at all transactions in Moody's European Securitization list of June 2003. The number of issues is 254, of which 185 have a Moody's "New Issue Report." It is this report that contains the information required for conducting the study, including a description of the underlying assets as well as the covenants relevant for the issue. Among the many other features of the issue, the report also contains the pricing of the tranches at the issue date and the name of the originator. Not every issue has a single originator.[9]

For 112 transactions we were able to identify the originator. We imposed the additional restriction that the originator is a listed company (else no stock price is available), and arrive at a sample of ninety-two transactions from thirty-one banks. We excluded the non-European banks, and finally have seventy-three transactions issued by twenty-seven banks. These issues are used for the event study and, later on, for the cross-sectional analysis.

Table 13.4 presents the descriptives of our final dataset. In the upper panel of table 13.4 one can see that the average size of transactions is small relative to the entire balance sheet, up to 2 percent of total assets. For repeat issuers this share of balance sheet assets adds up to 5–10 percent of

---

9. Several ABS products are managed arbitrage deals that pass through the cash flows of several originators at once.

total assets, and in some cases an even larger share of the total loan book. The average number of tranches over all transactions is about six. The lower panel refers to a subsample of the seventy-three issues, comprising fifty-one issues. It excludes repeat issues, that is, all transactions whose issue date is less than five months (100 days) after another issue by the same bank. This subsample will also be used later in the regression analysis. The basic model is an augmented event study estimation.

$$R_{i,t} = \alpha_i + \beta_i R_{m,t} + \gamma_{1,i} D_i^{event} + \gamma_{2,i} D_i^{otherevent} + \beta_i^\Delta D_i^{after} R_{m,t} + \varepsilon_{i,t};$$

$$t = -20, \ldots, +20$$

The dependent variable $R_{i,t}$, as well as the independent variable $R_{m,t}$, are daily log returns, the first being the bank's stock return, the latter being defined by the Dow Jones EUROSTOXX 50 index.[10] The dummy D^{event} captures the abnormal return over the event window. The window extends from day –20 to day +20 around the announcement date. Announcement dates were assumed to be the first public notification that could be identified in Lexis-Nexis, or in presale reports of the three major agencies.

The estimation uses a 200-days window, symmetrically around the event window. Thus for each event the time series extends over 240 trading days—approximately one year. Since we are interested in a possible change of systematic risk, the regression has a second variable capturing systematic risk, delta-beta (β^Δ), which is multiplied by a dummy, D^{after}, which equals 1 for the 100 days following the event window (–20, +20). The coefficient β^Δ measures the extent to which the after-event beta diverges from its preevent value. The null hypothesis sets β^Δ at zero.

The estimation is complicated by the fact that for many cases in our sample there are repeat issuers, and the interval between two consecutive announcement dates by the same issuer is frequently less than 100 days. Since a separate regression is run for every transaction, there is overlap among the estimation windows. In order to disentangle the effect of the original event from the effects of other events, we include a dummy "other event," $D^{otherevent}$, whose coefficient captures abnormal returns in a –20/+20 days window around each other event.

To deal with β^Δ in these frequent issue cases, we set the dummy D^{after} equal to 2 (3) for the second (third) subsequent overlapping event. Thus, we force β^Δ to be of the same order of magnitude for all successive and overlapping events.

In order to account for contemporaneous correlations between the regressors, we employ the Seemingly Unrelated Regression (SUR) methodology. Contemporaneous correlation between regressors is to be expected,

10. We also ran the regressions with excess returns, rather than returns, and found the same results.

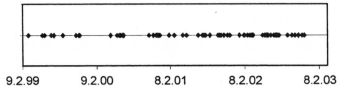

Fig. 13.5   Time series of announcement dates

Note: This figure plots the seventy-three announcement dates between January 1999 and September 2002.

since we observe some clustering of the event dates (see figure 13.5). The regression system is run in calendar time rather than in event time, so that contemporaneous correlations are properly accounted for.[11] To check the robustness of our results, the regressions were also run in event time, and as OLS regressions. All estimations yield qualitatively the same results.

The regression results are presented in table 13.5. While regression A.1 covers all seventy-three events, regression A.2 uses only the fifty-one events without overlap. Clearly, the announcement of a securitization does not generate abnormal stock returns. In regression A.1, the average values of the coefficients $\overline{\gamma}_1$ and $\overline{\gamma}_2$ are very close to zero and insignificant. In regression A.2, $\overline{\gamma}_1$ is higher but still insignificant. Thus, our conjecture that the announcement of securitizations does not yield significant abnormal returns is confirmed.

Securitization has, however, a rather impressive effect on the banks' average beta. Even though the relative increase in beta is rather modest, this is to be expected, given the small size of most securitizations relative to bank size. In regression A.1, beta increases in the postsecuritization period by 0.05, as shown by the coefficient of β^Δ. The coefficient is highly significant. This finding suggests that many banks engaged in securitizations increase their exposure vis-à-vis the market return. Our data, however, do not allow us to infer the sources of this increase in systematic risk.

In regression A.2, we look at the subsample of securitization events without overlap. Now the coefficient of β^Δ turns out to be much lower; also, the significance level is much lower. This sample underrepresents repeat issuers, that is, the large issuers. Thus, the beta increase after securitizations is much stronger for repeat issuers. These are more likely to systematically increase their risk after securitization.

The surprisingly strong increase in beta raises the question whether this finding may be biased. In particular, it is possible that the beta of the bank-

11. With 73×241 observations, there are enough degrees of freedom to estimate all coefficients in the SUR system. The regressions were also run in event time, without having a material effect. In fact, the results are even numerically very close.

Table 13.5   **Announcement effects: Regression results**

$$R_{i,t} = \alpha_i + \beta_i R_{m,t} + \gamma_{1,i} D^{\text{event}} + \gamma_{2,i} D^{\text{other event}} + \beta_i^{\Delta} D^{\text{after}} R_{m,t} + \delta_i (R_{b,t} - R_{m,t}) + \delta_i^{\Delta} D^{\text{after}} (R_{b,t} - R_{m,t}) + \varepsilon_{i,t}$$

	$\bar{\alpha}$	$\bar{\beta}$	$\bar{\gamma}_1$	$\bar{\gamma}_2$	$\bar{\beta}^{\Delta}$	$\bar{\delta}$	$\bar{\delta}^{\Delta}$
A.1 ($n = 73$)	−0.0003	0.7413	−0.0003	0.0003	0.05097		
w/ repeat issues	(0.982)	(0.000)	(0.360)	(0.456)	(0.003)		
A.2 ($n = 51$)	−0.0003	0.6597	0.0165		0.00175		
w/o repeat issues	(0.943)	(0.055)	(0.343)		(0.094)		
A.3 ($n = 73$)	0.0002	0.8230	−0.004	0.003	0.062	0.684	0.137
w/ repeat issues	(0.894)	(0.000)	(0.289)	(0.773)	(0.021)	(0.000)	(0.007)

Notes: This table reports the results of the event study relating to the announcement of collateralized debt obligation (CDO) issues. A calendar time seemingly unrelated regression (SUR) estimation of the determinants of issue banks' excess stock returns was employed. The first and third regression (A.1 and A.3) are time series estimations with seventy-three events over a window of 241 trading days. The second regression (A.2) has fifty-one events, excluding overlapping events by the same issuer (i.e., repeat issues). All regressions use data from the period January 1999 to December 2002. The dependent variable in all regressions is $R_{i,t}$, the daily log return of twenty-seven banks (from Datastream). The explanatory variables are $R_{m,t}$, $R_{b,t}$, D^{event}, $D^{\text{other event}}$, and D^{after}. $R_{m,t}$ is the log return on the DJ EuroStoxx and $R_{b,t}$ is the log return on the DJ Euro STOXX Bank. Both indexes are taken from Datastream. D^{event} equals one for the event window (-20, $+20$), where the event is the announcement date of the CDO issue, $D^{\text{other event}}$ equals one for all other event windows in the period (-120, $+120$), and D^{after} equals one for the period ($+20$, $+120$). If there is more than one other event, the dummy D-after is equal to 2 (3) for the second (third) subsequent overlapping event. Wald-statistics (p-values) are in parentheses.

ing industry increased over the sampling period and this effect accounted for the observed securitization impact on beta. In order to check for this possibility, we also estimated an augmented model

$$R_{i,t} = \alpha_i + \beta_i R_{m,t} + \gamma_{1,i} D_i^{\text{event}} + \gamma_{2,i} D_i^{\text{otherevent}} + \beta_i^{\Delta} D_i^{\text{after}} R_{m,t} + \delta_i (R_{b,t} - R_{m,t})$$
$$+ \delta_i^{\Delta} D_i^{\text{after}} (R_{b,t} - R_{m,t}) + \varepsilon_{i,t}$$
$$t = -20, \dots, +20$$

This regression includes as an additional regressor the excess bank index return $R_b - R_m$, defined as the log return of the European bank stock index minus the log market return.

In the augmented model, as shown in regression A.3 in table 13.5, the sensitivity of the single bank stock return with respect to the market return over the whole event window—the traditional beta—is now 0.82, whereas it is 0.68 for the excess bank index return.[12] Looking at the changes of these sensitivities after securitization, the traditional beta increases by a significant 0.062—essentially unchanged from regression A.1—whereas the sen-

---

12. Thus the market sensitivity increases from 0.74 (in regression A.1) to 0.82 (in A.3), due to the addition of the excess bank return index. The net sensitivity with regard to the market is 0.14, while it is 0.68 for the excess bank index.

sitivity with respect to the excess bank index return increases by 0.14, which is highly significant. Hence, taking both increases together, they are even more impressive than in the one-index model, A.1. This indicates again that on average the banks engaging in securitizations expand their risk taking.[13] Therefore, the increase in the traditional beta shown in regression A.1 does not appear to be driven by changes in the beta of the bank index return.

Given the increase of the traditional beta after securitization (regression A.1), we next ask whether this increase differs across types of transactions. For that purpose, we regress the bank-specific increases of β_i^Δ, as estimated in regression A.1, on a set of transaction-specific characteristics. The estimated model is:

$$\beta_i^\Delta = \alpha + \lambda_1 D_i^{\text{dynamic}} + \lambda_2 D_i^{\text{synthetic}} + \lambda_3 D_i^{\text{CLO}} + \lambda_4 D_i^{\text{CBO}} + \lambda_5 D_i^{\text{other}}$$
$$+ \lambda_{6-8} D_i^{\text{year}} + \varepsilon_i$$

The explanatory variables generate partitions of the sample. In particular, D^{dynamic} is a dummy variable that equals 1 for managed issues; that is, collateral portfolios that are being replenished over the life of the issue. $D^{\text{synthetic}}$ separates between synthetic and fully funded true sale issues, where the dummy equals 1 for synthetic issues. D^{CLO}, D^{CBO}, and D^{other} subdivide the sample into four categories according to the type of the underlying asset portfolio, as loans, bonds, mortgages (the reference group), and all others (e.g., credit card or leasing claims). The D^{year} dummies stand for the issue years, with 2002 as the reference year.

The cross-sectional analysis of β^Δ, reported in table 13.6, offers additional insight into what drives the increase in beta after securitizations. Among the structural characteristics, the dummy for managed issues, λ_1, is the only one that turns out to be significant. Since its sign is negative, it signifies that managed issues have a lower increase in systematic risk; that is, the bank may be less motivated to increase granularity in the aftermath of a securitization, or the bank may be more concerned to restrict the new risks to avoid early termination of the transaction, relative to static deals. The variables representing the type of underlying asset, such as CLOs or CBOs, remain insignificant altogether.

Clearly, these findings are explorative in nature, and they will have to be followed up by an integration of structural data concerning the collateral assets as well as balance sheet details of the bank.

---

13. We also employed alternative specifications of the banking industry model, using R_b as a regressor, rather than the difference of $(R_b - R_m)$, and using the error term from a first stage regression that relates R_b to R_m. All specifications lead to the same qualitative results. Furthermore, we also ran the regression in event time, and as a set of OLS-regressions, with very similar results for all specifications.

Table 13.6   **Announcement effects: Second-stage regression results**

$$\beta_i^\Delta = \alpha + \lambda_1 \cdot D_i^{dyn} + \lambda_2 \cdot D_i^{syn} + \lambda_3 \cdot D_i^{CLO} + \lambda_4 \cdot D_i^{CBO} + \lambda_5 \cdot D_i^{other} + \lambda_6 \cdot D_i^{99} + \lambda_7 \cdot D_i^{00} + \lambda_8 \cdot D_i^{01} + \varepsilon_i$$

α	λ_1	λ_2	λ_3	λ_4	λ_5	λ_6	λ_7	λ_8
0.061	−0.165	0.129	0.006	−0.111	−0.057	−0.282	0.172	−0.017
(0.65)	(0.02)	(0.16)	(0.95)	(0.45)	(0.62)	(0.01)	(0.04)	(0.83)
Adj. R^2	0.235							

Notes: This table reports the results of the event study relating to the announcement of CDO issues. A SUR estimation of the determinants of excess stock returns of the issuing banks was employed. The regression in this table is a cross-sectional estimation of the determinants of delta-beta from the regression A.1 in table 13.5, i.e. the change in systematic risk after an event. The explanatory variables are D^{dyn}, D^{syn}, D^{CLO}, D^{CBO}, D^{other}, D^{99}, D^{00}, D^{01}. D^{dyn} equals one for a managed issue, D^{syn} equals one for a synthetic issue. D^{CLO}, D^{CBO}, and D^{other} equal one when the collateral portfolio consists of loans, bonds, or other assets. Mortgage backed securities are the reference group. D^{99}, D^{00}, and D^{01} equal one for the issue year 1999, 2000, or 2001; *p*-values are in parentheses. As in table 13.5, the estimation is with seventy-three events over a window of 241 trading days. The regression uses data from the period January 1999 to December 2002.

13.4   Conclusions

In this paper we have analyzed the design of CDO-transactions and their impact on the default risk exposure of the originating bank. These risk effects are measured in two different ways: the impact on the bank's default losses and on its stock beta. The latter reflects the impact on the systematic risk in the stock market. Adverse selection and moral hazard problems, which are considered strong barriers to trading-default risks, are largely eliminated in a CDO-transaction by a substantial FLP of the originator. The size of this position increases with the average default probability of the underlying portfolio. Typically, only a small portion of default losses of the underlying portfolio is transferred in a CDO-transaction. In addition to the first-loss piece, tranching typically leads to a large senior tranche, which in the case of a fully funded transaction may be sold to investors so that the originator is protected against high default losses that otherwise might lead to financial distress.

The bank can adjust its policy to securitization in different ways. In one polar case it does not take new risks, in the other polar case it strongly expands its risk taking. The impact of securitization and reinvestment on the banks' default risk is illustrated in a simulation exercise that also illustrates the impact of default correlations on the bank's risk exposure. If the bank uses the securitization proceeds to expand its loan business, then its default risk tends to increase. This tends to translate also into an increase in its stock beta. On average, a beta increase is confirmed by our empirical findings. Our evidence suggests that many banks use the risk reduction achieved through securitization to take new risks. However, this finding has to be interpreted with care, given the size of the dataset and the length of the observation period.

Finally, we tentatively draw some conclusions about consequences of securitizations for financial markets. The risk transfer achieved by securitization depends as much on the way the issue is tranched as on the allocation of these tranches to different groups of investors. The tranching technique allows us to largely separate idiosyncratic risks from macro default risks. Assuming that the default risk of corporate loans depends on the relationship between the bank and its customers, tranching allows to allocate information-sensitive risks predominantly to the first-loss piece, and to a lesser extent to the mezzanine pieces, while the large senior tranches are largely free of these risks. In turn, extreme macro risks are borne predominantly by the senior tranches. The return on these tranches is effectively indexed to systemwide economic shocks. To the extent that loan securitizations replace the traditional "risk-free" deposit-financing of banks, one may conclude that both—bank lending and funding—are indexed to macro risks, making the banks less vulnerable.

To what extent these effects exist depends on the allocation of tranches to different types of investors. To realize an optimal risk sharing, the first-loss piece should be retained by the originating bank, because then its incentives as a lender are kept intact. In contrast, senior tranches should be allocated to remote investors, in order to improve the stability of financial markets. Remote investors are defined as investors who are in a better position to withstand macro shocks, so that their solvency is not endangered. In contrast, highly levered financial intermediaries without any hedge against macro shocks would be endangered, and the domino effects of insolvencies might destabilize the financial system. Figures published by banks and bank regulators indicate that financial intermediaries themselves buy the bulk of CDO tranches. It appears that originating banks often retain the nonsecuritized senior portion in synthetic deals. This indicates that the banking system as a whole is not effectively hedged against macro shocks. Financial stability would be improved if banks would neither invest in the senior tranches nor retain them, but sell them to more remote investors.

These tentative conclusions suggest a demand for more research along the lines we have presented in this paper. On the modeling side, the correlation structure between tranches of different seniority is relevant for CDO-bond portfolio management and for assessing financial system stability. For example, a change in the correlation between asset classes not only alters the default probabilities of tranches, but also the joint default probabilities of different tranches. The latter statistic is relevant for the analysis of contagion effects, as pointed out by Bae, Karolyi, and Stulz (2003) and Gersbach (2002). On the empirical side, more research is needed to find out how banks change their business policy in response to securitization. In addition, more evidence is required on the effective allocation of tranches to investor groups and on the expanded role of commercial banks as intermediaries between capital markets and the corporate sector, as discussed in Gorton and Pennacchi (1995). It appears that the securitization of bank loans provides an efficient new tool to combine the advantages of bank- and market-based financial systems.

References

Arrow, K. 1971. *Essays in the theory of risk bearing.* Markham.
Bae, K.-H., Karolyi, G. A., and R. M. Stulz. 2003. A new approach to measuring financial contagion. *Review of Financial Studies* 16:717–64.
Blanco, R., Brennan, S., and I. W. Marsh. 2005. An empirical analysis of the dynamic relationship between investment-grade bonds and credit default swaps. *Journal of Finance* 60:2255–81.
Calomiris, C. W., and J. R. Mason. 2004. Credit card securitization and regulatory arbitrage. *Journal of Financial Services Research* 26:5–27.
Cebenoyan, A. S., and P. E. Strahan. 2004. Risk management, capital structure and lending at banks. *Journal of Banking and Finance* 28:19–43.
Collin-Dufresne, P., Goldstein, R. S., and J. S. Martin. 2001. The determinants of credit spread changes. *Journal of Finance* 56:2177–2207.
Das, S. 2000. *Credit derivatives and credit linked notes.* 2nd ed. New York: Wiley.
DeMarzo, P. 2005. The pooling and tranching of securities: A model of informed intermediation. *Review of Financial Studies* 18:1–35.
Deutsche Bundesbank. 2004. Instrumente zum Kreditrisikotransfer: Einsatz bei deutschen Banken und Aspekte der Finanzmarktstabilität, *Monatsberichte* (April): 27–45.
Diamond, D. W., and R. W. Rajan. 2001. Liquidity risk, liquidity creation, and financial fragility: A theory of banking. *Journal of Political Economy* 109:287–327.
Elsas, R., and J. P. Krahnen. 2004. Universal banks and relationships with firms. In *The German financial system,* ed. J. P. Krahnen and R. H. Schmidt, 197–232. Oxford: Oxford University Press.
Fabozzi, F. J., Modigliani, F., Jones, F. J., and M. G. Ferri. 2002. *Foundations of financial markets and institutions,* 3rd ed. New York: Prentice Hall.
Franke, G., and J. P. Krahnen. 2004. Understanding CLO markets. Working Paper, preliminary draft, University of Konstanz.
Gale, D., and M. Hellwig. 1985. Incentive-compatible debt contracts: The one-period problem. *Review of Economic Studies* 52:647–63.
Gersbach, H. 2002. Financial intermediation and the creation of macroeconomic risks. CESifo Working Paper series no. 695, April.
Gorton, G., and G. G. Pennacchi. 1995. Banking and loan sales: Marketing non-marketable assets. *Journal of Monetary Economics* 35:389–411.
Greenbaum, S., and A. Thakor. 1987. Bank funding models: Securitization versus deposits. *Journal of Banking and Finance* 11:379–401.
Lockwood, L. J., Rutherford, R. C., and Herrera, M. J. 1996. Wealth effects of asset securitization. *Journal of Banking and Finance* 20:151–64.
Moody's Investor Service. 2002. Default and recovery rates of European corporate bond issuers, 1985–2001. July.

Ongena, S., and D. C. Smith. 2000. Bank relationships: A review. In *The performance of financial institutions,* ed. P. Harker and A. Zenios, 221–58. Cambridge: Cambridge University Press.

Plantin, G. 2003. Tranching. London School of Economics Working Paper.

Riddiough, T. 1997. Optimal design of asset backed securities. *Journal of Financial Intermediation* 6:121–52.

Standard & Poor's. 2002. Global cash flow and synthetic CDO criteria. *Standard & Poors Structured Research,* March 21.

Thomas, H. 2001. Effects of asset securitization on seller claimants. *Journal of Financial Intermediation* 10:306–30.

Townsend, R. M. 1979. Optimal contracts and competitive markets with costly state verification. *Journal of Economic Theory* 21:265–93.

Comment   Patricia Jackson

Franke and Krahnen consider the question of the effect on banks' risk profiles of the securitization of a portion of their assets through the collateralized debt obligation (CDO) market. The CDO market has grown rapidly over the past five years, and new issuance worldwide has probably reached some £100bn per annum; therefore, the question the authors pose is important.

Through a CDO the bank transfers some default risk on loans it has originated to the holders of securities while retaining part of the risk itself. The securitization is usually structured so that the first portion of any loss is covered by the originating bank. Franke and Krahnen find that the banks retain a sizeable portion of default risk, leaving the market with the tail risk—the risk of extreme events. In effect, the banks are retaining the risk portion that is easier to price into the original loan through the margin (the expected loss) plus some of the unexpected loss relating to more probable events, which is also easier to measure.

Franke and Krahnen estimate a loss distribution for different types of securitization pools and compare these with the size of the first-loss piece retained by the banks. The method used is to take information on the quality of the underlying loans as indicated by a rating agency and then use an S&P rating transition matrix to estimate the loss distribution. They assume a correlation coefficient of 0.3 for assets in the same industry.

They find that in a typical issue the first loss piece is between 2 percent and 10 percent of the issue volume. In the case of collateralized bond obligations (CBOs), where the securities are collateralized by bonds, the first-loss piece is on average 3.36 times the expected loss on the underlying portfolio, versus 1.34 times in the case of collateralized loan obligations (CLOs) collateralized by loans to small- to medium-sized enterprises (SMEs). The difference could in part reflect the fact that the distribution of losses on

SME portfolios may be tighter, with many more losses falling closer to the mean—because small companies fail in all points of the cycle, whereas failures of large companies are concentrated in recessions. The correlations may therefore be larger for bonds and large company loans than SMEs. However, the fact that the most junior-rated tranche of the CBO transactions is rated several notches higher than those in the SMEs does support the Franke and Krahnen view that, to a degree, the banks are absorbing less risk in the case of SME transactions.

The most important question tackled is the effect that securitization has on the overall risk profile of the sponsoring banks. Franke and Krahnen focus on various assumptions concerning the reinvestment of the funds raised from the securitization, assuming that the bank can reinvest the proceeds less the first-loss position (FLP). They find that the mean loss rate of the new portfolio (including the FLP in the securitization and the risk in the portfolio gained by reinvesting the funds from the securitization) is higher. But the skewness and kurtosis are lower, underling the point that securitization is enabling the banks to move extreme scenario risk into the market. Again, the banks are keeping the portion of risk for which it is easiest to price/set aside reserves and moving the rest into the market.

This would appear to reduce the risks of the banks and the banking sector. Banking crises generally occur when the sector is under overall pressure because of a severe macroeconomic downturn. But one important question beyond the scope of this paper is the extent to which banks might feel obligated to help support the securitization market, effectively moving the losses back onto the balance sheet.

Franke and Krahnen also point to evidence that much of the market in higher-rated tranches consists of sales to other banks. Thus, much of the extreme risk is not moving out of the banking sector. The effect on individual banks will, however, depend on the overall profile of their existing book.

To see the overall effect on the riskiness of banks carrying out the securitization it would also be necessary to consider the effect on risk relative to the capital held by the banks and also relative to the margin/provisions to cover expected losses. Under the current Basel Accord FLPs held by banks are deducted from capital; under Basel II, all tranches rated below BB will also be deducted. In effect, such risky tranches are treated as expected loss, which has to be covered dollar for dollar by capital. The market sets the total amount of capital required by a major internationally active bank, because more capital is needed than the Basel minimum to achieve an adequate rating, but the market probably relies to a degree on the Basel measurement approach and looks for an excess above it. In addition, rating agencies will be very aware of the amount and type of securitizations being carried out by individual banks. A bank might therefore be unable to reinvest as large a proportion of the receipts from securitization as is assumed in this paper, given the capital needed to back the first loss in the securitization, unless more capital is raised.

Franke and Krahnen use event studies to consider the market reaction to the announcement of securitizations, while acknowledging that the net impact of securitization on a bank's stock price is hard to predict. In addition to the factors mentioned in the paper, the size of the program relative to the bank's balance sheet would be important, as well as the likely effect on bank earnings. They find that securitization does not generate abnormal stock returns but it does increase the bank's beta. It is not fully clear why this is the case.

Discussion Summary

The general discussion focused on technical suggestions for the authors. *Gary Gorton* suggested that synthetic CLOs should be removed from the sample, as they have no effect on the leverage of the sponsor. *Til Schuermann* suggested that the authors focus on expected shortfall measures of loss in their modeling of individual securitizations. *Philippe Jorion* and *Hashem Pesaran* expressed concern about cross-sectional dependence in the pooled sample of CLOs, suggesting that different methods may be needed in estimation of standard errors. *Mark Carey* suggested that unlevered rather than levered betas be used in the computations.

Biographies

Kenneth C. Abbott is a managing director in the market risk department at Morgan Stanley.

Franklin Allen is the Nippon Life Professor of Finance at The Wharton School of the University of Pennsylvania, professor of economics in the College of Arts and Sciences at the University of Pennsylvania, and codirector of the Wharton Financial Institutions Center.

Torben G. Andersen is the Nathan and Mary Sharp Distinguished Professor of Finance at the Kellogg School of Management, Northwestern University, and a research associate of the National Bureau of Economic Research (NBER).

Thorsten Beck is a senior financial economist in the finance team of the Development Research Group of the World Bank.

Jeremy Berkowitz is an associate professor in the department of finance at the University of Houston.

Tim Bollerslev is the Juanita and Clifton Kreps Professor of Economics, Duke University, professor of finance at its Fuqua School of Business, and a research associate of the National Bureau of Economic Research.

Charles W. Calomiris is the Henry Kaufman Professor of Financial Institutions at Columbia Business School, and a research associate of the National Bureau of Economic Research.

Richard Cantor is managing director of the Credit Policy Research Group, which conducts default research and measures ratings performance for Moody's Investors Service.

Mark Carey is finance project manager in the Division of International Finance at the Federal Reserve Board and codirector of the NBER's Working Group on Risks of Financial Institutions.

Nicholas Chan is a managing director and senior research scientist at AlphaSimplex Group.

Peter F. Christoffersen is an associate professor of finance at McGill University and a research fellow at the Center for Interuniversity Research and Analysis on Organizations (CIRANO) and the Center for Interuniversity Research on Quantitative Economics (CIREQ).

Michel Crouhy is head of research and development and financial engineering at IXIS Corporate and Investment Bank (Groupe Caisse d'Epargne).

Asli Demirgüç-Kunt holds the joint appointment of senior research manager, in the World Bank's Development Economics Research Group, and senior adviser, operations and policy department, in the Bank's Financial Sector Vice-Presidency.

Francis X. Diebold is the W. P. Carey Professor of Economics at the University of Pennsylvania, professor of finance and statistics at its Wharton School, and a research associate of the National Bureau of Economic Research.

Darrell Duffie is the James I. Miller Professor of Finance at The Graduate School of Business, Stanford University.

Richard C. S. Evans is the chief risk officer in market risk at Deutsche Bank A. G.

Martin Feldstein is the George F. Baker Professor of Economics at Harvard University, and president of the National Bureau of Economic Research.

Patrick de Fontnouvelle is a vice president in the Supervision, Regulation and Credit Department at the Federal Reserve Bank of Boston.

Günter Franke is a professor of finance at the Center for Finance and Econometrics, University of Konstanz, and Center for Financial Studies, Frankfurt.

Douglas Gale is the Julius Silver Professor of Economics, New York University, and Extraordinary Fellow, Churchill College, Cambridge.

Peter M. Garber is global strategist at Global Markets Research, Deutsche Bank, and a research associate of the National Bureau of Economic Research.

Evan Gatev is an assistant professor of finance at Boston College.

Mila Getmansky is an assistant professor of finance at the Isenberg School of Management, University of Massachusetts, Amherst.

Gary Gorton is the Robert Morris Professor of Banking and Finance at The Wharton School of the University of Pennsylvania, professor of economics in the College of Arts and Sciences at the University of Pennsylvania, and a research associate of the National Bureau of Economic Research.

Shane M. Haas is a senior research scientist at the AlphaSimplex Group.

Philipp Hartmann is head of the Financial Research Division at the European Central Bank and a fellow of the Centre for Economic Policy Research (CEPR).

Patricia Jackson is a partner in the Risk Management practice at Ernst & Young, LLP.

John S. Jordan is a vice president at JP Morgan Chase.

Philippe Jorion is a professor of finance at the Paul Merage School of Business at the University of California, Irvine.

Jan Pieter Krahnen is a professor of finance at Goethe-University, Frankfurt, and director of the Center for Financial Studies, Frankfurt.

Paul Kupiec is associate director, Division of Insurance and Research, of the Federal Deposit Insurance Corporation.

Andrew Kuritzkes is a managing director at Mercer Oliver Wyman.

Hayne Leland is the Arno Rayner Professor of Finance and Management at the Haas School of Business, University of California, Berkeley.

Ross Levine is the Harrison S. Kravis University Professor and professor of economics at Brown University, and a research associate of the National Bureau of Economic Research.

Andrew W. Lo is the Harris & Harris Group Professor of Finance at the MIT Sloan School of Management, and a research associate of the National Bureau of Economic Research.

David M. Modest is a managing director of J. P. Morgan Chase.

James O'Brien is a senior economist in the Division of Research and Statistics at the Federal Reserve Board.

Loriana Pelizzon is an associate professor of economics at the University Ca' Foscari of Venice and SSAV.

M. Hashem Pesaran is a professor of economics at the University of Southern California and at the University of Cambridge, and a Fellow of Trinity College.

Eric S. Rosengren is the executive vice president in the Supervision, Regulation and Credit Department at the Federal Reserve Bank of Boston.

Marc Saidenberg is currently a managing director at Merrill Lynch & Company, but was at the Federal Reserve Bank of New York when this work was completed.

Pedro Santa-Clara is an associate professor of finance at the Anderson School of Management, University of California, Los Angeles, and a research associate of the National Bureau of Economic Research.

Anthony Saunders is the John M. Schiff Professor of Finance, and chairman of the department of finance, Stern School of Business, New York University.

Stephen Schaefer is a professor of finance at London Business School.

Til Schuermann is a senior economist at the Federal Reserve Bank of New York and a research fellow at the Wharton Financial Institutions Center.

Nicholas S. Souleles is an associate professor of finance at The Wharton School of the University of Pennsylvania, and a research associate of the National Bureau of Economic Research.

Stefan Straetmans is an assistant professor of finance at Maastricht University.

Philip E. Strahan is an associate professor of finance at Boston College, a research fellow at the Wharton Financial Institutions Center, and a faculty research fellow at the National Bureau of Economic Research.

René M. Stulz is the Everett D. Reese Chair of Banking and Monetary Economics at The Ohio State University, codirector of the NBER's Working Group in Risks of Financial Institutions and a research associate of the NBER.

Björn-Jakob Treutler is a consultant at the London office of Mercer Oliver Wyman, the financial services consulting firm.

Peter Tufano is the Sylvan C. Coleman Professor of Financial Management, senior associate dean and director of faculty development at Harvard Business School, and a research associate of the National Bureau of Economic Research.

Casper G. de Vries is chair of monetary economics in the faculty of economics at Erasmus University, Rotterdam.

Contributors

Kenneth C. Abbott
Bank of America Securities
9 West 57th Street
New York, NY 10019

Franklin Allen
Department of Finance
The Wharton School of the University
 of Pennsylvania
3620 Locust Walk
Philadelphia, PA 19104-6367

Torben G. Andersen
Kellogg School of Management
Northwestern University
2001 Sheridan Road
Evanston, IL 60208

Thorsten Beck
The World Bank
1818 H Street, NW
Washington, DC 20433

Jeremy Berkowitz
Department of Finance
University of Houston
Houston, TX 77204-6021

Tim Bollerslev
Department of Economics
Duke University
Box 90097
Durham, NC 27708-0097

Charles W. Calomiris
Columbia Business School
3022 Broadway, Uris Hall 601
New York, NY 10027

Richard Cantor
Moody's Investors Service
99 Church Street
New York, NY 10007

Mark Carey
Finance Project Manager
Division of International Finance
Federal Reserve Board
Washington, DC 20551 USA

Nicholas Chan
AlphaSimplex Group, LLC
One Cambridge Center
Cambridge, MA 02142

Peter F. Christoffersen
McGill University
Faculty of Management
1001 Sherbrooke West
Montreal, PQ Canada H3A 1G5

Michel Crouhy
IXIS Corporate and Investment Bank
47, quai d'Austerlitz
75013 Paris, France

Asli Demirgüç-Kunt
The World Bank
1818 H Street, NW
Washington, DC 20433

Francis X. Diebold
Department of Economics
University of Pennsylvania
3718 Locust Walk
Philadelphia, PA 19104-6297

Darrell Duffie
Graduate School of Business
Stanford University
Stanford, CA 94305-5015

Richard C. S. Evans
Deutsche Bank A.G.
1 Great Winchester Street
London EC2N 2DB England

Martin Feldstein
National Bureau of Economic
    Research
1050 Massachusetts Avenue
Cambridge, MA 02138-5398

Patrick de Fontnouvelle
Federal Reserve Bank of Boston
600 Atlantic Avenue
Boston, MA 02210

Günter Franke
Department of Economics
University of Konstanz
Box D 147
D-78457 Konstanz Germany

Douglas Gale
Department of Economics
New York University
269 Mercer Street
New York, NY 10003

Peter M. Garber
Deutsche Bank
60 Wall Street
New York, NY 10005

Evan Gatev
Carroll School of Management
Boston College
140 Commonwealth Avenue
Chestnut Hill, MA 02467

Mila Getmansky
Isenberg School of Management
University of Massachusetts, Amherst
121 Presidents Drive
Amherst, MA 01003

Gary B. Gorton
Department of Finance
The Wharton School
University of Pennsylvania
Philadelphia, PA 19104-6367

Shane M. Haas
AlphaSimplex Group, LLC
One Cambridge Center
Cambridge, MA 02142

Philipp Hartmann
European Central Bank
Kaiserstrasse 29
60311 Frankfurt Am Main Germany

Patricia Jackson
Ernst & Young LLP
1 More London Place
London SE1 2AF England

John S. Jordan
Algorithmics Incorporated
33 Whitehall Street, 26th Floor
New York, NY 10004

Philippe Jorion
Paul Merage School of Business
University of California at Irvine
Irvine, CA 92697-3125

Jan Pieter Krahnan
Center for Financial Studies
Mertonstr. 17-21
D-60325 Frankfurt am Main Germany

Paul Kupiec
Federal Deposit Insurance
    Corporation (FDIC)
550 Seventeenth Street, NW
Washington, DC 20057

Andrew Kuritzkes
Mercer Oliver Wyman
99 Park Avenue, 5th Floor
New York, NY 10016

Hayne Leland
Haas School of Business
University of California
545 Student Services Building #1900
Berkeley, CA 94720-1900

Ross Levine
Department of Economics
Brown University
Providence, RI 02912

Andrew W. Lo
Sloan School of Management
Massachusetts Institute of Technology
50 Memorial Drive
Cambridge, MA 02142-1347

David M. Modest
Azimuth Trust Company, LLC
162 Fifth Avenue, 8th Floor
New York, NY 10010

James O'Brien
Division of Research and Statistics
Federal Reserve Board
20th Street and Constitution Avenue,
    NW
Washington, DC 20551

Loriana Pelizzon
Department of Economics
University of Venice
Fondamenta San Giobbe 873
30121 Venice Italy

M. Hashem Pesaran
Faculty of Economics
University of Cambridge
Sidgwick Avenue
Cambridge CB3 9DD England

Eric S. Rosengren
Federal Reserve Bank of Boston
600 Atlantic Avenue
Boston, MA 02210

Marc Saidenberg
Merrill Lynch & Co.
4 World Financial Center, 22nd Floor
New York, NY 10080

Pedro Santa-Clara
Anderson School of Management
University of California, Los Angeles
110 Westwood Plaza
Los Angeles, CA 90095-1481

Anthony Saunders
Stern School of Business
New York University
44 West 4th Street
New York, NY 10012

Stephen Schaefer
Finance Department
London Business School
Regent's Park
London NW1 4SA England

Til Schuermann
Federal Reserve Bank of New York
33 Liberty Street
New York, NY 10045

Nicholas S. Souleles
The Wharton School
University of Pennsylvania
2300 Steinberg Hall—Dietrich Hall
Philadelphia, PA 19104-6367

Stefan Straetmans
Faculty of Economics and Business
    Administration
Maastricht University
P.O. Box 616
NL-6200 MD Maastricht
    The Netherlands

Philip E. Strahan
Carroll School of Management
Boston College
140 Commonwealth Avenue
Chestnut Hill, MA 02467

René M. Stulz
Fisher College of Business
The Ohio State University
2100 Neil Avenue
Columbus, OH 43210-1399

Björn-Jakob Treutler
Mercer Oliver Wyman
1 Neal Street
London WC2H 9QL England

Peter Tufano
Harvard Business School
Soldiers Field Road
Boston, MA 02163

Casper G. de Vries
Faculty of Economics
Erasmus University Rotterdam
PO Box 1738
3000 DR Rotterdam The Netherlands

Author Index

Subject Index